Street law

Practical law for South Africans

LEARNER'S MANUAL

Street law

Practical law for South Africans

THIRD EDITION

By
David McQuoid-Mason
(General Editor)

with Lindi Coetzee, Lloyd Lotz, Malebakeng Forere and Rowena Bernard

Illustrated by
Andy Mason
with Jeff Rankin, Grant Cresswell, Luke Molver and Themba Siwela

JUTA

First edition 1990
Second edition 2004
Third edition 2015

First Floor Sunclare Building, 21 Dreyer Street, Claremont, 7708

Production Coordinator: Deidre du Preez
Editor: Robyn Evans
Cover design: Drag and Drop
Proofreading: Sarah Johnston & Leila Samodien
Indexer & Glossator: Daphne Burger
Design and layout: Nicole de Swardt – Fly Creative

A special thank you to *Proudly South African* for the use of their logo

ISBN 978 0 70218 554 0

Printed by

Preface to Third Edition

In 1973 I established one of the first university legal-aid clinics in South Africa. Subsequently I had been considering introducing a programme of public legal education which would enable members of the public to enforce their legal rights and avoid conflicts with the law. In 1984, during a visitor's programme sponsored by the United States Information Service (USIS), I met Ed O'Brien of Georgetown University Law Faculty, Washington DC, a co-founder of the American street-law programme. I invited him to South Africa in 1985 and his trip was paid for by USIS. It was an inauspicious time as President PW Botha declared a state of emergency while Ed O'Brien was in the country conducting non-racial street-law workshops with me. He and I brainstormed a curriculum with a multi-racial group of high school teachers and pupils and then persuaded the president of the Association of Law Societies, Graham Cox, to provide financial backing for a pilot street-law programme for South Africa - the first such programme outside of the United States.

In 1986 a pilot street-law programme under Mandla Mchunu was set up at the University of Natal (Durban) to operate in five schools - according to the apartheid context: two African and two white schools and one Indian school. The programme was a success and soon expanded to 16 other universities with financial assistance from the Attorneys Fidelity Fund. The Fund continued to sponsor the programme until South Africa's transition towards democracy in the early 1990s, when funding ceased. I produced a series of five user-friendly cartoon-illustrated books for school children together with accompanying teacher's manuals. Initially I acted as national coordinator of the programme and was responsible for training the street-law coordinators at the different universities. Mandla Mchunu was subsequently appointed as the national street-law director at the Centre for Socio-Legal Studies (CSLS), University of Natal, which had been established in 1987.

After the release of Nelson Mandela in 1990, the South African street-law programme decided to introduce South Africans to the Universal Declaration of Human Rights. With assistance from an American civic education school teacher, Eleanor Greene, and field-testing by the 16 street-law coordinators, Ed O'Brien and I produced a workbook, together with an instructor's manual, in the South African street-law format, entitled *Human Rights for All.* I was the general editor and coordinator of the project which was done in partnership with Lawyers for Human Rights (of which I was Durban chairperson at the time) and Street Law Inc (then known as the National Institute for Citizen Education under the Law (NICEL)). An American version of the book was subsequently published in 1996.

In 1992, with assistance from the United States Agency for International Development (USAID) the CSLS in partnership with NICEL decided that it was necessary to introduce South Africans to the principles of democracy in preparation for the country's first democratic elections. The local street-law team met with the 26 NGOs involved in voter education in KwaZulu-Natal and we agreed to work together to produce a workbook on democracy. The NGO contribution was to help design the curriculum for the programme and to field- test the materials in their constituencies. Over a period of a year the CSLS coordinated the process and I was general editor of the book that was produced, together with an instructor's manual, entitled *Democracy for All.* There was consultation with, and field-testing by, the 26 NGOs and 16 street-law coordinators throughout the process. I worked as a writer and editor with a writing team consisting of two Americans (Ed O'Brien and Mary Curd Larkin of NICEL) and two South Africans (Mandla Mchunu of CSLS and Karthy Govender of the University of Natal). One spin-off from the book was the development by Chuck Scott and the CSLS of the *Democracy Challenge Game* which requires players to identify and define 13 different signposts of democracy using interactive techniques in a board game involving quizzes and debates. The game was field-tested in over 500 high schools in South Africa and has been translated into Swahili. It has also been adapted to embrace the Convention of the Rights of the Child in Nigeria.

In 1997 I began assisting the Ford Foundation, the Open Society Institute and Street Law Inc to develop street-law programmes and materials and provide workshop training in Eastern and Central Europe, Central Asia and the former Soviet Union. The countries involved in the project were Albania, Belarus, Croatia, the Czech Republic, Estonia, Hungary, Kazakhstan, Kyrgyzstan, Latvia, Macedonia, Moldova, Mongolia, Romania, Russia, Slovakia, Ukraine and Uzbekistan. The programme was aimed at assisting the countries to develop cadres of school teachers, law students and law teachers who could teach and develop indigenous curricula and materials on street-law, human rights and democracy for inclusion in the formal school curriculum. My experience in dealing with the transition from apartheid to democracy in South Africa resonated strongly with the countries that were undergoing the transition from communism and dictatorship to democracy. By the end of 2001 street-law, human rights and democracy materials had been published by Belarus, Croatia, the Czech Republic, Estonia, Kazakhstan, Kyrgyzstan, Latvia, Macedonia, Moldova, Mongolia, Russia, Slovakia, Ukraine and Uzbekistan. In addition *Human Rights for All* and *Democracy for All* were translated into Croatian, Mongolian and Russian. *Democracy for All* was also translated into French for use by Civitas International.

The street-law books, *Human Rights for All* and *Democracy for All* have also been used in street-law, human rights and democracy workshops in Egypt, Haiti, Lesotho, Zimbabwe, Zambia, Namibia, Mozambique, Tanzania, Uganda, Ghana, Nigeria, Morocco, Ethiopia, India and Bangladesh. In addition they have been used in British Commonwealth Secretariat human rights workshops in Tanzania, Lesotho, Uganda, Mozambique and in the annual African Human Rights Education camps in different parts of Africa. Street-law programmes in one form or another exist in Kenya, Uganda, Nigeria and Ghana.

The support given to the initial founding of the South African street-law programme by the Attorneys Fidelity Fund, and the subsequent funding of the South African *Democracy for All* street-law programme for the decade since 1992, primarily by the USAID, has paid handsome dividends. In 2003 Street Law South Africa (incorporated as an association in terms of s 21) was established. Street Law South Africa is in the process of applying to the POSLEC SETA (Police, Private Security, Legal, Correctional Services and Justice Sector Education and Training Authority) as a service provider to use the training materials produced in this *Street Law South Africa: Learner's Manual and the Educator's Manual.* It also intends to apply to the South African Qualifications Authority (SAQA) for approval of a street-law unit standard. These steps are being taken to ensure that Street Law South Africa becomes more self-sustaining and less dependant on donor funding.

The South African street-law programme has produced a valuable tool for the teaching of law, human rights and democracy to civil society, particularly school children, university students, school teachers, prison officials and police officers, as well as community groups. Aspects of it have been successfully replicated in a number of developing countries ranging from Africa, Asia and the Caribbean to Eastern and Central Europe, Central Asia and the former Soviet Union, as well as the United States itself.

David McQuoid-Mason
President, Commonwealth Legal Education Association
James Scott Wylie Professor of Law
University of KwaZulu-Natal
Durban

June 2015

Acknowledgements

Acknowledgements for the first edition of *Street Law* were due to the Association of Law Societies (ALS) and the Attorneys Notaries and Conveyancers Fidelity Guarantee Fund for financing the first street law projects; Graham Cox for enlisting the support of the ALS and the Attorneys Fidelity Fund and overseeing the project; Edward O'Brien, co-director of the National Institute for Citizen Education in the Law (NICEL), Washington DC, for introducing the concept to South Africa (with David McQuoid-Mason) and acting as a consulting editor; the pioneering American textbook *Street Law: A Course in Practical Law* 3 ed (1986), published by West Publishing Co, and NICEL, on which the South African *Street Law* books were based; and the Legal Resources Centre's *Advice Office Training Manual* (1986) for aspects of South African public interest law. Thanks were also due to the 1985 University of Natal legal-aid students who assisted in preparing an early *Street Law* draft; the 1986 legal-aid students for helping to field-test the materials in the pilot schools project; Mandla Mchunu for running the 1986 pilot project; Alan Rycroft for supervising the pilot project; and Anne Kroon of the Careers Information Centre for assisting in setting up the pilot project.

Acknowledgements for the second edition of *Street Law South Africa: Practical Law for South Africans* were due to the European Foundation for Human Rights which funded the project; the United States Agency for International Development (USAID) which provided funds for many years to keep the running after funding was no longer available from the ALS (now the Law Society of South Africa) and Attorneys Fidelity Fund; to Murray Wesson for assisting with the updating of some of the materials; and to the enthusiastic law students in the different parts of the country who over the past 18 years have provided, and continue to provide, the life-blood of the street-law programme. Last, but not least, acknowledgements are due to Isabelle de Grandpré who has admirably handled the difficult task of coordinating the publication of the second edition; Jess Nicholson who has done the layout for the new edition; and to Suloshini Pather of Juta who has unstintingly and enthusiastically supported the project.

Acknowledgements for this third edition of *Street Law South Africa: Practical Law for South Africans* are due to my co-authors Lindi Coetzee, Lloyd Lotz, Malebakeng Forere and Rowena Bernard; Melanie Reddy of the National Street Law Office for administrative support; Nicole de Swardt of *Fly Creative* for the lay out; Marlinee Chetty and Deidre du Preez of Juta & Company (Pty) Ltd for their help and encouragement to produce the third edition and Seanokeng Makgala of *Proudly South African* for the permission to use their logo.

David McQuoid-Mason
General Editor

CONTENTS

PART ONE

Introduction to South African law and the legal system

PART TWO

Criminal law and child justice

PART THREE

Consumer law

PART FOUR

Family law

PART FIVE

Socio-economic rights

PART SIX

Employment law

Street law

1. Introduction to South African law and the legal system

CONTENTS

PART ONE

Introduction to South African law and the legal system

1.1 Street law and law in general

Outcomes

After completion of this section learners will be able to:

1. Explain the purpose and meaning of Street law and law in general

Assessment criteria

1. An explanation is given of the purpose and meaning of Street law and law.
2. The relationship between law and everyday life is identified.
3. A set of facts is examined and a decision is taken on whether or not the accused were guilty of murder.
4. The relationship between law and morality is identified.
5. The reasons for having laws in society are identified.

1.1.1 What is Street law?

contact with the law

Street law tells people about laws that affect them in their everyday life 'on the street'. For example, every time a person buys something, rents a house, gets married or divorced, or is accused of a crime, he or she comes into contact with the law. Street law will help you understand how the law works and how it can protect you. It also explains what the law expects you to do in certain cases. It tells you about the different legal problems you should watch for and how you can solve them.

getting help to take action

Most people think that only the rich can win by using the law, and that it works against the poor. The law is confusing and it seems difficult to get help from lawyers without having money. Many people do not believe that poor people renting broken down houses can get a court to order the owner to fix them. They do not think that people who buy cars that do not work properly can force the garages which sold them the cars to make repairs or refund their money. Women who are beaten by their husbands probably do not know that they can use the law to prevent their husbands from assaulting them. Others probably do not believe that people assaulted by the police can get compensation for their injuries. It is important for people renting houses (called tenants) or the buyers of motor cars (called consumers), or the women beaten by their husbands, or the people injured by the police, to know about their legal rights and where they can get help to take action.

practical advice

Apart from telling you generally about why we need laws and about problems in criminal law, consumer law, family law, social and economic rights and employment law, the *Street Law Manual* will also give you advice you can use in practical situations: What to do when you are arrested. Where to get a lawyer. How to get your money back when a shop sells you something that does not work.

What to do if you are unfairly dismissed from your job. How old or sick people can get a pension. How to buy or rent a house. What parents and children are expected to do for each other.

Problem 1: The case of the silent radio

'as good as new'

Mrs Khumalo buys a second-hand radio from Ghetto Blasters Limited after the salesman had tested it for her. Her friend goes with her to the shop and hears the salesman tell her that it 'works well' and is 'as good as new'. Two days later the radio stops working and Mrs Khumalo takes it back to the shop.

radio was tested

The salesman refuses to do anything because the radio was tested by him when Mrs Khumalo bought it and it was working when she left the shop.

two days after she bought it, Mrs Khumalo's radio stopped working

Questions

1. What is the problem in this case?
2. If you were Mrs Khumalo what would you do?
3. What could her friend do to help her?
4. If this case went to court and you were the judge, what would you decide? Why?
5. Has anything like this ever happened to you or somebody you know? If so, what was done about it?

thinking about the law

Street law also encourages you to think about the law from all sides so that you can understand how law works. For example, you would be expected to give your reasons when discussing questions like: What is the meaning of the law? Why was the law made? Do you think it is a 'good' or a 'bad' law? What are the arguments in favour of the law? What are the arguments against the law? Should the law be left as it is or changed? How are laws changed? If you were the person making the law how would you word the law?

understanding the law

Before you are given advice on how to use the law it is necessary for you to understand such things as: The meaning of the word 'law'. Where South African law comes from. How law is made. The different kinds of law. How the courts work. The types of lawyers and how they can help. What happens when you go to court? Problems you may face when going to court.

Problem 2: A few general questions

Questions

1. What is the purpose of learning Street law?
2. Should only lawyers know about the law? Give reasons for your answer.
3. Do you know anyone who has got into trouble with the law? If so, what kind of trouble? Do you think that knowing about Street law would have helped them? How?

1.1.2 What is law?

rights and duties

It is not easy to answer the question: What is law? There are many definitions of law, but for our purposes, law can be defined as a set of rules used to control the behaviour of people in society. These rules tell people what they must do, what they may do and what they may not do. In other words they tell people about their legal 'rights' and 'duties'. They also tell people when they will be protected by the courts. This definition is not complete, however, because it does not answer questions like: Where do laws come from? Do we need laws? Are all laws written? Can laws be changed? If so, how? Are all laws fair? What is the difference between laws and 'morals' (ie whether something is right or wrong)? What is certain, however, is that the law affects nearly every part of our daily activities even if we do not realise it.

laws and morals

Problem 3: Did the law touch you today?

Questions

Make a list of all your daily activities (eg waking up, going to the toilet, bathing or showering, eating, going to school). Next to each activity state whether you think there are any laws affecting it. What do you think is the purpose of these laws? Would you change any of these laws? Give reasons for your answer.

punishment and compensation

The law is binding on people. This means that its rules must be followed. If a person does not follow the rules, he or she may be punished by the court or be made to pay another person compensation or made to do other things. It does not mean, however, that a law must be fair or just to be a law. In the past, South Africa's apartheid laws, which forced people of different races to live in different areas and attend different schools, were not fair and just.

some laws may be regarded as wrong

When studying the law we often have to think about the connection between laws and morals. Morals refer to behaviour that a particular society regards as right or wrong, and unless these morals have become part of the law, the courts cannot be used to enforce them. For example, it may not be moral for a person to tell a lie to another, but it will not generally be against the law (unless it was done to cheat someone out of their property or to insult them). Some laws, however, may be regarded as wrong by the majority of people in South Africa but they are still laws. For instance, many people think that the death penalty is moral, despite the fact that it is now unlawful. Similarly, many people think that laws that allow for abortion on demand are immoral. Other people, however, believe that these laws are justified. (These complex debates are discussed in Parts 2 and 4.)

Sometimes it may be difficult to decide whether an act that appears to be obviously unlawful should be regarded as immoral or wrong. Usually what most people regard as wrong has also been made illegal. For example, murder would generally be regarded as wrong by most people in South Africa.

Problem 4: The case of the shipwrecked sailors

no food no water

Three people Dan, Sam and Bob, who worked on a ship as sailors, were floating in a small boat after a storm sank their boat. The ship sank too soon for them to send a radio call for help. The three sailors were the only people who had not drowned. They had no food, no water and nothing to help them catch fish.

Bob, Dan and Sam agreed that one of them should be killed and eaten by the other two. But when it turned out to be him, Bob wasn't so keen anymore

if one died the others could eat him

The three men spoke about their problem: Dan, who knew about how ships travel, said they were about 1 600 kilometres from land, and that no ships were likely to pass near them. Sam, the ship's doctor, said that they could not live more than 30 days without food. They might be lucky and get some water from rain. He also said that if one of them died before the others, the other two could live for longer by eating the body of the dead person.

they killed and ate him

On the 25th day, Bob, who was very weak, suggested that the three should toss a coin and the loser should be killed and eaten by the other two. Dan and Sam agreed. Bob lost the toss and then refused to consent to being killed. Dan and Sam decided that Bob would die soon anyway and killed and began eating him.

on trial for murder

Five days later Dan and Sam were rescued by a passing ship and brought to land. They were then put on trial for murder. The law states: Any person who intentionally and unlawfully kills another is guilty of murder.

Questions

1. Should Dan and Sam be charged with murder?
2. If you were the lawyer for Dan and Sam what would be your arguments?
3. If you were the lawyer for the state (the prosecutor) what arguments would you make?
4. If they were found guilty (convicted), what should their punishment be?
5. What would be the purpose of convicting Dan and Sam?
6. What is the connection between law and morality in this case? Was it morally wrong for Dan and Sam to kill Bob? Was it morally wrong for Bob to change his mind after he lost the toss? Explain your answer.
7. Can someone act legally, but immorally? Can an act be morally right but unlawful?

the courts enforce the laws

The Constitution contains a Bill of Rights and is the supreme law of South Africa. Parliament is the main law making body in South Africa. Provided it acts within the Constitution and the Bill of Rights, Parliament can make new laws, change laws, give new rights or take people's rights away. In general, the courts enforce the laws that are made by Parliament. Parliament cannot, however, make laws that conflict with the Constitution. If Parliament makes a law that conflicts with the Constitution, certain courts, such as the Constitutional Court, have the power to rule that that law is invalid. In this way the courts protect peoples' rights.

unfair laws that conflict with the Constitution can be changed

Laws may act harshly on people. A law can be unfair and still be the law. Judges cannot change laws made by Parliament because they believe them unjust or unfair. However, certain courts in South Africa may change unjust or unfair laws that conflict with the Constitution.

Every society has recognised the need for some law even if the laws were not written – as was the case in South Africa before the European settlers arrived.

laws are necessary

People governing a society need rules to control the conduct of the community. Without laws there would be confusion, fear, and disorder. This does not mean that all laws are fair or even good; but imagine how people could take advantage of one another without laws or some set of rules.

Problem 5: Imagine there were no laws

imagine the chaos in a large city if there were no laws

Questions

1. If cities did not have traffic lights what would happen? What if they had traffic lights but no laws against going through a red light? What would happen?
2. What would happen if there were no laws against stealing?
3. Do you think people always need laws to make them do what is moral or fair?

1.2 Where law comes from, how it is made, and the different kinds of law

Outcomes

After completion of this section learners will be able to:

1. Demonstrate an understanding of where law comes from, how it is interpreted, and the different kinds of law.

Assessment criteria

1. An explanation is given of where South African law comes from and how it is made.
2. An explanation is given of how the Constitution operates.
3. Sets of facts are examined and decisions are taken on whether any rights in the Bill of Rights have been violated.
4. A set of facts in a case is examined and a decision is taken on whether the Constitutional Court should have abolished corporal punishment for juvenile offenders.
5. A set of facts is examined and a decision is taken on how the court would interpret the law.
6. A set of facts in a case is examined and a decision is taken on whether the judge calculated the damages correctly.
7. A set of facts is examined and a decision is taken on which acts were criminal and which were civil wrongs.

1.2.1 Where South African law comes from

pre-colonial law

Before the European settlers arrived at the Cape, the people of South Africa had their own law and rules. The pre-colonial rulers used *customary law* to govern the people. The law was based on traditions and customs.

law from Holland

In 1652 Jan Van Riebeeck arrived at the Cape. He brought with him the law of Holland. This was called *Roman-Dutch law*. For the next 150 years, Roman-Dutch law was the official law of the Cape.

law from England

In the early 1800s the British took over the rule of the Cape from the Dutch. They brought *English law* with them. This led to the influence of English law, but Roman-Dutch law remained dominant and continued to develop. However, the court procedure changed from the Dutch 'inquisitorial' system where the judges or magistrates ran the trials, to the English 'adversarial' system, where the lawyers run the trials and the judges or magistrates act as referees (see below para 1.4.2).

apartheid laws

In 1948 the National Party introduced apartheid, a political policy of racial segregation and discrimination. These laws were statute law made by the white minority Parliament and were not part of Roman-Dutch law or English law.

In 1990, Nelson Mandela was released from prison and the African National Congress and other organisations were unbanned. All political groupings then participated in the negotiation of a *Constitution* for South Africa. The drafters of the Constitution were influenced by the constitutions of many other countries. In 1993 the Interim Constitution with a Bill of Rights was passed, and it came into effect in 1994. In 1996 the final Constitution with a Bill of Rights was passed (see below para 1.2.2.1). South African law cannot conflict with the Constitution. If it does, it is invalid.

Constitution

The position in South Africa today is as follows:

Constitution

1. The Constitution is the supreme law of the country and all laws – customary law, common law and statute law – must be in line with the Constitution, otherwise the parts of the law that conflict with the Constitution will be declared invalid.

customary law

2. The application of customary law is usually limited to the courts of the chiefs and headmen, which operate in areas where communities still live according to customary law. Customary law is recognised in the Constitution but must be in line with it and the courts have sometimes taken note of indigenous concepts such as *ubuntu* (meaning 'humanity to others' or 'I am what I am because of who we all are').

Roman-Dutch law

2. Roman-Dutch law has remained the basis of the South African common-law system.

English law

3. English law has had an influence on South African law as it is today, especially in regard to court procedures and many of the statutes (see below para 1.2.2.3) that Parliament has passed regarding commercial transactions and court procedures.

South African law

4. South African common law is mainly Roman-Dutch with some English law and statute law (law made by Parliament) influences, and limited recognition of customary law.

statute law

5. Statute law is made by Parliament, the provincial legislatures and local authorities such as municipalities.

Problem 1: The origin of South African law

Questions

1 Where does South African law come from?
2. Which foreign legal system has had the greatest influence on South African law?
3. Do you think customary law is still important in South Africa? Give reasons for your answer.
4. What does the history of South African law tell us about where laws come from?

1.2.2 How South African law is made

In 1910, the four colonies of South Africa, the Cape Colony, the Orange Free State, Transvaal and Natal joined together to become the Union of South Africa. This created one central system of government with the former colonies as provinces. The central government was given the supreme law-making power.

levels of government

Under the 1996 Constitution, South Africa now has nine provinces: the Eastern Cape, Free State, Gauteng, KwaZulu-Natal, Mpumalanga, Northern Cape, Limpopo, North West and Western Cape. It also has three levels of government: national, provincial and local. At the national level, South Africa is governed by Parliament, which consists of the National Assembly and the National Council of Provinces. The provinces are governed by provincial legislatures. At the local level, municipal areas are governed by municipal councils.

legislation

While the Constitution is the supreme law of the country, each of the above bodies – Parliament, provincial legislatures and municipal councils – has the power to make laws. Laws passed by these bodies are called *legislation*. These laws are written. If a law is made by Parliament it is called a *statute* or an *act*. If a law is made by a provincial legislature it is called a *provincial* act. If a law is made by a municipal council it is called a *by-law*.

common law

If a specific matter is not governed by legislation then the *common law* applies. The common law is not made by Parliament, or any of the bodies mentioned, and is not written down in statutes. Instead, it comes mainly from Roman-Dutch law. We will discuss the Constitution, statute law and common law separately.

1.2.2.1 The Constitution

the Constitution is supreme

The Constitution sets out the basic laws according to which South Africa is governed. Before 1994, South Africa had a 'sovereign' Parliament. This meant that the courts, and ordinary people, could not challenge the laws made by Parliament. Since 1994, however, Parliament has not been sovereign. Instead, the Constitution is the *supreme law* of South Africa. This means that if Parliament makes a law that conflicts with the Constitution certain courts can declare these laws invalid.

the Constitution sets out how the country is governed

The 1993 Interim Constitution and the 1996 final Constitution were South Africa's first democratic Constitutions. Before 1994 (the year in which democracy was introduced) the rules according to which South Africa was governed were racist. For example, black people could not vote and people of different races had to live in different areas. South Africa's Constitution is now democratic; for example, all South Africans over the age of 18 may vote and all South Africans are guaranteed basic rights, such as the freedom to live where they want.

Most people are aware that the Constitution gives them basic human rights (see below). However, not everyone is aware that the Bill of Rights is only 1 out of 14 chapters in the Constitution. The remaining chapters mainly set out how the country should be governed. The Constitution describes the laws for the main branches of government: Parliament (which makes laws), the executive (which consists of the President and the Ministers and which executes laws) and the courts (which resolve legal disputes by interpreting the law). This is called the 'separation of powers' and is found in democratic countries to prevent dictatorship by making sure that the executive does not hold too much power. The Constitution also sets out laws for other important branches of government, such as the police and defence force, and independent bodies that protect human rights such as the Human Rights Commission and the Public Protector.

'separation of powers'

Problem 2: Some questions on the Constitution

Questions

1. What is meant by the 'separation of powers'. What are the main branches of government? Explain what each of them does. Why is the separation of powers important?
2. Do you feel that having a Constitution and a Bill of Rights makes any difference to your life? How do you think that your life may differ from what it might have been if you had lived when South Africa had a 'sovereign' Parliament? Give reasons for your answer.

Bill of Rights

The Bill of Rights sets out basic human rights. All South Africans are entitled to these rights. These rights protect citizens in their dealings with the state (eg the Bill of Rights gives rights to people who have been arrested – see Part 2). However, these rights also protect people in their dealings with one another (for instance, you cannot be fired from your job just because your employer does not like your race or because you are HIV positive). If legislation or any part of the common law violates a human right, certain courts may declare that law invalid.

The Constitution contains the following types of rights:

civil and political rights

1. Civil and political rights. These rights protect people against the state and against one another. Important examples of these rights in the Constitution are the rights to equality and freedom from unfair discrimination (including on the grounds of race, gender, sex, pregnancy, marital status, ethnic or social origin, colour, sexual orientation, age, disability, religion, conscience, belief, culture, language and birth); dignity; life; freedom and security of person; privacy; freedom of religion; belief and opinion; freedom of expression; freedom of association; freedom of movement and residence; and freedom of trade, occupation and profession (see below Bill of Rights).

economic and social rights

2. Economic and social rights. These rights require the state to take positive action to improve people's standards of living within its available resources. The Constitution includes a right to basic education. It also includes rights of access to adequate housing and access to health care services. This means that the state must take steps to realise these rights but is not expected to do so immediately.

environmental, cultural and developmental rights

3. Environmental, cultural and developmental rights. These rights relate to groups of people. For example, the Constitution contains a right to an environment that is not harmful to one's health or well-being. The Constitution says that this is also for the benefit of 'future generations.' The Constitution also provides for a right to language and culture.

The South African Bill of Rights

The following rights are found in the Bill of Rights in Chapter 2 of the South African Constitution:

1. The right to be treated equally and to be free from unfair discrimination (s 9).
2. The right to respect and protection of dignity (s 10).
3. The right to life (s 11).
4. The right to freedom and security of the person (s 12).
5. The right to freedom from servitude and forced labour (s 13).
6. The right to privacy (s 14).
7. The right to freedom of conscience, religion, thought, belief and opinion (s 15).
8. The right to freedom of speech, expression, artistic creativity and scientific research (s 16).
9. The right to assemble, demonstrate and petition peacefully and unarmed (s 17).
10. The right to freedom of association (s 18).
11. The right to join and campaign for a political party of choice (s 19).
12. The right to vote in secret (s 19).
13. The right to hold and keep citizenship (s 20).
14. The right to freedom of movement (s 21).
15. The right to choose a place of residence (s 21).
16. The right to enter, remain in and leave the country (s 21).
17. The right of every citizen to choose and practice their trade, profession or occupation freely – subject to regulation (s 22).
18. The right to fair labour practices (s 23).
19. The right to an environment that is not harmful to health or well-being (s 24).
20. The right not to be arbitrarily deprived of property (s 25).
21. The right of access to adequate housing within available resources (s 26).
22. The right of access to health care, food, water and social security (s 27).
23. The right of access to reproductive health care (s 27).
24. The right not to be refused emergency medical treatment (s 27).
25. The right of children to a name, nationality and parental care (s 28).
26. The right of children to security, basic nutrition and basic health and social services (s 28).
27. The right of children to be provided with a lawyer by the state in civil cases affecting children where the interests of justice so require (s 28).
28. The right to basic education and access to educational institutions (s 29).
29. The right to language and culture of choice (s 30).
30. The right not to be denied the right to enjoy one's culture, to practise one's religion and use one's language (s 31).

the Bill of Rights sets out basic human rights

31. The right of access to information (s 32).
32. The right to be treated fairly and to be given reasons by administrative bodies (s 33).
33. The right of access to independent and impartial courts (s 34).
34. The right to employ a lawyer and to be provided with a lawyer by the state in criminal cases where the interests of justice so require (s 35).
35. The right to be informed of reasons for arrest (s 35).
36. The right to remain silent and to be presumed innocent (s 35).
37. The right to be brought before a court within 4. hours of arrest (s 35).
38. The right to bail if the interests of justice permit, subject to reasonable conditions (s 35).
39. The right to a fair trial (s 35).

Problem 3: Which rights in the Bill of Rights were violated?

Consider each of the situations below and decide which rights in the Bill of Rights have been violated – give reasons for your answers:

1. An unemployed person is knocked down by a car in front of a private hospital and is seriously injured, requiring an urgent blood transfusion. The private hospital refuses to treat him because he has no money and says that he must be taken to a state hospital.
2. A foreigner who is legally employed and resident in South Africa is accused of theft and arrested. He is brought before a magistrate one week after his arrest and is refused bail.

3. A refugee who makes crafts while sitting on a pavement outside a supermarket is arrested by the police. The police confiscate his craft materials without giving him a receipt and tell him that he may no longer work there.

4. A domestic worker is dismissed from her job when her employer finds out that she has tested positive for HIV.
5. A baby is badly injured in a motor accident and requires an urgent blood transfusion. The baby's parents refuse to allow the baby to have a blood transfusion for religious reasons.

limitation of rights

All these rights are indivisible and may only be limited under certain circumstances. First, there must be a law that applies to all people. Second, that law must be reasonable and justifiable in an open and democratic society based on human dignity, equality and freedom. Finally, a right may only be limited if it serves an important goal, and there is no other way to achieve that goal that would limit the right less (eg there may be less cruel punishments than the death penalty or whipping of convicted persons).

Problem 4: A case about corporal punishment

corporal punishment is unconstitutional

The Criminal Procedure Act used to allow for juvenile criminals (ie criminals under the age of 18) to be whipped. However, in 1995, after the Interim Constitution was passed, the Constitutional Court, in a case called *S v Williams*, was asked to decide whether this type of punishment was unconstitutional. First, the court considered whether whipping violated any of the rights in the Bill of Rights. The court held that it violated the rights to dignity, not to be subjected to torture and not to be subjected to cruel, inhuman or degrading punishment. Next, the court asked whether the violation of these rights was justifiable. The court held that other, more humane (less cruel) forms of punishment could achieve the same goals as whipping. Also, whipping would not deter juveniles from committing crimes more than other forms of punishment. The court held therefore that whipping juvenile criminals was unconstitutional, and the relevant sections of the Criminal Procedure Act were removed.

Questions

1. What rights did the Constitutional Court say were violated by sentencing a juvenile criminal to be whipped?
2. Why did the Constitutional Court say that the violation of these rights was not justifiable?
3. Do you agree with the judgment of the court? Do you think juveniles should be whipped for certain crimes? Give reasons for your answer.

1.2.2.2 Common law

common law is not made by Parliament

The common law comes mainly from Roman-Dutch law, English law, and sometimes even ancient Roman law. The common law is the law not made by Parliament, a provincial body or a municipal council. Since 1994, in keeping with the spirit of the Constitution, the courts have also taken note of customary law and law brought to South Africa by other communities, such as the Islamic and Hindu communities. Like all law, the common law may not conflict with the Constitution. Judges are required to develop the common law to make it fit in with the Constitution. Judges in South Africa have developed the common law by interpreting and applying it to individual cases. Common law therefore develops from the rules made by judges in court decisions and written down in their judgments. Sometimes new decisions are taken by judges as to what the common law means. These decisions state how the law must be interpreted in future and are called 'precedents'.

judgments and precedents

The way in which the common law has been developed is written down in the decisions of judges in the High Court. In the High Court the people involved in a dispute (called the 'parties') each present their case by calling witnesses and arguing about the law. The judge then makes a decision about the case. This decision is called a judgment.

decisions by judges are called judgments

Problem 5: Statute law and common law

Questions

1 What is the difference between statute law and common law?
2. Who can change the common law?
3. Who can change the statute law?
4. If a town passes an unfair by-law, how do you think the law can be changed?

Is there a rule covering the facts?

A court decision or judgment is made in one of three ways:

1. The judges look at the law to see if there is a rule that covers the facts of the case. If there is a rule, they apply it to the case.
2. Sometimes there is no rule that covers the facts of the case. Then the judges must make a decision based on their own opinion. They do this by looking at the facts of the case and the existing law. The judgment sometimes includes a new rule of law. This is called a 'precedent'.
3. Sometimes there is a rule that covers the facts of the case, but it has always been applied in a particular way. A person may argue that the rule can be applied in a different way.

precedent

applying the rule differently

The judge must then decide if this new approach is correct. If the judge decides that the new approach is correct, he or she has given a new interpretation or explanation of the law. This judgment can also be called a precedent.

courts are guided by precedents

In law the courts are guided by precedents. A court must follow precedents set by courts that are higher than it. The highest courts in South Africa are the Supreme Court of Appeal (the highest court in all matters except constitutional matters) and the Constitutional Court (the highest court in constitutional matters). If a precedent has been set by the Supreme Court of Appeal in a non-constitutional case, only the Supreme Court of Appeal or Parliament can change that precedent. If, however, a precedent has been set by the Constitutional Court on lower courts must follow the decisions of higher courts

a constitutional matter, even Parliament may be bound by it and only the court itself can change it. Precedents set (ie cases decided) by the Constitutional Court and the Supreme Court of Appeal (in non-constitutional cases) must be followed by all the High Courts and magistrates' courts. Similarly, precedents set by the High Courts must be followed by the magistrates' courts.

Problem 6: A case of pain and suffering

Radebe and his friends threw stones at Hough and his friend. Hough went to fetch a gun

In 1949 a case called *Radebe v Hough* was argued in the Appellate Division. (The Supreme Court of Appeal was previously called the Appellate Division.) Radebe, an African, had been shot and injured by Hough, a white person. Radebe and some friends had thrown stones at Hough while they were out walking. Hough went to fetch a gun and he and his friend chased Radebe and his two friends into a room where shots were fired. Radebe was seriously injured. He was in hospital for 10 days and suffered severe pain in his private parts for three months. The Witwatersrand Local Division of the Supreme Court (now called the High Court) found Hough liable for assault and gave Radebe compensation of R32. The court took into account that Radebe was a poor man and an African for whom R32 in those days would have been a lot of money.

Radebe appealed to the Appellate Division saying that he had not been awarded enough damages. He also argued that it was wrong to take his race and the amount of money he earned (R4 a week) into account when compensating him for pain and suffering.

Hough argued that the courts in Southern Rhodesia (now Zimbabwe) and Natal (now KwaZulu-Natal) had previously said that poor people like Africans for whom a little money meant a lot should only receive a small amount in these cases. Hough argued that this was the correct approach in pain and suffering cases.

rich and poor suffer the same pain

The Appellate Division held that the earlier cases were wrong and that when giving damages for pain and suffering a court should not look at the race, or culture or financial position of the injured person. Both rich and poor people of different races and cultures suffer the same amount of pain if they are injured. The Appellate Division awarded Radebe R400 damages, a lot of money in those days. (Radebe was also entitled to his lost wages.)

Questions

1. What was the precedent set in this case?
2. Which courts have to follow this precedent?
3. Which courts would have to follow this precedent if it had been set by the KwaZulu-Natal Provincial Division of the High Court?
4. Which body can change a precedent made by the Supreme Court of Appeal?
5. If you were a judge, would you have decided in favour of Radebe's or Hough's argument? Give reasons for your answer.

1.2.2.3 Statute law

statute law is made by Parliament, provincial legislatures and municipal councils

Statute law is written law. It is made by Parliament, provincial legislatures and municipal councils. However, Parliament, provincial legislatures and municipal councils may not make laws about anything: The Constitution states what each body may make laws about. Parliament may make laws about almost any matter. There are some matters, however, such as provincial roads, that only provincial legislatures may make laws about.

all South Africans over the age of 18 years may vote

Parliament is the most important law-making body, and so we will focus on how it makes laws. A parliament should always consist of representatives of the community, chosen through free and fair elections that are held regularly, in which all adult citizens may vote. In the past, due to the South African government's apartheid policy, black people were not allowed to vote and were not represented in Parliament. Since 1994 all South Africans over 18 years of age have been entitled to vote, and have a say in who makes the laws that govern South Africa.

Bills are introduced by Cabinet Ministers

When a need for a law arises, a Bill is introduced in the National Assembly by the Cabinet Minister responsible for that topic. (Ministers run the different government departments). The Bill is debated by the members of the National Assembly, who may propose amendments to the Bill. Eventually, the members vote on whether the Bill should be passed.

the National Council of Provinces must approve all Bills

If the Bill is approved by the National Assembly it is referred to the National Council of Provinces for approval. The purpose of the National Council of Provinces is to ensure that the provinces have a say regarding national legislation that affects the provinces. The Bill is also debated, and voted on, in the National Council of Provinces. If it is rejected, and the two houses are in disagreement,

Bills signed by the President become Acts

the Constitution says how the dispute must be resolved. If the National Council of Provinces approves the Bill it is referred to the President, who signs it. The Bill then becomes a statute or an 'Act'. The Act must be in line with the Constitution, otherwise it or parts of it may be declared invalid by the Constitutional Court.

Acts are published in the *Government Gazette*

Acts are published in a Government newspaper called the *Government Gazette*. The statutes of South Africa are collected in *Butterworths Statutes of South Africa* and *Juta's Statutes of South Africa*, which are available in most university law libraries. Some examples of statute law are the Criminal Procedure Act of 1977, which sets out the procedures in the criminal courts, and the Consumer Protection Act of 2008, which protects consumers.

statutes may allow Ministers of government departments to make regulations

Sometimes a statute may give power to a person (eg a Minister) or a body (eg the Department of Correctional Services) to make 'regulations' (rules). These regulations are not written in the Act, but are published in the *Government Gazette* and other newspapers. The most important regulations can be found in most university law libraries. The regulations must not conflict with the Constitution or the Act. If regulations conflict with the Constitution they will be invalid.

Acts that conflict with the Constitution are invalid

As mentioned, if Parliament passes legislation that conflicts with the Constitution, which is the supreme law of South Africa, that law is invalid. To give effect to this principle, the Constitution states that certain courts may test legislation against its provisions. If legislation conflicts with the Constitution, those courts may declare the legislation invalid.

When a statute does not conflict with the Constitution, the courts must apply the statute. To do so, the courts must interpret the statute. Often, to do this, the courts must look at the intention of Parliament or the law-making body. The following problem shows the difficulty of deciding what a law intends.

Problem 7: No vehicles in the park!

Are skateboards, bicycles and prams also vehicles?

The town of Tandi has established a lovely park in its centre. The town council wishes to preserve the feeling of nature, undisturbed by city noise, traffic, pollution and crowding. It is a place where people can go and find grass, trees, flowers and quiet. In addition, there are playgrounds and picnic areas. At all entrances to the park, the following sign has been posted:

'NO VEHICLES IN THE PARK'

The law seems clear, but some disputes have arisen over the interpretation of the law. Interpret the law in the following cases, keeping in mind what the law says (called 'the letter of the law') and what the lawmakers intended (called 'the intent of the law' Note: The dictionary defines a 'vehicle' as something on wheels that carries people or things.)

Questions

1. John Reddy lost his legs in a car accident and uses a wheelchair. He wishes to use his wheelchair to visit the park in order to enjoy the garden and the quiet environment.

a place of peace and quiet

2. There are many rubbish bins in the park so that people can deposit litter there and keep the park clean. The sanitation department wants to drive in to collect the rubbish.
3. Two police cars are chasing a suspected bank robber. If one car cuts through the park, it can get in front of the suspect car and trap the robber between the police cars.

Are the police allowed to drive through the park?

4. An ambulance has a dying car accident victim in it and is racing to hospital. The shortest route is through the park.
5. Some of the children who visit the park want to ride their bicycles and skateboards there.
6. Mrs Dube wants to take her baby to the park in a pram.
7. A memorial to the town's citizens who died in the Second World War is being constructed. An army truck donated by the government is to be placed beside it.

1.2.3 Kinds of law

There are two main kinds of law: criminal and civil.

the state brings criminal cases to court

Criminal law controls how people in society behave and what they are expected to do. In South Africa the 'state' brings a legal action against a person charged with a crime. If he or she is found guilty by the court the person concerned can be imprisoned, fined (made to pay money), or punished in some other way. Therefore we can say: 'A crime is a wrong against the state for which the wrongdoer (criminal) is punished by the state'.

Civil law controls how individual people or groups of people behave towards each other. The state is generally not directly involved as a party to cases that result from disputes between private people. (It may, however, be involved as a party if it is suing, or being sued, like a private person for a wrongful act, for example, if government property is damaged, or a government official injures somebody without good cause.)

a civil case is usually brought by a private person

A civil case is usually brought by a person (called the 'plaintiff') who feels that he or she has been wronged (eg injured, or his or her property damaged) by another (called the 'defendant'). If the plaintiff wins the case, the defendant will usually be ordered by the court to pay compensation. Sometimes the court may also order a defendant to do, or stop doing, something (eg to deliver something he or she has sold, or to stop damaging the plaintiff's property).

Civil cases usually deal with actions for damage to property, injuries to people, consumer problems, employment troubles, family problems, etc. We can summarise this by saying: 'A civil wrong is a wrong against an individual for which the wrongdoer must pay compensation to the injured person'.

sometimes an act may be both a civil wrong and a crime

Sometimes a person's act may result in both criminal and civil actions. For example, a person who assaults (wrongfully and intentionally injures) someone can be prosecuted by the state and, if convicted, punished for committing a crime. (Crimes and criminal law will be discussed in Part 2.) He or she could be sued for damages by the person injured in the assault and made to pay compensation for medical expenses, lost wages and pain and suffering. The criminal action for assault will be brought in a different court from the one where the civil action for damages is heard.

Problem 8: The case of the juvenile delinquents

John and Peter are bored. For excitement they steal bicycles belonging to people at their school. They decide to go into town and on their way ride through a red traffic light. They go into a radio shop and use their savings to buy a small radio. The shopkeeper sells them a radio which he knows does not work properly. The radio works for a couple of hours and stops. John and Peter become angry and hurry back to the radio shop. On their way John knocks over an old woman and injures her. The boys go into the shop and angrily assault the dishonest shopkeeper.

Examine the pictures and answer the questions below. Give reasons for your answers.

1. John and Peter steal bicycles belonging to people at their school.

2. On their way to town they ride through a red traffic light.

3. The shopkeeper sells them a radio which he knows does not work properly.

4. The radio works for a couple of hours and then stops. They become angry.

5. On their way back to the shop John knocks over an old lady and injures her.

6. The boys go into the shop and angrily assault the dishonest shopkeeper

Questions

1. Which of these acts are unlawful?
2. List the acts that you think are crimes.
3. List the acts that you think are civil wrongs.
4. List the acts that you think may be both crimes and civil wrongs.

1.3 The courts and settling disputes outside of the courts

Outcomes

After completion of this section learners will be able to:

1. Demonstrate an understanding of how the courts and other dispute resolution mechanisms work

Assessment criteria

1. An explanation of the different courts in South Africa is given.
2. A decision is taken on how magistrates should be appointed.
3. A set of facts in a case is examined and a decision is taken on whether people were entitled to take the law into their own hands.
4. A stated problem is solved using negotiation, mediation and arbitration.
5. Sets of facts are examined and a decision is taken on the best method of resolving different disputes.

1.3.1 The different courts in South Africa

a civil court: clockwise from left: plaintiff, advocate for plaintiff, clerk, judge, judge's registrar, advocate for defendant, defendant

courts decide disputes

The courts are used to make people obey the law. They do this by deciding disputes brought to them. In civil cases they order compensation by law-breakers. In criminal cases they order punishment of law-breakers. Another function of the courts is to interpret and apply the law to individual cases. Sometimes when the higher courts make new decisions these are called 'precedents' (see above para 1.2.2.2).

There are the following courts in South Africa:

Constitutional Court

Constitutional Court: This court is the highest court in South Africa for constitutional matters and may only hear constitutional matters (see below para 1.3.1.1).

Supreme Court of Appeal

Supreme Court of Appeal: This is the highest court in South Africa in all matters except constitutional cases (see below). The court does not conduct trials, but only hears appeals (see below para 1.3.1.2).

High Courts

High Courts: These are the higher or superior courts which usually hear more serious criminal or civil cases. There are only a few High Courts. They do not hear as many cases as the magistrates' courts. They hear about 5 000 criminal cases a year. It is more expensive to bring an action in the High Court than in the magistrate's court (see below para 1.3.1.3).

magistrates' courts

Magistrates' courts: These are the lower or inferior courts which deal with less serious criminal and civil cases. There is usually a magistrate's court in every town. It is cheaper to bring cases in the magistrate's court than the High Court. Magistrates' courts may be divided into district and regional magistrates' courts. District magistrates' courts are presided over by ordinary magistrates. Regional courts are presided over by regional magistrates who hear more serious criminal and civil cases. District courts hear about 600 000 cases a year, while regional courts hear about 60 000 cases a year (see below para 1.3.1.4).

small claims courts

Small claims courts: These are the newest courts in South Africa and have been set up in a few of the major towns. These courts deal with small civil claims of less than R15 000.

courts of chiefs and headmen

Courts of chiefs and headmen: In rural areas, the chiefs and headmen of certain African communities have their own courts. These courts apply the customary law of the specific community.

We will look at each of these courts beginning with the Constitutional Court.

1.3.1.1 Constitutional Court

the Constitutional Court is the highest court in the country for constitutional cases

The Constitutional Court is in Braamfontein, Johannesburg. The court consists of 11 judges. It can only hear constitutional cases and issues connected with such cases. For constitutional cases, it is the highest court in South Africa. The Constitutional Court is, in part, a court of appeal and hears appeals against constitutional judgments of the High Courts and the Supreme Court of Appeal. However, there are certain issues that only the Constitutional Court can decide and, because no other court can hear these cases, it does not function as a court of appeal when hearing these. For example, only the Constitutional Court can decide on the constitutionality of an amendment to the Constitution. Finally, when a High Court or the Supreme Court of Appeal declares that an Act of Parliament, a Provincial Act or the conduct of the President is unconstitutional, the order will only come into effect once it has been confirmed by the Constitutional Court.

1.3.1.2 Supreme Court of Appeal

Supreme Court of Appeal

The highest court of appeal in all cases (except constitutional cases) is the Supreme Court of Appeal in Bloemfontein. This is a court of appeal only. It does not hear trials; it hears appeals from the High Courts. The court can decide appeals in constitutional cases. There are, however, certain cases that only the Constitutional Court can decide, eg although the Supreme Court of Appeal can declare an Act of Parliament, a Provincial Act or the conduct of the President unconstitutional, such an order will only take effect once it is confirmed by the Constitutional Court. All cases in the Supreme Court of Appeal are heard by three or five judges. These judges are appointed from the ordinary judges who sit in the High Courts. Decisions by the Supreme Court of Appeal must be followed by all the High Courts and magistrates' courts in South Africa.

the highest court in the country for non-constitutional cases

1.3.1.3 High Court

a High Court can hear any type of criminal or civil case

A High Court can hear any type of criminal or civil case. Usually, however, the High Court will only hear criminal cases that may result in serious forms of punishment (life imprisonment or longer or a fine of more than R400 000). A charge of treason must always be heard by the High Court. The High Court hears civil cases involving claims of more than R400 000. There are also certain civil matters that must be heard by a High Court (eg interpretation of wills, declaration of a person as insane). A High Court may also decide any constitutional matter, except for some matters that can only be heard by the Constitutional Court. A High Court can, however, rule on the constitutionality of an Act of Parliament, a Provincial Act or the conduct of the President. Such a ruling will only come into effect once it is confirmed by the Constitutional Court. High Courts also hear appeals and reviews from the magistrates' courts (see below para 1.3.1.7).

a High Court ruling that an Act is unconstitutional must be confirmed by the Constitutional Court

cases are heard by judges

All cases in High Courts are heard by judges. In the past all judges were appointed from senior advocates. However, in 1995 the first advocate who had not obtained senior status was appointed as a judge. In the same year the first attorney was appointed as a judge. University lecturers and magistrates may now also be appointed as judges. The President appoints judges on the advice of the Judicial Service Commission, an independent body established for this purpose.

Civil and criminal cases are usually only heard by one judge. However, if the case goes on appeal it must be heard by at least two judges.

judges may be helped by assessors

In complex matters a judge may be helped by one or two other people called 'assessors' who are not judges. Assessors are usually retired lawyers, magistrates and university lecturers who help the judge decide the facts – not the law. The judge decides the law.

Previously, there was a division of what was called the Supreme Court for each of the four provinces of South Africa. Under apartheid there was also a Supreme

Court in each of the so-called independent African 'homeland' states. There are now nine provinces and the 'independent' states no longer exist. However, in terms of the transitional arrangements of the Constitution each division of the former Supreme Court is now regarded as a High Court. The following High Courts exist:

High Courts in main cities

- Eastern Cape High Court (Bhisho)
- Free State High Court (Bloemfontein)
- Western Cape High Court (Cape Town)
- KwaZulu-Natal High Court (Durban)
- Eastern Cape High Court (Grahamstown)
- South Gauteng High Court (Johannesburg)
- Northern Cape High Court (Kimberley)
- KwaZulu-Natal High Court (Pietermaritzburg)
- Eastern Cape High Court (Port Elizabeth)
- North Gauteng High Court (Pretoria)
- Limpopo High Court (Thohoyandou)
- Eastern Cape High Court (Mthatha)
- North West High Court, Mafikeng (Mmabatho) and
- Polokwane Circuit Court of the North Gauteng High Court, Pretoria.

permission must be obtained to appeal from a High Court to the Supreme Court of Appeal

Before appealing to the Supreme Court of Appeal against a High Court decision the person wishing to appeal must get permission from the High Court that made the decision. The High Courts must follow the decisions of the Constitutional Court in constitutional cases and the decisions of the Supreme Court of Appeal in non-constitutional cases.

1.3.1.4 Magistrates' courts

magistrates' courts

There are nearly 350 magisterial districts in South Africa. The magisterial districts are served by more than 400 magistrates' courts involving more than 1 400 magistrates and 325 regional magistrates. Unlike the High Court judges, the powers of magistrates are limited. For example, they may not rule on the constitutionality of any legislation (statute) or the conduct of the President. Magistrates' courts may be divided into different groups: criminal courts and civil courts (regional and district).

1.3.1.4.1 Criminal courts

Regional magistrates' courts

regional magistrates' courts

The regional magistrates' courts have more power than the ordinary magistrates' courts. The regional magistrates' courts may hear all criminal offences, except treason. They may sentence a person to a maximum fine of R400 000 or imprisonment including life imprisonment. They usually hear cases involving serious crimes like murder, rape, armed robbery and serious assaults.

district magistrates' courts

District magistrates' courts

The district magistrates' courts have less power than the regional magistrates' courts. They may sentence a person to a maximum fine of R200 000 or three years' imprisonment. Some statutes may extend these powers (eg laws dealing with drug crimes). They may not try cases of murder, rape, and treason.

1.3.1.4.2 Civil courts

Regional magistrates' courts

regional magistrates' courts

In civil cases the regional magistrates can hear claims of up to R400 000. However, like district magistrates' courts, they cannot hear actions for interpretation of wills (documents saying how people want their property distributed after their death) and whether someone is insane. They can, however, hear divorce cases.

District magistrates' courts

district magistrates' courts

In civil cases the ordinary magistrates' courts cannot usually hear claims involving more than R200 000. They also cannot hear certain actions like divorce, interpretation of wills (documents saying how people want their property distributed after their death) and whether someone is insane.

In the magistrates' courts all matters are heard by magistrates. Magistrates are civil servants who are usually appointed from people who have worked as prosecutors and clerks in the Department of Justice. In the past magistrates were appointed by the Minister of Justice, mainly from the ranks of prosecutors. Since 1994 increasing numbers of magistrates have been appointed from private practitioners. In order to achieve greater independence, a Magistrates Commission has been established that deals with matters such as the appointment or removal from office of magistrates, and eventually all courts will fall under the Chief Justice.

Problem 1: How should magistrates be appointed?

Some people say that magistrates cannot give fair decisions because they are paid by the government. People also say that most magistrates have only worked as prosecutors and should spend some time doing ordinary legal work as lawyers. Others defend the system by saying that magistrates are trained to be independent. Furthermore, prosecutors get good experience in criminal cases, which is useful when they later sit as magistrates to decide the truth. Most ordinary lawyers do not do much criminal work.

Questions

1. Do you think that it is better for magistrates to be appointed by the Magistrates Commission instead of the Minister of Justice? Give reasons for your answer.
2. Give arguments in favour of the present system of appointing magistrates through the Magistrates Commission.

3. Give arguments against the present system of appointing magistrates.
4. Should the system be changed? Give reasons for your answer.

appeals

A person involved in a criminal or civil case can ask the High Court to examine the decision of the magistrate's court and decide whether it was correct. The person asks the High Court to change the decision of the magistrate's court. This is called an 'appeal'. If a person believes that the proceedings in the magistrate's court were unlawful or unfair, he or she can bring the case to the High Court. This is called a 'review'.

1.3.1.5 Small claims court

small claims courts

claims under R15 000

no appeals allowed

no lawyers allowed

Small claims courts were introduced in 1985. They allow people to go to court without lawyers for civil claims of not more than R15 000. Very few documents are needed. No lawyers are allowed to represent people bringing and defending claims in the small claims court. There is no appeal against a decision by the court. If the court has been biased or did not allow one of the parties to give his or her side of the case it can be taken on 'review'.

small claims court commissioners

do it yourself

In the small claims court, cases are heard by Commissioners who are appointed by the Minister of Justice. Commissioners are usually practising advocates and attorneys (see below para 1.4.1.2) who hear cases in the evenings after work. It is very cheap to go to the small claims court because people can bring or defend the cases themselves (see below para 1.5.2). Most claims in the small claims court usually involve consumer complaints, labour disputes (mainly involving unpaid wages), and damages for motor collisions.

The small claims court is much more informal than other courts. From left: the plaintiff, the commissioner and the defendant

1.3.1.6 Courts of chiefs and headmen

courts of chiefs and headmen

Chiefs' and headmen's courts – there are very few headwomen – have restricted civil and criminal jurisdiction. This means that there are limits on the type of cases they may hear. They apply the customary law of the community in question.

No legal representation is allowed. If a person involved in a case before one of these courts is unhappy with the decision, he or she may start again in, or appeal to, the magistrate's court.

special courts for disputes between Africans

Problem 2: Should there be separate traditional courts for Africans?

Questions

1. Do you think there should be separate traditional courts for Africans? Give reasons for your answer.
2. Should the system be changed? If so, how?

1.3.1.7 Trials, appeals and reviews

1.3.1.7.1 Trials

the court considers evidence

Trials are very different from appeals (see below). During trials the court listens to evidence from witnesses and sees physical evidence (like a weapon used to commit a murder), considers the evidence and decides which facts are in dispute. The judge or magistrate makes a decision called a 'judgment'. The losing party may be able to appeal to a higher court. The magistrates' courts and the High Courts act as trial courts.

1.3.1.7.2 Appeals

appeal to a higher court

In an appeal, the party who has lost in a trial court presents arguments asking the appeal court to change the decision of the trial court. The other party presents arguments supporting the decision of the trial court. The losing party can appeal to an appeal court only if the trial court has made a mistake about the facts or the law in the case.

a party should employ a lawyer when making an appeal

If a case is heard in a magistrate's court, it may go on appeal to the nearest High Court. From there, it may go on appeal to the Supreme Court of Appeal. Finally, if the case deals with a constitutional matter it may go on appeal to the Constitutional Court. Similarly, if a case is heard as a trial by a High Court (by one judge – not as an appeal) it may go on appeal to a 'Full Bench' of the High Court in the province concerned (ie three judges), and/or to the Supreme Court of Appeal and, if it is a constitutional matter, then to the Constitutional Court. In certain rare cases it is possible to go from a magistrate's court or High Court directly to the Constitutional Court, such as in urgent cases that are in the public interest. The Constitutional Court has to give permission for this to happen. Legal documents have to be drawn up for an appeal and a lawyer should be employed. The person who loses the appeal usually has to pay the costs of the party who wins. It is very expensive to take a case on appeal.

In general, however, the appeal process can be shown as follows:

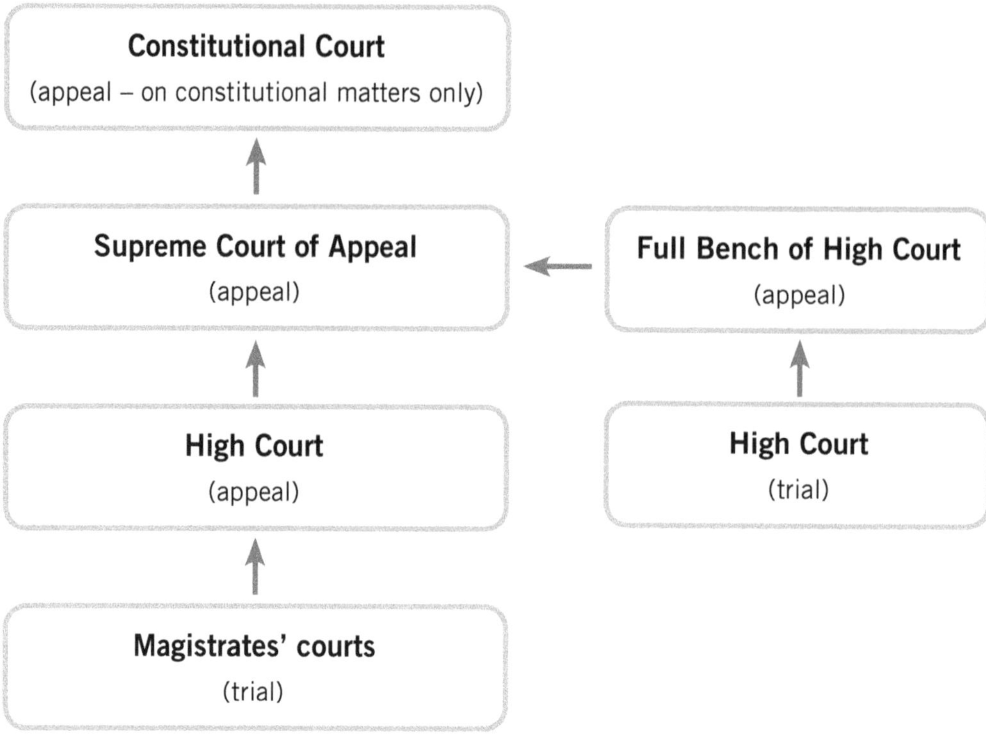

Case study: An appeal against a mistake by a magistrate

Mafu was arrested for breaking the curfew laws when his car broke down at night

In the case of *State v Mafu* in 1966, Mafu was charged with being in a public street when a curfew law said that nobody should be on the street at that time.

Mafu would have been home in time, but his car had broken down and the only way he could get home was to walk.

charged with breaking curfew laws

The Magistrate found Mafu guilty of breaking the curfew laws.

Mafu appealed to the Supreme Court (this is what the High Court used to be called) saying that the magistrate had made a mistake about the law, because the law does not expect a person to do something that is impossible. Because his car had broken down it was impossible for him to get home before the curfew.

The Appeal Court agreed with Mafu and he was found not guilty.

In most cases the courts will assist people who are expected to do something impossible. Usually the law does not make it a crime for people not to do something that is impossible.

1.3.1.7.3 Review

review by a higher court

If a person believes that the procedure followed in a magistrates' court or High Court was unfair (eg the magistrate or judge was biased), according to the law he or she can take the case on review to a higher court.

automatic review

In criminal cases where an accused without a lawyer is sentenced to a period of imprisonment of more than three months or a fine of more than R2 500 by a magistrate of less than seven years' experience, the sentence will be automatically reviewed by a judge. Sentences imposed on an unrepresented person by a magistrate of more than seven years' experience will only be automatically reviewed if they exceed six months of imprisonment or a fine exceeds R5 000. In review cases the clerk of the court must send the judge all the relevant documents.

Problem 3: Which court should be used?

1. Mary is caught shoplifting a cheap dress in Durban

2. John is charged with raping a woman in Pretoria

3. Govan murders his wife in Pietermaritzburg

4. Bheki buys a TV that does not work from a shop in Port Elizabeth for R5 000

5. Peter buys a car from a garage in Johannesburg for R50 000. It breaks down three days later

6. Vusi and Ernest, who live in a village in KwaZulu-Natal, have a dispute about who owns certain cows

Questions

Answer the following questions, giving reason for your answers.

1. Mary is caught shoplifting a cheap dress from a shop in Durban. In which court is she likely to appear? If she is convicted, to which court should she appeal?
2. John is charged with raping a woman in Pretoria. In which court will he appear? If he is convicted, to which court should he appeal?
3. Govan murders his wife in Pietermaritzburg. In which court will he appear? If he is convicted and wishes to appeal, which court should he approach?
4. Bheki buys a TV that doesn't work from a shop in Port Elizabeth for R5 000. If the shop refuses to refund his money, which court could he approach? Where can he appeal if he is not satisfied with the court's decision?

5. Peter buys a car from a garage in Johannesburg for R50 000. It breaks down three days later. Which court must he use to get his money back if the garage refuses to refund him? Where should he appeal if he is not happy with the court's decision?
6. Vusi and Ernest, who live in a village in rural KwaZulu-Natal, have a dispute about who owns certain cows. Which court should they approach about their problem? What can they do if they are not satisfied with the court's decision?
7. Maria, who lives in Cape Town, wishes to divorce her husband who also lives there. Which court should she use?
8. Sipho, a senior advocate in Kimberley, thinks that part of a statute conflicts with the Bill of Rights and is unconstitutional. He wants a court to rule that these parts of the statute are invalid. Which court should Sipho approach? If the court rules that the provisions in question are unconstitutional, will this ruling come into effect immediately? If Sipho is unhappy with the decision of the court, which courts can he appeal to?

1.3.2 Settling disputes outside of court

most problems can be settled without going to court

court procedures are slow and expensive

people taking law into their own hands will cause chaos

Many legal problems can be settled without going to court. Usually court procedures are slow and expensive. Most people solve their problems without going to court. If a person's dog barks all night so that a neighbour cannot sleep, the neighbour will usually complain to the owner before consulting a lawyer. It would be difficult to live in a society if people asked lawyers to go to court every time there was a problem or a dispute. However, it is often better for people to approach lawyers when a problem cannot be settled outside of court than to take the law into their own hands. If everybody took the law into their own hands there would be chaos in society. The law does, however, allow self-defence if a person is defending himself or his family from an immediate attack on them or their property (see below para 2.10.3).

Problem 4: If people took the law into their own hands

Questions

Consider what would happen to society if people took the law into their own hands in the following cases:

a shopkeeper sells a stove that does not work

1. Steven, a storekeeper, sold a stove which did not work to Paul. When Paul demanded his money back Steven refused to give it to him. Instead of getting legal help Paul burnt down Steven's store 'to pay him back for cheating people'. Do you think that Paul did the right thing? What else could Paul have done to get his money back? Where could Paul have got legal help?

a neighbour's dog attacks the other neighbour's chickens

2. Ahmed's dog keeps going onto Benny's property and attacking his chickens. Benny tells Ahmed to control his dog but Ahmed does nothing about it. Benny poisons Ahmed's dog. Do you think that Benny acted lawfully? What could Benny have done instead of killing the dog?

the police fail to arrest a drug dealer

3. People in a certain community know that Sharkie is involved in organised crime and sells drugs. They complain to the police but the police say that they cannot do anything because they have no evidence. The people concerned suspect that Sharkie is paying the police money not to investigate him. The people wait outside Sharkie's house one night and, when he comes out, they shoot and kill him. They say they were forced to take the matter into their own hands because the police were not doing anything. Were the actions of these people justified? What else could they have done?

a political party threatens to burn the house of people of another party

4. People from one political group in a township threaten to burn down the house of people belonging to another political group. The second group lays a complaint with the police. The police tell them that there is nothing that can be done as there is no proof that the first group will burn down the house. What should the second group do to protect themselves if the police cannot help them?

a driver shoots a hijacker

5. Logan is afraid that he might be hijacked so he buys a gun to protect himself. One day a man comes up to his car at a traffic light and pulls out a knife. He tells Logan to get out of the car. He also tells Logan that if he co-operates he will not be hurt. Logan pulls out his gun, shoots and kills the man. Were Logan's actions justified? Do you think people should carry guns to protect themselves?

a person kills another in self-defence

6. Bob is attacked by Dan who pulls out a knife and threatens to stab him. Bob tries to run away but Dan catches up. Bob picks up an iron bar and hits Dan on the head, killing him. Do you think that Bob is guilty of a crime?

There are a number of ways that people can solve disputes without going to court and without taking the law into their own hands. The most common ways are by 'negotiation', 'mediation' and 'arbitration'.

solving problems through negotiation can be a lot cheaper and more effective than going to court

1.3.2.1 Negotiation

people talk

attorneys may negotiate

a 'settlement' may be reached

Negotiation means that the people in dispute talk to each other about their problem and try to solve it by coming up with a decision which is acceptable to both sides. Sometimes people cannot settle a dispute on their own and hire attorneys to negotiate for them. For example, people involved in motor accidents sometimes hire attorneys to negotiate with insurance companies over payments for injuries or damage to their cars. People who hire attorneys to negotiate for them must approve any agreements made by the attorneys. Sometimes attorneys begin court proceedings and then try to work out a 'settlement' so that the case does not go to court. A settlement is an agreement between the parties to end a dispute. Most civil cases are settled this way, saving time and money. Poor people who cannot afford lawyers may ask legal aid clinics (see below para 1.4.1.4) to negotiate for them.

step 1: preparing for the negotiation

step 2: the negotiation process

Negotiation Guidelines

Step 1: Preparing for the negotiation

- Understand the facts and issues
- Decide what is the least and most you can expect
- What is not negotiable?
- What does the other side care about?
- What is in both your interests?

Step 2: The negotiation process

- Try to build a good relationship with the other side
- Be friendly and cordial
- Speak about what you would like (eg I think, I feel)
- Find out what the other side would like
- Brainstorm solutions or options to solve the problem
- Do not make unfair or unrealistic demands

- Do not become abusive, over-emotional or threatening
- Offer to give something away in exchange for something from the other side

step 3: moving and reaching an agreement

Step 3: Moving and reaching an agreement
- Identify your common interests
- Try to move the process if the other side does not
- Consider offering a compromise
- Try to make the agreement as fair as possible
- Use objective criteria to measure compliance with the agreement (eg give specific dates for when things will be done)

Problem 5: The case of Maria Mchunu

Consider the following facts in the Maria Mchunu case:

a wife is told her husband infected his girlfriend with HIV

Maria Mchunu is employed as a teacher and is married to Mondi Mchunu, who is a truck driver. They have three children. One day Maria receives a telephone call from a woman called Thandi who tells her that she has been Mondi's girlfriend for the past three years. Thandi says that she has just been told that she is HIV-positive and must have been infected by Mondi because she has had no other boyfriends.

the husband refuses to have protected sex and assaults his wife and children

Mondi returns home from a trip after having a few drinks with his friends. Maria tells him about the phone call from Thandi and says that she will not have sex with him again until he has an HIV/AIDS test and agrees not to see Thandi again. Mondi denies that Thandi is his girlfriend and that he had sex with her. Maria continues to accuse Mondi and he gets very cross and beats her up. Mondi also hits the three children who try to protect Maria. Maria tries to leave the house to go with the children to her family, but is locked in the bedroom by Mondi. Mondi later forces Maria to have unprotected sex with him, and he again beats her up when she tries to object.

the wife and children leave the house

the husband agrees to negotiate to get back his wife and children

The next day while Mondi is still asleep, Maria and the three children manage to leave the house and go to her parents' home. She and her children go to a clinic for medical treatment. The nurse refers them to you as a paralegal for advice. Maria says she still loves Mondi and wants to go back to him. She asks you to phone Mondi and to negotiate with him to make sure that he will not beat them again if they return home. You telephone Mondi who says that he still loves his wife and children. He denies that he had a relationship with Thandi but agrees to meet with you.

In twos, acting either as a paralegal representing Maria Mchunu or as Mondi Mchunu himself, try to reach a negotiated settlement by using the above Negotiation Guidelines.

1.3.2.2 Mediation

a mediator is a third person who acts as a 'go-between'

Mediation is an extension of negotiation. Mediation happens when a third person acts as a 'go-between' to help people who have a dispute to solve their problem themselves. The mediator does not make the decision for the parties to the dispute, the parties decide what their dispute is about and how they want it settled. The mediator's job is to control the process so that the parties in dispute are able to come to their own solution. For example, a parent who sees two children arguing over which TV programme to watch acts as a mediator when assisting the children to agree on a particular programme. Non-governmental organisations, paralegal advice offices and some newspaper columns often settle disputes by acting as mediators or go-betweens. Church leaders and social workers often act as mediators in their communities.

Steps in a Mediation

step 1: introduction

Step 1. Introduction
The mediator makes the parties relax and explains the rules. The mediator's role is not to make a decision but to help the parties reach an agreement. The mediator explains that he or she will not take sides.

step 2: telling the story

Step 2. Telling the story
Each party tells what happened. The person bringing the complaint tells his or her side of the story first. No interruptions are allowed. Then the other party explains his or her version of the facts.

step 3: identifying the facts and issues

Step 3. Identifying the facts and issues
The mediator attempts to identify facts and issues agreed upon by the parties. This is done by listening to each side, summarising each party's views, and asking if these are the facts and issues as each party understands them.

step 4: identifying alternative solutions

Step 4. Identifying alternative solutions
Everyone thinks of possible solutions to the problem. The mediator makes a list and asks each party to explain his or her feelings about each solution.

step 5: revising and discussing solutions

Step 5. Revising and discussing solutions
Based on the expressed feelings of the parties, the mediator revises possible solutions and attempts to identify a solution to which both parties can agree.

step 6: reaching agreement

Step 6. Reaching agreement
The mediator helps the parties reach an agreement with which both can live. The agreement should be written down. The parties should also discuss what will happen if either of them breaks the agreement.

students should be selected to play the roles of the parties or the mediator

Problem 6: Hospital workers v hospital management

the parties argue about searching the workers to prevent hospital thefts

the party leaders agree to mediation

Hospital workers object to being searched when leaving the hospital premises. The hospital is experiencing massive losses due to theft of drugs, food, equipment and bedding. Despite appeals to hospital workers to assist with preventing the losses, the thefts continue. In desperation the hospital management introduce compulsory searches of all hospital workers when they leave the hospital premises. The hospital workers declare a dispute with the management on the basis that the compulsory searches are an unlawful invasion of their constitutional right to privacy. The hospital maintains that the steps are reasonable and justifiable. Negotiations between the parties fail and they agree to mediation.

In groups of three acting as representatives of the hospital workers, mediators or representatives of the hospital management, conduct mediations using the above Steps in a Mediation in order to reach a decision.

1.3.2.3 Arbitration

Arbitration is often used when the parties to a dispute have tried unsuccessfully to resolve it by agreement through negotiation and mediation. Arbitration takes place when both parties to a dispute agree to have a third party ('an arbitrator') listen to their arguments and work out a decision. This means that the parties do not come to an agreement themselves, but that the arbitrator acts like a judge and makes the decision for them. The parties usually agree to follow his or her decision. The parties cannot appeal if they do not like the decision. The advantages of arbitration are that it is quicker, less expensive and less formal than a court case.

Arbitration guidelines

step 1: both sides prepare

Step 1: Both sides prepare
- Both sides should prepare to tell their stories from their point of view
- Each side should also have prepared questions to ask the other side about their story

step 2: the complaining side tell their story

Step 2: The complaining side tell their story
- The arbitrator asks the complaining side to tell their story first
- The arbitrator asks questions to ensure that the complaining side's story is clear and complete
- The other side questions the complaining side about their story

step 3: the other side tell their story

Step 3: The other side tell their story
- The arbitrator asks the other side to tell their story
- The arbitrator asks questions to ensure that the other side's story is clear and complete
- The complaining side questions the other side about their story

step 4: the arbitrator makes a decision after both sides have been heard

Step 4: The arbitrator makes a decision after both sides have been heard
- The arbitrator reviews the facts
- The arbitrator summarises the applicable law
- The arbitrator applies the law to the facts and makes a decision, giving reasons

Problem 7: Public Service health workers v Minister of Health

public service health workers strike for higher pay

The Public Service health workers have embarked on a nation-wide strike for higher pay. The workers are demanding an 8,5% increase and a housing subsidy of R1 000 per month. The Department of Health is offering a 5% increase and a housing subsidy of R700 per month.

the workers argue they have the right to fair labour practices

The Union and the workers argue that s 23(1) of the Constitution provides that everyone has the right to fair labour practices and this includes being paid a living wage. In any event s 23(2) provides that every worker has the right: (a) to form and join a trade union; (b) to participate in the activities and programmes of a trade union; and (c) to strike. They argue that by engaging in picketing of hospitals they are asserting their right to strike, and they deny that they are responsible the workers strike and picket

for using violence to prevent other hospital workers and patients from accessing the hospital entrances. They blame the violence and intimidation on criminals and government agents who are trying to discredit the strike. If they are not able to withhold their labour they have no other way of forcing the government to accede to their demands. Furthermore, the Department of Health has not signed a 'minimum service agreement' with the Union and therefore they and the health workers are not bound to provide such services at hospitals.

the Department of Health says the wages demanded are unaffordable

health workers are an 'essential service'

The Department of Health maintains that it cannot afford to offer any more as this will impact on service delivery because cuts will have to be made to other line items in the health sector. The Department also regards health workers as an 'essential service' and argues that it is illegal for them to go on strike (see below para 6.4.5.3). The Department claims that even though no 'minimum service agreement' has been signed with the Union in terms of the Labour Relations Act, the health workers must return to work because they are in violation of three provisions of the Constitution, viz (a) s 27(1)*(a)* which provides that everyone has the right of access to health care, including reproductive health care; (b) s 28(1)*(c)* which provides that every child has the right to basic health care services; and (c) s 27(3) which provides that nobody may be denied emergency medical treatment. These rights are being violated through the use of intimidation and aggressive picketing which prevents non-striking workers from working and ill patients from entering the hospitals.

the Department and the workers agree to arbitration

The Department of Health is considering approaching the Labour Court to obtain an order declaring that Public Service health workers are an 'essential service' and requiring them to return to work. Before doing so however the Department informs the Union and the workers that it is prepared to submit to arbitration in the matter. The Union and workers agree to arbitration.

In groups of three acting as representatives of the Public Service health workers, arbitrators or representatives of the Minister of Health, conduct arbitrations using the above Arbitration Guidelines in order to reach a decision.

1.3.2.4 Special provisions for labour disputes

the CCMA tries to resolve labour disputes

Labour law statutes require that an attempt must be made to resolve labour disputes (ie arguments between workers and employers) through negotiation, mediation or arbitration before going to court. For this reason the Commission for Conciliation, Mediation and Arbitration (CCMA) has been established (see para 6.10.1). The purpose of the CCMA is to try to resolve labour disputes through mediation and, if that is unsuccessful, arbitration.

the CCMA handles unfair dismissals

The CCMA also handles cases of unfair dismissal – where people think that they were dismissed from their job without good reason (see below Part 6). If a person thinks that he or she has been unfairly dismissed from his or her job, the person can visit the CCMA, which will be able to provide assistance free of charge. (The telephone number of the CCMA can be found in the telephone directory.)

Problem 8: Which is the best method of settling the dispute?

Consider each of the situations below and decide the best way of settling the dispute. In each case decide whether the problem would be best handled by an informal discussion between the parties, negotiation, mediation, arbitration, by going to court, or by some other method. Discuss the reasons for your answer.

Questions

1. A father agrees to pay all his daughter's university expenses but later changes his mind.
2. A tape recorder Zo buys stops working after two weeks and the salesperson refuses to get it fixed or give Zo his money back.
3. A town council will not repair a council house because it believes that the tenant (the person renting the house) caused the damage.
4. A trade union and an employer disagree over wages and conditions of employment.
5. A married couple want a divorce.
6. Mogani accuses Angela, a domestic worker, of having stolen things from her home and promptly fires her. Angela says that she did not steal the things in question. Angela says that she was unfairly dismissed and either wants her job back or to be compensated.

1.4 Lawyers and the adversary system

Outcomes

After completion of this section learners will be able to:

1. Demonstrate an understanding of how lawyers and the adversary system work.

Assessment criteria

1. An explanation is given of when people are likely to need a lawyer.
2. A set of facts is examined and a decision is made on when a lawyer will be required.
3. A decision is taken on whether South Africa should have a divided legal profession.
4. An explanation is given of the qualifications and nature of the work of the different branches of the legal profession.
5. A set of facts in a case is examined and a decision is taken on who qualifies for legal aid.
6. A role-play of a consultation between a lawyer and a client concerning a motor collision is conducted.
7. An explanation is given of how the adversary system operates.
8. A role-play is conducted of a consultation between a lawyer and a client who admits that she is guilty of murder, and a decision is made on whether the lawyer should defend her.

1.4.1 Lawyers

not all lawyers are in practice

There are over 24 500 lawyers serving about 54 million people in South Africa. Of these approximately 2 500 are advocates and about 22 000 attorneys. Most are in practice but others work for companies and the public service. A small number of lawyers work as university lecturers, judges, politicians and in public-interest law firms.

attorneys and advocates

a lawyer is necessary in court

legal advice can prevent problems

Most attorneys do not spend much time in court. The practice of law usually involves giving advice, drafting legal opinions, negotiating settlements, or otherwise providing out-of-court legal assistance. Some lawyers, however, especially advocates, spend a lot of time in court. If a person has to appear in any court, it is important that he or she gets legal advice and assistance. Every person who needs a lawyer should have the right to be represented in court by a lawyer. It is important to know if one needs a lawyer and if so, how to get one.

1.4.1.1 When do you need a lawyer?

Many people think of seeing an attorney only after they get into trouble, but sometimes the best time to see an attorney is before the trouble happens.

Advice on how to prevent legal problems is one of the most important services a lawyer can provide. People should think about seeing lawyers when they are:

1. Buying or selling a house;
2. Starting up businesses;

3. Thinking of marriage or divorce;
4. Making wills (documents saying who they want to give their property to when they die);
5. Signing important agreements ('contracts');
6. Handling accidents involving injuries or damage to property;
7. Needing bail and defending criminal charges;
8. Bringing civil actions in courts other than in the small claims court and a chiefs' and headmen's court (see above para 1.3.1.6); and
9. Trying to collect money owed to them if it cannot be claimed through the small claims court (see above para 1.3.1.5).

too expensive to see a lawyer every time a person has a legal problem

It would be expensive to see a lawyer every time a person has a legal problem. Sometimes a teacher, doctor, religious leader or friend may be able to help or advise. If a person cannot afford a lawyer he or she should contact a university law clinic or Legal Aid South Africa (see below para 1.4.1.4).

Problem 1: Is a lawyer necessary?

Each of the following examples involves a case where a lawyer may or may not be needed. For each case discuss the reasons why you or your family may or may not need an attorney.

Questions

1. Your father crashes into another car at a shopping centre and damages it. Your father's insurance company says it will pay out the cost of repairs to your father's and the other person's car.
2. You borrow your brother's car without his knowledge and he reports it to the police as stolen.
3. You buy a new stereo for R2 000. At a party one month later the receiver and speakers blow out. You go back to the store and they say that there is nothing they can do as the stereo only had a two-week guarantee.
4. Your brother decides to trade in his old car and buy another second-hand car.
5. Your friends are caught robbing a store and they tell the police that you helped plan the robbery.
6. Your parents want to get divorced.
7. Your parents want to make a will (a legal document saying to whom their property should go when they die).

1.4.1.2 Different types of lawyers

two main types of lawyers

In South Africa there are two main types of lawyers: attorneys and advocates. Advocates and attorneys do different work. They are also trained differently after they finish their university studies. In addition, attorneys may qualify as conveyancers (lawyers who transfer ownership of land or buildings) and notaries (lawyers who draw up and certify certain documents).

Previously, there were several law degrees offered at South African universities, which qualified people for different legal professions. These degrees have now been replaced by a four-year LLB degree available at all South African universities, which provides access to all branches of the legal profession.

1.4.1.2.1 Advocates

advocates spend more time in court

In contrast to attorneys (who spend most of their time in their offices) advocates do a lot of court work. Advocates can appear in any court in South Africa except the small claims court and traditional courts like chiefs and headmen's courts. Advocates must practise alone. They cannot enter into partnerships with each other but may be in-house advisers to firms of attorneys, business companies and firms, or work in public interest firms, like a Legal Resources Centre or a law clinic. (See below para 1.4.1.4.) Advocates do not get cases directly from clients; instead, attorneys bring cases to them.

advocates cannot have partners

advocates need an LLB degree

People who want to become advocates must go to university for at least four years to get an LLB degree. People who pass the LLB degree, and wish to join a practising group of advocates, must then serve a one-year period of 'pupillage.' This involves working under a practising advocate in an advocate's office, called 'chambers.' Pupils must also attend, and help with, a number of court cases. During this time pupils are not paid any wages. In addition to completing a pupillage, pupils must also pass a Bar Examination. People who do not wish to practise as members of a bar association may, however, be admitted as advocates after passing their LLB degree and do not need to complete a pupillage or write a Bar Examination. In order to be admitted as an advocate a person must apply to the High Court.

advocates wishing to join a bar must do 'pupillage' and pass a bar examination

Previously, only advocates could appear in the High Court, the Supreme Court of Appeal and the Constitutional Court. Attorneys could not appear in these courts and could only appear in the magistrate's court. Nowadays, some attorneys can appear in these courts (see below). In general, however, South Africa still has a *divided profession*, based on the English system of barristers (like advocates) and solicitors (like attorneys). Many other countries do not have these distinctions and it may also change in South Africa one day.

1.4.1.2.2 Attorneys

Attorneys spend most of their time collecting money from people who do not pay debts, transferring properties (see below para 1.4.1.2.3), drawing up legal documents like agreements and wills, handling claims for personal injuries and damage to property, and doing commercial work. Some attorneys also specialise in a specific areas of law such as motor accident claims, family law, commercial law, tax law, labour law, etc.

most attorneys do not spend time in court

Most attorneys only have right of appearance in the magistrate's court, and cannot appear in the higher courts. However, certain senior attorneys have been allowed to appear in the High Court. Most attorneys do not spend much time in court and some attorneys may never go to court.

an attorney instructs an advocate about the details of a case before going to court

law graduates wishing to become attorneys must serve articles of clerkship

they must also attend a practical training course and pass an admission examination

To become an attorney a person must go to university for at least four years to get an LLB degree. After a person has passed the LLB degree he or she must work for two years at a private law firm, a public interest law firm (eg the Legal Resources Centre, see below para 1.4.1.4.4), a law clinic (see below para 1.4.1.4.3) or a legal aid justice centre (see below para 1.4.1.4.2) and attend a practical training course or school. During this time the person is an 'articled clerk'. If the person has completed a five-month practical legal training school course, he or she need only work as an articled clerk for one year. If the person does the 'sandwich' 5-week practical legal training courses, he or she must complete two years' articles of clerkship. Clerks are paid for their work, but not as much as when they qualify and work as attorneys. To qualify as an attorney, a person must pass an Attorney's Admission Examination. Once the person has completed the above requirements he or she may apply to the High Court to be admitted as an attorney.

some attorneys may appear in the higher courts

As mentioned, in the past attorneys could not appear in the High Court, Supreme Court of Appeal or Constitutional Court. Nowadays, most attorneys still do not have right of appearance in these courts. However, attorneys may apply to the Registrar of a High Court to be granted a right of appearance. If the application is successful, the attorney may appear in the High Court, the Supreme Court of Appeal and the Constitutional Court.

In the past the *divided profession* (ie a rigid distinction between attorneys and advocates) was criticised because it was too expensive for most clients. Nowadays, the distinction is not as rigid because some attorneys can do the court work that only advocates were allowed to do in the past. Some people argue that, if attorneys can now appear in the higher courts, there is no reason to maintain the division between attorneys and advocates. They argue that there should just be lawyers, who would do all the work that attorneys and advocates used to do. They further argue that this would also make legal services cheaper. Others argue that, although the divided profession is more expensive, clients get a better legal service if there are advocates who specialise in court work, especially in the High Court. The Legal Practice Act calls all lawyers 'legal practitioners'.

arguments for and against the divided profession

Problem 2: The divided profession

Questions

1. Why do you think South Africa has a divided legal profession consisting of advocates and attorneys when most countries in the world do not?
2. What are the advantages and disadvantages of a divided legal profession?
3. Do you think that it is a positive development that certain attorneys are now allowed to appear in the High Court? Give reasons for your answer.
4. Given that certain attorneys can now appear in the High Court, do you think that the division between attorneys and advocates should be kept? Give reasons for your answer.
5. Should the provisions of the Legal Practice Act do away with the distinction between advocates and attorneys? Give reasons for your answer.

1.4.1.2.3 Conveyancers

conveyancers deal with immovable property

Conveyancers are attorneys who have passed a special examination in conveyancing, which deals with how to prepare documents for the transferring of land or immovable property, and the registration of mortgage bonds. The work of a conveyancer is to prepare for registration of certain legal documents called deeds of transfer, title deeds and mortgage bonds (see below para 5.6.4.11).

1.4.1.2.4 Notaries public

notaries draw up and certify documents

Notaries public are attorneys who have passed a special notaries examination. The work of a notary public is to draw up (and make sure that the proper people sign) certain legal documents like contracts entered into before marriage (called 'ante-nuptial contracts', see below para 4.2.2.2), or other documents called notarial deeds or bonds.

1.4.1.3 How to find a lawyer

find somebody who knows a lawyer

The best way to find a lawyer is probably to ask a friend who has had a similar problem and who used a lawyer to solve it. Otherwise ask an employer, clergyman, school teacher or some professional person who may know a lawyer. Attorneys are also listed in the 'Yellow Pages' of the telephone book.

1.4.1.3.1 Finding an attorney

ask a clergyman, teacher, employer or some professional person to help you find a lawyer

law societies

Previously, each of the four provinces of South Africa had a law society, which was responsible for controlling the conduct of attorneys. South Africa now has nine provinces but there are, at present, still four law societies. These are the Cape Law Society (Cape Town), the Law Society of the Free State (Bloemfontein), the KwaZulu-Natal Law Society (Pietermaritzburg) and the Law Society of the Northern Provinces (Pretoria). There is also the Law Society of South Africa in Pretoria which is a co-ordinating body.

local associations of lawyers

Some law societies have published directories of attorneys. These are available from the secretary of the local law society and contain a list of names, addresses and services of most attorneys in the main towns in the province. There are also local associations of lawyers as well as organisations like the Black Lawyers' Association and the National Association of Democratic Lawyers who may have lists of their members. Another way to find a lawyer is simply to look in the Yellow Pages. A commercial publisher, Hortors, also publishes a list of all the attorneys and advocates in South Africa.

paying for advice

Before an attorney takes a case he or she will usually ask for money as a deposit towards fees. Some attorneys, however, give a reduced rate for their first consultation. For example, some attorneys may charge a reduced fixed rate for the first half-hour interview. If you consult a lawyer you should find out if the reduced rate applies and, if not, what rate will apply. (For people who cannot afford lawyers' fees, see below para 1.4.1.4.) Attorneys may also take certain cases (eg motor accident or medical negligence cases) on a speculative or contingency basis, which means that the client will only pay the attorney if the attorney wins the case.

1.4.1.3.2 Finding an advocate

Advocates join a 'bar' in a particular city and are controlled by a 'bar council'. Advocates work in groups and are usually found in the same building.

Bar councils

bar councils and societies of advocates

There is a bar council or society of advocates in each of the main cities: the Cape Bar Council in Cape Town; the Eastern Cape Society of Advocates which has members in Grahamstown and Port Elizabeth; the Northern Cape Society of Advocates in Kimberley; the Free State Society of Advocates in Bloemfontein; the Society of Advocates, KwaZulu-Natal in Durban; the KwaZulu-Natal Bar Council in Pietermaritzburg; the Pretoria Bar Association; the Johannesburg Bar; the North-West Bar Association in Mafikeng; the Bisho Society of Advocates; and the Transkei Society of Advocates in Mthatha.

General Council of the Bar

advocates are employed by attorneys

There is also a General Council of the Bar in South Africa which is a co-ordinating body for the different provincial bar councils. There is also an 'Independent Bar' consisting of advocates who have not joined the different bar councils. As we have seen, advocates are employed by attorneys on behalf of a client and some attorneys will know who the good advocates are. Clients may, however, ask for a particular advocate if they think that this advocate will handle the case best.

Problem 3: Some questions about the legal profession

1. What is the main work of attorneys? In which courts may attorneys appear?
2. What work is done by conveyancers and notaries public?
3. What is the main work of advocates? In which courts may advocates appear?
4. If you want to become an advocate or attorney what qualifications do you need?
5. If you need an advocate or attorney how would you find one?
6. As mentioned there was a time when judges were appointed solely from the ranks of senior advocates. However, judges are now appointed from other branches of the legal profession such as attorneys, magistrates and law lecturers. Do you think that this is a good thing? Give reasons for your answer.

1.4.1.4 People who cannot afford lawyers

In certain cases people have a constitutional right to be represented by a lawyer. A person who cannot afford a lawyer may consult (a) Legal Aid South Africa, (b) a university legal aid clinic, (c) a Legal Resources Centre office; or (d) a paralegal advice office.

1.4.1.4.1 Constitutional right to a lawyer

before 1994 no constitutional right to a lawyer

Before the Interim Constitution came into effect in 1994 a person accused of a crime had no constitutional right to a lawyer at the expense of the state, although there was a limited common law right to counsel. Very often, however, accused people could not afford to hire lawyers.

substantial injustice

constitutional right to legal aid in criminal cases

The Constitution says that an accused person must be given legal representation at the expense of the state if a 'substantial injustice' would otherwise result. When deciding whether a 'substantial injustice' will result if legal representation is not provided, the courts have said the following factors should be taken into account: (a) the complexity of the case (ie whether it is a complicated or difficult case); (b) the severity of the potential sentence – how serious the results of sentence are likely to be (eg the person may be sentenced to imprisonment or lose his or her job); (c) the ignorance and inability of the person to represent himself or herself; and (d) the indigence of the accused (ie the person does not have the money to hire a lawyer to represent him or her).

people who cannot afford a lawyer may obtain legal aid

1.4.1.4.2 Legal Aid South Africa

the 'means test'

Legal Aid South Africa is a state-funded but independent body that provides legal services to poor people in South Africa who qualify for legal aid. Legal Aid South Africa uses a 'means test' to decide how much a person may earn to qualify for legal aid. Accordingly Legal Aid South Africa will find a lawyer for a person who earns less than R5 000 per month after tax as a single person, or R5 500 per month after tax for a household where people live with each other for at least four nights a week. The person receiving legal aid will pay nothing. In exceptional cases Legal Aid South Africa may give legal aid to a person who earns more than these amounts. For example, in deserving cases a legal aid justice centre head may give legal aid to a person earning R1 000 more than the maximum allowed by the 'means test', while the head of a regional legal aid office may authorise legal aid to be given to a person who earns R2 000 more than the 'means test'.

'substantial injustice' if no legal representation

Legal aid in criminal cases: As previously mentioned (see above para 1.4.1.4.1), according to the Constitution people who are accused of crimes must be given legal aid if they cannot afford a lawyer and a 'substantial injustice' will arise if the state does not provide them with a lawyer. Legal Aid South Africa interprets a 'substantial injustice' to mean that an accused person who cannot afford a lawyer is likely, if convicted, to be sentenced to (a) a period of imprisonment of three months without the option of a fine or (b) if granted the option of a fine (instead of three months' imprisonment), will be unable to pay the fine within two weeks of being sentenced. In the case of detained people a 'substantial injustice' means that they are unable to afford the cost of consulting with a lawyer and they reasonably need to do so in relation to their continued detention. More than 90% of Legal Aid South Africa's budget is spent on criminal cases because of the requirements of the Constitution and the fact that Parliament does not provide sufficient money to cover more civil cases.

90% of legal aid money spent on criminal cases

legal aid for children in civil cases

Legal aid in civil cases: The Constitution provides that a child under the age of 18 years must be provided with a lawyer at state expense if a 'substantial injustice' will arise if the child is unable to afford the cost of his or he own lawyer in a civil case affecting that child. This has been provided for by Legal Aid South Africa. However, there are certain cases for which people cannot get legal aid (eg for driving, speeding or parking offences; cases involving defamation, insults, invasion of privacy, seduction and adultery; and cases where the person can go to the small claims court). Certain people also cannot get legal aid (eg people intentionally unemployed). People wishing to get a divorce may sometimes be refused legal aid if they have previously received legal aid to get a divorce. As has been mentioned before, less than 10% of Legal Aid South Africa's budget is spent on civil cases because of the protection given to arrested, detained and accused persons by the Constitution. Parliament at present does not give Legal Aid South Africa enough money to do more civil cases. Many civil cases involving damages suffered by people (eg to their property or bodies) may be taken on a 'contingency basis' by lawyers. This means that the lawyers will take the case free and will only claim their fees if they win the case for their clients. Cases for damages of less than R15 000 may be brought in the small claims court (see above para 1.3.1.5).

legal aid excluded for certain civil cases

Problem 4: Some questions on legal aid

1. Should most of the budget of Legal Aid South Africa be spent on criminal cases? Give reasons for your answer.

2. Should Parliament provide more money for civil legal aid? Give reasons for your answer.

justice centres throughout the country

Legal Aid South Africa deals with over 400 000 cases a year and has set up 64 justice centres and 64 satellite justice centres in most of the larger cities and towns in the country. Justice centres are 'one-stop-shops' that provide a full range of legal services to poor people whose cases qualify for legal aid. The justice centres in the large rural towns supervise Legal Aid South Africa satellite offices in the smaller rural towns in their areas. The satellite offices have fewer lawyers than the justice centres and operate in small rural towns where there are magistrates' courts.

justice centres in main cities and towns

In *Gauteng* there are justice centres in Alexandra, Benoni, Germiston, Johannesburg, Krugersdorp, Pretoria, Soweto, Tembisa, Soshanguve, Vereeniging and Witwatersrand University; in the *Western Cape* in Athlone, Bellville, Caledon, Cape Town, George, Malmesbury, Stellenbosch, Vredendal and Worcester; in *KwaZulu-Natal* in Durban, Empangeni, Ladysmith, Newcastle, Pietermaritzburg, Pinetown, Port Shepstone, Umlazi, Verulam and Vryheid; in the *Eastern Cape* in Aliwal North, Butterworth, East London, Graaff-Reinet, Grahamstown, King Williams Town, Mthatha, Port Elizabeth, Queenstown, and Uitenhage; in the *Free State* in Bethlehem, Bloemfontein, Botshabelo, Kroonstad, Phuthaditjhaba and Welkom; in the *North West* in Ga-Rankuwa, Klerksdorp, Lichtenburg, Mafikeng, Potchefstroom, Rustenburg and Vryburg; in the *Northern Cape* in Colesberg, Kimberley and Upington; in *Mpumalanga in* Ermelo, Middelburg, Nelspruit and Witbank; and in *Limpopo* in Makhado, Modimolle, Polokwane, Thohoyandou and Tzaneen.

justice centres are like law offices

where there are no justice centres the magistrate's court will assist with legal aid

Justice centres are like law offices with lawyers and paralegals who can help poor people with their cases if they qualify for legal aid. The justice centres are staffed by qualified lawyers acting as public defenders in the regional courts, and by candidate attorney public defenders under the supervision of qualified lawyers in the magistrate's courts. The candidate attorney public defenders help accused people who are charged in the district magistrate's courts (see above para 1.3.1.4). If there is no justice centre or satellite justice centre in your town you should go to the local magistrate's court and ask for the legal aid officer. There should be a legal aid officer at each magistrate's court.

Is there a justice centre or magistrate's court in your area?

attorneys can help to get legal aid

If people approach an attorney's office and qualify for legal aid (ie earn less than R5 000 per month after tax if they are single or R5 500 after tax if they are part of a household), they should ask the attorney to help them apply for legal aid. If people have difficulty in obtaining legal aid they should approach their nearest university legal aid clinic. If the problem will affect many people (like violations of people's constitutional rights) a Legal Resources Centre may help.

Problem 5: Who qualifies for legal aid?

In each case say whether you think the person can get free legal assistance or legal aid. Give reasons for your answers. What else can the person do?

Questions

1. Mr Bona, who earns R5 000 per month and is married with four dependent children, parks his car in a no parking zone and is told to pay a R500 fine.
2. Mrs Green, who has been deserted by her husband and earns R4 500 per month, wishes to get a divorce. There are five children from their marriage, all of whom are dependent on her as her husband is unemployed.
3. Mr Samuels bought and paid for some furniture from a shop. The furniture was not delivered. He later hears that a whole lot of people paid for furniture that was not delivered by the same shop. Mr Samuels is unmarried, with no children and earns R6 000 per month.
4. Mr Khuzwayo visits an attorney's office because he is being sued for R10 000 by a person into whose car he crashed. The attorney asks Mr Khuzwayo for a R2 000 deposit to defend the case. Mr Khuzwayo only earns R4 000 per month and supports a wife and child. He cannot afford to pay the deposit.
5. Mrs van der Merwe, who is married with two children and earns R3 200 a month, says that she has been defamed by her neighbour and wishes to sue her for damages. Her husband earns R2 300 a month.

1.4.1.4.3 University law clinics

law clinics help poor people

Most universities in South Africa now have law clinics. The clinics will usually help people who fall within the income limits set by Legal Aid South Africa. They do not, however, exclude people for other reasons set out by Legal Aid South Africa (see above para 1.4.1.4.2). Law clinics are staffed by practising attorneys or advocates and senior law students who work under the supervision of qualified lawyers. At present law students cannot go to court but can assist qualified lawyers to prepare for court, give advice, write letters and negotiate settlements for poor people. Law clinics often take on civil cases to fill the gap left by Legal Aid South Africa, which does not have enough money to do more civil cases. You may contact your nearest university to see if it has a law clinic.

assistance from law students

1.4.1.4.4 Legal Resources Centres

Legal Resources Centres deal with problems affecting large numbers of people

Legal Resources Centres are public interest law firms that usually deal with problems that affect large numbers of people in the community. They do not deal with cases affecting individual people unless the case will impact on many other people as well. The Legal Resources Centres are staffed by highly trained advocates and attorneys who specialise in human rights and constitutional law problems. They have won some very important cases in the Constitutional Court, Supreme Court of Appeal and High Courts that have helped to improve the living conditions of thousands of marginalised and poor people in South Africa.

There are Legal Resources Centres in Johannesburg, Durban, Cape Town, Pretoria and Grahamstown.

1.4.1.4.5 Paralegal advice offices

paralegal advice offices

Paralegal advice offices in South Africa are run by non-governmental organisations, citizens' advice bureaux, and many local organisations. In rural areas they have been established by bodies like the Community Law and Rural Development Centre in KwaZulu-Natal. Many of the offices are assisted by university law clinics, Legal Aid South Africa, the Legal Resources Centres and other bodies. Advice offices are staffed by persons who can give advice, and where necessary refer clients to lawyers. Some of the very important cases won by the Legal Resources Centre were first identified by staff in paralegal advice offices. Although the staff are not qualified lawyers they are often paralegals who have experience in helping with specific legal problems.

Are there any paralegal advice offices in your area?

questions to ask your lawyer

Advice on what to ask your lawyer

Once you have found a lawyer who seems prepared to take your case, you should get answers to the following questions:

1. What is the lawyer's fee?
2. Has the lawyer ever handled a case like yours before? If so, what were the results?
3. Will the lawyer provide you with copies of all correspondence and documents prepared on your behalf?
4. Will the lawyer keep you informed of any new developments in your case? Will the lawyer explain things to you in simple language?
5. How much personal attention will you get? If the lawyer is a member of a firm, is he or she the person who will actually handle your case?

if not satisfied consult another lawyer

If you are not satisfied with the lawyer's answers, you should consult another lawyer.

Problem 6: The case of the car crash

Mac Sono's Golf crashed into the rear of Tim Smith's Mazda

Tim's car was damaged

On 1 January 2012 Tim Smith was driving along Margaret Mncadi Avenue (Victoria Embankment) in Durban. Tim slowed down when he approached the traffic light on the corner of Margaret Mncadi Avenue and Field Street, when a 2005 Golf owned by Mac Sono hit his car in the rear.

Mac was given a ticket

Tim's 2008 Mazda was smashed in as far as the back seat. Fortunately nobody was injured. Tim took his car to a panel beater who said that it would cost R20 000 to fix.

Mac said that the Mazda's brake lights were not working. Therefore he did not know that Tim was slowing down. Mac was given a ticket for speeding and negligent driving.

Mac's insurance company offers to pay half

Mac's insurance company offers to pay Tim R10 000. It says the accident was also Tim's fault because the Mazda's brake lights were not working. Tim is uncertain whether to accept R10 000. He consults a lawyer.

Role-play

Role-play an interview between Tim and the attorney. Students playing the role of the attorney should ask all the questions they think an attorney should ask. Students playing the role of Tim should answer the attorney's questions and give any other information they think the attorney will need. If necessary they should also ask the attorney the questions mentioned in the box above.

1.4.1.5 Working with your attorney

you must be able to trust your attorney

Trust is the foundation of the attorney-client relationship. You must be able to trust your attorney. To help you, the attorney needs to know everything about your problem. To encourage clients to speak freely to their lawyers, the law grants them an attorney-client privilege. This means that whatever you tell your attorney is secret and cannot be told to anyone without your permission.

you make the decisions

Working with an attorney also means that you have to make decisions. A good attorney will give you advice, but you must make the final decision. For example, you must decide whether or not to sue, or to accept or reject an offer of settlement.

1.4.1.6 Problems with lawyers

complaints may be investigated by the local law society

If people have problems with attorneys or advocates they can contact the secretary of the local law society or bar council to find out the procedure for laying a complaint. They could also ask their local legal aid clinic to advise them as to the procedure. Once a formal complaint is made the law society or bar council will investigate. If the law society or bar council finds that the lawyer has acted 'unprofessionally' it may apply to the High Court to stop the lawyer practising.

if an attorney steals a client's money there is a special fund, called the Attorneys' Fidelity Fund, to which the client may apply for compensation

compensation if money is stolen

If an attorney steals a client's money there is a special fund to which the client may apply for compensation (eg if an attorney receives money from an insurance company for a client but does not pay the money to the client). This fund is called the Attorneys, Notaries and Conveyancers' Fidelity Guarantee Fund and each year all attorneys have to contribute to it. There are special procedures for claiming against the fund. The person complaining must first use the normal legal procedures to recover the money before approaching the Fund. The Fund will not, however, compensate clients who have lost money because their attorneys have been careless. Here the client will have to ask another lawyer to help them recover the money. The secretary of your local law society can explain the procedure for claiming against the fund. Other lawyers and law clinics may also assist with such claims.

help from the law society or law clinics

1.4.2 The adversary system

trials are like contests in the US and Commonwealth countries which use the 'adversary system'

In South Africa, as in England, most Commonwealth countries and the United States, trials in courts are run like contests between the parties involved. This is called the 'adversary system'. The idea of the 'adversary system' is for the judge or magistrate to decide the truth after listening to each side presenting its case. Under the 'adversary system' the prosecutors or lawyers run the cases and the judge or magistrate acts as a referee.

the United States and England have 'jury' trials

In the United States and England a 'jury' made up of 6–12 ordinary citizens decides the facts in some cases. In South Africa the judge or magistrate tries to find the truth while parties bring witnesses to speak in their favour (ie give 'evidence') and present arguments as to why they should win. They also try to show the court that the other side's witnesses are not telling the truth or are mistaken.

in continental and civil law countries the 'inquistorial system' is used for trials

In the 'inquisitorial system' which applies to most countries in Western and Eastern Europe and South and Central America, as well as French and Portuguese-speaking African countries, judges or magistrates try to find the truth by asking all the questions themselves and getting involved in the arguments. The lawyers usually only ask their questions after the judge has completed his or her questioning of each witness. In South Africa the judge or magistrate is not allowed to do this except in the small claims court.

in South Africa the judge or magistrate is not allowed to get involved in the arguments between the parties

guilty 'beyond reasonable doubt'

In South Africa in criminal cases the state (represented by the 'prosecutor'), has to prove that the accused person is guilty 'beyond a reasonable doubt'. This means that if the court has any doubt that the accused is guilty it must let the person off by finding the person 'not guilty'.

proof 'on a balance of probabilities'

In civil cases the person bringing the action (the 'plaintiff') must prove his or her case 'on a balance of probabilities'. This means that the plaintiff must prove to the court that his or her story is more likely than that of the other party (the 'defendant'). If the court does not believe that the plaintiff's story is more likely the plaintiff will lose the case.

criminal and civil trials are heard separately

The difference between the amount of proof needed in criminal and civil cases means that criminal and civil cases cannot be heard in the same court at the same time. This is because although people may be found not guilty in a criminal case (eg assault), they may still have to compensate the victim. This will happen if the injured people can show that their stories are more likely than those of the accused – even though the facts are not proven 'beyond a reasonable doubt'.

The adversary system is often criticised for being a battle between lawyers who are only aiming to win, and not interested in finding the truth or being fair. It is said that the inquisitorial system is more likely to get to the truth because the judge or magistrate has all the statements of the witnesses in advance, so that they the pros and cons of the adversary system

cannot change their stories when giving evidence. Under the adversary system the judge or magistrate does not have access to any written statements unless they are handed in as 'exhibits'. As a result, some argue that because under the adversary system the evidence is tested through 'cross-examination' by lawyers (see below para 1.4.2.2), the court has a better chance of finding the truth than by methods where the court asks most of the questions.

Problem 7: Questions on the adversary system

1. Do you think that the 'adversary system' is a better way of finding the truth than the 'inquisitorial system' where the judge or magistrate asks all the questions? Give reasons for your answer.
2. Do you agree or disagree with the statement: 'It is better that 10 guilty persons go free than one innocent person be found guilty.'

1.4.2.1 Should lawyers defend 'guilty' people?

Problems arise when lawyers are consulted by clients who confess to having committed crimes and want to be defended. What should lawyers do in this situation?

Problem 8: What should the lawyer do?

Mina admits stabbing the man, and says she is not sorry for what she did

Mina stabs to death a man who had called her and her mother prostitutes. The previous day the man had tried to persuade Mina to sleep with him. The next day she pretended to allow the man to kiss her. She then stabbed him in the heart. Mina is not sorry for what she did because she felt very insulted by the man's actions. Mina is in jail, being interviewed by a lawyer who is deciding whether or not to take her case.

Questions

1. Role-play the interview between the lawyer and Mina to decide whether or not the lawyer will agree to represent Mina.
2. If you were a lawyer would you represent Mina at her trial for wrongfully killing the man? Give reasons for your answer.

1.4.2.2 Steps in a trial under the adversary system

Under the adversary system the following steps usually occur in a trial, whether it is a criminal or civil case. (We will look in more detail at civil and small claims cases below in paras 1.5.1 and 1.5.2.)

opening statements

1. The case may begin with brief opening statements by the people bringing and defending the action. Both sides briefly tell the court what their case is about.

prosecutor's or plaintiff's case

2. The person bringing the action (the 'prosecutor' in a criminal case, the 'plaintiff' in a civil case) tries to prove his or her claim by calling witnesses to support the claim. This is known as 'evidence'.

evidence-in-chief

3. The prosecutor or plaintiff (or plaintiff's lawyer) will ask his or her witnesses to tell the court what they know about the case. This is called 'evidence-in-chief'.

cross-examination

4. The defence (the 'accused', or the accused's lawyer, in a criminal trial; the 'defendant' or the defendant's lawyer in a civil trial) then has a chance to question the prosecutor's or plaintiff's witnesses. This is called 'cross-examination'. Cross-examination is aimed at obtaining the truth by breaking down the story of unreliable witnesses or by showing that they are confused or perhaps not telling the truth.

re-examination

5. The prosecutor or plaintiff (or plaintiff's lawyer) can then clear up any questions asked by the defence by getting the witnesses to explain what their answers meant. This is called 're-examination'.

prosecutor or plaintiff closes case

6. When the prosecutor or plaintiff (or plaintiff's lawyer) thinks that enough evidence has been led to win the case, he or she will close the case for the prosecution.

witnesses for defence case

7. The defence (the accused or defendant, or defendant's lawyer) then calls its witnesses and leads evidence to show that it is doubtful that the accused has committed the crime or that the defendant is not responsible for what is claimed.

cross-examination

8. The prosecutor or plaintiff (or plaintiff's lawyer) then has a chance to cross-examine the defence's witnesses.

re-examination

9. The defence may then re-examine the witness to explain any answers that upset the defence's case.

defence closes case

10. When the defence thinks that it has raised doubts concerning the case against the accused in a criminal case or in a civil case has shown that its story is more likely than that of the plaintiff, the defence will close its case.

closing arguments

11. Each side then has a chance to tell the court about the case. The prosecutor or plaintiff (or plaintiff's lawyer) will sum up the case and explain why the state or plaintiff should win. The accused or defendant (or defendant's lawyer) will then argue why the accused should be found not guilty or why the plaintiff should lose the case.

judgment

12. The judge or magistrate will then give a judgment. In a criminal case the judge or magistrate will find the accused guilty or not guilty. In a civil case the judge or magistrate will find that the plaintiff has or has not proven his or her case.

The following is a summary of the steps in an adversary trial:

Opening Statement

prosecutor's/ plaintiff's case

Prosecutor's/Plaintiff's Case

Evidence by prosecutor's/plaintiff's witnesses
Cross-examination by defence
Re-examination by prosecutor/plaintiff
Prosecutor/plaintiff closes case

---

defence case

Defence Case

Evidence by accused's/defendant's witnesses
Cross-examination by prosecutor/plaintiff
Re-examination by defence
Defence closes case

Argument

Prosecutor/plaintiff argues why he or she has proved his or her case
Defence argues why prosecutor/plaintiff has not proved his or her case

---

judgment

Judgment

1.5 Civil courts and small claims courts

Outcomes

After completion of this section learners will be able to:

1. Demonstrate an understanding of how the civil courts and small claims courts work.

Assessment criteria

1. An explanation is given of how the civil courts and small claims courts work.
2. A decision is taken on which courts it is necessary to employ a lawyer in.
3. A set of facts in a case is examined and a decision is taken on what steps will be taken in a civil case involving an assault on a worker by a foreman.
4. Sets of facts in a series of scenarios are examined and a decision is taken in each on whether the case should be heard in the small claims court.
5. A role-play involving a consumer claim in a small claims court is conducted and a decision is made on whether the consumer should recover his money.

judges and magistrates are 'referees'

In para 1.4.2 above we saw how the civil and criminal courts in South Africa use the adversary system. We also saw how judges or magistrates do not play an active role in court. They are 'referees'. They do not help the parties win their cases, but are there to make sure that the rules of evidence and the proper procedures are followed. The rules of evidence state how information may be used to prove or disprove a case, and what people may or may not say in a civil or criminal court.

court proceedings can be difficult

People should be given a chance to present their cases fairly and to question people who give evidence against them. Many court proceedings, however, can be difficult. Just because people are innocent does not mean that the court will find in their favour if they do not have a lawyer. People defending a criminal case, or bringing or defending a civil case, should employ a lawyer to assist them. The only situation where it is not necessary to employ a lawyer is in the small claims court.

Problem 1: When lawyers may and may not be necessary

1. Do judges and magistrates help people who bring and defend actions in court? What should these people do?
2. In which court is it not necessary to employ a lawyer?

1.5.1 Civil courts

The steps taken in a civil case are different from those in a criminal case. In a civil case there is usually a dispute between two people about money (eg because of a broken contract, damage to property or injury to someone). As we have proof 'on a balance of probabilities'

mentioned, in a civil case the people bringing the action must prove their case '*on a balance of probabilities*'. This means that the plaintiff must prove that his or her story is more likely than that of the other parties.

1.5.1.1 Examples of civil cases

There are several different types of civil cases. Here are some examples:

tinned fish makes Nathan sick

1. Nathan Naidoo buys a tin of fish from A.J. Bazaars. There is something wrong with the fish and he becomes sick. Under the civil law the manufacturer of the tinned fish, or possibly A.J. Bazaars, may have to pay Nathan Naidoo's medical bills and other damages (eg pain and suffering and lost wages while he was sick).

Sam wants to 'eject' Frank from his flat

2. Sam Garfield, a landlord, wants Frank Mhlanga, a tenant, to leave the flat he is renting. Frank Mhlanga and his family are disturbing the neighbours and not paying the rent. Sam Garfield can apply to court for an order to make Frank Mhlanga pay the unpaid rent. He can also ask the court for an order to make Frank Mhlanga and his family leave the flat. This is called an 'ejection' or 'eviction' order.

Dora wants a divorce

3. Dora Hendricks wants to end her marriage because her husband, Henry Hendricks, always gets drunk, cannot hold down a job, and beats her up. She sues her husband for divorce.

Kobus calls a shopkeeper 'a crook'

4. Kobus Van Zyl accuses a storekeeper of being 'a crook' in front of his customers. The shopkeeper can sue Kobus Van Zyl for defamation for harming his reputation. If he succeeds, Kobus Van Zyl will have to pay the shopkeeper damages.

1.5.1.2 Steps in a civil case

Mr Brown owes Mrs Green R30 000

Mr Brown owes Mrs Green R30 000 for the price of a second-hand car bought from her. The car's engine seizes up after two weeks and Mr Brown refuses to pay Mrs Green. This is what will happen if Mrs Green wishes to bring a civil action against Mr Brown:

Mrs Green consults a lawyer

1. Mrs Green ('the plaintiff') goes to a lawyer and asks for help to claim her R30 000. The lawyer takes a statement and then writes a letter to Mr Brown setting out the claim and demanding payment of the money within a certain number of days. This is called a *letter of demand*.

letter of demand

a summons is sent

2. If there is no reply to the letter of demand the lawyer draws up a *summons*. The summons is a document issued by the court setting out the details of Mrs Green's (the plaintiff's) claim. It also tells Mr Brown ('the defendant') that he must defend the case within a certain number of days or judgment will be given in favour of Mrs Green. (If Mr Brown does not reply a judgment will be given even though he was not present in court.)

Mr Brown has a choice

3. Mr Brown, when he receives the summons, can do one of the following:
   (a) Defend the claim.
   (b) Admit that the money is owed and agree to pay.
   (c) Try to settle the case after discussing it with Mrs Green's lawyer.

Mr Brown defends the case

4. Mr Brown can defend the claim by himself or his lawyer completing a form called a '*Notice of Intention to Defend*' which is on the back of the Summons. Mr Brown or his lawyer must take copies of the notice to court for stamping and then give a copy to Mrs Green's lawyer.

Mr Brown should employ a lawyer

5. Defending a civil case involves complicated legal documents called '*pleadings*'. It is therefore advisable for Mr Brown to employ a lawyer. It is nearly impossible for a non-lawyer to defend a civil case in the magistrate's or Supreme Court. It is, however, easy for people to defend cases in the small claims court because lawyers are not allowed. However, the amount claimed in the small claims court may not be more than R15 000 (see below para 1.5.2.).

the lawyers draw up 'pleadings'

6. After the 'Notice of Intention to Defend' has been sent, Mrs Green's and Mr Brown's lawyers set out the facts in dispute in pleadings which have to be drawn up according to the rules of the court.

Mr Brown could settle the case

7. At any time during the pleadings (or even during the trial), Mr Brown can still decide to *settle* the case out of court. He does this by agreeing to pay the amount claimed or by persuading Mrs Green to accept less.

evidence is given

witnesses are examined

8. If Mrs Green and Mr Brown do not settle the dispute, there will be a *trial* (a court case). At the trial the parties will present their cases to court. This is done by giving their evidence, and calling witnesses. As in criminal cases, witnesses may be *cross-examined* and *re-examined*. (See above para 1.4.2.)

the attorneys try to persuade the court

9. When they think they have led sufficient evidence, the attorneys for Mrs Green and Mr Brown will close their clients' cases. They will try to persuade the court that their client should win.

the magistrate gives a judgment

10. The magistrate will decide whether Mrs Green has proved her case. If she proves her case 'on a balance of probabilities', judgment is given in her favour. If Mrs Green does not prove her claim, judgment is given in favour of Mr Brown.

the loser may appeal

11. If Mrs Green or Mr Brown thinks that the magistrate made a mistake when applying the law, he or she can take the case on appeal to the High Court (see above para 1.3.1.7).

the case may go on review

12. If the loser feels that the magistrate was biased or prevented him or her from presenting the case properly, the case may be taken on review to the High Court (see above para 1.3.1.7). It is, however, expensive to take a case on appeal or review to the High Court.

if a defendant ignores a summons default judgment may be given in favour of the plaintiff

Note: Sometimes the defendant receives a summons to appear in court, but ignores it. If the defendant does nothing, the plaintiff can still go to court without the defendant and ask the court to give a judgment in his or her favour. Judgment will then be given against the defendant even though he or she was not in court. This is called a '*default judgment*' and the defendant automatically loses the case.

1.5.1.3 Enforcing a judgment

the defendant may pay in instalments

If the plaintiff wins the case and the defendant cannot pay, the latter can offer to pay in instalments. The plaintiff may agree to this. If, however, the defendant property may be attached and sold

still fails to pay after the judgment has been given, the plaintiff can ask the court to issue a *'warrant of execution'*. This is a document which authorises the *'sheriff of the court'* (a court official) to go to the defendant's home and *'attach'* property sufficient to cover the amount of the judgment plus the sheriff's fees. This means that the attached property can be taken and sold by the sheriff of the court. The amount of the debt plus legal costs will be paid to the plaintiff out of the proceeds of the sale. The rest of the proceeds, if any, will be paid to the defendant.

costs may exceed the debt

Therefore, if Mrs Green had won her case against Mr Brown and Mr Brown had still not paid, she could get a warrant of execution against Mr Brown's property for R30 000 plus legal costs. The sheriff may, for example, attach a television set, motor car, radio, refrigerator, furniture or other property sufficient to pay the outstanding debt and costs. The legal costs would include Mrs Green's attorney's fees for going to court, the court costs, and the cost of the sheriff of the court. Sometimes these costs add up to more than the original debt.

the sheriff of the court may 'attach' property sufficient to pay the outstanding debt and costs

a 'financial inquiry' may be held

money may be deducted from the defendant's salary

If the defendant does not have sufficient property that can be sold to pay off the plaintiff's claim, the plaintiff may ask the court to enquire into the defendant's financial position. The defendant can then be ordered to pay a certain amount each month, or have a certain amount deducted from his or her salary each month by the employer and sent to the plaintiff. If the defendant refuses to obey the court order he or she can be arrested for contempt of court. It is sometimes very expensive to enforce a judgment and it is usually necessary to employ a lawyer to do so.

steps in a civil case

Summary: Steps in a civil case

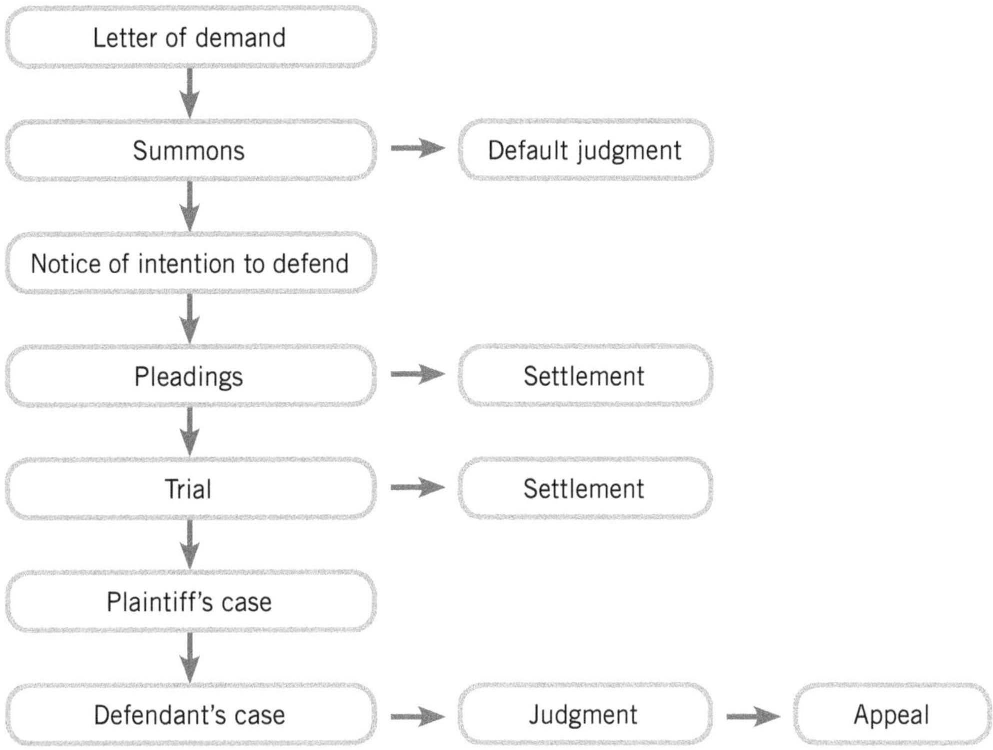

Problem 2: The case of the assaulted worker

Mr Dlamini is a worker at Henry's Construction. One day Mr Dlamini and the foreman have an argument. The foreman assaults Mr Dlamini. Mr Dlamini wants to claim R25 000 damages from the foreman. The foreman refuses to pay him. Mr Dlamini goes to a lawyer to help in claiming the money.

Questions

1. What will Mr Dlamini's lawyer do?
2. What happens if the foreman ignores his lawyer's actions?
3. What procedure will be followed if the case goes to court?
4. What will happen if the foreman fails to defend the case after he has received a summons?
5 What do you think could be done if the foreman refuses to obey a judgment telling him to pay Mr Dlamini?
6. What could the foreman do if he was unhappy about losing the case after it had been to court?

1.5.2 Small claims courts

claims of less than R15 000

As previously mentioned, the aim of the small claims courts is to allow people to bring claims for less than R15 000 cheaply and quickly (see above para 1.3.1.5). Small claims courts, however, cannot hear certain cases (eg divorce, interpretation of wills, whether people are insane, defamation, malicious prosecution, wrongful imprisonment, seduction and breach of promise to marry). The small claims court may also not hear cases that the Commissioner thinks involve difficult questions of law and should be heard by a magistrates' court.

1.5.2.1 Examples of small claims cases

Many of the cases heard in the small claims court are similar to those heard in the ordinary civil courts, except they are for less than R15 000. For example:

Mavis is dismissed by her employer when she complains about not being paid

Ahmed's second-hand stove burns out after one month

Mali is assaulted by John at a football match

James drives negligently and crashes into Ethel's car

1. Mavis is employed as a domestic worker for R2 000 per month. He employer does not pay her for three months. When Mavis complains, she is dismissed. Mavis may claim against her employer for R6 000 in the small claims court.
2. Ahmed buys a second-hand stove for R2 500. It works for one month and then burns out. Ahmed may claim against the seller in the small claims court.
3. Mali is assaulted by John at a football match. Mali requires five stitches in his cheek. Mali wishes to sue John for R4 000 pain and suffering and R2 000 lost wages. Mali may sue in the small claims court.
4. James drives negligently and crashes into Ethel's car causing R18 000 damage. Ethel may sue James in the small claims court – if she is prepared to reduce her claim to R15 000 by abandoning R3 000.

Very few legal documents are needed, and no lawyers can appear, in the small claims court. The 'adversary system' (see above para 1.4.2.2) does not apply as the Commissioner asks all the questions. The steps for bringing actions in the small claims court are much simpler than those in the ordinary civil courts.

1.5.2.2 Steps in a small claims case

Mabel buys a stove that does not work

Mabel Shabangu buys a paraffin stove from P. Stores for R4 500. After two weeks the stove stops working. P. Stores refuses to replace it or give Mabel Shabangu her money back. The following steps would occur if Mabel Shabangu wished to sue in the small claims court:

Mabel sends a letter of demand

1. Mabel Shabangu (the 'plaintiff') must first send a *letter of demand* by registered post or delivered by hand to the owner of P. Stores (the 'defendant'). P. Stores must be given 14 days to reply. (A letter of demand form can be obtained from the clerk of the small claims court.)

P. Stores do not reply

2. If P. Stores does not reply to the letter of demand, Mabel can take a copy of the letter of demand, and proof that it was sent (eg a registered slip from the post office) to the *clerk of the small claims court* and ask him or her to issue a summons.

the clerk of the court issues a summons

3. The clerk of the small claims court will fill in a summons form and tell Mabel to *serve* it on P. Stores. This means that Mabel must take the summons to the owner of P. Stores at his or her home or place of work. If Mabel does not want to take the summons herself she can ask the *sheriff* of the magistrates' court to serve the summons. The summons gives P. Stores 10 days to pay the plaintiff's claim. It also mentions a date after the 10 days when P. Stores will have to appear in the small claims court if the claim is not settled.

a 'statement of defence' may be handed in

4. If P. Stores wishes, a *statement of defence* may be handed to the clerk of the small claims court but this is not necessary. The owner of P. Stores may mention his or her defence at the court appearance.

the Commissioner asks all the questions

5. At the trial the *Small Claims Commissioner* (who is like a judge or magistrate, except that he or she asks all the questions) will explain the court procedure to the parties and ask all the questions. If one person wishes to ask the person a question the question must be asked through the Commissioner.

witnesses are questioned, evidence is led

6. Both Mabel Shabangu and P. Stores may call witnesses to support their cases. The witnesses will be questioned by the Commissioner. The parties should also bring any documents involved in their case (eg an invoice or receipt), which could be used as proof. The amount of proof required is the same as in ordinary civil cases (ie proof 'on balance of probabilities').

the Commissioner hears sufficient evidence

7. When the Commissioner has heard sufficient evidence to decide the case the trial can be stopped and judgment given. The Commissioner does not have to listen to all the witnesses if he or she thinks it is not necessary.

no appeal, only review

8. The Commissioner gives almost the same judgments as a magistrate or judge, but the Commissioner's judgment *cannot be taken on appeal*. As in criminal and civil cases the Commissioner's judgment can be taken on *review* if he or she was biased or does not give each party a fair hearing (eg does not allow one of them to tell his or a story).

default judgment may be given

9. If P. Stores do not appear in the small claims court the Commissioner can give a *default judgment* in favour of Mabel Shabangu.

The same method of enforcing a judgment can be used as is used in an ordinary civil case (see above para 1.5.1.3).

steps in a small claims case

Summary: Steps in a small claims case

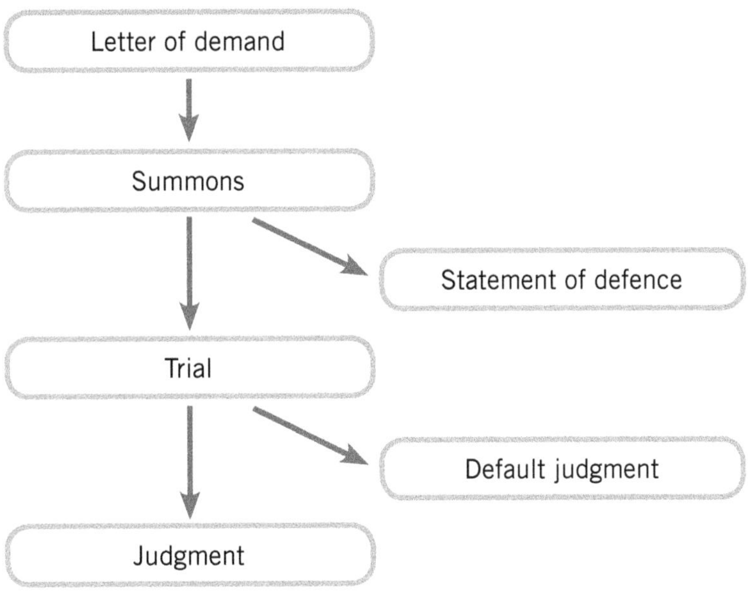

Problem 3: The case of the cheap tape recorder

Tom's tape recorder stops working

Tom, who is 22 years old, buys a cheap tape recorder for R1 000 from a store called Tapes Galore owned by Sam. The tape recorder stops working and ten days later Tom tries to exchange it. The sales invoice has the following words typed at the bottom: 'This product is fully guaranteed for 5 days from the date of purchase. If defective, return in original box for credit towards another purchase.'

Tapes Galore refuse to help

Tapes Galore refuse to give Tom his money back or exchange the tape recorder and Tom brings an action in the small claims court. He has already sent a registered letter of demand and a summons. The store has ignored both. The shop owner and salesman appear in the small claims court on the day of the hearing.

Questions

Role-play the small claims court hearing.

Evidence:
Tom has the sales invoice for R1 000 paid to Tapes Galore, and the broken tape recorder. He claims to have thrown away the box the tape recorder originally came in.

Witnesses for Tom:

'the salesman talked me into buying'

(a) Tom says: 'The salesman talked me into buying a Super Sound Special tape recorder for R1 000. The tape recorder was given to me in a cardboard box. I was told that it had a five-day guarantee. When I got home I found that the tape recorder did not work. I did not take it back immediately because my mother was sick. I have the receipt and broken tape recorder as proof and I want my money back.'

'when he tried to record it did not work'

(b) Thandi (Tom's sister) says: 'When Tom came home with the new tape recorder he was very excited. But when he tried to record it did not work. I told him to take it back to the store and ask for a refund.'

Witnesses for Tapes Galore:

'it worked alright'

(a) Victor (the salesman) says: 'I sold Tom the tape recorder. I know that it worked alright because we never have trouble with Super Sound Special tape recorders straight from the factory. I think Tom dropped the tape recorder and broke it on the way home. Maybe he broke it during the 10 days he had it.'

'must be returned in the original box'

(b) Sam (the owner): 'We have never had a complaint about a Super Special Sound. We never give refunds unless the tape recorders are returned within five days in the packaging in which we sell them. The guarantee says they must be returned in the original box. I agree with Victor that Tom probably did not bring it back in the box because he damaged the box when he dropped it.'

Further reading

1.1 Street law and law in general

Grimes R, McQuoid-Mason D, O'Brien E & Zimmer J 'Street Law and Social Justice Education' in Frank S Bloch (ed) *The Global Clinical Movement: Educating Lawyers for Social Justice* (2011) Chapter 15

Kleyn D & Viljoen F *Beginner's Guide for Law Students* 5 ed (2011) Chapter 1

Maisel P & Greenbaum L *Introduction to Law and Legal Skills* (2001) Chapter 2

McQuoid-Mason D & Palmer R *African Law Clinicians Manual* (2013) Chapter 3

R v Dudley and Stevens [1884] 14 QBD 273 (DC).

1.2 Where law comes from, how it is made, and the different kinds of law

Currie I & De Waal J *The Bill of Rights Handbook* 5 ed (2005)

Kleyn D & Viljoen F *Beginner's Guide for Law Students* 5 ed (2011) Chapter 2

Maisel P & Greenbaum L *Introduction to Law and Legal Skills* (2001) Chapter 4

Radebe v Hough 1949 (1) SA 380 (A)

S v Mafu 1966 (2) SA 240 (E)

S v Williams 1995 (3) SA 632 (CC)

1.3 The courts and settling disputes outside the courts

Kleyn D & Viljoen F *Beginner's Guide for Law Students* 5 ed (2011) Chapter 11

Maisel P & Greenbaum L *Introduction to Law and Legal Skills* (2001) Chapters 5 and 6

1.4 Lawyers and the adversary system

Kleyn D & Viljoen F *Beginner's Guide for Law Students* 5 ed (2011) Chapters 8 and 12

1.5 Civil courts and small claims courts

Kleyn D & Viljoen F *Beginner's Guide for Law Students* 5 ed (2011) Chapter 6

Street law

2. Criminal law and child justice

CONTENTS

PART TWO

Criminal law and child justice

2.1 The meaning, nature and causes of crime

Outcomes

After completion of this section learners will be able to:

1. Explain the meaning, nature and causes of crimes.

Assessment criteria

1. An explanation is given of what a crime is.
2. A set of facts is examined and a decision is taken on whether a person's act or failure to act is a crime.
3. Causes of crimes are identified.
4. Ways of preventing and reporting crimes are identified.
5. A set of facts is examined and a decision is taken on whether or not to report a crime.
6. A set of facts is examined and a decision is taken on which parties should be held criminally liable.
7. A set of facts is examined and a decision is taken on which actions by people can be regarded as crimes.
8. An explanation is given of the types of behaviour that can take place prior to the commission of a crime.

Criminal law deals with acts that are regarded as 'crimes' by society. Child justice concerns the criminal law as it affects children, and how the courts deal with children accused of crimes.

2.1.1 What is 'crime'?

a wrong against the state

As we mentioned in Part 1, a crime is a wrong against the state for which the criminal is punished by the state. Criminal law attempts to control how people behave. It therefore forbids certain types of behaviour. Anyone who breaks the criminal law may have committed a 'crime'. In order to force people to follow the criminal law, the state uses threats of punishment.

'crime' is difficult to define

It is not easy to provide a single definition of all types of behaviour that are considered 'criminal'. This is because what is considered criminal is determined by many different values – moral, social and legal. Some crimes (eg murder, theft and rape) have been recognised by different societies for thousands of years. Usually, however, it is the ruling authority that labels conduct as 'criminal'. In South Africa for instance, Parliament, provincial legislatures and local authorities make these decisions.

moral and social influences

What is regarded as a crime will therefore be influenced by the moral and social values of those in power. In democratic countries, such as South Africa, these values are usually based on what the majority of people regard as right or wrong.

If this is the case, the aims of the lawmakers are the same as those of society. The criminal law can then function so as to protect society from anti-social conduct (eg acts that threaten life and property, individual freedom and our system of government).

In countries that are not democracies (such as South Africa during the apartheid era) the values of those in power do not reflect the values of the majority.

In apartheid South Africa, this resulted in types of behaviour being labelled 'criminal' that were not regarded as such by most people (eg someone of the 'wrong' race living in a segregated neighbourhood).

Constitution includes the Bill of Rights

In order to protect the rights of South Africans, and to protect these types of laws from being passed again, we now have a Constitution that includes a Bill of Rights. If a criminal law (either common law or statute) conflicts with the Bill of Rights, certain courts have the power to declare that law invalid (see above para 1.3.1.1).

Problem 1: If you were a lawmaker

Questions

Imagine you are a lawmaker and decide for each of the following whether the person's act or failure to act should be a crime. If you think it should be a crime, decide whether it should be ranked as 'very serious (vs)', 'less serious (ls)' or 'petty (p)'. Rank each according to what you think should be a crime, not what the law says is a crime. Give reasons for your decisions:

Zol is a drug addict

Xolani is a pickpocket

Jan robs a bottlestore

Sheila is a prostitute

1. Zol is a drug addict who sells dagga and mandrax.
2. Xolani pickpockets a person's wallet containing R100.
3. Jan robs a bottle store at gunpoint.
4. Midas, a rich lawyer, refuses to pay income tax because he does not support the government's policies.
5. Pam leaves a shop with change for R20 after she gave the cashier R10. The cashier mistakenly thought that Pam gave her a R20 note.
6. Sheila approaches a man for the purposes of prostitution.
7. Ming refuses to wear a crash helmet while riding a motorcycle.
8. A factory makes a river dirty with chemicals from a laboratory.
9. Max gets drunk and kills a child while driving too fast through a school zone.
10. Jane sees a friend shoplifting but does not report her.
11. Romeo asks Juliet to go out for a date, and, when she refuses, swears at her.
12. A shopkeeper cheats by not paying his value-added tax (VAT) to the government.
13. Zola is a Rastafari and smokes dagga because it is part of her religion.
14. Devan carries his own gun and shoots someone who is stealing his car, despite the fact that his life is not in danger.
15. William smokes a cigarette in a restaurant that does not have a smoking area.
16. A youth political leader chants 'kill the boer' and a national police commissioner tells police officers 'shoot to kill'.

crime takes many forms

Crime takes many forms. It may be a youth snatching a handbag, or a gang robbing a bank. It may be a person taking someone else's car for a joyride, or a gang of car thieves stealing it for resale. It may be a teenager selling dagga to school friends in the playground, or an organised gang who have a countrywide drug network. Professional people who are usually regarded as 'respectable' may also commit crimes. For example, a lawyer who steals his clients' money from his trust fund, an accountant who helps his client cheat on tax, or a businessman who overcharges, fixes prices or illegally takes money out of the country.

2.1.2 The nature and causes of crime

South Africa has a very high crime rate

In South Africa the high crime rate is a major issue that affects all of us. Of particular concern is the high rate of violent crime in South Africa.

Although most South Africans agree that crime is a problem, there is very little agreement on why the crime rate is so high. Some of the reasons given are poverty, inequality, unemployment, lack of education, breakdown in family structures and morals and the influence of television and films. People also say that the police and the justice system are ineffective, so that there is little chance of criminals being caught or punished. Others argue that the Bill of Rights in the Constitution gives too many rights to criminals and that the death penalty should be reintroduced.

poverty, inequality, unemployment and lack of education are related to crime

No one of these factors, considered on its own, is able to provide an explanation for South Africa's high crime rate. There is evidence that poverty, inequality, unemployment and lack of education are related to crime. But many wealthy family breakdowns and a decline in moral standards

countries also have problems with crime. There are also countries that are far poorer than South Africa but which have low crime rates and very little violent crime. Family breakdowns, and a resulting decline in moral standards, may contribute to the crime rate but cannot be the sole cause.

improving the police and justice system may reduce crime

It is true that improving the police force and the justice system may help reduce the crime rate. However, South Africa has limited resources, so this will not be an easy task. This also does not explain why South Africa's crime rate is so high in the first place.

there is no evidence that the death penalty deters people from committing crimes

There is no evidence that the death penalty deters (ie discourages) people from committing crimes. There are also many countries that have a Bill of Rights, but which also have low crime rates. Indeed, many people think that South Africa's history of colonialism and apartheid, which involved widespread human rights violations, has created a culture in which human life is not respected. This, in turn, gives rise to violent crime. Other people think that changing the Bill of Rights will worsen, not improve, this situation.

more than one cause of crime

There is not a *single* cause of crime. Instead, a *number* of factors mentioned above – such as poverty, unemployment and a culture of disrespect for human life – contribute to South Africa's high crime rate. There is, in other words, more than one cause of crime.

The causes of crime

poverty, unemployment, lack of education

growing population, breakdown in family structure

breakdown in parental guidance and morals

ineffective police protection

the influence of television and films

racial discrimination and disrespect for the law

Problem 2: The causes of crime

Questions

1. Can you suggest causes of crime not mentioned above?
2. Rank the causes of crime in the text and on your list from the most important to the least important. Discuss your ranking.

2.1.3 Victims of crime

crime affects everybody

Crime affects everybody. It results in lost money, damaged lives, frightened people and suffering. Victims of crime are of all races, and include rich and poor, young and old. Very often the victims of crime who suffer most are the weakest people in society – the young, the old, and the poor.

In some countries the state helps victims of crimes by paying compensation to people who are injured by criminal acts. This has not yet been done in South Africa, although the government is looking at providing victims of crimes with more rights and has introduced a 'Victim's Charter'. In South Africa the victim of a crime who, as a result, has lost money or had property damaged, can ask the court to order the criminal to pay back the value of the money or property. This is called 'compensation' or 'restitution'.

compensation and restitution for victims

'Compensation' means being given money for the thing stolen or damaged. 'Restitution' means returning the thing stolen. The victim at the criminal trial – not the prosecutor – must ask the court for the compensation or restitution, otherwise the court will not order the criminal to pay the money or hand over the property.

Service Charter for Victims of Crime in South Africa
If you have been a victim of crime the following rights, as contained in the Constitution and relevant legislation, will be upheld in your contact with the criminal justice system:

1. The right to be treated with fairness and with respect for dignity and privacy:
   - You have the right to be attended to promptly and courteously, treated with respect for your dignity and privacy by all members of any department, institution, agency or organisation dealing with or providing a service to you.
2. The right to offer information:
   - You have the right to offer information during the criminal investigation and trial.
3. The right to receive information:
   - You have the right to be informed of your rights and of how to exercise them.
4. The right to protection:
   - You have the right to be free from intimidation, harassment, fear, tampering, bribery, corruption and abuse. If you are a witness, you must report any such threats to the police or senior state prosecutor.
5. The right to assistance:
   - You have the right to request assistance and, where relevant, have access to available social, health and counselling services, as well as legal assistance which is responsive to your needs.
6. The right to compensation:
   - You have the right to compensation for loss of or damage to property suffered as a result of a crime being committed against you.
7. The right to restitution:
   - You have the right to restitution in cases where you have been unlawfully dispossessed of goods or property, or where your goods or property has been damaged unlawfully.

Crime prevention:

Some simple crime prevention rules

Mugging, bag-snatching, housebreaking and robbery are crimes that many people worry about. We can all help to fight crime. People can learn how to protect themselves. To do this people have to know how to prevent crime and what to do if they are victims of crime. Here are some simple crime prevention rules:

Report suspicious activity to the police

1. **General:** Report suspicious activity to the police. The police cannot help if they are not informed.
2. **When away from home:** Lock all doors and windows when going out. Leave a light on at night. Do not leave a key above a door, under a mat, or a note on the door.

3. **When at home:** Lock all doors leading to the outside of the property. Never let strangers into the house without checking their identity or making sure about the reasons for their visit.
4. **When on the street:** Beware of high crime areas. Dark deserted streets, parking lots, garages and bus stops are all high crime areas. Do not carry much money with you. Do not 'flash' money in public. Beware of people asking directions or brushing up against you. If somebody follows you, enter the nearest occupied residence or building and ask for help. Always walk on the side of the road facing oncoming traffic. If anyone in a car tries to stop you run in the direction opposite to the way the car is going.
5. **Safety on public transport:** Stand close to others when waiting for a bus or taxi. In dark or deserted areas stand close to occupied or well-lit places. If anyone on a bus acts suspiciously or attempts to interfere with you or other people, notify the driver.

Stand close to others when waiting for a bus or taxi

6. **Car safety:** Make certain the car is in good working order with safe tyres and enough fuel. Check the car to make sure nobody is hiding in it. When driving or riding in a car keep the doors locked. Cars should be parked in attended parking areas and well-lit areas where there are car guards at night. Packages or personal items should not be left so that people can see them in the car. If you are attacked in a car, sound the hooter until help arrives. In high crime areas you should drive or ride with your windows closed.
7. **Identify your property:** The serial numbers of all valuable items such as radios and hi-fi sets, computers, cell phones, Ipods, Ipads, watches, television sets, bicycles, electrical appliances, tools, etc should be recorded and the list kept in a safe place. This will help the police to identify the items if they are stolen.
8. **Children:** Children should not enter unknown vehicles (eg cars, minibuses or lorries) or premises or accompany unknown adults to lonely places. Children should write down the registration number of a vehicle where the driver has stopped or taken their friends for a 'joy ride'. Use a pencil or stone to write on the pavement or draw the number in the sand. Tell parents, instructors or the police about adults who loiter around school playgrounds or follow children about. Children should not accept gifts or lifts from strangers.

Children should not accept gifts or lifts from strangers

9. **Rape:** Women who are attacked should try to escape. Sometimes they can talk themselves out of danger or pretend that they are insane or stupid or are HIV positive. They may be able to successfully resist, but this must be done carefully and quickly to throw the attacker off balance. Do not appear to be looking directly at the rapist but try to notice a definite mark of identity (eg colour of hair, eyes, a scar, speech problem, etc). This will help the police to catch the rapist. After being raped a woman should not change her clothes or wash before she has been examined by a doctor to make sure that no evidence is lost – otherwise the rapist may get away with his crime.
10. **Going on a trip:** When away on a trip, cancel any deliveries (eg newspapers). Ask a neighbour to collect the mail. Arrange for some lights to be turned on at night (eg by a friend or a time switch). If possible ask a friend to stay in your house while you are away. In some neighbourhoods you can ask the police to check your property once a day. If the house has a burglar alarm tell the security company that you are going away and, if somebody is staying in your house, the name of that person.

When away on a trip cancel all deliveries

11. **Single women:** Women living alone should list only their last name and first initial on their mailbox in a block of flats and in the telephone directory.

If you become a victim

1. **Safety first:** If you become a victim of a crime, remember that your safety comes first. Most burglars and robbers will run away if they can, so do not try to stop them. Although you should try to identify them, do not let them see that you are looking at them as they may attack you if they think that you could subsequently identify them to the police.
2. **Do not resist:** You may be injured or killed. If you cannot run away, sit down so you do not get knocked down.
3. **Call the police as soon as you can:** Do not wait. The longer you wait, the more likely it is the criminal will get away. Most burglaries occur when no one is at home. But if you arrive home and suspect there is a burglar inside do not go in. Go to a neighbour's house and call the police immediately. Always keep the panic button within reach if you live in a house that has a burglar alarm. Press it immediately if suspicious strangers enter the premises.

How to report a crime

If you are a victim or a witness to a crime, you should do the following:

1. Stay calm.
2. Call the police immediately.
3. Always report a crime, even though the law does not require you to do so. If you do not report it, the police cannot help. Someone else may become a victim.
4. Tell the police who you are, where you are, and what happened.
5. If anyone is hurt ask the police to call an ambulance.
6. When the police arrive tell them exactly what you saw. Try to remember what the suspect looked like: age, height, clothing, face (eg eyes, hair, freckles, scars, etc). Was the suspect driving a car? If so try to remember the make, model, colour, registration number, and direction of travel. Try to write down this information before the police arrive. The police will take a statement.
7. You may be asked to make a complaint or give evidence in court. Remember, if you do not help the police the criminal may hurt somebody else.

Should crimes be reported?

A person who is not involved in a crime, before or after it is committed, is generally not legally required to report it to the police. Most people, however, report crimes because they believe that it is in the interests of society to do so. Many people criticise those who witness crimes and do not report them as selfish or uncaring individuals. The laws in some countries require witnesses to report crimes to the police. In these countries failure to report a crime may result in the witness being prosecuted.

Problem 3: Preventing and reporting crimes

Questions

1. Do you know anybody who has been the victim of a crime? What was the crime? How did it affect the person?
2. List and discuss at least four things you can do to protect yourself.
3. One afternoon at about 4 pm you see a white truck stop in front of your neighbour's house. Two strange men get out of the truck and walk to the back of the house. You are suspicious because you know your neighbours are away on holiday. What will you do?
4. If you call the police about the incident in 3 above, what will you say? Role-play a telephone call between yourself and the police.
5. Have you ever witnessed a crime? What happened? What did you do?
6. Do you think that witnesses to crimes should be legally obliged to report crimes? Give reasons for your answer.

2.1.4 What makes an act a crime?

elements of crimes

All crimes have certain 'elements'. Elements are the conditions that make an act a crime. A crime is only committed if all the elements are present. For example, robbery is the unlawful taking of another's property with the intention of stealing it, carried out with force or threats of force. Therefore the elements of robbery are (1) unlawful taking of another's property, (2) the intention to steal and (3) the use of force or threats of force (see below para 2.6.4).

If someone picks your pocket without your knowledge, the person cannot be convicted of robbery. This is because the person did not use force or threats of force, which are an essential element for robbery. The person would, however, be guilty of theft, because the elements of theft do not include force or threats of force (see below para 2.6.3).

act and intention

Most crimes require an act and an intention. Criminal intention means that the person intended to commit the crime and knew that his or her act was wrongful. Criminal intention involves knowing and wilful action. If, however, a person acts because of a mistake or some other innocent reason, there is no criminal intention. For example, if a hunter accidentally shoots another hunter who is mistaken for an animal, no crime is committed because there was no criminal intention. If, however, the hunter was careless, he or she may be guilty of culpable homicide (see below para 2.2.1.2).

liability

Some crimes are strict liability offences that do not require criminal intention. Strict liability offences make the act itself a crime even if the person does not intend to commit a crime. For example, a café owner who stores or sells fresh food which becomes dirty in the café.

intention and motive

Intention is different from motive. Motive is the reason why a person commits a crime. For example, in murder, the motive is the reason why a person kills someone (eg out of hatred, for revenge, or to steal). A good motive can never justify a criminal act. A person may rob the rich to pay the poor, but his or her action will still be unlawful. A single act can be both a crime and a civil wrong (see above para 1.2.3). For example, if John punches Ben, the state can prosecute John for assault and Ben can sue John civilly for damages. In most cases an act cannot be a crime unless, at the time it was committed, the law said that the act was a crime.

2.1.5 People who may be charged with crimes

'parties' to crimes

'perpetrators' and 'co-perpetrators'

A 'party' to a crime is a person involved in the crime. The criminal who actually commits the crime is called the 'perpetrator' (eg the person who fires the gun in a murder). A person who helps the perpetrator is called a 'co-perpetrator' and may also be charged as a perpetrator to the crime. An example of a co-perpetrator would be a person who drives the getaway car in a bank robbery or a person who keeps a lookout during the robbery.

'accomplice'

A person who orders the crime or who helps the perpetrator commit the crime (eg supplies the gun or car for a bank robbery, or helps to plan the robbery), but is not present, is known as an 'accomplice'. He or she can usually be charged with the same crime and may receive the same punishment as the perpetrator.

'accessory after the fact'

A person who after learning that a crime has been committed helps the perpetrators avoid capture or escape is known as an 'accessory after the fact'. An example would be where a person helps a murderer dispose of a body or hide other evidence. An accessory after the fact is not charged with the main crime (eg murder) but may be charged with a separate crime (eg obstructing the course of justice). This person is not a party to the main crime because he or she only comes into the picture after the crime has been committed. An accessory after the fact will usually receive a lesser sentence than the perpetrator.

a person who orders, plans or helps commit the crime, but is not present at the scene of the crime, is called an 'accomplice'

the criminal who commits a crime is called the 'perpetrator'. A person who helps the perpetrator is called the 'co-perpetrator'

a person who helps the perpetrator avoid capture is called an 'accessory after the fact'

Problem 4: The bank robbery

Joe and Mary decide to rob the branch of a bank. Their friend Carl, an employee at the bank, helps by telling them when the branch will not be very busy and when it will have the most money. Mary drives a van to the bank and keeps a lookout while Joe goes inside and holds up the teller. Joe and Mary later meet a friend, Bob, who was not involved in the robbery. After hearing about it, Bob agrees to lend them his car so that they can drive to another town. David, a former school friend of Joe's and Mary's, witnesses the crime but does not tell the police, even though he recognises the robbers.

Do you think that (1) Joe, (2) Mary, (3) Carl, (4) Bob and (5) David can each be charged with a crime? If so, name the crimes. Should each be charged? Give reasons for your answer.

Questions

2.1.6 Crimes of omission

an omission may sometimes be a crime

Most crimes happen when a person commits an act that is against the law. Sometimes, however, a person may be criminally liable for failing to do something. This failure to act is called an 'omission'. In most cases the law does not make it a crime if a person fails to do something, but in a few cases it does. For example, a failure to fill in an income tax form or to stop after being involved in a car accident would be a crime of omission.

legal duty to act

Generally people are not liable for 'mere omissions' where there is no legal duty on them to act. If, however, there is a legal duty on them to act they may be criminally (and civilly) liable. Usually there is only a legal duty if there is some link or relationship between the person who fails to act and the person or thing injured by the omission. For example:

1. Where there was some previous conduct by the person who caused the dangerous situation (eg A pushes B, who cannot swim, into a river).
2. Where the person who failed to act was in control of dangerous property (eg A has a hole in his shop floor which he does not fix and B is injured when she steps into it).
3. Where there is 'a special relationship' between the person who fails to act and the person injured (eg a father fails to rescue his drowning child).
4. Where a person holds a public office (eg a police officer who fails to prevent a crime).
5. Where a statute requires a duty to act, (eg a doctor must report child abuse).
6. Where the 'legal convictions of the community' would be 'outraged' if the person did not act, ie members of society would be very upset if the person did nothing (eg where an off-duty lifesaver does not rescue a drowning child in a swimming pool).

Problem 5: Was there a duty to act?

Questions

In each case say whether you think there was a legal duty on the person to act. Was the failure to act a crime? Give reasons for your answer.

Busi watches a blind man walk over a cliff

1. Busi sees a blind man walking towards the edge of a cliff. Busi does nothing and the blind man is killed when he falls onto the rocks below.

Eunice pays no attention to the drowning child

2. Eunice, a bystander, sees a child drowning in a puddle of water. Eunice walks on and the child drowns.

Ndaba fails to warn Vuka about a live electricity cable

3. Ndaba, an electrician's assistant, is told to warn his fellow workers about a dangerous 'live' electricity cable lying on the floor. Ndaba fails to warn Vuka who is electrocuted and killed.

Jacob fails to rescue his drowning wife

4. Jacob sees his wife fall into a river. Jacob fails to rescue her and she drowns.

Donald, a doctor, passes by an accident victim

5. Donald, a doctor, sees that Graham has been injured in a motor accident but does not stop to help him.

Francisco, a factory owner, does not observe safety regulations

6. Francisco, a factory owner, fails to place a safety fence around a machine. He is required to do so by statute. Silvia is injured when her hand is caught in the machine.

2.1.7 Preliminary crimes

There are certain types of behaviour that take place before a crime is committed but which are still regarded as complete crimes in themselves. These offences, called 'incitement', 'attempt', and 'conspiracy', are aimed at giving the police the chance to prevent the crime from being committed. Each offence can be punished even if the harm never occurs.

incitement

Incitement happens when a person encourages another to commit a crime. This encouragement can be done in any way and the person accused will be liable as long as he or she tries to persuade the other person to commit the crime. An example would be where Jannie wishes to kill his wife Hettie, and asks Piet to do it for him. Even if Piet refuses to do the killing, Jannie has committed the crime of incitement.

attempt

Attempt occurs where a person intends to commit a crime and takes steps towards committing it. An attempt to commit a crime is in itself a crime even if the attempted crime is not committed. For example, Krish intends to shoot and kill Ali. He fires at Ali but misses him. Krish could be charged with the attempted murder of Ali. Mere preparation to commit a crime, however, would not be enough. For instance, if Krish went to buy a gun so that he could shoot Ali, this would be mere preparation, not an attempt.

conspiracy

Conspiracy is an agreement between two or more persons to commit a crime. The law punishes the act of conspiring to commit a crime even though the crime itself is not committed. The crime of conspiracy is aimed at preventing criminal activity by groups of people and has often been criticised as a threat to freedom of speech and association. An example of a conspiracy would be where Vusi persuades Bheki to help him rob a bank. If Bheki agrees to help Vusi with the bank robbery both are guilty of conspiracy to commit robbery, even if the robbery is never carried out.

Problem 6: Which crimes have been committed?

Questions

Decide whether any of the following people would be liable for the crimes of incitement, attempt and conspiracy. Give reasons for your answers.

1. Lionel, a bank teller, works out a foolproof way to steal money from his bank. He takes two weeks to make up his mind to steal the money. The day before he intends to steal the money he tries to persuade his girlfriend Dora, who also works at the bank, to join him.
2. Graham, an expert pickpocket, is caught while trying to pickpocket money from Sarah. He pleads not guilty and says that he cannot be convicted because Sarah did not have any money on her.
3. Vernon and Mdlolo decide to rob a bottle store. They meet in a bar and discuss their plans. Vernon leaves to buy a gun and Mdlolo goes off to steal a car for use in their getaway. Vernon is arrested as he walks out of the gunshop with his new gun. Mdlolo is arrested while stealing a car.
4. Annie decides to burn down her shop in order to be paid out by an insurance company. She spreads petrol around the building. She is arrested while leaving the shop where she had gone to buy a box of matches.

2.2 Crimes against people

Outcomes

After completion of this section learners will be able to:

1. List and explain the different crimes against people.

Assessment criteria

1. The elements of murder and culpable homicide are identified.
2. A set of facts is examined and a decision in made on whether the person was guilty of murder or culpable homicide.
3. Active euthanasia is distinguished from passive euthanasia.
4. A decision is made on whether active euthanasia should be regarded as a crime.
5. The legal position regarding suicide is explained.
6. The crime of assault is defined.
7. Common assault is distinguished from assault with intent to do grievous bodily harm.
8. A set of facts is examined and a decision is made on the kind of assault that has taken place.
9. Criminal insult (*crimen injuria*) is defined and discussed, with examples.
10. Kidnapping is defined and discussed.

The most important crimes against people are homicide (involving murder and culpable homicide), assault and rape. These are all very serious crimes and a person found guilty of them may receive a heavy sentence. The law, however, takes into account the particular facts of each case when deciding how to punish a guilty person. It also recognises that although in some cases the person's conduct appears to be a crime, there may be some lawful excuse for the act.

2.2.1 Homicide – the unlawful killing of a person

a very serious crime

South African society regards homicide or the unlawful killing of one human by another as one of the most serious of all crimes. The Constitution guarantees everyone the right to life. It is also a civil wrong to kill another person and the dead person's family can sue the killer for compensation. A person who is found guilty of homicide may receive a very heavy sentence – even life imprisonment.

justifiable homicide

Sometimes, however, a killing may be justified ('justifiable homicide') and not regarded as a crime. For example, the killing of an enemy soldier in wartime, or the killing of a person in self-defence. There are two crimes involving homicide or the unlawful killing of another human being – murder and culpable homicide. These are defined below.

2.2.1.1 Murder

Murder is the most serious form of homicide. In South Africa it used to carry the death penalty, unless there were special reasons why it should not be imposed. Nowadays, the heaviest sentence that can be imposed is life imprisonment or several life imprisonments.

unlawful and intentional killing

Murder is defined as 'the unlawful and intentional killing of another human being'. An intentional killing means that the murderer killed the person on purpose (ie directed his or her mind to kill the person) and knew that what he or she was doing was wrong at the time. The killing is unlawful if there is no justification for it. An example of justification is self-defence. It is not justified to kill people you hate, or because you do not agree with their politics or religion.

foreseeing the risk of death

An intention to kill includes a situation where a person knows that his or her act or failure to act might cause the risk of death to another person but does not care whether or not somebody is killed. This is known as eventual intention. For example, A fires a gun at B in a crowded street and kills C who is standing nearby. If A foresaw the risk of death to C or any other people in the street and did not care whether or not he killed them, he would be guilty of murder. The judge in the Oscar Pistorius case took a different approach which has been criticised.

Previously, the death sentence had to be imposed in cases of murder, except if there were extenuating circumstances (ie special facts that the courts could take into account to reduce the sentence). In its very first case the Constitutional Court ruled that the death sentence is unlawful.

life imprisonment

Parliament has, however, passed legislation that gives minimum sentences for cases of murder. In serious cases of murder (where, for example, the murder was planned or premeditated), the convicted person must be sentenced to life imprisonment. In less serious cases of murder the court must impose a sentence of no less than 15 years. In passing sentence, the court may also take into account whether or not the person is a first offender.

These sentences must be imposed unless there are 'substantial and compelling circumstances' why they should not be. 'Substantial and compelling reasons' has a similar meaning to extenuating circumstances (ie special facts that justify a lesser sentence).

2.2.1.2 Culpable homicide

negligent killing

Culpable homicide is usually regarded as a less serious form of homicide. Here the person who kills the other does not intend to do so. Culpable homicide is defined as the 'unlawful negligent killing of another person'. Negligence occurs where a person is careless, because he or she ought to have foreseen the chance of harm to another and should have taken steps to prevent the harm from happening. Negligence, therefore, deals with how people ought to have behaved, not with what they intended to do. A common form of culpable homicide arises from motor collisions where drivers do not intend to kill people but do so as a result of their negligent or careless driving.

Problem 1: The case of the jealous husband

Nico decides to shoot his wife who has run away with another man. He drives to her lover's house. On the way Nico's car knocks over a woman who suddenly steps into the road. Nico stops immediately and rushes to help the woman, who is already dead. Nico is very upset until he discovers that the woman is his wife.

Questions

1. If Nico was driving at a safe speed and the collision was unavoidable, is he guilty of a crime? Give reasons for your answer.
2. If Nico was driving too fast and the collision was avoidable, is he guilty of a crime? Give reasons for your answer.
3. If Nico deliberately drove over the woman even though he did not know that she was his wife, is he guilty of a crime? Give reasons for your answer.

Problem 2: The Oscar Pistorius trial

Oscar Pistorius, the famous Olympic and Paralympic runner with no legs – known as the 'Blade Runner' – shot and killed his model girlfriend, Reeva Steenkamp, on Valentine's Day in 2013. Reeva was in the enclosed toilet in the en suite bathroom at Oscar's home at the time of the shooting. Neighbours had heard shouting and screaming before Oscar fired four shots into the bathroom door. Oscar claimed immediately after the shooting, and during his trial, that he thought that there was a burglar in the bathroom. He said that because he had no legs he was vulnerable and that is why he always carried his gun. At the time he fired the shots he thought that the burglar was coming out of the bathroom to harm Reeva and him. He did not check if Reeva was still in bed before going towards the bathroom and did not know that she was in there. The bathroom door was locked and after the firing the shots he had to break down the door to enter it. To his horror he found that he had shot Reeva. Oscar was charged with murder and his trial was broadcast on TV in South Africa and throughout the world.

Questions

1. As the prosecutor what would your arguments be to support the charge of murder?
2. As the defence lawyer what would your arguments be to defend Oscar?
3. As the judge what would your judgment be?

2.2.1.3 Mercy killing (euthanasia) and suicide

'passive euthanasia' (eg withdrawing treatment from a very sick person who cannot be cured and allowing the person to die naturally from the disease or illness that is killing him or her) is not usually regarded as murder by the law

euthanasia

Euthanasia or 'mercy killing', is a crime and usually takes place when very sick people ask a doctor or friend to kill them to 'put them out of their misery'.

active euthanasia

'Active euthanasia' takes place if a person does something positive to kill the other person (eg by giving people an injection or pills that kill them, or shooting them) – even if the other person asks to be killed – and is regarded as murder. It has been suggested that euthanasia should be allowed where the person is so ill that he or she will soon die anyway.

passive euthanasia

'Passive euthanasia' takes place where people who are so ill that they are about to die are allowed to die naturally and is not usually regarded as a crime. For example, withdrawing treatment from a very sick person who cannot be cured and allowing the person to die naturally from the disease or illness that is killing him or her is not regarded as murder by the law. In such cases, however, the person must be given pain-relieving care.

active euthanasia is murder

The law regards 'active euthanasia' as murder. The court may, however, decide that the circumstances amount to 'substantial and compelling reasons' (ie special facts that justify a lighter sentence) and pass a lighter sentence than it normally would.

suggestions regarding doctor-assisted suicide

More than 10 years ago the South African Law Commission suggested that doctor-assisted suicide should be allowed in cases where patients who are terminally ill or suffering from unbearable pain ask a doctor to help them die. The Commission recommended three options regarding doctor-assisted suicide: (a) the law should stay as it is so that doctor-assisted suicide is murder; (b) doctor-assisted suicide should be lawful provided a number of conditions concerning a proper consent are satisfied, the decision is made by the patient together with his or her doctor, and the doctor's opinion regarding the terminal illness is confirmed by an independent doctor; or (c) a number of conditions concerning a proper consent are met and the patient's request for doctor-assisted suicide is confirmed by an ethics committee. These suggestions are still being considered by the government.

seriously ill patients may refuse medical treatment

Seriously injured or very ill people who are still able to think clearly may insist that they do not want to receive medical attention so that they can die. Allowing them to die would be 'passive euthanasia' and is not usually a crime.

attempted suicide is not a crime

Attempted suicide, where people try to kill themselves, used to be a crime, but it is no longer a crime in South Africa. Usually a person who attempts suicide is given medical help and referred to a psychological counsellor. A person who helps another to commit suicide may be guilty of murder. For example, two lovers, A and B, enter into a 'suicide pact' in which A supplies the pills for an overdose. If A lives and B dies, A will be guilty of murdering B.

Helping to kill someone in a 'suicide pact' is murder

Problem 3: People who kill themselves or ask others to kill them

Questions

1. Should people who are in great pain and have only a short time to live be allowed to ask others to kill them to end their suffering? Should people who kill them be charged with a crime? Give reasons for your answer.
2. Which of the South African Law Commission's recommendations concerning doctor-assisted suicide do you think should be adopted by the government – options (a), (b) or (c)? Give reasons for your answer.
3. Should attempted suicide be a crime, like it used to be? Should the person who does not die in a 'suicide pact', but helped to kill the other person, be guilty of a crime?

2.2.2 Assault

physical attack or threat of attack – injury is not necessary

Assault is an unlawful and intentional physical attack or the threat of an attack upon another person. At the same time the threatened person must believe that he or she is in immediate danger. For example, if Titus points an unloaded gun at Mary, it would be an assault if Mary believed that the gun was loaded. Assault can be defined as 'the unlawful and intentional use of force on another or making another believe that force is about to be immediately applied to him or her'. Actual injury is not necessary, but the person must have acted unlawfully and intentionally.

lawful assaults are allowed

Several 'assaults' are lawful, for instance: (a) a person defending himself or herself against an attack by another; (b) reasonable punishment of a child by a parent; (c) a policeman using reasonable force during an arrest; (d) some sports competitions, as long as it is within the rules of the game (eg rugby and boxing matches); and (e) medical treatment or surgical operations. For the crime of assault there must be proof of intention – negligence or carelessness is not enough. The use of force in an assault may be direct or indirect. An example of a direct assault would be where one person punches another. An example of an indirect assault would be where a person injures another by derailing a train or making someone fall off a bicycle.

direct and indirect assaults

common assault

The least serious form of assault is 'common assault' where a person does not intend to injure another seriously. However, the court would regard the crime as much more serious if a person were to assault another with the intention of committing some other crime, (eg murder, robbery, rape, and housebreaking). The same applies where a person assaults another 'with intent to do grievous bodily harm'. An assault with the intent to do grievous bodily harm means that the harm that is likely to occur is very serious and the intention is to cause more than the light injuries that usually result from a common assault. For example, if a person uses a dangerous bush knife to slash at another and slightly cuts the other's wrist, it will still be assault with intent to do grievous bodily harm. But if a person does not intend to injure another seriously, even though in fact the person is badly injured, it will only be common assault. For example, if Jack slaps William on his back and the latter slips and falls into the path of a passing motor car, which causes severe injuries, it will still be common assault.

grievous bodily harm

Many assaults result from arguments between people who know or are related to each other. Usually they lose their tempers – often under the influence of alcohol or jealousy – and end up using violence.

Problem 4: The wife's revenge

Devi pours hot oil over Shan's body while he is asleep

Questions

family violence

Devi and Shan have an unhappy marriage. They often quarrel with the result that Devi is frequently assaulted and injured by Shan.

Shan starts a quarrel with Devi

Shan is badly burned

However, she does not report Shan to the police. One day Shan comes home drunk and starts another quarrel with Devi. She becomes very angry and runs out of the bedroom before he can hit her. Shan sinks into a drunken sleep. Devi heats up some cooking oil in a pot and carries it to the bedroom. The oil is very hot but not boiling. She pours the hot oil all over Shan's body, but not on his face. Shan is badly burned and has to go to hospital for a week.

1. Devi is charged with assault. Argue as prosecutors.
   Argue as defence lawyers.
2. If you were the magistrate, would you find Devi guilty of a crime? If so, which?
3. Assume that Shan had beaten up Devi before he went to sleep and she had grabbed the hot oil during the fight and thrown it at him. If you were the magistrate, would you find her guilty of a crime? Give reasons for your answer.

2.2.3 *Crimen injuria* (criminal insult)

2.2.3.1 Introduction

crimen injuria means a criminal insult

The crime of *crimen injuria* (or criminal insult) refers to the unlawful, intentional and serious violation of the dignity or privacy of another person. The exact meaning of dignity has never been defined by the courts but it includes 'self-respect', 'mental tranquillity' (mental peace) and how people feel about themselves. Criminal insult may overlap with assault, because an act that violates bodily security may also violate dignity. However, a charge of *crimen injuria* will be laid only if the violation of dignity is more serious than the violation of bodily integrity (eg if X spits in Y's face). Another example is where a man kisses a woman without her consent – this may amount to either assault or *crimen injuria*. Indecent assault was often also *crimen injuria*. Where a person's privacy is invaded (eg a man watches a woman taking a shower without her knowing) it may also be *crimen injuria*. The importance of respecting people's dignity is also provided for in the Constitution. The Constitution provides that 'everyone has the inherent dignity and the right to have their dignity respected and protected'. The protection of dignity can be seen as preventing people from having their dignity harmed by words or conduct that is insulting and disrespectful.

indecent assault is often *crimen injuria*

The behaviour of the perpetrator must be unlawful and intentional. This means that the perpetrators must have directed their minds to commit the crime and must have known at the time that their conduct was unlawful. Negligence is not sufficient, as the crime must be committed intentionally. *Crimen injuria* that violates a person's dignity or privacy can be committed by either words or deeds (what is done). The crime can be committed in many different ways, for example: (a) by the indecent exposure of a person's body in the presence of others; (b) by communicating to somebody else a message inviting or suggesting sexual immorality or impropriety (incorrectness); or (c) a man sending indecent photos to a woman, etc. However, a mere declaration of love or affection in situations where there is no suggestion of sexual immorality or impropriety is not usually considered to be a violation of the dignity of the recipient – even if it is unwelcome or irritating. The use of vulgar or abusive words may amount to a violation of dignity if the situation is sufficiently serious (eg swearing at a police officer or calling a person 'a kaffir' or 'white trash'). The crime can also be committed by an omission, eg where a police officer on duty sees a man invading a woman's privacy by peeping through her window while she is having a shower, but fails to stop the man from continuing with his behaviour.

perpetrators must act intentionally not negligently

using vulgar or abusive words may be *crimen injuria*

Some of the things that people do that are regarded as *crimen injuria* under the common law are now also covered by the Sexual Offences Amendment Act (see below para 2.3.3).

Crimen injuria may take the form of: (a) violations of dignity; (b) violations of privacy; (c) stalking (see below para 2.2.3.5); and (d) criminal defamation – although this is not a closed list and there may be other forms. Some people have suggested that criminal defamation should no longer be a crime because it interferes with freedom of speech and a civil action should be sufficient in defamation cases.

crimen injuria takes many forms

2.2.3.2 Violations of dignity

In order to decide whether there has been a violation of another person's dignity, both a subjective and an objective test are applied. A subjective approach refers to how the harmed person himself or herself feels about the violation. An objective approach refers to how a reasonable person in the position of the harmed person would have felt about the violation. The subjective test is that Y must

test for a violation of dignity is subjective and objective

(a) be aware of X's offending behaviour, and (b) feel degraded or humiliated by it. Dignity, self-respect and mental tranquillity describe subjective aspects of a person's personality (how they feel about themselves). An individual's self-respect is closely connected with his or her social position and moral values. However, the crime can also be committed against young children or mentally defective people. Although such people may not be able to understand the nature of X's conduct and may not feel degraded by it, the courts would take an objective approach to decide how an ordinary person would have felt about such behaviour. The fact that the person subjectively did not feel degraded or humiliated would not be a defence to the crime if the person was not mentally competent (eg an insane person or a child). However, where an ordinary reasonable person would not be upset at X's behaviour, a court will not convict X of the crime. The law generally applies the objective 'reasonable person test' to decide if a crime has been committed: if Y happens to be so timid or hypersensitive that he or she feels insulted by behaviour that would not be an insult to a reasonable person, the law does not assume that the crime of crimen injuria has been committed.

crimen injuria may be committed against young children or mentally defective persons who do not know that it is happening

2.2.3.3 Violations of privacy

violations of privacy and dignity are different

Criminal insults based on invasions of privacy have different rules to those for violations of dignity because it is not necessary to show that Y was aware of X's harmful conduct. A person's privacy may be invaded in a number of ways, eg (a) X peeps through a window at Y undressing; (b) X opens a letter addressed to Y; (c) X spies on Y's private life in his home in an unjustified manner by using cameras, binoculars, telescopes or 'bugging devices', etc. In cases of unjustified invasions of privacy, as opposed to cases where Y's dignity is violated, it does not matter whether Y is aware of the invasion or not.

2.2.3.4 Violations must be serious

people are expected to experience minor insults to their dignity

The violation of dignity or privacy must be serious. What is serious enough to cause criminal liability depends upon the thoughts and conduct of a particular community at a particular time and in a particular place, and is decided by an objective test. However, most people are expected to experience minor or small insults to their dignity in their everyday life without getting too upset about them. The seriousness of the violation will depend upon such things as:

the seriousness of the violation depends on a number of factors

(a) the relationship between the parties;
(b) the age and sex of the parties;
(c) the persistence of the conduct complained of (ie how long it lasted);
(d) the amount of publicity attached to the conduct (ie did other people know about the behaviour?);
(e) the relative social positions of the two parties;
(f) the fact that the insult is aimed at a public official such as a traffic officer or policeman who is acting in his or her official capacity; or
(g) the fact that the insult was racist.

The courts have held that it is crimen injuria to call a woman a 'bitch' or to call anyone a 'kaffir' or 'white trash' where the words are used with the intention of hurting the other person's feelings.

Problem 5: Was it a violation of dignity or a violation of privacy?

Questions

Divide into small groups and decide whether the following situations are sufficiently serious cases of violations of dignity or privacy to amount to *crimen injuria.*

1. People in a rural village mock and insult a mentally disabled person who is very short by calling him a 'tikoloshe' and 'village idiot'.
2. A complete stranger writes a 'love' letter to a woman he sees in a restaurant in which he says that he would like to marry her and have children with her.
3. A woman spies on men in a football team taking a shower in a sports club. The men do not know that she is spying on them.
4. A mother opens a love letter addressed to her teenage daughter by her married boyfriend.
5. A weightlifter gets upset when a spectator at a competition shouts out that he is a 'moffie' (ie gay person).
6. A senior police officer says that the police officers at a police station are behaving like 'baboons'.

2.2.3.5 Stalking

stalkers use unlawful means to harass their victims

Stalkers are people who use unlawful means to harass their victims. For example, a stalker may make rude or threatening telephone calls, threatening the victim and his or her family with violence or damage to their property. Victims of such conduct can obtain a court order to protect them or lay a criminal charge of assault against the stalker. However, stalkers may try to avoid arrest and prosecution by behaving in a way that seems to be harmless and entirely lawful when looked at by itself. These acts are done individually, at different times and in different places.

people being harassed or stalked can get a protection order

The Protection from Harassment Act provides for the granting of a protection order against harassment or stalking. In terms of the Act a person who is being harassed or stalked may apply to court for a protection order against the perpetrator. The court may not refuse to issue a protection order or to impose any condition or make any order, which it has the power to impose or make – provided that the complainant is not in possession of or not in the process of applying for a protection order against harassment or stalking under the Domestic Violence Act. A protection order issued by the court may order the perpetrator not to harass or not to seek the help of other persons to commit harassment or stalking. The court may also issue a warrant of arrest with the protection order.

The court issuing the protection order may order the station commissioner of a police station to investigate the case in order to institute criminal proceedings against the person.

different forms of stalking

The following are forms of stalking: (a) communicating; (b) surveillance; (c) manipulative behaviour; (d) culturally inappropriate courtship behaviour; (e) indecent exposure; (f) threats and violence; (g) litigation abuse; (h) cyber stalking; (i) gang stalking; and (j) indirect stalking.

2.2.3.5.1 Communicating

includes following a person about

Communicating includes: (a) making constant telephone calls (including rude, obscene or 'silent' calls); (b) sending written messages such as letters, faxes, e-mails, text messages; (c) using graffiti; (d) making rude or obscene gestures to the victim; or (e) sending 'romantic' (eg flowers or sweets), strange (eg weird objects), perverted (eg pornographic objects) or sinister (eg an object soaked in blood) gifts to the victim.

2.2.3.5.2 Surveillance

Surveillance includes: (a) following the victim from place to place by car or on foot; (b) waiting at the victim's house, school, workplace or some other place where the victim often goes; (c) trespassing on the victim's property; (d) continuously watching or spying on the victim; (e) contacting people who know the victim to get information about him or her; (f) searching public or personal records for information about the victim; (g) getting someone else to watch the victim; (h) using video cameras or recording equipment to monitor the victim; (i) tapping telephones or using listening devices; or (j) reading the victim's letters or e-mails. Surveillance also includes more unusual behaviour, such as: (i) going through the victim's rubbish to learn more about the victim's life; (ii) repeatedly entering the victim's personal space (eg home, car or office); (iii) leaving behind some evidence to make the intrusion obvious; or (iv) taking things from the victim (such as some of the victim's clothing).

2.2.3.5.3 Manipulative behaviour

Manipulative behaviour includes bringing an unjustified legal action against the victim, or threatening to commit suicide in an attempt to get the victim to take notice.

2.2.3.5.4 Culturally inappropriate courtship behaviours

Culturally inappropriate courtship behaviours includes conduct such as repeatedly asking for sex or continuously asking for dates after the victim has said that this is unwelcome.

2.2.3.5.5 Indecent exposure

Indecent exposure includes behaviour such as repeatedly 'flashing' at the victim (ie a person exposing their private parts to a victim). This is sometimes done in such a way as to make the exposure seem accidental.

2.2.3.5.6 Threats and violence

Threats and violence can include: (a) making clear threats of physical or other harm; (b) property damage (such as slashing tyres on the victim's car); (c) actual physical attacks (eg minor assaults that leave abrasions or bruises intended to frighten the victim, assaults which can cause serious injury, or sexual assaults); (d) killing pets; (e) threatening family members or friends of the victim; or (f) even situations where the stalker threatens to harm himself or herself.

2.2.3.5.7 Litigation abuse

Litigation abuse involves using the legal system to harass a victim by continuously bringing unjustified legal actions or applications for protection orders or laying unjustified criminal charges against the victim.

2.2.3.5.8 Cyber stalking

cyber stalking involves using electronic media

Cyber stalking refers to using electronic media such as the Internet to pursue, harass or contact the victim, such as: (a) repeatedly sending unwanted e-mails which are abusive, threatening or obscene (rude); (b) sending computer viruses to the victim; (c) pretending to be the victim online and sending abusive e-mails in the victim's name; (d) putting the victim's name on online sex forums; (e) inviting persons online to call the victim; or (f) inviting people online to come to the victim's home.

2.2.3.5.9 Gang stalking

Gang stalking refers to stalking by many different perpetrators, or to situations where one perpetrator gets others to help carry out stalking activities (eg members of gangs sometimes use other gang members or friends to watch the victim or to intimidate the victim).

2.2.3.5.10 Indirect stalking

Indirect stalking includes using third persons to carry out the stalking behaviour (eg using third parties to deliver gift packages to victims) or indirectly intimidating or threatening the victim by making contact with the victim's employer, children or other family members.

2.2.3.6 Criminal defamation

criminal defamation may be unconstitutional

Criminal defamation is the unlawful and intentional publication of words or behaviour about another which tends to injure his or her reputation. Defamatory words or conduct may take the form of written or spoken words or acts or omissions which lower a person's reputation in the eyes of others. In criminal defamation cases the defamation must be serious and usually reflects upon the person's moral character. However, as previously mentioned, criminal defamation undermines freedom of speech and it is likely that the Constitutional Court will find that it is unconstitutional, as people who are defamed may sue civilly.

2.2.4 Kidnapping

kidnappers violate a person's freedom of movement

The crime of kidnapping is committed by taking away a person's freedom of movement, or taking away control over a child by a parent or carer. This is usually done by force but need not be. It can also be done by cheating or cunning (eg if X pretends to be a photographer's assistant who has to fetch a little girl from her school to photograph her). The crime can also be committed even though there is no physical removal (eg where Y is hidden or imprisoned where she lives). Kidnapping is not the same as abduction: abduction is committed against the authority of parents or carers over a child, while kidnapping is committed against a person's freedom of movement and applies to adults or children.

kidnapping of children is a crime against parents and carers and the children

The conduct of the alleged kidnapper must be unlawful. The law recognises that the crime can also sometimes be committed against a person who consents to his or her removal (eg Y, a child who is 16 or 17 years old). However, X may still be convicted of kidnapping because he violated the control over Y by her parents or carers. Where a child does not consent, or because of her age cannot legally give a valid consent, and the parents or carers do not consent, the crime is committed against both the parents' or carers' control and the child's freedom of movement.

it is not a crime for a parent to kidnap their own child

Parents cannot commit the crime of kidnapping their own children. Therefore, if a father who is divorced from his wife removes their child from her care in order to keep her in his own care, he does not commit the crime of kidnapping. This is true even if the court has awarded the custody and control of the child to her mother. However, the father may be convicted of contempt of court if he has gone against a court order. Taking away a person's freedom may sometimes be justified, for example where a police officer lawfully arrests someone, or by the consent of the person removed – provided such person is able to give a lawful consent (eg is not a child).

the kidnapper must know that the kidnapped person has not consented or cannot consent

In order to be guilty of kidnapping the accused person must have directed his or her mind to kidnap the person and know that his or her conduct is unlawful. Thus, X must know that Y has not consented to the removal of Y and, if Y is a child, that her parents or carers have not consented to Y's removal. X need not intend to deprive Y permanently of her freedom of movement; it is sufficient if he or she intends to release Y upon payment of a ransom.

Problem 6: Was it kidnapping?

Questions

Divide into small groups and decide whether the people in the following cases can be convicted of kidnapping:

1. A 15-year-old girl runs away from home to live with her 23-year-old boyfriend.

2. A father forces his daughter to live secretly in the basement of his house so that he can have sex with her. He tells his wife that the daughter has run away from home.
3. The son of a politician is taken from school by the followers of a rival politician and hidden in the rival politician's house for one hour. When the boy's father agrees to support the motion of the rival politician in Parliament, the boy is released.

2.3 Sexual crimes

Outcomes

After completion of this section learners will be able to:

1. List and explain the different sexual offences.

Assessment criteria

1. The legal definition of rape and compelled rape is explained.
2. A set of facts is examined and a decision is made on whether the people were guilty of rape.
3. The procedures that should be followed after a rape attack are explained.
4. Some questions about rape are answered.
5. An explanation is given of sexual assault, compelled sexual assault and compelled self-sexual assault and a set of facts is examined and a decision is made on whether the people were guilty of sexual assault.
6. An explanation is given of sexual crimes against children.
7. A set of facts is examined and a decision is made on whether the people were guilty of statutory rape of children.
8. A set of facts is examined and a decision is made on whether the people were guilty of statutory sexual assault of children.
9. A set of facts is examined and a decision is made on whether the people were guilty of sexual exploitation of children.
10. A set of facts is examined and a decision is made on whether the people were guilty of sexual grooming of children.
11. The duty to report sexual offences against children is explained.
12. An explanation is given of sexual offences against mentally disabled persons and the duty to report sexual offences against them.
13. A set of facts is examined and a decision is made on whether the people were guilty of attempt, conspiracy, incitement or inducing another person to commit a sexual offence.
14. An explanation is given of the services available to victims of sexual assault and compulsory testing of sex offenders.
15. Other sexual offences are identified.
16. Trafficking of persons for sexual purposes is explained.
17. A set of facts is examined and a decision is made on whether the people were guilty of trafficking of persons for sexual purposes.

2.3.1 Rape

rape is no longer a gender-specific crime

According to the Sexual Offences Amendment Act, any person who unlawfully and intentionally commits an act of sexual penetration (ie where someone enters part of another person's body) with a complainant without his or her consent commits rape. According to this definition, rape is no longer a gender-specific crime – the victims as well as the perpetrators can be men or women. The conduct of the alleged rapist must be unlawful and the alleged rapist must have had the intention to rape the other person. This means that the accused person must know that the other person had not consented to sexual penetration.

sexual penetration

In the Sexual Offences Amendment Act, sexual penetration means any of the following acts:

1. any act which causes penetration to any extent whatsoever by the genital organs (private parts) of one person into or beyond the genital organs, anus (backside), or mouth, of another person;
2. any act which causes penetration to any extent whatsoever by any other part of the body of one person or, any object, including any part of the body of an animal, into or beyond the genital organs or anus of another person; or
3. any act which causes penetration to any extent whatsoever by the genital organs of an animal, into the mouth, or down the throat, of another person.

common-law definition of rape held to be unconstitutional

The Sexual Offences Amendment Act does away with the common-law definition of 'penetration' in rape cases which used to mean the penetration only of a female's private parts (vagina) with a male's private parts (penis). Before the case *Masiya v Director of Public Prosecutions*, common-law rape could only be committed by a male on a female, and only where the male had penetrated the woman's vagina without her consent. In the *Masiya v Director of Public Prosecutions* case the Constitutional Court found that the common-law definition of rape was not unconstitutional, but that it needed to be extended to include penetration of a female's anus by a male penis.

it is no defence that a woman has had multiple sexual partners

The fact that a woman has had intercourse with a number of other men in the past or is a prostitute is no defence to a charge of rape. A girl under the age of 12 years can never consent to sexual intercourse, and the Sexual Offences Amendment Act deals specifically with sexual crimes against children (see para 2.3.6). A husband can be convicted of raping his wife.

Problem 1: Was it rape?

Questions

Divide into small groups and decide whether the people in the following cases can be convicted of rape. Give reasons for your answers.

1. A man forces his penis into a woman's mouth without her consent.

2. A man pushes his finger into another man's anus.
3. A man forces a prostitute to have sex with him from behind against her will.
4. A woman forces an artificial penis into another woman's vagina against her will.
5. A man puts his tongue in a women's vagina against her will.

2.3.2 Compelled rape

many rapes are not reported

forcing somebody to rape another is 'compelled rape'

In terms of the Sexual Offences Amendment Act, it is a crime to compel (force) a third person to rape a male or female victim. The person who forces the third person to rape the victim does not commit an act of sexual penetration but can be convicted of compelled rape. Compelled rape is committed by any person of any gender, who unlawfully and intentionally forces a third person, without the consent of that person, to commit an act of sexual penetration with a victim, without the consent of the victim. The crime is committed without the consent of both the third person and the victim. For example, a hijacker forces a man to have sex with his female passenger before releasing them after he has used a gun to steal the man's car.

Is there a rape crisis advice centre or hospital rape crisis centre in your area?

report rapes to the police

Anyone who has been raped and wishes to lay a charge with the police should contact their nearest rape crisis centre or report the crime to the police as soon as possible after it happens.

If a rape victim wishes the police to investigate she or he will have to give the police a statement and have an examination by a district medical officer (a government doctor). However, it is not necessary to go to the police first.

post-exposure prophylaxis

The victim may go directly to a hospital or rape crisis centre before laying a charge with the police. Hospitals may not turn away people who have been raped as they have a right to emergency medical treatment and may need PEP.

After a rape attack

1. Go to a safe place and call the police.
2. Keep the evidence (eg traces of hair, skin or blood, clothing threads, etc from the attacker) intact by not changing clothes or washing until after there has been a medical examination – otherwise evidence may be lost.
3. Get medical treatment directly from a hospital or ask the police to arrange for an examination.
4. Do not shower, take off your clothes, or disturb the scene of the crime, until after you have spoken to the police and have been examined by a doctor.
5. Contact a rape crisis advice office or hospital rape crisis centre if there is one in your area.

Problem 2: Some questions about rape

Questions

1. Only a small percentage of rape cases are reported to the police. Why do you think this is? What can be done to encourage more people to report rape cases?
2. Should the defending lawyer in a rape case be allowed to question the victim about her or his past sexual relations with other people? Give reasons for your answer.
3. Do you agree with the law that allows husbands to be charged with raping their wives? Give reasons for your answer.
4. What should a person do if she or he is the victim of rape?

2.3.3 Sexual assault

the common-law crime of 'indecent assault' has been replaced by 'sexual assault'

The Sexual Offences Amendment Act has repealed the common-law crime of indecent assault. The crime of indecent assault has been replaced by a new statutory offence of sexual assault which prohibits all forms of sexual violence without consent. Sexual assault happens when a perpetrator unlawfully and intentionally sexually violates a victim without his or her consent. A sexual violation does not include an act of sexual penetration but covers the following acts:

sexual assault usually involves contact with, not penetration of another

1. any act which causes direct or indirect contact between the genital organs or anus of one person or, in the case of a female, her breasts, and any part of the body of another person or an animal;
2. any act that causes direct or indirect contact between the genital organs or anus of one person or, in the case of a female, her breasts, and any object, including any object resembling or representing the genital organs or anus of a person or animal;
3. any act that causes direct or indirect contact between the mouth of one person and the genital organs or anus of another person, or a female's breasts;
4. any act which causes direct or indirect contact between the mouth of one person and the mouth of another person;
5. any act which causes direct or indirect contact between the mouth of one person and any other part of the body of another person, other than the genitals or anus of that person or a female's breasts, which could (a) be used in an act of sexual penetration; (b) cause sexual arousal or stimulation; or (c) be sexually aroused or stimulated thereby;
6. any act which causes direct or indirect contact between the mouth of one person and any object resembling the genital organs or anus of a person, or a female's breasts, or an animal;
7. any act which causes direct or indirect contact between the mouth of the victim and the genital organs or anus of an animal;

8. any act which causes the masturbation of one person by another;
9. any act which causes the insertion of any object resembling or representing the genital organs of a person or an animal, into or beyond the mouth of another person.

sexual assault includes making a person believe that he or she will be sexually violated

It is not only the actual sexual violation without the consent of the victim that is the crime of sexual assault: a person who unlawfully and intentionally makes a victim believe that he or she will be sexually violated, is also guilty of sexual assault.

Problem 3: Was it sexual assault?

Questions

Divide into small groups and decide whether the people in the following cases can be convicted of sexual assault. Give reasons for your answers.

1. A woman pushes her breasts up against a strange man in a lift.
2. A man rubs a cool drink bottle against the private parts of a woman at a party.
3. A man kisses the breasts of a woman through the top of her bikini at the beach.

4. A man kisses a strange woman on the mouth at a music festival.
5. A woman gets aroused while nibbling the ear of a sportsman in a bar.
6. A man forces a woman to suck on a banana and to pretend that she is sucking a penis.

2.3.4 Compelled sexual assault

forcing a person to sexually violate another is compelled sexual assault

The Sexual Offences Amendment Act makes it a crime for one person to force another person to sexually violate a victim. The person who compels the other person to violate the victim is guilty of the crime of compelled sexual assault. This is so even though the person who compels another to sexually violate the victim does not physically sexually assault or violate the victim himself or herself.

there must be no consent between the parties

Compelled sexual assault is committed by a person who unlawfully and intentionally compels a third person, without consent, to sexually violate the victim, without the victim's consent. The crime is only committed where there is no consent by both the victim and the third party. If both parties consented, no crime is committed. The victim and the perpetrator may be of either gender and may be a child, an adult or a mentally disabled person. Marriage or any other relationship between the perpetrator and the victim will not be a defence to a charge of sexual assault.

marriage is not a defence

2.3.5 Compelled self-sexual assault

Compelled self-sexual assault is where a person compels a victim to perform any act of sexual violation on the victim himself or herself. As in the case of compelled sexual assault the victim may be a person of either gender and may be a child, an adult or a mentally disabled person.

forcing a victim to perform a sexual violation on himself or herself

The crime of compelled self-sexual assault is committed when a person compels the victim, without the victim's consent, to engage with him-or herself in masturbation, or any form of sexual arousal or sexual act. Compelling the victim, without his or her consent, to engage in any act which has or may have the effect of sexually arousing or sexually degrading the victim, or compelling the victim to penetrate in any manner whatsoever his or her own genital organs or anus will also amount to the crime of compelled self-sexual assault.

2.3.6 Sexual crimes against children

2.3.6.1 Statutory rape

statutory rape

In statutory rape cases the child often has consensual sexual penetration (ie sexual penetration by agreement) with the perpetrator. The Sexual Offences Amendment Act creates the crime of statutory rape for acts of consensual sexual penetration with children subject to the following conditions:

sex with an under-age child

1. A person who commits an act of sexual penetration with the consent of a child under the age of 18 years is guilty of consensual penetration of a child (statutory rape) but may raise a defence.
2. A person who commits an act of sexual penetration with the consent of a child under 12 years old is guilty of consensual penetration of a child (statutory rape) and cannot raise any kind of defence.
3. A person who commits an act of sexual penetration with the consent of a child of 12 years or older but under the age of 16 years is guilty of consensual sexual penetration with a child, but may raise the defence that: (a) he or she was deceived by the child into believing that the child was 16 years or older and (b) he or she reasonably believed that the child was 16 years or older. As mentioned above this does not apply if the child was under 12 years of age.

Perpetrators and victims may be male or female. If both people involved in the act were 12 years or older but under the age of 16 years at the time the alleged the National Director of Public Prosecutions must consent to prosecutions of children 12 to 16 years old

offence was committed, the prosecution must be authorised in writing by the National Director of Public Prosecutions. If the authorisation is given, both people involved in the act will be charged with consensual sexual penetration with a child. The National Director of Public Prosecutions may not delegate his or her power to authorise the prosecution.

finding children between 12 and 15 years who together have 'consensual sexual penetration' guilty is unconstitutional

In the *Teddy Bear Clinic for Abused Children v Minister of Justice and Constitutional Development* the Constitutional Court said that the section in the Act referring to children under 16 years of age are discriminatory and unconstitutional. The court gave the example of a first child who is between 16 and 17 years of age having 'consensual sexual penetration' with a second child aged 12 to 15 years of age, where only the first child commits a crime. However, where the first child and the second child are both 12 to 15 years of age, both are guilty of an offence. The result is that if two younger children engage in 'consensual sexual penetration' they may both be prosecuted, but if one child has sex with an older child between 16 and 17 years, only the older child can be prosecuted. The Constitutional Court held that imposing criminal liability on children under 16 years of age was unconstitutional.

Problem 4: Was it statutory rape?

Questions

Divide into small groups and decide whether the people in the following cases can be convicted of statutory rape, and if so, who. Give reasons for your answers.

1. A 20-year-old man who has 'consensual sexual penetration' with a sexually mature girl aged 11 years who looks much older and who tells him that she is 16 years old. Because of her appearance and what she says, the man believes her.
2. A boy aged 14 and a girl aged 13 have 'consensual sexual penetration'.
3. A 15-year-old boy tells a 30-year-old woman that he is 18 years old and she believes him and has 'consensual sexual penetration' with him.
4. A boy who is 16 years of age has 'consensual sexual penetration' with a girl who is 15 years of age.

consensual sexual violation with a child

2.3.6.2 Statutory sexual assault

The Sexual Offences Amendment Act creates the crime of statutory sexual assault, which is an act of consensual sexual violation with a child. This crime is committed when a person commits an act of sexual violation with a child with the consent of the child. The victims and perpetrators may be male or female.

if both are children the National Director of Public Prosecutions must authorise the prosecution

If both people involved in the act were children at the time the alleged offence was committed, the prosecution must be authorised in writing by the National Director of Public Prosecutions. If the authorisation is given, both people involved in the act will be charged with consensual sexual violation of a child. The National Director of Public Prosecutions may not delegate his or her power to authorise the prosecution. However, the *Teddy Bear Clinic* case also decided that this was unconstitutional (see above para 2.3.6.1).

Statutory sexual assault must be committed intentionally and unlawfully and there are two possible defences – provided the victim was not under 12 years of age:

defences to statutory sexual assault

1. It is a valid defence to a charge of statutory sexual assault to show that: (a) the child deceived the alleged offender into believing that he or she was 16 years or older at the time of the alleged commission of the offence; and (b) the alleged offender reasonably believed the child to have been 16 years or older at time. This defence is the same as that for statutory rape.
2. It is a valid defence to a charge of statutory sexual assault to show that both accused persons were children and the age difference between them was not more than two years at the time of the alleged defence. This defence is not available in cases of statutory rape.

Problem 5: Was it statutory sexual assault?

Questions

Divide into small groups and decide whether the people in the following cases can be convicted of statutory sexual assault. Give reasons for your answers.

1. A 22-year-old man touches the private parts of a sexually mature girl aged 11 years who looks much older and who tells him that she is 16 years old. Because of her appearance and what she says, the man believes her.
2. A boy aged 14 and a girl aged 13 stimulate each other by touching their private parts.
3. A 15-year-old boy tells a 35-year-old woman that he is 18 years old and she believes him and touches his private parts.

2.3.6.3 Sexual exploitation of children

The Sexual Offences Amendment Act creates six offences dealing with the sexual exploitation of children: (a) sexual exploitation of children; (b) being involved in the sexual exploitation of children; (c) furthering the sexual exploitation of children; (d) benefiting from the sexual exploitation of children; (e) living from the earnings of the sexual exploitation of children; and (f) promoting sex tours.

2.3.6.3.1 Sexual exploitation of children

engaging the services of a child for a sexual act

The Sexual Offences Amendment Act creates the crime of sexual exploitation of children when (a) a person unlawfully and intentionally engages the services of a child, (b) with or without the consent of such child, (c) for financial or other reward, for favour or compensation to either the child or a third person (d) for the purpose of engaging in a sexual act with the child. It is a crime if the perpetrator commits a sexual act with the child. It is also a crime if the sexual act does not take place, but the services of the child were obtained. The crime is based on unlawfully and intentionally engaging the services of the child for sexual acts.

2.3.6.3.2 Being involved in sexual exploitation of children

offering the services of a child for a sexual act to third persons

Under the Sexual Offences Amendment Act the crime of being involved in sexual exploitation of children happens when a person (a) intentionally and unlawfully offers the services of a child for sexual acts to a third person, (b) with or without the consent of such child, (c) for financial or other reward, favour or compensation and (d) to either the alleged perpetrator, the child or another person. The crime is based on unlawfully and intentionally offering the services of the child for sexual acts. The crime is committed in the following situations:

1. By inviting, persuading or inducing the child to allow the third person to commit a sexual act with the child;
2. By participating in, being involved in, promoting, encouraging or facilitating the commission of a sexual act with the child for purposes of the commission of a sexual act with the child by a third person; or
3. By detaining the child, whether under threat, force, coercion, deception, abuse of power or authority, for the purposes of the commission of a sexual act with the child by a third person.

2.3.6.3.3 Furthering the sexual exploitation of children

intentionally allowing a third person to commit a sexual act with a child

Under the Sexual Offences Amendment Act the crime of furthering the sexual exploitation of a child happens: (a) where a primary care-giver, parent or guardian of the child intentionally or knowingly allows a third person to commit a sexual act with such child, with or without the consent of the child; or (b) where a person who owns, leases, rents, manages, occupies or has control over any movable property (eg a car) or immovable property (eg a house), intentionally or knowingly allows such property to be used to commit a sexual act with a child by a third person, with or without the consent of the child. The crime is based on intentionally or knowingly allowing a third person to commit a sexual act with a child. Thus any care-giver, parent or guardian who intentionally allows his or her girl child to be kidnapped in terms of the *ukuthwala* custom (see below para 2.3.6.3.7) may be found guilty of furthering the sexual exploitation of a child.

2.3.6.3.4 Benefiting from the sexual exploitation of children

intentionally receiving financial or other rewards from a sexual act with a child

Under the Sexual Offences Amendment Act the crime of benefiting from the sexual exploitation of a child is committed by a person (a) who intentionally receives financial or other reward, favour or compensation for the commission of a sexual act with a child by a third person (b) with or without the consent of such child. The crime is based on intentionally receiving benefits from a sexual act with a child. Therefore, parents or guardians who intentionally allow their girl children to be abducted in terms of the *ukuthwala* custom in exchange for *lobolo* may be convicted of benefiting from the sexual exploitation of children.

2.3.6.3.5 Living off the earnings of the sexual exploitation of a child

intentionally living off the earnings of a child from sexual acts with third persons

The Sexual Offences Amendment Act provides that a person is guilty of the offence of living from the earnings of the sexual exploitation of a child (a) who intentionally lives wholly or in part on reward, favour or compensation for the commission of a sexual act with a child by a third person , (b) with or without the consent of such child, The crime is based on intentionally living wholly or partly on the earnings of a child arising from sexual acts with third persons.

2.3.6.3.6 Promoting child sex tours

promoting tours to facilitate sexual acts with a child

The Sexual Offences Amendment Act also deals with the problem of child sex tourism by creating the crime of promoting child sex tours. The Act provides that (a) a natural or juristic person (non-human entity like a company) (b) who makes or organises any travel arrangements for third persons, (c) whether the third persons are resident in or outside South Africa, (d) with the intention of facilitating the commission of any sexual act with a child, (e) whether the act is committed or not, (f) is guilty of the offence. Furthermore, a person (including a juristic person) who prints or publishes, in any manner, any information that is intended to promote or facilitate a sexual act with a child, is also guilty of the offence of promoting child sex tours.

2.3.6.3.7 The cultural practice of 'ukuthwala'

traditionally a romantic mock abduction

Ukuthwala literally means 'to carry away' or 'to carry something'. It is traditionally a romantic mock abduction or an irregular proposal to an unmarried woman (girl) by a man who intends to marry her. The customary practice of *ukuthwala*, which involves the abduction of a girl by a suitor or his friends to force her family to enter into marriage negotiations with them, is still common amongst some sections of the Xhosa and Zulu people. *Ukuthwala* must be distinguished from the common-law crime of abduction. To be a customary law wrong *ukuthwala* must take place without the consent of the girl's guardian. It may take place prior to the payment of *lobolo* or after the partial or full payment of *lobolo*. Where the parents or guardians consent to the abduction it will be a breach of the Sexual Offences Amendment Act provision dealing with furthering the sexual exploitation of a child. Where *lobolo* has been paid and the parents consent to the abduction it will be a breach of the provision dealing with benefiting from the sexual exploitation of a child. The SA Law Commission is investigating whether a new statute should be introduced to make *ukuthwala* a crime.

ukuthwala involving a child is a crime under the Sexual Offences Act

Problem 6: Was it sexual exploitation of children?

Questions

Divide into small groups and decide whether the people in the following cases can be convicted of sexual exploitation of children. Give reasons for your answer.

1. A 60-year-old man meets a street child aged 11 years and invites him back to his flat to have sex for which he will pay the boy R100. The boy agrees to go with him.
2. A tourist asks a taxi driver where he can find some young girls to have sex with. The driver says that he knows of a house where there are young girls under the age of 14 years who have sex with adult men for R300 a time. The taxi driver offers to take the tourist there.
3. In a rural area the parents of a 12-year-old girl accept *lobolo* of three goats from a 50-year-old man who says that he wants to marry their daughter. The girl wishes to continue her schooling and does not want to get married. Her parents help the man to take her to his house where he keeps her and forces her to have unprotected sex with him.

2.3.6.4 Sexual grooming of children

it is difficult to decide where grooming starts and where it ends

The Sexual Offences Amendment Act creates the crimes of (a) promoting the sexual grooming of children and (b) sexual grooming of children. Grooming is difficult to define. There is no agreement amongst psychologists and other experts about what grooming means because it covers a wide variety of behaviours and situations. It is also difficult to decide exactly when the grooming process starts and when it ends. When considering the grooming process, the courts have taken into account the role and purpose of the gifts and favours which were given to the victim. In one case the court found that the accused's conduct in making the complainant a consenting party to video recordings of herself created an improper closeness between them. The accused's tactics of relaxing the rules of the institution where the girl was staying and buying her presents were calculated to remove her will to resist his sexual demands when he eventually made them.

2.3.6.4.1 Promoting the sexual grooming of children

The crime of promoting the sexual grooming of a child is committed in the following circumstances:

methods of promoting sexual grooming of children

(a) Where a person manufactures, produces, possesses, distributes or facilitates the manufacture, production or distribution of an article which is exclusively intended to facilitate the commission of a sexual act with or by a child;
(b) Where a person manufactures, produces, possesses, distributes or facilitates the manufacture, production or distribution of a publication or film that promotes or is intended to be used in the commission of a sexual act with or by a child;

(c) Where a person supplies, exposes or displays (i) any article which is intended to be used in the performance of a sexual act; (ii) child pornography or pornography; or (iii) a publication or film – with the intention to encourage, enable, instruct or persuade such third person to perform a sexual act with a child; and

(d) Where a person arranges or facilitates a meeting or communication between a third party and a child by means from, to or in any part of the world, with the intention that the third party will perform a sexual act with such child.

2.3.6.4.2 The crime of sexual grooming of children

The crime of sexual grooming of a child is committed by a person (the perpetrator) who:

supplying, exposing or displaying articles to encourage a child to engage in sexual acts

(a) supplies, exposes or displays to a child (i) an article which is intended to be used in the performance of a sexual act; (ii) child pornography or pornography; or (iii) a publication or film – with the intention to encourage, enable, instruct or persuade such child to perform a sexual act;

committing any acts to encourage a child to engage in sexual acts

(b) commits any act with or in the presence of, or describes the commission of any act to or in the presence of, a child with the intention to encourage or persuade such child or to reduce any unwillingness on the part of such child to (i) perform a sexual act with the perpetrator or a third person; (ii) perform an act of self-masturbation in the presence of the perpetrator or a third person or while the perpetrator or a third person is watching; (iii) be in the presence of or watch the perpetrator or a third person while either such perpetrator or such third person performs a sexual act or an act of self-masturbation; (iv) be exposed to child pornography or pornography; (v) be used for pornographic purposes; or (vi) exposes his or her body, or parts of the body to the perpetrator or a third person in a manner which violates or offends the sexual dignity of the child;

communicating with a child in order to commit a sexual act with the child

(c) arranges or facilitates a meeting or communication with a child by any means from, to or in any part of the world, with the intention that the perpetrator will commit a sexual act with such child;

(d) have met or communicated with a child by any means from, to or in any part of the world, invites, persuades, seduces, induces, entices or coerces such child:
   (i) to travel to any part of the world in order to meet the perpetrator with the intention to commit a sexual act with the child; or
   (ii) during such meeting or communication or any subsequent meeting or communication to (aa) commit a sexual act with the perpetrator; (bb) discuss, explain or describe the commission of a sexual act; or (cc) provide the perpetrator, by means of any form of communication including electronic communication, with any image, publication, depiction, description or sequence of child pornography of the child himself or herself or any other person; or

(e) after meeting or communicating with a child by any means from, to or in any part of the world, intentionally travels to meet or meets such child with the intention of committing a sexual act with the child.

2.3.6.5 Exposure or display of child pornography or pornography to children

Under the Sexual Offences Amendment Act it is a crime to unlawfully and intentionally expose or display the following material to a child, either with or without the consent of the child:

exposing a child to images or visual presentations of a sexual nature

(a) any image, publication, depiction, description or sequence of child pornography or pornography;
(b) any image, publication, depiction, description or sequence containing a visual presentation, description or representation of a sexual nature of a child, which may be disturbing or harmful to, or age-inappropriate for children as mentioned in the Films and Publications Act, or in terms of any other law;
(c) any image, publication, depiction, description or sequence containing a visual presentation, description or representation of pornography or an act of an explicit sexual nature of a person 18 years or older, which may be disturbing or harmful to, or age-inappropriate for children as mentioned in the Films and Publications Act, or in terms of any other law.

2.3.6.6 Using children for, or benefiting from, child pornography

The Sexual Offences Amendment Act is aimed at protecting children from involvement in child pornography. The Act creates two offences: (a) using a child for child pornography; and (b) benefiting from child pornography.

2.3.6.6.1 Using a child for child pornography

using a child to create or produce images or depictions of child pornography

The Sexual Offences Amendment Act provides that the crime of using a child for child pornography is committed by a person who (a) unlawfully and intentionally uses a child, (b) with or without the child's consent, (c) for the purposes of creating, making or producing or in any manner assisting to create, make or produce any image, publication, depiction, description or sequence in any manner whatsoever of child pornography. The Act states that it will not be a valid defence, in a visual representation, that the perpetrator believed that the person shown in the representation, was, or was depicted as being, 18 years or older unless the perpetrator took all reasonable steps to establish the age of that person. In addition, the perpetrator must have taken all reasonable steps to ensure that where the person was 18 years or older, the representation did not depict that person as being under the age of 18 years.

2.3.6.6.2 Benefiting from child pornography

The Sexual Offences Amendment Act provides that the crime of benefiting from child pornography is committed by a person who knowingly and intentionally gains financially from, or receives any favour, benefit, reward, compensation or any other advantage as a result of any of the acts that are regarded as using a child for child pornography in terms of the Act.

Problem 7: Was it sexual grooming or using children for, or benefiting from, child pornography?

Questions

Divide into small groups and decide whether the people in the following cases can be convicted of sexual grooming of children or using children for, or benefiting from, child pornography. Give reasons for your answer.

1. Parents make a video of their 6 and 7-year-old daughters in the nude and sell it to a syndicate on the Internet.
2. A person shows children how to use a vibrator to sexually stimulate themselves.
3. Street children are invited to a person's flat, given food and shown videos of children having sex with each other.

4. A 55-year-old man gives lots of gifts to a 14-year-old school girl and asks her 'to be nice' to him.
5. A 60-year-old man exposes his private parts to a group of street children playing in a park.

2.3.6.7 Compelling or causing children to witness sexual offences, sexual acts or self-masturbation

The Sexual Offences Amendment Act has created three offences which relate to children witnessing certain acts of a sexual nature: (a) compelling or causing a child to witness a sexual offence; (b) compelling or causing a child to witness a sexual act; and (c) compelling or causing a child to witness self-masturbation.

2.3.6.7.1 Compelling or causing a child to witness a sexual offence

the child witnesses a sexual offence

The Sexual Offences Amendment Act provides that a person who (a) unlawfully and intentionally, (b) whether for sexual gratification of that person or a third person or not, (c) compels or causes a child, (d) without the consent of the child (e) to be in the presence of or to watch the perpetrator or third person (e) while he or she commits a sexual offence, (f) is guilty of the crime of compelling or causing a child to witness a sexual offence. Here the child witnesses a sexual offence.

2.3.6.7.2 Compelling or causing a child to witness a sexual act

the child witnesses a sexual act, not a sexual offence

The Sexual Offences Act provides that a person who (a) unlawfully and intentionally, (b) whether for sexual gratification of himself or herself or a third person or not, (c) compels or causes a child, (d) without the consent of the child, (e) to be in the presence of or to watch the perpetrator (f) while he or she engages in a sexual act with a third person (g) or while the third person engages in a sexual act with another person (h) is guilty of the crime of compelling or causing a child to witness a sexual act. Here the child witnesses a sexual act, not a sexual offence.

2.3.6.7.3 Compelling or causing a child to witness self-masturbation

the child witnesses self-masturbation

The Sexual Offences Act provides that a person who (a) unlawfully and intentionally (b) compels or causes a child, (c) without the consent of the child, (d) to be in the presence of or watch the perpetrator or third person (e) while he or she engages in an act of self-masturbation (f) is guilty of the crime of compelling or causing a child to witness self-masturbation. Here the child witnesses self-masturbation.

2.3.6.8 Exposure or display of, or causing exposure or display of genital organs, anus or female breasts to children (flashing)

no offence if it is part of a legitimate cultural practice

The Sexual Offences Amendment Act provides that a person who (a) unlawfully and intentionally, (b) whether for his or her own or a third person's sexual gratification or not, (c) whether with or without the consent of the child, (d) exposes or causes the exposure of the genital organs, anus or female breasts of such person or third person to a child, (e) is guilty of the crime of exposing or displaying the exposure or display of genital organs, anus or female breasts to a child. However, this offence will not be committed by a person who commits such acts as part of a legitimate cultural practice that is not unconstitutional.

2.3.6.9 Trafficking in children

Under the Children's Act it is a crime to use children for commercial sexual exploitation. Commercial sexual exploitation of a child means the procurement of a child to perform sexual activities for money or other reward. This includes acts of prostitution or pornography. It does not matter whether the reward is claimed by, payable to or is shared with the (a) procurer, (b) the child, (c) the parent, (d) the care-giver of the child, or (e) any other person. Commercial sexual exploitation also includes the trafficking of a child for use in sexual activities, including prostitution or pornography. The Act provides that no natural or trafficking by any means is illegal

juristic person (eg a company) or a partnership may traffic a child or allow a child to be trafficked. Trafficking of children means recruiting, selling, supplying, transporting, transferring, harbouring (keeping) or receiving children. This applies to trafficking of children in South Africa by any means (including the use of threats, force or other forms of coercion, abduction, fraud, deception, abuse of power or the giving or receiving of payments or benefits to get the consent of a person having control of a child; or because of their vulnerability) for the purposes of exploitation. It also includes the adoption of a child through illegal means.

a child or person in control of a child may not consent to trafficking

It is no defence that a child who is a victim of trafficking or a person having control over the child has consented to the intended exploitation or the adoption of the child through illegal means; or that the intended exploitation of a child did not occur. The Children's Act prohibits behaviour which assists trafficking in children such as the lease or sub-lease of, or allowing any, room, house, dwelling or establishment to be used for the purpose of keeping a child who is a victim of trafficking. No such person may advertise, publish, print, broadcast, distribute or cause the advertisement, publication, printing, broadcast or distribution of information that suggests or indicates trafficking by any means, including the use of the Internet or other information technology.

2.3.6.10 Duty to report sexual offences against children

persons with knowledge of sexual offences against children must report it to the police

The Sexual Offences Amendment Act creates an obligation to report sexual offences against children. Any person who has knowledge that a sexual offence has been committed against a child must report this information to the police. Failure to report such knowledge will make the person guilty of a crime and he or she will be liable on conviction to a fine or to imprisonment of a period not exceeding five years or to both a fine and such imprisonment. The only exception would be where it would not be in the child's 'best interests' as stated in the Constitution and the Children's Act.

property owners and occupiers must report sexual offences against children

In terms of the Children's Act, it is a crime for any person who is the owner, lessor, manager, tenant or occupier of any premises on which commercial sexual exploitation of a child has occurred, to fail to immediately report this information to the SA Police Service. The Act also states that all Internet service providers operating in South Africa have a duty to report to the SA Police Service any site on their servers that contains information about behaviour that assists in the trafficking of children.

ukuthwala must be reported to the police

While there are strong pressures on public officials, rural doctors, healthcare professionals and others to respect cultural practices, where such practices undermine fundamental human rights in the Bill of Rights, and are contraventions of the Sexual Offences Amendment Act, there is a legal duty on them to report practices such as *ukuthwala* to the police. A similar duty is imposed on traditional health practitioners and traditional leaders by the Children's Amendment Act. The failure to report ill-treatment of children in terms of the Sexual Offences Amendment Act and the Children's Amendment Act, is punishable as crime.

2.3.7 Sexual offences against mentally disabled people

mentally incompetent persons cannot consent to sexual acts

Mentally incompetent persons cannot consent to sexual acts such as sexual penetration or sexual violations because they do not understand the nature and effect of what they are consenting to. They are in a similar position to children under the age of 12 years, who may not legally consent to sexual acts.

mentally incompetent persons have the same protection as children under 12 years regarding sexual acts

Mentally incompetent persons have the same protection as children under the age of 12 years regarding sexual acts to which they cannot legally consent. The types of crimes committed against children also apply to mentally incompetent persons with allowance being made for mental disability rather than age. These include: (a) sexual exploitation of persons who are mentally disabled; (b) sexual grooming of persons who are mentally disabled; (c) exposure or display of or causing exposure or display of child pornography or pornography to persons who are mentally disabled; and (d) using persons who are mentally disabled for pornographic purposes or benefitting from using such persons.

The identical duties are placed on the same categories of people regarding the reporting of sexual acts against mentally disabled persons as are placed on people who know about sexual offences against children. Failure to report such crimes against mentally disabled persons may also result in punishment.

2.3.8 Attempt, conspiracy, incitement or inducing another person to commit a sexual offence

The Sexual Offences Amendment Act makes it a crime for any person to (a) attempt; (b) conspire with any other person; or (c) aid, abet, induce, incite, instigate, instruct, command, counsel or procure another to commit a sexual offence in terms of the Act. A person who is found guilty of any of these crimes may be given the same punishment as a person convicted of actually committing the sexual offence itself.

Problem 8: Was it an attempt, conspiracy, incitement or inducing another person to commit a sexual offence?

Questions

Divide into small groups and decide whether the people in the following cases can be convicted of attempting, conspiring, inciting or inducing another person to commit a sexual offence. Give reasons for your answer.

1. A man arranges for some foreign women to act as sex workers in his house. He redecorates and furnishes the house to make it comfortable for clients and the sex workers. However, before the sex workers can begin work the man is arrested by the police.

2. A woman arranges visas for women to come to South Africa to work as sex workers. The woman is arrested by the police when she goes to the airport to meet the first group of sex workers.

3. A man stops his car and offers a sex worker R500 to have sex with him. The woman gets into his car. As the man drives off he is stopped by the police who have been watching the behaviour of sex workers in the neighbourhood.

2.3.9 Services for victims of sexual assault and compulsory testing of sex offenders

many rapes are not reported

Many rapes are not reported because women and men are too shy or ashamed to report the crime to the police. Some rape survivors are also reluctant to go through the agony of describing the rape during the trial. Others have fears about what their family and friends will think if they find out about it.

rape crisis centres have been established

To assist people who have been raped, 'rape crisis advice centres' and at some hospitals 'rape crisis centres' have been established. These advice centres help rape survivors lay charges at police stations, provide psychological counselling and give them emotional support during the court case. The hospital crisis centres provide rape victims with a caring environment when they undergo medical examinations for treatment and the collection of evidence concerning the rape.

2.3.9.1 Access to PEP

access to PEP is free

In terms of the Sexual Offences Amendment Act, rape survivors can access free 'post exposure prophylaxis' (PEP) – which means taking 'anti-retroviral drugs' that may stop them from being infected with HIV, at a state facility if the rape is reported and a charge has been laid within 72 hours (three days) of when the alleged rape took place. Afterwards the anti-retroviral drugs must be taken for 28 days by the rape survivor.

2.3.9.2 Compulsory testing of sex offenders for HIV

Many rape survivors want to know whether the person who raped them has HIV. If the rapist has been arrested or his whereabouts are known, rape survivors often ask why the rapist cannot be tested. In the past the law did not allow for the testing of people accused of rape unless they consented to the test. A person's constitutional right to bodily integrity and privacy is violated if his or her blood is tested for HIV without his or her informed consent, except when this is allowed by reasonable and justifiable legislation. Given the high incidence of sexual violence and HIV in South Africa, the compulsory testing of alleged sex offenders for HIV without their consent is likely to be regarded as reasonable and justifiable, provided that confidentiality is protected.

application must be made to magistrate

The Sexual Offences Amendment Act provides that within 90 days after the alleged sexual offence any victim or any interested person on behalf of a victim, may apply to a magistrate for an order that the alleged offender be tested for HIV and that the results of the test be disclosed to the victim or interested person, and to the alleged offender.

The Act also provides that at any stage – even after 90 days – the investigating police officer may apply to a magistrate for an order that the alleged offender be tested for HIV and that the results of the test be disclosed to the victim or interested person, and to the alleged offender.

interested persons may apply on behalf of victims

An application for compulsory testing by an interested person must have the written consent of the victim, unless the victim is: (a) under the age of 14 years; (b) mentally disabled; (c) unconscious; (d) a person in respect of whom a curator has been appointed in terms of a court order; or (e) a person whom the magistrate is satisfied is unable to provide consent. The application for compulsory HIV testing must be made as soon as possible, to a magistrate of the magisterial district in which the sexual offence is alleged to have occurred.

2.3.10 Other sexual offences

2.3.10.1 Trafficking in persons for sexual purposes under the Sexual Offences Amendment Act

Until a special act on trafficking in persons as required by the United Nations has been passed by Parliament in South Africa, the Sexual Offences Amendment Act at present makes it a crime both to traffic in persons for sexual purposes and to be involved in trafficking in persons for sexual purposes.

2.3.10.1.1 Meaning of trafficking

'trafficking' is widely defined

'Trafficking' means the supply, recruitment, procurement, capture, removal, transportation, transfer, harbouring (keeping), sale, disposal or receiving of a person, within or across the borders of South Africa, by:

(a) a threat of harm;
(b) the threat or use of force, intimidation or other forms of coercion;
(c) abduction;
(d) fraud;
(e) deception or false pretences;
(f) the abuse of power or of a position of vulnerability, to the extent that the complainant is inhibited from indicating (reluctant to show) his or her unwillingness or resistance to being trafficked, or unwillingness to participate in such an act; or
(g) the giving or receiving of payments, compensation, rewards, benefits or any other advantage.

the conduct must be in order to commit an act of a sexual nature

In addition, for 'trafficking' the above acts must be done for the purpose of any type of exploitation, grooming or abuse of a sexual nature of such person, including the commission of any sexual offence or any offence of a sexual nature in any other law against such person or performing any sexual act with such person, whether committed in or outside the borders of South Africa.

2.3.10.1.2 The crime of trafficking in persons for sexual purposes

The crime of trafficking in persons for sexual purposes is committed by any person who traffics another person without consent.

2.3.10.1.3 The crime of involvement in trafficking in persons for sexual purposes

The crime of involvement in trafficking in persons for sexual purposes is committed by any person who for sexual purposes:

(a) orders, commands, organises, controls or directs trafficking;
(b) performs any act which is aimed at committing, causing, bringing about, encouraging, promoting, contributing towards or participating in trafficking; or
(c) incites, instigates, commands, aids, advices, recruits, encourages or procures any other person to commit, bring about, promote, perform, contribute towards or participates in trafficking.

2.3.10.1.4 Meaning of 'consent' and 'coercion' in trafficking

voluntary or uncoerced agreement

'Consent' means voluntary or uncoerced agreement (ie an agreement that is not forced on a person).

Examples of when a victim does not voluntarily or without coercion agree to being trafficked include:

(a) where the victim submits or is subjected to the trafficking as a result of any one or more of the means mentioned in the definition in para 2.3.10.1.1 above; or certain victims are incapable of consenting

(b) where the victim is incapable in law of appreciating the nature of the act, including (i) where the victim, at the time of the commission of such act, is asleep; (ii) unconscious; or (iii) in an altered state of unconsciousness, including under the influence of any medicine, drug, alcohol or other substance, to the extent that the victim's consciousness or judgement is negatively affected.

Problem 9: Was it trafficking for sexual purposes?

Questions

Divide into small groups and decide whether any of the cases below amounted to trafficking for sexual purposes. Give reasons for your answers.

1. A woman from Thailand is told that she will be employed as a secretary when she arrives in South Africa. However, when she arrives her passport is taken away by the people who meet her and she is told that she has to be prepared to 'entertain' men in order to pay back the cost of her airfare and accommodation. She is forced to work in a 'men's club' which provides prostitutes for rich clients.
2. A woman from the Philippines agrees to come to South Africa to work as a sex worker for five years, after which she hopes to have saved enough to go home and buy a house. At the time that she was recruited she knew that she would be required to work as a prostitute.

2.4 Domestic violence

Outcomes

After completion of this section learners will be able to:

1. Explain what is meant by domestic violence.

Assessment criteria

1. The different types of domestic violence are identified.
2. The duty to report child abuse and children in need of care and protection is explained.
3. The duty to report abuse of older persons in the home and elsewhere is explained.
4. A set of facts is examined and a decision in made on whether the abuse must be reported to the authorities.

2.4.1 Domestic violence

domestic violence takes many different forms

Many crimes committed against women and children such as rape and assault take place in the home. It was for this reason that the Domestic Violence Act of 1998 was introduced. The Act applies to crimes against males and females and recognises that domestic violence takes many different forms in a wide range of relationships. The Act includes all people in intimate relationships – including same-sex relationships, people who live together, those who do not stay together, as well as those abused by any family member, for example mothers who live in fear of their sons. Domestic violence is defined as:

1. Physical, sexual, emotional, verbal, psychological or economic abuse;
2. Intimidation, harassment, stalking, damage to property, entry into a person's property without consent (where he or she is not staying with the abuser); or
3. Any other controlling behaviour against the person that can cause harm to his or her safety, health or well-being (see below para 4.2.4).

The Children's Amendment Act and the Older Persons Act impose duties on certain people to report abuse of children and older persons.

2.4.2 Duty to report child abuse

child abuse includes abuse causing physical injury, sexual abuse or deliberate neglect

The Children's Amendment Act defines child abuse as including abuse causing physical injury, sexual abuse or deliberate neglect of children. The Act provides that any correctional official, dentist, homoeopath, immigration official, labour inspector, legal practitioner, medical practitioner, midwife, minister of religion, nurse, occupational therapist, physiotherapist, psychologist, religious leader, social service professional, social worker, speech therapist, teacher, traditional health practitioner, traditional leader or member of staff or volunteer worker at a partial care facility, drop-in centre or child and youth care centre who on reasonable grounds concludes that a child has been abused in a manner causing physical the Act imposes a mandatory duty on certain people to report child abuse

injury, sexually abused or deliberately neglected, must report such conclusion in the prescribed form to a designated child protection organisation, the provincial department of social development or a police official. The Act imposes a mandatory duty (ie the person has no choice) on the designated categories of persons to report instances of abuse or neglect to the relevant authorities. Failure to comply is a criminal offence and may also result in civil liability for damages if the child concerned suffers further injury as a result of failure to report.

the Act provides for discretionary reporting of a child in need of care and protection

The Children's Amendment Act also provides for discretionary reporting (ie a person can choose whether to report or not) by anyone who on reasonable grounds believes that a child is in need of care and protection, and may report that belief to the provincial department of social development, a designated child protection organisation or a police official. The reporting duty regarding children in need of care and protection is discretionary and there is no criminal liability for deciding not to report that a child is in need of care. However, where a failure to report that a child needs care and protection results in foreseeable harm to the child it may be a breach of a common-law duty on the person concerned to prevent such harm (eg because of a special relationship such as that between doctor and patient), and the injured child may institute a civil action for damages. Persons who report child abuse or neglect, or that a child is in need of care in line with the Act, must justify their conclusion or belief to the relevant provincial department of social development, a designated child protection organisation or a police official, and if they do they will not be liable for any civil action if the report was made in good faith.

reports made in good faith are protected by law

2.4.3 Duty to report abuse of older persons

older persons are those over 60 years of age

The Older Persons Act defines an older person as a male of 65 years of age or older and a female of 60 years of age or older – although to bring the definition into line with the Constitution and old age pensions the definition should refer to all persons over 60 years of age. The Act provides that any person who is involved with an older person in a professional capacity and who on personal observation concludes that the older person is in need of care and protection must report such conclusion to the director-general of social development.

Problem 1: Was there a duty to report?

Questions

Divide into small groups and decide whether the people in the following cases have a duty to report the abuse. Give reasons for your answer.

1. A doctor sees a 1-year-old girl who is full of bruises. The parents say that the child keeps falling down the stairs.
2. A mother confesses to a priest that her husband continually beats their six-year-old boy until he is 'black and blue'.

3. A traditional leader knows that the men in his community practice *ukuthwala* with young girls under the age of 12 years, with the consent of the girls' parents, in order to cure themselves of HIV infection.
4. A school teacher discovers that a 13-year-old school girl who continually misses classes does so because her parents cannot afford to look after her and she spends nights on the streets being picked up by 'sugar daddies'.
5. A doctor discovers that his patient, who is a 70-year-old granny, is forced by her family to give them her pension and to go begging at traffic light intersections.

2.5 Cyber crimes

Outcomes

After completion of this section learners will be able to:

1. Explain what is meant by cyber crimes.

Assessment criteria

1. The different types of cyber crimes are identified.
2. Some sexting terms are listed and explained.
3. A set of facts is examined and a decision in made on whether the conduct was cyber bullying.
4. How a person may be protected against cyber crime is explained.
5. A set of facts is examined and a decision in made on whether what was posted on Facebook violated a person's human rights.

2.5.1 Cyber bullying

2.5.1.1 Introduction

cyber bullying occurs inside and outside school

Cyber bullying is the use of information technology on computers and cell phones to harass, threaten, embarrass, or target another person. Examples of cyber bullying are to send a person cruel text messages or to post nasty comments about a person on eg Facebook or Twitter. Bullying is no longer restricted to only occurring on the school grounds during school time. The increased use of information technology by persons allows acts of cyber bullying to happen 24 hours a day. Bullying is a form of abuse. It involves repeated acts over time, with the more powerful individuals or groups abusing those who are less powerful. Cyber bullying is normally not a once off event. There is normally a repeated attack against the person targeted.

It is strongly recommended that schools should include cyber bullying as a form of misconduct in their codes of conduct for learners. The codes of conduct should state that the school may take disciplinary action against the wrongdoer even where the cyber bullying happens off school grounds where it has a harmful effect on the victim while at school.

Cyber bullying can take many forms and can happen in a number of ways such as: (a) instant short messaging; (b) password stealing; (c) blogs; (d) websites; or (e) sexting.

2.5.1.2 Instant short messaging

Cyber bullying takes place when a person sends hurtful and hateful SMSes to another person. It includes text wars where a large number of children gang up against another young person and send him or her thousands of text messages that require the person to download data when opening the message. This results in the victim getting a large cell phone bill. Another example is where a person is sent a death threat using instant short messaging.

2.5.1.3 Password stealing

Password stealing happens when a person steals another person's password and then pretends to be that person or locks the person out of his or her account. Cyber bullying occurs if the person pretending to be another does things that harm the other person's dignity or reputation or prevents him or her from using his or her account.

2.5.1.4 Blogs

Blogs allow a person to send a message to a large number of people at once using an online journal. When used in cyber bullying blogs invade another person's privacy or say things that will damage the person's reputation or dignity.

2.5.1.5 Websites

Cyber bullying can also happen where a person creates a website that is aimed at insulting another person. Sometimes personal information about the victim is put on the website that makes it much easier for such a person to be contacted and insulted.

2.5.1.6 Sexting

Sexting refers to sending images with rude messages, nude or sexually explicit photos. This could happen where a person takes a picture of someone nude in the change rooms and then circulates it via e-mail, mms, WhatsApp, BBM, YouTube etc.

Terms to know if you are monitoring sexting

Banana	Penis
CD9 or Code 9	Parents are around
DUM	Do you masturbate
DUSL	Do you scream loud?
FB	F***buddy
FMLTWIA	F*** me like the whore I am
GNOC	Get naked on camera
IF/IB	In the front or in the back
GYPO	Get your pants off
MOS	Mom over shoulder
NIFOC	Nude in front of computer
PIR	Parent in room
PAW	Parents are watching
PAL	Parents are listening

Case study: The school administrators who were cyber bullied: *Le Roux v Dey*

In *Le Roux and Others v Dey* a learner at a school searched the Internet and found a photograph of two gay body builders on the Internet. The two body builders were in a compromising position in the photograph indicating that they were involved in some sexual activity. The learner then cut and pasted the faces of the principal and the deputy principal onto the faces of the body builders. He further covered the genitals of each bodybuilder with the school badge. He sent the manipulated photograph to a friend who distributed it further. The picture spread rapidly. Another learner printed the photo and pasted it on the school notice board. The deputy principal sued the learners for damages. The court held that everyone should in terms of the Constitution of the Republic of South Africa have their rights to dignity and privacy respected. The court held that a joke at the expense of someone is likely to be interpreted as defamatory. It found that the manipulated photograph ridiculed and humiliated the deputy principal. The court ordered the learners to pay damages to the deputy principal.

2.5.1.7 Internet polling

Cyber bullying can happen where teenagers create an Internet poll inviting fellow teenagers to vote on something that harms another person's dignity or reputation (eg 'Who is the biggest slut in grade 9?').

2.5.1.8 Interactive gaming

Cyber bullying happens when children who play interactive games online are intentionally locked out of playing the games by the bullies. Cyber bullies can also go into chat rooms and spread nasty rumours about other children.

Problem 1: Was it cyber bullying?

Questions

Divide into small groups and decide whether the people in the following cases can be convicted of cyber bullying. Give reasons for your answer.

1. A boy sends another boy an SMS telling him that if he does not stop going out with a particular girl he will 'fix' him so he cannot go out with her anymore.
2. A girl uses another girl's password to download pornography from the Internet, knowing that it is against school's rules and that the first girl will be punished by losing her Internet access as a result.
3. A boy uses his blog to say that the boy who has been going out with his ex-girlfriend is gay.

a boy is embarassed by being named 'stud of the year' by some girls

4. A girl sends out an Internet message inviting other girls to nominate and send photographs of boys for the 'Stud of the Year Award'. Some of the boys nominated and whose photographs are posted are embarrassed, upset and angry.

2.5.1.9 Human rights that have to be considered when faced with cyber bullying

2.5.1.9.1 The right to dignity

the rights to dignity and privacy have to be balanced against the right to freedom of expression

The Constitution provides that everyone has inherent dignity and the right to have their dignity respected and protected. The right to human dignity requires all of us to acknowledge the value and worth of human beings as members of society. The right to dignity is linked with other human rights (eg equality and privacy). The right to a good name and reputation forms part of the right to dignity. The right to dignity is linked to cases that involve the law of defamation. Very often in issues relating to defamation, the right to dignity and the right to privacy have to be balanced against the right to freedom of expression.

2.5.1.9.2 Freedom of expression

The Constitution provides that everyone has the right to freedom of expression, which includes:

(a) freedom of the press and other media;
(b) freedom to receive and impart information or ideas;
(c) freedom of artistic creativity; and
(d) academic freedom and freedom of scientific research.

hate speech is excluded from freedom of expression

However, propaganda for war, incitement to violence and advocacy of hatred that is based on race, ethnicity, gender or religion are excluded from freedom of speech.

Freedom of expression includes all conduct that seeks to communicate and covers the use of social media, such as Facebook, MySpace, and Twitter.

2.5.1.9.3 Right to privacy

The Constitution provides that everyone has the right to privacy, which includes the right not to have:

(a) their person or home searched;
(b) their property searched;
(c) their possessions seized; or
(d) the privacy of their communications infringed.

people have the right to decide who has information about them

The right to privacy guarantees people the right to control all private information about themselves. A person's right to privacy will be invaded if somebody publishes a photograph of that person without his or her permission. It will also infringe a person's right to privacy if a person listens to private conversations or where somebody hacks into another's personal information and discloses such information to somebody else. Sending photographs through e-mail or cell phones or posting them on social media websites (eg Facebook) also invades the right to privacy. It is no defence to prove that the photograph actually makes the person look good in the eyes of others. It would not, however, be an invasion of privacy if the person consented to having their photographs posted or circulated to others.

2.5.1.10 Protection from Harassment Act

a protection order against harassment

The Protection from Harassment Act provides for the granting of a protection order against harassment similar to that granted to protect against domestic violence. The definition of harassment includes (a) engaging in verbal, electronic or any other communication aimed at a particular person by any means, (b) whether or not conversation ensues; or (c) sending, delivering or causing the delivery of letters, telegrams, packages, facsimiles, electronic mail or other objects to the person or leaving it where it will be found by or given to, or brought to the attention of, the person. A person who is being harassed may apply to court for a protection order against the perpetrator and the court may also issue a warrant of arrest with the protection order. A person who goes against a protection order or a condition of a protection order can be charged with a criminal offence and, if convicted, can be fined or sent to prison for a maximum of five years.

The court issuing the protection order may order the station commissioner of a police station to investigate the matter with the view to instituting criminal proceedings against the person. The victim of harassment may also lodge a criminal complaint of *crimen injuria* with the police (see above para 2.2.3).

Protecting yourself against cyber crime

1. Places like Facebook, MySpace and Twitter are public spaces.
2. Make sure you do not post anything that you do not want the world to know.
3. Avoid posting your address, contact details or specific whereabouts.
4. Make sure that you report harassment, hate speech and inappropriate content to your Internet service provider, or to your social media provider.
5. Do not post anything that will embarrass you later.

6. Think twice before posting photographs or information that you would not want your parents or friends to see.
7. Do not lie about your age.
8. Make sure you create a strong password that you update regularly – strong passwords are usually at least eight characters with a number and a special character such as an '&' or '@'.
9. Keep different passwords for different online accounts.
10. If a phisher gains access to your e-mail account he or she can request that your password be sent via a 'forgotten password' feature.
11. Make sure that you are on an authentic website when logging into your social media account.
12. If you are asked to log into your account for a second time you may have been redirected to a phishing site.
13. If you receive an e-mail asking you to verify your account and/or giving you a time limit to respond you can assume that the e-mail is fraudulent and is part of a phishing scam – do not respond to such an e-mail in any way.
14. Do not click on unknown links embedded in an e-mail.
15. Install anti-virus and anti-spyware filters, and be sure to keep your operating system updated with the latest patches and firewall software.
16. If a person is attacking you in an electronic public forum, block that person (eg on Facebook you can unfriend a person who is harassing you).
17. Customise your privacy settings to reflect the amount of information you want to share with your online friends.
18. Parents and older people should get their children or young friends to teach them the basics of online social media.

Problem 2: The story of Desiree

Desiree becomes the laughing stock of the school and commits suicide

Desiree is a grade 8 learner. She is struggling at school and is not part of the 'popular girls' group. Desiree signs up to Facebook and invites some of the young people she knows to become her friends on Facebook. Cassandra, a fellow grade 8 learner who does not like Desiree, posts the following on Facebook: 'Did you know that Desiree is a lesbian?' This rumour spreads like wildfire in the school. James befriends Desiree on Facebook telling her that the only way she can get rid of the rumour is to be friends with him. Desiree and James have a number of very personal chats. Unbeknown to Desiree, James copies and pastes all their private discussions into his chats with his friends. Desiree becomes the laughing stock of the school. When Desiree finds out about this she is so distraught that she commits suicide.

Questions

Divide into groups and discuss the following:

1. Identify the human rights that Cassandra infringed when she posted on Facebook that 'Desiree is a lesbian'. Give reasons for your answers.
2. Cassandra claims that she is exercising her freedom of expression when she posts comments on Facebook. Discuss whether you think Cassandra's right to freedom of expression allows her to say nasty things about Desiree.
3. Identify the rights that James infringed when he shared the content of Desiree's private conversations with him with the rest of his friends. Give reasons for your answers.
4. You are selected on a committee to draft a plan of action explaining what learners and teenagers can do to protect themselves and their friends from cyber bullying. In your groups list a number of things that can be done to prevent or address cyber bullying.

2.6 Crimes against property

Outcomes

After completion of this section learners will be able to:

1. List and explain the crimes against property.

Assessment criteria

1. The different crimes against property are identified.
2. A set of facts is analysed and a decision is taken on whether any crimes against property have been committed.
3. The elements of arson; malicious injury to property; theft; robbery and housebreaking are explained.

Crimes against property include cases in which property is destroyed (eg arson and malicious injury to property), and those in which property is stolen or otherwise taken without the consent of the owner (eg theft, robbery, housebreaking, receiving stolen property and unauthorised borrowing).

2.6.1 Arson

setting fire to buildings

Arson is the unlawful setting on fire of buildings or immovable structures (eg houses or factories), with the intention of causing damage to another person's property. A person can only be convicted of arson if the structure actually burns and is damaged by the burning, even if the damage is slight. For instance, if only the area where the fire was started is charred and the building did not burn it would still be arson. Otherwise it may be attempted arson. For example, if a person pours petrol on the floor of a building and is caught before he or she can set it alight, the crime will be attempted arson.

attempted arson

during the struggle for democracy many people had their homes destroyed by arson

burning homes or public buildings

People who burn down others' homes, or public buildings like schools or offices, will be guilty of arson. A person, however, who burns a structure that is not immovable, like a motor car, would probably be charged with malicious injury to property (see below para 2.6.2).

2.6.2 Malicious injury to property

vandalism

Malicious injury to property occurs when someone unlawfully damages property with the intention of causing injury to another person's property. Malicious injury to property is often called 'vandalism'. A difficult question is what is meant by 'damage.' Is it damage if something is not broken but merely dismantled? Some cases say that the original form of the thing must have been changed. Others say that there must have been financial loss. In general, however, it seems that a 'common-sense' test must be applied regarding what is 'damage' and each case must be decided on its own facts.

malicious injury to property is often called 'vandalism'

2.6.3 Theft

Theft is the unlawful taking control of another person's property with the intention of stealing it. Usually the thief takes control of the property by removing the property from the possession of the owner or the person who has a right to it.

theft is the unlawful taking control of another's property with the intention of stealing it

stealing, shoplifting and pickpocketing

The intention to steal means the intention permanently to deprive the owner of his or her rights over the thing stolen. Shoplifting is a common example of theft. Here goods are unlawfully taken from a shop (without paying), with the intention of permanently depriving the shopkeeper of the goods. Pickpocketing is another example of theft.

2.6.4 Robbery

Robbery is theft carried out with force or threats of force. Robbery therefore involves two wrongs, theft of the property and the use or threatened use of force against the other person. The force or threatened force must be used with the intention of taking the thing away.

the use of force to steal

The difference between theft and robbery can be shown as follows. A pickpocket who secretly takes your wallet from your pocket is guilty of theft. The 'mugger' who knocks you down and then takes your wallet by force is guilty of robbery. If a person is found guilty of robbery, and it is the first time that that person has committed the crime, he or she must be sentenced to a minimum of 15 years' imprisonment. A second offender must be sentenced to at least 20 years' imprisonment and a third offender to at least 25 years' imprisonment. However, these sentences may be reduced if special circumstances are shown by the convicted person (eg he or she stole because his or her family was starving).

robbery involves the threat or use of force

breaking and entering

2.6.5 Housebreaking (burglary)

'entry' means entering or inserting an instrument into the premises in order to steal

The crime of housebreaking with intent to commit a crime occurs when a person breaks into and enters a house, shop, storeroom or similar structure with the intention of committing a crime inside the premises. 'Breaking' does not mean damage, but the removal of some obstruction that stops the burglar from entering, for example, opening a half-closed door or window to allow entry. 'Entry' means that the person enters the premises or inserts into the premises any part of his or her body or any instrument so that he or she can get control of something in the house (eg placing one's hand or a fishing rod through a window to steal clothes). The intention of the burglar must not only be to break and enter, but also to commit some crime (eg arson, malicious injury to property, theft, robbery, and rape or, sometimes, some unknown crime).

intention to commit a crime

2.6.6 Receiving stolen property

a person who buys property which he or she suspects is stolen commits a crime

A person who receives or buys property that he or she knows, or has reason to believe, is stolen, commits the crime of receiving stolen property. This applies to property that is obtained for the profit of the receiver or is held on behalf of a thief. It also applies where the receiver assists somebody who holds stolen property.

In most cases the receiver will also be guilty of theft. Technically a receiver is also an accessory after the fact of theft (see above para 2.1.5). A person cannot be found guilty of receiving unless he or she knew or suspected that the goods were stolen and did nothing to discover the truth.

2.6.7 Unauthorised borrowing

borrowing property without consent

The crime of unauthorised borrowing is committed where a person intentionally removes property from the control of the owner or person in charge without consent. The most common example is where a person takes a car for a joyride without the owner's consent or takes it believing that the owner would not consent. A person will not be guilty of unauthorised borrowing, however, where the owner lends the car for one purpose and it is used for another. For example A lends B his car to go shopping and B goes to the beach. There is a similar crime of driving an owner's car on the road without his or her consent.

Problem 1: Which crimes have been committed?

Questions

Analyse the following facts and decide which crimes (if any) have been committed:

1. Paul climbs through an open window into Pam's bedroom and takes her radio.
2. Sarel tries to burn down Sannie's house but the fire does not take and merely burns the carpet and scorches the floor.
3. Zo sees that Zube's door is half open. He pushes it open and goes into Zube's bedroom in order to look for money. Zube surprises him and calls the police.
4. Ashwin sets fire to Ansie's car because she won't go out with him.
5. Bobby borrows Betty's bicycle without asking her in order to go to the shop. He returns it two hours later.
6. Vuka threatens to punch Vicky if she does not hand over her purse.
7. Ishmael gives Ismeralda a stolen ring for her birthday.

2.6.8 Other crimes against property

There are several other crimes against property: for example, extortion ('blackmail'); fraud (a false statement causing harm to another); forgery (making a false document that harms another) and uttering (using a false document to harm another); and trespass (going onto somebody's property without their consent).

2.7 Crimes against the state

Outcomes

After completion of this section learners will be able to:

1. List and explain the crimes against the state.

Assessment criteria

1. Crimes against the state are identified and explained.
2. The reasons why the state recognises these crimes are identified.
3. A set of facts is analysed and a decision is taken on which crime against the state has been committed.

Most states recognise offences such as high treason, public violence and sedition. These crimes exist in order to protect the structures and institutions that the state uses to govern. These crimes also exist because people should use lawful means, such as elections, if they want to change or influence the government. Since the destruction of the World Trade Towers in New York by terrorist groups flying aircraft into the buildings on 11 September 2001 there has been an increase in anti-terrorism laws around the world. South Africa has introduced the Protection of Constitutional Democracy against Terrorism and Related Activities Act (see below para 2.7.5).

2.7.1 High treason

allegiance or loyalty to the state

High treason occurs when a person who owes allegiance to a state commits an unlawful act with the hostile intention of overthrowing the state or forcing the state to do something. The courts regard a person as owing allegiance to the South African state if he or she is a citizen, is not a citizen but intends to live here indefinitely, or even if he or she is merely resident in South Africa. Such a person will owe allegiance to the state whether or not he or she agrees with the policies of the government. A person does not, however, owe allegiance if he or she is merely a temporary visitor.

2.7.2 Public violence

unlawful disturbance

Public violence takes place when a number of people act together unlawfully and intentionally commit disturbances that are so serious that they become dangerous to the rest of the community. The disturbances must have been intended forcibly to disturb the public peace or security or to invade the rights of others.

2.7.3 Sedition

Sedition occurs when a number of people join together unlawfully with the intention of defying, undermining or challenging the authority of the government.

2.7.4 Sabotage

Sabotage is the crime of intentionally endangering public safety, polluting water supplies, or disrupting essential services or industries or the movement of land, sea or air traffic, or attempting to do so.

2.7.5 Terrorism

controversial provisions

South Africa's anti-terror legislation is the Protection of Constitutional Democracy against Terrorist and Related Activities Act 33 of 2004. The Act was introduced to bring South Africa's extensive collection of apartheid-era security laws into line with the Constitution and South Africa's international obligations.

terrorist activity

A terrorist activity as defined in the Act can be roughly summed up as any act that may cause damage to property and is intended to disrupt public service. The definition therefore includes law breakers who in the normal meaning of the word would not be terrorists but who act in a way that disrupts public services or causes damage to property.

duty to report suspected terrorists

The Act places an obligation on citizens to report 'as soon as possible' the presence of people suspected of committing a terrorist act. A failure to report on the presence of such persons is a crime under the Act. The Act also creates a number of new offences and penalties as set out by twelve United Nations and African Union conventions. The Act also contains a clause that states that a person suspected of aiding or funding terrorist activity has to disprove that he or she is doing so. This provision is against the presumption of innocence provision in the Constitution.

detention without trial conflicts with the Constitution

The Act also provides for 14-day detention of anyone when there is reason to believe he or she possesses or is withholding information about any offence in terms of the Act. Such a person can be interrogated until he or she has satisfactorily replied to all questions under interrogation. This would effectively lead to detention without trial and is in direct conflict with the Constitutional right to a fair trial. Critics of the Act say that some of its provisions are similar to those that existed under apartheid and are unconstitutional.

Protection of Information Act

More recently, Parliament has passed the Protection of State Information Act (popularly known as the 'Secrecy Act') which seeks to prohibit the publication of certain information about public officials or affairs that the state and its organs think should not be published. Critics are worried that this will allow public officials to cover up corruption, while the state says that it is necessary for the security of the state.

Problem 1: Crimes against the state

Questions

1. Members of a right-wing organisation conspire to overthrow the government through an armed uprising. What can they be charged with? Why?
2. The crime of public violence takes different forms in various countries. Do you think that the authorities are justified in prosecuting people who forcibly disturb the peace or security of others, or invade their rights? Give reasons for your answer.
3. Sedition is also a crime found in most countries. Should people who join together to defy, undermine or attack the authority of a government be prosecuted? Give reasons for your answer.
4. Members of a right-wing organisation blow up a number of railway lines in Soweto. What can they be charged with? Why?
5. Since the destruction of the World Trade Centre in New York in 2001 many countries have introduced anti-terrorism laws. Do you think that it was correct for South Africa to do the same? Give reasons for your answer.

2.8 Crimes against morality involving sexual conduct

Outcomes

After completion of this section learners will be able to:

1. Explain the crimes against morality involving sexual conduct.

Assessment criteria

1. The crimes against morality are identified and questions about them are answered.
2. Incest as a crime is explained.
3. An explanation of prostitution is provided.
4. An explanation of bigamy is provided.
5. An explanation of bestiality is provided.
6. The crime of sexual acts with a corpse is explained.
7. The legal position regarding abortion is explained.
8. The legal position relating to drug offences is explained.
9. Arguments about whether there should be crimes against morality are advanced.
10. Some questions on the rights of gays and lesbians are answered.

crimes against morality may involve sexual acts between consenting adults

Some crimes, particularly those relating to sexual relations between consenting adult partners, are regarded as crimes against morality rather than wrongful acts committed against the individuals concerned. This is because many people may not believe that such conduct should be made criminal because it is done between consenting adults. In other words they see such crimes as 'victimless', because it is society, rather than individual people, which is 'harmed' by them.

sex and drugs

Probably the most controversial crimes against morality are those relating to sex and drugs. The crimes relating to sex include incest, prostitution, bigamy, bestiality and sexual acts with corpses, while those relating to drugs include possession of, and dealing in, drugs. Furthermore, since democracy in South African there has been a considerable change concerning attitudes towards abortion and gay and lesbian people.

2.8.1 Incest

sex between people who are closely related

Incest is provided for in the Sexual Offences Amendment Act, which states that persons who may not lawfully marry each other because of (a) their blood relationship, or (b) because they are related by marriage or (c) because of their adoptive relationship, will be guilty of the crime of incest if they unlawfully and intentionally have sexual penetration with each other with consent. Prohibited blood relationships are (i) ascendants and descendants in the direct line (eg parents or children) and (ii) 'collaterals' (ie blood relatives not in the direct prohibited relationships by marriage or adoption

line) that are related to their common ancestor in the first degree of descent (eg brothers and sisters). Prohibited relationships by marriage are those in the ascending and descending line (eg parents-in-law or children-in-law). Prohibited adoptive relationships include adoptive parents and their adoptive children. If a child is to be prosecuted for incest the Director of Public Prosecutions must authorise it and may not delegate this authority.

2.8.2 Prostitution

doing sexual acts for money

The Sexual Offences Amendment Act provides that any person who unlawfully and intentionally engages the services of a person who is 18 years or older for a sexual act, for financial or other reward, favour or compensation is guilty of engaging the sexual services of a person of 18 years or older. The same applies to a person who engages such sexual services with a person of 18 years or older for financial reward, favour or compensation to a third person. In both cases the person who engages the sexual services is guilty of a crime, whether or not the sexual act takes place.

prostitutes and their clients may be prosecuted

Similar provisions apply to people who unlawfully and intentionally engage the services of a person who is under 18 years of age for a sexual act, for financial or other reward, favour or compensation.

previously prostitutes not their clients were prosecuted

This is different from the past, where it was a crime for a person to have a sexual act with another person for reward, but not a crime to give the reward in return for the sexual act. The result was that the law was directed at prosecuting prostitutes and not their customers. However, the majority of the Constitutional Court in *S v Jordan* stated that customers of prostitutes could be found guilty of being an accomplice or of incitement or conspiracy regarding the crime committed by the prostitute. As pointed out above, this has now been changed by the Sexual Offences Amendment Act, which makes it a crime for people to engage the sexual services of another for reward.

2.8.3 Bigamy

a married person 'marries' somebody else

bigamy applies to marriages and civil unions

Bigamy occurs where a person already legally married to somebody else enters into a 'marriage' or 'civil union' with another person. Parliament has passed laws that allow men who marry according to African customary law to have more than one wife (see para 4.1.5). In addition, the crime of bigamy does not apply to people married according to Hindu or Muslim rites.

2.8.4 Bestiality

sexual acts with animals

According to the Sexual Offences Amendment Act, a person is guilty of bestiality when he or she unlawfully and intentionally commits an act which causes penetration by the genital organs of the person into or beyond the mouth, genital organs or anus of an animal. In the case of *S v M* the court confirmed the constitutionality of the crime of bestiality and regarded the behaviour covered by the crime as against the legal convictions of the community. Bestiality can also be an act which causes penetration by the genital organs of an animal into or beyond the mouth, genital organs or anus of the person. In addition, a person is guilty of bestiality when he or she unlawfully and intentionally commits an act of masturbation of an animal (unless such act is committed for scientific reasons or breeding purposes) or of masturbation with an animal.

2.8.5 Sexual acts with a human corpse

The Sexual Offences Amendment Act states that a person who unlawfully and intentionally commits a sexual act with a human corpse is guilty of the crime of committing a sexual act with a corpse. At common law it is a crime to interfere with a corpse.

2.8.6 Abortion

2.8.6.1 When is termination of pregnancy illegal?

a foetus is a potential human being

Abortion is the unlawful termination of a woman's pregnancy. It is the ending of a pregnancy before the child is born. Although the foetus (the unborn baby inside the mother) is not, legally speaking, a human being, it is a potential human being and some people regard the destruction of a foetus as ethically and morally wrong.

conflict between the mother's right to choose and the foetus's right to life

People have different ideas about whether the law should allow or prohibit abortion. There is a conflict between the right to life of the foetus and the right of the mother to decide whether she wishes bear a child. The Constitution provides that everyone has the right to bodily integrity and privacy, which means that women may do what they want with their bodies, including ending a pregnancy subject to certain limits. For example, as a pregnancy progresses there are also good practical reasons for allowing the lawful termination of a pregnancy for more restrictive reasons (eg where the child to be born would suffer from a severe mental or physical handicap or the mother's life is at risk). Another justification is that the pregnancy should be legally ended when it is the result of rape or incest. There are also arguments that the prohibition of legal abortions forces women to seek 'backstreet' abortions performed by people not properly qualified, which often causes the women to suffer severe injury or death (see below para 5.6.8).

2.8.6.2 The crime of unlawful abortion

South African law recognises that a lawful abortion may take place under certain conditions in terms of the Choice on Termination of Pregnancy Act. However, it is a crime to terminate a pregnancy outside of the conditions specified in the Act or for any person who is not a doctor or a midwife (a nurse who delivers babies) to end a pregnancy.

Stages for legal termination of pregnancy

First 12 weeks

request of the mother

During the first 12 weeks the abortion may be performed by a doctor or a midwife at the request and with the consent of the mother.

13th to 20th week

From the 13th to 20th week the pregnancy may only be terminated by a doctor, after consultation with the pregnant woman, on the following grounds specified in the Act, where:

limited grounds

- In the opinion of the medical practitioner, the continuation of the pregnancy would bear a risk of injury to the woman's physical or mental health.
- In the opinion of the medical practitioner, if the pregnancy were to continue, there is a substantial risk that the foetus would suffer from severe physical or mental abnormality.
- In the opinion of the medical practitioner, the continuation of the pregnancy would severely affect the social or economic conditions of the woman.

After 20 weeks

more restrictive grounds

After 20 weeks the pregnancy may only be terminated where, in the opinion of the doctor, after consulting another doctor or a midwife, the woman's life is in danger or there would be severe malformation of the foetus.

Problem 1: Crimes against morality

Questions

1. Should society protect people from 'harming' themselves? Should people be allowed to do what they like with their lives? Give reasons for your answer.
2. What is the difference between people harming themselves by taking drugs like alcohol and cigarettes and using a drug like dagga?
3. Should people be punished for having sex as prostitutes if they do it in the privacy of their homes? Give reasons for your answer.
4. Should children who sell sexual favours in exchange for money, sweets, drinks, videos or a 'good time' be prosecuted for prostitution? Give reasons for your answer.
5. Should incest be a crime? Give reasons for your answer.
6. Take a stand on whether or not prostitution should be legalised.

Problem 2: The rights of gays and lesbians

sodomy was a common-law crime

There was a time when, in South Africa, the law criminalised the conduct of gay men. Under the common law, it was a crime for men to engage in sodomy (ie anal intercourse) or 'unnatural sexual acts.' Parliament also passed a statute called the Sexual Offences Act 23 of 1957. This act made it a crime for one man to commit any act which was intended to stimulate sexual passion or give sexual gratification to another man at any gathering where more than two people were present.

crime of sodomy held unconstitutional

In the case of *National Coalition for Gay and Lesbian Equality v Minister of Justice*, the Constitutional Court was asked to declare the crime of sodomy and the crime created by the Sexual Offences Act unconstitutional (the common-law offence of 'unnatural sexual acts' had already been declared unconstitutional). The court noted that the Bill of Rights says that everyone has the right to equality, which includes the right not to be unfairly discriminated against by the state. The Bill of Rights also says that the state may not discriminate on the ground of 'sexual orientation' (ie whether a person is sexually attracted to men or women or both). In addition, the Bill of Rights recognises the rights to privacy and dignity.

The Constitutional Court held that the criminal offences mentioned above in the Sexual Offences Act discriminated against gay men without justification and thus violated the right to equality. In addition, they violated the rights to dignity and equality without justification. The court therefore declared the offences unconstitutional.

Questions

1. What offences criminalised the conduct of gay men?
2. What rights did the Constitutional Court say were violated by these offences?
3. Do you agree with the decision of the Constitutional Court? Give reasons for your answer.
4. Do you think that gays and lesbians should be allowed to marry and adopt children?

2.9 Crimes involving alcohol and drugs

Outcomes

After completion of this section learners will be able to:

1. List and explain the crimes of abusing alcohol or possessing or dealing in illegal drugs.

Assessment criteria

1. Offences in terms of the National Road Traffic Act are identified and explained.
2. Offences in terms of the Drugs and Drug Trafficking Act are identified and explained.
2. The reasons why the state recognises these crimes are identified.
3. A set of facts is analysed and a decision is taken on which crimes involving drugs and alcohol have been committed.

alcohol abuse may lead to domestic violence

Crimes involving drugs and alcohol are not always 'victimless' as they may have severe consequences for other people (eg driving under the influence of alcohol may cause accidents). For example, alcohol abuse may lead to domestic violence and other crimes involving violence. In addition drugs other than alcohol they may seem to be 'victimless' because they only affect the person who takes them, but they may also have a harmful effect on other people such as family members and friends.

2.9.1 Driving under the influence of alcohol

sitting in the driver's seat of a car while drunk on a public road with the engine running is a crime

The National Road Traffic Act provides that it is a crime if a person drives a vehicle or sits in the driver's seat of a vehicle with its engine running on a public road, while under the influence of intoxicating liquor or a drug having a narcotic effect. When an intoxicated person is charged with occupying the driver's seat while the engine of the vehicle is running, the person must be sitting and his or her act must be voluntary. Therefore, if X is found sleeping while occupying the driver's seat when the engine is running, the person does not commit a voluntary act and does not contravene the law. It does not matter whether the vehicle is unable to move because of some mechanical fault, or whether X is prevented by external factors (eg a heavy storm) from driving the car.

it is not necessary for a person to drive like a drunk person

It is not necessary to prove that the person was drunk when he or she drove the car, or that the person in fact drove like a drunken person, or that the person's driving was 'erratic' (not regular) or that the person drove the car negligently. It is sufficient to prove that the person was affected by alcohol or a drug to the extent that his or her usual driving skill and judgement were reduced or badly affected.

other alcohol-related crimes

There are other alcohol-related crimes, such as selling alcohol to persons under the age of 18 years and drinking in public on streets in certain towns and cities. Also the consumption of alcohol may sometimes be a defence to crime (eg where people are so drunk that they do not know what they are doing), and at other times it may be a mitigating (making the crime less serious – eg where a person had not experienced the effect of alcohol before) or aggravating factor (making the crime more serious – eg where people know that they become violent if they consume alcohol) (see below para 2.10.4.3).

2.9.2 Drug offences

use, possession or sale of drugs is prohibited

The Drugs and Drugs Trafficking Act makes it a crime to possess or deal in certain drugs. The Act defines three kinds of undesirable drugs: (a) dependence-producing substances; (b) dangerous dependence-producing substances (eg coca leaf, morphine, and opium and opium opiates); and (c) undesirable dependence-producing substances (eg dagga, heroin and mandrax). The Act makes it an offence to possess, or deal in, these substances. Dealing in drugs means selling drugs to other people and is regarded as a more serious crime than merely possessing them.

accused persons are presumed to be innocent

Previously, the Act stated that if a person was found in possession of more than 115 grams of drugs or dagga, he or she was presumed to be a dealer. This meant that instead of the state having to prove beyond a reasonable doubt that the accused was a dealer, the accused would have to prove to the court that he or she was *not* a dealer. These provisions were later declared unconstitutional by the Constitutional Court because the Bill of Rights guarantees all people the right to be presumed innocent when accused of a crime. This means that the state must prove all the elements of crime that the accused is alleged to have committed beyond a reasonable doubt – the accused does not have to prove that he or she is innocent – the accused only has to raise a doubt in the mind of the court that one of the elements of the crime has not been satisfied (see below para 2.10).

2.9.2.1 Unlawful possession or use of drugs

dangerous dependence-producing drugs may only be bought from a pharmacist with a prescription from a doctor

Use or possession of drugs is not treated in the Drugs and Drug Trafficking Act as two separate offences, but as a single crime. The Act provides that no person shall use or have in his or her possession any dependence-producing substance or any dangerous or undesirable dependence-producing substance, unless there are statutory grounds of justification (ie where an Act of Parliament allows it). For example, a patient is allowed to buy certain dangerous, dependence-producing drugs from a pharmacist with a prescription from a doctor.

2.9.2.2 Unlawful dealing in drugs

an accused person must have acted intentionally

In order for a person to be convicted of unlawful dealing in drugs, his or her conduct must be unlawful. Intention on the part of the accused person is an element of the unlawful dealing in drugs. The person must know that the substance is listed in the Act and that his or her behaviour amounts to 'dealing in' the substance, and that his or her conduct is unlawful.

The ordinary meaning of 'dealing in' usually means to buy and sell, but it may also mean doing business or carrying out a commercial contract. For example, if a person charged with unlawful dealing in dagga is found in possession of a large quantity of dagga and is unable to give a reasonable explanation, the conclusion will be that such person was dealing in dagga. This is common sense and does not involve any legal presumption of dealing.

it is unlawful to supply, manufacture, sell or cultivate illegal drugs

The Act also provides for an extended meaning of 'dealing in' by stating that it includes 'any act in connection with the transhipment, importation, cultivation, collection, manufacture, supply, prescription, administration, sale, transmission or exportation of the drug'. 'Supply' covers only activities relating to the giving of drugs to others and not to the obtaining of drugs. This means that an agent or other person, who gets drugs for a buyer, is not guilty of dealing in such drugs but only of possessing them. 'Manufacture' refers to 'the preparing, extraction or producing of the substance' (eg where a person makes the drugs ready for use by others).'Selling' is linked to 'sale' in the definition of 'dealing in' which includes 'to offer, advertise, possess or expose the drug for sale, to dispose of it, whether for consideration or otherwise, or to exchange it'. 'Cultivate' means to grow drug plants, or to stimulate or promote their growth. A person who buys dagga for his or her own use from another does not perform an act in connection with the 'supply' or 'sale' of dagga, and is therefore not guilty of dealing in dagga but only of possessing it.

dagga may not be used for religious reasons

In *Prince v President, Cape Law Society* it was argued that the Drugs and Drug Trafficking Act was in conflict with the constitutional right to freedom of religion by not granting Rastafari an exemption to possess and use dagga for religious purposes. The Constitutional Court held that Rastafaris could not be allowed to possess and use dagga for religious purposes.

Problem 1: Was it a crime involving alcohol or drugs?

Questions

Analyse the following facts and decide which crimes involving alcohol or drugs (if any) have been committed:

1. A man who has been drinking heavily climbs into the driver's seat of his car in a parking zone in the street. He switches on the engine but falls asleep before he can drive off. The police find him bent forward, asleep with his head on the steering wheel and the car's engine running.
2. A university student buys a bottle of beer and walks down the road drinking it on his way to the university residence where he stays.
3. Some students are found smoking dagga in a park.

4. A woman looks after a pot plant given to her by her daughter. She does not know that the plant is a dagga plant and is arrested by the police when they raid her house looking for her daughter.

5. A Rastafari smokes dagga for religious purposes.
6. A traditional healer prescribes dagga to cure a patient's illness.

2.10 Defences to crimes

Outcomes

After completion of this section learners will be able to:

1. Identify and explain the different defences to crimes.

Assessment criteria

1. Defences to crimes are identified.
2. A situation when no crime has been committed is identified.
3. A set of facts is examined and a decision is made on whether the person used reasonable force to prevent a crime.
4. An explanation is given of when a criminal act is committed, but excused or justified.
5. An explanation of private defence and necessity is given.
6. Lack of criminal responsibility is explained.
7. A set of facts is examined and a decision is made on whether there was a defence to each of the crimes.

proof 'beyond a reasonable doubt'

For a person to be found guilty in a criminal case, the prosecutor must prove all the elements of the crime 'beyond a reasonable doubt' to show that the accused committed the crime in question. The accused need not present a defence but can simply force the state to prove its case. All the accused has to show is that there is doubt concerning one of the elements of the crime and he or she will be entitled to be found not guilty. Thus there are a number of possible defences in a criminal trial: These are (a) no crime has been committed; (b) the accused did not commit the crime; (c) the accused committed the crime but the act was justified or excused; or (d) the accused committed a criminal act but is not legally responsible.

2.10.1 No crime has been committed

no unlawful act or no criminal intent

The accused may establish his or her innocence by showing that no unlawful act was committed or there was no criminal intent. For example, there would be no unlawful act if an accused charged with having an unlicensed firearm was carrying a gun that had a valid licence, or in a rape case the woman was of legal age and consented. Likewise there would be no criminal intent if the accused mistakenly took someone else's property or was under 10 years of age. (According to the Children's Act children less than 10 years cannot form the intention to commit a crime – see below para 2.10.4.1.)

2.10.2 Accused did not commit the crime

an alibi

Even though a crime has been committed the accused can show that he or she did not commit the crime by proving that he or she was somewhere else at the time. This is called an 'alibi'. The accused could also indicate that he or she did not commit the crime by showing that he or she was mistaken for somebody else who was the real criminal.

2.10.3 Accused committed a criminal act but the act is excused or justified

Here an accused's act will be excused or justified if he or she acted out of private defence, defence of property, defence of other people, necessity or duress (eg was forced by someone to commit the crime).

2.10.3.1 Private defence

reasonable force must be used

Private defence includes self-defence, defence of property or defence of other people. A person who is unlawfully attacked by another may use reasonable force in self-defence. The same may be used to protect one's property or another person against an immediate attack. Private defence cannot be used against the use of lawful force by another (eg a police officer making an arrest). The force used in private defence must be reasonable and must stop once the attack ends. If there is a way for the threatened person to run away instead of fighting, he or she should do so. In exceptional cases, if killing the attacker is the only way of protecting oneself, one's property or another, then deadly force may be used. The courts, however, are very strict on the use of deadly force.

the force used in private defence must be reasonable and must stop once the attack ends

2.10.3.2 Necessity

harming an innocent person

Necessity is like private defence except that usually the accused person's act harms an innocent third person, whereas in private defence it is aimed against a guilty person (eg A acts out of necessity when he steals food from B to feed himself or his family when he or the family are starving).

Problem 1: The use of force to prevent crimes

Questions

1. Petrus keeps a gun in his home as protection against intruders. One night he hears a noise in his lounge and sees a man stealing his radio. The burglar sees the gun and runs to the window. Petrus fires at the man's back and kills him before he can escape. Petrus is charged with unlawfully killing the burglar. Would you find him guilty or not guilty? Give reasons for your answer.
2. The owner of a shop sees a shoplifter stealing a tape recorder. Can the owner use force to prevent the crime? Give reasons for your answer.

2.10.3.3 Duress

forced to commit a crime

Duress happens when a person is forced to commit a crime in order to prevent greater harm to him- or herself or close relatives. The defence allows the criminal act to be excused because the accused is not acting of his or her free will. Usually the accused or a member of his or her immediate family is threatened with death or serious bodily injury. For example, John kidnaps Paul's daughter and threatens to kill her unless Paul steals money from his employer.

2.10.3.4 Other excuses

Other defences that excuse criminal conduct are impossibility (eg where a person's car breaks down in a no-stopping lane on a freeway); and obedience to orders (eg where a soldier obeys a lawful command). Others are statutory authority (eg where a police officer may use force to arrest a person); and consent (eg where a person consents to an 'assault' like a medical operation).

2.10.4 Accused committed a criminal act but is not criminally responsible

An accused may not be criminally liable for committing a crime because he or she could not form the intention to commit the crime. This occurs, for example, as a result of youth or insanity.

2.10.4.1 Youth

children under 10 years of age

The Child Justice Act amends the common law regarding criminal capacity of children. A child who commits an offence while under the age of 10 years does not have criminal capacity and cannot be prosecuted for that offence. Children aged 10–14 years are also presumed to be unable to form a criminal intent, but this can be challenged by the prosecution proving beyond reasonable doubt that the child did have criminal intent. The state will have to prove beyond a reasonable doubt that at the time of the criminal conduct the child had the psychological capacity for insight and self-control.

children between 10 and 14

Children over the age of 14 years are treated as adults, but their youth will be taken into account when deciding what form of proceedings should be followed in their case (see below para 2.14), and if they are sentenced for a crime. They can also be dealt with by the children's courts if they were under 18 years of age (see below para 2.14.8).

children over the age of 14

2.10.4.2 Insanity

insanity is a defence

A person who is mentally disabled and commits an offence may be regarded as not being responsible for his or her actions. This is because the law recognises that someone who is mentally ill may not have formed the intention to commit the crime and should not be punished. In order to successfully raise the defence of insanity it has to be shown that the accused could not tell the difference between right and wrong, or could tell the difference between right and wrong but could not act in accordance with this appreciation. The court looks at the accused's state of mind at the time when the offence was committed.

If the court finds that a person was legally insane at the time of the offence, that person will not be convicted and will not be sent to prison. He or she will, however, be committed to a mental institution.

Other defences that exclude criminal intention are provocation (eg where people become so angry that they do not know what they are doing); and, sometimes, mistake (eg where a person does not intend to break the law).

2.10.4.3 Intoxication

South African law previously said that a person who is drunk on alcohol or high on drugs (ie intoxicated), and commits an offence when in that state of mind, is not criminally responsible for his or her actions and will not be convicted or go to jail. Many people were unhappy about this so Parliament passed a Criminal Law Amendment Act to change the law.

The Act refers to people who are so intoxicated that they cannot tell the difference between right and wrong, or can tell the difference but cannot act in accordance with this appreciation. If a person commits an offence when in such an intoxicated state of mind, he or she will be guilty of an offence and will be punished as if he or she had committed the crime while sober. In fact, the law says that the court may impose an even harsher sentence on the person who was intoxicated than it would have on a sober person who committed the same crime.

Problem 2: What defences are available?

Questions

What defences, if any, would be available to accused persons in the following cases? Give reasons for your answers.

1. A gang tells a 17-year-old boy that if he does not help sell drugs he and his family will be assaulted.
2. An 8-year-old boy throws stones which break a person's window, while his 13-year-old brother smashes down the door.
3. A man, suffering from a mental illness, kills his wife and family.
4. A husband comes home drunk and severely assaults his wife.
5. During a heated argument a man insults a stranger by telling him that his mother was a prostitute. The stranger gets very angry and punches the man in the face.
6. A woman mistakenly takes somebody else's bundle of clothes from a laundromat. At the time that she took the bundle she thought that it contained her clothes.

2.11 Powers of the police and bail

Outcomes

After completion of this section learners will be able to:

1. Understand the powers of the police and what constitutes bail.

Assessment criteria

1. The powers of the police to question are explained.
2. The aim of arrest is explained.
3. A set of facts is examined and a decision made on what a person should do when stopped and questioned by the police.
4. The powers of the police to arrest with or without a warrant are explained.
5. A set of facts is examined and a decision made on whether the arrest was lawful.
6. A set of facts is examined and a decision made on whether the police were entitled to use deadly force.
7. A set of facts is examined and a decision made on whether a citizen's arrest could be made.
8. The rights of arrested people from the time of arrest are explained.
9. A distinction is drawn between police bail and court bail.
10. An explanation is provided on what to tell the court when applying for bail in court.
11. A set of facts is examined and a decision made on whether a person should be granted bail.

In the past, apartheid legislation granted the South African Police Service very wide powers. For many people in South Africa, the police acted in the interests of an illegitimate government instead of serving the community as a whole.

police are to ensure the safety and security of persons and property

Since the end of apartheid, the police have had to change the way in which people see them. Today they have to exercise their power in a way that respects the rights of people in the Constitution. As a result, the law now says that the purpose of the police force is to: (a) ensure the safety and security of persons and property in South Africa; (b) uphold and safeguard the fundamental rights of every person as guaranteed by the Constitution; (c) ensure co-operation between the police and the communities they serve; and (d) to respect the needs of victims of crime.

2.11.1 Powers of the police to question

answering questions

The police have the power to question anyone without arresting them. But whether the person is obliged to answer the police's questions depends on the following circumstances:

2.11.1.1 Persons suspected of committing or trying to commit crimes or thought to be able to give evidence about crimes

asking for identification

If a police officer reasonably suspects that someone has committed or tried to commit a crime, or if he or she thinks that a person may be able to give evidence about a crime, the police officer may ask that person to give his or her full name and address. Before answering, the person may ask the police officer for his or her identity document, showing his or her name and photograph. If the police officer refuses, the person need not give his or her name and address. Even a plain clothes police officer must carry an identity document.

If, however, the police officer does identify him – or herself the person must give his or her name and address. Failure to do so may result in a fine or imprisonment.

consult a lawyer

The person stopped need not answer any other questions and cannot be forced to do so by the police. The police should also tell such a person that he or she need not say anything. The person may, however, agree to answer further questions or to do so if his or her lawyer is present. (If possible, it is advisable to consult a lawyer before deciding.) In some cases it may be wise for the person simply to answer the police officer's questions, especially if the person knows that he or she has done nothing wrong. This is because the police officer can then find out what he or she needs to know and the person can go on his or her way.

making a statement

A police officer may also ask the person to go to the police station to make a statement. The person has a right to refuse to go. The police officer may then decide to arrest the person (see below para 2.11.2). The Constitution says that a person who has been arrested has a right to remain silent, and must be informed of this right. This means that the arrested person can refuse to make a statement, or refuse to make a statement unless his or her lawyer is present. Alternatively, he or she may decide to make a statement in the hope of being released sooner.

2.11.1.2 Persons driving cars, motorcycles, or other vehicles

name and address

The police may ask a driver to stop at any time. The driver must stop the vehicle. The police may ask the driver to give his or her name and address. The driver must give his or her name and address.

driver's licence

The police may ask the driver to produce his or her driver's licence. The driver must show the police his or her driver's licence.

Failure by a driver to stop a vehicle, give his or her name and address, or present a drivers' licence at the request of the police, may result in the driver being prosecuted for committing a crime.

2.11.1.3 Assaults by the police

if assaulted by the police

The police are not allowed to assault people for failing to answer questions or refusing to make statements. They may, however, sometimes use force against people who resist arrest (see below para 2.11.2.4). If a person is assaulted he or she should tell a senior police officer and, as soon as possible, a lawyer. The assaulted person should also tell the magistrate when he or she appears in court. The person should insist on seeing a doctor as soon as possible after the assault.

Problem 1: The second-hand clothes arrest

Mr Msomi refuses to answer questions

A man in plain clothes stops Mr Albert Msomi while he is walking down the street with a box full of second-hand clothes that have been given to him by his employer. The man says he is a policeman and asks Mr Msomi to give him his full name and address. He also asks Mr Msomi where he obtained the clothes. Mr Msomi refuses to give his name and address until the policeman identifies himself. The policeman gets angry with Mr Msomi and takes him to the police station for questioning.

the plain-clothes policeman tells Mr Msomi that he is being cheeky and takes him to the police station for questioning

Questions

1. Role-play the incident between the policeman and Mr Msomi in the street, and at the police station.
2. Is Mr Msomi required by law to answer any questions? Why might he decide to answer questions? Give reasons for your answer.

3. If you were Mr Msomi, what would you have done?
4. Should people have the right to refuse to answer questions by the police? Give reasons for your answer. If people have the right to keep quiet, should the police tell them about it? Give reasons for your answer.

2.11.2 Powers of police to arrest

ordinary powers of arrest

The powers of the police to arrest a person are carefully controlled by law, specifically the Criminal Procedure Act. The Constitution also gives several important rights to people who are arrested or detained.

2.11.2.1 Aim of arrest

arrest must be lawful

Usually a person may only be arrested in order to be taken to court on a criminal charge or as a suspect in a criminal investigation. An arrest for any other purpose is unlawful. For example, an arrest with the purpose of frightening or intimidating a person is illegal. An arrest is a serious interference with a person's freedom. Therefore an arrest is only lawful when it is allowed by law and follows proper procedures. People may be arrested with or without a document called a 'warrant of arrest', depending on the circumstances.

2.11.2.2 Arrest with a warrant

arrest must follow proper procedures

A warrant of arrest is a document that gives a police officer the power to arrest a person and bring him or her before a court. A magistrate or judge must issue the warrant of arrest. There must also be a reasonable suspicion that the person to be arrested committed the crime in question. A person who is arrested with a warrant of arrest has the right to ask the police officer to see the warrant. The police officer must then show the person the warrant of arrest. The person arrested is also entitled to a copy of the warrant. Whether or not the person asks to see the warrant the police officer must tell the person why he or she is being arrested.

the right to see the warrant

2.11.2.3 Arrest without a warrant

reasonable suspicion

A police officer may only arrest a person without a warrant if the police officer witnesses a crime or if he or she is acting upon a 'reasonable suspicion' that the person committed a serious crime. (Serious crimes include treason, sedition, murder, culpable homicide, rape, indecent assault, robbery and arson). A reasonable suspicion is a reasonable belief based upon some facts. Where a policeman relies upon information by another person he or she must have a reasonable suspicion that a crime has been committed. In this case the informer must be reliable.

person actually committing the crime

Usually the police arrest a person without a warrant when they do not have time to obtain a warrant because the person is actually committing a crime. For example, the police receive a report about a bank robbery. A police officer sees a woman who fits the description of the bank robber waving a gun and running away from the bank. The police officer would be acting on a reasonable suspicion if he or she stopped the woman and arrested her. What is reasonable depends upon the facts of each case. However, a 'reasonable suspicion' must be more than a mere suspicion – it must be based on reasons. If a police officer arrests a person without a warrant, the officer must tell the person why he or she is being arrested.

action for unlawful arrest

If the police arrest a person unlawfully, the person may bring an action against them for unlawful arrest. Unlawful arrest may happen if the police fail to obtain a warrant of arrest when one is required, or did not have a 'reasonable suspicion' for an arrest without a warrant, or had no lawful reasons for the arrest (eg it was done to intimidate the person). Persons who are unlawfully arrested may sometimes recover damages from the police who arrested them, or the Minister of Police.

Problem 2: Were the arrests lawful?

the police arrest a person suspected of robbery without a warrant of arrest

Questions

1. One night the police receive an anonymous phone call that a man at a specified address was involved in a large robbery. Although it is late at night the police go directly to his house. They do not have a warrant of arrest but tell the man that they are arresting him without a warrant, because they suspect that he was involved in a robbery. Was the arrest lawful? Give reasons for your answer. If it was not lawful, what can the man do?
2. A VW Beetle has been stolen. The police at the Lesotho/South Africa border post receive a police report that a vehicle matching the description of the Beetle, driven by people who resemble the suspects, is driving rapidly towards the South African border. The police do not have time to get a warrant and they arrest the driver of the vehicle and his passengers on their arrival at the border post. Was the arrest without the warrant lawful?

the police arrest two young men on suspicion of robbery

2.11.2.4 Method of arrest

The apartheid government passed a law that gave the police wide powers to kill people who, on being arrested, resisted arrest or tried to run away. This law was often criticised. Parliament has changed the law, so that the police are required to use force in line with the rights and values of the Constitution.

force must be 'reasonably necessary and proportional'

The new law deals with the situation in which the police are trying to arrest someone (the 'suspect'), and the suspect resists arrest or tries to run away. The law says that if the suspect cannot be arrested without the use of force, the police may use force, but only such force as is 'reasonably necessary and proportional in the circumstances.' This means that the police cannot use any more force than they need to in order to arrest the suspect. They may only use force that is necessary.

use of deadly force

In addition, the police may only use 'deadly force' (ie force intended to kill someone or cause serious bodily harm) in two situations:

self-defence or necessity

1. The force must be necessary to protect the police officer making the arrest, or any other person, from death or serious bodily harm. The use of deadly force is only allowed as a type of self-defence or necessity where the suspect is about to kill or seriously injure someone else.

committing a crime using life-threatening force

2. The police may use deadly force when the suspect is actually committing the crime. The crime must, however, be of such a nature that it involves the use of life threatening violence, or a strong likelihood that it will cause serious bodily harm. An example might be if the police catch a suspect in the middle of an armed robbery or hijacking, and it seems likely that the suspect is about to use life-threatening violence.

Problem 3: The case of the fleeing car thieves

fighting, damaging property, public violence, escaping arrest

The police see two men steal a car. They pursue the men out of the city until they catch up with them. The two men jump out of the stolen car and run away from the road. The police shout at the men that they are under arrest and that they should stop running away. The police also fire several warning shots. When the men do not stop running they fire shots at the men and kill them.

1. Were the actions of the police lawful? Does the law allow the police to kill people in situations such as this?
2. Assume that one of the men had pulled a gun out of his pocket and pointed it at one of the policemen who was trying to make the arrest. Would your answer change? Give reasons for your answer.
3. Assume that the police had found the two men 'hijacking' the car. One had a gun pointed at the driver of the car, and it seemed likely that he was about to pull the trigger. Would your answer change? Give reasons for your answer.

2.11.2.5 Unlawful arrest

grounds for unlawful arrest

An arrest will be unlawful where:

1. There are no reasonable grounds for suspecting that the person has committed a crime.
2. The purpose of the arrest is not to take the person to court to stand trial, but merely to intimidate the person.
3. The person is not told why he or she is under arrest, and the person is not caught committing the crime.

As we have seen, if the arrest was unlawful the arrested person may sue the police officer and/or the Minister of Police for damages. A person wishing to sue the police should immediately consult a lawyer, a legal aid justice centre, Legal Resources Centre or a legal aid clinic (see above para 1.4.1.4).

2.11.2.6 Unlawful use of force

The use of force by a police officer is unlawful, and constitutes an assault, in the following situations:

grounds for unlawful use of force

1. where the arrest itself is unlawful;
2. where the person being arrested did not resist arrest or try to escape; or
3. where the policeman used more force than is permitted by law.

A person who has suffered an assault from unlawful use of force by the police may:

1. lay a charge of assault against the police officer concerned;
2. sue the police officer responsible and/or the Minister of Police for damages.

2.11.2.7 Citizen's arrests

private people helping the police

Citizens or private people may arrest people who commit or attempt to commit serious crimes in their presence or whom they reasonably suspect of having committed serious crimes. Private citizens may also arrest people who fight in their presence or whom they reasonably believe to be escaping arrest for any offence. The owner, a person lawfully living on a property, or a person in charge of a property, or any person authorised by them, may arrest people committing crimes on the property or in connection with the property.

Citizen's arrests are always done without a warrant. It is therefore necessary for the arresting person to tell the person arrested that he or she is being arrested. If this is not done, people being arrested may think that it is an assault and may lawfully defend themselves. If a citizen lawfully arrests a person he or she may use the same amount of force as the police.

Any male person over 16, and under 60, years of age may be called on to help the police to arrest someone and must then do so. Failure to help may result in criminal prosecution.

Problem 4: The use of force by private citizens

1. Sam and Jovu, two workers in a clothing factory, have a fight in the street. Sam beats up Jovu. Although Jovu was not seriously injured he did not report to work for two days. On his return he told the foreman about the fight. The foreman waited for Sam as he checked in for duty in the morning. He then tried to arrest Sam for assaulting Jovu. Sam ran away. The foreman shot him in the leg. Sam was so badly injured that his leg had to be cut off.
   Was the foreman entitled to arrest Sam and to shoot him when he ran away? Give reasons for your answers.
2. Two 17-year-old youths are surprised by a night watchman while they are breaking into a shop. As they try to run away the night watchman fires six shots, injuring them both seriously.
   Was the watchman entitled to shoot the youths? Give reasons for your answer.

2.11.3 Rights of arrested people

2.11.3.1 On arrest

The Constitution gives some very important rights to people who are arrested:

right to be informed

1. An arrested person has the right to be informed of the reason for his or her arrest.

right to remain silent

2. An arrested person has the right to remain silent. This means that an arrested person does not have to give any information to the police except his or her name and address. This also means that the police cannot force an arrested person to make a confession. When the police arrest a person, they must tell that person that he or she has this right and the consequences of not remaining silent (ie that what is said may be used against the arrested person at a trial).

legal representation

3. An arrested person has the right to choose, and consult with, a lawyer. He or she also has the right to be provided with a lawyer by the state, if 'substantial injustice' would otherwise result (see para 1.4.1.4.1). In addition, an arrested person must be informed of these rights when arrested.

must be brought to court within 48 hours

4. An arrested person has the right to be brought before a court as soon as is reasonably possible, but not later than 48 hours after the arrest. However, a person arrested on a Thursday or Friday afternoon need only be brought to court on the following Monday, although in urgent cases application may be made for bail on the weekend.

An arrested person who is denied any of the above rights may bring a civil action against the police officer who performed the arrest and/or the Minister of Police.

If the police arrest a person in a manner that violates these rights, or any of the rights in the Bill of Rights, any evidence that the police get by arresting that person may be excluded by the court. For example, if the police arrest people but do not inform them of their right to silence, and then threaten them so that they are scared and make a confession, the court may exclude the confession at their trial. This means that the court will not look at that evidence when deciding whether the person is guilty. (For a more detailed discussion, see below para 2.12.1).

2.11.3.2 Bail

bail payment is a deposit

The Constitution says that everyone who is arrested has the right to be released from detention if the interests of justice permit, subject to reasonable conditions. This is a reference to 'bail'. Bail is a fixed sum of money paid to the state. It is paid to allow the arrested person to be released from prison. It is paid as a deposit to make sure that the person will come to court during the trial. If the person does not arrive in court on the date of the trial, and as long as the trial lasts, the money paid as bail will kept by the state.

The bail will be returned if the person appears in court. There are two kinds of bail: (a) police bail and (b) court bail.

2.11.3.2.1 Police bail

if the charge is not serious

The police may sometimes release a person on bail decided by them if the charge is not serious. Police bail cannot be given for serious crimes like treason, sedition, public violence, murder, culpable homicide, rape, kidnapping, childstealing, robbery, assault with a dangerous weapon, arson, housebreaking, theft of more than R200, illegally selling gold or diamonds and crimes related to drugs. Police bail also cannot be given to people who attempt to commit these crimes or to anyone encouraging others to commit them.

release on warning

The police may also release a person 'on warning', (by warning the person when to appear in court), without demanding that he or she pay an amount as bail.

release of children into the care of parents

If the arrested persons are under 18 years old a senior police officer may release them 'on warning' into the care of their parents. The parents will be told when to bring the children to court. The decision to release on bail is made by the police. The police must give the person released on bail a receipt for any bail paid. If bail is refused the person will have to wait until he or she is taken to court. Then the person can apply to the magistrate for bail.

2.11.3.2.2 Court bail

ask for bail

If a person is brought to court and the case is postponed, the accused should ask to be released on bail. An accused who does not ask for bail may have to remain in prison until the trial is over. In granting and setting bail the magistrate will consider factors such as whether the accused is likely to: (a) endanger anyone; (b) avoid attending the trial; (c) intimidate witnesses; (d) destroy evidence; (e) undermine the criminal justice system; or (f) disturb public peace and security. The accused must persuade the magistrate that he or she will not do any of these things.

'prisoner's friend'

After listening to the accused and the prosecutor the magistrate will say how much bail must be paid. He or she may also refuse bail. Accused people may pay the money at court, or their family or friends may pay it at the prison. The prison officials must help accused people contact their family or friends, if they are not in court. Most courts have a person called a 'prisoner's friend' who may also help with contacting friends or relatives. The person who pays the bail must obtain a receipt. This person may be given back the bail money after the trial ends.

If the magistrate refuses bail or sets an unreasonably high amount of money the accused may appeal to the High Court.

Bail: What to tell the court

People wishing to apply for bail must tell the court that they want to apply for bail. The magistrate may not always ask them if they want bail. When applying for bail they should tell the court:

1. Where they live and how long they have lived there.
2. Whether they are married and live with their family.
3. Whether they have children to support.
4. Where they work, what type of work they do, and how long they have had their present job.
5. How much they earn each week or each month.
6. How much bail money they can afford.

2.11.3.3 When people are released

release 'on warning'

Sometimes people may be released without having to pay bail. This is called release 'on warning' and is often applied to young accused people who are released into the custody of their parents. Release 'on warning' means that the accused is warned by the magistrate, or police officer in the case of 'police bail', to return to court on the day of the trial.

deciding to release

When deciding whether the accused is likely to return to court, the magistrate, or police officer, will consider facts such as: (a) the type of crime and how it happened; (b) the accused's family and community ties; (c) the accused's financial and employment situation; and (d) the accused's previous criminal record (if any). A magistrate allowing bail may make the accused promise to carry out certain conditions (eg report to a police station once a week, surrender a passport, or not leave the area without notifying the police). Some people argue that it should be made more difficult, not easier, for accused persons to be released on bail. They say statistics show that many accused people commit crimes while they are out on bail. The court should take into account the danger to the community when setting bail.

arguments against bail

arguments for bail

People who favour release on bail say that it prevents accused persons being punished before they are found guilty by a court. In the past, statistics have shown that only 25% of accused persons who were kept in prison before trial received a prison sentence by the court once they were found guilty. Other arguments in favour of bail are that: (a) it prevents first-time accused persons mixing with hardened prisoners in jail; (b) it gives accused people more time to prepare their cases; and (c) it saves the state money because fewer people will have to be looked after in prison if they are let out before their trials. (There are usually about 60 000 prisoners a year waiting to go to trial in South Africa.)

Problem 5: Should an accused be let out on bail?

Questions

1. The following three people have been arrested and charged with different crimes. If you were the magistrate, which people would you release on bail? Give reasons for your answer. Which conditions would you apply to those you would release?
   Choose from one of the following options and give reasons for your decision: (i) bail (decide on amount); (ii) release on warning (no money required); (iii) bail plus conditions (decide on the amount and the conditions); or (iv) stay in prison (during trial).
   (a) Jannie is 22 years old and is caught by the police while breaking into a house and stealing a camera, jewellery and tools. Jannie rents a room in a boarding house. He is unemployed and has no family. He has a grade six education and has five previous convictions. He was found guilty of theft on three occasions before he was 18 years old and sent to a reformatory. Since then he has served two short sentences for housebreaking.
   (b) Moona, a 44-year-old businessman, is arrested at King Shaka International Airport after returning from India via Mauritius. He is found in possession of 1 000 Mandrax tablets (illegal drugs). Moona owns a large house in Westville and is married with a wife and five children. He has a BComm degree and owns a number of businesses in

Durban that sell videos and films. He travels overseas three times a year. Moona has two previous convictions: one for selling banned videos and the other for not paying value-added tax (VAT).

(c) Vuma, who is 19 years old, is arrested for stabbing Karabe to death during an argument about a girl friend. Vuma lives with his parents in the family home in Soweto. He has completed his matriculation examination, and hopes to go to university. Vuma is unemployed and has not previously been in trouble with the law.

2. Should an arrested person be kept in prison before trial? Do you think it should be easier or more difficult to get out of prison before trial?

Problem 6: The case of the unlucky couple

Logan and Sandy see burglars in the act of stealing school equipment

After an evening at the movies, Logan and Sandy decide to park in the grounds behind Marula School. While there they see two men loading school equipment into a truck. Realising that the men are burglars Logan starts the car and drives into the main street.

At the same time a burglar alarm is set off at the local police station and constables Van der Merwe and Sibiya head for the school in a squad car. The police turn into the main road near the school just as Logan's car is speeding away.

Questions

1. Role-play the situation. As constables Van der Merwe and Sibiya, decide what you would say and how you would act towards Logan and Sandy if you stopped them. As Logan and Sandy, decide what you would say and how you would act towards the police.

2. If the police chase after Logan would they have a 'reasonable suspicion' for arresting Logan and Sandy?
3. How do you think constables Van der Merwe and Sibiya would act once they had stopped Logan? How do you think Logan and Sandy would act?
4. What could Logan and Sandy do if they were mistakenly arrested as burglars? What could they do if they were abused or mistreated by constables Van der Merwe and Sibiya?

What to do if you are arrested

1. Do not struggle with, or swear at, the police even if the police have made a mistake.
2. Give the police your name, address and telephone number – otherwise keep quiet. You must also show your identity book if asked to do so. Do not discuss your case with anyone and do not sign any statements about your case.
3. As soon as possible after you arrive at the police station ask if you can telephone a lawyer. If you do not know a lawyer, telephone your family or a friend or relative and explain: (a) where you are; (b) what you are charged with; and (c) what your bail will be (if you know). If you or they cannot afford a lawyer tell them to apply for legal aid for you (see above para 1.4.1.4).
4. If you are released on bail ask for your bail receipt and find out when you are due in court. Never be late for, or miss, a court hearing. If you do not arrive on time a warrant for your arrest may be issued. You may also lose your bail money if you do not go to court on the day of the hearing.
5. Do not talk about your case to anyone except your lawyer – if you have one. Be honest with your lawyer otherwise he or she will find it difficult to help you. Ask for your lawyer to be present if you are being questioned or told to attend an 'identity parade'. (An 'identity parade' is a line-up of people – including the suspect – at which witnesses try to identify the person or persons they thought they saw commit the crime).

2.12 Search and seizure

Outcomes

After completion of this section learners will be able to:

1. Understand the legal principles applicable to search and seizure.

Assessment criteria

1. The powers of the police to search and seize property are explained.
2. A set of facts is examined and a decision taken on whether the evidence should be admitted.
3. Searches with and without warrants are explained.
4. A set of facts is examined and a decision made on whether the searches carried out were legal.
5. The powers of the police to stop and search vehicles at roadblocks are explained.

2.12.1 The powers of the police to search and seize property

the right to privacy

There are many laws that authorise searches and seizures, the most important of which is the Criminal Procedure Act. These laws limit the right to privacy and must be justified under the limitation clause in the Constitution. The Constitution says that everyone has a right to privacy in relation to his or her body, home, property and communications. Sometimes, however, the state needs to collect information about its citizens. For example, it is necessary for the police to collect information (ie evidence) about criminals in order to protect society against crime.

evidence may not be used if it would make a trial unfair

The Constitution regulates how the police may collect evidence. It says that if the police obtain evidence in a manner that violates any right in the Bill of Rights, that evidence may not be used in court if it would make the 'trial unfair or otherwise be detrimental to the administration of justice'. 'Detrimental' means 'harmful'. 'Administration of justice' refers to the system – of police, prosecutors and courts – whereby the criminal law is enforced.

the 'exclusionary rule'

The rule that evidence may not be used in court because it was obtained in violation of the Bill or Rights is called the 'exclusionary rule'. People who agree with the exclusionary rule say that it is necessary to protect people's rights and prevent the police acting unlawfully. People who disagree with the exclusionary rule say that it lets dangerous criminals go free. There are also arguments about how the exclusionary rule, as stated in the Constitution, should be interpreted.

Problem 1: A case involving the exclusionary rule

In the case of *S v Naidoo*, five people had robbed the SBV business premises in Westmead, KwaZulu-Natal of R43 million. During the robbery one of the robbers had used a cell phone. After the robbery the police approached MTN and Vodacom and obtained the numbers of the cell phones that had been used in that area on the night in question, and the numbers of the land-lines that had been called from those cell phones. The police then obtained permission from a judge to monitor or listen to conversations on the land-lines. By doing so, they identified two of the robbers, arrested them and recovered R5,4 million.

However, when the police applied to court for permission to monitor the land-lines they had relied upon information that was untrue and misleading. The police had therefore misled the court and monitored the land-lines illegally. At the trial, when the police tried to give evidence of the telephone conversations that they had recorded and the R5,4 million that was recovered, the advocate for the accused argued that this evidence should not be admitted by the court. His argument was that it had been obtained in a manner that violated the right to privacy in the Bill of Rights and should therefore be excluded in terms of the exclusionary rule set out in the Constitution.

The court asked whether the admission of the evidence would be harmful to the administration of justice (ie the system of police, prosecutors and courts). It held that the right to privacy is fundamental. To allow the evidence to be admitted would give the public the impression that the courts tolerate illegal methods of investigation and human rights violations, on the part of the police. This would bring the administration of justice into disrepute (ie people would think less of it). The court therefore excluded the evidence.

Questions

1. If you were the advocate for the accused, what arguments would you have used?
2. If you were the prosecutor, what arguments would you have used?
3. Do you agree with the court's decision? Give reasons for your answer.
4. Some people argue that not admitting the evidence brought the administration of justice into disrepute, because the public was given the impression that the courts are soft on criminals. What do you think of this argument?

There are two methods of searching and seizing in South Africa, one with a warrant and the other without a warrant. Provided the police follow the correct procedures (see below paras 2.12.1.1 and 2.12.1.2) in relation to each of these methods, the court will not regard the right to privacy as having been infringed, and the evidence may be used in court. If the correct procedure is not used, the evidence may be excluded.

2.12.1.1 Searches with a warrant

reasonable suspicion

A search warrant is a court order obtained from a magistrate who has been persuaded that there is 'a reasonable suspicion' that a crime has been committed and that he or she should allow the search of a person or a place. A police officer must persuade the magistrate that there is a reasonable suspicion that justifies the search. If a magistrate decides to issue a search warrant, the warrant must describe the person or place to be searched and the particular things to be seized.

time limit

The search must be carried out within the time stated in the warrant. A search warrant does not necessarily allow a general search of everything in the place mentioned. For example if the police are searching for stolen bicycles it would be unreasonable for them to look in desk drawers or other small places where a bicycle could not be hidden.

the right to examine the warrant

Only the people and property mentioned in the warrant may be searched and only things mentioned in the search warrant may be seized. A person who is about to be searched or whose property is about to be searched may demand to see the search warrant.

entry of private property

Another type of search warrant gives the police power to search any property. This is issued if the police believe that: (a) the internal security of South Africa is threatened by a meeting on the property; (b) a crime has been committed; or (c) a crime is being planned on the property. Many people think that that this type of warrant is unconstitutional, at least insofar as it relates to 'internal security'. They argue that the notion of 'internal security' is too vague to justify the infringement of rights caused by the warrant.

2.12.1.2 Searches without a warrant

grounds for searches without a warrant

The police are generally required to obtain a search warrant, but the law recognises situations where searches may be made without a warrant. These are where:

1. The aim of a search may be destroyed by a delay in obtaining a search warrant.
2. A person has been lawfully arrested. Here the police may search the person and the area near the person for any evidence that may be destroyed.
3. A person voluntarily agrees to the search. A person need not agree to a search even if the police ask for permission.
4. The search is by customs officials at borders, airports and harbours. They may search any person or luggage without a warrant or a reasonable suspicion.
5. The police are manning a roadblock (see below para 2.12.1.4). Here the police may search all vehicles.

Sometimes a police officer reasonably suspects that a person on a property has information that can help an investigation. The police officer may enter the property without a warrant to question the person and take a statement. Unless, however, the law allows the police do so, a police officer cannot enter any private house to ask questions or take a statement without the consent of the occupier.

policemen may not search females

Policemen may search males, but not females. Only policewomen may search women or the search may be conducted by any other women asked to do so by the police.

unlawful search and seizure

Anybody who is unlawfully searched or abused during a search or has property unlawfully seized may sue the Minister of Police and the guilty police officer. The same applies where property is destroyed or damaged during an unlawful search or seizure by the police. If the police have obtained evidence in a manner that violates any of the rights in the Bill of Rights, the court may exclude that evidence from the trial. Any person who has been unlawfully searched or abused during a search or whose property has been unlawfully seized should immediately contact a lawyer or, if they cannot afford a lawyer, a legal aid justice centre, the Legal Resources Centre or a university law clinic (see above para 1.4.1.4).

2.12.1.3 Demanding entry and the use of force

demand entry

If the police wish to search any property they should first loudly demand entry and state why they wish to search the property. However, if announcing their intention to enter would defeat the aim of the search, the police need not do so. The police should, however, identify themselves.

reasonable force

During a search the police may use reasonable force to overcome resistance to the search or entry to property. For example, they may break down doors and windows. But the police must first demand to be let into the property. They must also state the reason for the search. If this is not done the search may be unlawful.

actions against the police

If there is an unlawful search a criminal charge may be laid against the offending police officer. Both the police officer and the Minister of Police could also be sued for damages. In addition, as mentioned, in terms of the exclusionary rule, the evidence obtained could be excluded at the trial.

Problem 2: Searches by the police

Questions

Here are some examples of searches made by the police. Read each example, and then decide whether the search was legal or not. If the search was not legal, what should the person do? Give reasons for your answers.

1. A policeman comes to Elsa's house. He explains that he has heard that her son, Hendrik, aged 9 years, has stolen a bicycle. The policeman asks Elsa if he can look around Hendrik's room. He says that he has no search warrant. Elsa allows him to search. A BMX bicycle is found in Hendrik's room.
2. The police, acting upon the information of an informer, obtain a search warrant to search Brad's premises for stolen cars. The police come to his house and claim that they have a warrant to search his premises for stolen cars. When Brad asks to see the warrant they refuse to show it to him, push him out of the way, and enter his home. The police conduct a thorough search of his entire home. Among other places, they search his dressing table drawers and his refrigerator.
3. A warrant is issued for Raj's arrest. The police find him at his home. Although no search warrant has been obtained, the police search the entire home and garage. They find several hand-grenades in the garage.

the police force their way into Muzekile's house

4. A number of crimes have recently been committed in Muzekile's township. The police have no reason to search Muzekile or her house, or to believe that she has ever committed a crime. They come to the door and ask if they can search her house. They have no search warrant. Muzekile says 'No'. The police force their way in and find nothing.

2.12.1.4 Roadblocks

the police may search the vehicle without a search warrant

While carrying out their duties the police have the power to order a car or any other vehicle to stop. They can do this by signalling the driver to stop, or by erecting a road sign, or a roadblock. The police may search the vehicle without a search warrant. They may seize any of the following articles:

1. Any article believed to have been used in committing a crime.
2. Any article that is intended to be used to commit a crime.
3. Any article which can be used as evidence that a crime has been committed.

Problem 3: The car that failed to stop

Questions

The police are alerted to look out for a motor car stolen by some escaped prisoners. They fire on a car which fails to stop when directed to do so. The car they fire on is not the same make or colour as that described in the police alert. Do you think that the force used in this case was lawful? Give reasons for your answer.

a fine or prison for failing to stop

If a person fails to stop at police roadblock he or she can be imprisoned for up to three months or fined.

2.13 The criminal trial and sentencing process

Outcomes

After completion of this section learners will be able to:

1. Demonstrate an understanding of the criminal trial and sentencing process.

Assessment criteria

1. The procedures to be followed in a criminal process are explained.
2. A set of facts is examined and a decision made on what steps will be taken during an arrested person's trial.
3. The different types of sentences are identified.
4. A set of facts is examined and a decision made on what would be an appropriate sentence.
5. The arguments for and against the death penalty are explained.
6. The meaning of vigilantism is explained.
7. A decision is taken on the effectiveness of community policing forums.

2.13.1 The criminal process

2.13.1.1 Right to a fair trial

rights of accused people to a fair trial

The Constitution says that every accused person has the right to a fair trial. This involves a number of rights, including the right to: (a) be informed of the charge in enough detail to be able to prepare a defence; (b) have time and facilities to prepare a defence; (c) a speedy and public trial; (d) be present when tried; (e) remain silent; (f) choose and be represented by a lawyer; and, (g) if the accused cannot afford a lawyer, to have a lawyer provided at state expense if 'substantial injustice would otherwise result' (see above para 1.4.1.4.1). If the accused is denied any of these rights he or she may be able to take the court's decision on review (see above para 1.3.1.7.3).

right to legal assistance

legal aid

The Constitution also says that an accused person must be informed of his or her right to choose and be represented by a lawyer, or have a lawyer assigned by the state if substantial injustice would otherwise result. An accused person may also apply for legal aid (see above para 1.4.1.4.2). If an accused person is not represented by a lawyer during a trial, the magistrate must inform the person of his or her right to be represented by a lawyer and to apply for legal aid.

refusal to have a lawyer

If the accused chooses not to be represented by a lawyer, the magistrate must inform him or her of his or her rights throughout the trial, (eg the right to silence and the right to cross-examine witnesses). This is to ensure that the accused is aware of his or her rights and that the trial is as fair as possible.

In spite of the provisions in the Constitution, many people who appear in court are not represented by lawyers. Unrepresented accused do not usually know much about the law and, even when they are informed of their rights, they are not able to put up a good defence. Therefore, it has been said that despite the rights set out in the Constitution, for many people accused of crimes, the ideal of a fair trial is still far away.

2.13.1.2 The overcrowded prisons

overcrowding

It is often said that South Africa's prisons are grossly overcrowded and that in 2013 the daily average number of prisoners was about 160 000, whereas there was only accommodation for about 112 000 prisoners. As has been mentioned, it has been suggested that about 48 000 of these are awaiting trial prisoners of whom only about 25% will ever receive a term of imprisonment. It costs about R118 500 a year to house just one prisoner. Alternative plans have been suggested to relieve the overcrowding in the prisons, including building new prisons that are run by the private sector. These have proved to be much more expensive than those run by the state. At one stage a previous Director-General of Prisons had become so desperate to solve the overcrowding problem that he had suggested that prisoners should be housed in disused mine shafts!

Problem 1: Making the prison population smaller

Questions

1. How do you think the large number of people waiting for trials and sentenced to imprisonment in South Africa can be reduced?
2. What are the arguments for and against making sure that every accused person who may be sent to prison if found guilty is given a lawyer?
3. If you were a lawmaker, would you introduce a law to change the present position of prisoners waiting for trial and those sentenced to prison? Give reasons for your answer. If you were to introduce a new law, what would it say?

2.13.2 The criminal trial

2.13.2.1 After the arrest

In para 2.11.3.1 we discussed the steps after arrest in a criminal case. These can be summarised as follows:

rights of arrested suspects

1. People suspected of crimes (*suspects*) are *arrested* by the police and taken to the police station. The police must inform suspects of: (a) the reason for their arrest; (b) their right to silence; (c) their right to choose, and consult with, a lawyer; and, (d) their right to be provided with a lawyer by the state if 'substantial injustice would otherwise result'. (See above para 2.11.3.1.) At this stage suspects are only required to give their names and addresses to the police.

charge

2. People arrested must be *charged* before a magistrate in the magistrate's court within 48 hours of the arrest. When, however, a person has been arrested on a Thursday or Friday afternoon, he or she may only be brought before court on the Monday after the weekend.

legal representation

3. When accused persons come before a magistrate, they must be informed of their right to legal representation and their right to have a lawyer assigned to them at state expense if 'substantial injustice' would otherwise result. Accused persons who come before a magistrate may also ask to be released until the trial (ie they may ask for bail). If the accused does not ask for bail, the magistrate must ask the accused whether he or she wants the question of bail to be considered. (Note: If accused persons are charged with less serious crimes – such as trespassing or theft of an item worth less than R200 – they may ask for bail at the police station before they are taken to court (see above para 2.11.3.2).

pleading

4. Before the case comes to trial accused persons will be asked to plead by the magistrate. This means that they must say whether they plead 'guilty' or 'not guilty'.

pleading guilty

5. Where the accused persons plead guilty the magistrate asks (except where the crime is not very serious) why they have pleaded guilty. The accused must then explain fully why they think that they are guilty. If the magistrate is satisfied that the accused are guilty, he or she may find them guilty on what they have said. There is no need for a further trial. If the magistrate is not satisfied that they are guilty, he or she will enter a plea of 'not guilty'.

pleading not guilty

6. Where the accused persons plead not guilty, the magistrate may ask the reason for their plea. The accused need not tell the court anything. If the accused, however, wish to do so they should give only short reasons (eg they did not commit the crime, or were defending themselves). They should not go into detail because it may later harm their case when the trial is heard.

2.13.2.2 The trial

opening statements

1. Where the accused pleads not guilty the prosecutor will begin by calling witnesses for the State to prove that the accused committed the crime. The prosecutor does not have to, but may, make an opening statement beforehand in which he or she explains what the prosecution will prove.

evidence-in-chief

2. The prosecutor will ask each witness to tell the court what he or she knows about the case (ie to give their 'evidence-in-chief').

cross-examination

3. After each prosecution witness's evidence-in-chief, the accused (or the defence lawyer) will have a chance to ask each witness questions (called 'cross examination'). The aim of cross-examination is to obtain evidence from the witness to support the accused's case, or to show that the witness is uncertain, not telling the truth, or confused.

re-examination

4. After cross-examination of each of the State's witnesses by the accused (or defence lawyer) the prosecutor may ask the witnesses further questions (called 're-examination'). The aim of re-examination is to clear up or explain

answers that were made to look untrue or unreliable in cross-examination by the accused or the defence lawyer. The court may also ask questions to clear up evidence which is not clear, but may not cross-examine witnesses.

prosecutor closes State's case

5. After the prosecutor has called all the state witnesses and each has been cross-examined and re-examined, the prosecutor closes the State's case. This means that the prosecutor thinks that he or she has proved every element of the State's case beyond reasonable doubt and it is the turn of the accused to present his or her case.

witnesses for defence

6. If the prosecution's case was weak, the accused (or the defence lawyer) may ask the court to dismiss the charge on the basis that the prosecution had not proved a case to answer. Otherwise the defence may, but does not have to, make an opening statement. The defence then calls its witnesses to give their evidence-in-chief for the defence. The first witness to be called will be the accused – if he or she is going to give evidence. This is so that the accused will tell the truth and not change his or her story to agree with what the other defence witnesses say. The accused can decide not to give evidence (see below para 2.13.2.3).

cross-examination is to find out whether a witness or the accused is telling the truth

cross-examination and re-examination

7. After the accused has given his or her evidence the prosecutor may cross-examine. Thereafter the defence lawyer may re-examine the accused. The same procedure is followed for each defence witness. The prosecutor may cross-examine each witness and then the accused (or the defence lawyer) may re-examine each witness. The court may also ask questions but not cross-examine the accused or witnesses.

close of defence case

8. After all the defence witnesses have been called, cross-examined, and re-examined, the accused (or the defence lawyer) closes the case for the defence. This means that the defence does not intend to call any more witnesses.

summing up

9. The prosecutor sums up the State's case, giving reasons why the accused should be found guilty.

judgment

addresses on sentence

sentence

appeal

review

10. The accused (or the defence lawyer) then presents argument, giving reasons why the accused should be found not guilty.
11. The magistrate then gives a judgment. We will assume that the magistrate finds the accused guilty (ie convicts the person). If the magistrate found the accused 'not guilty' the latter would be 'acquitted'.
12. The magistrate gives the accused (or the defence lawyer) a chance to say why the accused should get a reduced sentence. The prosecutor may also say why the sentence should be increased.
13. The magistrate then sentences the accused (see below para 2.13.3).
14. If the accused is unhappy with his or her conviction and/or sentence, he or she could *appeal* to the High Court (see above para 1.3.1.7.2).
15. If the accused thought that the trial was unfair (eg the magistrate was biased or the accused was not given a chance to call his or her witnesses or to get legal representation), he or she could take the case on *review* to the High Court (see above para 1.3.1.7.3).

Note: A person may only be found guilty of a crime if the State proves every element of the alleged crime 'beyond a reasonable doubt'.

Summary: Steps in a criminal case

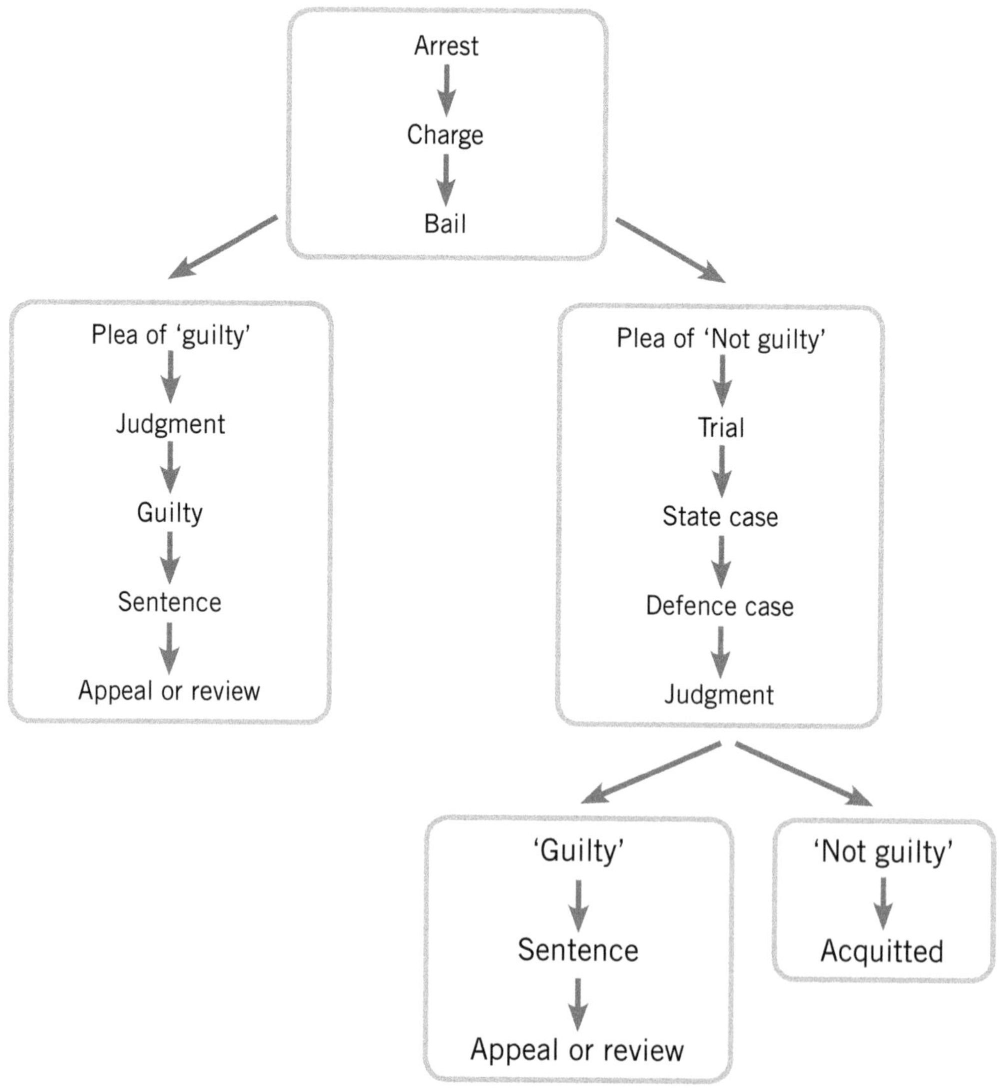

Problem 2: The case of the stolen car

Roy Rajah returns to where his car was just in time to see it being driven off by Jay

Jay Naidoo leaves his car keys in his 2003 red BMW. When he comes back an hour later, he mistakenly gets into a different red BMW. The car also has keys in it. Jay Naidoo does not notice that it is a different car and drives away. The owner of the car, Roy Rajah, returns to where he parked his car just in time to see it being driven off by Jay. Roy goes to the police station to report that his car has been stolen. The police find Roy's car at Jay's house. They arrest Jay and keep him in custody.

Questions

1. Role-play the police and Jay at the house and at the police station.
2. How soon will Jay appear in court?
3. What should Jay do when he first appears in court?
4. What procedure will be followed during Jay's trial?
5. Do you think that Jay was guilty of a crime?
6. What may Jay do if he is found guilty of stealing the car?

2.13.2.3 Right to remain silent

the right to remain silent

The Constitution gives every accused person the right to remain silent, not to testify at his or her trial and not to be forced to give self-incriminating evidence. This means that an accused person cannot be forced to give evidence at his or her trial, and cannot be forced to give evidence which might make the court find him or her guilty of a crime. The accused person can, however, choose not to make use of these rights, in which case he or she will give evidence.

The Criminal Procedure Act says that witnesses in a criminal case cannot be forced to answer questions that may make them liable to a criminal charge. Another provision, however, says that witnesses for the prosecution (ie the State) must answer all questions even if they are likely to make them guilty of a crime (ie are incriminating). The court, however, must tell State witnesses that if they answer all the questions honestly even if they are incriminating, they will not be prosecuted.

Problem 3: Giving evidence and being defended

1. Do you think it is right that an accused need not give evidence in a criminal case? Give reasons for your answer.
2. If you were a defence lawyer, what do you think would be the advantages and disadvantages of allowing an accused person to give evidence?
3. If you were a judge or magistrate, what would you think if an accused did not give evidence?
4. Do you think that it is necessary for innocent accused people to be defended in court by lawyers? Give reasons for your answer.

2.13.3 The sentencing process

after the accused is found guilty

The 'sentencing process' happens after the accused has been found guilty and the court decides on the punishment. Once the accused has been found guilty, he or she will be sentenced by the judge or magistrate.

a sentence can affect a person's life for many years

The sentence is very important because it can affect the accused person's life for many years afterwards. The Criminal Procedure Act gives a number of sentencing options. Usually, however, judges and magistrates have a choice about the type, length and conditions of the sentence. In deciding this, the court will take into account the accused's earlier criminal record, and his or her social, medical, educational and employment background, as well as recommendations for sentencing by the prosecution and defence lawyers.

2.13.3.1 Types of sentences

sentencing options

Depending upon the court's attitude to punishment and what the judge or magistrate thinks is in the best interests of society and of the criminal, the magistrate or judge may choose from one or more of the following sentences:

discharge without penalty

1. Caution and discharge: This is one of the most lenient sentences. Here the criminal is warned that he or she should not commit the offence again and is discharged without any penalty. Although the sentence is like an 'acquittal' (a 'not guilty' decision), it is recorded by the Criminal Bureau as a 'previous conviction' (ie the accused has previously been found guilty of a crime).

sentence conditionally delayed

2. Postponed sentence: The court may delay the passing of sentence for up to five years on condition the criminal agrees to do or not do certain things.

At the end of the period laid down by the court, if the criminal is not convicted of any crime and has carried out the conditions, he or she will be 'discharged'. This has the same effect as if the accused had been found 'not guilty', except that it is recorded as a 'previous conviction'.

sentence conditionally suspended

3. Suspended sentence: Here a sentence is given but the convicted person is not required to serve all or part of it, provided he or she is not guilty of a similar crime during the period of the suspension. For example, a person may be sentenced to five years' imprisonment, four years of which is suspended on condition that the accused is not convicted of a similar crime during the next five years. This means that the criminal may only serve one year in jail if the condition is carried out. A condition for suspending a sentence may be community service where a criminal may be ordered to spend so many hours a week, or on weekends doing 'community service' instead of some other sentence. For example, a person may be ordered to help out at a hospital, old age home or children's home.

community service

money paid to the court

4. Fine: A fine is the amount of money that a criminal must pay to the court. Sometimes a convicted person may have to pay a fine in addition, or as an alternative, to a period in prison.

money paid to the victim

5. Compensation and restitution: Where the crime has caused damage or loss of property (including money), the victim may ask the court to order the criminal to pay compensation for the lost property or money, or to return the property ('restitution'). A compensation or restitution order is often combined with a suspended sentence.

a fixed period of time in prison

6. Imprisonment: Here the criminal is sentenced to a period of time in prison. The minimum sentence is four days – unless the court sentences a person 'until the rising of the court'. This means that the criminal is allowed to go free when the court rises to leave the courtroom. It is a very lenient sentence. The maximum sentence is life imprisonment. Some serious crimes such as murder, rape and armed robbery have minimum sentences which have to be imposed unless there are special circumstances why they should not. A separate sentence may be given for each charge ('count') of the crime (eg convicted persons could get more than one life sentence if they murdered more than one person).

periodical imprisonment

7. Periodical imprisonment: A court may sentence a convicted person to a certain number of hours in prison a week or on week-ends for a total of not less than 100 hours and not more than 2 000 hours (eg 10 week-ends of 20 hours each).

rehabilitation

8. Committal to an institution: A criminal who is addicted to alcohol or drugs and who is a danger to peace may, in addition to any other sentence, be detained at a rehabilitation centre.

correctional supervision of the offender

9. Correctional supervision: This is the supervision of the offender with the view to correcting the wrongdoer and the wrongdoing. It is described as a community-based form of punishment. Examples of correctional supervision are house arrest, monitoring and community service.

2.13.3.2 The death penalty

death sentence

In South Africa, the courts used to be able to give the death sentence for 11 crimes, ranging from murder and rape to robbery and housebreaking. The death sentence was most often given for murder, for which it was compulsory if there were no 'extenuating circumstances' (special facts justifying a reduced sentence). For a while, South Africa had one of the highest execution rates in the Western world. Between 1980 and 1988 there were an average of 120 executions per year (one every three days). Many people regarded the death sentence as a political tool of the oppressive apartheid government.

In 1990, however, FW de Klerk began the process of reform that ended the apartheid era. One important step he took was to suspend, or place a 'moratorium' on executions. In 1995, the question of whether the death penalty is constitutional was the first case to be heard by the newly established Constitutional Court.

Problem 4: The death penalty case

The Constitutional Court was asked to decide whether the death penalty is constitutional in the case of S *v Makwanyane*.

arguments in favour of the death penalty

The lawyers who argued that there should be a death penalty said that it was important because it deterred (ie discouraged) people from committing violent crimes. They also said that most South Africans want the death penalty, which means that it will satisfy the public need for retribution (ie revenge) against criminals. In addition, it was argued that the death penalty did not violate the right not to be subjected to cruel, inhuman and degrading punishment. (This right is in the Bill of Rights.) This, they argued, was because the death penalty exists in many other countries. It cannot therefore be an example of cruel, inhuman or degrading punishment.

arguments against the death penalty

The lawyers who argued that the death penalty should be declared unconstitutional said that it violated the rights to life and dignity, and the right not to be subjected to cruel, inhuman or degrading punishment. (All these rights are in the Bill of Rights.) They also argued that the death penalty was 'arbitrary in its imposition.' This means that whether a person gets the death penalty often depends on the judge who decides the case. It also depends on whether the accused person can afford a good lawyer. Given the degree of economic inequality in South Africa, many South Africans cannot afford good lawyers. This, it was argued, was unacceptable, given that the death penalty is an extreme punishment. In addition, there is always a possibility of error (ie a chance that the wrong person will be sentenced to death). If a mistake is discovered later, there is no way that it can be undone.

All 11 judges of the Constitutional Court gave separate judgements. They all agreed that the death penalty is unconstitutional, and that people may no longer be sentenced to death in South Africa. The Court held that the death penalty violates certain rights in the Constitution – the rights to life, dignity and not to be subjected to cruel, inhuman or degrading punishment – and that this infringement cannot be justified. The court agreed that the death penalty is unacceptably 'arbitrary in its imposition'. In addition, it said that there is no evidence that the death penalty deters (ie discourages) violent crime. In countries where the death penalty has been introduced, the number of violent crimes has not decreased. Several judges also argued that the death penalty is contrary to the indigenous concept of *ubuntu* because one person's life is worth no more than that of another person. The court acknowledged that most South Africans would want the death penalty to be kept, but said that public opinion should not take the place of the duty of the court to interpret and apply the Constitution.

no evidence death penalty discourages violent crime

Some questions on the death penalty case:

Questions

1. What arguments were given for keeping the death penalty?
2. What arguments were given for declaring that the death penalty is unconstitutional?
3. What did the Constitutional Court eventually decide, and what were its reasons?
4. Do you agree with the decision of the court? Give reasons for your answer.
5. Take a stand: Do you think that there should, or should not, be a death penalty in South Africa? What are your reasons?

2.13.3.3 Aims of sentencing

Sentences in criminal cases are used for a number of reasons including retribution, deterrence, rehabilitation and incapacitation.

revenge

1. Retribution: Retribution is said to be the main reason for punishment. It takes the form of revenge to pay back the criminal for his or her wrongful act. Retribution is used by the courts to show society's disapproval of what the criminal has done.

discouragement

2. Deterrence: In the case of deterrence the court takes into account that the punishment may deter (discourage) the criminal from committing another crime in future. It may also act as an example to deter other people from committing crimes.

encourage responsibility

3. Rehabilitation: Rehabilitation is based on the idea that criminals can be helped to overcome the social, educational or psychological problems that caused them to commit crimes. They can be encouraged to become responsible members of society. For example, the criminal may be given job training or psychological treatment while in prison.

protecting society

4. Incapacitation: Incapacitation applies when the criminal is put in prison (or sentenced to death in countries that still have the death penalty). Here the court decides it is necessary to protect society by separating the criminal from the community. While locked up the criminal will no longer be a threat to the safety of the community.

When sentencing a criminal the court usually has one or more of these aims in mind.

Aims of sentencing

retribution is a form of revenge for the criminal's wrongful act

punishment may deter people from committing crimes

rehabilitation may help criminals to become responsible members of society

incapacitation protects society by separating the criminal from the community

Problem 5: How would you have sentenced the criminal?

Questions

How would you sentence the criminal in the following cases? What sentence would you choose? What is the aim of the sentence chosen by you?

1. Petrus Pekhani, who is 18 years old, is found guilty of assault with the intention to cause grievous bodily harm. He stabbed an elderly night watchman in the back while the watchman was on duty. The watchman was left paralysed for the rest of his life. Petrus said that he did not do it, as he was not there. Because he did not admit doing it the court did not know what his motive was. After his conviction Petrus still insists he was not there and therefore is not sorry for what had happened.
   Petrus comes from a broken home. He did not know his father. His mother works as a domestic servant and lives on her employer's property. Petrus lives with an uncle in Umlazi. His uncle says that Petrus is a good scholar and has passed grade 7. Lately, however, he has become involved with a gang of older boys. He has been in trouble once before. At the age of 16 years he was found guilty of stealing from a motor car and was sentenced to a brief period of imprisonment.

   Petrus is found guilty of assault

   Petrus says he did not do it

   he became involved in a gang

   he had a previous conviction

2. Jopie van Vuuren, aged 56, is an accountant who managed his own second-hand car firm. Over 18 months he obtained R400 000 from several banks to cover the prices of cars that he said he sold to customers. This was false. He drew up a number of fraudulent credit agreements and no sales were made. He had hoped to repay the money to the banks when his business improved, but he became bankrupt. There is only enough in his business to pay the banks R20 000 of the R400 000 lent to him. Jopie is found guilty of fraud. He is sorry for what he has done and has co-operated with the police.
   Jopie had been chairman of a child welfare society and is respected for his welfare work. He also goes to church regularly. His trial takes place two years after his arrest. In the meantime he finds work as a bookkeeper. He earns just enough to support himself and his wife aged 54 years. His wife is ill and cannot work. His employer says Jopie is a good worker and that he will keep him on even though Jopie has been convicted.

   Jopie draws up fraudulent documents to get money

   he is found guilty of fraud

   he works as a bookkeeper to support his sick wife

3. Read the Oscar Pistorius case in para 2.2.1.2 above and decide if you were the judge who found him guilty of culpable homicide what his sentence should be.

   Oscar's case

2.13.4 Vigilantism

vigilante action

Vigilantism means that people take the law into their own hands. It has been used by some communities in South Africa to fight crime in their neighbourhoods. Such communities say that vigilante violence fills a gap left by police inefficiency, corruption and collaboration with criminals. Vigilantism may exist as a single or spontaneous incident or as planned action. People who participate in vigilantism see it as a means of achieving justice. Those who are opposed to it say that if people take the law into their own hands society will be ruled by the 'law of the jungle', because there are no safeguards to make sure that accused persons are presumed innocent until proved guilty and to ensure that they will receive a fair trial.

examples of vigilantism

Examples:

1. A woman is ordered to throw the first stone at her alleged rapist before a crowd stones him to death.
2. A youth accused of murder was sentenced to death by 'necklacing'. His hands were tied behind his back with wire and it was decided that he should be stabbed once by each man present and stoned by the women. A tire was placed around his neck, petrol was poured over it and he was set alight.
3. Members of a crowd of about 200 people began shouting for the man accused of stabbing a girl to be flogged. The people's court judge ordered the man to pack his belongings and leave the area.
4. Gugu Dlamini of KwaMashu, near Durban, was stoned, kicked and beaten to death by a mob who accused her of degrading her neighbourhood by disclosing that she was HIV positive.

Is vigilantism fighting crime?

Rather than getting rid of crime, vigilantism has been seen as being motivated by personal benefit and in some instances by crime itself. According to the South African Police Service many cases of vigilantism reveal charges against the vigilantes that include murder, assault, robbery, stock theft, kidnapping, housebreaking, theft and arson. These are purely criminal charges and do not happen only when fighting crime. Regardless of the motive, vigilante violence is a crime because it infringes on human rights and undermines the Constitution.

vigilantism is used to fight crime when the police are inefficient

The criminal justice system faces a huge problem because using the police to arrest and prosecute vigilantes takes away essential resources needed to fight other crimes. It also makes it more difficult to deal with the 'real' criminals.

On the one hand, vigilante violence is understood as criminal activity because it breaks the law and is seen as part of the 'crime problem' faced by South Africa. On the other hand, vigilantism itself is explained as fighting crime because of an inefficient police force. The following can be used to reduce vigilantism:

1. Addressing the real and practical failings of the criminal justice system;
2. Prioritising and tackling vigilantism as a form of crime; and
3. Educating the public and authorities about the workings of the criminal justice system (eg so that people understand the difference between an accused person being released on bail and being acquitted of a crime).

Problem 6: A vigilante case study – a murder accused has his bail paid by vigilantes

vigilantes pay for bail to get an accused person released so that they can kill him

Residents of a Pietermaritzburg squatter camp each paid R20 to bail out of prison a man accused of murder. Johannes Dube left jail thinking relatives had paid his R4 000 bail. Instead he walked into the hands of the residents of Oliver Tambo squatter camp in The Grange, Pietermaritzburg. They dragged him before a people's court and sentenced him to death. He was stabbed and had petrol poured over him before a tyre was placed around his neck and set on fire. One of the men who paid Dube's bail said, 'I donated R20 when I heard what was going to happen to him. The idea of paying bail for criminals and then killing them is liked by everyone. We want them to know that we will get them in the end. We don't trust the police and the justice system.'

Questions

1. Were the actions of the Oliver Tambo squatter camp residents right or wrong? Give reasons for your answer.
2. Does the Constitution allow people to take the law into their own hands?

2.13.5 Community policing forums

community policing forums or CPFs

A community policing forum (CPF) means an organisation established in terms of the South African Police Service Act. A CPF is a group of people from different communities and police representatives who meet to discuss safety problems in their communities. A CPF also aims at ensuring police accountability, transparency and effectiveness in the community. CPFs were introduced in South Africa during the period of transition from apartheid to democracy. CPFs play an important role in assisting the police. CPFs are intended to help establish the legitimacy of state institutions – the SAPS in particular.

perceptions of CPFs

There are many debates about whether people should or should not work with the police to fight crime. These debates also extend to whether or not people should work with CPFs. Some suggest that CPFs, like the police, are actively part of the crime problem because they collaborate with criminals. Others see CPFs as useful in encouraging the community to assist the police in fighting crime.

Problem 7: Questions on community policing forums

Questions

1. Is there a community policing forum (CPF) in your area? If not, do you know of an area where there is a CPF?
2. Do you think that CPFs can help in fighting crime? Give reasons for your answer.

2.14 Child justice

Outcomes

After completion of this section learners will be able to:

1. Explain what is meant by child justice.

Assessment criteria

1. An explanation is given of who is regarded as a child in conflict with the law.
2. An explanation is provided on what is meant by the criminal capacity of children.
3. A set of facts is examined and a decision made on whether a child can be charged with a crime.
4. An explanation is given of how probation officers assess children in conflict with the law.
5. An explanation is given of a preliminary inquiry and how it works.
6. An explanation is given of how diversion works and the different types of diversion.
7. A set of facts is examined and a decision made on whether the child should be diverted out of the criminal justice system.
8. An explanation is provided regarding the operation of child justice courts.
9. The different sentences that are usually used for children in conflict with the law are identified.
10. A discussion is held on whether children in conflict with the law should be rehabilitated or punished.
11. A set of facts is examined and a decision made on whether or not the proceedings should be stopped and the child referred to a children's court.

2.14.1 Introduction

a child is a person under 18 years of age

A child is defined as any person under the age of 18 years. In the past children in conflict with the law were managed in much the same ways as adult offenders. During the apartheid-era children were arrested and detained in prisons for long periods of time while awaiting trial. The law prior to the Child Justice Act contained a presumption that children between the ages of 7 years and 14 years do not have criminal capacity and the prosecution had to prove that they had such capacity before they could be convicted of a crime. It was assumed that children between 7 years and 14 years do not know the difference between right and wrong. This has now been changed where the Child Justice Act provides that children between the age of 10 years and 14 years do not have criminal capacity unless this is proved by the prosecutor.

the prosecutor must prove that children 10–14 years have criminal capacity

children can only be detained as a last resort

In terms of the Constitution, a child has the right not to be detained except as a measure of last resort (eg where it is unavoidable). If a child in conflict with the law is detained he or she should be detained for the shortest appropriate period of time and must be kept separately from detained persons over the age of 18 years. The manner and conditions in which children are kept must take into account separate from adults

the child's age. When children are detained they must be kept separately from adults, and boys must be separated from girls.

Child Justice Act applies to children under 18 years of age when the crime was committed

The provisions of the Child Justice Act apply where a child in conflict with the law is under the age of 10 years at the time the alleged crime is committed or is 10 years or older but under the age of 18 years when he or she was handed a written notice, or served with a summons or arrested for the crime. Where a child was under the age of 18 when the alleged offence was committed, but is now 18 years or older but still under the age of 21, the Director of Public Prosecutions may direct that a preliminary enquiry be held and that the case be diverted (ie the case is taken out of the usual criminal proceedings) in terms of the provisions of the Child Justice Act. The provisions of the Criminal Procedure Act still apply except where the provisions of the Child Justice Act provide for something different.

guidelines for a preliminary inquiry

The following are suggested as guidelines for the Director of Public Prosecutions to consider when deciding whether a preliminary enquiry must be held where a child was under the age of 18 when the alleged offence was committed, but is now 18 years or older but still under the age of 21: (a) the seriousness of the offence; (b) the child's age at the time of commission of the crime; (c) the child's previous convictions; (d) the need to obtain an assessment from a probation officer; and (e) how common the type of crime is within society.

2.14.2 Criminal capacity of children

meaning of criminal capacity

A person will have criminal capacity if he or she is mentally able to be held legally liable for his or her unlawful conduct. This means that the child must be proved to be mentally able to appreciate what he or she was doing was wrong and must be able to act in accordance with such appreciation.

a child under 10 years of age lacks criminal capacity

The Child Justice Act amends the common law regarding criminal capacity of children. A child who commits an offence while under the age of 10 years does not have criminal capacity and cannot be prosecuted for that offence. A child who is 10 years or older but under the age of 14 years is presumed to lack criminal capacity, unless the State proves that he or she has criminal capacity. The State will have to prove beyond a reasonable doubt that at the time the crime was committed the child had the psychological capacity to understand and appreciate that what he or she was doing was wrong.

2.14.2.1 Children under 10 years

children under 10 years of age may not be arrested

A police officer may not arrest a child under the age of 10 years. Such a child must be handed over to his or her parents or an appropriate adult (eg a carer). Where there is no parent or appropriate adult available or it is not in the best interest of the child to be handed over to the parent or appropriate adult, the child must be sent to a suitable child and youth care facility. The police officer must then immediately notify the probation officer that a child suspected of committing an offence is under the age of 10 years.

2.14.2.2 Children older than 10 years

probation officer must do an assessment

Children who are 10 years and older but under 14 are presumed to lack criminal capacity. Every child who is 10 years or older and who is alleged to have committed a crime and who is required to appear at a preliminary inquiry in respect of that offence must, before his or her first appearance at the preliminary inquiry, be assessed by a probation officer. The probation officer must decide whether it would be advisable to appoint an expert who will be required to conduct an assessment of the thinking ability of the child and his or her moral, emotional, psychological and social development.

Problem 1: The case of the jealous child

Questions

Damon is 8 years old and very jealous of his parents. One day he thinks that his younger brother and sister are receiving too much attention. Damon takes his father's loaded gun out of the cupboard and shoots his brother and sister so that he can have his parents' full attention. Damon's brother and sister die from their wounds.

Will Damon be found guilty of murder? Give reasons for your answer. Do you think the law should punish him? Give reasons for your answer. If you think that children under 10 years should be punished by law, what words would you put in a statute to make them responsible?

2.14.3 Assessment

The Child Justice Act provides that the purpose of an assessment by a probation officer is to:

purpose of an assessment by a probation officer

(a) establish whether a child may be in need of care and protection in order to refer the child to a children's court;
(b) estimate the age of the child if the age is uncertain;
(c) gather information relating to any previous conviction, previous diversion or pending charge in respect of the child;
(d) make recommendations regarding the release or detention and placement of the child;
(e) where appropriate, establish the prospects for diversion of the matter;
(f) in the case of a child under the age of 10 years, establish what measures need to be taken in terms of the Act;
(g) in the case of a child who is 10 years or older but under the age of 14 years, suggest whether or not expert evidence would be required;
(h) decide whether the child has been used by an adult to commit the crime in question; and
(i) provide any other relevant information regarding the child which the probation officer thinks may be in the best interests of the child or which may advance any objective which the Act intends to achieve.

a child must be assessed before appearing before a preliminary inquiry

Every child who is alleged to have committed a crime must be assessed by a probation officer, unless the assessment is not required. Assessment by the probation officer may not be required if the assessment will not be in the best interest of the child. A probation officer who is notified by a police official that a child has been handed a written notice, served with a summons or arrested must assess the child before the child appears at a preliminary inquiry (see below para 2.14.4) within the prescribed time periods. A probation officer who was notified by a police official that a child under the age of 10 years has been dealt with must make arrangements to assess the child within seven days of the notification.

2.14.3.1 Duties of the probation officer at assessment

duties of probation officer during assessment

The probation officer must do the following:
(a) explain the purpose of the assessment to the child;
(b) inform the child of his or her rights in the prescribed manner;
(c) explain to the child the immediate procedures to be followed; and
(d) inquire from the child whether or not he or she intends acknowledging responsibility for the crime in question.

probation officer may consult with other persons during assessment

The probation officer may, at any stage during the assessment of a child, consult with any person who may provide information necessary for the assessment, including a prosecutor, police official or diversion service provider. The probation officer may, at any stage during the assessment, consult privately with any person present. The probation officer may consult any person who is not at the assessment and who has any information relating to the assessment, but if additional information is obtained, the child must be informed accordingly.

where more than one child has committed a crime

Where a child is accused with another child or other children, the probation officer may conduct the assessment of the children simultaneously if this will be in the best interests of all the children concerned. The probation officer must encourage the participation of the child during the assessment.

Role of a probation officer
- Compile an assessment report with recommendations.
- Draw up a plan of action appropriate to the child.
- Record the results of the assessment and the decisions made.
- Submit the report to the prosecutor within prescribed period.

Problem 2: The case of the cruel boys

Sam, aged 10 years, and Vusi, aged 12 years, are suspected of attempting to kill Marie, an 18-month-old girl. It is alleged that they poured boiling water and oil over Marie's body, then smeared her body with chilli powder and put a cloth in her mouth to stop her from crying. She was then covered with a blanket and left of the floor. Luckily Marie did not die and she was found by her mother when she came home from work.

Questions

1. Assume that you are the investigating police officer in the case. What would you do with Sam and Vusi?

2. Assume you are the probation officer to whom Sam and Vusi are referred for an assessment. What would you do?

2.14.4 Preliminary inquiry

an informal pre-trial procedure

The Child Justice Act creates a new procedure to help with the management of children in conflict with the law called a 'preliminary inquiry'. A preliminary inquiry is an informal pre-trial procedure which is inquisitorial (ie the inquiry magistrate asks the questions). It may be held in a court or any other suitable place. A preliminary inquiry must be held for every child who is alleged to have committed a crime – except where (a) the case was diverted by a prosecutor; (b) the child is under the age of 10 years; or (c) the case has been withdrawn. Every child who is suspected of committing a crime must be assessed by a probation officer before the preliminary inquiry. As mentioned (see above para 2.14.3), the assessment report must contain a recommendation to the magistrate at the preliminary inquiry about the suggested management of the child.

a preliminary inquiry is the same as a first appearance before a lower court

A preliminary inquiry must be held within 48 hours of arrest if a child is arrested and remains in detention, or within the time periods specified in a written notice or a summons. A child's appearance at a preliminary inquiry is regarded as his or her first appearance before a lower court. The preliminary inquiry will have to assist in deciding whether the child may be dealt with outside the criminal justice system.

Aims of a preliminary inquiry

The aims of a preliminary inquiry are to:

(1) consider the content and recommendations of the assessment report of the probation officer, especially regarding: (a) the age estimation where the child's age is uncertain; (b) whether the child had criminal capacity if the child is 10 years or older but under the age of 14 years; (c) whether the criminal capacity of the child must be determined by a suitably qualified person; and (d) whether a further and more detailed assessment of the child is needed;
(2) decide whether the case can be diverted before plea;
(3) identify a suitable diversion option;
(4) decide whether the case should be referred to a children's court;
(5) ensure that all available information regarding the child, his or her circumstances and the crime are considered in order to make a decision on diversion and placement of the child;
(6) ensure that the views of all persons present are considered before a decision is taken;
(7) encourage the participation of the child and his or her parent or an appropriate adult in decisions concerning the child; and
(8) decide whether the child should be released or placed pending the conclusion of the preliminary inquiry or the appearance of the child in a child justice court or the referral of the matter to a children's court.

chaired by an 'inquiry magistrate'

The preliminary inquiry is chaired by a magistrate who is neutral, but who can use an 'inquisitorial approach', meaning that he or she is more active than is usual in a criminal case. The magistrate, called the 'inquiry magistrate', gets more involved and can ask questions and require additional information necessary for him or her to make the required decisions.

inquiry is attended by magistrate and prosecutor, child accused, parent or appropriate adult and probation officer

In addition to the inquiry magistrate and prosecutor, the persons who must attend the preliminary inquiry are: the child; the child's parent or an appropriate adult; and the probation officer. The preliminary inquiry is not open to the general public. If a diversion order is likely to be made, a diversion service provider identified by the probation officer should be present at the preliminary inquiry. The inquiry magistrate may exclude any person from attending the preliminary inquiry if that person's presence is not in the best interests of the child or undermines the inquisitorial nature and objectives of a preliminary inquiry.

held within 48 hours

The Act provides that a preliminary inquiry must be held within 48 hours of a child's arrest. If the child has been handed a written notice or served with a summons, then it must be held within the time periods set out in the written notice or summons.

2.14.4.1 Orders made at the preliminary inquiry

diversion order

There are two orders that are made at the preliminary inquiry. The first is a diversion order which is made if the child is diverted in terms of the Act. If the child is 10 years or older but under 14 years of age, the inquiry magistrate must first be satisfied that the child has criminal capacity. The second is an order that the case be referred to the child justice court for plea and trial. If such an order is made, the inquiry magistrate must refer the child to Legal Aid South Africa for legal representation if the child does not already have a legal representative.

referral to child justice court

2.14.5 Diversion

removal from formal court procedures

In terms of the Child Justice Act 'diversion' means diversion of a case involving a child away from the formal court procedures in a criminal case. As mentioned previously, the Constitution provides that a child has the right not to be detained except as a last resort. Diversion involves the referral of cases away from criminal court procedures. Diversion can be done in three ways:

(a) by the prosecutor diverting minor offences;
(b) at the preliminary inquiry, through an order by the inquiry magistrate; and
(c) during a trial in the child justice court, through an order of court.

child must admit liability

The Act is in favour of diversion for all cases involving child offenders who voluntarily acknowledge their liability for the offence and where there is sufficient evidence to prosecute. The Act does not create a right to diversion. The court may make a diversion order and may even develop an individual diversion option that meets the requirements of the particular matter.

The objectives of diversion are to:

objectives of diversion

(a) Deal with a child outside the formal criminal justice system;
(b) Encourage the child to be accountable for the harm he or she has caused;
(c) Meet the particular needs of the individual child;
(d) Promote the reintegration of the child into his or her family and community;
(e) Provide an opportunity to those affected by the harm to express their views on its impact on them;
(f) Encourage the rendering to the victim of some symbolic benefit or the delivery of some object as compensation for the harm;
(g) Promote reconciliation between the child and the person or community affected by the harm caused by the child;
(h) Prevent stigmatising the child and prevent the adverse consequences flowing from being subject to the criminal justice system;
(i) Reduce the potential for re-offending;
(j) Prevent the child from having a criminal record; and
(k) Promote the dignity and well-being of the child, and the development of his or her sense of self-worth and ability to contribute to society.

2.14.5.1 Different diversion options

The Child Justice Act creates a legal framework for many diversion options that include:

school attendance order

(a) A compulsory school attendance order that requires a child to attend school every day for a specified period of time. School attendance must be monitored by a specified person;

family time order

(b) A family time order that requires a child to spend a specified number of hours with his or her family;

good behaviour order

(c) A good behaviour order that requires the child to abide by an agreement made between the child and his or her family to comply with certain standards of behaviour;

peer association order

(d) A peer association order that requires a child to associate with persons or peers who can contribute to the child's positive behaviour or to stop associating with certain specified persons or peers;

reporting order

(e) A reporting order that requires a child to report to a specified person at a time or at times specified in the order so as to enable that person to monitor the child's behaviour; and

supervision order

(f) A supervision and guidance order placing a child under the supervision and guidance of a mentor or peer in order to monitor and guide the child's behaviour.

There are two levels of diversion, namely Level 1 and Level 2:

2.14.5.1.1 Level 1 diversion options

simple plans

Level 1 diversion options can be described as simple plans or agreements that include requirements such as supervision and guidance; compulsory school attendance or not going to a certain place; and apologising and restitution (giving back) to a victim. A diversion order given to a child under the age of 14 years may not last longer than twelve months. Where the child is 14 years or older, the order may not last longer than 24 months. It is possible to give a diversion order for a longer period but then the reasons for giving a longer order must be entered on the record of the proceedings.

Level 1 diversion options apply to Schedule 1 offences in the Criminal Procedure Act

Level 1 diversion options apply to Schedule 1 offences and include:

(a) An oral or written apology to a specified person or persons or institution;
(b) A formal caution, with or without conditions;
(c) Placement under a supervision and guidance order;
(d) Placement under a reporting order;
(e) A compulsory school attendance order;
(f) A family time order;
(g) A peer association order;
(h) A good behaviour order;
(i) An order prohibiting the child from visiting, frequenting or appearing at a specified place;
(j) Referral to counselling or therapy;
(k) Compulsory attendance at a specified centre or place for a specified vocational, educational or therapeutic purpose;
(l) Symbolic restitution to a specified person, persons, group of persons or community, charity or welfare organisation or institution;
(m) Restitution of a specified object to a specified victim or victims of the alleged offence where the object concerned can be returned or restored;
(n) Community service under the supervision or control of an organisation or institution, or a specified person, persons or group of persons identified by the probation officer;
(o) Provision of some service or benefit by the child to a specified victim or victims;
(p) Payment of compensation to a specified person, persons, group of persons or community, charity or welfare organisation or institution where the child or his or her family is able to afford this; and
(q) Where there is no identifiable person, persons or group of persons to whom restitution or compensation can be made, provision of some service or benefit or payment of compensation to a community, charity or welfare organisation or institution.

a combination of diversion options may be used

A combination of the above diversion options may also be used. In addition to the diversion options, a prosecutor, an inquiry magistrate, or a presiding officer in a child justice court, may develop an individual diversion option which meets the objectives of diversion and, where applicable, the minimum standards.

Schedule 1 Offences for Level 1 Diversions

1. Theft and receiving stolen property that does not exceed R2 500;
2. Fraud, extortion, forgery and uttering or corruption where the amount does not exceed R1 500;
3. Malicious injury to property, where the amount does not exceed R1 500;
4. Common assault;
5. Perjury;
6. Contempt of court;
7. Blasphemy;
8. Compounding;
9. *Crimen injuria*;
10. Defamation;
11. Trespass;
12. Public indecency;
13. Engaging sexual services of persons 18 years or older;
14. Bestiality;
15. Acts of consensual sexual penetration (statutory rape), sexual assault (statutory sexual assault) and acts of consensual sexual violation with certain children;
16. Illegal possession of dependence-producing drugs that do not exceed R500 in value;
17. Any other statutory offence where the maximum penalty is imprisonment for a period of no longer than three months or an equivalent fine; and
18. Any conspiracy, incitement or attempt to commit any offence referred to in Schedule 1.

2.14.5.1.2 Level 2 diversion options

Level 2 diversion options apply to Schedule 2 and 3 offences in the Criminal Procedure Act

Level 2 diversion options apply to offences referred to in Schedules 2 and 3. Apart from the Schedules, the difference between Level 1 and Level 2 diversion options is the time periods applicable. Where there are time periods applicable, a diversion order for a child under 14 may not exceed 24 months and for a child 14 years or older may not exceed 48 months in duration. An order exceeding the time period may be given, but the reasons must be entered on the record of the proceedings. In addition to Level 1 options, Level 2 options include:

(a) Compulsory attendance of vocational, educational or therapeutic programmes, which may include a period of temporary residence;

(b) Referral to intensive therapy to treat or manage problems that have been identified as a cause of the child coming into conflict with the law, which may include a period or periods of temporary residence; and

(d) Placement under the supervision of a probation officer on conditions which may include restriction of the child's movement outside the magisterial district in which the child usually resides without the prior approval of the probation officer.

family group conference or victim-offender mediation

A magistrate who is required to make diversion an order of court, an inquiry magistrate or child justice court may order a child to appear at a family group conference or a victim-offender mediation or order any other restorative justice option in the place of any of the Level 1 or Level 2 diversion options or in combination with any of the Level 1 or 2 diversion options. In addition to the diversion options, a prosecutor, an inquiry magistrate, or a presiding officer in a child justice court, may, after consideration of all available information, develop an individual diversion option which meets the objectives of diversion and, where applicable, the minimum standards.

Schedule 2 Offences for Level 2 Diversion

1. Theft and receiving stolen property exceeding R2 500;
2. Fraud, extortion, forgery and uttering or corruption for amounts exceeding R1 500;
3. Robbery, other than robbery with aggravating circumstances;
4. Malicious injury to property, where the amount involved exceeds R1 500;
5. Assault, involving grievous bodily harm;
6. Public violence;
7. Culpable homicide;
8. Arson;
9. Housebreaking with the intent to commit an offence;
10. Administering a poisonous or noxious substance;
11. Allowing a newborn baby to die;
12. Abduction;
13. Sexual assault, compelled sexual assault or compelled self-sexual assault without grievous bodily harm;
14. Compelling or causing persons 18 years or older to witness sexual offences, sexual acts or self-masturbation;
15. Exposure or display of or causing exposure or display of child pornography or pornography;
16. Incest and sexual acts with a corpse;
17. Exposure or display of or causing exposure or display of genital organs, anus or female breasts to any person ('flashing);
18. Violating a dead body or grave;
19. Defeating or obstructing the course of justice;
20. Intimidation;
21. Any offence relating to criminal gang activities;
22. Animal cruelty;
23. Illegal possession of dependence-producing drugs valued at over R500 but less than R5 000;
24. Any other statutory offence where the maximum penalty is imprisonment for a period of no longer than three months but less than five years or an equivalent fine; and
25. Any conspiracy, incitement or attempt to commit any offence referred to in Schedule 2.

Schedule 3 Offences for Level 2 Diversion

1. Treason;
2. Sedition;
3. Murder.
4. Extortion, with aggravating circumstances;
5. Kidnapping;
6. Robbery with aggravating circumstances or involving the taking of a motor vehicle;
7. Rape or compelled rape;
8. Sexual assault, compelled sexual assault or compelled self-sexual assault involving grievous bodily harm;
9. Sexual exploitation of children, sexual grooming of children and using children for or benefiting from child pornography;
10. Exposure or display of or causing exposure or display of child pornography or pornography to children intended to facilitate or promote sexual exploitation or sexual grooming of a child or the use of a child for purposes of child pornography or to benefit from child pornography;
11. Compelling or causing children to witness sexual offences, sexual acts or self-masturbation;
12. Sexual exploitation of persons who are mentally disabled, sexual grooming of persons who are mentally disabled, exposure or display of or causing exposure or display of child pornography or pornography to persons who are mentally disabled or using persons who are mentally disabled for pornographic purposes or benefiting from it;
13. Trafficking in persons for sexual purposes and involvement in trafficking in persons for sexual purposes;
14. Terrorism;
15. Racketeering and involvement in organised crime;
16. Genocide, crimes against humanity and war crimes;
17. Illegally dealing in or smuggling of ammunition, firearms, explosives or armaments or possession of firearms, explosives or armaments;
18. Illegally dealing in any dangerous dependence-producing substance or any undesirable dependence-producing substance;
19. Any offence of a serious nature if it is alleged that the offence was committed by a person, group of persons, syndicate or any enterprise, acting in the execution or furtherance of a common purpose or conspiracy;
20. Illegally possessing dependence-producing drugs exceeding R5 000 in value;
21. Any other statutory offence where the maximum penalty is imprisonment for a period of longer than five years or an equivalent fine; and
22. Any conspiracy, incitement or attempt to commit any offence referred to in Schedule 3.

The following factors must be considered when a diversion option is selected:

(a) The diversion option must be at the appropriate level;

(b) The child's cultural, religious and linguistic background;
(c) The child's educational level, cognitive ability and domestic and environmental circumstances;
(d) The proportionality of the option recommended or selected, to the circumstances of the child, the nature of the offence and the interests of society; and
(e) The child's age and developmental needs.

Problem 3: The case of the drug-taking school children

Hope High School has a problem with drugs at the school. The school asks the SAPS to carry out drug searches at the school. Fifty learners are searched and urine tests for drugs are carried out on 25 of the children. Five learners test positive for dagga and two test positive for heroin. Three other children are found in possession of dagga. The police arrest all 10 children, who are between the ages of 15 and 17 years of age. Assume that the cases are not diverted by the prosecutor and a preliminary inquiry is held.

Questions

1. Who may attend the preliminary inquiry?
2. Assume that you are the presiding officer at the preliminary inquiry. Would you consider diverting the matter? Provide reasons for your answer.
3. Assume that you decide to divert the matter. Which diversion options would you consider in this case?

2.14.5.2 Diversion at the child justice court

diversion may be made at any time before the end of a case

The Act provides that a matter can be diverted at any time before the conclusion of a case. When a diversion order is made at the child justice court, the proceedings are postponed pending the child's compliance with the diversion order. The court must warn the child that any failure to comply with the diversion order may result in any acknowledgment of responsibility being recorded as an admission in the event of the trial being proceeded with. After a probation officer has informed the court that a child has successfully complied with the diversion order and the court is satisfied it has been complied with, then the court must make an order to stop the proceedings.

2.14.5.3 Diversion register

The Director-General: Social Development must, in consultation with the Director-General: Justice and Constitutional Development and the National Commissioner of the South African Police Service, establish and maintain a register of children in respect of whom a diversion order has been made.

The register must include:

(a) The personal details of each child;
(b) Details of the offence in relation to which the diversion order was made;
(c) The diversion option or options as described in the diversion order; and
(d) Particulars of the child's compliance with the diversion order.

persons who may have access to the diversion register

The purpose of the register is to keep a record of particulars in respect of children whose matters are diverted from the formal criminal justice system. The register may be accessed by probation officers when assessing a child, by police officials when performing functions in terms of the Act, or by presiding officers, members of the national prosecuting authority or other court officials, when considering diversion at a preliminary inquiry and during proceedings at a child justice court. The information contained in the register will also facilitate research relating to the effectiveness of diversion and trends relating to diversion. Access to the register must be limited to persons or organisations requiring the information for the purposes of diversion.

2.14.6 Child justice court

2.14.6.1 Child justice courts and conduct of trials involving children

a child justice court is any court that deals with a child

The child justice court is not a separate court. It is any court that deals with a child who is alleged to have committed an offence and applies the provisions of the Child Justice Act to the case regarding the child. Where a child and an adult are charged together in the same trial in respect of the same set of facts, a court must apply the provisions of the Child Justice Act in respect of the child and the Criminal Procedure Act in respect of the adult.

Before a child tells a child justice court whether he or she will plead guilty or not guilty, the presiding officer must:

(a) Inform the child of the nature of the allegations against him or her;
(b) Inform the child of his or her rights; and
(c) Explain to the child the further procedures to be followed in terms of the Child Justice Act.

the best interests of the child must be protected

A child justice court must ensure that the best interests of the child are protected during these proceedings. The court may get additional information from any person involved in the proceedings. The court must, during all stages of the trial, especially during cross-examination of a child, ensure that the proceedings are fair and not unduly hostile and are appropriate to the age and understanding of the child. No person may be present at any sitting of a child justice court, unless his or her presence is necessary in connection with the proceedings of the child justice court or the magistrate has granted him or her permission to be present.

the child must be assisted by a parent, guardian or appropriate adult unless it is not in its best interests

The child must be assisted by his or her parent, guardian or appropriate adult in a child justice court. However, if they cannot be found, the magistrate can do away with this requirement if it is in the best interests of the child, or is not prejudicial to the administration of justice. If, however, the parent, guardian or appropriate adult fails to attend after being warned to be there, he or she can be found guilty of an offence and fined or imprisoned for period of up to three months. The parent, guardian or appropriate adult can also apply to be exempted from attending the court proceedings (eg if he or she would lose his or her job) and if granted, the magistrate must exempt him or her in writing. If the child is not assisted by a parent, guardian or appropriate adult, the magistrate can, in exceptional circumstances, appoint an independent observer to assist the child.

2.14.6.2 Postponements in the child justice court

all trials of children should be concluded speedily

A child justice court must conclude all trials of children as speedily as possible and must ensure that postponements are limited in number and time. Where a child is being detained in prison, a child justice court may not, before the beginning of a trial, postpone the proceedings for a period longer than 14 days at a time. Where a child is in detention in a child and youth care centre, a child justice court may not, before the beginning of a trial, postpone the proceedings for a period longer than 30 days at a time. Where a child has been released, a child justice court may not, before the beginning of a trial, postpone the proceedings for a period longer than 60 days at a time.

postponement of bail applications

Where the bail application of a child has not been finalised the child justice court may postpone the bail proceedings or bail application to any date or court, for a period not exceeding seven days at a time. The bail application may be postponed on the terms that the court may deem proper if:

1. The court is of the opinion that it has insufficient information or evidence to reach a decision on the bail application;

2. The prosecutor informs the court that the case has been or will be referred to the director of public prosecutions for written confirmation that he or she intends to charge the accused child with committing a crime referred to in Schedule 5 or 6 of the Criminal Procedure Act (ie serious crimes similar to those in the Schedule 3 offences that apply to Level 2 diversions);
3. It appears to the court that it is necessary to provide the State with a reasonable opportunity to obtain important evidence that may be lost if bail is granted or to identify bodily features of the accused (eg prints and bodily features); or
4. It appears to the court that it is necessary in the interests of justice to do so.

2.14.6.3 Diversion during the trial at the child justice court

a child justice court that makes a diversion order must postpone the proceedings

A child justice court may, at any time before the conclusion of the case for the prosecution, divert the matter. A child justice court that makes a diversion order must postpone the proceedings, pending the child's compliance with the diversion order, and warn the child that any failure to comply with the diversion order may result in any acknowledgment of responsibility being recorded as an admission if the trial is proceeded with. The child justice court must, on receipt of a report from the probation officer that a child has successfully complied with the diversion order, and if the child justice court is satisfied that the child has complied, make an order to stop the proceedings. This means that the child is not found guilty and the case cannot be re-instated in court.

If the child does not successfully carry out the conditions of the diversion order, the case continues in the child justice court and any acknowledgement of responsibility may be recorded as an admission for the purposes of the trial.

Problem 4: The hungry boy

Thami's parents do not care for him

Thami is 12 years old and lives at home but spends most of his time with his friends because his parents are never at home. He says his parents do not care about him. They tell him to go to school. He is regularly absent from school. Thami is arrested for breaking the window of a parked car and stealing money from the handbag lying on the seat. He says he was hungry and has no other way of getting money. He also claims that the police beat him up after he was caught. His mother says she is very angry with him because she thought he was at school, and that he no longer listens to her. She says she has to work because if she stays at home with him they would not eat. 'Already there is very little money for food.'

Questions

1. Is Thami a good candidate for diversion? Motivate your answer.
2. Assume that you are a magistrate and decide Thami must be diverted. Which diversion options will you consider?

2.14.7 Sentencing

sentences that can be imposed on children

The Criminal Procedure Act provides that a court must, after convicting a child, pass sentence in accordance with the Act. The types of sentences provided for in the Act are divided into two basic categories – custodial and non-custodial sentences. The range of sentences includes:

- Community-based sentences, including the diversion options;
- Restorative justice sentences, such as family group conferences and victim offender mediation, which result in a recommendation which may be confirmed or altered by the court;
- Correctional supervision as provided for in the Criminal Procedure Act;
- Suspended sentences, with or without conditions, for a period not exceeding five years;
- Penalties in lieu of a fine or imprisonment, such as symbolic restitution or the payment of compensation; and
- Custodial sentences to a child and youth care centre or prison.

factors to be taken into account when sentencing children

These are all similar to those sentences already available in South African law (see para 2.13.3). There are, however, other sentences that can be used for children. Where a child is convicted of committing a criminal offence, the court must take the following factors into account when deciding on the most appropriate sentence, namely:

- The best interest of the child;
- The provisions of the Constitution;
- International law;
- The 'traditional approach' to sentencing which requires a sentencing court to look at the seriousness of the offence, the character of the accused and the interests of society;
- The purpose of punishment; and

- Youthfulness, which is recognised as a mitigating factor in common law for reducing sentences.

punishment must be in line with the Constitution

In the case of *Brandt v S* the judge said that the traditional purpose of punishment, in respect of children, has to be developed to be in line with the South African Constitution. The purpose of punishing child offenders must be aimed at re-integrating the child back into society. When a court imposes a sentence on a child offender the court must be guided by certain principles, namely:

1. Proportionality;
2. Best interest of the child; and
3. The least possible restrictive deprivation of the child's right to liberty.

2.14.7.1 Objectives of sentencing

The Child Justice Act sets out the objectives of sentencing, which are to:

- Encourage the child to understand the implications of his or her actions and to be accountable for the harm caused;
- Promote an individualised response which balances the circumstances of the child, the nature of the offence and the interests of society;
- Promote the reintegration of the child into the family and community;
- Ensure that any necessary supervision, guidance, treatment or services which form part of the sentence assist the child in the process of reintegration; and
- Use imprisonment only as a measure of last resort and only for the shortest appropriate period of time.

These objectives go further than the constitutional and international law requirements regarding detention, but are closely aligned with the objectives of the Act itself.

2.14.7.2 Probation officers' pre-sentence reports

pre-sentence reports required

The courts have consistently said that pre-sentence reports by probation officers are necessary for sentencing purposes. The Child Justice Act now requires that a child justice court must request a pre-sentence report from the probation officer before imposing a sentence. Should the court decide to impose a sentence different from the one recommended in the pre-sentence report, the Act provides that the reasons for doing so must be recorded. The court can do away with a pre-sentence report if the child is convicted of a minor offence referred to in Schedule 1 (see above para 2.14.5.1.1), or the delay in obtaining one would cause undue hardship or prejudice the child. However, if the child is to be sentenced to a child and youth care centre or prison, the case cannot be finalised without a pre-sentence report.

2.14.7.3 Correctional supervision

imposed on children 14 years of age or older

Correctional supervision in terms of the Criminal Procedure Act may be imposed on a child of 14 years of age or older. However, correctional supervision linked to a period of imprisonment may not be applied to children under 14 years of age as they cannot be sentenced to prison.

2.14.7.4 Sentence to a child and youth care centre

Under the Child Justice Act, when considering a sentence involving compulsory residence in a child and youth care centre, a child justice court must consider the following:

factors to consider when sentencing a child to a compulsory residence

- Whether the offence is of such a serious nature that it indicates that the child has a tendency towards harmful activities;
- Whether the harm caused by the offence indicates that a residential sentence is appropriate;
- The extent to which the harm caused by the offence can be apportioned to the culpability of the child in causing or risking the harm;
- Whether the child is in need of a particular service provided at a child and youth care centre;
- The seriousness of the offence, with regard to the amount of harm done or risked through the offence and the culpability of the child in causing or risking the harm;
- The protection of the community;
- The severity of the impact of the offence on the victim;
- The previous failure of the child to respond to non-residential alternatives, if applicable; and
- The desirability of keeping the child out of prison.

The above factors must be taken into account and guide the court when it considers sentencing a child to residence in a youth care centre. These factors can also guide the probation officer when compiling sentencing recommendations for the pre-sentence report.

therapeutic programme

There are two types of sentences to a child and youth care centre. The first is the sentencing of a child to compulsory residence in a child and youth care centre which provides a therapeutic programme referred to in the Children's Act. A sentence like this may be imposed for a period not exceeding five years or for a period which may not exceed the date on which the child in question turns 21 years of age, whichever date is the earliest. This is essentially the same as the old sentence to a reform school.

sentence of imprisonment after stay in child and youth care centre

The second applies when a child justice court convicts a child of an offence referred to in Schedule 3 to the Child Justice Act (see above para 2.14.5.1.2) and which, if committed by an adult, would have justified a term of imprisonment exceeding 10 years. In such cases the court may, if substantial and compelling reasons exist, in addition to a child and youth care sentence, sentence the child to a period of imprisonment, which is to be served after completion of the stay in the child and youth care centre. After completion of the time at the child and youth care centre, the child must be brought before the child justice court. The manager of the child and youth care centre must submit a report to the court on the child's progress regarding whether the objectives of sentencing have been achieved and the possibility of the child's reintegration into society. The court then has to decide, if it is in the interests of justice, either to:

sentencing options for child justice court

- Confirm the sentence and period of imprisonment originally imposed, upon which the child must immediately be transferred from the child and youth care centre to the specified prison;
- Substitute that sentence with any other sentence that the court considers to be appropriate; or
- Order the release of the child, with or without conditions.

2.14.7.5 Sentence to prison

imprisonment for children over 14 years

In terms of the Child Justice Act a sentence of imprisonment may only be imposed on a child who is 14 years and older at the time of being sentenced. The Act provides that when considering the imposition of a sentence involving imprisonment, the child justice court must take the following factors into account:

factors to be taken into account

- The seriousness of the offence, with regard to the amount of harm done or risked through the offence and the fault of the child in causing or risking the harm;
- The protection of the community;
- The severity of the impact of the offence on the victim;
- The previous failure of the child to respond to non-residential alternatives, if applicable; and
- The desirability of keeping the child out of prison.

prison sentences for a child over 14 years must be as a last resort

The Act provides that a child justice court may not impose a sentence of imprisonment on a child who is under the age of 14 years at the time of being sentenced for the offence. When the court sentences a child who is 14 years or older at the time of being sentenced for the offence, the court must only do so as a measure of last resort and for the shortest appropriate period of time. However, if a child is 14 years of age or older the child can only be sentenced to imprisonment if the child is convicted of an offence referred to in:

- Schedule 3 (see above para 2.14.5.1.2);
- Schedule 2 (see above para 2.14.5.1.2), if substantial and compelling reasons exist for imposing a sentence of imprisonment; or
- Schedule 1 (see above para 2.14.5.1.1), if the child has a record of relevant previous convictions and substantial and compelling reasons exist for imposing a sentence of imprisonment.

minimum sentences for children aged 16 and 17 years are invalid

These children may be sentenced to imprisonment for a period not exceeding 25 years. In terms of the Act, minimum sentences apply to children aged 16 years or older. The Constitutional Court in *Centre for Child Law v Minister of Justice and Constitutional Development and Others* has stated that minimum sentences are invalid for children aged 16 and 17 years old. When a child is sentenced to direct imprisonment, the child justice court must subtract the number of days that a child may have spent awaiting trial in a child and youth care centre or prison (if any) from the period of imprisonment imposed.

Problem 5: How would you sentence Barend?

Barend, aged 16 years, is convicted in the child justice court. He broke into the house of an elderly lady, aged 83, while under the influence of alcohol. He raped her and stole her cell phone and R500 cash. He was convicted of rape and theft. Barend has no previous record of criminal activity or diversion. His parents both abuse alcohol and show very little interest in him. There is evidence that Barend was sexually abused by his uncle from the age of nine years. Assume that you are the magistrate.

Questions

1. Which factors would you take into account before sentencing Barend?
2. What would be an appropriate sentence for Barend? The victim indicated that she does not want to meet Barend.
3. What should the purpose of the sentence be in this case?

criminal records for children cause problems in later life

Even though the public cannot attend juvenile cases and the newspapers cannot report the names of juvenile criminals, their criminal records can still cause problems later on in life. For example, when people are looking for work, or applying for positions of trust or official documents, they may have to mention whether or not they have been found guilty of crimes. If they have been found guilty they may find it difficult to obtain a job or a position of trust.

2.14.8 When criminal proceedings are stopped and the child referred to a children's court

If it appears to the magistrate during proceedings in a child justice court that a child is a child in need of care and protection, the proceedings must be stopped and the court must refer the case to the children's court (see below para 4.3.3.2).

Children in need of care and protection

Children in need of care and protection are those where:

1. The child has no parents or guardian.
2. The child has been abandoned and has no means of support.
3. The child behaves in a way that cannot be controlled by his or her parents or the people in whose care he or she is.
4. The child lives or works on the streets or begs for a living.
5. The child is addicted to a dependence-producing substance and is without support to obtain treatment for such dependency.
6. The child has been exploited or lives in circumstances that expose him or her to exploitation.
7. The child lives in or is exposed to circumstances that may seriously harm his or her physical, mental or social well-being.
8. The child may be at risk if returned to the care of his or her parent, guardian or care-giver because there is reason to believe that the child will live in or be exposed to circumstances which may seriously harm his or her physical, mental or social well-being.
9. The child is being maltreated, abused, deliberately neglected or degraded by a parent, guardian, care-giver or family member, someone who has parental responsibility over the child or someone under whose control the child is.
10. The child may also be in need of care and protection if he or she is a victim of child labour or is in a child-headed household.

parents whose habits may seriously injure the physical, mental or social well-being of the child may be declared unfit to have custody of children

Problem 6: Would you stop the proceedings?

Questions

If you were the magistrate in a child justice court in the following cases, would you stop the proceedings and refer the case to the children's court? Give reasons for your answer.

15-year-old Gawie robs an old lady at knife-point

1. Gawie, aged 15 years, is accused of robbing an 80-year-old woman by threatening her with a knife. Gawie's parents are never at home and he has been allowed to do what he likes since he was a small child. He continually misses school and stays out on the streets with gangs of much older boys. He robbed the old lady while he was with a gang of 19-year-old boys.

17-year-old Sue is a prostitute

2. Sue, aged 17 years, spends her nights walking around the city streets where she earns 'pocket money' by being a prostitute. Her parents allow her to stay out late at night without asking questions. During the day both her parents work and she stays at home and smokes dagga with her friends. Sue dropped out of school when she was 14 years old and her parents have never taken an interest in her education. She was arrested in a police raid on prostitutes in the city streets.

Further reading

2.1 The meaning, nature and causes of crime

Burchell J *Principles of Criminal Law* 3 ed (2005)

McQuoid-Mason D, Lotz L & Natsylishvili A *Criminal Law: Student Book* (2009)

Milton JRL *South African Criminal Law and Procedure (Volume II) Common Law Crimes* 3 ed (1996)

2.2 Crimes against people

Burchell J *Principles of Criminal Law* 3 ed (2005)

McQuoid-Mason D, Lotz L & Natsylishvili A *Criminal Law: Student Book* (2009)

Milton JRL *South African Criminal Law and Procedure (Volume II) Common Law Crimes* 3 ed (1996)

2.3 Sexual crimes

McQuoid-Mason D 'The Children's Amendment Act and the Criminal Law (Sexual Offences and Related Matters) Amendment Act: Duty to Report Child Abuse and Sexual Offences against Children and Mentally Disabled Persons' 2008 SA *Med J* 929–931.

Criminal Law (Sexual Offences and Related Matters) Amendment Act 32 of 2007

Masiya v Director of Public Prosecutions, Pretoria and Another 2007 (5) SA 30 (CC) – the Constitutional Court found that the common-law definition of rape was not unconstitutional, but that it needed to be appropriately adapted and that it had to be extended to include acts of non-consensual, intentional penetration of a penis into a female's anus.

S v Geldenhuys 2009 (1) SACR 1 (SCA) – it was held, while it was possible that certain children of 12 years of age might be regarded as competent to make rational decisions about their sexual activity this did not mean it was unconstitutional to set the age of consent higher than 12. It was further held that the state is both constitutionally and internationally obliged to protect its children from all forms of abuse and that, by setting the legal age of consent to sexual activities above the age of 12 years, is in line with these obligations.

Teddy Bear Clinic for Abused Children and Another v Minister of Justice and Constitutional Development and Another 2014 (2) SA 168 (CC).

2.4 Domestic violence

Children's Act 38 of 2005

Domestic Violence Act 116 of 1998

Older Persons Act 13 of 2006

Minister of Safety and Security v Carmichele 2004 (3) SA 305 (SCA) – the Supreme Court of Appeal held that the respondent owed a legal duty to the appellant to take reasonable steps to prevent an escaped serial rapist from causing her harm.

S v Baloyi 2000 (2) SA 425 (CC) – the Constitutional Court held that the Constitution imposes a direct obligation on the state to protect the right of all persons to be free from domestic violence.

2.5 Cyber crime

Currie I & De Waal J *The Bill of Rights Handbook* 5 ed (2005)

http://kidshealth.org/parent/positive/talk/cyberbullying.html (accessed on 6 September 2011)

http://www.character.org/bullyprevention (accessed on 6 September 2011)

http://www.stopcyberbullying.org/how_it_works/direct_attacks.html#im (accessed on 6 September 2011)

http://www.collegeotr.com/college_otr/word_of_the_week_sexting_16399 (accessed on 7 September 2011)

http://www.esarcasm.com/347/25-more-sexting-acronyms-parents-should-know/ (accessed on 7 September 2011)

Constitution of the Republic of South Africa, 1996

Protection from Harassment Act 17 of 2011

Le Roux v Dey 2010 (4) SA 210 (SCA) – learners found liable for manipulating and electronically posting a photograph that ridiculed and humiliated the deputy-principal of a school by falsely showing him to be involved in naked homosexual activity with the school principal.

National Coalition for Gay and Lesbian Equality v Minister of Justice 1999 (1) SA 6 (CC)

2.6 Crimes against property

Burchell J *Principles of Criminal Law* 3 ed (2005)

McQuoid-Mason D, Lotz L & Natsylishvili A *Criminal Law: Student Book* (2009)

Criminal Procedure Act 51 of 1977

2.7 Crimes against the state

Burchell J *Principles of Criminal Law* 3 ed (2005)

McQuoid-Mason D, Lotz L & Natsylishvili A *Criminal Law: Student Book* (2009)

Criminal Procedure Act 51 of 1977

Protection of Constitutional Democracy against Terrorist and Related Activities Act 33 of 2004

Protection of State Information Act 43 of 2013

2.8 Crimes against morality involving sexual conduct

Burchell J *Principles of Criminal Law* 3 ed (2005)

McQuoid-Mason D, Lotz L & Natsylishvili A *Criminal Law: Student Book* (2009)

Choice of Termination of Pregnancy Act 92 of 1996

Choice of Termination of Pregnancy Amendment Act 38 of 2004

Christian Lawyers Association of South Africa v Minister of Health 2005 (1) SA 509 (T); 2004 (4) All SA 31 (T) – minor's ability to consent to termination of pregnancy independently.

S v Jordan 2002 (6) SA 642 (CC) – the majority of the Constitutional Court confirmed the criminality of prostitution (sex for reward). It also stated that the customer of the prostitute may be guilty of being an accomplice or of incitement or conspiracy regarding the offence of the prostitute.

S v M 2004 (3) SA 680 (O) – the court confirmed the constitutionality of the crime of bestiality and correctly regarded the conduct covered by the crime as against legal convictions of the community (*boni mores*).

2.9 Crimes involving alcohol and drugs

Burchell J *Principles of Criminal Law* 3 ed (2005)

McQuoid-Mason D, Lotz L & Natsylishvili A *Criminal Law: Student Book* (2009)

Criminal Procedure Act 51 of 1977

Drugs and Drug Trafficking Act 140 of 1992

National Road Traffic Act 93 of 1996

Prince v President, Cape Law Society 2002 (2) SA 794 (CC) – the Constitutional Court held that the Drugs and Drug Trafficking Act was not in conflict with the Constitutional right to freedom of religion by not granting Rastafari exemption to possess and use dagga for religious purposes.

2.10 Defences to crimes

Burchell J *Principles of Criminal Law* 3 ed (2005)

Child Justice Act 75 of 2008

Children's Act 38 of 2005

2.11 Powers of the police and bail

Burchell J *Principles of Criminal Law* 3 ed (2005)

Criminal Procedure Act 51 of 1997

2.12 Search and seizure

Boezaart T (ed) *Child Law in South Africa* (2009)

Burchell J *Principles of Criminal Law* 3 ed (2005)

Mofokeng L *Legal Pluralism in South Africa: Aspects of African Customary, Muslim and Hindu Family Law* (2008)

Criminal Procedure Act 51 of 1977

2.13 The criminal trial and sentencing process

Burchell J *Principles of Criminal Law* 3 ed (2005)

McQuoid-Mason D, Lotz L, Natsylishvili A *Criminal Law: Student Book* (2009)

Criminal Procedure Act 51 of 1977

South African Police Services Act 68 of 1995

S v Makwanyane 1995 (3) SA 391 (CC) – dealt with the constitutionality of the death penalty: the court abolished the death penalty and described the rights to life and dignity as the 'most important of all human rights, and the source of all other personal rights in the Bill of Rights'.

2.14 Child justice

Coetzee L (ed) *Child Justice Act: Training Manual* (2nd Draft) (2009)

Gallinetti J *Getting to know the Child Justice Act* (2009)

Brandt v S [2005] 2 All SA 1 (SCA) – indicated that the traditional purpose of punishment, in respect of children, has to be re-appraised and developed to be in line with the South African Constitution.

Centre for Child Law v Minister of Justice and Constitutional Development and Others 2009 (6) SA 632 (CC) – a judgment declaring that minimum sentences are invalid for children aged 16 and 17 years old.

DPP, KwaZulu-Natal v P 2006 (1) SACR 243 (SCA) – a 14 year old girl convicted of a brutal murder committed when she was 12 years old, was give a sentence of seven years imprisonment suspended for 5 years on condition that she is not convicted of a crime of violence and 36 months correctional supervision involving house arrest in the care and custody of her mother, except for attendence at school, a NICRO rehabilitation project, medical visits, etc.

Weber v Santam Versekeringsmaatskappy Bpk 1983 (1) SA 381 (A) – the court held that when determining capacity the test is subjective, whereas the test is objective when determining fault. When a child is found to have criminal capacity, the negligence or otherwise should be determined in accordance with the ordinary reasonable person.

Street law

3. Consumer law

CONTENTS

PART THREE

Consumer law

3.1 Consumer protection

Outcomes

After completion of this section learners will be able to:

1. Identify and explain the protection afforded to consumers in South Africa.

Assessment criteria

1. A decision is taken on whether a person was a wise consumer.
2. An explanation is given on how to prevent consumers from becoming victims of dishonesty and fraud.
3. The main statutes protecting consumers and the common-law protection of consumers are listed.

3.1.1 Introduction

we are all consumers

A person may buy sweets or cold drinks at a café, catch a bus or taxi to school or visit a movie house. A person who does any of these is a consumer of food, drink, transport and entertainment. A consumer is a person who buys or uses goods or services bought from another. We are all consumers because at some time everyone buys or uses goods and services.

entering into a contract

When a seller agrees to sell, and the consumer agrees to pay for goods and services, they have entered into a contract. Every time a person buys something, he or she agrees to pay for it. The seller in return agrees to sell the item. If sweets or drinks are sold they must be fit to eat or drink. If there is an argument between the seller and the buyer the law will decide what should be done.

if a person buys a soft drink, hamburger or bunny chow from the local take-away, he or she makes a contract

'let the buyer beware'

An important saying in consumer law is 'let the buyer beware'. This means that the buyer must be on the lookout when he or she buys something from someone in case there is something wrong with it. This does not mean, however, that sellers must be honest

consumers must be informed

sellers can cheat or sell goods that do not work, or services that are useless. The seller must be honest. But the consumer must be on guard against dishonesty. Therefore, the best protection for consumers is to be informed about the goods or services they are buying. They must also be informed about their rights as consumers. If a consumer makes a bad buy there are various ways of putting things right. Often this can be done by consumers themselves without going to lawyers. This part will help you become a more informed consumer, and better able to recognise, avoid, and solve consumer problems.

3.1.2 Buying on the spur of the moment

impulse buying

Have you ever stood in line to pay for something at the grocery store and, while waiting, you are tempted to buy some of the chocolates or sweets that are displayed in front of the tills? This is referred to as impulse buying. Impulse buying is when you buy something that you did not plan on buying when you entered the shop. Shops spend a lot of time planning the layout of the store. How the store smells, what music they are playing and where they place certain items are all things the stores do to make sure they tempt you to buy more things.

How to avoid buying on the spur of the moment:

1. Make a list of the items you need and the shops that you are going to visit in order to buy those items.
2. If you are thinking of buying a big item, eg a car or television, which will cost a lot of money, wait a couple of days, weeks or months before you decide.
3. If you have to take your children with you to the shop, learn to say no. Get them involved in writing your shopping list at home and then make a game of finding the stuff on the list inside the shop. That might distract them from the other things around them in the shop.
4. Browsing in a shop can be disastrous. If you do not have the self-discipline to browse without buying, then rather go to the shop with a specific purpose and leave after accomplishing your purpose.
5. Paying with debit and credit cards often allows you to spend more than you have. Try paying cash for what you are buying.

Problem 1: Were you a wise consumer?

Questions

1. Make a list of five products or services you have bought in the last week. For each item explain why you decided to buy that particular product or service.
2. Do you think that you were a wise consumer?
3. Have you ever had a problem with these or any other goods or services you have bought?

The law says that, generally, contracts need not be in writing, except for important contracts like buying a house, standing surety for someone else's debts (ie guaranteeing that you will pay off a debt if he or she does not) or entering into long leases, credit agreements or contracts of apprenticeship. Where the law states that the contract must be in writing, such a contract will not be valid until it has been written down and signed by the parties. Where the law does not require the contract to be in writing, the contracting parties can still decide to put the contract in writing. If the parties intend that the contract must first be in writing before it will be valid, there will be no contract until it is in writing. Where the parties only intended to put the contract in writing to prove the terms of the contract, the contract will be valid even before it was put in writing. The Electronic Communications and Transactions Act of 2002 (ECTA) allows electronic alternatives to writing and signature for some agreements. Section 12 of the ECTA provides that a requirement in law that a document or information must be in writing will be met if the information is contained in a data message and the information is stored in a format that will be accessible in future.

electronic signature for some agreements (ECTA)

Problem 2: Some questions about consumers

Questions

Read each of the statements below. Decide whether you (a) strongly agree; (b) agree, (c) are undecided; (d) disagree; or (e) strongly disagree with each statement. There are no right or wrong answers.

1. Children (people under 18 years of age) should not be able to make contracts without the approval of their parents or guardians.
2. Contracts should always be in writing.
3. Consumers should never buy items, except a house or car, unless they can pay the full price in cash at the time of buying.
4. Sellers who trick consumers into buying things should be sent to prison.
5. Most consumers are not affected by radio and television advertising.
6. A car dealer who gives a loan to buy a car should be able to take the car back if the buyer misses a payment.
7. The government should prohibit the sale of anything that is harmful to consumers.

3.1.3 Watch out for dishonesty and fraud

Have you received an e-mail or SMS telling you that someone has found a very rich, long-lost relative from whom you inherited millions, or you have won a lottery for which you had never bought a ticket, or won a competition that you had never entered? You could not have won a lottery if you had not bought a lottery ticket. You should delete such messages immediately and not respond to them. Remember, if it is too good to be true, it probably is not true.

too good to be true

If you are told that you have won a prize it must not cost you anything to receive the prize. You cannot be asked to pay the costs and taxes to deliver the prize to you.

If you need to do business with someone, make sure that you get references and follow up on those references to make sure that the person and his or her work is reliable.

3.1.4 How are consumers protected?

The United Nations (UN) recognises that consumers are often in a weak bargaining position. It has developed guidelines for countries to deal with consumer protection. The UN encourages countries to adopt a strong consumer protection policy in accordance with the economic, social and environmental conditions of the country. In line with its international obligations the South African government has taken steps to protect South African consumers.

the United Nations (UN) recognises that consumers are often in a weak bargaining position

In this Part we will be looking at two laws that are aimed at protecting consumers: the Consumer Protection Act of 2008 and the National Credit Act of 2005, as well as the common-law protection of consumers for situations where their transactions are not covered by statute. Here the common law of contract and 'delict' (civil wrongs) will protect consumers and third parties injured by consumer transactions and impose obligations on the providers of goods and services.

15 March is World Consumer Rights Day.

3.2 Consumer Protection Act of 2008

Outcomes

After completion of this section learners will be able to:

1. Identify and explain the protection given to consumers in South Africa by the Consumer Protection Act (CPA).

Assessment criteria

1. An explanation is given of the different rights of consumers under the Consumer Protection Act (CPA).
2. A decision is taken on whether a consumer was discriminated against.
3. A decision is taken on whether a person can 'opt out' of direct marketing.
4. A solution is recommended to problems relating to discrimination against consumers.
5. Advice is given to a supplier on 'bundling' of products.
6. A decision is taken on whether cancellation of an agreement can take place.
7. Advice is given to a consumer on whether a contract may be cancelled.
8. A decision is taken on whether a consumer can insist that broken goods be replaced.
9. A recommendation is provided about a consumer's duties in relation to goods sent in the post that were not ordered.
10. Labelling on products is analysed for correctness.

the Consumer Protection Act aims to promote fair marketing

the CPA only applies to transactions in the 'ordinary course of business'

The way in which we buy products or services has changed over time. In the past you went to a shop to buy what you needed. It is now also possible to buy goods over the Internet. The Consumer Protection Act (CPA) aims to promote fair marketing of consumer products and services. It prohibits unfair marketing and unfair business practices. The purpose of the CPA is to protect the interests of all consumers. It provides remedies for consumers who are, or who have been, abused or exploited. The CPA is applicable to transactions that involve the marketing of goods and services to the consumer. The CPA further regulates the relationship, transactions and agreements between consumers, producers, suppliers, distributors, importers, retailers, service providers and intermediaries of those goods and services. The CPA applies to transactions and marketing. A transaction is an agreement for the supply of any goods or services in exchange for consideration (payment) in the ordinary course of business. The purposes of the CPA are to:

- Improve consumer awareness and information;
- Encourage responsible and informed consumer choice and behaviour; and
- Promote consumer confidence, empowerment and the development of a culture of consumer responsibility, through individual and group education, vigilance, advocacy and activism.

As previously mentioned, the Consumer Protection Act applies only to consumers of any goods or services to whom such goods or services are marketed in the ordinary course of the supplier's business. This means that it does not apply to transactions that are not done in the course of such business, eg people who are not involved in the business of buying and selling or leasing goods or services. The common law will apply when the contracting parties are private persons who are not conducting business as suppliers and manufacturers of goods and services. In such cases the consumer will have to rely on the common law remedies (see below para 3.4).

common law applies when the contracting parties are private persons

3.2.1 What are my rights as a consumer?

The Consumer Protection Act (CPA) provides consumers with eight rights:

the CPA protects eight rights

1. The right to equality
2. The right to privacy
3. The right to choose
4. The right to the disclosure of information
5. The right to fair and responsible marketing
6. The right to fair and honest dealing
7. The right to fair, just and reasonable terms and conditions
8. The right to fair value, quality and safety.

The CPA also provides protection for consumers who pay in advance for goods or services.

3.2.2 The right to equality

certain consumers may not be favoured unfairly compared with other consumers

The CPA protects the right to equality of consumers. The right to equality means that suppliers may not unfairly limit access to goods and services for certain consumers, nor may they unfairly favour certain consumer groups when they market, sell or distribute their goods or services. A supplier is also not allowed to unfairly provide low quality goods to certain consumers and high quality goods to other consumers. This would be discriminatory. If you have received goods of a poor quality you may question the quality of the goods and services that you have received by complaining to the person who sold them to you.

the equality provisions of the Constitution apply

Equality requires that people in similar situations be treated the same. The CPA sets out the grounds upon which a supplier is not allowed to discriminate and provides the reasonable grounds when differential treatment is allowed. The listed grounds in the equality clause of the South African Constitution are applicable. The Constitution provides that everyone is equal before the law and has the right to equal protection of the law. No one may be discriminated against on the ground of race, gender, sex, pregnancy, marital status, ethnic or social origin, colour, sexual orientation, age, disability, religion, conscience, belief, culture, language and birth. The provisions of the Promotion of Equality and Prevention of Discrimination Act of 2000 are relevant to this discussion. The Act provides inferior services may not be provided to persons from one race group

that no person may unfairly discriminate against any person on the grounds of race. Service providers may not provide inferior services to any racial group compared to what is being provided to other race groups. Access to opportunities, including access to services or contractual opportunities for providing services, must not discriminate against any racial groups. Service providers must eliminate obstacles that unfairly limit or restrict persons with disabilities from enjoying equal opportunities with able-bodied persons.

it is not unfair discrimination to discriminate against minors in certain circumstances

Exceptions to the prohibition on discrimination against consumers are contained in the CPA. It will not be unfair discrimination if the supplier refuses to provide a service to a minor or where the supplier requires the minor to prove that he or she is acting with the permission of the parent or guardian. Suppliers will not be discriminating if they state that a place or service is only to be used by minors or persons who have reached a certain age. It will also not be unfair discrimination if the supplier decides to give access to a place only to males or females.

A supplier will be discriminating unfairly if:

1. The supplier treats consumers differently compared to other consumers in terms of the CPA;
2. The differential treatment is based on one of the listed grounds in the Constitution; and
3. The supplier, when called upon to do so, has refused or failed to offer an alternative reasonable and justifiable explanation for the difference in treatment.

persons discriminated against can sue in the Equality Court

The CPA allows an accredited consumer protection group or any person who is acting for himself or herself or on behalf of someone else to institute an action in the Equality Court. The Human Rights Commission or the Commission for Gender Equality may also institute an action.

suppliers may not charge unfair prices

The right to equality for consumers also means that suppliers may not charge unfair prices for goods and services. Consumers must be treated equally, no matter what their gender, race or socio-economic status is, or where they stay.

A person who feels that he or she has been discriminated against as a consumer may lay a complaint with the National Consumer Commission. If the claim is justified the Commission will refer the matter to the Equality Court.

Problem 1: Was the consumer unfairly discriminated against?

Questions

Read the statements below and decide whether unfair discrimination against a consumer has taken place:

1. A local liquor shop places a sign above its entrance that reads: 'This store will not sell any alcohol or tobacco products to persons under the age of 18.'
2. Thando, a black man, applies for a loan from a bank. Thando earns R3 500 a month and has a good credit history. Thando is informed that he does not qualify for the loan based upon his income. However, Thando does not realise that the bank has not been strictly enforcing its policy, and has been allowing white customers with lower income to qualify for the loans.

3.2.3 The right to privacy

junk mail invades our privacy

The CPA protects the right to privacy of consumers. The right to privacy means that people may not intrude into another person's private life or get private information about a person without the person's consent. The right to privacy of consumers is invaded if, without their consent, junk mail or things they do not want are sent to them, or other people get private information about them such as their address, how much they earn, what their buying habits are, etc.

A common example of when the right to privacy of consumers is invaded is when sellers, charitable organisations and others use direct marketing to contact them in their homes.

direct marketing is done when people are contacted in their homes

The CPA controls the use of direct marketing. Direct marketing occurs when suppliers contact potential customers individually in their homes in order to promote their goods and services. An example of direct marketing is where you are phoned by a cell phone company that tries to convince you to enter into a contract with them. Another example is where somebody contacts you on the phone or through the post to make a donation.

direct marketing can be done by a person coming to see you personally

Direct marketing can be done by a person coming to see you personally or sending you information through the post, or you could be contacted electronically such as by telephone, fax, SMS, wireless computer access, email or any similar technological device.

you have the right to opt out of direct marketing

opt-out register

The CPA gives you the right to protect your privacy and confidentiality by refusing unwanted SMSes, telephone calls, letters, spam or e-mails. You have the right to 'opt out' of unsolicited direct marketing by blocking the relevant supplier. ('Unsolicited' means that you have not asked people to contact you.) You can have your details recorded in the Opt-out Register. ('Opt out' means that you can ask that you must not be contacted by anyone about direct marketing.) Once your details are recorded, the suppliers may not contact you. The Opt-out Register allows consumers to contact their telephone operator to record a preference to opt out of direct marketing in the National Directory Database (NDD).

direct marketers may not share your details with others

The main aim of the NDD is to stop unsolicited marketing regarding any calls made from within South Africa. Once you have opted out, a direct marketer may not share your details with any other person. However, if the e-mails originate outside of South Africa, the country where the e-mail originates might not have similar laws that allow persons to opt out of direct marketing.

Marketing companies who break the rules can be prosecuted.

Direct Marketing Association of South Africa
The Direct Marketing Association of South Africa has a National Opt-out Register. If you add your details to the Register you will not be contacted by any supplier who is a member of the Direct Marketing Association. You can opt out by visiting http://www.dmasa.org/dmasa/dma_optout.php and completing your details online. Within 28 days of opting out, no direct marketing telephone calls should occur.

put a 'no adverts' sign on your mail box

If you wish to stop direct marketers from placing unwanted promotional material in your post box you must put a sign on your post box that indicates that you do not wish to receive any direct marketing material. An example would be to place the notice 'No Adverts' outside on your mail box.

restricted times

No direct marketing is allowed on Sundays or public holidays, Saturdays before 09:00 and after 12:00 and all other days between 19:00 and 08:00 the following day. It is, however, possible that you can agree to be contacted during these times.

Problem 2: Opting out from being contacted by direct marketers

Questions

Divide into groups of not more than five. Read the statements below and suggest possible solutions to the questions asked:

1. A person knocks on your door at 20:00 in the evening. He asks you to make a donation to a shelter for abused women. He says that you will win a fantastic prize if you make a donation. Do you think that you can opt out of a request for this kind of donation?

a person knocks on the door and says that you can win a fantastic prize if you make a donation

2. Assume that you can opt out of the request for a donation. Discuss what would be the most effective way of stopping the organisation from coming to your house to request donations.
3. You receive a large number of unwanted junk e-mails in your inbox. It is really frustrating you. Discuss what you can do to stop receiving these e-mails.

3.2.4 The right to choose

The right to choose means that consumers may shop around for the best price. Consumers cannot be forced to enter into additional agreements with suppliers from whom they bought goods or services. For example they cannot be forced:

1. To enter into 'bundling' agreements;
2. To extend fixed-term contracts;
3. To pay for repairs they did not authorise;
4. Not to change their mind;

5. Not to cancel reservations, advance bookings or orders;
6. To keep defective goods; or
7. To pay for unordered goods.

3.2.4.1 Bundling

The CPA controls the use of 'bundling'. 'Bundling' happens when a supplier joins two products together in order to sell them as one unit (eg a company offers you a television set and a PlayStation to buy as a single unit). There is usually a special price that makes it cheaper to buy the products together than when you buy them individually. Sometimes 'bundling' involves getting a low value or free product together with a high value product (eg some cheap bedding for free if you buy a mattress). Normally the price of the 'free' product has already been added to the price that you are being charged (eg giving away a free cell phone when you take out a cell phone contract). The CPA also prohibits suppliers from forcing consumers to enter into agreements with third parties, unless the suppliers can prove the benefits of these additional goods or services.

sometimes 'bundling' involves getting a low value or free product together with a high value product

3.2.4.2 Fixed-term contracts

a fixed-term contract is one that lasts for a certain period of time

The CPA gives consumers certain protection where they have entered into fixed-term agreements. A 'fixed-term contract' is a contract which lasts for a certain period of time (eg where you agree to take out a 12-month membership at your local gym or you enter into a 24-month contract with a cell phone service provider). The right to choose also allows you to cancel a fixed-term contract once it ends without being charged a penalty. If you wish to cancel a fixed-term contract, you must give the supplier 20 business days' notice, in writing, that you are cancelling it. Depending on the nature of the business a supplier might charge a reasonable penalty when cancelling reservations, bookings or orders.

may not last longer than 24 months

Where the fixed-term contract is not cancelled the contract will continue on a monthly basis. Usually a fixed-term contract may not last longer than 24 months unless the consumer agrees to a longer period and the supplier can show that it is to the financial benefit of the consumer.

consumers must be notified regarding the termination date

Where a consumer enters into a fixed-term contract (eg a gym contract or a cell phone contract), the consumer may cancel the contract at the end of the term of the contract. Between 40 and 80 days before the contract ends the supplier must notify the consumer of the date of termination of the contract. The supplier must also notify the consumer of any changes that would apply should the consumer wish to renew the contract. The duty is then on the consumer to notify the supplier that he or she wishes to cancel the agreement. If the consumer fails to notify the supplier of his or her intention to cancel the agreement, the contract will continue on a month to month basis on the new terms.

suppliers may only charge a reasonable cancellation penalty

The CPA provides that upon cancellation of a fixed-term contract the consumer will remain liable to the supplier for any amounts owed to the supplier in terms of the agreement up to the date of cancellation, and the supplier may impose a reasonable cancellation penalty to compensate for the agreement not continuing for its intended fixed term and must credit the consumer with any amount that remains the property of the consumer. The supplier may not charge an amount that would not make it worthwhile for the consumer to cancel the fixed-term contract. In order to decide what a reasonable charge would be for cancellation, the supplier must take the following factors into account:

1. The amount the consumer will still be liable for up to the date of cancellation;
2. The value of the transaction up to cancellation;
3. The value of the goods which will remain in the possession of the consumer after cancellation;
4. The value of the goods that are returned to the supplier;
5. The duration of the consumer agreement as initially agreed;
6. Losses suffered or benefits accrued by the consumer as a result of the consumer entering into the agreement;

7. The nature of the goods and services that were reserved or booked;
8. The length of notice of cancellation provided by the consumer; and
9. The practice of the relevant industry.

Problem 3: Simpiwe wishes to cancel his gym contract

Questions

Divide into groups of not more than five. Read the case study below and advise Simpiwe:

Simpiwe takes out a contract for a gym membership with Muscle Power Gym for a period of 24 months. Eight months after taking out the gym membership Simpiwe decides that he cannot afford the gym membership any longer. He writes a letter to the gym in which he gives 30 days' notice of his intention to cancel his gym membership. Muscle Power Gym writes him a letter accepting his cancellation and informing him that they are charging him 60% of the fees that he would have paid for the rest of his membership contract as a reasonable charge for cancellation of the membership. Discuss whether you think the charge of 60% is a reasonable charge for the cancellation.

3.2.4.3 The need for authorisation of repairs or maintenance

consumers are entitled to a quotation before repairs are made

The CPA gives consumers the right to not be charged for repairs they did not agree to. A person who hands in goods for repairs or maintenance has the right to obtain a quotation from the supplier before the supplier starts with the repairs. A supplier may not charge a person for the quotation. A consumer cannot be forced to pay for repairs that were done without his or her approval before the repairs were started. If a supplier is required to do some work before making a quotation, the consumer must agree that the supplier can charge for such work. If there is no such agreement, the supplier may not charge for the work.

Problem 4: The case of the costly quotation

Questions

Divide into groups of not more than five. Read the case study below and advise Mavis if she has to pay the R800.

Mavis takes her car to Sammy's Service Station. The mechanic tells her that the car needs a tune-up and estimates the cost at R500. Mavis tells the mechanic to go ahead with the tune-up, but when she returns to fetch the car the bill adds up to R800.

3.2.4.4 Consumers changing their minds using a 'cooling-off' period

cancellation within 5 working days

The CPA gives consumers a 'cooling-off' period if they wish to change their mind after buying goods or services under a direct marketing agreement. Where a consumer enters into an agreement as a result of direct marketing, the consumer has the right to cancel the agreement within five business days. This is referred to as a 'cooling-off' period. The consumer does not have to provide reasons for the cancellation and may not be charged any penalties. The supplier must return any payment received from the consumer within 15 business days of receiving the notice of cancellation. Direct marketers must inform their customers of the right to cancel the agreement within the 'cooling-off' period.

Problem 5: Noluthando buys some waterless cooking pots

Questions

Divide into groups of not more than five. Read the case study below and advise Noluthando if she has a remedy:

Noluthando is approached at her house by Tembeka. Tembeka tells her that she is selling the most amazing waterless pots. Noluthando signs a contract to purchase one of these expensive pots. The next day Noluthando comes to see you. She informs you that she ordered the waterless pot on the spur of the moment without considering whether she can afford it. She now tells you that she cannot afford the pot and wants to know if she can cancel the agreement.

3.2.4.5 Consumers cancelling advance reservations, bookings or orders

a reasonable cancellation fee

The CPA gives consumers the right to cancel any advance reservations, bookings or orders. A supplier may request a deposit for advance reservations, bookings or orders. When a consumer cancels an advance reservation or booking, the supplier may impose a reasonable charge for the cancellation of the booking. An example of an advance booking would be where a person reserves a ticket on an airline to fly at some future date. Later the person's plans change and she is no longer able to take the flight that she booked. When the passenger cancels the booking the airline may charge her a reasonable fee for the cancellation.

3.2.5 Consumers' right to examine or choose goods

a reasonable chance to inspect the goods

The CPA provides that suppliers must allow consumers a reasonable opportunity to inspect goods that have been purchased or delivered. Consumers may return goods that were not examined by them before delivery. If consumers deliberately or through gross negligence lose or damage property or goods, the supplier has the right to charge them for loss of, or damage to, such property or goods. A consumer has the right to ask for unopened goods (ie goods still sealed in their packages) and cannot be forced to take goods on display or goods that have been opened. Where consumers buy goods after being shown a sample, they may reject the goods if they are not the same as the samples that they thought that they were buying.

3.2.6 Consumers' right to return defective goods

return the goods within a reasonable period

The CPA protects consumers against defective goods. If there is something wrong with the goods that consumers have bought they may return the goods within a reasonable period and ask for a full refund. The CPA provides that a consumer has the right to receive goods that are suitable for the purpose for which they were bought. Any products that consumers buy must be of good quality, in working order and free of any defects. The CPA says that when consumers buy something the manufacturer, importer, distributor and retailer gives them an implied (unspoken) warranty that the goods they receive are quality goods fit for the purpose for which they were bought. Where the defect in the goods appears within six months from the date of purchase, the purchaser may return the goods without any penalty to the seller. The consumer and not the seller may decide whether the goods must be replaced, repaired or the money paid for them returned to the consumer.

Problem 6: The case of the faulty TV set

Questions

Divide into groups of not more than five. Read the case study below and advise the Thodis if they have a remedy.

Mr and Mrs Thodi see an advertisement in the newspaper for brand-new colour television sets on a sale at Sharky's Radio and TV Shop. They buy a new TV for R5 000. After a few weeks the TV loses its picture. A TV service mechanic tells them that the tube has blown and that the repairs will cost R1 000.

a few weeks after they bought it the Thodis' TV set loses its picture

Problem 7: The case of the defective cell phone

Questions

Divide into groups of not more than five. Read the case study below and discuss whether the supplier is correct:

You renew your cell phone contract. Upon renewal of the contract you get a brand-new cell phone. The suppliers tell you that if anything is wrong with the cell phone in the first seven days after the date you bought it, they will give you a new phone. On day 10 after you bought the phone, the phone freezes and you cannot get it to work. The suppliers tell you that they will send your phone to be repaired and that they cannot give you a new phone. Discuss whether you think the suppliers are correct.

3.2.6.1 Unordered goods

unordered goods do not have to be returned

The CPA provides that consumers may not be charged for unordered ('unsolicited') goods that are sent to them. The consumer may (but does not have to) return unordered goods or services to the suppliers at their risk and expense. If the consumer wishes to send the goods back he or she can write 'Return to sender' on the unopened package or envelope and post it back to the supplier. If the consumer decides not to send it back where the supplier informs him or her that it was sent by mistake, the consumer is entitled to keep the unordered goods or services after 20 business days if the supplier does not collect it before then. The duty is on the supplier to collect the goods, not on the consumer to send them back.

Problem 8: The case of the unwanted books

Questions

Divide into groups of not more than five. Read the case study below and decide whether the books must be paid for:

The Reader's Friend sends you a set of books that you have not ordered. Included in the package is a letter that says if you keep the books longer than 10 business days you will be responsible for paying the price of the books into the bank account of The Reader's Friend and if you do not wish to keep the books you must return the books to The Reader's Friend within 10 days of receiving the books. Discuss whether The Reader's Friend can claim the money for the books from you if you do not send the books back.

3.2.7 The right to be given information

The right to information includes the right to:

1. Be told the price of goods and services;
2. Be given information in plain and understandable language;
3. Have products properly labelled;

4. Be told whether goods are 'grey goods' (ie goods without a manufacturer's guarantee or warranty) or reconditioned;
5. Receive receipts or invoices for things bought; and
6. Information about who go-betweens ('intermediaries'), agents and brokers are representing.

3.2.7.1 Information about the price of goods and services

the price of goods and services must be displayed

The CPA makes sure that consumers know the prices of goods and services. The prices of goods and services must be shown to consumers. A seller is not allowed to put out any goods for sale without showing the price of those goods. A price is properly shown if a written label containing the price is attached to the goods. It will also be sufficient if the price is in a catalogue (ie a magazine advertising the goods), and the catalogue is made available to the consumer.

if two prices are shown consumers can demand the lower price

If a person is buying something that has more than one part or unit, he or she may ask what the price of each part or unit is. If a consumer asks about the unit cost he or she will make sure that he or she avoids any hidden costs. The supplier must say how long any promotion that is advertised will last. If a brochure or catalogue does not say how long the promotion will last, the consumer may insist on buying the goods or services at the advertised price. Where the supplier shows two different prices, the consumer can demand to pay the lower price.

3.2.7.2 The right to information in plain and understandable language

not all contracts have to be in writing

The CPA makes sure that contracts that are in writing use plain and understandable writing. There is no general rule that contracts have to be in writing. It is possible to enter into a contract verbally (by speaking). Where contracts are made in writing the contracts must be in plain and easily understandable language. For it to be in plain language the ordinary consumer for whom the contract is intended, with average literacy skills and little experience as a consumer of goods or services, must be able to understand the words in the contract. This means that difficult lawyer's language must be removed from contracts and replaced with language that an ordinary person will understand. An example of a plain language sentence would be: 'If I break any of my promises in this document, you can demand that I immediately pay everything that I owe'.

3.2.7.3 Product labelling

may not change, hide, remove or damage trademarks and other product labelling

The CPA protects consumers against misleading labelling and makes sure that they are given sufficient information in labels on products. The supplier may not mislead the consumers about the contents of the packaging or goods attached to the products (eg regarding the ingredients of juices or food). Suppliers and service providers must show the name of the producer and the product's number and make sure things are labelled. Suppliers are not allowed to change, hide, remove or damage trademarks and other product labelling. Imported goods must show the country of origin and other information such as expiry dates.

indicate 'genetically modified' ingredients

Producers, suppliers and importers are required to show the presence of any 'genetically modified' ingredients. For example, plants are genetically modified if farmers add a foreign 'gene' (eg part of another plant) to the plants. A gene is something in plants or animals (including humans) that decides how they will develop as they grow. Foreign genes are usually used to improve or correct defects in plants or animals (eg a farmer might add a foreign gene to tomato plants to make ripened tomatoes last a long time without becoming soft).

state country of origin

The labels on textiles, shoes, clothing and leather goods must state clearly the country in which they were made, produced or put together. If a product is made locally using imported material the labels must say: 'Made in South Africa from imported materials'. If goods were put together or made in South Africa the labels must state 'Made in South Africa'.

It is important to understand the different date stamps that appear on food, especially the 'use by' and 'best by' date stamps.

date stamps

a 'use by' date

People or firms that make food must put date stamps on their food. Certain foods do not have to have a date stamp (eg honey, unprocessed and unpacked meat such as fresh meat in a butchery, fresh fruit and vegetables, vinegar and sweets). Foods with a limited 'shelf-life' (ie foods that will go bad if they are not used soon after being bought) or foods that can cause food poisoning if not stored correctly must carry a 'use by' date. A 'use by' date means the date by which the food must be used, otherwise it will not be healthy to use it. It is illegal to sell, re-label or donate any food that has passed its 'use by' date.

a 'best before' date

Food that has a longer shelf-life must have a 'best before' date on it. A 'best before' date shows the date when it is best to eat the food. The food can still be eaten after the 'best before' date as long as it is not used after the 'use by' date. It is not illegal for a shopkeeper to keep these products on the shelf after the 'best before' date, as long as it is before the 'use by' date. However, keeping products on the shelf after they have reached the 'best before' date is not recommended.

Problem 9: Did the shopkeepers break the law?

Questions

Divide into groups of not more than five. Discuss the following:

1. You go to the supermarket and pick up a carton of orange juice. The label says that it is 100% pure orange juice. When you read the ingredients you notice that the juice contains orange and apple juice and some preservatives. Discuss whether you think the orange juice is correctly labelled.
2. You go to Discount Sweets. On the shelf you find chocolates. The 'best before' date on the chocolates is three months ago. The 'use by' date will be in one month's time. Discuss whether you think that the shopkeeper has done anything wrong by keeping chocolates on the shelf after their 'best before' date.

3.2.7.4 'Grey' or reconditioned goods

not imported by official suppliers

The CPA protects consumers against being misled about 'grey' goods. Companies in foreign countries may allow a company in South Africa to be the official importer of their goods to South Africa. 'Grey goods' are foreign goods that are imported by a supplier in South Africa which is not the official importer and supplier appointed by the foreign company. These goods are not illegal. However, if grey goods are brought into the country, the official supplier in South Africa appointed by the foreign company will refuse to recognise the warranty or guarantee that usually goes with the goods. A supplier who sells 'grey goods' must advertise and show that the goods are being imported without the approval or licence of the registered trade mark owner (eg the foreign company that made the goods).

advertisements must indicate 'grey' or reconditioned goods

Where 'grey' goods have been reconditioned, rebuilt or remade, suppliers must put up a notice explaining this so that it can be clearly seen by all consumers. Notices must be put on the goods and advertisements where consumers are likely to see them. The notice must be of a size that can be easily seen by consumers. If consumers buy 'grey' or reconditioned goods the supplier must explain to them what it means and must draw their attention to the notice appearing on the goods.

3.2.7.5 Receipts and invoices for things bought

Consumers have the right to demand receipts or invoices for all goods or services bought by them.

3.2.7.6 Information about go-betweens ('intermediaries') such as brokers, sales representatives and estate agents

The CPA requires 'intermediaries' to give consumers certain information. 'Intermediaries', such as brokers, sales representatives and estate agents are required to tell the consumer whom they represent. An 'intermediary' is someone consumers may demand 'identification'

who acts as a 'go-between' and links people together (eg estate agents link sellers and buyers of houses). People who deliver goods or services or who install things must wear a name badge or identification. Consumers may demand identification from the deliverers, installers and others, before allowing them to deliver or install goods or products.

Problem 10: Something to do in your community

Questions

1. Go to your favourite clothing or shoe shop. Study the label on a piece of clothing or on the box of a pair of shoes. Explain if the label contains the information required by the Consumer Protection Act.
2. Go to a furniture or electronic appliance shop and inquire if they supply 'grey' goods.

3.2.8 The right to fair and responsible marketing

The right to fair and responsible marketing involves topics such as protection against:
1. False and misleading advertising;
2. 'Bait' marketing;
3. Fake 'free' offers;
4. Misleading claims in catalogues;
5. Misleading promotional offers;
6. Unsupported customer loyalty programmes;
7. Misleading promotional competitions; and
8. 'Referral' selling.

3.2.8.1 False and misleading advertising

The CPA prohibits the use of false and misleading advertising.

advertisements affect consumers greatly

Advertising has a great effect on the behaviour of consumers. Advertisements make consumers want the products advertised. They tell consumers what to eat, how to dress, where to travel, when to shop, how to look, how to feel better, etc.

Problem 11: Some questions about advertisements

Questions

1. Give an example of an advertisement you have seen or heard that appeals to you. Why does it appeal to you? Would you buy the thing advertised? Give reasons for your answer.

2. Give an example of an advertisement you have seen or heard that you think is unhelpful, confusing, or misleading. What is wrong with the advertisement? Would you buy the thing advertised? Give reasons for your answer.

useful advertisements

Some advertisements are useful, for example, those that tell consumers about new goods or services, or provide useful information about the things advertised. The main purpose of advertisements, however, is to sell things. While advertisements can be helpful, they can also be misleading and confusing.

Certain advertisements mislead by saying things that do not tell consumers much about the product or service. In a few cases, advertisements tell lies. Others try to make consumers buy things they do not really need or want. Many advertisements play with our feelings, rather than give us useful factual information.

many advertisements play with our feelings

an 'invitation to do business'

According to our law an advertisement is an 'invitation to do business' rather than an offer to sell something at the price advertised. This means that at common law you cannot sue a shop that advertises goods at one price and then tells you that the price is wrong or that it has run out of stock. (Reputable shops, however, do not do this. They will say in their advertisement 'for as long as stocks last' or give the number of things the shop has for sale.)

false or misleading advertisments

A false advertisement is one that does not tell the truth. A misleading advertisement is one that confuses or misleads consumers. False and misleading advertisements may be reported to the local inspector at the Department of Trade and Industry. A consumer may have a common-law action for damages if an advertisement fraudulently makes him or her lose money. Consumers suing for fraudulent misrepresentation must show that the seller intentionally cheated them. The Advertising Standards Authority may stop advertisements that are false or misleading. It may also make advertisers change their advertisements.

3.2.8.2 Puffing

obvious exaggeration is legal

Sometimes what seems to be a misleading advertisement is really 'puffing'. 'Puffing' is a type of advertising that is an exception to the rule about misleading advertising. 'Puffing' refers to advertisements that are based on the seller's opinion or taste, or some obvious exaggeration. They are called puffing because the advertisers 'puff up' their products (eg 'the Scimitar is the best car in the world'). It is sometimes difficult to see the difference between false and misleading advertisements and puffing. Therefore consumers should examine advertisements carefully. If an advertisement is merely an opinion or obvious exaggeration, it is puffing and legal. If, however, it appears to be factual, and is false or misleading, it is illegal.

Problem 12: Is the advertisement puffing or false and misleading?

Questions

Decide whether the following, if untrue, are false or misleading advertisements or merely puffing:

1. 'Hand-sewn dresses', which are machine sewn.
2. 'Henry's famous hamburgers'
3. 'Jump higher, run longer with Jaguar Jogging shoes.'
4. 'Lose two to five kilograms in a week or less with Body-Less.'

buying things we don't really need

The problem for many consumers is not that they are misled by false or misleading advertisements, but that they are influenced to buy things they do not really want or need. Many of these advertisements appeal to people's feelings or emotions. For example, some advertisements connect the things advertised with popular images such as the family, motherhood, wealth and sex appeal. They are aimed at persuading consumers that buying the product will make them similar to the person in the advertisement.

the art of persuading customers

The different methods used include the following:

1. The 'bandwagon' approach: everybody buys it, so you should too.
2. The 'celebrity' appeal: famous people use it, so you should too.
3. The 'expert' approach: professional people recommend it, so it must be good.
4. 'Seeing is believing': ordinary people use it successfully; so should you.
5. Advertisements that make you feel happy or good: when you want to feel good you will think of the product.

most consumers buy well-known brands

Some advertisers do not care what information consumers have about their products. They just want consumers to buy their brand or make. They know that most consumers buy well-known brands, even though local or shop brands may cost less and be of the same quality.

Whatever methods are used, consumers should learn to separate the product from the people and images used in the advertisements.

Problem 13: To whom do the advertisements appeal?

Questions

Read and examine each of the following advertisements and decide:

1. Which method of making people buy the product is used in each advertisement?
2. What important information is missing from each advertisement?
3. To whom is the advertisement trying to appeal: children, adults, women, men, or other people?

3.2.8.3 Bait marketing

'Bait' marketing occurs when a person enters a shop to buy something that it advertised as cheap but is then persuaded to buy something more expensive.

the advertised product is not available

The CPA prohibits the use of bait marketing. Bait marketing is when a supplier advertises something and when the consumer arrives at the shop, the advertised product is not available. The supplier then tries to persuade the consumer to buy something else.

'loss leaders' are not illegal

'Bait and switch' is a commonly used technique, especially in stores selling items such as major electrical appliances, radio equipment or television sets. The line between aggressive selling and 'bait and switch' is not always clear. Shops often advertise 'loss leaders'. These are items advertised at low prices in order to attract customers to the shop. Loss leaders are not illegal. In addition a salesperson that merely shows a customer a better quality, more expensive item, is not necessarily engaged in 'bait and switch'. However, when the seller either purposely exaggerates the faults in the cheaper product, or has no stock of the advertised item and tries to switch the customer to higher priced goods, 'bait and switch' is present.

'bait and switch' may be subtle

Selling techniques using 'bait and switch' may be subtle. For example, in the United States a major television appliance store had inexpensive black and white sets (that had been advertised as bait) badly connected to provide a less clear picture. The more expensive sets to which customers were switched had clear pictures and were placed in a comfortable viewing room.

consumers are vulnerable

Bait and switch methods give sellers a strong advantage over consumers who are not on their guard. Consumers are already in the shop and expecting to buy something. If they are disappointed with the bait product, consumers are unlikely to go out and examine prices at other shops. They are likely to stay in the shop and buy something else. A shop that uses bait and switch methods may be prosecuted for misleading advertising, but this may be difficult to prove.

suppliers may not mislead

Suppliers are not allowed to mislead consumers regarding pricing, the nature, properties, advantages or uses of goods or services advertised if such goods or services are not actually available for buying or ordering.

Suppliers are obliged to mention any limitations or conditions regarding the availability of goods or services when advertising such items, and must honour them.

Problem 14: The case of the TV switch

Mr and Mrs Brown see an advertisement in a newspaper that says: 'Come to Flare for the cheapest flat screen LCD TVs in town'. The salespeople in the shop have been told to try selling a flat screen LED TV to every customer who calls in after seeing the advertisement. If consumers do not want the LED flat screen TVs, the sales staff should try to sell the more expensive LCD TV before showing the customer the cheaper advertised model.

Questions

1. Role-play a conversation between Mr and Mrs Brown and one of the salespeople.
2. Have you ever experienced a situation like this? If so, how did you handle it?
3. What are the advantages and disadvantages for shops of this type of selling?

3.2.8.4 Fake 'free' offers

'free' samples used to make consumers buy more

The CPA prohibits the use of fake 'free' offers. Fake 'free' offers happen when a supplier offers a consumer a 'free' sample of something and then assumes that the consumer will keep buying more of it unless the consumer says he or she does not want it. For example, a pharmaceutical company may offer a consumer a 'free sample' of their new diet product. In order to receive the 'free sample' the consumer must provide the supplier with their credit card details. In the fine print it says that if the consumer does not return the free sample within 30 days the consumer agrees to receive a monthly order of the product and that the pharmaceutical company may automatically take money from the consumer's bank account each month.

Suppliers are not allowed to use fake 'free' offers to promote any goods or services or make consumers automatically enter into agreements for the supply of goods or services.

3.2.8.5 Buying goods from a catalogue

The CPA controls the buying of goods from catalogues, which takes place when consumers order goods by telephone, fax or postal order after looking through a catalogues may not mislead

catalogue. Catalogues may not be misleading and must include information about the supplier as well as how the goods will be delivered; the cancellation, return, exchange and refund policies of the supplier; and how complaints can be made.

Problem 15: The case of the wrong racquet sent by mail order

Garp orders a tennis racquet from a mail order house which advertises things for sale in its catalogue. The advertisement includes a photograph of a metal tennis racquet. Two weeks later Garp receives a wooden racquet in the post.

Role-play a telephone conversation beween Garp and the manager of the mail order house when Garp telephones to complain about receiving a wooden racquet.

Garp complains over the telephone when he receives a wooden racquet by mail order instead of a metal one

3.2.8.6 Promotional offers

people may not make false promotional offers

The CPA controls the use of 'promotional offers'. A promotional offer is an offer or promise of any prize, reward, gift, free goods or services, reduction in price or concession (eg a benefit) whether or not the person accepting the offer has to enter into an agreement to buy something. An example of a promotional offer is where consumers are required to collect sets of coupons or stamps which, once complete, can be used to collect a reward. People may not make promotional offers with the intention of not fulfilling them or fulfilling them in a different way from what was originally offered.

Problem 16: The case of the wrong bicycle

Harry reads about a 'special offer' for a 'Chief' bicycle in the newspaper. He rushes to Ron's Speed Shop but the bicycle is out of stock. The shop, however, promises to deliver the bicycle to Harry's house the following week if he pays the price of R800 in advance. Harry pays the money and a week later the bicycle arrives. When Harry unpacks the bicycle he sees that it is a 'Chuffer' instead of a 'Chief'.

Questions

1. Is there anything Harry could have done differently when he paid for the bicycle?
2. What steps do you think Harry should have taken after discovering the mistake? Role-play Harry complaining to Ron.
3. If this happened in your community, and Ron's Speed Shop refused to exchange the bicycle, who could Harry contact for help?

Harry orders a 'Chief' bicycle he sees in a catalogue – but when the bicycle is delivered it is a 'Chuffer'

3.2.8.7 'Customer loyalty programmes'

reward for buying things from the same supplier

The CPA controls the use of 'customer loyalty programmes' that reward consumers for buying things, very often from the same person or business. Consumers are offered points, discounts, coupons, etc. in exchange for agreeing to join in the programme. An example of a customer loyalty programme is an airline's 'frequent flyer' programme that rewards its passengers with free 'miles' every time they fly with the airline. Once passengers have collected sufficient 'miles' they can exchange them for discounted flights, even though they will have to pay the airport taxes and a carrier charge on the tickets. Another example is where a shop gives consumers a card that looks like a credit card. Every time the consumers buy something, their card is 'swiped' and they earn points. The points can be used later to get a discount on things bought in future from the same shop.

When suppliers offer loyalty programmes they must be able to provide what was offered.

3.2.8.8 'Promotional competitions'

The CPA strictly controls the use of 'promotional competitions' that are used to create an interest in a product or service. A 'promotional competition' is any competition, game, scheme, arrangement, system, plan or method of distributing held during the usual business of supplier

prizes by consumers drawing lots or taking chances (eg like a lucky dip). The competition must be held during the usual business of the supplier in order to promote a producer, distributor, supplier or the sale of any goods or services. It does not matter whether a person in the competition has to show any skill or ability before being awarded a prize.

no fee for participation

Prizes may include gifts, rewards, free goods or services, a reduction in price, increasing the quantity or quality of goods or services or another discounted or free thing. People who participate in promotional competitions may not be required to pay, either directly or indirectly, for their participation. The participant may also not be asked to buy goods and services at a price that is more than what is usually charged. If the competition requires the participants to enter the competition electronically (eg by sending an SMS to a given number) the cost of electronically transmitting the entry cannot be more than R1,50. People who participate in a competition must be given a chance to refuse to have their photographs used for marketing or to be present at the draw for the prizes.

refuse to have photos used

Problem 17: The competition to win a car

Honest Joe's Cars launch a competition with the main prize being a luxury Scimitar C200. Participants can enter the competition by sending an SMS with their full names and surname to 34277. The rules state that the SMS entry will cost R10 and free SMSes do not apply.

Discuss whether you think this competition complies with the Consumer Protection Act.

3.2.8.9 'Referral selling'

giving name of other consumers

The CPA protects consumers against 'referral selling'. 'Referral selling' happens when suppliers ask consumers to give them the names of other consumers in exchange for some benefit. The CPA states that a supplier may not offer a person a discount on goods or services on condition the person provides the supplier with the names of other consumers.

3.2.9 The right to fair and honest dealing

The CPA ensures that consumers have protection against unfair and dishonest dealing such as:

1. Unacceptable behaviour;
2. False and misleading representations;
3. Fraudulent schemes and offers;
4. Pyramid, Ponzi, multiplication and other fraudulent schemes;
5. Substituted goods being used to change terms of agreements of sale; and
6. Over-selling and over-booking.

3.2.9.1 Unacceptable behaviour

no assaulting or harassing of consumers

The CPA protects consumers against unacceptable behaviour that is unfair and unethical. A person is not allowed to behave in a way that is unreasonable or unacceptable (eg unethical). Suppliers must not assault consumers, put pressure on them, harass them or use unfair tactics to sell goods or services to them. Nor may they use these methods to force consumers to buy anything, to collect payments owing for goods or services or to get back goods sold.

debt collectors may not threaten consumers with violence to force them to pay their debts

no taking advantage of vulnerable people

In addition it would be unacceptable for a supplier to knowingly take advantage of the fact that a person has a physical or mental disability or is illiterate, ignorant or unable to understand the language in an agreement. It is also unacceptable to take advantage of vulnerable people such as children, old people and those who are sick.

3.2.9.2 False or misleading representations

no misleading or tricking of consumers

The CPA protects consumers against false or misleading statements by suppliers. Suppliers may not mislead or try to trick consumers. They may not use confusing or misleading statements when referring to goods or services or their benefits. Consumers have the right to assume that suppliers have the legal right or authority to supply or lease goods or products that are on sale or promoted by the suppliers.

Problem 18: Were the representations false or misleading?

1. Debra buys a dress after telling the shop assistant that she plans to wash it in a washing machine. The shop assistant replies: 'That's fine. The material

can be washed any way you like.' The dress shrinks after being washed in a washing machine. It would not have shrunk if it had been washed by hand. Debra complains to the shop assistant.

(a) Role-play a conversation between Debra and the shop assistant when Debra complains.

(b) Was the representation by the shop assistant false and misleading?

Debra's dress shrinks after being washed in a washing machine

2. Ivan, a shop assistant, tells Buti: 'This is the best camera on the market. It will last for years.' Six months later the lens falls out and breaks because it is faulty. Buti complains to Ivan.

   (a) Role-play a conversation between Buti and Ivan when Buti complains.

   (b) Was the representation by Ivan false and misleading?

the lens falls out of Buti's camera and breaks six months after he bought it

3.2.9.3 Fraudulent schemes and offers

producing fake money

The CPA ensures that people cannot harm consumers by knowingly doing things with the intention of defrauding others. No one may produce fake money or say that they can increase a sum of money, through scientific or other ways. People may also not knowingly become involved in fraudulent or unlawful financial dealings.

3.2.9.4 Pyramid, Ponzi, multiplication and other fraudulent schemes

The CPA protects consumers against pyramid, Ponzi, multiplication and other fraudulent schemes.

3.2.9.4.1 Pyramid schemes

A pyramid scheme is where a person makes one payment as an initial investment and is paid compensation for the recruitment of other participants. The investor is paid from money that is invested by people that he or she has recruited.

'excellent returns' – more than banks give

Pyramid schemes are a type of consumer abuse that happens often in South Africa. Usually, a person tells consumers that, if they invest money in the business, they will receive excellent returns. For example, consumers are told that if they invest money they will receive double their money back the next week or that they will receive a higher interest rate than the rate that investors would get from a bank. People are attracted to this because the returns are far greater than those given by normal banks. In addition, at the beginning, the person in charge usually does give consumers the excellent returns promised. This encourages more people to get involved, and encourages people to put money back into the scheme.

the person in charge disappears

In order to sustain these schemes new members have to be recruited continuously. However, the scheme cannot go on forever because the business will eventually not be able to pay money back to everyone involved. Usually, once a lot of money has been put into the scheme, the person in charge disappears with the money. Those people who had money in the scheme when the business disappeared lose out, often with devastating consequences for them and their families. Only a few people benefit, namely those who put money in at the beginning and never again. It is obvious that this is not worth the risk.

Tips to avoid a pyramid scheme:

1. Avoid any plan that offers to reward you if you recruit new members.
2. Beware of promises about high profits or claims about miracle products.
3. Beware of any promise to double or treble your money.
4. Be careful of claims that you will make more money by recruiting new members instead of the sales you make.
5. Don't pay money or sign contracts in high-pressure situations.

1
10
100
1 000
10 000
100 000
1 000 000
10 000 000

3.2.9.4.2 Ponzi schemes

promise of unrealistically high returns

A Ponzi scheme is where a person hands over a sum of money and is promised unrealistically high returns on the investment with little or no risk taken by the investor. A person investing in a Ponzi scheme is not required to find new investors but is paid from money received from persons investing later. In a Ponzi scheme the investor is not told that their payments will come from the money invested by new investors.

3.2.9.4.3 Multiplication schemes

high interest rates

A multiplication scheme is where the supplier offers the investor interest rates of 20% and above the South African Reserve Bank's regulated repo rate.

3.2.9.4.4 Chain letter schemes

re-selling advice

A chain letter scheme is a direct or electronic mail promotion that sells advice on how to make money by simply re-selling that advice to other people.

How a chain letter works

1. A friend sends you a letter in the mail that contains the names and addresses of 10 people.
2. The friend informs you in the letter to send R10 to each of the first five people on the list.
3. You are then instructed to delete the name and information of no 1 on the list and to add yourself as number 10.
4. Thereafter you must mail the new list to 10 friends.
5. By the time you become number 5 on the list there will be thousands of people each sending you R10.

The CPA prohibits persons from participating in these schemes or any other fraudulent schemes or scams.

Problem 19: Arno and his pension package

Questions

Arno is 56 years old. He has worked at the Post Office for 38 years. At the end of the month he is retiring. He will be receiving a pension pay-out of R300 000. He does not know what to do with the money. He is offered the following choices:

1. He has been banking with Lebowa Bank for the last 25 years. They offer to put his money in the money market. He will be paid monthly interest of 8%.
2. The People's Trust investment business approaches him and promises that if he invests the money with them they will treble his money in 42 days, provided he brings them 10 more investors.
   - (a) Role-play a meeting between Arno and the representative from the investment business.
   - (b) Where do you think Arno should invest his money?

3.2.9.4.5 Substitution of goods

protection against substituted goods or services

The CPA protects consumers against suppliers who substitute goods or services by requiring the suppliers to treat these as changes to existing agreements and not as grounds to enter into new agreements. Suppliers must deliver to consumers amended sales agreements or records, describing the substituted goods, without making other changes to the original agreements or records (eg by changing the price).

3.2.9.4.6 Over-selling and over-booking

protection against over-selling and over-booking

The CPA also protects consumers against over-selling and over-booking. Suppliers are required to honour the supply of goods or services regarding the dates, times and other particulars mentioned in reservations or bookings. Where suppliers do not honour such dates, times and other commitments, consumers may demand refunds for full amounts paid for such commitments or reservations, together with interest, at fixed rates, from the dates of payment until they get their money back.

Problem 20: 'Sorry ma'am, the flight has been over-booked'

Divide into groups of not more than five and discuss the following case study:

A woman is flying to Johannesburg from Cape Town to attend her son's wedding. When she tries to check in at the airport the airline staff member says to her: 'Sorry ma'am, the flight is over-booked'.

1. What can the woman do?
2. What should the airline do?

3.2.10 The right to fair, just and reasonable terms and conditions

terms must not be unfair, unjust or unreasonable

The right to fair, just and reasonable terms and conditions means that they must not be unfair, unreasonable or unjust. The CPA states that suppliers may not force consumers to agree to terms and conditions that are unfair, unreasonable or unjust.

written notice of risks

Before a consumer enters into an agreement the suppliers must give the person written notice of clauses in the agreement that affect the supplier's liability to the consumer. The effects of these risks to the consumer must be drawn to their attention in a way that they can easily be seen by the consumer and the consumer must accept them.

free copies of agreements

Consumers are entitled to get free copies or free electronic access to copies of agreements, even if they have not yet entered into such agreements. The free copies should include a breakdown of the financial obligations of consumers under the agreement. Where the agreements are not in writing, suppliers must still keep proper records of them.

3.2.10.1 Examples of unfair, unjust or unreasonable terms and conditions in agreements and contracts

The CPA states that suppliers are not allowed to include terms and conditions in agreements that:

prohibited terms and conditions

1. Are against what the CPA says must be done by suppliers;
2. Mislead or deceive consumers;
3. Make consumers accept fraudulent behaviour by the supplier;
4. Directly or indirectly take away the rights of consumers provided for in the CPA;
5. Take away the suppliers' obligations or duties in terms of the CPA;
6. Limit or exempt suppliers of goods or services from liability for any loss, directly or indirectly due to the gross negligence of the suppliers or anyone acting for or controlled by the suppliers;
7. Make consumers carry the risk of any losses;
8. Make consumers pay for damage to goods on display, even if there is no fault by them;
9. Force consumers to enter into additional agreements;
10. Force consumers to falsely state that before the agreement was made, no representations or warranties were made by the supplier or anyone on behalf of the supplier; or
11. Force consumers to lose any money paid to the supplier when the law says they can get the money back.

certain conditions must be pointed out

A term or condition in a contract will be unfair if it is very one-sided in favour of anyone except the consumer. The CPA states that the supplier must point out certain notices and terms and conditions of contracts to consumers before a contract is entered into and before the consumer is expected to pay anything.

Problem 21: 'The fantastic Firebird'

Javu goes to Shifty's Car Sales to a buy a Firebird sports car. A salesperson shows him a Firebird and says: 'This fantastic Firebird is a bargain. There is absolutely nothing wrong with it. You will never find a better second-hand Firebird anywhere.' Javu buys the car on credit and signs a credit agreement. He pays a deposit of R3 000 and agrees to pay the balance in monthly instalments of R2 000 over 24 months.

The credit agreement has the following clause:

'The purchaser hereby acknowledges that he has carefully inspected the car, that he purchases it as it stands, and that the owner gave no warranties nor made any representations whatever as to the condition or performance of the car'.

1. Role-play the salesperson selling the car to Javu, and Javu signing the agreement.
2. If something goes wrong with the car could the salesperson say that Javu is bound by the clause? Why or why not?

Javu signs a credit agreement to buy the fantastic Firebird

investigation or court action

Consumers who are unhappy about unfair, unjust or unreasonable terms and conditions in contracts or agreements may ask the National Consumer Tribunal to investigate. If they are not satisfied with the result of the National Consumer Tribunal's investigation into unreasonable, unjust or unfair behaviour by the suppliers, they may bring an action in court.

3.2.11 The right to fair value, quality and safety

The CPA states that consumers have a right to fair value, quality and safety, which includes the right to:

1. Demand quality service;
2. Safe, good quality goods;
3. An implied warranty of quality;
4. A warranty on repaired goods;
5. Receive warnings about risks;
6. Make suppliers get rid of waste that cannot be thrown away as ordinary garbage or rubbish; and
7. Have products monitored for safety or to be recalled.

3.2.11.1 The right to demand quality service

service on time

According to the CPA the right to quality service means that services should be provided on time and if not, consumers should be given reasonable notice of any unavoidable delays. Consumers are entitled to expect high quality services and that the use, delivery or installation of goods will be free of defects.

refund for sub-standard services

Suppliers must make good any defects in the quality of services performed or goods supplied. Otherwise they must refund the consumers a reasonable amount of the price paid for sub-standard services performed and sub-standard goods supplied.

the CPA protects the right of consumers to demand quality service

3.2.11.2 The right to safe, good quality goods

Consumers are entitled to receive goods or services that are of good quality, in good working order and free of any defects, and that comply with any applicable standards (eg like those from the South African Bureau of Standards (SABS)).

3.2.11.3 The right to an implied warranty of quality

goods to be returned within 6 months of delivery

The producer or importer, distributor and retailer (ie everyone involved as suppliers) each warrant (guarantee) that the goods comply with the required standards and are safe, of good quality and durable (long lasting). Consumers are allowed to return goods to suppliers, without penalty and at the suppliers' risk and expense, within six months after delivery of the goods, if the goods are not of good quality, unsafe or defective. Suppliers must refund, repair or replace the failed, unsafe and defective goods.

goods to be replaced within 3 months after repairs

Suppliers must replace goods or refund the consumer the price paid for the goods within three months after repairs have been done, if the repaired goods are found to be defective, have failed or are unsafe.

Problem 22: What should the buyer and seller do?

Divide into groups of not more than five and decide what the buyer and seller should do in the following cases:

1. Trusty's Second Hand Cars sells Vos a used car for R50 000. On his way home the brakes fail. Luckily Vos does not have an accident. It will cost Vos R2 000 to have the brakes fixed.
2. Natie buys a 'whistling kettle' from Sally's Supermarket for R300. The kettle is supposed to whistle when water boils. Natie puts the kettle on the stove. After 10 minutes the water boils but the kettle does not whistle. A kettle that does not whistle would cost R200.

3.2.11.4 The right to a warranty on repaired goods

Suppliers must guarantee the parts and labour used to repair goods for three months after the date of repair, or a longer period if the supplier states this in writing.

suppliers must guarantee the parts and labour used to repair goods

Guarantees will not apply if consumers are found to be misusing or abusing goods or property, while under the guarantee.

3.2.11.5 The right to receive warnings about risks

unusual risks

Suppliers must tell consumers about any unusual risks or risks that consumers would not expect, as well as risks that could result in serious injury or death.

dangerous goods

Labelling on products must warn consumers about any dangerous or unsafe goods, and provide the consumers with adequate instructions for the safe handling and use of those goods.

3.2.11.6 The right to make suppliers get rid of waste that cannot be thrown away as ordinary garbage or rubbish

Suppliers are responsible for accepting and getting rid of waste that is unsuitable for being thrown away as ordinary garbage or rubbish in terms of the law (eg expired medicines bought at a pharmacy).

3.2.11.7 The right to have products monitored for safety and recalled

recall of dangerous goods

Certain industries have provisions in their codes for the return or recall of dangerous, unsafe or defective goods. Consumers have the right to expect that the relevant industries will monitor their products for safety and where necessary ensure that consumers are warned and dangerous products are recalled (eg when cars have dangerous defects the manufacturers must recall them).

3.2.12 Strict liability for harm caused to consumers

The CPA provides that any producer, importer, distributor or retailer of a good is strictly liable for any harm caused wholly or partly as a result of (a) supplying any unsafe goods; (b) a product failure, defect or danger in any goods; or (c) inadequate instructions or warnings provided to the consumer regarding any danger linked to the use of such goods.

They are liable to consumers even if there is no negligence by them – except if:

(a) They were following a government law or regulation;
(b) The defect or danger was not in the product at the time that it was supplied;
(c) Another person is liable (eg a manufacturer);
(d) The person selling the product was following the instructions of the person who provided them with the goods – the last person would then be liable; or
(e) The claim for damages is brought more than three years after the death or injury of the person harmed;

The CPA provides that the harm for which a person may be liable to a consumer includes: (a) the death or injury of any person; (b) an illness of any person; (c) any loss or physical damage to any property – movable or immovable (eg a house); or (d) any other monetary loss suffered by the consumer as a result of the above. Consumers must bring their action within three years.

Problem 23: Can the consumer claim damages?

Divide into groups of not more than five and decide whether the consumer in each case can recover damages.

1. Mrs Tshabalala buys boerewors from a butchery. She suffers food poisoning after cooking and eating the boerewors. As a result she has to visit a doctor and is off work for two days. Mrs Tshabalala complains to the butcher.

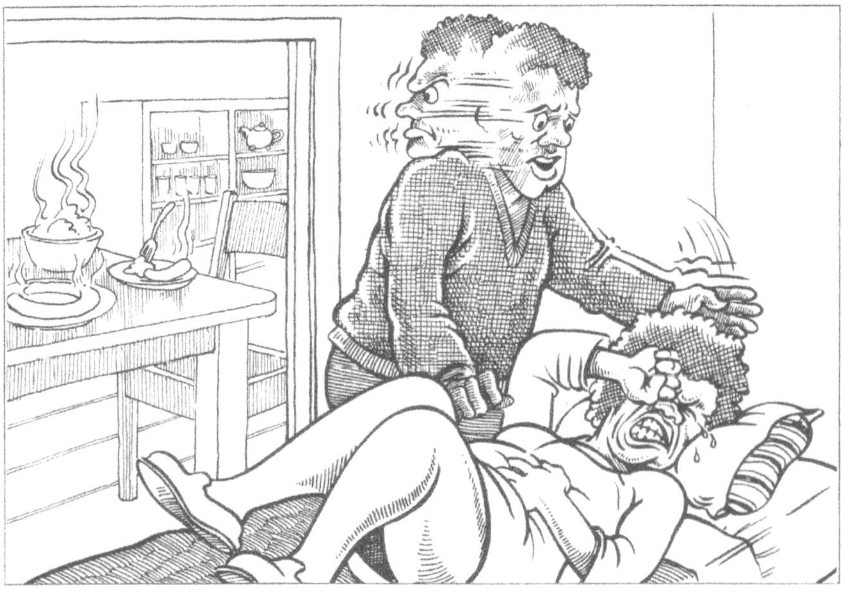

Mrs Tshabalala suffers food poisoning after eating some boerewors

2. Mr Smit buys an electric drill from Jerry's General Store. When he switches on the drill he is electrocuted and has to go to hospital for a week. He is off work for a further week. Mr Smit complains to the manager of Jerry's General Store.

When Mr Smit switches on the drill he is electrocuted

3. Mrs Nair buys a new sofa from Queen's Quality Furnishers. When she sits on the sofa it collapses. Mrs Nair is not injured but her tea set worth R1 000 is broken. The tea set was on the coffee table next to the sofa. Mrs Nair complains to the owner of Queen's Quality Furnishers.

Mrs Nair's new sofa collapses, causing her R1 000 tea set to be broken

3.2.13 Payments in advance

The CPA provides protection for consumers who pay in advance for goods and services such as in the case of:

1. prepaid certificates, credits and vouchers;
2. prepaid services; and
3. lay-bys.

3.2.13.1 Prepaid certificates, credits and vouchers

protection for consumers buying goods or services in advance

The CPA protects consumers where suppliers accept payment from them in exchange for a prepaid certificate, card, credit, voucher or similar device and agree to provide goods or services to anyone who presents the prepaid certificate, care, voucher or similar device. An example is where people can buy prepaid electricity cards. (However in such cases a prepaid electricity meter would first have to be installed in the consumer's home.)

> **Note:** Municipalities that are not metropolitan municipalities have been exempted from complying with the provisions of the Consumer Protection Act.

Any money on a prepaid certificate remains the property of the person who possesses the certificate until it has been exchanged for goods or services.

expires when used or after 3 years

A prepaid certificate, card, voucher or credit will only expire on the date on which its full value has been used for goods or services. If the full amount has not been used it will expire three years after the date on which it was issued or a longer period that the supplier has agreed to.

conflicting rules seem to apply to mobile phones

In respect of mobile phone contracts there is a conflict between the Consumer Commission's interpretation of section 63 and the interpretation of Cellular Service Providers. The National Consumer Commission is of the view that the prepaid data and airtime credited to a consumer must only expire when they are used up, or after three years from the date on which the prepaid data value is credited to the consumer. The mobile phone companies claim that when customers purchase data bundles, funds are deducted from their airtime in return for access to data bundles. So they are deemed to have exchanged the value of their prepaid airtime for access to data bundles. The companies claim that there is a difference between a voucher and a product bought by that voucher and that the three-year expiry rule refers to vouchers and not to products purchased with vouchers. This difference of interpretation has not been cleared up. The National Consumer Commission is still in discussion with service providers. Since there is a difference in the interpretation, the Consumer Tribunal or the courts should be approached by a consumer organisation for a ruling on the interpretation of section 63.

Problem 24: Buying a prepaid 1 gig data bundle

A consumer buys a prepaid 1 gig data bundle from her service provider. She receives the following message: 'Your account has been successfully recharged. Your data bundle will expire on the last day of the next calendar month'.

Discuss in groups of not more than five whether this is in line with the CPA.

3.2.13.2 Prepaid services

The CPA provides that prepaid services and access to services is where a consumer agrees to pay a one-time or periodic (eg every month) membership monthly charges can be made against a lump sum payment in advance

fee or a certain amount for services or access to services that will be provided more than 25 business days after the payment was made. The supplier of these services may charge against the prepaid amount once each month in advance in proportion to the amount that is held. For example, if payment of R1 200 has been made for a year, each month the supplier can deduct one-twelfth of the amount, ie R100 a month.

40 days' notice

If a supplier is going to close a facility that provides the service for which the consumer has prepaid and will not be providing an alternative, the supplier must give the consumer 40 business days' written notice of the intention to close the facility. The supplier must then pay back any money due to the consumer within five business days after closing the facility.

Problem 25: The two-year gym membership

Zintle takes out a two-year membership at the Aquatic Swimming Academy. In terms of the agreement Zintle will receive swimming lessons at the academy twice a week for two years. Zintle paid the full two-year membership fee of R8 400 upfront. Discuss the following questions

1. Who does the R8 400 belong to?
2. When can Aquatic Swimming Academy charge against the R8 400?
3. Assume that 12 months after Zintle entered into the agreement the Aquatic Swimming Academy decides to close down. Advise them what their responsibilities to Zintle are.

3.2.13.3 Lay-bys

goods set aside until full price paid

A lay-by is an agreement where the seller agrees to keep goods aside for a consumer until the consumer has paid the full price. In exchange the consumer pays a deposit and the rest of the price in periodic (eg monthly) instalments.

money paid belongs to the consumer

Any money that the consumer pays to a supplier remains the property of the consumer until the goods have been delivered. The supplier may not treat the money as property of the supplier until the goods have been delivered. Before delivery of the goods the supplier will be responsible for any damage to, or loss of, the goods.

What happens if a consumer has paid in full for the goods and the supplier cannot supply them anymore?

The consumer has the right to decide whether the supplier must:

1. Give the consumer similar goods to the goods that were originally chosen; or
2. Refund the consumer's money with interest if it is not the fault of the supplier that the goods cannot be delivered; or
3. Refund double the amount that the consumer paid where it is the supplier's fault that the goods cannot be delivered.

'termination penalty'

The supplier may charge the consumer a 'termination penalty':

1. Where the consumer ends the agreement before fully paying for the goods; or
2. Where the consumer fails to complete the payment for the goods within 60 business days after the agreed date.

no 'termination fee' for death or illness cancellation

The supplier must inform the consumer at the beginning of the agreement that a termination fee will be charged if the agreement is ended or the goods are not fully paid for. After deducting the termination penalty the supplier must refund any balance of the amount paid to the consumer. Where the consumer could not complete the payment because the consumer died or was hospitalised, the supplier may not charge a termination fee.

The termination fee charged by the supplier may not be more than 1% of the full price of the good.

Problem 26: The untimely death of Eunice

Questions

Eunice paid a deposit on a dress and a pair of shoes at Get Fashions. She intended wearing the outfit to her daughter's wedding. The supplier agreed to keep the goods for Eunice until she paid the full amount. One day Eunice was killed when the taxi she was travelling in collided with another vehicle. She had one instalment outstanding on her lay-by agreement.

Divide into groups of five and discuss whether Get Fashions can force Eunice's daughter to pay the balance of the price of the wedding outfit. If not, can Get Fashions charge a 'termination fee'? Give reasons for your answers.

3.2.14 Where to go for help

If consumers have a problem, the first step is always to approach the supplier. If an agreement cannot be reached with the supplier, the complaint can be referred to:

1. A provincial consumer affairs office;
2. A consumer court;
3. A small claims court if the complaint involves trying to get back less than R15 000;
4. The Consumer Tribunal of the National Consumer Commission; or
5. An ordinary court.

3.2.14.1 National Consumer Commission

protecting consumer rights

The National Consumer Commission is responsible for taking practical steps to protect and advance the interests of consumers. This includes protecting the rights of consumers to safety, information, choice, the right to recourse and the right to a fair settlement of just claims.

3.2.14.2 Provincial consumer affairs offices

When consumers have a complaint about a contract, the quality of a product or a service and cannot solve the problem after complaining to the business concerned, the consumer may approach the local provincial consumer affairs office.

The provincial consumer affairs offices were established in each province to provide consumers with protection, information and advice.

provincial consumer affairs offices

Contact numbers for provincial consumer affairs offices

Eastern Cape – 045 808 4000; Free State – 051 400 4852; Gauteng – 011 355 8000; KwaZulu-Natal – 031 310 5300; Limpopo – 015 293 8300; Mpumalanga – 013 752 3761; North West – 018 387 7700; Northern Cape – 053 839 4000; and Western Cape – 0800 007 081

A number of self-regulatory organisations also assist consumers with complaints.

self-regulated consumer complaint bodies

Contact details for self-regulated consumer complaint bodies

Advertising: Advertising Standards Authority of South Africa (ASASA); tel: (011) 781 2006; info@asasa.org.za; **Banking:** The Ombudsman for Banking Services; tel: 0860 800 900 (ShareCall); e-mail: info@obssa.co.za; **Broadcasting:** Broadcasting Complaints Commission; tel: 011 325 5755; e-mail: bccsa@nabsa.co.za; **Competition:** Competition Commission; tel: (012) 394 3200; e-mail: ccsa@compcom.co.za; **Consumer Organisations:** South African National Consumer Union; tel: 012 428 7122; e-mail: info@sancu.co.za; **Credit Bureaus:** Credit Information Ombud; tel: 0860 662 837; e-mail: ombud@creditombud.org.za; **Credit including Micro-lending:** National Credit Regulator; tel: 0860 627 627; e-mail: complaints@ncr.org.za; **Debt Collectors:** Debt Collectors Council; tel: 012 8049808/3402; e-mail: info@debtcol-council.co.za; **Debt Counsellors:** National Credit Regulator; tel: 0860 627 627; e-mail: complaints@ncr.org.za; **Electricity, Gas and Petroleum:** National Energy Regulator of South Africa (NERSA); tel: 012 401 4600; e-mail: info@nersa.org.za; **Financial Services/Investments:** Financial Services Board; tel: 0800 110 443/0800 20 20 87; e-mail: info@fsb.co.za; Office of the Ombud for Financial Services Providers; tel: 012 470 9080/012 348 3428; e-mail: info@faisombud.co.za; **Furniture:** Furniture Traders' Association; tel: (011) 789 6770/1; **Government officials/departments:** The Public Protector; tel: 012 366 7143/0800 11 20 40 (toll free); e-mail: customerservice@pprotect.org; The National Consumer Commission: tel: 012 761 3200; e-mail: complaints@thencc.org.za; **Hospitals:** Department of Health (government); provincial Department of Health; Hospital Association of South Africa (private); tel: 011 784 6828; e-mail: contact@hasa.co.za; **Housing:** Estate Agency Affairs Board; tel: 087 285 3222; e-mail: eab@eaab.org.za; **Insurance:** Ombudsman for Long-Term Insurance; tel: 021 657 5000/0860 662 837 (ShareCall); e-mail: info@ombud.co.za; Ombudsman for Short-Term Insurance: tel: 011 726 8900/0860 726 890; e-mail: info@osti.co.za;

Medical: Council for Medical Schemes; tel: 012 431 0500; e-mail: information@medicalschemes.com; Health Professions Council of South Africa: tel: 012 338 9300/1; e-mail: info@hpcsa.co.za; South African Medical Association: tel: 012 481 2000; e-mail: online@samedical.org; South African Dental Association: tel: 011 484 5288; Toll Share: 0860 110 725; website: www.sadanet.co.za; **Motor industry:** Motor Industry Ombudsman; tel: 0861 164 672; e-mail: info@miosa.co.za; **Pension Funds:** Pension Funds Adjudicator; tel: 012 346 1738/012 748 4000; e-mail: enquiries@pfa.org.za; **Press:** Press Ombudsman; tel: 011 484 3618/3612; e-mail: johanr@ombudsman.org.za; **Standards:** South African Bureau of Standards; tel: 012 428 7911; website: www.sabs.co.za; National Regulator for Compulsory Specifications: tel: 0800 214 719; e-mail: nrcs@nrcs.org.za; **Telecommunications:** Independent Communications Authority of South Africa (ICASA); tel: 011 566 3000; e-mail: info@icasa.org.za; **Tourism:** Tourism Grading Council of South Africa; tel: 011 895 3108; e-mail: enquiries@tourismgrading.co.za.

3.2.15 Steps consumers should take when complaining

The following steps should be taken when consumers identify a problem and wish to complain:

1. Approach the supplier to find a solution.
2. If the supplier fails to solve the problem, refer the case to the applicable ombud's office.
3. If the amount involves a money claim of less than R15 000, use the small claims court (see above para 1.5.2).
4. If the supplier is a financial institution like a bank, the problem will be resolved, depending on the type of service, by the Financial Services Ombudsman, the Ombudsman for Banking Services or the Financial Advisory and Intermediary Services (FAIS) Ombudsman.
5. If the credit provider is not a financial institution and the CPA applies, then the matter will be referred to either the consumer court or an alternative dispute resolution (ADR) agent.
6. If the dispute is resolved, the ombudsman or consumer court or ADR agent may record the resolution in the form of an order and submit it to court or the Consumer Tribunal for it to be made a consent order.

Problem 27: Who would you contact?

Divide into groups of five and decide how you would deal with the following problems. Which agencies would you contact? Why?

1. You buy your brother a toy you saw advertised in a magazine as long-lasting and very strong. The first time it is dropped the toy breaks. To whom would you complain?

the first time the toy is dropped it breaks

2. You buy a meat pie and when you bite into it a cockroach jumps out. You are very angry and want to complain to someone.

when you bite into your pie a cockroach jumps out

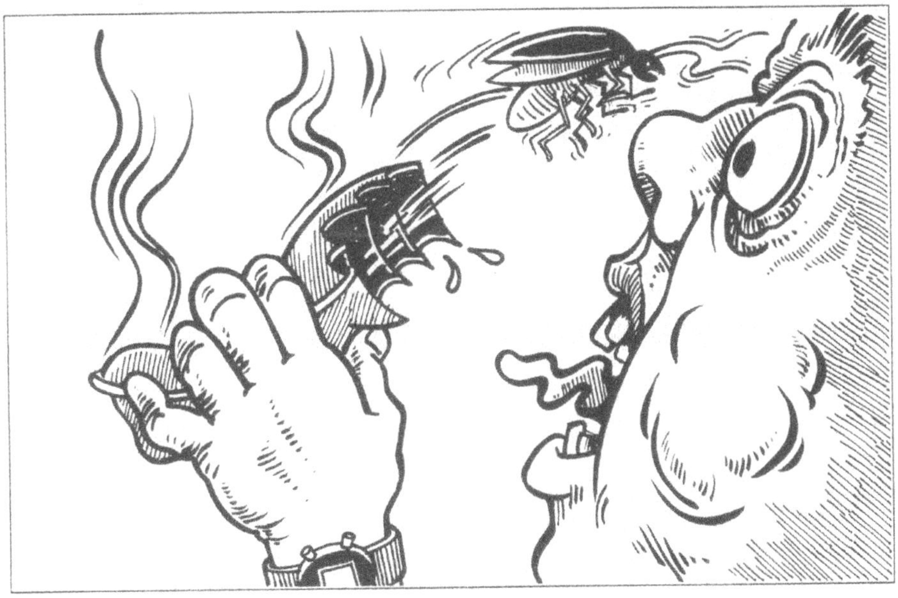

3. You become ill after eating a tin of fish bought from a local supermarket. You know of several friends who also became sick after eating this make of canned fish. You complain to the supermarket but they do nothing.
4. Your parents buy a brand-new refrigerator with a 5-year guarantee and an 'SABS' mark on it. After only three weeks the fridge fails to freeze, and your parents want another.
   (a) What should you do?
   (b) How can they make sure that the next one will work?

after only three weeks the fridge fails to freeze

5. You order a correspondence course on maths and science for the matriculation examination. The course material is delivered so late that you cannot write the matriculation examinations in maths and science. The correspondence college threatens to sue you for the fees. Where could you complain?
6. You book a train ticket from Durban to Johannesburg with a travel agent. When you arrive at the station, the train is full and no booking has been made. You want your money back from the agent.
7. Your parents buy a new car, but it keeps having mechanical problems. What can they do?

3.3 Credit buying and credit agreements

Outcomes

After completion of this section learners will be able to:

1. Demonstrate an understanding of the law relating to consumer credit.

Assessment criteria

1. The advantages and disadvantages of credit are identified.
2. A decision is taken on whether credit should be given to a specific person.
3. A decision is made on which costs may be charged when credit is incurred.
4. A decision is made on the type of credit that is provided in a specific transaction.
5. A decision is made on whether a consumer's rights were infringed.
6. How repossession works is explained.
7. What creditors may or may not do if debtors do not pay their debts is explained.
8. Sets of facts are examined and decisions are made on whether the debt collection was lawful, immoral or illegal.

3.3.1 Introduction

creditors and debtors

interest and finance charges

Buying on credit means that people buy goods or services now but with an agreement that they will pay for it later. It also means borrowing money now in exchange for a promise to repay it in the future. The person who lends the money is the 'creditor'. The person who borrows the money is the 'debtor'. Debtors must usually pay creditors a certain amount of money in addition to the amount that they lend. This is called 'interest' or 'finance charges'.

'wise consumers'

Consumers should be encouraged to become 'wise consumers' when using credit. For example, most car buyers would probably visit several dealers before deciding to buy a car, but many consumers do not shop around for credit.

different types of credit

Credit can be used in many different ways to buy things. For example, people buy homes through bank loans; meals at restaurants are often paid for by credit cards; and cars, furniture and equipment are often bought by paying for them in instalments under a credit agreement.

Some consumers think that it is a good idea to 'buy now, pay later' when prices are rising. This, however, often leads to people using more credit than they can afford. A consumer may not be imprisoned for failing to pay his or her debts.

many people buy on credit because they are unable to pay the full price of goods or services immediately

Many people buy on credit because they are unable to pay the full price of goods or services when they receive them. This means that the buyer may have the goods and use them before paying the full price. The debtor may pay a small deposits and instalments

amount of money at the time the item or product is bought. This is called a 'deposit'. The rest of the price (the balance') is paid off in small amounts (eg six months, one year or two years). Previously in South Africa these types of agreements were called hire-purchase agreements. Hire-purchase agreements very often exploited the debtors. Debtors had to sign standard contracts that protected the seller and severely limited the rights of the buyer. In the past credit providers very often gave persons credit who could not afford to pay it back.

In South Africa many consumers make use of credit when they may not have a large sum of money available to buy furniture or a car. A consumer may not be able to pay for clothes in cash on the date that he or she buys them and would want to open a clothing account at one of the well-known chain stores. A consumer may not be imprisoned for failure to pay his or her debts.

3.3.2 National Credit Act of 2005

exploitation of consumers

The government recognised that there were various problems with people buying on credit. These problems included reckless behaviour by credit providers, exploitation of consumers by some (a) micro lenders (people who give small loans to consumers who need to borrow money); (b) debt administrators (people who help consumers who are having problems in paying off their debts); (c) debt collectors; and (d) others who lend money without taking into account the borrower's ability to pay back the money they borrow or need to pay their accounts.

regulation of credit granting

The National Credit Act of 2005 (NCA) was introduced to protect consumers who buy on credit. The Act promotes a fair, transparent, competitive, sustainable, responsible, efficient, effective and accessible credit market. The NCA regulates almost every aspect of credit granting in South Africa.

what the NCA covers

The NCA applies to (a) mortgage bond agreements to buy houses (see below para 3.3.7.6); (b) buying movables (eg furniture or a car) on credit; (c) pawn transactions (see below para 3.3.7.1); (d) personal loans; (e) overdraft facilities from banks; and (f) guaranteeing the payment of someone else's debts (see below para 3.3.6.3).

what the NCA does not apply to

The NCA does not apply to (a) a policy of insurance or credit extended by an insurer solely to maintain the payment of premiums on a policy of insurance; (b) a lease of immovable property; or (c) a transaction between a stokvel and a member of that stokvel in accordance with the rules of that stokvel (see below para 3.3.7.9).

The NCA also introduces new concepts into our law, eg affordability test, reckless granting of credit and debt counselling.

When a person tries to borrow money from a bank or other financial institution, the bank or financial institution must first conduct a test (assessment) to make sure that the consumer can afford to repay the loan. The consumer will have to provide full details of his or her monthly income and expenditure. The bank or financial institution must disclose to the consumer the instalment amount, the number of instalments, total amount of all the instalments including interest, fees and insurance, whether there will be any final residual or balloon payment, the interest rate that is being charged and the amount charged for other credit costs. It is very important that a consumer carefully reads the credit agreement that he or she is signing to try and avoid problems in the future.

all financial charges must be disclosed

3.3.2.1 Buying for cash or on credit?

In a cash transaction payment occurs immediately. No interest is charged on a cash transaction. One should always try to pay cash for things like food.

the extra cost of buying on credit

Before buying on credit consumers should decide whether it is worth buying something before they have saved enough to pay for it. Do they really need the item or product? Is it worth the extra price of the 'interest' or 'finance charges'?

the trap of 'easy credit'

Many people use credit but do not know that it costs more to buy on credit than for cash. This is because sellers charge for credit. This is also why sellers encourage consumers to buy on credit. 'Easy credit' means that consumers pay more in the long run.

before buying on credit, decide if you really need the item

Problem 1: Using credit

Questions

1. Make a list of things that you, your friends, or your family, have bought on credit.
2. What are the advantages and disadvantages of using credit to pay for: (a) clothing for a special party; (b) university fees; (c) a car to drive to work; and, (d) a holiday?
3. Write out some rules that will help you to decide when to use credit.

Advice on using credit

1. Credit costs money. Do not buy on credit items you do not need or want. Do not be persuaded by high-pressure salespeople.
2. Work out how much credit you can afford. It should not be more than 20% of your take-home wages or salary.
3. Shop around for credit to obtain the best deal.
4. Before signing a credit agreement read it. Make sure you understand the whole contract. Read the small print.
5. Do not sign contracts that have blank spaces.
6. Do not sign contracts that make you pay a large sum of money at the end. You may not be able to pay the last amount, and may lose everything.
7. Once you have signed a credit agreement, keep a copy in a safe place. Keep receipts for every payment so that you can prove what you have paid if something goes wrong.

3.3.2.2 Your rights as a consumer of credit

Under the National Credit Act (NCA) consumers have the right: (a) to apply for credit; (b) not to be unfairly discriminated against; (c) to be given reasons if credit is refused; (d) to information in one of the official languages; (e) to information in plain, understandable language; (f) to receive documentation; (g) to receive a statement of account; (h) to confidential treatment of information; (i) to challenge the accuracy of credit information; (j) to obtain a quote before incurring credit; (k) to terminate a lease or instalment sale agreement during the cooling-off period; and (l) to give back certain goods.

3.3.2.3 The right to apply for credit

credit may be refused if the consumer cannot afford it

Every adult has the right to apply for credit. This right does not mean, however, that you can force a credit provider to give you credit. A valid reason for refusing a consumer credit would be that the credit provider, after considering the application, came to the conclusion that the consumer cannot afford the credit.

3.3.2.4 The right not to be unfairly discriminated against

The Constitution of the Republic of South Africa provides that every person is equal before the law and has the right to equal protection and benefit of the law. No person may be discriminated against on the ground of race, gender, sex, pregnancy, marital status, ethnic or social origin, colour, sexual orientation, age, disability, religion, conscience, belief, culture, language and birth.

consumers may not be unfairly discriminated against

The National Credit Act prohibits credit providers from discriminating against consumers on one of the grounds in the Constitution. The NCA provides that no discriminatory criteria may be used when determining the cost of credit, the terms and conditions under which credit is granted, the grounds that will be used to enforce an agreement and the reason for reporting credit information to the credit bureau. Where a consumer is refused credit the consumer is entitled to be given reasons why the credit is being refused. If the credit provider fails to give reasons, a court of law may assume that the credit provider unfairly discriminated against the consumer.

The credit provider must not discriminate when deciding:

1. Whether the consumer can afford the credit;
2. The terms and conditions of awarding credit;
3. The cost of credit; and
4. Whether to continue, enforce or terminate an agreement.

minors may be refused credit

It would not, however, be unfair discrimination on the ground of age where a credit provider refuses to grant credit to a minor under the age of 18. The rights are provided to adults who are persons older than 18.

consumers may not be punished for enforcing their rights

Where a consumer exercises any of his or her rights provided by the NCA, the credit provider is not allowed to discriminate against such a consumer. The credit provider may not punish a consumer for relying on his or her rights. The provisions of an agreement may not be altered to the disadvantage of the consumer and the credit provider may not terminate, enforce or suspend a credit agreement because the consumer exercises his or her rights.

Problem 2: Was Nosethu unfairly discriminated against?

Nosethu is a domestic worker. She applies for a loan from S Bank for a personal loan of R2 000. She gives them proof of her income of R3 500 per month. S Bank has a policy not to provide loans to black domestic workers.

Discuss whether in your opinion S Bank must be allowed to implement such a policy.

3.3.2.5 The right to be given reasons if credit is refused

A consumer whose application for credit was refused may ask the credit provider to give reasons why the application for credit was refused. A credit provider must give reasons in writing why the application for credit was refused.

You may also request reasons from the credit provider where:

1. The credit provider offers you a lower credit limit than the one you applied for.
2. The credit provider refuses your request to increase your credit limit.
3. The credit provider refuses to renew a credit card.

Problem 3: Cameron applies for a personal loan

Cameron applies for a personal loan of R10 000 from B Bank. The bank informs him that it will only lend him R5 000.

Divide into groups of not more than five and explain to Cameron what his rights are.

3.3.2.6 The right to information in one of the official languages

consumers can choose their language

A consumer has the right to receive information in an official language that the consumer reads or understands. This does not force the credit provider to make information known in all 11 official languages. The credit provider must allow the consumer to choose the language in which he or she wants to receive information. The National Credit Regulator will approve at least two official languages in which documents may be supplied.

3.3.2.7 The right to information in plain and understandable language

You should not require the services of a lawyer to understand the documents that the credit provider gives you. A credit provider must make sure that its documents are understandable to consumers with average literacy skills and minimum credit knowledge.

3.3.2.8 The right to receive documentation

consumers may choose how documents are delivered

The consumer may choose how the documents should be delivered. The following methods are available:

1. The credit provider may hand a copy over in person to the consumer at the business premises of the credit provider.
2. The credit provider may hand a copy over at an address chosen by the consumer, provided the consumer pays the expenses of handing it over at an address that is different from the business premises of the credit provider.
3. The credit provider may post the copy to the consumer in the mail.
4. The credit provider may fax a copy to the consumer.
5. The credit provider may e-mail a copy to the consumer.
6. The credit provider may make a copy available for downloading from a printable webpage.

an original and a copy free of charge

Where the NCA requires a special method of delivery of documentation the credit provider is forced to use that method. The original documentation and a first additional copy must be given to the consumer free of charge. A consumer must request additional copies in writing. The credit provider may charge a fee if the consumer requests another copy after receiving a first additional copy.

3.3.2.9 The right to receive a statement of account

regular statements of account

The general rule is that the consumer must receive monthly statements of accounts. If it is a mortgage bond the credit provider must give the consumer a statement every six months. A statement must be sent every two months where the credit agreement is an instalment agreement, lease or a secured loan.

The consumer and credit provider may agree to reduce how often the statement of accounts must be sent, but cannot agree to more than three months between each statement.

disputed accounts must be investigated

If the consumer disputes the correctness of the statement of account, the consumer may notify the credit provider in writing that entries on the account are incorrect. If the credit provider receives notification of a dispute from the consumer, the credit provider must investigate it and reply to the consumer. The credit provider may not enforce a disputed entry on an account until the investigation has been completed.

early settlement

A consumer has the right to settle an account earlier than agreed without giving notice to the credit provider. Where the consumer wants to pay off or settle the account, the consumer may ask the credit provider for a statement that contains the settlement amount. The credit provider must deliver such an account within five days of receiving the request and it will be binding on the credit provider for five days after its delivery.

Problem 4: Tiaan wants to pay off his bank loan early

Tiaan bought a car that he financed through a loan from the bank. He agreed that he would pay the purchase price over 60 monthly instalments. He has paid 30 of the 60 instalments. He has just received an inheritance from his late grandmother and is now in a position to pay off the balance that he owes on his car.

Divide into groups of not more than five and explain Tiaan's rights to him.

3.3.2.10 The right to confidential treatment of information

Any person who receives personal information in terms of the NCA about a consumer is forced to protect the secrecy of that information. Personal information is information about a person that is not generally known to others.

Problem 5: Marelize's personal credit information is disclosed to her son's school

Marelize applies to open an account at Uptown Fashion Designers. The agreement is that Marelize will pay her outstanding account at the end of every month. They further agree that if she fails to pay the full outstanding balance of her account, Uptown Fashion Designers may charge interest on the unpaid balance. To qualify to open the account Marelize provides Uptown Fashion Designers with details of her monthly income and expenditure. Marelize applies for admission of her 7-year-old son, Tommy, to Mopani Primary School. The headmaster of Mopani Primary School knows the manager of Uptown Fashion Designers. He asks the manager to provide him with details about Marelize's income and expenditure so that he can determine whether she will be able to afford paying school fees at Mopani Primary School. The manager of Uptown Fashion Designers gives the school copies of all Marelize's personal information. Advise Marelize whether any of her rights were infringed.

3.3.2.11 The right to challenge the accuracy of credit information

credit bureau must check their information

Credit bureaus and the National Register of Credit Agreements (NRCA) have information about the creditworthiness of individuals. The information held includes information about the person's credit history, income, assets and liabilities. A credit bureau is forced to check the accuracy of the information.

consumers may inspect credit bureau information about themselves

A credit provider must tell a consumer if it is going to submit any negative information about the consumer to the bureau. A consumer may inspect the information held by the bureau once a year without any charge. If you feel that the information held by the credit bureau is not accurate you must lodge a complaint with the bureau or with the National Credit Regulator.

credit repair

There is a difference between requesting credit repair and challenging credit information. Credit repair refers to the situation where the consumer has paid off a debt that created the negative listing and then approaches the credit bureau to remove the information proving that he or she has paid off the debt concerned.

challenging credit information

Challenging credit information is where a consumer logs a dispute with the credit bureau or the National Credit Regulator. The credit bureau must then take steps to find evidence in support of the negative information it has on its records. The credit bureau may not charge the consumer for seeking this evidence. Such an investigation must be completed within 20 business days. If the credit bureau cannot verify the information it will remove the negative information, but if it finds credible evidence, the information will be retained in the records and a copy of the evidence must be provided to the consumer.

Problem 6: Neville checks his personal information in the credit bureau

Neville approaches the credit bureau with a request to see the information that the bureau has on his creditworthiness. During his inspection he finds that a plumbing company has informed the credit bureau that Neville is a slow payer. Neville says that he does not owe the plumbing company any money.

Divide into groups of not less than five and explain to Neville what his rights are.

3.3.2.12 The right to obtain a quote before incurring credit

quotes set out all the terms, conditions and costs of an agreement

It is always good to shop around with different credit providers before asking for credit. The NCA forces the credit provider to give the debtor a quote before entering into the agreement. The quotation will set out the terms and conditions of the agreement and the full cost of the agreement, including all fees such as the on-road costs, radio, initiation fee, the instalment amount, the number of instalments, total amount of all the instalments including interest, fees, insurance, whether there will be any final residual or balloon payment, the interest rate that is being charged and the amount charged for other credit costs. Consumers can obtain quotes from different credit providers and compare the quotes to find out which one will be the cheapest. The quotation is binding on the credit provider for five days.

Problem 7: Sally is not given a quotation

Sally goes to Honest Joe's second-hand car dealership. She sees a Volkswagen City Golf. On the window of the car the sale price of R85 000 is painted. Sally tells Jaftha, the sales person, that she is unable to pay cash for the car and would have to buy it in terms of a credit agreement. Jaftha gives her a contract to sign. After signing the contract she gets a statement from Jaftha where the following items were added: on road costs R950, radio R2 500, initiation fee R150. Sally says that she was not told that she would have to pay extra for the radio. She also says that she did not receive a written quotation. Jaftha claims that he did not have to give her a quotation because the price was painted on the windscreen of the car.

1. Were any of Sally's rights infringed?
2. Explain to Jaftha what he must do in future to make sure that consumers' rights are not infringed.

3.3.2.13 The right to terminate a lease or instalment agreement during the cooling-off period

cancellation within 5 business days

Where a contract was entered into at any place which is not the business premises of the credit provider, the consumer has a right to cancel the agreement within five business days from the date of signing this agreement.

Problem 8: Mrs Hemraj buys a vacuum cleaner

Mrs Hemraj signs a credit agreement, but, after discussion with her husband, realises that they do not need the 'Super Sucker'

One evening Arthur Goldmouth, a vacuum cleaner salesman, calls at the Hemraj's house with a 'Super Sucker' vacuum cleaner. He says: 'It is the world's greatest vacuum cleaner and can be bought for only a R400 deposit and R250 a month for 12 months. Mrs Hemraj is so impressed that she signs a credit agreement. That night, when Mr Hemraj comes home from work, Mrs Hemraj and he discuss whether they really need the 'Super Sucker'. They decide that they do not want it.

1. What must the Hemrajs do if they wish to cancel the agreement?
2. What must Arthur do if the Hemrajs decide to cancel the agreement?

3.3.2.14 The right to give back certain goods

sale proceeds of returned goods deducted from consumer's account

The consumer who enters into a lease, instalment agreement or a secured loan has the right to notify the credit provider that he or she wishes to return the goods so that they can be sold to settle the consumer's account. Once the consumer returns the goods they will be valued, sold and the proceeds will be deducted from the consumer's account.

consumer advised of value of returned goods

Where a consumer has voluntarily returned goods to the seller, the seller must inform the consumer of the approximate value that he will get for the returned goods within 10 days of the consumer returning the goods. Such a consumer will then be aware of the price that the seller will sell the goods for. Where the consumer is not happy with the price, the consumer can choose to pay the arrears on the account and demand that the goods be returned to him or her. In such a case the consumer can sell the goods himself of herself to try and obtain a higher price.

Where the seller notified the consumer of the price that he or she can get for the goods and the consumer does not respond, the seller must sell the goods for the balance may be claimed from consumer

best reasonable price. The seller can credit the money obtained for the goods to the consumer's account. If the money that the goods are sold for is not enough to cover the whole of the outstanding debt, the seller may claim the balance from the consumer.

Problem 9: Michelle is retrenched

Michelle bought an LCD television set from Kunzima Furnishers a year ago. She paid a deposit and agreed that she would pay the balance of the purchase price off in monthly instalments. It was a condition of the agreement that Kunzima Furnishers would remain the owner of the LCD television set until Michelle finished paying the purchase price. Michelle comes to see you. She says that she has been retrenched and can no longer afford the television set. She wants to know from you whether she can give the television set back to Kunzima Furnishers.

Divide into groups of not more than five and explain to Michelle whether she can return the television set to them.

3.3.2.15 The right to seek help from a debt counsellor

when in arrears consumers are given 10 days to find a debt counsellor

Where the consumer's account is in arrears and the consumer has not voluntarily surrendered or returned the goods, the seller must inform the consumer of the right to seek help from a debt counsellor (see below para 3.3.9), alternative dispute resolution agent, consumer court or ombudsman in terms of the National Credit Act (see above para 3.2.15). A consumer is given 10 business days to seek this help. Where the consumer is in default for at least 20 business days, the seller may apply to court for an order that entitles the seller to repossess the goods. The seller must notify the consumer in writing of the estimated value of the goods within 10 business days of attaching the goods.

pay overdue amounts to get reposssessed goods back

Where the goods are repossessed the consumer may reinstate the agreement by paying all overdue amounts and get the repossessed goods back. Where the creditor has sold the goods after attaching the goods in terms of a court order, the consumer will not be able to reinstate the agreement. Where the consumer does not reinstate the agreement the seller will sell the goods in execution and deduct the proceeds from the amount that the consumer still owes. If the amount that was received for the goods is not enough to settle the consumer's account, the seller may recover the shortfall from the consumer.

Case study: The unlucky consumer

Marina buys a second-hand car under a credit agreement for R20 000. She pays off R8 000 but then falls behind in her instalments. The seller obtains a court order to repossess the car. After repossession the car is sold at a public auction for R4 000 (after expenses). So far the seller has received the R8 000 paid off plus R4 000 from the auction, ie a total of R12 000. Marina originally owed R20 000. She now owes R8 000 (ie R20 000 - R12 000). Even though the seller keeps the money Marina has paid, and repossesses the car, Marina still owes R8 000. She has neither the car nor the money she had paid, and must pay the seller another R8 000.

Marina loses the car, her deposit, and must pay the seller R8 000

3.3.3 Affordability assessment

A credit provider may not agree to provide a consumer with credit unless the credit provider has carried out an affordability test on the consumer. The affordability assessment will help to decide whether the consumer will be able to afford his or her repayments.

3.3.3.1 Duties of the credit provider

The credit provider must assess the following:

1. Whether the consumer understands the risk, costs, rights and obligations in terms of the credit agreement;
2. How reliable the consumer is, by obtaining a credit report from a credit bureau to see how the consumer repaid previous credit; and
3. The consumer's income and expenditure.
4. Whether after deducting all the monthly expenses the consumer will still be able to pay the monthly instalment.

consumers who tell lies are not protected by the NCA

If the credit provider comes to the conclusion that the consumer cannot afford the repayments, the application for credit must be refused. If the consumer lies on the application for credit and does not disclose all his or her expenses, the consumer will lose the protection given by the National Credit Act. If the consumer's application for credit is refused he or she has the right to ask the credit provider to provide him or her with the reasons why the application failed.

reckless credit agreements

If a credit provider fails to do the affordability assessment, the credit provider can be guilty of entering into a reckless credit agreement. A credit provider can lose all or part of the money that it forwarded to the consumer if the credit granting is reckless.

It will not be reckless credit granting if the credit provider can prove that the consumer did not answer questions truthfully during the affordability assessment.

buying more than you can afford on credit could lead to financial difficulties

3.3.3.2 When an affordability assessment is not required

situations when affordability test not required

The credit provider is not forced to do an affordability test for the following credit situations:

1. A school or student loan, but the granting of credit has to be recorded in the National Register of Credit Agreements;
2. An emergency loan (eg loans granted when there has been a death or someone is very ill or where someone unexpectedly loses his or her income);
3. A public interest credit agreement, usually declared by a government Minister where there is a natural disaster;
4. A pawn transaction;
5. An incidental credit agreement; or
6. A temporary increase in a credit limit.

3.3.4 Obtaining credit

information required in credit applications

Any shop or bank that gives credit to a consumer wants to be sure that the money will be repaid. When deciding whether to give credit to a buyer, the seller or person giving credit will want to know the following:

reliable

1. Is the consumer a reliable person? For example, does he or she have a permanent address and a good job?

steady income

2. Does the consumer have a steady income or wage? Will he or she continue to have this income or wage in the future?

enough money

3. Does the consumer earn enough money to pay off the amount lent as credit?

good record

4. Does the consumer have a good record of paying off other accounts and loans?

Creditors ask these questions to make sure that they get their money back. They will not give loans to people who will not pay back their money. However, banks are not forced to do an affordability test for a student loan – although such loans must be recorded in the National Credit Register.

Problem 10: If you were the credit manager

if you were the credit manager would you give credit to these people?

Questions

Divide into groups of not more than five and decide, if you were the credit manager for a bank, whether you would give credit to the following people. Give reasons for your answer.

1. Tilly has three children and receives R1 500 per month maintenance from her ex-husband. She is unemployed. She lives in a council house. Her rent, food and other expenses come to R1 400 per month. Tilly asks the manager to lend her R300 to buy a second-hand stove.
2. Jannie is a handyman who does odd jobs to earn a living. He does not always have a steady income but usually earns about R2 000 a month. Each month he pays out R600 on food, R700 on rent, R300 on a car and R200 on his television set. He has no money in the bank. Jannie would like to borrow R3 000 to buy a motorcycle and calls in to ask the manager for a loan.
3. Shadreck, 23 years, is in the final year of his BComm degree. He has done well in all his university examinations and plans to study law after completing his BComm. Until recently his parents have paid his fees. They can no longer afford to do so. Shadreck wants to borrow R12 000 for his university fees until he can obtain a scholarship. He has never borrowed money before. He plans to repay the loan after he completes his law degree, which will take him another two years. Shadreck calls in to see the manager.

What information must be supplied when applying for credit?

1. Proof of income, eg payslip.
2. Details of the consumer's other debts. The consumer must disclose all the debts that he or she owes and must give the details of all his or her other accounts.
3. Household budget.
4. Details of other credit agreements, eg where the consumer bought a car or furniture in terms of a credit agreement he or she must provide the details of those agreements.
5. If the consumer is married in community of property, the consumer's spouse needs to give written consent.
6. Certified copy of the consumer's identity document or passport.
7. Proof of residence. An example of this would be one of the consumer's utility bills (eg telephone account or municipal account that shows his or her street address).
8. Details of whether the consumer can provide security for repayment of the credit (eg is there a policy that the consumer can cede to the credit provider as security that the consumer will repay the credit?)

3.3.5 Costs of credit

shop around

Consumers should shop around for credit to see where they can obtain the best deal. The National Credit Act (NCA) contains very strict provisions on the cost of credit.

If a consumer enters into a credit agreement the following costs can be charged:

3.3.5.1 Service fee

A service fee is an amount that the credit provider charges the consumer for the cost of maintaining a credit agreement.

3.3.5.2 Interest

maximum rates

The NCA sets out the maximum interest rate that may be charged by credit providers. Interest is calculated taking into account the Reserve Bank's repurchase rate (repo rate). The repo rate affects the interest rates charged by commercial banks in South Africa.

variable or fixed rate

Interest can be charged at a variable (changing) or fixed rate of interest. If it is variable the interest rate changes every time the Reserve Bank changes the repo rate. A fixed interest rate does not change during the duration of the agreement. It remains fixed. If the consumer's account is in arrears, the credit provider is not allowed to charge the consumer a higher interest rate or a penalty interest rate.

3.3.5.3 Initiation fee

once-off fee

This is a once-off fee that the credit provider can charge the consumer when a credit agreement is entered into. This amount can only be charged if the consumer's application for finance or credit is approved.

3.3.5.4 Default administration charges

failing to pay an account

A default administration fee is a fee that the credit provider charges to cover the costs that the credit provider incurs when the consumer fails to pay his or her account (eg the cost of a registered letter the credit provider has to send you to inform you that your account is behind and to demand that you pay the amount owing so far).

3.3.5.5 Collection costs

less than double the capital amount the consumer still owes

Collection costs are the costs that the credit provider may charge when having to take steps to recover payment from the consumer. The maximum collection costs that may be charged may not be more than double the capital amount that the consumer still owes. For example, if the consumer bought a television on credit for R5 000 and has paid off R2 000 of the capital so that there is R3 000 remaining to be paid, when the consumer falls behind with her account, the collection costs may not be more than R6 000. The maximum that the consumer can be required to pay is R3 000 (outstanding capital) and R6 000 (total collection costs – double the amount owing).

3.3.5.6 Credit insurance

credit insurance

A credit provider is allowed to insist that the consumer takes out a life insurance policy that covers the outstanding debt for the duration of the credit agreement. The credit provider can provide the consumer with optional credit insurance, but the consumer is not forced to take out the insurance offered by the credit provider. The consumer may take out his or her own life insurance and provide proof of the life insurance to the credit provider. The total amount of the life insurance cannot be more than the value of the item or product that the consumer bought. For example, if the consumer bought a car and the purchase price of the car is R60 000 the insurance cannot be for more than R60 000. A car reduces in value. Every year the insured amount must be reduced to take into account the amount by which the car has reduced in value (depreciated). If the consumer takes out life insurance that is being offered by the credit provider, the credit provider is not allowed to charge any fee or commission for arranging the insurance.

insurance not to be more than value of purchase price

3.3.6 Types of credit

credit agreement

There are several types of credit that can be used by people who cannot afford to pay cash for goods or services. For example, people may borrow money from banks or enter into credit agreements. They may also use their bank credit card that allows them to borrow money, pay accounts, and buy things on credit.

A very common method used by people who cannot afford to pay cash for things is to sign a credit agreement with a seller or finance company. This is often used by people who buy furniture, cars, television sets, hi-fis, stoves, refrigerators, etc.

The National Credit Act (NCA) covers a broad range of transactions. It includes loans and other credit from banks, mortgages, overdrafts, credit cards, vehicle finance, any other personal finance, furniture finance, clothing accounts, any other type of credit from retailers, micro-loans, pawn transactions and any other type of credit or loan provided to a consumer.

3.3.6.1 Credit agreements

seller owns goods until last payment by buyer

A credit agreement is an agreement where goods are sold or services given in return for money paid over a period of time. Credit agreements in which the buyer has the item or product, but the seller keeps ownership of it until the buyer has made the last payment, used to be called 'hire-purchase agreements'. Credit agreements include a credit facility, a credit transaction, a credit guarantee or any combination of a credit transaction, guarantee or facility. An example of a credit agreement is when you buy a car from a credit provider and the purchase price is financed through a bank. The bank agrees that you pay the purchase price off in instalments. There is a provision in the contract that the bank remains the owner of the car until you have paid off the price. Where the consumer is married in commuity of property the credit provider (seller) cannot enter into a credit agreement with the consumer unless the spouse of the consumer signed the contract or gave written permission that his or her spouse may enter into the credit agreement.

3.3.6.2 Credit facilities

instalments paid over time

A credit facility is when a credit provider (seller) agrees to provide goods or services to the consumer (buyer) and agrees that the consumer can pay later or agrees that the consumer can pay the costs in instalments over time. Interest is charged on the balance of the price that is paid later. Examples of credit facilities are credit cards, overdraft facilities on your cheque account at the bank, clothing accounts and accounts held at other shops.

3.3.6.3 Credit guarantees

surety for payment by another

A credit guarantee is where a person agrees to pay the obligations of another consumer in terms of a credit facility or a credit transaction (eg where a consumer signs surety for payment of another person's loan with the bank, which means that the consumer promises to pay the bank if the other person fails to pay back the loan).

3.3.7 Credit transactions

types of credit transactions

A credit transaction includes: (a) a pawn transaction; (b) an incidental credit agreement; (c) an instalment agreement; (d) a lease of movable goods agreement; (e) a low income housing agreement; (f) a mortgage agreement; (g) a school loan; (h) a secured loan or (i) any other agreement – but not a credit facility or credit guarantee – where payment of the amount owed by one person is delayed and interest is charged.

3.3.7.1 Pawn transactions

property kept as security until money loan repaid

A pawn transaction is where a consumer gives a person (like a pawnbroker) some of his or her property to keep as security for the repayment of money that the person lends to him or her. It is a condition of the agreement that if the consumer does not repay the amount that he or she borrowed before the end of a certain period (eg three months), the pawnbroker is allowed to sell the property left with him or her to recover the money that the consumer owes the pawnbroker. An example of a pawn transaction would be where a woman takes her engagement ring worth R5 000 to the pawnshop. The pawnshop agrees to lend her R3 000. They further agree that the pawnshop will keep the ring for three months. During these three months the woman can repay the loan and get her ring back. If after the three months she has not paid back the loan, the pawnbroker can sell the ring to recover the money that the woman owes him and give her any money left over.

3.3.7.2 Incidental credit agreements

failure to pay within an agreed period

An incidental credit agreement is where a consumer buy goods or services and the supplier informs the consumer that if payment is not made within 20 business days a late payment fee or interest will be charged, or where the supplier indicates the amount by which the price of goods increases if payment is not made within 20 business days. An incidental credit agreement includes those agreements where interest is charged if the debtor fails to pay within an agreed time period (eg 30 days). Examples are cell phone accounts, doctor's and dentist's accounts.

3.3.7.3 Instalment agreements

payment delayed over a period of time

An instalment agreement involves the sale of movable goods where payment of the purchase price is delayed and is to be paid in small amounts over a period of time. Interest is charged and the consumer is given possession of the goods immediately. The consumer may get ownership of the goods either: (a) immediately – but the seller has the right to re-possess the goods if the consumer fails to pay or satisfy his or her obligations; or (b) only when the consumer has fully paid for them in terms of the agreement.

3.3.7.4 Lease of movable goods

consumer becomes owner at end of lease

A lease of movable goods is an agreement in terms of which temporary possession of movable property (eg a car) is given to the consumer. The consumer is given the right to use the property and the consumer pays for the use of the property in small amounts over a period of time or part or all of the payment is delayed for any period during the agreement. Interest must be paid to the credit provider. At the end of the agreement the consumer becomes the owner of the goods.

3.3.7.5 Low income housing agreements

housing development plan

A low income housing agreement is provided in terms of a housing development plan, housing assistance or any other measure that is designed to provide access to housing or to repair existing housing and infrastructure for historically disadvantaged people, low-income earning people and communities, and remote, isolated or low density populations and communities, or other people who cannot independently provide for their own housing needs.

3.3.7.6 Mortgage bond agreements

loan to buy a house giving the lender security registered on the property

A mortgage bond agreement is an agreement a consumer enters into when he or she wants a loan to buy a house. When the consumer applies to the bank for a loan to buy a house, the bank will usually only give the loan if a mortgage bond is registered over the title deeds of the property the house is on. (Title deeds are the documents that show who is the owner of the property.) This means that if the consumer does not pay what he or she owes the bank, the bank can get a court order to sell the consumer's property and recover what the consumer owes it from the money from the sale. Any money left over will be paid back to the consumer.

3.3.7.7 School loan agreements

payment of school fees delayed

A school loan agreement is a credit agreement in which money is paid to a primary or secondary school for school fees or related costs for the benefit of the consumer's child or other dependent. It may also be an agreement where the primary or secondary school agrees to delay the payment of all or part of the school's fees or related costs until the consumer can afford to pay it.

3.3.7.8 Secured loan agreements

loan with security to guarantee repayment

A secured loan agreement is an agreement in which one person lends money to another person and keeps or receives (a) a pledge (ie property is handed over); or (b) cession of the title to any movable property (ie a document proving ownership of property is handed over) as security for the repayment of all money owing in terms of the agreement. An example would be where the consumer gives an insurance policy to the credit provider to be security for repayment of the loan that the credit provider gives him or her. If the consumer does not pay the amounts he or she owes, the credit provider can surrender the policy and recover the money that the consumer owes.

3.3.7.9 Stokvels

members take turns to use the money

A stokvel is a formal or informal financial scheme to which members contribute money in order to help each other with entertainment, social, economic or other activities. Members of the stokvel take turns in using the money contributed to the scheme.

members share the profits

A stokvel consists of two or more members, each of whom agree to support the others to achieve certain objectives. This is done by members contributing to a pool of money, which is then used to give credit to its members. The members share in the profits and elect the people to manage the scheme. The members also make up their own rules for how the scheme works. As previously mentioned, the NCA does not apply to a transaction between a stokvel and a member of that stokvel in accordance with the rules of that stokvel because a stokvel is not a credit agreement.

3.3.7.10 Student loan agreements

payment of university fees delayed

A student loan agreement is a credit agreement in which money is paid by the credit provider to a tertiary institution (eg a university or college) as payment of the education fees of the consumer or the consumer's dependents. A student loan agreement may also be where the tertiary institution delays payment of all or part of the consumer's education fees or related costs until he or she is able to pay for them.

Problem 11: Identify the type of credit

Questions

Divide into groups of not more than five and decide what type of credit is involved.

Aphelele wants to buy a house

1. Aphelele is interested in buying a house. She goes to see the house. First-time home owners who earn between R3 501 and R7 000 a month qualify to buy these houses. The government will provide a subsidy to assist Aphelele to buy the house. The subsidy is not enough to pay the full purchase price. F Bank agrees to give Aphelele a home loan to finance the balance of the purchase price. F Bank says that it will give the home loan on condition that a mortgage is registered over the title deed of the house to secure the balance that Aphelele owes the bank. Aphelele will have to pay R750 per month for a period of five years. The bank will charge interest on the outstanding amount. Identify whether this type of transaction is a form of credit that has to be in line with the provisions of the National Credit Act.

'friends who care'

2. Seni, Thando, Dennis and Luvoyo agree to pay R1 000 per month into a fixed deposit account of 'Friends who care'. The fixed deposit account is held at S bank. The group is charged service fees by the bank and the bank agrees to pay them a fixed interest rate. The members of 'Friends who care' agree that if a member or relative of 'Friends who care' passes away the group will make a contribution towards payment of the burial costs of the deceased. What types of transaction have Seni, Thando, Dennis and Luvoyo entered into?

Melanie wants a personal loan

3. Melanie approaches S bank for a personal loan of R10 000. S bank indicates that it will grant the loan to Melanie provided she gives security for the repayment of the loan amount. Melanie has an insurance policy that has a surrender value of R12 000. Advise Melanie what type of credit agreement she can enter into.

Zintle buys a TV set in instalments

4. Zintle buys an LCD television from Honest Furniture store for R8 500. She agrees to pay a deposit of R850 and the balance of the purchase price in monthly instalments. Honest Furniture will charge interest on the

outstanding purchase price. What type of agreement are Zintle and Honest Furniture entering into?

Stoffel applies for a student loan

5. Stoffel goes to university. His parents are too poor to pay for his student fees. He applies for a loan to National Student Financial Aid Scheme (NSFAS). The NSFAS agrees to pay for his studies for the next four years. It is a condition of the agreement that after four years Stoffel has to repay the amount borrowed from the NSFAS in monthly payments, including interest. What type of credit is involved in this transaction?

3.3.8 Clauses that may no longer be included in credit agreements

prohibited clauses

The National Credit Act prohibits the inclusion of certain clauses in credit agreements. These are where the consumer:

1. Consents to the jurisdiction of a court in a town other than the one where the consumer lives.
2. Consents to a judgment by the court without a hearing.
3. Consents to a court order that allows the creditor to force the consumer's employer to deduct a certain amount of money from the consumer's wages each month before paying the balance of the wages to the consumer.
4. Is required to pay all the legal fees that the credit provider is liable for – the consumer can only be made to pay the fees set out in the Magistrates' Courts Act, 1944.

3.3.9 Debt counselling

legal action to recover money

If a consumer fails to pay his or her debts as agreed, the credit provider will take legal action to recover the money that is owed. When the credit provider takes legal action to recover overdue accounts, collection costs and penalty interest are added to the consumer's outstanding balance.

rearranging repayment of debts

The NCA provides for debt counselling. Through debt counselling a consumer may rearrange the repayment of his or her debts. A consumer will have to go to a registered debt counsellor to have a debt review done. A debt review means that the debt counsellor will help the consumer to work out what his or her monthly income and expenditure is and how much he or she owes. Together the consumer and debt counsellor will try to arrange how the debtor can pay his or her debts and make an offer of payment in instalments to the people and firms to whom the debtor owes money.

A registered debt counsellor will have an A4 certificate of registration and will have stickers on his or her office doors and windows that show the counsellor has been registered. The consumer must supply the debt counsellor with copies of his or her payslip and statement of accounts. A debt counsellor can only charge R50 for the debt review application.

The debt counsellor will review the consumer's financial affairs and decide whether the consumer is over-indebted. A consumer is said to be over-indebted if the consumer is unable to pay all his or her monthly expenses.

consumers who owe too much could find themselves in serious financial trouble

no more direct dealings with creditors by consumers

If you are over-indebted your debt counsellor may make a proposal to the magistrate's court that you be placed under debt counselling and you will not deal directly with your creditors. Your debt counsellor will negotiate with your creditors to re-arrange the amounts that you pay each creditor. The purpose of debt counselling is to give a debtor the chance to repay his or her debts over a longer period of time. While you are under debt counselling your creditors will not take legal action against you. Some might even agree to write off some of the debt. You may not incur further debts while you are under debt counselling. If your debts were rearranged and you have paid all your debts in terms of the rearrangement, your debt counsellor must give you a 'clearance certificate' within seven days from the date you paid the last amount.

3.3.10 Reckless credit granting

consumers must answer all credit grantor's questions truthfully

When applying for credit a consumer must answer all questions truthfully. The consumer must make available all information requested by the credit provider. A credit provider is not allowed to enter into a credit agreement unless the credit provider takes steps to find out whether the consumer knows and understands the risks and costs of incurring the proposed debt. Before deciding to grant credit the credit provider must take into account the consumer's income and expenditure and the previous repayment history of the consumer.

credit grantors must do a proper assessment of a consumer's financial position

If the credit provider grants a consumer credit without taking these things into account the credit agreement will be reckless. If a court concludes that a credit agreement is reckless it may set aside the rights of the credit provider and the obligations of the consumer in terms of the agreement. If the credit agreement results in the consumer being over-indebted, the court may suspend the reckless agreement to a date in the future or the court may restructure the agreement. When restructuring the agreement the court may order that the consumer does not have to make any payments in terms of the agreement, or that the consumer may not be charged interest, and determine that the credit provider may not enforce its rights in terms of the agreement. If, however, it appears that the consumer lied or withheld information from the credit provider, the consumer may not rely on the protection afforded in connection with reckless credit granting.

a clearance certificate

If the consumer's debts are re-arranged and the consumer pays his or her obligations in terms of the re-arrangement, the debt counsellor must give the consumer a clearance certificate within seven days from the date of the last payment.

Problem 12: What should Odette do?

Read the following case study and the answer the questions below.
Odette is a secretary at Livingstone High School. She earns R7 500 per month. After deductions she gets approximately R5 800. She has accounts with Woolworths, Sportscene, Truworths, Jet and Edgars. Her monthly instalments to these shops are R4 000. She rents a flat and pays R1 500 per month rent. She has a daughter who goes to a government school. The school fees are R300 per month. She complains to you that she does not have enough money left over after she has paid her debts to buy food and pay her and her daughter's taxi fare to and from work and school.

Questions

1. What would you advise Odette to do?
2. Assume you think Odette might qualify for debt counselling. Explain to her the process that she must go through in order to be placed under debt counselling.
3. She tells you that when she opened an account at one of the well-known shops six months ago they only asked for her identity document and a copy of her payslip. She was not asked any information about her monthly expenses. Explain to Odette whether the retail shop has done anything wrong.
4. Explain to Odette if there are steps she can take against the retail shop.
5. Would your answer be different if the shop asked Odette detailed questions about her income and expenditure and Odette lied on the form?

3.3.11 How repossession works

if the buyer cannot pay the instalments

Sometimes buyers may not be able to pay their instalments. They can then ask the seller to give them more time to pay. The seller may agree to their request but does not have to. If the seller does not, he or she may demand that the missing instalments are paid, or the goods are returned. If the buyer does not pay the missing instalments or return the goods, the seller may repossess them. Sellers who wish to repossess goods, however, cannot just walk onto the property of the buyer and repossess the goods. This would be illegal. Sellers who do this may be criminally liable for trespass, housebreaking, invasion of privacy or malicious injury to property if anything is damaged (eg a door lock broken). In such cases a buyer should complain to the police.

rules for repossession

Legally, sellers may only repossess goods in two situations:

1. If the buyer consents (eg signs a 'voluntary repossession' or 'consent' form); or
2. The seller obtains a court order.

'voluntary repossession'

A 'voluntary repossession' or 'consent' form is an agreement by the buyer to allow the seller to repossess the goods. If the buyer does not agree to hand back the goods the seller must approach the court for a repossession order. Before obtaining a court order the seller must send the buyer a letter saying that he or she has breached the agreement. The seller should demand payment of the missing instalments within 30 days. If the buyer has previously missed instalments on two or more occasions, the seller need only give the buyer 14 days to pay. If the buyer then fails to pay the missing instalments, the court will make a repossession order and a court official will repossess the goods. (The court official in the magistrates' court is called the 'sheriff of the magistrates' court'. The official in the High Court is called the 'sheriff of the High Court'.) If the buyer still fails to pay, the goods will be sold at a public auction (see above para 1.5.1.3).

a repossession order against the buyer

seller must keep goods for 30 days

If the seller repossesses the goods without a court order, or without the consent of the buyer, the seller must keep the goods for 30 days before selling them. If, during the 30-day period, the buyer pays the missing instalments, the seller must return the repossessed goods and the credit agreement will continue.

buyer may have to pay balance after repossession

If, after repossession, the value of the goods is less than what the buyer still owes, the buyer will have to pay the seller any amount will owing. This happened in the case of 'the unlucky consumer' (see above para 3.3.2.15).

Consumers should be very careful about buying things on credit if they cannot afford to pay the instalments. In most cases they will lose the money paid and the thing bought. In a very few cases the seller has to refund the buyer. This only happens if the value of the goods sold and the amount of money paid are more than the amount owing. This may sometimes happen if only the last instalment has not been paid. Usually, however, if the goods are repossessed the buyer will still end up paying off the balance.

3.3.12 What creditors may or may not do if debtors do not pay

creditors must use lawful means

Creditors may use a number of methods for collecting money from consumers who are unable or unwilling to pay their debts. Creditors are allowed to take action to collect money or property owed to them – provided they use lawful means to do so. Sometimes debt collectors use unlawful methods. These often cause family problems, loss of jobs and invasion of consumers' rights.

3.3.12.1 Immoral and illegal methods of collecting debts

fake summonses

Consumers should not be intimidated by immoral methods like the use of fake summonses – supposedly issued by the courts, and threats to inform local shopkeepers and employers about their debts.

unlawful methods of debt collection

Consumers should also not allow creditors to use unlawful methods like:

(a) Threats of intimidation and harassment;
(b) Debt collectors calling at night or when people are out of their homes, and taking away goods;
(c) Illegal repossessions of goods not bought under a credit agreement;
(d) Illegal repossessions of goods bought under a credit agreement where creditors have not followed the provisions of the National Credit Act; and
(e) Threats to have debtors arrested or imprisoned.

prescription

A debt collector may not collect a debt that is older than three years. This is called prescription. There are, however, requirements that must be complied with before the debt will be regarded as prescribed.

For prescription to apply the consumer must not have:

(a) Made a payment on the debt;
(b) Signed an acknowledgement of debt agreeing that the consumer owes the debt;
(c) Admitted that the debt is still owed;
(d) Had legal proceedings to enforce payment of the debt instituted against the consumer; or
(e) At any time given a promise to pay the debt.

3.3.12.2 Remedies for immoral or illegal methods of debt collection

'invasion of privacy'

Creditors who use these methods can be taken to court for 'invasion of privacy', which happens when a person unlawfully interferes with the private life of another person. Threats of violence against consumers are regarded as assaults (see above para 2.2.2) and may be reported to the police. If creditors or their agents enter a consumer's property without the consumer's consent or a court order they may be charged with trespass (see above para 2.6.8). Trespass occurs when people go onto other people's property without their consent. Creditors or

trespass

their agents may also be guilty of housebreaking if they open a window or door to enter a house (see above para 2.6.5). If they break down a door, or break a window or door lock to enter, they will be guilty of the crime of malicious injury to property (see above para 2.6.2). Consumers whose homes or properties are entered without their consent should report the guilty people to the police and charge them with committing a crime.

report crimes to the police

Consumers whose property has been illegally repossessed may claim it back again. They should first complain to the person who repossessed it before resorting to legal action (see above paras 3.2.13 and 3.2.14).

Problem 13: The case of the missing motorcycle

when Willem goes outside to get onto his motorbike, he finds it is not there

Willem purchases a second-hand motorcycle from Price Busters for R9 000. He pays a deposit of R1 800, and signs a credit agreement to pay monthly instalments of R300 for 24 months. He pays instalments for 12 months. During the 13th month he has to pay funeral expenses and fails to pay the instalment on the motorcycle. Three weeks later Willem goes outside his house and finds the motorcycle gone. Price Busters have sent a man in the middle of the night to repossess it. Willem is not given notice that the motorcycle will be repossessed.

Questions

1. Role-play Willem complaining to the manager of Price Busters.
2. Was Price Busters legally entitled to repossess the motorcycle? Give reasons for your answer.
3. What can Willem do to get back the motorcycle?

3.3.12.3 Lawful methods of debt collection

court order of consent

If a creditor has a court order, or the consent of the debtor, he or she may enter property to repossess goods sold under a credit agreement (see above para 3.3.11). Goods not sold under a credit agreement may not be repossessed – the only person who can take these goods away is the sheriff (see above para 1.5.1.3).

Problem 14: Were the actions of the creditor lawful, immoral or unlawful?

1. Sofala buys some furniture under an instalment agreement for R5 000. She falls ill for a month and fails to pay her instalments for three months. Sofala's house is broken into while she is at work. The door and lock are damaged. The furniture she bought under the instalment agreement and a radio she paid for in cash are 'repossessed' by the seller without her consent or a court order. Are the 'repossessions' lawful, immoral or unlawful? Why do you say so? Role-play a conversation between Sofala and the seller.

Sofala's creditor breaks into her house and removes her furniture

2. Vloog fails to pay his television account for two months. He had promised to pay the full price in cash within one month of buying it. Vloog is sent a document with the words 'Summonsed' printed on the top. The document, which is not issued by the court, says that if Vloog does not settle his account immediately, a court order for his arrest and detention will be obtained. Do you think that the document is lawful, immoral or unlawful? Role-play a conversation between Vloog and the owner of the television shop.

3. Lucy is telephoned by the credit manager of a clothes shop. He tells Lucy that if she does not settle her account of R3 000 he will tell her employer. Do you think that the credit manager's threat is lawful, immoral or unlawful? Give reasons for your answer. Role-play a telephone conversation between Lucy and the credit manager.
4. Arvin owes R2 000 to a computer shop. The owner tells him that unless he pays immediately she will tell all other computer shops that he is a person who does not pay his debts.
   Do you think that the owner's threat is lawful, immoral or unlawful? Give reasons for your answer. Role-play a conversation between Arvin and the shop owner.
5. A debt collector threatens to assault Ferdie if he does not settle his video recorder account in full within five days.
   Is the threat lawful, immoral or illegal? Give reasons for your answer. Role-play a conversation between Ferdie and and the debt collector.

a debt collector threatens to assault Ferdie

6. Greg does not pay his furniture account and the shop obtains a default judgment against him for R6 000. Greg ignores all the other court documents given to him by the sheriff of the court. While Greg is at work the sheriff goes to his house with a warrant of execution (see above para 1.5.1.3) and removes his furniture and his fridge.
   Was the sheriff's action lawful, immoral or unlawful? Give reasons for your answer. Role-play a conversation between Greg and the sheriff.
7. Dambuza does not pay his shoe account of R1 500 for two months. While at work he is asked to call in at the shoe shop during his lunch break. When he calls in at the shop the manager takes away his shoes and socks!
   Was the manager's act lawful, immoral or unlawful? Why or why not? Role-play a conversation between Dambuza and the manager of the shoe shop.

the manager of the shop takes away Dambuza's shoes and socks

3.4 Common-law protection of consumers

Outcomes

After completion of this section learners will be able to:

1. Demonstrate an understanding of the common-law protection of consumers when statute law does not apply, particularly under the law of contract.

Assessment criteria

1. The common-law protection of consumers, when statute law does not apply, is explained.
2. The requirements for a valid contract at common law are explained.
3. A decision is taken on whether or not a contract has been entered into.
4. Different types of terms and conditions in contracts that may sometimes exclude liability are identified.
5. A decision is taken on whether a person may enter into a contract.
6. Five types of contracts that must be in writing are listed.
7. An explanation is given on what should be done before entering into a written contract.
8. Decisions are made on whether breach of contract has occurred.
9. The court's powers when a breach of contract occurs are explained.
10. A set of facts is examined and a decision is made on what order the magistrate should give.
11. Sets of facts are examined and decisions taken on whether or not the persons breaching the contracts are liable.

contracts not covered by the CPA or the NCA

The common law protects consumers who are not covered by the statutes that protect consumers. For instance, contracts between people who are not manufacturers, suppliers or distributors in the buying and selling of goods and services may not be covered by the Consumer Protection Act or the National Credit Act, but may be covered by the common law.

common law of contract and delict

The common law of contract and 'delict' (civil wrongs) will protect consumers and impose obligations on the providers of goods and services where statute law does not apply. Where such people have entered into agreements they will be governed by the common law of contract regarding the agreement, and the common law of delict if they or 'third parties' (see below para 3.4.2.9) wish to sue for damages for harm caused to them. This section will deal mainly with the common law of contract which affects contracts that are not governed by statute.

offer and acceptance

People in law include natural people (human beings) and legal persons (eg companies). In a contract one person offers to do something and the other person most contracts are verbal

accepts the offer. (For example, Sipho offers to sell his second-hand car to Barnard for R135 000 and Barnard accepts the offer.) A contract may be in writing but most contracts are verbal. A person will be making a contract if he or she buys a soft drink, hamburger or bunny chow from the local take-away. If one person does not carry out the promise, the other person may have a legal claim against the first person. Consumers should understand how a contract is made and how it may affect their rights.

3.4.1 Requirements for a contract

an agreement between two or more people

For a proper contract, there must be an agreement between the people about what each person must do under the contract. This means there must be an offer by one person and an acceptance by the other. The offer must be serious, and definite, not vague. It must be made to a particular person or group of persons. Sometimes it can take the form of an offer of reward to anyone who does what is required (eg offer a reward for finding a lost child or animal). The person accepting the offer must let the other person know that he or she is accepting it. Sometimes the person making the offer says how it must be accepted (eg in writing or by doing something).

offer of reward

mentally incompetent persons cannot enter into contracts

The people making the contract must have the legal power to enter into it. For example, children under the age of 7 years, or people who are mentally ill or very drunk or drugged cannot enter into contracts. Where a person is so drunk that she does not understand that she is entering into an agreement or where she does not understand the terms of the contract, such a contract will be regarded as void. The courts will not enforce agreements to do something illegal, immoral contracts or contracts against public policy (eg an agreement to steal or an agreement preventing a person from marrying). The courts will not enforce contracts that are impossible to carry out. For example, where the item to be sold had been destroyed at the time the contract was made there is no proper contract, as when a person sells a house that had been washed away in a flood before the contract was made.

illegal or immoral contracts cannot be enforced

When Jacob says to Krish, 'I will sell you my motorbike for R10 000', there is an offer. When Krish says 'OK', or when he pays the R10 000, or when he signs an agreement to pay R10 000, there is acceptance. They have agreed on the exact terms of the contract.

an advertisement is an invitation to do business

An advertisement, however, is not an offer to contract. It is just an invitation to do business. Consumers should not rush into contracts. They should make sure that they understand and agree with all the terms before they accept an offer. Otherwise it may be too late for them to change their minds.

Problem 1: Is there a contract?

Questions

For each of the following situations decide whether a contract has been concluded. Give reasons for your answers.

1. A small child is lost and the parents offer a reward of R1 000 to anyone who finds her. Chiman finds the child and claims the reward.

Chiman finds the child and claims the reward

2. Lindiwe says to Thandi, 'I am going to sell my bicycle for R4 000.' Thandi replies, 'OK. Here is the money. I'll take it.'
3. Fanie's father promises to give him R2 000 when he turns 18. On his eighteenth birthday he asks for the money.
4. Standing on the side of a river where a log connects the one side of the river to the other John says to Piet: 'I'll give you R100 if you walk across that log'. Piet says nothing but starts walking across the log.

Piet starts walking across the log . . .

5. Sam offers Charles R440 to steal four hubcaps for his car. Charles steals the hubcaps, brings them to Sam, and asks for the money.
6. Dan sells Peggy his car, but does not know at the time that it had been destroyed by fire.
7. Tom says to Anne, 'I will buy your car, if it suits me'. Anne agrees to this.
8. Dave and Deepak agree that Deepak will not marry Dave's sister. Deepak then proposes to Dave's sister, and Dave goes to court in an attempt to stop Deepak going through with the marriage.
9. Lindi goes to a party with friends where she gets drunk. When she wakes up the next morning she cannot remember what happened at the party. Her friend tells her that she agreed to sell her diamond ring to Fenner for R2 000 so that he can get engaged.

3.4.2 Conditions that limit the liability of people in contracts

contracts that contain conditions

Sometimes contracts have conditions in them that say that a person will not be liable if he or she does not carry out the contract properly. This means that the wrongdoer cannot be sued by an innocent person who is harmed when something is not done, or something does not work properly. These conditions are usually found in 'as is' sales and notices, or on tickets, receipts or invoices.

3.4.2.1 'As is' sales

'voetstoots' or 'as is'

Very often a contract says that something is sold 'as is' or 'voetstoots'. This means that the buyer buys the thing with all its faults and cannot cancel the contract if something is wrong with the thing sold. The only time a buyer may cancel the contract and recover damages for a thing sold 'as is', is where the seller knew that there was something wrong with it when it was sold and did not tell the buyer.

Sales between individuals in their private capacity can still have this type of clause (eg Razina sells her car to Christelle and between them they agree that the sale will be voetstoots) which is covered by the common law.

consumer protection

The Consumer Protection Act of 2008 (CPA) regulates the use of this type of clause in a contract, but as previously mentioned, the CPA only applies when the party is acting in the ordinary course of their businesses. The CPA is applicable when a consumer enters into an agreement with a business (see above para 3.2).

Problem 2: Is the buyer bound by the terms and conditions?

Questions

Study the following case. Role-play the conversation and decide whether the buyer is bound by the terms and conditions in the following contract:

Frikkie sells his car to Ntombi. The car is sold 'as is' but Frikkie knows that the car has a faulty gear-box. The gear-box stops working and Ntombi tells Frikkie that she wishes to cancel the contract and get her money back. Frikkie says that he is not liable because he sold the car 'as is'. Role-play Ntombi complaining to Frikkie and Frikkie's reply.

3.4.2.2 'Implied warranties'

common-law protection against defective goods and services

A guarantee that is regarded as having been given by a seller who says nothing about a guarantee is called an 'implied warranty'. The *common law* protects consumers who buy damaged or defective goods, or unsatisfactory services that are not covered by the Consumer Protection Act. 'Defective' goods are goods that have something wrong with them. Unsatisfactory service may sometimes be given by doctors, lawyers, mechanics, electricians, plumbers, dry cleaners, builders, etc.

3.4.2.3 Guarantee against hidden faults

protection against hidden defects

The common law states that the seller of goods must tell the buyer about any hidden faults in the goods. If the seller does not do this, he or she will be responsible for any hidden or 'latent' faults that exist. Lawyers call this the 'implied warranty against latent defects'.

For example, Peter sells Mary a waterproof watch for R800. The law regards Peter as having guaranteed that the watch is waterproof. If the watch does not work after it gets wet it is said to suffer from a hidden fault or defect. Peter will be responsible for the hidden fault and will have to take back the watch and return Mary's R800. Mary may, however, agree to let Peter give her another watch that works properly. If Mary would still have bought the watch but would have paid less for it (eg R600), if she had known it was not waterproof, she could ask for the price to be reduced to R600. This means that she could claim a R200 refund from Peter.

goods must be fit for purpose

The implied warranty against latent defects is implied by law even though the seller does not mention that the goods are guaranteed. The law states that there is an implied guarantee by the seller that the goods do not have any defects that make them unfit for their purpose. If, however, the seller and buyer agree that the implied guarantee against hidden defects will not apply to the contract (eg where the things is sold 'as is'), the buyer cannot complain if a fault arises (see above para 3.4.2.1).

3.4.2.4 No guarantee against obvious faults

Where a person buys goods that have an obvious fault, not a hidden fault, he or she cannot complain about the defect – for example, where the buyer should have seen that there was clearly something wrong with the thing (such as it was the wrong size or colour).

if the buyer should have seen there was clearly something wrong with the thing bought, he or she cannot complain about the defect

3.4.2.5 What can be done about goods with hidden faults?

At common law where a consumer buys goods that have a hidden fault he or she may do the following:

the buyer may cancel

1. If the goods are so faulty that if the buyer had known about the defect, he or she would not have bought the goods, the buyer may cancel the sale, return the goods, and get back the price paid. As a favour the consumer may allow the seller to exchange the goods, but the seller cannot insist that this is done.

the buyer may pay less

2. If the buyer would still have bought the goods if he or she had known about the faults, but would have paid less money, the buyer may ask the seller to reduce the price.

court order to carry out contract

3. If the buyer still wants the seller to carry out the contract, the buyer may ask the court to order the seller to do what he impliedly promised (ie that the goods are fit for the purpose for which they were sold). The courts usually do not like ordering people to do things if it is easier to give the other person compensation. Sometimes, however, if the goods sold are very special, such as a painting by a particular artist, the court may order the seller to deliver the painting, instead of paying back the money paid.

Problem 3: What should the buyer and seller do?

Questions

Role-play the following situations: (a) Decide whether the seller is regarded as having given an implied warranty. (b) Is the buyer entitled to a full refund or a reduced price? Give reasons for your answer.

1. Jack sells his used car to Vos for R15 000. On his way home the brakes fail. Luckily, Vos does not have an accident. It will cost Vos R1 000 to have the brakes fixed. Vos complains to Jack.
2. Winnie buys a red skirt from Dorothy for R300. When she arrives home and wears it with her other clothes she decides that the skirt should have been orange. Winnie asks Dorothy to exchange it.

3.4.2.6 Guarantee against having the goods taken away

'implied warranty against eviction'

At common law the seller is also regarded as guaranteeing that the goods will not be taken away from the buyer by somebody else. This means that there is an implied guarantee by the seller that nobody else will have the right to take the goods away from the buyer. Lawyers call this the 'implied warranty against eviction'. Here 'eviction' means that somebody will take the goods away. If the goods are taken away the buyer is entitled to a refund from the seller.

For example, Diva sells Satie a stolen ring for R500. If the owner of the stolen ring claims it back from Satie, Diva's guarantee that the ring will not be taken away by somebody else has been broken. Satie will be entitled to get back the R500 she gave Diva.

The implied warranty against eviction is sometimes broken when a person buys a car from a dishonest seller who bought it under an 'instalment agreement', but did not pay it off (see above para 3.3.7.3). In this case the seller is entitled to claim the car back from the person who innocently bought it from the dishonest seller.

3.4.2.7 'Exemption clauses'

prevent buyer suing seller

At common law consumers may lose their protection under the implied warranties if the seller makes an 'exemption clause' a condition of the sale. An 'exemption clause' is a condition in a contract that prevents the buyer suing the seller, or provider of the service, if something goes wrong, or there is a hidden fault in the thing sold (see above para 3.4.2.1).

For example Cynthia buys an electric iron from Krish, her neighbour, who is not a commercial trader. The iron is sold 'as is', or 'with all faults', or 'voetstoots'. This means Cynthia buys the thing with whatever is wrong with it, and may not claim a refund or a reduced price from Krish if something goes wrong – unless Krish knew that it had hidden faults. If so, he cannot use the exemption clause to take away Cynthia's common-law rights. She will be entitled to cancel the sale or obtain a reduced price in terms of the implied warranty against hidden defects (see above para 3.4.2.3).

If, however, Krish ran a business as a dealer in goods or the iron was bought under a credit agreement, such exemption clauses may not be used in terms of the Consumer Protection Act (see above para 3.2.10.1).

3.4.2.8 'Express warranties' or 'guarantees'

form part of contract

An 'express warranty' or a 'guarantee' is a statement usually made in writing or by words or acts that forms part of the contract. For example, when goods are sold the seller may 'guarantee' or 'warrant' that the goods have certain qualities. These warranties are different from 'implied warranties' because they are included in writing, words or acts. Usually express warranties or guarantees take away the protection given to consumers by the implied warranties.

guarantees are terms in contracts

In a private sale between people who are not involved in marketing, and which is not covered by the Consumer Protection Act, an express warranty in writing happens when, for example, the seller tells the buyer that he or she will guarantee the thing for one year and gives this statement to the buyer in writing. If the buyer accepts the guarantee, this usually means that the seller promises to give back the buyer's money or have the thing repaired free of charge if something goes wrong within a year. The details of what the guarantee will cover should be spelled out in writing. If the thing breaks down after one year the buyer will not refund the buyer's money or repair the thing. At common law without the 'guarantee' the buyer would have up to three years to claim.

refund for breach of express warranty

An express warranty that arises from an act would happen where a person buys a vacuum cleaner from another private person after seeing a demonstration of it cleaning a very dirty carpet. This would be an express warranty that the vacuum cleaner can clean very dirty carpets. If the vacuum cleaner did not clean very dirty carpets, the buyer could take it back to the seller and ask for a refund of the price.

'puffing' is not an express warranty

Express warranties are usually statements made about things that have been bought. However, not everything a seller says about the goods is a warranty or guarantee. If a seller's statement is only an opinion or an obvious exaggeration, it is regarded as puffing (see above para 3.2.8.2) and cannot be relied on: for example, the seller says: 'This washing machine is amazingly good and efficient.' However, if the seller says: 'This lawnmower will not break for two years', this is an express warranty. Many express warranties or guarantees limit the buyer's rights under the common law. This is done to prevent sellers having to pay consumers who are injured or have their property damaged by faulty goods. (For what can be done about these types of warranties or guarantees when the contract is covered by the Consumer Protection Act, see above para 3.2.15).

3.4.2.9 Where a consumer or 'third party' consumer is harmed by a faulty product

'third parties' do not buy the goods or services

At common law under the law of delict (civil wrongs) a consumer or 'third party' consumer may recover damages if he or she suffers personal injury, damage to property or economic loss as a result of a defective product or service. A 'third party' consumer is a consumer who does not buy the item. He or she may be injured when using the item, or when somebody else uses it. For example, a member of the buyer's family may be poisoned by bad food, or a visitor injured by an exploding TV set, bought by the buyer.

the third party must prove fault

In the above situations, if they are not covered by the Consumer Protection Act (eg if the goods or services are provided by persons who are not involved in the business of providing goods or services), the consumer may only claim damages from the seller if he or she can prove fault by them. The consumer would have to prove that the seller knew that the item had a fault, or should have foreseen that it was defective. The same applies to 'third party' consumers who use the dangerous thing sold.

warranty limits do not apply to third party consumers

A guarantee or warranty taking away common-law rights does not apply to third party consumers. This is because they do not have a contract with the seller. A warranty or guarantee is part of the contract of sale between the buyer and the seller. It only applies to the people who agreed to the contract.

Problem 4: Can the third party consumer claim damages?

Questions

Role-play each of the following situations. (a) Decide whether the third party consumer can claim damages. Give reasons for your answers. (b) If so, what damages do you think the third party would be able to claim?

1. Frans buys an electric lawnmower from his neighbour Koos. The cord is faulty and his son Robbie is electrocuted. Robbie has to go to hospital for two days and is off work for a week. His hospital expenses amount to R3 000 and his lost wages to R700. Frans complains to Koos.
2. Hluka buys a gas lamp from his friend Hansa who says that he is selling it to him 'as is'. Hluka's wife is badly burned when the gas lamp explodes. Hluka asks Hansa to pay his wife's medical expenses.

3.4.3 Minors and contracts

persons under 18 years of age

A minor is a person under 18 years of age. That is a person below the age of legal majority. A minor does not need anyone's permission if he or she enters into a contract where he or she incurs only rights, eg accepting a donation. Where the minor will incur both rights and responsibilities in a contract, such a minor would require the assistance of his or her parents or guardian when concluding the contract. A minor who enters into a contract without the consent of his or her parent or guardian does not have to keep to the terms of the contract. If, however, the minor acted fraudulently (eg pretends to be an adult), the person harmed by the minor's action may sue for damages. Minors who cancel contracts must usually return the goods or things that they bought. The reason for the rule allowing unassisted minors to cancel contracts is to prevent people taking advantage of them because of their age and inexperience.

minors entering into contracts must be assisted by a parent or guardian

economically independent

It is also possible that a minor can be regarded as emancipated. In *Sesing v Minister of Police* the court held that a minor is emancipated when the parent or guardian agrees, either expressly or tacitly, that the minor can act as an economically independent person.

The rule about minor's contracts makes it difficult for young people to obtain credit from shops without their parent's or guardian's assistance. If a parent or guardian helps a minor by signing a credit agreement then the contract will normally make the parent(s) liable for the payments. If minors enter into contracts for reasonably priced essential things like food, clothing, shelter and medical aid, their parents or guardians will be liable – even though they did not assist when the contracts were made. This is because these things are regarded as 'necessities' and essential for the minor's welfare.

'necessities'

If a parent or guardian enters into a contract for a minor that is to the minor's disadvantage the minor may cancel the contract when he or she turns 18. The cancellation must be done as soon as the minor becomes 18. If the minor continues to make payments after turning 18 the court may decide that the minor has agreed to the contract.

parental assistance for young people

The Children's Act of 2005 recognises child-headed households. If the department of Social Development recognises a home as a child-headed household where a child over the age of 16 years has assumed the role of a care-giver in respect of the rest of the children in the house, then that child must be allowed to contract without seeking permission from the supervising adult.

16-year-old child-headed households

Problem 5: The case of the unassisted minor

Syd, who is 16 years old, agrees to buy a motorbike on credit for R10 000 from Flash Bikes. He agrees to pay the money off in monthly instalments over two years. His parents do not assist Syd when he makes the contract. Syd's parents do not even know that he has bought the motorbike.

Syd's father does not even know that he has bought the bike

Questions

1. Is Syd bound by the contract to buy the motorbike?
2. Must Syd pay the R10 000?
3. What must Syd do if he wants to keep the motorbike? What must he do if he wishes to cancel the contract?
4. Assume that Syd wishes to cancel the contract. Role-play a meeting between Syd and the owner of Flash Bikes to discuss the cancellation of the contract.

3.4.4 Married persons

marriages in community of property

If persons get married in South Africa without entering into a contract, the couple is regarded as married in community of property (see below para 4.2.2.1). This means that the assets and liabilities of each spouse are joined together and become one estate. It is important to remember that persons who are in a same-sex relationship can also get married or enter into a civil union (see below para 4.1.4.3). Where persons of either gender are married in community of property, both spouses will require the consent of the other spouse when entering into certain contracts. For example, if one of the spouses wants to buy a house he or she must get the written consent of the other spouse.

ante-nuptial contract

Where a couple entered into an ante-nuptial agreement before they got married they may be married out of community of property (see below para 4.2.2.2). In this case the assets and debts of a spouse belong to that spouse. Persons married out of community of property can enter into any agreement without the permission of the other spouse.

3.4.5 Written and spoken contracts

most contracts need not be in writing

Contracts may be written or spoken. Most contracts need not be in writing and nearly all daily contracts are entered into merely by using words (eg buying from shops, using transport, eating at restaurants, going to the movies). Many contracts happen by word of mouth or even behaviour (eg by handing over a bus fare or taxi fare or paying to go to a movie). Where the law requires a contract to be in writing the Consumer Protection Act regulates what can and cannot be in a document. (see above para 3.2.10.1)

3.4.5.1 Contracts that must be in writing

certain contracts need to be in writing

Certain contracts must be in writing in order to be enforced in a court of law. If such a contract is not in writing the courts will not be able to help people enforce the terms of the contract.

For example the following contracts must be in writing and signed by the contracting persons (a) buying or selling a house; (b) a lease for 10 years or longer; (c) credit agreements; (d) marriage contracts that persons enter into if they wish to be married out of community of property; and (e) contracts of apprenticeship.

proving written contracts is easier

A written contract is much easier to prove than a spoken contract. It is always better to put a contract in writing. If it is not in writing it is difficult to prove that a person promised to do something. Usually if there is a written contract the court will not listen to evidence of promises made before the contract was signed. The court will, however, hear evidence if the contract is not clear, or one of the people was tricked into signing it by the other.

Advice on written contracts

1. Never sign a contract that has blank spaces.
2. Never sign a contract to get rid of an irritating salesperson.
3. Never sign a contract without obtaining a copy of it.
4. Never sign a contract unless all the promises are included in writing and the total amount of money to be paid is clearly stated.
5. Never sign a contract unless you have read and understood everything in it. If necessary, take it to a lawyer, legal aid clinic or citizen's advice office and have it explained.

Problem 6: The case of the broken promise

Mr Wilson does not send a written acceptance

Mr Wilson promises to sell his house to Mr Brown for R450 000. Mr Brown sends a written offer to Mr Wilson but Mr Wilson does not send a written acceptance. Instead Mr Wilson sells his land to Mr Green for R600 000. Mr Brown is upset with Mr Wilson for breaking his promise and visits him at his home.

Questions

1. Role-play the meeting between Mr Brown and Mr Wilson.
2. Was there a legally binding contract between Mr Brown and Mr Wilson? Give reasons for your answer.

3.4.6 Breaking a contract

breach of contract

If a contract is broken it is known as a 'breach of contract'. A breach of contract happens when one person fails to do what he or she promises to do under the contract. A person may breach a contract by carrying out the contract too late. For example, if a seller does not deliver goods to the buyer on the agreed day, and the delay is not due to the buyer's fault, the seller has breached the contract. A breach may also happen where a person says or does something that makes it clear that he or she will not carry out his or her part of the contract, for instance, where a person promises to sell something to one person but sells it to another instead. There may also be a breach where some of the contract takes place, but something else agreed to is not carried out. This might happen, for example, where certain goods are ordered by a customer and the seller sends poor quality goods.

one party does not do what he or she promised to do

if a seller does not deliver goods to the buyer on the agreed day, the seller has breached the contract

Problem 7: Was there a breach of contract?

Has there been a breach of contract in the following cases? Give reasons for your answer.

1. Andy promises to sell his car to Bob, who agrees to buy it. Andy sells the car to Chris.
2. Fast Furnishers agree to deliver a bedroom suite to Harriet within two weeks of her signing an agreement. The undertaking to deliver is included in the written agreement. The bedroom suite is delivered a month after she signed the agreement.
3. Freddy undertakes to deliver first grade potatoes to Rosemary's Restaurant. Instead he delivers third grade potatoes.

3.4.6.1 What happens if a contract is breached?

The law helps an innocent party if a contract has been breached. This may take the form of 'specific performance', an 'interdict', damages or cancellation of the contract and damages.

legal remedies

3.4.6.1.1 Specific performance

Specific performance happens when a court orders the person who broke the contract to do what he or she promised (eg a painter is ordered to finish painting a house). The court may refuse to grant an order for specific performance if:

impossibility

1. It is impossible for the person who broke the contract to do what was promised.

compensation

2. Payment of money is a better way of compensating the person and will do justice to the injured party.

unreasonableness

3. It would be unreasonable or unjust to make the person who broke the contract, carry out the contract. If a court orders specific performance, it compels the person who broke the contract to perform what he or she undertook to perform in terms of the contract. If that person ignores the court order he or she may be guilty of 'contempt of court'. Contempt of court may result in the person who is disobeying the court order being fined or jailed.

contempt of court

3.4.6.1.2 Interdict

preventing someone from doing or forcing someone to do something

An interdict is a court order preventing the wrongdoing person from doing something (eg stopping a person from selling a car to B because he had agreed to sell it to A), or making the wrongdoing person do something (eg remove an illegal wall from his neighbour's property). Again, failure to obey an interdict may lead to a charge of contempt of court.

3.4.6.1.3 Damages

financial compensation

An innocent person may decide to keep to the contract, even though it is not carried out properly, and sue for damages. This means that the person does not cancel the contract. Instead he or she sues for any loss suffered as a result of the contract not being carried out properly. For example, where a suit is damaged by dry cleaners the customer may keep the suit and sue for the loss in its value. The damages claimed must be the type of damages that the parties would have expected if the contract had been breached.

a person may decide to sue for damages caused as a result of the contract not being carried out properly

3.4.6.1.4 Cancellation and damages

sometimes innocent persons may cancel contracts

An innocent person may cancel the contract if the wrongdoing person failed to carry out an important part of the contract. Once the contract is cancelled nobody is required to carry it out. The innocent person may also due for damages.

(For example, where a service station fails to repair a taxi on time and causes the owner to lose the fares of passengers, the owner can sue for damages. He or she would have to prove the value of the passenger fares that were lost.)

Problem 8: What should the court order?

Questions

Read the following cases and decide what you would order if you were the magistrate. Give reasons for your judgment.

1. Harold agrees to repair Roberta's house for R10 000. Roberta pays him a deposit of R2 000. Harold does nothing about the repairs.
2. Fanyana buys a brand-new stereo from Sound Waves for R5 000. When it is delivered the stereo has a large scratch across the top.
3. Koos uses his motorbike for deliveries. He takes it to Sammy's Service Station for repairs and tells them that he needs it the next day for deliveries otherwise he will lose money. The motorbike is returned the next week and is still not properly repaired. Koos loses R500 in delivery commission.
4. Paruk buys a car from Jadwat for R40 000. Before the car is delivered he hears that Jadwat also sold it to Norma. Jadwat is about to deliver the car to Norma and Paruk wants to stop him.

3.4.6.2 When does a contract end?

A contract ends when: (a) each party does what he or she promised to do; (b) both parties agree to end the contract; (c) there is a breach of the contract and a cancellation; or, (d) one of the parties dies.

3.5 Cars and the consumer

Outcomes

After completion of this section learners will be able to:

1. Understand the legal rules applicable when buying a car.

Assessment criteria

1. The steps a wise consumer should follow when buying a car are explained.
2. Advice is given to a consumer about the things that should be done when test driving a car.
3. A distinction is drawn between warranties and guarantees.
4. An explanation is given on what to do when buying a car from a private seller.
5. The transfer documents that are necessary for a consumer to transfer ownership of a car are listed.
6. The different types of vehicle insurance are explained.
7. A description is given of how a 'no claim bonus' works.
8. A set of facts is examined and a decision made on the liability of the insurance companies of the different parties involved in a motor accident.
9. An explanation is given of what to do and not to do in the case of an accident.

3.5.1 Introduction

car buying involves many areas of the law

A motor car is usually one of the most expensive purchases a consumer will ever make, apart from when he or she buys a house. The buying, owning, repairing, and selling of motor cars involves many areas of the law. In this section we will also apply some of the other things that we have learnt about consumer law, such as shopping around, entering into contracts, watching out for warranties and guarantees and using credit to buy motor cars. The very important problem of insurance will also be discussed briefly. We have used the word 'car', but what is said in this chapter also applies to other vehicles such as motorcycles, minibuses, bakkies, trucks, buses, etc.

3.5.2 Buying a car

what to look for

When shopping around for a new or used car, a consumer should look for the following: (a) a reasonable price; (b) reliability and economy; (c) safety; and (d) a good warranty or guarantee.

classified advertisements

visit websites, eg Autotrader, Gumtree and OLX

The best way that a consumer can be sure of paying a reasonable price for a car is to read the 'classified part' (headed 'Cars for Sale') of the newspapers or search websites on the Internet, eg Autotrader, OLX or Gumtree. The newspaper advertisements will usually tell you the age and price of the cars. You can then compare ages and prices

dealers and private sellers

see who has driven the car

shopping around

compare the ages and prices of the different cars. Usually cars sold by 'dealers' will be more expensive than those sold by private people. This is because dealers add a profit on to the price they pay when buying the car from the previous owner. The advantage of buying from reputable dealers, however, is that they are compelled by the CPA to give you a warranty or guarantee with the car. A private person will not usually give you a written guarantee, but you can rely on your common-law rights (see above para 3.4). When you buy a car from a private person, you know who has driven the car if the seller was the only owner. When you buy from a dealer you do not usually meet the previous owner, and have to rely on what the dealer says about the car. Another way of checking prices is to visit a few dealers' showrooms and compare the prices and condition of similar cars sold by them. The Internet also provides an easy way of comparing car prices without travelling around. Many dealers have a website which you can access and compare prices. You will soon have an idea as to what would be a reasonable price for the type of car that you wish to buy.

3.5.3 A reasonable price

discounts

Consumers shopping for a car should realise that very often it is possible to obtain large discounts when buying a new or used car. In the case of new cars, the discounts will depend upon the time of year the consumer buys the car, and whether there have been any special manufacturer's bonuses for the car dealers or whether the old shape of the car is being replaced with a new shape and design. Consumers buying cars should always ask the sales person whether or not they will be given a discount. Some car dealers try to impress buyers by offering to give them a free tank of petrol, but this is worth very little compared with a reasonable discount.

hidden costs

In addition to the price of the car there are a number of hidden costs. These may include, for example, VAT, finance charges, insurance costs, number plate costs and licensing fees (also referred to as 'on road costs'). These costs should be taken into account by consumers when deciding whether they can afford to buy a car.

3.5.4 Reliability and economy

check reliability

repair costs

logbooks and service records

Reliability means that the car will not break down. Therefore money will not have to be spent on repairs. Economy means that the car will be cheap to run because it does not use much petrol and oil, and does not have to be serviced very often. New cars should be reliable and the car dealer should be able to tell you what the petrol consumption should be and how often the car should be serviced. It is difficult to check how reliable and economical a second-hand car is. The best way of doing this is to ask for a copy of the car's petrol logbook (if one has been kept), and the service record of the car. The service record is usually stamped by the garage each time a motor car is serviced there. A careful consumer should also ask for the garage service invoices to check what work was done on the car.

service invoices

running costs

work out your running costs

Consumers should try to work out how much it would cost them to run the car each month. This can be done by looking at the petrol log-book, the service record, and the repair invoices of the car. The average monthly cost could be worked out by adding up the amount spent each year on petrol, oil, repairs, insurance and licensing, and dividing the total figure by 12. For example, if the person spends R12 000 a year on petrol, oil, repairs, insurance and licensing, the monthly cost of running the car is R1 000.

Problem 1: Gerhard's dream

Questions

Gerhard dreams about buying a GT Sprint motor car. He saves R8 000 towards buying it. He sees an advertisement by A1 Autos for 'Good used cars. All cars like new'. Gerhard calls in at A1 Autos' premises and examines the cars. Eventually he sees a GT Sprint car that he likes. The car costs R40 000.

1. Make a list of things that Gerhard should do or think about before going to A1 Autos.
2. In addition to the price, make a list of the other costs Gerhard should take into account before buying the car.
3. Where can Gerhard obtain information about the costs in 2 above?
4. Taking into account the lists you have made, role-play a discussion between Gerhard and the A1 Autos salesperson selling the GT Sprint.
5. Assuming that Gerhard is buying from a private person, role-play a discussion between Gerhard and the private seller.

changing gears

testing brakes

Test driving a used car: What to look for

When test driving a motor car, you should check the following:

1. Before driving off you should check that the gears move easily from reverse to first, and through the other gears. Then test the gear changes while driving. Watch out for strange noises and gears that are 'rough' or 'grate' when you change them.
2. Test the brakes by going up to about 55 km/h and then slowly pressing down on the brake pedal. If it goes down without slowing the car, or goes down quite far without slowing the car, the brakes are faulty.
3. If the car pulls to one side when you apply the brakes it may mean a fault in the brakes or suspension.

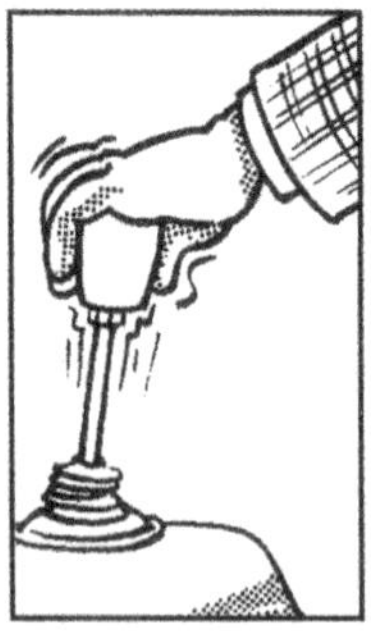

changing gears

testing the brakes

testing steering

4. Find an empty parking area and test the steering by driving slowly and moving the steering wheel from side to side. If it does not turn the car immediately the steering may be worn. Try driving about 35 km/h and allowing the car to steer itself. If the car goes off to one side there may be wheel alignment problems.

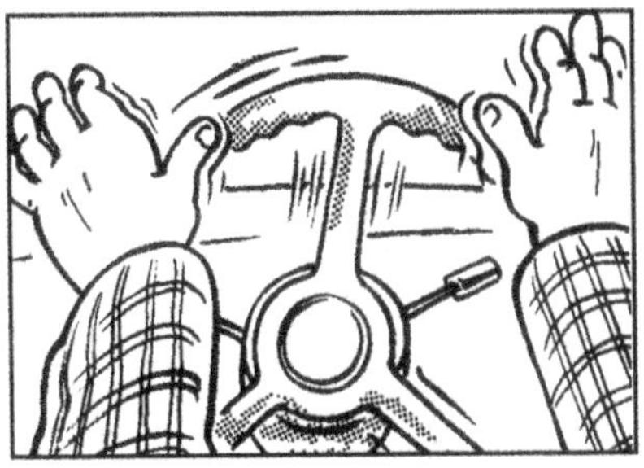

testing the steering

testing shock absorbers

5. Drive the car on a bumpy road. If it moves from side to side or bounces too much the shock absorbers may be faulty. Also listen for loud rattles and other strange noises.

checking for leaks

6. Park the car for a short while, then drive it forward. Check for any leaks (eg oil, water, brake fluid).

testing the shock absorbers

checking for leaks

Important:
The best way of checking a used car is to ask an organisation like the AA (Automobile Association) to do it for you. They will charge you a lower price if you are a member of the AA and more if you are not a member of the AA, but will give you a full report on the car, including a checklist of faults. There are AA testing workshops in most large towns.

Buying a used car: What to look for
When buying a used car you should check the following:

A. Mechanical parts

engine and oil

1. Is the engine clean and the engine oil clear? Are there oil leaks?

battery

2. Are the battery terminals clean, or corroded by acid?

exhaust

3. Is the exhaust smoke black, blue or white when you start the engine? White smoke is all right, black smoke may mean there is a carburettor problem, blue smoke may mean the engine is worn.
4. Is the exhaust noisy? If so, it should be fixed.

engine number

5. Is the engine number on the engine block the same as on the registration papers? If not, the car may be stolen.

engine and oil

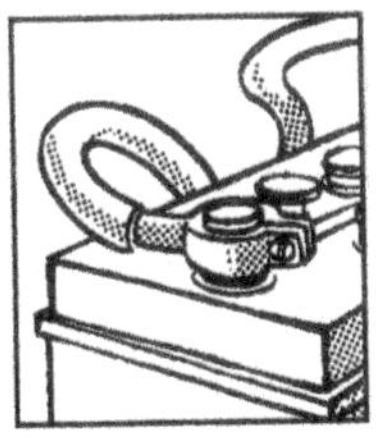

battery

exhaust

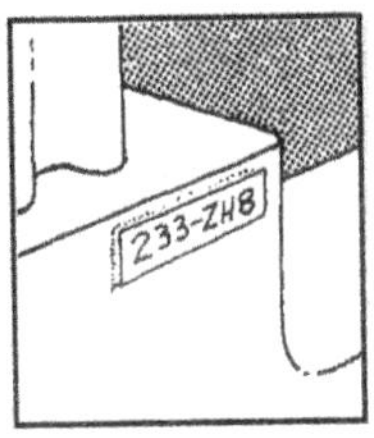

engine number

6. Are the tyres worn evenly? Is there enough tread on the tyres? If not they should be replaced.
7. When you shake the front wheels from side to side they should not be too loose.

suspension

8. Is the suspension in order? If you push down on the car above each mud-guard, the car should go down and then bounce back to its original position. If it does not there is something wrong with the suspension or springs.

lights and indicators

9. Do all the lights and indicators work? Are there any cracks in the glass covering the lights?

gauges

10. Do the oil, temperature, fuel and speedometer gauges work?

windscreen wipers

11. Do the windscreen wipers and hooters work?
12. Does the steering wheel feel loose when you turn it?

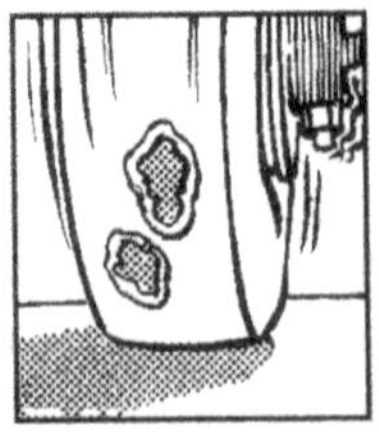
wheels and tyres

suspension

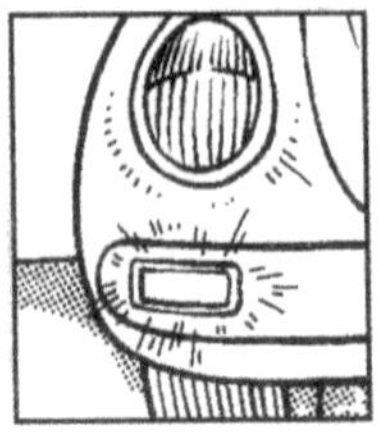
lights and indicators

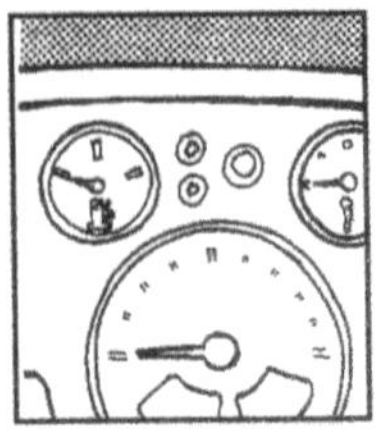
gauges

windscreen wipers

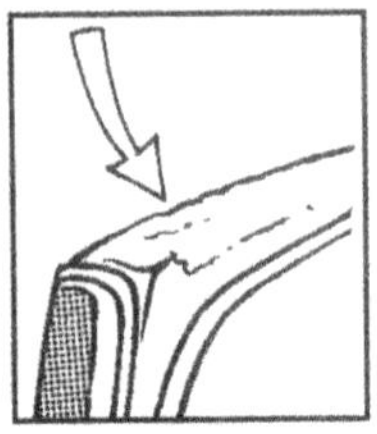
repainted surfaces

upholstery

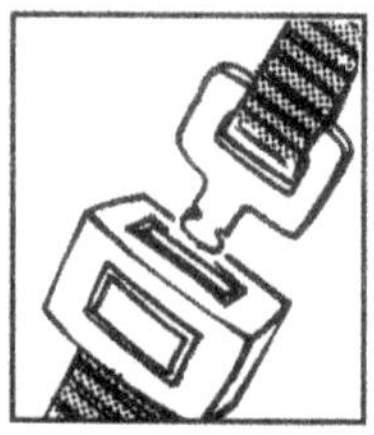
seat belts

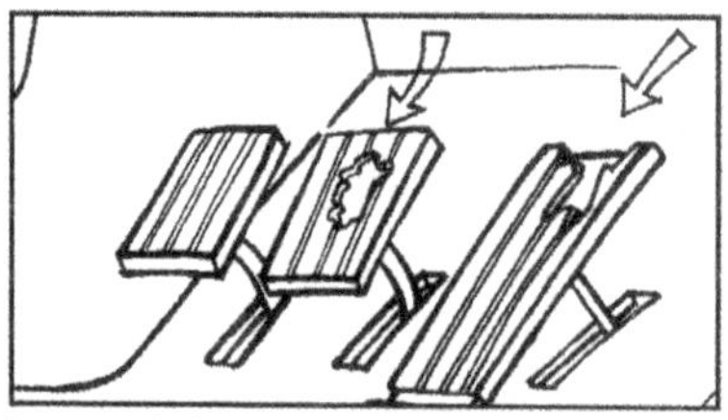
foot pedals

B. Bodywork

1. Is there any rust? The best place to look is at the bottom of doors, and the edges of the boot and bonnet. Also look inside the boot to see if it has rust, which might show that it leaks.

repainted surfaces

2. Are there uneven paint surfaces or paint 'ripples'? These may show that the car has been repainted because it was involved in an accident, or because rust has been taken out. Ask the seller why it was repainted.
3. Do the windscreen and windows have any cracks or scratches that make them difficult to see through?

upholstery

4. Are the seats in good condition? Are the seats torn or worn? Do the seats sag? Do they slide backwards or forwards easily? If there are seat covers check underneath to see if the upholstery is torn or worn.

seat belts

5. Are the seat belts in good condition? Do they adjust easily? Are they torn? Are they clean?
6. Is the steering wheel cracked? If it has a steering wheel cover, ask the seller to remove the cover so that you can check for cracks.

foot pedals

7. Are there rubber covers on the foot pedals? If so, are they too worn or too new? If so, ask why.

3.5.5 Safety

think about safety

safety checks

Many consumers fail to think about safety when buying cars. Safety is important because of the high accident rate in South Africa. When buying a car, a consumer should test drive it (see above box 'Test driving a used car'), in order to check things like: (a) how much can be seen from the driver's seat (eg check for blind spots, windscreen glare in strong sunlight, and repositioning of mirrors; (b) whether all the controls can be reached while sitting in the driver's seat while the seat belt is fastened; and, (c) the amount of protection given to the driver and passengers by the bumpers and safety belts.

3.5.6 Warranties and guarantees

compare guarantees: Will the dealer be able to repair?

paying for extra protection

When buying a motor car consumers should compare warranties and guarantees, and check whether the dealer would be able to make any necessary repairs. The CPA now gives all consumers a statutory guarantee of at least six months against defects if the car is bought from a dealer. This is in addition to any warranty or guarantee given by the dealer or manufacturer. Most warranties for new cars cover parts (except batteries and tyres), eg for one to three years, or 100 000 kilometres, whichever comes first. Some manufacturers offer to give an extended warranty if the buyer is prepared to pay more. Other warranties may be given by manufacturers of products that are used in car engines. Many warranties and guarantees are the same, but consumers should make sure that they read and fully understand the protection provided – if any. The CPA also offers protection to a consumer as the terms of the warranty are subject to the restrictions placed on excluding consumers' rights in terms of the common law and the CPA.

used car warranties

conditions in warranties

when buying a car from a dealer, the consumer is protected by the CPA

in a private sale the consumer is not protected by the CPA

Private sellers of used cars may also give warranties. For example a warranty or guarantee for a used car may be for one or two months or 2 000 or 4 000 kilometres, from the date it was bought. Sometimes, however, a warranty or guarantee may not be given. If a warranty is not given the consumer is protected by the common law. A consumer who feels more comfortable with a warranty should ask for a written warranty to be included with the sale of the motor car. Consumers should not sign warranties they have not read or which take away all their common-law rights. They should read warranties carefully because they may not be able to use them if they do not carry out the conditions (eg if the owner fails to service the car 'properly' by taking it to a service station instead of a registered dealer), as required by the warranty. Unlike the case of buying the car from a dealer, in a private sale the consumer is not protected by the CPA. Consumers should also make sure that the warranty and any other promises are written down. The warranty and other written promises by the seller should be kept in a safe place.

a car bought 'as is' from a private seller is bought with all its faults

When buying a used car, consumers should remember that if it is bought 'as is' they are buying it with all its faults. This is the case when the car is bought from a private seller, but if the car is bought from a dealer the CPA restricts the CPA restricts the ability of the dealer to sell the car 'as is'

what does 'good condition' mean?

hidden defects

the ability of the dealer to sell the car 'as is'. The dealer may only do so if (a) the defects have been brought to the attention of the consumer and (b) the consumer has expressly agreed to accept it in that condition. Also, if the seller says that the car is 'in good condition' this merely means that it is in good condition for a used car. It does not mean that there are no defects. If the seller says the car is in 'a good mechanical condition' and it is not, the seller will be liable for the cost of putting the car into a good mechanical condition. Before buying a used car, a buyer should consult the AA and ask them to inspect the car for defects. A roadworthy certificate (COR) does not guarantee that there are no defects in the motor car.

Problem 2: Phewa and the minibus

Phewa goes to Babu's Used Bargains to buy a minibus. The saleslady says: 'This is the best minibus on the market. It will give you many years of good service.'

The price is R60 000 but the saleslady says that she will be able to arrange for a R3 000 discount. She says that Babu's will let him sign a credit agreement and sell him the necessary insurance. Babu's will also guarantee to make any repairs to the engine – not caused by bad driving – for a period of 30 days or 2 000 kilometres, whichever comes first. Phewa is very excited about buying the minibus.

Questions

1. What should Phewa do before agreeing to buy the minibus?
2. If you were Phewa, would you take the minibus for a test drive? Give reasons for your answer. If Phewa took it for a test drive what should he look out for?
3. Did the saleslady make any promises to Phewa or were her words merely 'puffing'?
4. Role-play the conversation between Phewa and the saleslady.

3.5.7 Buying from private sellers

common-law protection

has the seller paid the previous owner in full?

When buying a car from a private seller, a consumer is not protected by the Consumer Protection Act, but is protected by the common law (see above para 3.4). Such consumers should always make sure that the private seller has paid the previous owner the full purchase price. If not, the consumer may have to hand the car back to the previous owner. The consumer would then have to try to recover the price paid from the dishonest private seller. Many consumers have bought cars from private sellers and then had them repossessed by credit agreement sellers because the private seller had not paid off the full price.

taking over payments

Sometimes a credit seller will allow a new buyer to take over the payments from the previous buyer. The new buyer will then have to enter into a credit agreement with the previous seller.

obtain the seller's name and address

all promises in writing

organising the paperwork

Consumers buying from private sellers should also make sure that they have the full address and telephone number of the seller. If the seller works, they should also obtain his or her work address and telephone number. Any promises or guarantees should be put in writing; otherwise the consumer has to rely on the common law. It is a good idea to make sure that the car has a certificate of roadworthiness (COR) when buying from a private seller. Cars bought from private sellers are usually cheaper than those bought from dealers. It is also often easier to obtain copies of the petrol log-book, service record and repair invoices from private sellers than dealers. The disadvantage of buying from a private dealer is that consumers may have to organise all the transfer documents themselves, but this is not difficult. A buyer could ask the seller to do all the paperwork.

Problem 3: Car dealers v private sellers

Questions

1. What are the advantages and disadvantages of buying cars from used car dealers?
2. What are the advantages and disadvantages of buying cars from private sellers?
3. Make a list of the things you would do when buying a used car from a private seller, which you would not have to do when buying from a dealer.

Documents necessary to transfer a car

The following documents are necessary to transfer a car into a buyer's name:

1. A registration certificate which gives the type, colour, make, model, licence registration number (on licence plate), engine number of the car, and the name, address, identity number and telephone number of the owner.
2. A certificate of roadworthiness (COR), which is obtained from accredited garages and the local traffic department and lasts for 60 days (two months). It can be obtained by buyers or sellers, but consumers should ask the seller to obtain it in case expensive repairs have to be done.
3. A change of ownership form that must be completed by both the seller and the buyer.
4. A detailed invoice and receipt for money paid to the seller. The invoice should mention the make of the car, year, licence plate number and the price paid. The receipt should show the amount paid and should be signed by the seller.
5. The car's licence disc that will be on the windscreen, and it should be up to date.

Important: Before signing any transfer documents, make sure that the seller is the owner of the car, and has paid off the previous purchase price.

3.5.8 Transfer documents

change of ownership

certificate of roadworthiness (COR)

When a car is sold the seller and buyer must complete transfer documents. These record the change of ownership and the date of sale. They must be signed by both the seller and the buyer. The buyer has to obtain a certificate of roadworthiness (COR) for the car, unless the seller has already done so. There are testing centres in most towns and cities for examining the safety of motor vehicles and issuing CORs. CORs are valid for 60 days and must be handed in by the buyer when registering the car in his or her name.

requirements for COR

When a car is tested for a COR the examiners will check the following: brakes; lights, including indicators; windscreen wipers; engine number; tyres; body work, the underneath of the car; steering mechanism; exhaust system; silencer system; shock absorbers; wheel bearings; and windscreen. A COR, however, does not mean that the car has not defects. Some of the defects mentioned above may not be checked. Even though a car has a COR you should carry out the checks mentioned above in the box (see above para 3.5.4).

buying from a dealer

When a consumer buys a car from a used car dealer the transfer documents and the COR are organised by the dealer. The consumer merely has to sign the transfer papers. Dealers who sell cars that have certificates of roadworthiness usually advertise them 'with COR'.

Problem 4: Anil wants to take ownership of a car

Questions

Anil, after carefully checking a used sports car, decides to buy it. He wants to pay the full price in cash. Because he is buying the car from Jason, a private person, Anil decides to do all the paperwork himself.

1. Make a list of all the documents Anil will need.
2. Role-play Anil checking the documents with Jason.

3.5.9 Insuring a car

'premiums', 'cover' and 'policies'

Every person who buys a car should make sure that it is insured. Insurance companies provide compensation when people are injured or property is damaged. People who take out insurance have to pay the insurance company a certain amount of money each year. This money is called a 'premium'. The protection given by an insurance company is called 'cover'. The contract between an insurance company and a consumer is called a 'policy'. The person covered by an insurance policy is called the 'insured'.

insurance against injury or death

Insurance companies protecting people against injuries may give cover for medical bills, lost wages, pain and suffering and disfigurement (where a person's body becomes deformed). If the insured person dies an insurance company third party insurance

may pay medical and funeral expenses, and compensate the people who were supported by the dead person. A life policy may also pay out a lump sum to a named person on the death of an insured person. Most motor accident insurance policies provide compensation for injury and death. The Road Accident Fund creates a system of automatic 'third party' insurance for all motor vehicles in South Africa (see below para 3.5.9.1).

damage to cars and property

Insurance policies dealing with damage to cars or property cover consumers for (a) fire and theft (see below para 3.5.9.3); (b) balance of third party (see below para 3.5.9.2); and (c) comprehensive insurance (see below para 3.5.9.5).

Problem 5: Some questions on insurance

Questions

1. Do you think people should take out insurance against accidents? Give reasons for your answer.
2. What compensation is given by insurance companies that cover people for injuries or death caused by accidents?

3.5.9.1 Automatic ('third party') motor vehicle insurance

funded by fuel levy

The Road Accident Fund Act creates a system of automatic 'third party' motor vehicle insurance. The insurance is automatic. This means that the owner of the vehicle does not have to do anything to get the insurance. Instead, a levy is placed on all fuel. The funds generated by this levy are then put in the 'Road Accident Fund' (RAF) and used to pay insurance claims.

insurance for other people involved in an accident

The automatic insurance provided to motor vehicles is 'third party' insurance. 'Third party' insurance covers people other than the driver of an insured vehicle. It does not apply only to people actually injured in car accidents.

It also applies to people who suffer loss as the result of the death of a breadwinner. The RAF will compensate a third party for any loss caused by the driving of a motor vehicle. This loss must, however, have been caused by death or bodily injury.

cases where the Road Accident Fund will not pay out

The RAF is only liable if the driver of the car was at fault. This means that the driver must have been negligent (ie he or she did not observe the standard of care that a reasonable person would have observed), or have intentionally caused the accident. An example of negligence would be if the driver did not intend to cause an accident but was driving too fast.

'third party' sues the RAF

The third party will sue the RAF for money. The third party does not sue the driver of the insured vehicle. This does not mean that drivers who cause accidents avoid paying for them. If the RAF pays out it can then claim what it paid to the third party from the driver who was at fault.

the Road Accident Fund will not pay out if the driver was drunk or on drugs

consult the RAF or a lawyer if injured in an accident

People injured in a motor collision may contact the RAF directly. If they are not happy with how the RAF is handling their claim they should contact a lawyer for help to make a claim against the RAF. They should, however, find out how much the lawyer will charge them. This is because some lawyers take advantage of people making RAF claims by taking a lot of the money eventually paid by the RAF. Lawyers will usually take RAF claims without charging an initial fee in the hope of recovering their fees later if the claim is successful.

Problem 6: Some questions on motor accidents

Questions

1. Describe an accident in which you or people you know were involved. What happened? Were you or they compensated by an insurance company? Give reasons for your answer.
2. Assume that you caused an accident and the driver of the other car was so badly injured that he or she could never walk again. Who do you think would have to compensate her if your car was not insured? Why?
3. Do you think that it would be fair if injured people could only obtain compensation if the person who caused the accident was able to pay? Why or why not?

3.5.9.2 Balance of third party insurance

insurance against damage to property

Ordinary third party insurance (see above para 3.5.9.1) only covers injury to and death of third parties – not damage to property. Balance of third party insurance, however, covers damage to the property of third parties. It must be taken out and paid for by the car owner. It covers not only damage to people's cars but also to property such as walls, buildings or windows.

3.5.9.3 Fire and theft insurance

damage by fire or loss through theft

A person who takes out insurance against fire and theft will be compensated if the car is damaged by fire or stolen. The insurance company must decide whether the car is worth repairing. If not, the insured person will be given an amount equal to what the car could have been sold for (ie its market price).

3.5.9.4 Balance of third party, fire and theft insurance

no cover for damage caused by someone else

This is a mixture of fire and theft insurance and balance of third party insurance. Therefore if your car is damaged by fire or theft you will be compensated. Also if you damage another person's car or property, the insurance company will pay out the owner. If, however, your car is damaged by somebody else or in some other way you will not be covered. The best way to insure your car against all possible damage, including fire and theft, is to take out comprehensive insurance.

3.5.9.5 Comprehensive insurance

the most complete form of insurance

Comprehensive insurance is the most expensive type of insurance. It gives all the benefits of balance of third party, fire and theft insurance as well as cover against damage to the insured's car, no matter how the damage is caused. This applies even if the driver of the insured car caused the damage. It also covers injuries to passengers and third parties.

no cover for wear and tear

Comprehensive insurance, however, does not cover repairs for wear and tear due to age. It does usually include the cost of towing the car from the scene of a motor accident. Extra insurance can be taken out to include things like protection against unrest, riots and disturbances. Otherwise these are not usually covered.

when insurance companies will not pay out

Most insurance policies will not pay out (a) if the car is driven by a person who does not have a driver's licence; (b) if the car is driven by a person who is under the influence of alcohol or drugs; (c) where the car is competing in some kind of motor sport; or (d) the car is being used for hire (eg a pirate taxi). If a 'lift club' is using the car, the premium will be slightly increased. A lift club is an agreement in which people give each other or each other's children lifts in each other's cars.

it is very risky not to insure a car

[Note: Many young people do not insure their cars because it is very expensive. However, accidents occur every day on South African roads and people who are uninsured are taking a great risk. Consumers should not buy cars they cannot afford to insure.]

Problem 7: The crash in the rain

Questions

Driving in the rain, Micky tries to pass a slow-moving truck just as the traffic light changes from green to orange. Micky thinks that if he goes fast enough he will be able to get through the light before it changes to red. Suddenly an on-coming van driven by Donald turns immediately in front of him. Micky puts his foot on the brakes but nothing happens. Micky's car smashes into the van. Micky is slightly injured but Donald is seriously injured. Micky's car and Donald's van are badly damaged and have to be repaired. Micky's car will cost R18 000 to repair and Donald's van R14 000.

Both cars are covered by the Road Accident Fund. Micky has balance of third party insurance, but Donald is not insured.

1. Who do you think should be responsible for paying the medical bills and car repairs resulting from this accident?
2. Assume that Micky and Donald consult their attorneys. Role-play Micky's and Donald's attorneys negotiating a settlement.

3.5.9.6 'Excesses' on insurance policies

'excesses' must be paid by the insured person in addition to what the insurance company pays

Usually insurance companies require an insured person to pay an 'excess' on the first part of a claim. An excess is the amount that must be paid by the insured if he or she wishes to claim under the policy. For example, an insurance policy may say that the motorist must pay the first R1 000, or in the case of a young person (usually under 25 years), R2 000. This is to stop insured people claiming small amounts from their insurance companies. It also means that insurance companies pay out less on larger claims.

For instance, if an insured claims R4 000 and the excess is R1 000, the insurance company will only pay out R3 000. Likewise if the insurance company had to pay a third party R4 000, the company would pay out R3 000 and the insured R1 000.

Problem 8: The crash in the rain: some more questions

Questions

Re-read 'The crash in the rain'. Assume that both Micky and Donald had comprehensive insurance cover. Also assume that Micky was at fault.

1. Whose insurance company should pay for Donald's hospital and car repair expenses?
2. Whose insurance company should pay for Micky's hospital and car expenses?
3. Role-play the attorneys of Donald's and Micky's insurance companies negotiating a settlement.
4. Assume that Micky has to pay a R1 000 excess. How much would Micky's insurance company pay Donald? Why?

3.5.9.7 No claim bonuses

a discount on the premiums

A'no claim bonus' is given to insured people who do not claim against their insurance companies. It is a discount on the premiums an insured person has to pay for insurance. A no claim bonus is given to drivers who have a good record of safety and have not caused accidents. After about four years good drivers may receive a discount of up to 40% on their original premium because they have not claimed against their insurance companies. For example, if the premium is R400, the driver may be given a discount of 40% (R160) and only have to pay R240 to receive the same insurance cover. Drivers may lose their no claim bonuses if they claim against their insurance companies. Most companies, however, will not immediately cancel a no claim bonus. They may reduce the no claim bonus if the insured makes a single claim. Sometimes a motorist will have to decide whether it is worth claiming if there is a risk of losing a no claim bonus. Therefore if the claim is small it might not be worth claiming against the insurance company and losing a no claim bonus. It is possible to take out extra insurance so that if the insured does not claim he or she will not lose the no claim bonus. This can be done by paying an extra premium to the insurance company.

a no claim bonus may be lost when a person claims from the insurance company

Advice on buying car insurance

1. Learn about the different types of car insurance and find out how much they cost before making a decision.
2. Find out whether the insurance company will give you a 'no claim bonus' if you do not have any accidents. Also ask whether the company will increase the premiums if you cause an accident and claim.
3. Find out if you will have to pay a higher premium because you are young. Will the insurance company still charge a higher premium even though you are young with a good driving record?
4. Ask whether the insurance company will charge less if you are insured under your parents' policy and not under your own policy.
5. Find out what 'excess' or extra amount you will have to pay before the insurance company pays out a claim.

3.5.10 What to do in the case of an accident

common sense

If a person is involved in an accident, there are certain things that should, and should not, be done. Many of these are common sense, but because accidents upset people emotionally it is useful to know what to do in advance.

3.5.10.1 Things that should be done

do not move the cars

If anyone is killed or seriously injured, the police or a traffic officer and an ambulance should be called immediately. People should not move the cars until ordered to do so by the police or traffic officer. If, however, the cars are completely blocking the road they may be moved provided their positions are clearly marked on the road. People involved in accidents must stop.

in the case of injury call the police and an ambulance immediately

get details of drivers and witnesses

All drivers involved in an accident should exchange: (a) names, addresses and telephone numbers; (b) driver's licence numbers; (c) car registration numbers; (d) the makes, models and years of the cars; (e) the names, addresses and telephone numbers of the insurance companies; (f) third party token numbers; and, (g) the names, addresses and telephone numbers of any witnesses. It is also useful to have a list of the registration numbers of the witnesses' cars so that the witnesses can be found later if necessary. Take photos with your cellphone.

write down a description of what happened

All important information should be written down as soon after the accident as possible while it's still fresh in your mind. This information should only be given to your attorney or insurance company. A plan of the accident should be drawn showing: (a) the width of the road; (b) the position of any traffic lights and intersections; (c) the position of the cars before they crashed, when they crashed, and after they crashed; and, (d) the directions in which the cars were travelling.

report to the police within 24 hours

contact your insurance company

The accident must be reported to the nearest police station within 24 hours and you must take your driver's licence with you. After an accident you should contact your insurance company as soon as possible. The company will then ask you to call in and make a statement. Failure to tell your insurance company within a certain period of time (eg within a few days) may mean that the company will not pay out for the damage caused. You may then have to pay for the damage yourself. You should obtain quotations for repairs from three or more panel-beaters and service stations approved by your insurance company.

get repair quotations

If your car is not insured and has been damaged, you should obtain quotations for repairs from three or more panel-beaters and service stations. These quotations can be used to work out how much to claim if the person causing the accident does not agree to pay you. (For what happens when you sue somebody in a civil case see above para 1.5.1.)

3.5.10.2 Things that should not be done

do not admit fault

The following things should not be done: (a) do not say how much your insurance company will pay out; (b) do not say that you are guilty; (c) do not say that your insurance company will take care of everything; and, (d) do not sign any paper that says you were not injured – some motor accident injuries can only be noticed days afterwards. It is essential that you do not say that you are liable for the accident otherwise your insurance company may refuse to pay out on the claim. You may then have to pay it yourself.

let the insurance company deal with the case

Your insurance company should deal with all telephone calls and letters from the other parties involved. If the accident was serious and people were injured it may be wise to ask a lawyer to handle all telephone calls and letters. People who are injured can usually claim from the Road Accident Fund (see above para 3.5.9.1).

Problem 9: The motorcycle accident

Questions

One day, while riding home from town, Sabelo's motorcycle was hit from behind by Kippie's bakkie. The accident occurred as Sabelo went through a traffic light which was changing from green to orange. Nobody was injured in the accident. While Sabelo was speaking to Kippie, he noticed that Kippie's eyes were bloodshot and his breath smelt of alcohol.

1. Make a list of the information that Sabelo should write down.
2. What should Sabelo do next? Why?
3. Role-play a conversation between Sabelo and Kippie at the scene of the accident.

Sabelo's motor cycle is hit from behind by Kippie's bakkie

Further reading

1.1 Contracts

Boezaart T *Child Law in South Africa* (2009) p 197

Hutchison D et al *The Law of Contract in South Africa* (2009)

Children's Act 38 of 2005

Joubert WA *The Law of South Africa* 2 ed, Vol 5 Part 1 (2010)

Sesing v Minister of Police 1978 (4) SA 742 (W) 745

1.2 Consumer Protection

Consumer Protection Act 68 of 2008 and Regulations in terms of the Consumer Protection Act 68 of 2008

Electronic Communications and Transactions Act 25 of 2002

Department of Trade and Industry *Your Guide to Consumer Rights and How to Protect Them*

Van Eeden E A *Guide to the Consumer Protection Act* (2009)

Van Eeden E A *Commentary on the Consumer Protection Act 2008* (2011)

Badler H *What are my consumer rights?* http://www.bizcommunity.com/Article/196/160/17811.html accessed on 11 October 2011

Joubert WA *The Law of South Africa* 2 ed, Vol 5 Part 1 (2010)

http://www.michalsons.co.za/grey-goods-under-the-consumer-protection-act/8162 accessed on 13 January 2012

http://www.southafrica.info/services/consumer/consumer.htm accessed on 11 October 2011

1.3 Consumer Protection Act of 2008

Consumer Protection Act 68 of 2008 and Regulations in terms of the Consumer Protection Act 68 of 2008

Electronic Communications and Transactions Act 25 of 2002

Department of Trade and Industry *Your Guide to Consumer Rights and How to Protect Them*

Van Eeden E A *Guide to the Consumer Protection Act* (2009)

Van Eeden E A *Commentary on the Consumer Protection Act 2008* (2011)

Joubert WA *The Law of South Africa* 2 ed, Vol 5 Part 1 (2010)

Badler H *What are my consumer rights?* http://www.bizcommunity.com/Article/196/160/17811.html accessed on 11 October 2011

http://www.michalsons.co.za/grey-goods-under-the-consumer-protection-act/8162 accessed on 13 January 2012

http://www.southafrica.info/services/consumer/consumer.htm accessed on 11 October 2011

3.4 Credit buying and Credit Agreements

National Credit Act 34 of 2005 and Regulations in terms of the National Credit Act 34 of 2005

Promotion of Equality and Prevention of Unfair Discrimination Act 4 of 2000

South African Schools Act 84 of 1996

Campbell N & Logan S *The Credit Guide: Manage your Money with the National Credit Act* (2008)

Joubert WA *The Law of South Africa* 2 ed, Vol 5 Part 1 (2010)

Scholtz JW et al *Guide to the National Credit Act* Service Issue 2

Bregman R & Logan S (Law Society of South Africa) *The National Credit Act 43 of 2005 A Basic Guide for Attorneys*, http://www.un.org/esa/sustdev/publications/consumption_en.pdf accessed on 11 October 2011

Goodwin-Groen RP *The National Credit Act and its Regulations in the Context of Access to Finance in South Africa*, http://www.amfisa.org.za/Downloads/Finmark%20Trust%20paper%20on%20NCR.pdf accessed on 30 April 2012

http://www.ncf.org.za/services/complain.html accessed on 11 October 2011

http://www.ncf.org.za/main.php?include=about/history.html&menu=menus/about.html accessed on 11 October 2011

http://www.un.org/esa/sustdev/publications/consumption_en.pdf accessed on 11 October 2011

http://www.investorwords.com/620/bundling.html#ixzz1jJywG2tc accessed on 12 January 2012

http://www.southafrica.info/services/consumer/consumer.htm accessed on 11 October 2011

http://www.ncf.org.za/services/complain.html accessed on 11 October 2011.

National Credit Regulator v C Bornman and Others case no NCT/656/2010/57(1)(a)(c)(P), National Consumer Tribunal (unreported)

Nedbank v National Credit Regulator 2011 (3) SA 581 (SCA)

Wesbank v Papier 2011 (2) SA 395 (WCC)

Street law

4. Family law

CONTENTS

PART FOUR

Family law

4.1 The family, marriage, and civil unions

Outcomes

After completion of this section learners will be able to:

1. Demonstrate an understanding of the different types of marriages, civil unions and families in South African law.

Assessment criteria

1. The meaning of 'family' is explained.
2. An explanation is given as to why the nuclear definition of the family is not a good definition of the modern South African family.
3. Different types of marriages and civil unions are identified.
4. A set of facts is given and a decision made on who can and cannot marry or enter into a civil union.
5. A set of facts is given and a decision made on whether or not the marriages or civil unions are valid.
6. A description is given of how a marriage or a civil union is entered into.
7. The requirements for entering into a valid marriage or civil union are given.
8. The customary marriage is explained.
9. The status of Muslim and Hindu marriages is explained.

4.1.1 The family

family members

Most of us are members of a family and affected by family law. We become members of a family by birth, marriage, adoption, foster care or living together. Children who are adopted by a family are legally regarded as the natural children of their adoptive parents even though they may not be related to them by blood. Children in foster care are brought up by a family but are not legally regarded as the natural children of their foster parents.

the role of family life

Family law includes such topics as marriage, civil unions, husbands and wives or civil union partners, parents and children, foster care and adoption, divorce and death.

Family law is the area of the law that deals mainly with the family. There are two main traditional areas of family law which will be dealt with this book. The first is the law of unions, which was known as the law of husband and wife. It is now called the law of unions because partners in a marriage are no longer limited to husbands and wives – the concept also extends to same-sex partners in civil unions. The law of unions includes such topics as engagement, formalities for marriages or civil unions, the consequences of marriages and civil unions; and the mechanisms for the dissolution of marriages or civil unions. The other is the law of parental rights and responsibilities, which was known as the law of parent and child. This branch of the law deals with parental rights and responsibilities of parents themselves, children, extended family members and third parties in exercising those rights. The main topics in this area are foster care and adoption.

4.1.1.1 What is a family?

Before studying family law it is important to understand what is meant by 'a family'. Family is used in both the wide and narrow sense. In the wide sense (extended family), it includes all the blood relatives or people who have become related because of adoption, marriage, a civil union and other forms. In the narrow sense, it refers to the nuclear family (spouses or partners and their children).

extended families

Before the development of large towns and cities most people in South Africa lived in 'extended' families. This meant that children, their parents and sometimes grandparents, uncles, aunts and cousins all lived together in one home or in small communities on farms or in small villages.

nuclear families

During the twentieth century there was a move away from rural areas to cities and many extended families were broken up. People began to form nuclear families. A nuclear family is one where just the parents and their children live together without other relatives. Young couples from different families get married or enter into civil unions and set up their own small family, which usually includes only themselves and their children.

However, in rural areas, the extended family is still a very common form of family. There are also extended families in the South African Indian community.

4.1.1.2 The modern family

new types of families

In recent times the traditional type of family has changed. Even in urban areas, the nuclear family is becoming less common. Many married women now go out to work, and many couples have fewer children or no children at all. More children are born of unmarried parents (before the coming into force of the Children's Act, a child whose parents were not legally married was known as an 'illegitimate' or an 'extra-marital' child), and more couples are divorced, which has increased the number of 'single-parent' families. Some couples also choose to live together, without getting legally married or entering into a civil union – this is known as cohabitation.

religious marriages

Previously, the traditional definition of the family did not recognise that many couples in South Africa are not married in terms of the marriage laws made by Parliament. Instead, they are married under Muslim or Hindu religion or custom or indigenous customary law. In addition, the definition did not recognise that many couples of the same sex live together in homosexual or lesbian relationships, and raise children. In other words, the definition did not recognise the diversity of South Africa.

constitutional guarantees

The Constitution, however, guarantees freedom from discrimination. It also says that Parliament may pass laws that recognise marriages and families formed under any tradition or religion. The Constitution recognises that South Africa is a diverse country. Since 1994, the legal definition of the family has begun to change so that it does not reflect only the Western nuclear conception. These changes are discussed in this book.

Due to these many changes it is difficult to define the typical South African family. Nonetheless, the family may be broadly defined as people who live together as a unit and care for and support one another.

the extended family is more common among people living in the country, although it has been disrupted by the system of migrant labour

in the past the traditional modern family usually had a working father, a mother working in the home and dependent children

Problem 1: What is a family?

Questions

1. Is it possible to give a definition of a family? If so, what would it be?
2. Is the Western nuclear definition of the family a good definition of the family in South Africa? Why or why not?
3. Is there such a thing as an 'ideal' family? If so, how would you describe it?

4.1.2 Marriage

Marriage has traditionally been defined as a contract entered into in front of a 'marriage officer', between a man and a woman, in which they agree to live together as husband and wife. As mentioned, since the passing of the Constitution, this definition has changed to take account of the diversity of South Africa. The traditional definition does not, for example, recognise that many South Africans are in same-sex relationships, or in marriages concluded under Muslim or Hindu religion, or customary law. The Civil Union Act now allows same-sex partners to enter into a civil union, which has the same consequences as a marriage.

4.1.3 Civil unions

same-sex couples can now enter into a civil union

A civil union is defined as the monogamous (having only one spouse), voluntary union of two people who are at least 18 years of age, which is solemnised and registered in terms of the procedures set out in the Civil Union Act. This means same-sex partners can now 'marry'. A civil union includes a marriage or a civil partnership. The civil union partners themselves may decide whether they wish their civil union to take the form of a marriage or a civil union partnership. The requirements for, and the consequences of, a civil union in a form of marriage or partnership are exactly the same. Also, apart from the fact that a civil union may be entered into by same-sex partners, the requirements for and consequences of, a civil union and those of a civil marriage are identical.

requirements of a civil union

children under 18 years may not enter into civil unions

As a civil union is a contract just like the civil marriage, both parties to a civil union must have the capacity to act. All the legal requirements for the conclusion of a civil marriage (see below para 4.1.4.3) apply to the civil union, except regarding the position of minors: While civil marriages and customary marriages allow minors to enter into such marriages with the written consent of their parent(s) or guardian(s) and the Minister of Home Affairs where applicable, the Civil Union Act does not provide for any exception to the rule that only persons who have already reached 18 years can enter into a civil union. This means a minor cannot enter into a civil union even if he or she obtains the necessary consent. It could be argued that this difference between minors wishing to enter into a civil marriage/ customary marriage and those wishing to enter a civil union could be considered unconstitutional, but this has not yet been decided by the courts.

the consequences of a civil union are the same as for marriage

The legal consequences of civil marriages apply equally to civil unions. For example, a person in a civil union cannot enter into another civil union or customary marriage or civil marriage with another person while the first civil union still exists. Also, parties to a civil union are obliged to support and maintain each other. The matrimonial property system (community of property or out of community of property) is governed by the same rules that apply to civil marriages. Civil unions are ended in the same way as civil marriages (see below para 4.5.2).

the common-law definition of marriage held to be unconstitutional

As already mentioned, same-sex couples could not marry previously because under the common law marriage was defined as the monogamous (single) voluntary union of two people of the opposite sex. Because the Bill of Rights in the Constitution gives all people the right to equality, in 2006 the Constitutional Court in the case of *Minister of Home Affairs v Fourie* declared the common-law definition of marriage and the marriage formula in the Marriage Act unconstitutional to the extent that it excludes same-sex couples from the status, benefits and responsibilities given to heterosexual (men and women) couples. The Constitutional Court suspended the declaration to give Parliament an opportunity to correct the unconstitutional parts of the Act. Parliament then passed the Civil Union Act.

4.1.4 Marriages and civil unions

Marriages and civil unions have many aspects: personal, social, economic and legal. We will discuss the legal aspects of marriage and civil unions in this section. Learners will learn about the steps necessary for a person to get married or enter into a civil union, the requirements for a legal marriage or civil union and the different types of marriages or civil unions.

Problem 2: Getting married or entering into a civil union

Questions

1. Marriage or civil unions involve many aspects. How important do you think the following are for a successful marriage or civil union: happiness, children, money, sexual relations, religious factors, common interests, romance, relationships with in-laws, age differences, or other factors? Rank these in order of importance with number 1 as the most important.
2. Make a list of all the questions you think you should ask yourself before deciding to get married or enter into a civil union.
3. Do you think that any of the questions in 2 above involve the law? If so, which?
4. Role-play a conversation between a couple who intend to get married or enter into a civil union in which they discuss what they expect from each other.

contract of 'engagement'

Before people marry or enter into a civil union they usually enter into a contract of 'engagement'. An engagement is an agreement to marry or enter into a civil union. If either person breaks this agreement without a good reason he or she can be sued by the other for breach of promise. The person who breaks the agreement may have to pay damages to the other person.

4.1.4.1 Who can marry or enter into a civil union?

rights and duties in marriages and civil unions

Marriage or a civil union is a contract between two people, a man and a woman or a man and a man or a woman and a woman in which they agree to live together as spouses or civil union partners. Like other contracts, marriage or a civil union creates certain rights and duties for each partner. But unlike other contracts, the marriage or civil union contract cannot be changed or ended without the approval of the court. This is because the state has an interest in the marriage or civil union relationships of its citizens. For this reason every person who gets married or enters into a civil union must meet certain requirements. For example, a person who is married to, or has entered into a civil union with, somebody else cannot marry or enter into a civil union again until the first spouse or partner dies, or until the first marriage or civil union has been ended by a court order. A person who marries or enters into a civil union with another while an earlier marriage or civil union still exists is guilty of the crime of bigamy (see above para 2.8.3). An exception to this is where a person is married according to customary law, because customary marriages allow more than one wife (see below para 4.1.5).

marrying or entering into a civil union again may only happen after the death or divorce of a spouse or partner

marriage or civil unions between relatives

The law also forbids marriages or civil unions between close relatives. For instance, people who marry or enter into a civil union, or have sexual relations, with their children, parents, grandparents, brothers, sister, aunts, uncles, nieces, or nephews are guilty of the crime of incest (see above para 2.8.1). First cousins, however, may marry, or enter into a civil union with, each other.

age is the most common barrier which prevents young people from getting married

barriers to marriage or civil unions by young people

Age is the most common barrier which prevents young people from getting married or entering into a civil union. Our common law says that a boy under the age of 14 and a girl under the age of 12 cannot marry because they only reach puberty at that age. Thereafter, they can only marry with their parents' consent. However, in terms of the Marriage Act, boys under 18 and girls under 15 years cannot enter into a valid marriage contract unless they have written consent from the Minister of Home Affairs. Even if the Minister consents, in all cases where one of the parties is a minor (ie under the age of 18), the consent of both parents (or if one parent is dead, of the surviving parent) to the marriage is necessary. If the parents unreasonably refuse to give their consent to the marriage, the minor may ask the High Court for consent. It is not clear whether these provisions apply to civil unions. (See above para 4.1.3.)

Problem 3: Restrictions on certain people marrying or entering into civil unions

Questions

1. Which relatives are not allowed to marry, or enter into a civil union with, each other?
2. William is 16 and Miro is 15. Can they be legally married? If so, whose consent do they need?
3. Why do you think there is a minimum age for getting married? Should there be any age requirements, and, if so, what should they be?
4. Tom and Angela, both aged 16 years, entered into a civil marriage with the permission of the Minister of Home Affairs and they are happily married. Pauline and Bridgette, also both aged 16 years, love each other dearly, and want to take their relationship to the next level and enter into a civil union marriage. Will the law allow them to? Can they also get permission from the Minister of Home Affairs? If not, do you think it is fair, given that Tom and Angela married at age 16?
5. Females are allowed to get married at a younger age than males. Why do you think the age requirement is different for males and females? Is this fair? Give reasons for your answer.

4.1.4.2 When a marriage or a civil union is invalid (not legal)

annulment of marriage or a civil union

When a couple go through a wedding or civil union ceremony without meeting the requirements for a legal marriage or civil union, the marriage or civil union may be declared invalid. In legal language this is referred to as an 'annulment' or a 'declaration of nullity'. When a marriage or civil union is annulled or declared invalid, the court makes an order which sets aside the marriage or civil union as if it never existed. None of the effects of marriage or a civil union apply if the marriage or civil union is annulled. There is a distinction between an annulment of a marriage or civil union and a divorce (see below para 4.5.2.1). The grounds for an annulment of a marriage or civil union are not limited but may include the following:

grounds for annulment

1. Where one of the couple is, or both are, below the required age and there is no consent by the Minister of Home Affairs (eg where the boy is under the age of 18 and the girl under 15). It is not clear whether this applies to civil unions because it may be unconstitutional to limit such unions to persons over 18 years of age.
2. Where one of the couple is, or both are, under the age of 18 and do not have their parents' consent.
3. Where the parties are too closely related to each other.
4. Where the one party was forced to marry against his or her will (ie there was no consent).
5. Where the wife was pregnant by somebody else at the time of the marriage and the husband did not know.
6. Where one of the parties is already married to somebody else.
7. Where one of the parties is incapable of having sexual intercourse (is impotent).

Problem 4: Was the marriage or civil union valid?

Questions

Discuss whether the following marriages are valid. Give reasons for your answers.

1. Jaggie, 17 years old, marries Linda, 16 years old, after their parents consent to the marriage.
2. Gladys, 16 years old, marries Das, 22 years old, without her parents' consent.
3. Pius, 23 years old, enters into a civil union with his cousin Thomas, 22 years old.
4. Dawn, 16 years old, marries Cuthbert, 21 years old, with her parents' consent. Dawn did not want to marry Cuthbert, but her parents assaulted her until she agreed to marry him.
5. Shirley, 25 years old, enters into a civil union with Diana, 28 years old. Shirley is pregnant by Pieter at the time of the civil union but does not tell Diana.
6. Theresa, 28 years old, married Ndou, 30 years old, even though she is already married to Humphrey.
7. Wolfgang, 32 years old, marries Hilda, 25 years old, but is unable to have sexual intercourse with her.

Wolfgang is unable to have sexual intercourse with Hilda

4.1.4.3 Getting married or entering into a civil union

legal competence, consent, formalities

A couple who wish to get married or enter into a civil union must: (a) be legally competent to marry or enter into a civil union with each other; (b) have consented to the marriage or civil union; and, (c) have gone through a marriage or civil union ceremony with the proper formalities. The marriage or civil union ceremony must be conducted by a marriage officer. Before the ceremony can take place the following must happen:

1. The couple must produce their identity documents.
2. A minor must produce the written consent of his or her parents or guardian.
3. A boy under the age of 18 or a girl under the age of 15 must produce the written consent of the Minister of Home Affairs.
4. A divorced or a widowed person must produce proof of the divorce or death of his or her former partner.
5. If the couple have entered into an 'ante-nuptial contract' (see below para 4.2.2.2) they must produce proof of this.

civil and religious marriage ceremonies

The ceremony may be a civil one carried out by a magistrate, a special justice of the peace, or a commissioner. In addition, the Minister of Home Affairs may appoint any officer in the public, diplomatic or consular service as a marriage officer. A religious ceremony may also be carried out by a minister of religion who is a marriage officer authorised to carry out marriages according to the Christian, Jewish, Hindu or Muslim faith or the rites of any other religion.

These marriages differ from marriages conducted under Hindu or Muslim religion by a person who is not an authorised marriage officer because such marriages are not legally valid. Thus a marriage may take place either by a civil or religious ceremony provided it is performed by an authorised marriage officer. Parliament has also passed legislation that recognises marriages entered into by Africans under African customary law as valid (see below para 4.1.5).

4.1.4.4 Requirements for a valid marriage or civil union

requirements for a valid marriage or civil union

In order for there to be a valid marriage or civil union, each spouse must:

1. Be above the minimum age for marriage or civil union or have the written permission of the relevant Minister in the case of marriage;
2. Be single, divorced or widowed;
3. Not be too closely related to the other spouse or partner either by blood or marriage;
4. Not be a mentally disordered person;
5. Have his or her parents' or guardian's consent in the case of marriages involving minors; and
6. Have the marriage or civil union ceremony performed by an authorised marriage officer.

4.1.5 Customary marriages

A customary marriage is a marriage entered into not in terms of common law or the Marriage Act or religion. Rather, it is entered into according to customary law under the Recognition of Customary Marriages Act. Customary law refers to the customs and usages of traditionally observed practices among the indigenous African peoples of South Africa, and which form part of the culture of those people. Not all African people marry under customary law, but many do. An African customary marriage is conducted without a marriage officer. It is usually witnessed by the relatives of the spouses and a representative of the local chief who acts as an 'official witness'.

customary marriage is conducted without a marriage officer

A customary marriage does not only lead to a husband and wife relationship. It also creates a legal relationship between the families of the spouses. Both families undertake rights and duties as a result of the marriage.

relationship between families

Previously, according to customary law, a woman in a customary marriage was always a 'minor'. This meant that she could not own property, enter into contracts or sue anyone without being assisted by her husband. In addition, customary law allows a man to have more than one wife provided he obtains approval from the court of a written contract that will regulate the matrimonial property system of his future marriage.

in customary law a man may have many wives

Because customary marriages allowed a man to have more than one wife, the common law regarded them as invalid. Parliament had also given customary marriages only limited recognition in the past. This changed when Parliament passed a statute called the Recognition of Customary Marriages Act. The Act

customary marriages recognised

recognises the validity of customary marriages. It changed aspects of both customary law and the common law. The main features of the Act are that:

'lobolo' acceptable

1. It recognises customary marriages as valid marriages, provided they are concluded in accordance with customary law procedures and are registered. This means that the payment of 'lobolo' is acceptable.

both parties must consent

2. Both parties must consent to the marriage. It creates greater equality between men and women in customary marriages. For example, women in these marriages are no longer minors and may own property, contract and appear in court unassisted.

in community of property

3. A customary marriage, where there are only two parties, is a marriage in community of property, unless the parties enter into an ante-nuptial contract in terms of the Matrimonial Property Act (see below para 4.2.2.1).

further customary law marriage requirement

4. When a man wants to enter into a further customary marriage, the court needs to approve a contract which provides for a fair distribution of the property. (This also creates greater equality for women in customary marriages, as the court will not allow an unfair contract.)

irretrievable breakdown

5. A customary marriage can only be ended by a court of law on the grounds of irretrievable breakdown (or death). The court will make the necessary orders regarding maintenance and care of any minor children.

civil-law marriage

6. If there are only two parties to a customary marriage the parties can contract it in terms of the civil law.

more than one wife

7. According to customary law a man may have more than one wife, but a woman may only have one husband.

4.1.6 Muslim and Hindu marriages

4.1.6.1 Muslim marriages

marriage by rites and legal marriages

Muslim marriages are not recognised in South African common law because they allow a man to marry more than one wife. If, however, spouses married according to Muslim rites are also married by a religious leader who is a marriage officer or go through a civil law ceremony, the marriage will be recognised by the state. The husband, however, would not be able to marry any other women according to civil law.

limited recognition of Muslim marriages

legal duty of support

Since the passing of the Constitution, South African courts have begun to extend limited recognition to Muslim marriages. For example, the courts have held that a Muslim marriage creates a contract between the spouses which is binding on both of them. In 1999, the Supreme Court of Appeal held that a Muslim marriage imposes a legal duty on a husband to support his wife. In 2008, the Cape Provincial Division (now the Western Cape High Court) extended the Intestate Succession Act (dealing with people who die without making wills – see below para 4.6.4.2) and the Maintenance of Surviving Spouses Act to spouses in Muslim polygynous marriages. The court found the exclusion of surviving spouses in Muslim polygynous marriages unconstitutional. This was confirmed by the Constitutional Court.

This does not mean that Muslim marriages have now been given full recognition – they have only been recognised by the courts in certain limited situations, depending on the facts of each case. Parliament is presently considering whether it will extend full recognition to Muslim marriages, as it has to customary marriages.

4.1.6.2 Hindu marriages

Hindu marriages

The common law also does not recognise Hindu marriages if the religious leader who conducted the ceremony was not a marriage officer. At present, Parliament has not passed any laws regarding these marriages.

limited recognition of Hindu marriages

legal duty of support

As with the Muslim marriages, the South African courts have begun to extend limited recognition to Hindu marriages. For example, in 2009 the court held that the word 'spouse' in the Intestate Succession Act includes the surviving partner in a monogamous (single) Hindu marriage. There is no constitutional reason for distinguishing between Muslim and Hindu marriages. For example, spouses in Hindu marriages should also be able to make claims in terms of the Intestate Succession Act if their spouses die without making a will. They can also claim compensation for loss of support under the Maintenance of Surviving Spouses Act and use the Maintenance Act to enforce the duty of their spouse or ex-spouse to support them and their children.

Problem 5: What should the law say?

Questions

1. The Recognition of Customary Marriages Act says that men in customary marriages may have more than one wife, whereas women in customary marriages may not have more than one husband. Do you think that this law is fair? Give reasons for your answer.
2. Do you think that Muslim and Hindu marriages should be fully recognised as valid marriages? If so, do you think that Muslim marriages in which the husband may have more than one wife, but a wife may not have more than one husband should also be recognised? Give reasons for your answer.

4.2 Husbands and wives and civil union partners

Outcomes

After completion of this section learners will be able to:

1. Demonstrate an understanding of the automatic consequences of marriage or civil union.
2. Explain the difference between marriages and civil unions in community of property and marriages and civil unions out of community of property (with and without accrual).
3. Demonstrate an understanding of the roles of spouses and civil union partners in the family.
4. Demonstrate an awareness of the problem of domestic violence.

Assessment criteria

1. The duty of support, including the duty to contribute to household necessities, is explained.
2. A set of facts is examined and a decision is taken on whether one spouse or civil union partner is legally responsible for certain things bought by the other spouse or union partner without his or her consent.
3. The meaning of a marriage or civil union 'in and out of community of property' and 'ante-nuptial' contract are explained.
4. A description is given of how the 'accrual' system works.
5. An explanation is given of what can be done by married couples or civil union partners who wish to change their type of marriage or union.
6. A set of facts is examined and a decision made on how accrual takes place between spouses or civil union partners.
7. The roles of husbands and wives and civil union partners in the family are identified.
8. An awareness is created that domestic violence is a problem among all sections of South Africa's population.
9. The provisions of the Domestic Violence Act are explained.
10. A set of facts is examined and a decision made on how an instance of domestic violence should be handled.

the traditional marriage arrangement

Traditionally, marriage was regarded as an arrangement by which the husband supported the family and the wife looked after the home. The husband was regarded as the head of the family and had a duty to look after his wife and children. The law therefore gave the husband the legal right to decide how and where the family should live and how the family's money should be spent.

the changing position of wives

Nowadays, the idea that the husband is the only breadwinner and the wife spends all her time at home is no longer true. Today, more and more married women are working outside the home and husbands and wives are beginning to share family responsibilities. The same applies to civil union partners.

the 1984 Matrimonial Property Act

The Matrimonial Property Act deals with the property of married people and civil union partners. In this part, we will look at things in a marriage or civil union that do not change; things in a marriage or civil union that may change depending upon how the parties are married – whether in or out of community of property; and the problem of domestic violence.

today more wives work and husbands share in family duties

4.2.1 Things in a marriage or a civil union that do not change

A marriage creates certain rights and duties for the husband and wife and this applies equally to civil union partners. Rights are things that spouses may expect to be done for each other. Duties are things that spouses must do for each other. These rights and duties cannot be changed, irrespective of the wishes of the parties. They remain the same for couples married or in civil unions in community of property, or out of community of property with an ante-nuptial contract (see below paras 4.2.2.1 and 4.2.2.2).

rights and duties of husbands and wives and civil union partners

A married couple, or a couple in a civil union, have a legal duty to live together, to act as husband and wife or civil union partners towards each other and to support each other. During the marriage or civil union the spouses or partners are expected to give what support they can to the 'joint household' (what the family needs to live together). This does not refer only to money. For example, the spouses or partners owe each other companionship, love, affection, comfort, sexual intercourse and maintenance. Both spouses or partners contribute to the joint household, but in different ways.

4.2.1.1 The duty of support

The duty of support is the duty to provide enough for the family to live on. Both

both spouses or civil law partners must provide support to each other

spouses or civil law partners owe this duty of support to each other, according to what each can afford. This means that if both spouses or partners work, each must contribute according to what he or she earns. Alternatively, if only one spouse or partner works, then the duty of support falls on that spouse or partner.

duty to provide 'household necessities'

The duty of support involves providing the other spouse or partner, and the family, with food and clothing, medical and dental care and the other 'household necessities' of family life. A 'necessity' is something a family needs in order to live at its usual standard of living. If a spouse or partner on whom a duty of support falls fails to provide these necessities, the other spouse or partner may buy them and make his or her spouse or partner pay. If, however, one spouse or partner is unable to work, the other spouse or partner will be responsible for providing the necessities, whether or not that spouse or partner is usually the breadwinner.

maintaining a reasonable standard of living

As mentioned, the things or services regarded as household necessities must be of the standard reasonably required to keep the family at the level at which they are used to living. What is reasonable depends upon factors such as the social status of the family, the income of the breadwinner and the standard of living of the family in the past. Therefore what is necessary for one family may not be the same for another. For example, a rich family is likely to live at a higher standard than a poor family. Usually, one spouse or civil union partner cannot force the other to pay for items that were bought without his or her knowledge. If, however, a duty of support falls on a spouse or partner, he or she may be forced to pay for necessities, even if he or she did not know that they were being bought.

Problem 1: The case of the unpaid bills

Dino is very angry with Betty for buying groceries, clothes and a hi-fi on his account

Dino and Betty have been married for six years. They both work, and each earns R36 000 a year. They have problems paying their bills and often fight over money. One day Betty goes shopping and charges Dino's account with groceries, clothes for the children, and a hi-fi costing over R5 000. Dino is very angry and tells Betty that he is not going to pay for them.

Questions

1. Role-play the conversation between Dino and Betty.
2. Is Dino legally responsible to the sellers for the groceries, clothes and hi-fi?
3. Suppose Dino was out of work and charged the above items to Betty's account without telling her. Would Betty have to pay the accounts?
4. Do you agree or disagree with the following statement: 'Husbands should have to support their wives, but wives should not have to support their husbands?' Give reasons for your answer.

A spouse's or civil partner's right to buy household necessities and make the other spouse or partner pay for them exists from the time of the marriage or civil union and continues for as long as they live together. The right also continues if the household breaks up due to the fault of the spouse or partner on whom a duty of support falls.

right to buy necessities a consequence of the marriage

The spouse's or civil partner's right to make his or her husband, wife or partner responsible for necessities exists whether the parties are married in or out of community of property (see below paras 4.2.2.1 and 4.2.2.2). This is because these rights and duties cannot be changed no matter how the spouses are married or what the terms of the partners' civil union are.

4.2.2 Things in a marriage or civil union that may change, depending upon how the spouses were married or entered into the civil union

Some things may be different in different marriages or civil unions, depending upon how the spouses were married or what the conditions of their civil union were. Spouses in a marriage or union may choose their marriage or civil union to be in community of property or out of community of property by entering into an ante-nuptial contract, with or without the accrual system.

4.2.2.1 Marriages or civil unions in community of property

If two people get married or enter into a civil union, their marriage or union is automatically in community of property, unless they have specifically decided that they would rather have their relationship governed by an ante-nuptial contract. What 'community of property' means is that the property and debts of each spouse, from before the marriage or union, are put together in what is called a 'joint estate'

'joint estate'. Everything obtained by the spouses after the marriage or union also becomes part of the joint estate. The couple share all the profits and losses of the marriage or union, which increase or decrease the joint estate. The husband and wife or union partners then have equal shares in the undivided joint estate, even if they did not – and do not – contribute equally to it.

equal share of joint estate

marital power before 1984

the Matrimonial Property Act of 1984

marital power abolished

Before 1984, a marriage in community of property gave the husband 'marital power'. This meant that the husband acted as his wife's guardian and she was treated as a minor (ie a person under 18 years of age). The wife could not enter into contracts, or sue or be sued without her husband's assistance. In 1984, Parliament passed the Matrimonial Property Act. This law abolished the marital power for all marriages in community of property entered into after 1984. In 1993, the marital power was abolished for all marriages, regardless of when they were entered into. This means that marital power no longer exists in marriages in community of property, whether they were entered into before or after 1984. Since 2006 the same has applied to civil unions.

equal management of joint estate

Both spouses or civil union partners now have equal powers of management over the joint estate. However, the written consent of the other spouse or partner is needed when one spouse or partner wishes to deal with certain types of property that belong to the joint estate. These types of property are:

1. Immovable property (eg land and buildings);
2. Stocks and shares, insurance policies, mortgage bonds and investments in finance houses;
3. Jewellery, coins, stamps, paintings and other assets, used mainly as investments;
4. The withdrawal of money held in the other spouse's or civil union partner's name in a bank or post office savings bank;
5. The entering into of certain credit agreements;
6. The buying of immovable property; and
7. The guaranteeing of other people's debts.

when consent of the other spouse or civil union partner needed

Consent is also required in a number of other situations, but need not be in writing. These situations involve:

1. Dealing with furniture and assets that belong to the joint estate;
2. Receiving money due to the other spouse or civil union partner or the joint estate; and
3. Certain donations to other people.

If one of the spouses or civil union partners unreasonably refuses consent, the other spouse or partner may apply to the High Court for assistance.

effect of absence of consent

If a spouse or civil union partner enters into an agreement for which he or she needs the consent of the other spouse or partner, but does not get that consent, the agreement is null and void (ie it has no effect). This may be very unfair to the person who attempted to enter into the agreement with the spouse or partner who did not get the consent: He or she might lose out without having done anything wrong. So, the law says that if that person did not know, and could not reasonably have known that the person should have had consent from the other spouse or civil union partner, the agreement is valid and enforceable (ie it has legal effect).

If the spouses or civil union partners are married in community of property when the marriage or civil union ends because one of the spouses or partners dies, the spouse or partner that survives is entitled to half of the joint estate. What happens to the other half depends on what the deceased spouse or partner said in his or her will, or, if he or she did not have a will, what the law says about people who die without wills (see below para 4.6.4.2). If the marriage or civil union ends because the spouses or civil union partners get divorced, the estate is also divided (see below para 4.5.2.5).

Problem 2: What can Jacobus and Edward do?

Questions

Assume that Jacobus and Edward are partners in a civil union that is in community of property. Answer the following questions:

1. Edward has been offered a new job and has been asked to sign a contract of employment by his future employer. Can he do so without Jacobus' assistance?
2. Edward wants to sell some furniture. Does he need Jacobus' consent? If so, what sort of consent does he need?
3. Jacobus wants to sell a flat that is the property of the joint estate. Does he need Edward's consent? If so, what sort of consent does he need?
4. Assume that Jacobus does sell the flat without Edward's consent. The person to whom he sells it – Martin – knows that Jacobus is in a civil union, and knows that Edward has not consented to the sale. Is the agreement to sell the flat valid and enforceable?

4.2.2.2 Marriages or civil unions out of community of property with an ante-nuptial contract

purpose of ante-nuptial contract

An ante-nuptial contract is an agreement entered into between spouses or civil union partners before marriage or a civil union.

separate estates

The main purpose of the ante-nuptial contract is to make a different matrimonial property system apply to the marriage or civil union instead of the normal community of property. This means that the spouses or civil union partners own and control their property separately. They do not need the consent of the other to enter into agreements, or to deal with their own property. Women in these types of marriages are not subject to the marital power of their husbands – they always have full legal capacity. They can enter into contracts on their own and can sue or exclusion of marital power

be sued without the assistance of their husbands. The same applies to civil union partners – neither is subject to the marital power of the other.

Both spouses or civil union partners are still subject to the 'duty of support' and are legally obliged to contribute to the necessities of the household according to their financial means (see above para 4.2.1.1).

types of ante-nuptial contracts

disadvantage of separate estates

Since 1984, there have been two types of ante-nuptial contracts, those with accrual (see below para 4.2.2.2.1) and those without accrual (ordinary, standard form of ante-nuptial contract). Previously, when a marriage out of community of property ended, each spouse kept his or her own property and profits, and was responsible for his or her own losses. This had obvious disadvantages for the spouse, usually the woman, who had chosen not to work, but to stay at home and care for the children of the marriage. Because this spouse had not worked, she also had not made money or gained property. Therefore, on divorce, she was often left with very little, despite the fact that she had contributed to the family and marriage for many years.

introduction of the 'accrual system'

accrual: an increase in property and possessions

To solve this problem, Parliament introduced something called the 'accrual system'. Since 1 November 1984, the accrual system has been automatically included in a marriage by ante-nuptial contract, unless the couple specifically decides that it should not be. The word 'accrual' means an 'increase'. While the marriage or civil union lasts each spouse controls his or her own separate estate. When the marriage or civil union ends, any increase in the value of both estates is shared by the parties equally. Both spouses or civil union partners may, however, agree in the ante-nuptial contract to keep their property separate so that the accrual system does not operate. If the parties do not enter into an ante-nuptial contract, the marriage or civil union is automatically in community of property.

the accrual system takes into account the fact that the spouses or civil union partners continually add to their property and possessions

4.2.2.2.1 How accrual works

'commencement values'

1. Before the marriage or civil union each spouse or civil union partner states the value of his or her property. These values are called the 'commencement values' and are usually included in the ante-nuptial contract.

additions to property

2. During the marriage or civil union additions take place to each of the spouse's or civil union partner's property. Usually inheritances and donations (including those between spouses or civil union partners) do not form part of the accrual, unless the ante-nuptial contract says that they do.

in case of recklessness

3. If one of the spouses or civil union partners spends money wildly or is reckless with his or her property, thereby affecting the other spouse's or partner's right to share in the accrual, the other spouse or partner may apply to the High Court for an order for an immediate division of the accrual. The court may also order that accrual no longer applies to the marriage or civil union.

when the marriage or civil union ends

4. When the marriage or civil union ends through death or divorce, the value of each spouse's or civil union partner's property before the marriage (the commencement value) is compared with the value at the end of the marriage or civil union. The commencement value may be adjusted to compensate for inflation. For example, if the commencement value of a spouse's or civil union partner's property was R100 000 in 1992 it may be worth R1 100 000 in 2011.

equal shares

5. The total accrual in the spouses' or civil union partners' estates is added together and then shared equally between them.

gifts deducted

6. Any gifts between the spouses or civil union partners are deducted from their properties before the accrual is shared between them.

Case study: Salim and Shirley share the accrual

Salim and Shirley were married in January 1997 and entered into an ante-nuptial contract that did not exclude the accrual system. At the time of the marriage the commencement value of Salim's estate (property) was R30 000, while the value of Shirley's estate was R6 000. They divorced in December 2010. At the date of the divorce Salim's estate was worth R900 000, while Shirley's was worth R180 000. Salim's estate has increased by R870 000 (R900 000 – R30 000), and Shirley's by R174 000 (R180 000 – R6 000). The total accrual for their estates is therefore R1 044 000 (R870 000 + R174 000). This must be shared equally between them. As a result, Salim and Shirley each receive R522 000 in addition to the commencement value of their estates.

Problem 3: Jerry and Ansie decide to divorce

Jerry and Ansie were married in December 1996. Before their marriage they entered into an ante-nuptial contract that excluded community of property.

The ante-nuptial contract also mentioned that Jerry would bring property worth R60 000 into the marriage, while Ansie would bring in property worth R15 000. The ante-nuptial contract did not mention the accrual system. Jerry and Ansie decided to obtain a divorce in July 2010. By then Jerry's property is worth R500 000 and Ansie's R120 000.

Questions

1. Role-play Jerry and Ansie discussing how the divorce will affect their property.
2. Does the accrual system apply in their case? Give reasons for your answer.
3. If the accrual system does apply, how will the increases in the value of Jerry's and Ansie's properties be shared between them?

4.2.2.2.2 Forfeiture of benefits and forfeiture of accrual

where a spouse is guilty of causing the divorce

If one of the spouses or civil union partners is guilty of causing a divorce, the innocent spouse or partner may ask the court to make an order stating that the guilty spouse or partner must forfeit (lose) any benefits he or she may have received from a marriage or civil union in community of property or under an ante-nuptial contract. This means that the guilty spouse or partner will not receive a half-share of the property from a marriage or civil union in community of property or any gifts promised under an ante-nuptial contract. The court may also order that a guilty spouse or civil union partner may not benefit from an accrual where the accrual system operates.

Problem 4: Would you order forfeiture of benefits?

Ranji has an affair with Yasmin which causes Zoobie to divorce him

Questions

Ranji, who married Zoobie in 1990 without an ante-nuptial contract, has an affair with Yasmin, which causes Zoobie to divorce him. Zoobie, who is wealthy, brought property worth R5 000 000 into the marriage, while Ranji only brought in R500 000. Zoobie asks the court to order forfeiture of benefits against Ranji.

If you were the judge would you order forfeiture of benefits? Give reasons for your answer.

4.2.2.3 How couples may change their type of marriage or civil union

application to the High Court

If a husband and wife or civil union partners want to change the type of marriage or union they have, they may apply to the High Court, asking for the court to let them do so. The husband and wife or civil union partners must apply to the High Court together. They must also explain the type of marriage or civil union they want in a document called a 'notarial contract' and submit this to the court. The court will only allow the change if the couple convinces the court of the following:

1. There must be good reasons for the change;
2. All people to whom the couple owe money must also have been told that the couple want to make the change; and
3. The court must be convinced that the change will not be unfair to anyone.

Summary of effect of different types of marriages

Community of property	Community of profit and loss	Divorce
Each spouse has half-share in undivided joint estate.	Profits and losses made by each spouse increase or decrease joint estate.	Power of court to change division of estate.
Marriage in community of property (ie without ante-nuptial contract)		
Yes. Property and debts of spouses before marriage/civil union go into joint estate. Each spouse has half-share in undivided joint estate.	Yes. Each spouse has half-share of profits and losses of joint estate.	Each spouse receives half-share unless there is forfeiture of benefits.
Marriage out of community of property (ie with ante-nuptial contract)		
No. Usually each spouse keeps property owned at time of marriage/civil union.	No. Accrual system applies automatically unless excluded in ante-nuptial contract. At end of marriage/civil union each spouse entitled to half-share of profits of marriage.	Accrual applies if not excluded by ante-nuptial contract.

4.2.3 Decisions in marriages and civil unions

division of responsibilities

Married life or life in a civil union involves many important decisions and responsibilities. It requires co-operation, sharing and division of the work done by the spouses or civil union partners. How far the responsibilities of the marriage or union are divided, however, depends upon the individual spouses or partners. In most marriages and unions spouses or partners make important decisions based on what they decide between themselves. Traditionally, however, in marriages the law gives the husband most of the power to make decisions in the family. This does not apply to civil unions.

old-fashioned laws and customs

Today there is more sharing of responsibilities in marriages and civil unions. Employment outside of the home has given many women new status and independence. Modern men are also more likely to help with the housekeeping and bringing up the children. Despite this, many old-fashioned laws and social customs still remain which affect marriage relationships. For example, because women traditionally use their husband's names, most people believe that the law requires a wife to take her husband's name. In fact the law says that a wife may, but need not, take her husband's surname.

modern men are more likely to help with housekeeping and bringing up children

Problem 5: What do you think should be the roles of husbands and wives and civil union partners?

Questions

Consider each of the following statements and decide whether you agree or disagree with them. Give reasons for your answers.

1. The wife or female partner in a civil union should take care of the house and children, and the husband or male partner should provide the family income.
2. When a woman marries she should keep her own name and not change it to that of her husband.
3. Married women or women in civil unions should only work if they have no young children.
4. As the head of the household, the husband or male partner in a civil union should be the only person with the right to choose where the family should live.
5. Husbands and wives or partners in a civil union should share everything equally regardless of who owns or pays for the things.

4.2.4 Domestic violence

a serious problem

Domestic violence (ie violence in families) is a very serious problem in South Africa (see above para 2.4.1). Studies show that domestic violence occurs in families across the population, regardless of race and class. Very often domestic violence results in serious injury or death. There are a limited number of cases where women assault men but in the vast majority of cases men abuse women. For instance, approximately 31 000 court orders were issued in the Western Cape between 1993 and 1997 to stop instances of family violence. Of these, 98% were issued to women, and only 2% to men.

most cases of spouse abuse involve husbands abusing their wives

the Domestic Violence Act

In an attempt to deal with this problem Parliament has passed the Domestic Violence Act. This law applies not only to men and women in civil marriages or civil unions. It also protects people who are, or have been, in the following types of relationships:

people protected

1. People married according to any law, custom or religion. This means that the law protects people in Hindu, Muslim and customary marriages;
2. People living together as if married or in civil unions;
3. People who are parents of the same child or who have had parental responsibility for the same child;
4. People related to one another;
5. People who are engaged, or merely 'dating' or 'going out'; and
6. People sharing the same residence (ie flat or house).

definition of domestic violence

The Act also defines domestic violence very broadly to include the following types of behaviour:

1. Physical assault (eg hitting or kicking someone);
2. Sexual abuse;
3. Emotional, verbal and psychological abuse (when one person does not physically or sexually abuse another but uses other means to make that person feel bad about themselves);
4. Economic abuse (when one person on whom there is a duty of support withholds that support);
5. Intimidation (frightening another person);
6. Harassment (not leaving another person alone);
7. Stalking (following another person);
8. Entering someone's residence (eg house or flat) without asking that person first; and
9. Any other form of behaviour that is abusive.

how people can protect themselves

The Domestic Violence Act says that if a person is in one of the relationships listed above, and is being abused in any one of the ways described above, she or he may take the following steps:

1. The victim of abuse (the 'applicant') may apply to a magistrate's court or family court for a 'protection order'. Someone else may also apply on behalf of the victim.
2. If the court thinks that the applicant might be a victim of domestic violence it will issue an 'interim protection order'.
3. This order will be given by the sheriff of the court to the person whom the applicant has said is abusing him or her. It will ask this person to come to court within 10 days. It will also tell the person to stop abusing the victim.
4. If the person does not come to court on the day given in the interim protection order, the court will make the interim protection order final. If the person does come to court, the court will listen to the evidence on both sides and then make a decision about whether to make the protection order final.
5. If the protection order is made final it will tell the abuser to stop abusing the victim. At the same time as the court issues the protection order it will issue a warrant of arrest (see above para 2.11.2.2) for the abuser which will be kept by the person who is being abused. However, it will be suspended and will only come into effect if the abuser does not obey the protection order.

6. If the abuser abuses the applicant again, the applicant does not have to go to court. He or she can phone the police and mention that he or she has a protection order. The abuser will then be arrested and will either get a fine or go to prison for as long as five years.

Note: It must be remembered that a person who commits domestic violence may also be guilty of crimes under the common law. For example, a husband who hits his wife may be guilty of 'assault' (or assault with intent to do grievous bodily harm) (see above para 2.2.2) or, if he kills her, he may be guilty of 'murder' (see above para 2.2.1).

Diagram showing procedure under Domestic Violence Act

diagram showing procedure under Domestic Violence Act

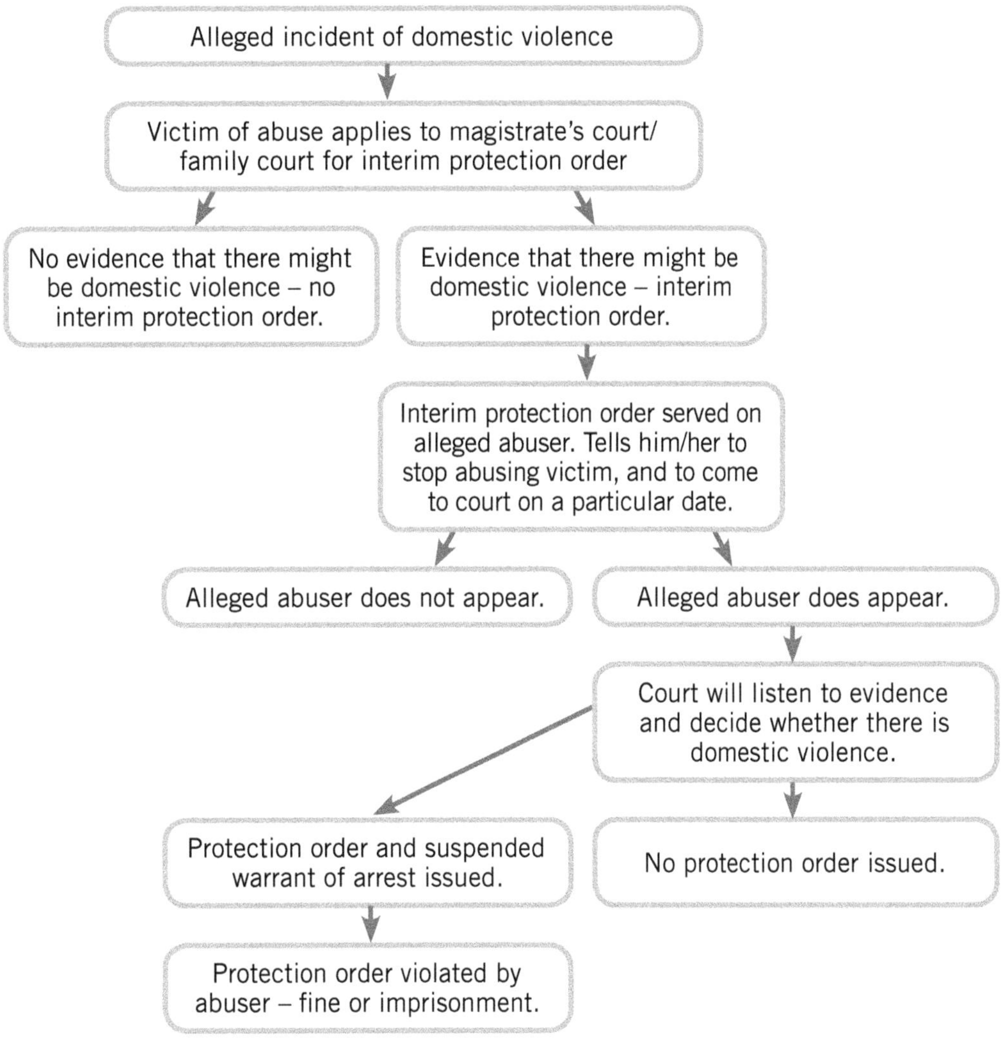

duty of police to help

Many people in South Africa think that violence in families is a 'private matter' and that other people, such as the police, should not get involved. In the past, the police were often reluctant to interfere. However, the Domestic Violence Act has changed this by saying that the police must help a victim of domestic violence. The police must also help such a person get medical treatment and shelter (if he or she needs these), and explain to the victim the procedures available under the Domestic Violence Act.

Problem 6: A case of domestic violence

Late one night you hear screams, bangs and crashes. You look out and see your neighbour, Mrs Swart, being slapped and punched by her husband as she tries to walk out of the door. Before she can run away Mr Swart pulls her back into the house and slams the door. You hear breaking glass, more screams and running around. You know that Mr Swart has a drinking problem and that this is not the first time he has beaten up his wife.

1. If you were the neighbour, what would you do? Would you call the police? If you would, what would you tell them? If you would not call the police, explain why not.
2. Suppose you are a police officer and you receive a call that Mr Swart is beating up his wife. When you and a fellow officer arrive at the Swarts you find that Mrs Swart is cut, bruised and beaten up. Do you think that this is an instance of domestic violence as defined by the Domestic Violence Act? Role-play you and your colleague talking to the Swarts.
3. Acting as the police, decide what you would do in this situation. What are your duties under the Domestic Violence Act in relation to Mrs Swart? What would you do about Mr Swart? Would you arrest him?
4. Acting as Mr Swart, decide how you would react to the police in this situation. Acting as Mrs Swart, decide how you would react. What are your options under the Domestic Violence Act? What procedures would you have to follow? In addition to any remedies under the Act, would you also lay a criminal charge for assault against your husband? Would you stay in the house or try to go somewhere else?
5. Suppose you are a magistrate and Mrs Swart has applied for a protection order. Would you grant one? What would the protection order ask Mr Swart to do?
6. Suppose that Mrs Swart lays a charge of assault and as a magistrate you find Mr Swart guilty, would you sentence him to prison, or would you take some other action?
7. What programmes are available in your community to help abused women? Are there places where abused women can go if they decide to leave home?

4.3 Parents and children

Outcomes

After completion of this section learners will be able to:

1. Explain and appreciate the relationship between parents and children.
2. Explain when a child is a 'child in need of care and protection'.
3. Explain the law relating to the termination of pregnancy.

Assessment criteria

1. The legal responsibilities of parents and children are identified and explained.
2. The meanings of 'care' and 'guardianship' are explained.
3. An explanation is given of the position of children born of married parents, children born of unmarried parents, and children of customary marriages.
4. A set of facts is examined to create awareness of the parental duty to support children and the reciprocal obligation owed by children.
5. Sets of facts are examined and decisions made on when parents are responsible for wrongs done by their children.
6. Sets of facts are examined and decisions made on what things children may do without their parents' assistance.
7. Ways in which children become independent of their parents are identified.
8. A description is given of when a child can be regarded as being a 'child in need of care and protection'.
9. Sets of facts are examined and decisions taken on whether the parents are guilty of ill-treatment or abandonment of children.
10. A set of facts is examined and a decision made on whether neighbours should become involved in child abuse and child neglect cases.
11. The conditions under which a pregnancy may be terminated are explained.
12. The conflicting rights involved in the choice to terminate a pregnancy are identified.

children's rights in the Constitution

The laws affecting children have undergone dramatic changes in recent years because of the special protection given to children in the Constitution. In 2005, the Parliament passed the Children's Act, which protects the rights of the child extensively. In addition to the other rights in the Constitution every child has the right:

1. To a name and nationality from birth;
2. To a family or parental care or alternative care when removed from the family environment;
3. To basic nutrition, shelter, basic health care and social services;

4. To be protected from maltreatment, neglect, abuse and degradation;
5. Not to be subjected to social, cultural and religious practices which are detrimental to the child's well-being. To this end, the following are prohibited:
   (a) Genital mutilation or circumcision of female children;
   (b) Circumcision of boys under the age of 16 years, except where it is done for religious or medical purposes;
   (c) Virginity testing of children under the age of 16 years;
6. To be protected from exploitative labour practices;
7. Not to be required to perform work that is inappropriate for a person of that child's age or that will place a risk on the child's well-being;
8. To have a lawyer and not to be detained except as a measure of last resort;
9. Not to be used directly in armed conflict, and to be protected in times of armed conflict.
10. To have access to information on health promotion and the prevention and treatment of ill-health and diseases, sexuality and reproduction.

child's responsibilities

Every child has responsibilities, appropriate to the child's age and ability, towards his or her family, community and the state.

child's best interests come first

parents' legal duties to their children

In addition the Constitution and Children's Act provide that a child's 'best interests' must always take priority (must be the most important thing) in every situation involving a child. What this means is that if there is a conflict between the child's interests and a parent's right in any given case, the child's interests must come first. In modern law the emphasis has shifted from the rights of the parent to the interests of the child. However, parents still have the right and duty to raise their children and are given extensive control over their children.

4.3.1 Responsibilities between parents and children

When people become parents they have certain legal duties towards their children. Parents must provide sufficient support for their minor children to survive. A minor child is a person under 18 years old. This support includes necessities such as food, clothing, accommodation, medical and dental expenses, and education. It may include more, depending on how much money the parents have, and the needs of their children. Although many people think that the duty to support applies only to the father, the law says that it applies to both parents. The parents must share the duty of support between them according to how much they each earn.

Eddy denies he is the father and refuses to marry Mana or support the child

Problem 1: The case of the unworthy father

Questions

Mana, who is 16 years old, has a baby. She claims that Eddy, aged 17, is the father. Eddy denies he is the father and refuses to marry Mana or support the child.

Should the law require Eddy to marry Mana if he is the father? Should the law require Eddy to provide support for the child? Why or why not?

children are expected to obey the 'reasonable' orders or requests of their parents

Just as the law requires parents to support their children, children are expected to obey the reasonable orders or requests of their parents. What is a reasonable parental order? Certainly children do not have to obey parents who order or ask them to commit illegal acts such as robbing a café. Nor must they obey an order to do something that seriously harms their physical or mental health, such as staying in a locked room for a week without food. However, parents are entitled to ask children to do things like helping with the housework or the garden.

what parents may decide

As long as parents do not abuse or neglect their children, the law gives them wide powers over their children. Parents have the right to control the lives of their children. For example, they may decide:

1. Where their children should live;
2. With whom they should or should not associate;
3. How they should be educated;
4. What religious training they should receive; and
5. How their health should be cared for.

Parents may even decide:

1. What time their children should come home at night;
2. Whether they should work; and
3. Whether they should go out with children of the other sex.

'parental power'

This is known as 'parental power'. Parents have parental power when they have 'care' and 'guardianship' of their children. However, parental power over a child is not absolute and weakens as the child approaches 18. As children approach majority, important questions arise. For example, can a parent decide with whom a child should or should not associate? Some may argue that a parent has a right in certain circumstances to decide whom a child may associate with and where the child may spend his or her time. It must not be forgotten, however, that children, like their parents, also have the other constitutional rights such as the right to privacy and dignity (see above para 1.2.2.1). We can therefore say that the parents' rights to make decisions for their children must give way to the children's rights to make their own decisions when they are mature enough.

child participation

However, when parents make major decisions involving their child, they must consider any views and wishes expressed by the child – bearing in mind the child's age, maturity and stage of development.

4.3.1.1 Care

providing a home and care

Care involves such things as:

1. Providing a home for the children;
2. Feeding and supporting the children;
3. Looking after the day-to-day needs of the children;
4. Educating the children; and
5. Generally ensuring that the best interests of the child is the paramount (most important) concern in everything affecting the child.

where the parents are married

While parents are married to each other or are in a civil union and live together they share the care of their children. (For the position of children born to married parents – see below para 4.3.1.4.) When they separate or divorce, one parent is usually given care of the children.

where the child is born of unmarried parents

This may be either the father or the mother, depending on what is best for the child. In some cases, the parents may not be married to each other, in which case the child is referred to as the child born of unmarried parents. If the child is born of unmarried parents, the mother has care over of the child, but the father may apply to the High Court for care to be given to him.

4.3.1.2 Guardianship

guardianship of children

A parent or any person who has guardianship over the child must assist or represent the child in administrative, contractual and other legal matters. Guardianship involves such things as:

1. Looking after the property of the children;
2. Acting on the children's behalf when they enter into contracts;
3. Acting on the children's behalf in court cases; and
4. Consenting to the marriages of the children.

equal guardianship where the child is born of married parents

As far as children born of married parents are concerned, both parents have equal guardianship of the children born of their marriage or civil union. A court may, however, decide that only one parent should have guardianship. In general, parents may exercise their guardianship without getting each other's consent. But for certain matters – such as the child marrying or being adopted – the consent of both parents is necessary.

how a non-parent can become a guardian

power of the High Court to appoint a guardian

There are two ways in which a person who is not the parent of the children may become their guardian. First, if one parent is dead, or if a court has ordered that one parent cannot exercise guardianship of the children, the other parent (ie the guardian) may appoint someone in his or her will to act as the guardian. Second, the High Court as the 'upper guardian' of all minors has the power to appoint someone who is not the parent of the children as their guardian. For example, if both parents desert their children or become mentally unfit to look after them, the High Court may appoint a legal guardian to look after them.

In the case of children born of unmarried parents, the guardianship of the guardianship of children born of unmarried parents

children is usually with the mother. If the mother is a minor (under 18), then her parents become guardians of her children, but she still has care over them. The biological father has no automatic right of guardianship, but may apply to the High Court for guardianship of the children. This will be given only if it is in the best interests of the children. In addition, an unmarried biological father can have parental rights (guardianship) over the child:

1. If, at the time of the child's birth, the father is living with the mother in a permanent life-partnership; or
2. If, whether or not he has lived with the mother, the father:
   (a) Consents to be identified as the father or applies successfully to be identified as the father of the child or pays damages in terms of customary law for fathering the child;
   (b) Contributes to the child's upbringing for a reasonable period; and
   (c) Contributes towards expenses in connection with the maintenance of the child for a reasonable period.

All the requirements under 2 above must be satisfied before an unmarried father may be given parental rights over a child.

natural and legal guardians

There is an important difference between a natural guardian and a legal guardian. Natural guardians (ie parents) have a legal duty to support their children. Natural guardians must use their own money to support the children. Legal guardians (ie persons appointed as guardians by the court or in a will) have no such duty. Legal guardians do not have to use their own money to support the children. The children's natural parents must support them. Both types of guardians, however, must look after the children's property.

guardians' duty of support

Problem 2: Parental control over children

Decide in the following situations whether the parents have the legal authority to make the decisions involved. What rights do you think the children should have in each situation? List arguments in favour of: (a) the parents, and (b) the children.

1. Mr Khuzwayo disapproves of the lifestyle of his 18-year-old son, Bart. Bart attends university, but moves out of the university residence into a house rented by a group of his friends. Mr Khuzwayo then refuses to pay for Bart's accommodation, food, clothing and university fees. Role-play a conversation between Bart and his father.
2. Christina, aged 17, wishes to marry Stoffel, a 25-year-old accountant, but her parents refuse to give her permission to marry. Role-play a conversation between Stoffel, Christina and her parents.
3. Rama, a 16-year-old student, does not want to move to a new city with his parents. He wants to finish his university education with his friends. His brother and sister are happy to move and agree to go with their parents. Role-play a conversation between Rama and his parents.

4.3.1.3 Are parents responsible for the wrongs of their children?

The law states that parents are not responsible for the wrongs of their children unless the parent:

1. Allowed the child to do the wrongful act;
2. Asked or ordered the child to do the wrongful act;
3. Asked the child to carry out a task as a 'servant' and the child did the wrongful act while carrying out the task; or
4. Ought to have foreseen that the child might have done the wrongful act and should have taken steps to prevent it.

if parents influence the child to commit a crime

Parents, however, will be ordered to pay compensation to the victims of crimes by their children if they had influenced them to commit the crime. The same applies to any other person who has custody of a child who commits a crime after being influenced by that person.

children may be sued

If the parent is not responsible the child may be sued by the injured person or the person whose property is damaged. When children are sued, however, they must be assisted by their guardians. In terms of the Child Justice Act children under the age of 10 years cannot be held legally liable for wrongs done by them (see above para 2.14.2.1).

Problem 3: Are the parents responsible?

Decide in the following situations whether the parents are legally responsible for the wrongs of their children. Give reasons for your answers.

Questions

1. Barend carelessly allows his 3-year-old daughter Engeltjie to run into the street. Andrew tries to avoid her and crashes his car into a wall. Luckily neither Engeltjie nor Andrew is injured, but Andrew's car is written off. Is Barend responsible for the damage to Andrew's car? Give reasons for your answer. Role-play a conversation between Andrew and Barend.
2. Gladys asks her 11-year-old son Goodwill to ride his bicycle to the store to buy some groceries for the home. On his way to the store Goodwill rides his bicycle too fast and knocks over Premjee, who is standing on the pavement. Premjee is injured and has to go to hospital. Is Gladys legally responsible for the injuries suffered by Premjee? Give reasons for your answer. Role-play a conversation between Gladys and Premjee.

Lennie hits a cricket ball through Sophie's window

3. Lennie, aged 9 years, and his friends play cricket in Lennie's back yard. Lennie hits the cricket ball out of the yard and it smashes a window in Sophie's house. Are Lennie's parents responsible for the broken window? Give reasons for your answer. Role-play a conversation between Sophie's and Lennie's fathers.

4.3.1.4 Children born of married parents and children born of unmarried parents and those born in or out of civil unions

children of married parents

Children are born of married parents if their parents were married at the time they were conceived or born or became married any time after that. When a child is born of married parents both parents get equal guardianship of the child. Both parents then have rights and duties in relation to that child. The same applies to children born of a civil union.

unmarried parents

Children are born of unmarried parents if their parents were not married at the time they were born and do not marry later. In terms of the common law the mother of a child becomes its natural guardian. The same applies to children born of parents not in a civil union who do not subsequently enter into a civil union.

natural father may apply for rights over his child born of a woman to whom he is not married

the natural father must support his child born of a woman to whom he is not married

However, since 1997 the father of a child born of unmarried parents may ask the High Court to grant him equal guardianship of the child. Alternatively, the court may decide to grant either the mother or father sole guardianship of the child. If a parent does not have guardianship he or she may also ask the High Court to be given care or access. In making these decisions the court is guided by what is in the best interests of the child. Even if a parent does not get guardianship of a child, he or she still has an obligation to support the child. How much each parent must contribute depends on how much each parent earns. This is called the duty of support (see below para 4.3.2). If one parent refuses to support the child in accordance with what he or she can afford, the other parent may get an order from the maintenance court to force him or her to support the child. This is called a maintenance order (see below para 4.5.3.2).

children born of unmarried parents no longer discriminated against

There was a time when the law discriminated against children who were born of unmarried parents and they were referred to as 'illegitimate'. For example, previously an 'illegitimate' child could inherit property from his or her mother even if she had not made a will, but could only inherit from his or her father if the father had made a will. This rule did not apply to children born of married parents – so-called 'legitimate' children. Nowadays, children born of unmarried parents or parents who have not entered into a civil union enjoy the same rights as children born of married parents or parents in a civil union. Children born of unmarried parents or parents not in a civil union may therefore inherit from their fathers, even if the father has not made a will. The Children's Act does not refer to 'illegitimate' or 'legitimate' children and uses the phrases 'children born of unmarried parents' and 'children born of married parents'. These terms should be taken to apply equally to children born of parents out of or in a civil union.

Problem 4: Some questions on the position of children born of unmarried parents or parents not in a civil union

Questions

1. Do you think the law is correct in saying that children born of married parents and children born of unmarried parents should be treated equally? Give reasons for your answer.
2. Do you think that it is fair that guardianship of a child born of unmarried parents is automatically given to the mother, whereas the father has to apply to court for equal guardianship? Give reasons for your answer.
3. Do you think that it is fair that a natural father has to pay maintenance for his child born of a woman to whom he is not married, but may not act as its guardian or carer? Give reasons for your answer.

4.3.1.5 Children of customary marriages

children of customary marriages are legitimate

Because customary marriages are now recognised as valid marriages (see above para 4.1.5), the children of these marriages are recognised as children born of married parents under South African law (although, as mentioned, being a child not born of married parents no longer carries serious consequences for children). Traditionally, under customary law the children's natural father was the guardian and had the duty to support them. Even if the father died, or was unfit to be a guardian, the mother could not become the guardian of the children. Instead, the father's eldest son, who was usually the heir, would become the children's guardian. If there were no sons then the father's eldest male relative became the guardian of the children. This is because women in customary marriages were always regarded as being minors (ie people under the age of 21 – nowadays people under the age of 18 years) regardless of their age.

guardianship of children under traditional customary law

equal guardianship of children in the modern law

It is unlikely that this is still the position in customary law marriages. This is because the Recognition of Customary Marriages Act (see above para 4.1.5) says that men and women in customary marriages are now equal in all respects, except that a man may still have more than one wife. The important point is that women in customary marriages are no longer minors. Although the issue has not been decided by a court, it is likely that the position in customary marriages is the same as for civil marriages (ie both parents have equal guardianship).

It must be noted that in a case of divorce, the court may make an order regarding guardianship of a minor child of the customary marriage. This means the court may award guardianship to the mother if it is in the best interests of the child.

4.3.2 The duty of support

4.3.2.1 When parents must support their children

different standards of living

Parents have a legal duty to feed and clothe their family, as well as to provide a home, medical care and education for their children. This duty, however, is different for each family depending upon the family's standard of living. For example, a rich person's child will have a right to a higher standard of living and more expensive education than a poor person's child.

children may sue their parents

The law states that children whose parents do not provide them with a reasonable standard of care may sue their parents for failing to care for them properly. This may happen if their parents are living together but neither does anything to support the children. If a child is not properly supported by its parents the court may order the child to be taken into care (see below para 4.3.3.2). For example, the child may be sent to a foster home or children's home or handed over to the care of a relative. Fortunately very few children ever have to sue their parents for proper support.

a rich person's child will have a right to higher standard of living and a better education than a poor person's child

support depends on the parents' standard of living

The support that parents owe to their children is not just to provide the bare necessities of life. The support that must be provided depends upon the standard of living of the parents and their position in the community. In some cases a child may be entitled to university or other higher education, even if the child is an adult. There is no legal duty, however, upon parents who cannot afford to support their children because they are poor or ill. Parents in this situation may qualify for support from social welfare agencies (see below para 5.3). The duty of parents to support their children ends when they become self-supporting.

4.3.2.2 When children must support their parents

adult children have a duty to support their parents

The law also expects adult children to support their parents if the parents need support and the children can afford to do so. Because the duty of support applies to parents and children, and children and parents, children must support their parents if the parents cannot support themselves and the children can afford to support them. Parents of minor children, however, may not use their children's earnings except to support the children. Even then they must use their own money if the children do not earn enough money to support themselves. Parents who use their children's earnings without providing any support for the children may be ordered by a court to refund the money to the children.

Problem 5: The case of the rich son

Questions

Jan, 40 years old, is the owner of a successful business. His mother, aged 60 years, retires from her job at the end of the year. Her small savings and pension payments will not be enough for her to continue renting her house. She could move to an old age home but would prefer to stay in the house.

1. Does Jan have a legal duty to support his mother? Give reasons for your answer.
2. Role-play a conversation between Jan and his mother.
3. Should the law require adult children to support their parents when the parents need help? Give reasons for your answer.

4.3.2.3 When children become independent

The duty of parents to support their children ends when the children become independent. Children may become independent in a number of ways, such as (a) when the child turns 18 years of age (ie becomes an adult); (b) when a child marries; and (c) when a child is 'emancipated'.

4.3.2.3.1 When a child turns 18 years of age

full legal capacity

When a child reaches the age of 18 years he or she becomes an adult and acquires full legal capacity. The person may then enter into contracts without assistance from a parent or guardian. He or she may also sue and be sued without assistance. The parents' duty of support, however, only ends if the child reaches 18 years of age and is self-supporting. Therefore a parent may be legally obliged to support a sick or crippled adult child over the age of 18 years if the child is unable to support itself.

4.3.2.3.2 When a child marries

a minor child becomes a 'major' through marriage

When a minor child marries he or she automatically becomes a 'major'. A major is a person over the age of 18 years and who has full legal capacity. A minor person who becomes a major after marriage remains a major even if he or she divorces or becomes a widow/widower before the age of 18 years. Therefore a divorced woman who is under 18 years of age remains a major, no matter how she was married.

financial independence of minor children

4.3.2.3.3 When a child is 'emancipated'

Minor males or females under the age of 18 years may become financially independent of their parents. This is called 'emancipation'. The minors must prove to court that they can earn enough money to live independently of their parents. They may then enter into contracts, and bring and defend court cases by themselves, but will not have full legal capacity.

Problem 6: Is Martie a major?

when Martie refuses to have an affair with her employer he dismisses her

Questions

Martie, aged 17 years, has earned her own living as a shop assistant for two years. She lives with her mother and father. She pays them for food and accommodation. When she refuses to have an affair with her employer he stops paying her wages and dismisses her. She is owed two months' wages and wishes to sue her employer. Does Martie need her father's assistance to bring the action for her wages? Give reasons for your answer.

4.3.2.4 Things children may do without their parents' assistance

The law allows children to do some things without their parents' assistance. For example:

1. Children aged 7 years may operate a post office savings account and open a savings account at a bank.
2. Children aged 16 years may open and control an investment account in a building society.
3. Children aged 16 years may make a will (see below para 4.6.4.3).

4. Children aged 14 years may witness a will (see below para 4.6.4.3).
5. Children aged 12 years who are sufficiently mature may consent to medical treatment.
6. Children aged 12 years who are sufficiently mature and assisted by their parents or guardian may consent to a surgical operation.
7. Children aged 12 years may consent to HIV testing where it is in their interests.
8. Children under the age of 12 years who are sufficiently mature may consent to HIV testing where it is in their interests.
9. Children aged 12 years may buy or access condoms on request.
10. Children aged 12 years may access contraceptives without their parents' or guardians' or care-giver's consent.
11. Children of any age may consent to an abortion (termination of pregnancy) provided they understand the nature and effect of what they are consenting to (see below para 4.3.4).

For the legal position of minors who enter into contracts with or without their parents' assistance, see above para 3.1.3.1.

Problem 7: Can the child act without assistance?

Questions

Decide in the following situations whether the children can do what they want to do without the assistance of their guardians. Give reasons for your answers.

1. Jody, aged 17 years, wishes to have her nose straightened by a plastic surgeon.
2. Salie, aged 12 years, wishes to open a building society account.
3. Khotso, aged 8 years, wishes to open a post office savings account.
4. Vish, aged 14 years, has inherited a lot of money and wants to make a will leaving it to his sister.
5. Paulus, aged 15 years, is asked to witness a will.
6. Thandi, aged 13 years, wants to have an abortion.
7. Shanti, aged 14 years, wants her doctor to prescribe the 'pill' so that she does not fall pregnant.
8. Busi, aged 15 years, wishes to have an HIV test without her parents knowing about it.

4.3.3 Children in need of care and protection

laws protecting children

The courts do not like interfering with the relationship between parents and children. Although the law tries to avoid being involved in disputes within families, the Children's Act protects children against ill-treatment and abandonment by their parents.

4.3.3.1 Removal to 'place of safety'

if there is no suitable parent or guardian

Any policeman, social worker or authorised officer (eg a person authorised in writing by the children's court) may remove a child to a 'place of safety' if he or she has reason to believe that the child has no suitable parent or guardian, or that it is in the interests of the child that he or she be taken to a place of safety (eg if the child's parents are unfit or unable to look after the child).

4.3.3.2 Children's court inquiry

'in need of care'

If a child is taken to a place of safety, the next step is an enquiry in the 'children's court' (see above para 2.14.8) to decide whether the child is 'in need of care'. The law says that a child is in need of care if:

1. The child has no parents or guardian;
2. The child has been abandoned and has no means of support;
3. The child behaves in a way that cannot be controlled by his or her parents or the people in whose care he or she is;
4. The child lives or works on the streets or begs for a living;
5. The child is addicted to a dependence-producing substance and is without support to obtain treatment for such dependency;
6. The child has been exploited or lives in circumstances that expose him or her to exploitation.
7. The child lives in or is exposed to circumstances that may seriously harm his or her physical, mental or social well-being;
8. The child may be at risk if returned to the care of his or her parent, guardian or care-giver because there is reason to believe that the child will live or be exposed to circumstances which may seriously harm his or her physical, mental or social well-being;
9. The child is being maltreated, abused or deliberately neglected or degraded by a parent, guardian, care-giver or family member, someone who has parental responsibility over the child or someone under whose control the child is; or
10. The child may also be in need of care and protection if he or she is a victim of child labour or is in a child-headed household.

what may happen to a child in need of care

If the children's court is satisfied that the child is in need of care (ie if one or more of the above conditions exist) the court has a number of options, which are not limited to the following:

1. Order that the child be placed in an alternative place of care, including an order placing the child in temporary safe care or in the care of a court-designated foster parent or youth care centre or court-designated facility.
2. Order that the child be returned to the person under whose care the child was before the child was placed in temporary safe care if the court finds that that person is a suitable person to provide for the safety and well-being of the child.
3. Order that the child be sent to a youth care centre if the court finds that the parent or care-giver cannot control the child or if the child displays criminal behaviour.

4. If the child has no parent or care-giver or has a parent or care-giver who is unable or unsuitable to care for the child, the court may order that the child be placed in:
   (i) Foster care with a suitable foster parent;
   (ii) Foster care with a group of persons;
   (iii) Temporary safe care, pending an application for and finalisation of the adoption of the child;
   (iv) A child and youth care centre – as a last resort.
5. Order that the child be taken care of in a partial care facility at the expense of a person under whose care the child was placed but who had no time to care for the child, as a result of which the child became in need of care and protection.
6. Order that the child receive appropriate treatment at state expense if the court finds that the child is in need of medical, psychological or other treatment.
7. Order that the child be admitted as an inpatient or outpatient to an appropriate facility if the court finds that the child is in need of treatment for addiction to a dependence-producing substance.
8. Interdict a person from maltreating, abusing, neglecting or degrading the child or from having contact with the child, if the court finds that –
   (i) The child has been or is being maltreated, abused, neglected or degraded by that person;
   (ii) The relationship between the child and that person is detrimental to the well-being or safety of the child; or
   (iii) The child is exposed to a substantial risk of imminent harm.

The Act also creates criminal offences where parents or caregivers have abused or exploited their children. For example, any parent or person having care over a child who ill-treats or abandons that child or allows him or her to be ill-treated is guilty of an offence and may be fined.

Problem 8: Which are cases of children in need of care?

Questions

Examine each of the following situations and decide whether you think the child is in need of care or whether the parent or parents have been guilty of ill-treatment or abandonment. Give reasons for your answer. If you decide the child is in need of care, indicate what type of care you think is the most suitable for each situation.

1. Kristel, an unmarried mother, goes to work and leaves her two children, Klaas aged 7, and Pixie aged 3, at home unattended.
2. Jason beats his 12-year-old son, Isaac, until he is 'black and blue'.

Ray tells Carla that she can do anything she wants to

3. Ray, a single parent, tells his 14-year-old daughter, Carla, that she may stay out all night or do anything else she wants, as long as she does not bother him.
4. Thulani spanks her 4-year-old son, Khala, until he cries.
5. Nazeer and Shaida refuse to allow their 16-year-old son, Ahmed, to go out alone with girls.
6. Amos, aged 13, lives with his two sisters aged 9 and 6 respectively. In addition, he lives with his 90-year-old great-grandmother who can no longer do anything for herself. Amos has to bath and dress his grandmother and feed her.
7. Noleen and Paul have a 15-year-old daughter, Mary, with cerebral palsy. Noleen and Paul have exhausted all their money caring for their disabled child, and they now have nothing to spend on Mary's well-being.
8. Thandeka, after being divorced by her husband who left her for a younger woman, continually shouts and swears at her 14-year-old daughter, Cindy.

4.3.3.3 When parents punish their children

reasonable punishment

children may sue their parents for unreasonable assault

Parents have a right and a duty, when their children misbehave, to punish them and to correct their behaviour. Parents may use a reasonable amount of physical force to punish their children. But a parent who goes beyond what is reasonable or acts out of spite may be sued civilly and criminally (see above para 1.2.3). A child who is unreasonably punished may sue his or her parents for damages for assault. Parents who unreasonably or spitefully punish their children may be criminally prosecuted under the common law or the Children's Act.

4.3.3.4 Reporting of child abuse and neglect

most child abuse cases are not reported

One of the problems with child abuse and neglect is that many cases are not reported. Most people are reluctant to interfere in the family affairs of others. The Children's Amendment Act, however, requires every dentist, medical practitioner, duty to report child abuse

nurse, social worker, teacher and any person who works at a children's home or place of safety to report suspected cases of child abuse. If a person employed in one of these jobs does not report a suspected case of child abuse he or she may be guilty of a crime.

After child abuse is reported several questions arise:

1. What should the police do when faced with a child abuse case?
2. What should the courts do?
3. Should the child be returned home or removed from the parents' care?
4. Should parents found guilty of child abuse be fined, sent to prison, or given some other punishment?

Problem 9: The case of the beaten boy

Questions

Assume that you look through a window and see Mr Sadie of the family next door beating his 10-year-old son, Robert. The boy is screaming and in obvious pain.

1. What would you do? Would you call the police? Give reasons for your answer.
2. Role-play a visit by the police to the Sadie's home. What should the police say and do?
3. If Mr Sadie is taken to court for continually beating and injuring Robert, what should the court do? Do you think child abuse should be a crime that is punished with imprisonment for the guilty parent? Give reasons for your answer.
4. Some people may say that a child learns to be violent when he or she is the victim of violence. Do you agree? Give reasons for your answer.

4.3.4 Termination of pregnancy

termination of pregnancy is a controversial issue

Termination of the pregnancy involves the expulsion of a foetus from a pregnant woman. It is a controversial question whether women should be allowed to terminate their pregnancies and, if so, under what conditions. Previously, under apartheid, the Abortion and Sterilization Act only allowed termination of pregnancy in very limited cases such as: (a) where the woman had been raped or was the victim of incest, (b) the continued pregnancy would endanger the life of the woman, or (c) where the child, when born, would be seriously physically or mentally handicapped.

the Choice on Termination of Pregnancy Act

However, after democracy in South Africa, Parliament passed the Choice on Termination of Pregnancy Act, which makes terminations of pregnancy far more widely available than previously. The Act divides a woman's 9-month pregnancy into three periods of time:

when termination of pregnancy may take place

1. During the first 12 weeks a woman may terminate her pregnancy upon her own choice.

2. From the 13th week to the 20th week a woman may terminate her pregnancy if a doctor believes that:
   (a) The continued pregnancy will injure the woman's physical or mental health;
   (b) The foetus will suffer from physical or mental abnormality;
   (c) The pregnancy resulted from rape or incest;
   (d) The continued pregnancy will significantly affect the social or economic circumstances of the woman.
3. From the 20th week a woman may only terminate her pregnancy if a doctor believes that the continued pregnancy:
   (a) Will endanger the woman's life;
   (b) Will result in a severe malformation of the foetus;
   (c) Will pose a risk of injury to the foetus. Nowadays, abortions can be obtained at some state hospitals (where they are free) or at many private hospitals and private clinics established for this purpose.

provision for counselling

The Act also says that counselling must be made available for a woman or a girl who wants to terminate the pregnancy, both before and after the termination of the pregnancy. However, this counselling is not compulsory and must not try to tell the woman whether or not she should terminate her pregnancy. If the woman is a child she will be advised to talk to her parents, guardians, family members and friends. However, she does not have to do this and the termination of pregnancy will go ahead if she chooses not to. This means that, if a woman wants to terminate her pregnancy, whether she is a child or not, she does not have to get the consent of anyone, including the father of the child or her parents.

pregnant minors may consent on their own to a termination of pregnancy

foetus has no right to life

When the Act was passed many people regarded it as a victory for women's rights. However, some religious groups and opposition political parties have argued that it infringes the right to life. In *Christian Lawyers Association of South Africa v Minister of Health*, the High Court held that a foetus does not have the right to life. The court held that a foetus is not a person in the sense of a being entitled to constitutional rights until it has been born alive. Also, the Bill of Rights says that everyone has the right to make decisions concerning reproduction, which, the court said, includes the right to terminate pregnancy on demand.

Problem 10: Termination of pregnancy on demand

Questions

1. Do you agree with the provisions in the Choice on Termination of Pregnancy Act which allow for termination of pregnancy on demand in the first 12 weeks of pregnancy? Give reasons for your answer. If you do not agree with the Act, how would you change it?

2. Do you think that counselling before and after termination of pregnancy should be compulsory? Give reasons for your answer.
3. Do you think that a woman should have to get the consent of the father of the child before terminating a pregnancy? Give reasons for your answer.
4. Do you think that pregnant children under the age of 18 years should need to get their parents' consent before terminating their pregnancy? Give reasons for your answer.

4.4 Foster care and adoption

Outcomes

After completion of this section learners will be able to:

1. Demonstrate an understanding of the law relating to foster care and adoption.

Assessment criteria

1. An explanation is given of what foster care means.
2. The rights and duties of foster parents are explained.
3. The rights and duties of a child's natural parents when a child has been placed in foster care are identified.
4. The meaning of adoption and how an adoption order is made are explained.
5. A set of facts is examined and a decision made on whether an adoption order should be cancelled.
6. A set of facts is examined and a decision made on whether people of different races or of the same sex should be allowed to adopt children.
7. A simulated hearing of the South African Law Commission is conducted to illustrate the problems that may arise if all adopted children are allowed to know who their natural parents are.
8. The effect of adoption is explained.

4.4.1 Foster care

foster care is ordered by the children's court

foster care may be with family or non-family members

Foster care is an order for alternative care of a child that is made by the children's court. A child is in foster care where he or she has been placed in the care of a person who is not his or her parent or guardian. When neglect or child abuse is proved against parents, a court may order an ill-treated child under 18 years of age to be removed from care of the natural parents and placed in a foster home for a period of two years or until the child reaches the age of 18 years. Court orders concerning foster care distinguish between foster care with non-family foster parents and family foster parents. With regard to non-family foster parents, the court orders an initial period of two years in a foster home. After the child has been in a foster home for two years, the children's court may order that the child remain in foster care until 18 years of age. In this period, there will be no further regular social work supervision or reports. However, social workers will visit the child once every two years. In a case of foster care with a family member, the children's court may from the outset order that the child remain in a foster care until 18 years. The children's court may give such an order if the child has been abandoned, orphaned or the purpose is to attempt to reunite the child with its parents. In this case, the social worker will visit the child once in every two years. An appropriate type of foster care must be chosen to ensure that it is in the best interests of the child. The government has set up a committee to review the present foster care system.

4.4.1.1 The rights of foster parents

foster parents take over care and control of the child

Foster parents are people who care for a child who is not their natural child. The effect of a foster care order is to take away the child's natural parents' rights of control and care of the child. These rights are handed over to the person in charge of a foster home or the foster parents. However, guardianship vests in the parents and is not transferred to the foster parents. The natural parents keep their common-law rights to visit their child at all reasonable times unless the court says they may not.

discipline and reasonable punishment

foster parents may not deal with property, marriage or employment affecting the child

In addition to any other rights that the children's court may award to the foster parents in an order of foster care, the foster parents are also given the right to discipline the foster child, to choose which school the foster child should attend, and to punish the child – provided the punishment is reasonable. Foster parents do not, however, have the right: (a) to deal with the child's property; (b) to consent to the child's marriage; (c) to consent to a medical operation or treatment where there is a serious danger to the life of the child – unless there is no time for anyone else to consent; or (d) to consent to the child getting a job.

4.4.1.2 How foster parents are selected

welfare organisations place children in foster homes

The prospective foster parents must be fit and proper persons to be entrusted with the foster care of the child in accordance with a social worker's assessment. In addition, the prospective parents must be willing and able to undertake, exercise and maintain the responsibilities of such care. They must also have the capacity to provide an environment that allows for the growth and development of the child. This does not mean that the foster parents must have a good income – even poor people can be foster parents and they can apply for social grants to help maintain the child. The Children's Act further requires the children's court to consider the social worker's report on the cultural, religious and linguistic background of the child. The report must also include information on the availability of a suitable person with a similar background to that of the child who is willing and able to provide foster care the child.

providing similar homes for foster children

Foster parents can never be the parents or guardians of the children placed in their care. This is because in the past, state grants have been abused and have been paid out to foster parents who were actually obliged to pay maintenance for the child. The children's court may place a child in a foster care: (a) with a person who is not a family member of the child; (b) with a family member who is not a parent or guardian of the child; or (c) in a registered cluster foster care scheme. Cluster foster care schemes are a new concept in South Africa, and usually take the form of a non-profit organisation managing a scheme registered with the Department of Social Development.

cluster foster care schemes

visits from social workers

After the foster child moves into his or her foster parents' home, the family is often visited by the social workers that placed the child. People who act as foster parents and need assistance may receive a monthly maintenance allowance for each foster child from the government.

after a child has been placed in foster care, the foster family is often visited by social workers

4.4.1.3 Duties of foster parents

to provide food, clothing and education

Foster parents who have been put in charge of a child by a court order have a duty to provide the child with food, clothing and education. Natural parents who have voluntarily placed their child with foster parents and were not ordered to do so by a court may remove the child at any time. In such cases the natural parents are also entitled to visit the child at all reasonable times.

the court may order natural parents not to visit

Where the child was removed by a court order the natural parents have to obey the conditions laid down by the court. For example, if the natural parents are a bad influence on the child, the court may order that they may not visit him or her. They may also have to pay maintenance for the foster child.

4.4.1.4 End of foster care

ending of foster care

Foster care comes to an end if: (a) the child is returned to his or her natural parents or is transferred to a home; (b) the foster child is adopted; (c) the foster child turns 18 years old – unless it is necessary for the child to remain in foster care in order to complete his or her education or training; or (d) two years have lapsed after the foster care order was made and it was not extended for a further period.

if a foster child runs away, he or she may be arrested

If a foster child runs away from the custody of his or her foster parents the child may be arrested without a warrant of arrest (see above para 2.11.2.3) by a police officer or social worker. The child will be asked to explain to the presiding officer in the children's court why he or she ran away. The child may or may not be returned to the foster parents, depending upon his or her reason for running away.

Problem 1: Natural parents and foster parents

Questions

1. Ertjies, who is 10 years old, is given to his aunt and uncle by his parents to be brought up as a foster child. They were not ordered to do so by the court. What rights and duties do his aunt and uncle have? What rights do his natural parents have?
2. The court orders Dolly, a 12-year-old girl, to be removed from the care of her unmarried mother and placed in foster care. This was done because her mother is a prostitute and allows her to mix with other prostitutes. If you were the children's court magistrate, would you allow Dolly's natural mother to visit her? Give reasons for your answer.

4.4.2 Adoption

adopted children have the same relationship as natural children

Adoption is a placement in the permanent care of a person with a view: (a) to protecting and nurturing the child by providing a safe, healthy environment with positive support; and (b) to connecting the child to other safe and nurturing family relationships for a lifetime. A child who is adopted has the same legal relationship with their adoptive parents that a natural child has with his or her parents and his or her parents' relatives.

4.4.2.1 Who may be adopted

Only a child can be adopted. However, not every child can be adopted – the child concerned must be adoptable. An adoption social worker must make an assessment to determine whether the child is adoptable.

children must be adoptable

A child is adoptable if the adoption is in the best interests of the child and the child is living under any of the following circumstances:

(a) The child is an orphan and has no guardian or care-giver who is willing to adopt him or her;
(b) The whereabouts of the child's parent or guardian cannot be established;
(c) The child has been abandoned;
(d) The child's parent or guardian has abused or deliberately neglected the child, or has allowed the child to be abused; or
(e) The child is in need of permanent alternative placement.

4.4.2.2 Who may adopt

Who may adopt a child?

Any of the following people may adopt a child: (a) a married couple; (b) partners in a civil union; (c) partners in a permanent domestic life-partnership; (d) other persons sharing a common household and forming a permanent family unit; (e) a widower; (f) a widow; (g) a divorced or unmarried person; (h) a married person whose spouse is the parent of the child; or (i) a partner in a civil union whose partner is the parent of the child. The latter two could happen when a person has a child with one person, and then marries or enters into a civil union with someone else. The same applies to a person whose domestic life-partner is the parent of the child or a biological father of a child born outside of marriage or a civil union. Previously, the mother of a child born outside of marriage or a civil union could put the child up for adoption without getting the consent of the father. This law has now been changed. If the mother of a child born out of marriage or a civil union wishes to put the child up for adoption, she must get the consent of the father, and he is able to apply for adoption of the child. A foster parent also can adopt a foster child.

father of an illegitimate child may adopt the child

foster parents may adopt foster children

conditions for adoption

In order to adopt a child the person wishing to adopt the child:

(a) Must be over the age of 18 years;
(b) Must be a South African citizen or permanent resident – adoptions by non-South Africans or non-South African residents are allowed but are governed by a different set of rules applied to inter-country adoptions;
(c) Must be fit and proper to be entrusted with full parental rights and responsibilities in respect of the child and must be willing and able to undertake, exercise and maintain those rights and responsibilities; and
(d) Must have been properly assessed by the social worker to ensure that he or she is a fit and proper person.

People wishing to adopt a child may not be disqualified because of their financial status. Any person who adopts a child may apply for social assistance where necessary.

religious and cultural background

While the adoption social worker may take into account the cultural and community diversity of the adoptive child and the people who wish to adopt the child, such people may not be refused permission to adopt a child because of their culture or the community they come from.

4.4.2.3 Consent

consent of parents

The child can only be adopted if: (a) each parent has consented to the adoption – whether the parents are married or not; or (b) any other person who is a guardian of the child has given consent; and (c) the child has given consent if he or she 10 years or older or if below 10 years of age, the child is of sufficient maturity and stage of development to understand the implications of such consent.

mature children must consent

In the case of a child born outside of marriage, the natural father's consent is not required where he has failed to acknowledge that he is the father of the child. In most cases, however, the parents' consent has to be obtained.

adoption of foster children

In the case of a foster child being adopted by a person who is not the foster parent, the foster parent has to state in writing that he or she does not wish to adopt the child. However, this is not necessary if, within a month, the foster parent has provided no indication of whether he or she would rather adopt the child.

when consent of parent or guardian not required

consent not required for adoption of orphans

Generally, there are some cases where consent of the parent or guardian is not needed for adoption and such cases include where the parent or guardian: (a) is unable to give consent because of mental disability; (b) has abandoned the child or the whereabouts of the parent or guardian cannot be established or the identity of the parent or guardian is not known; (c) has abused or deliberately neglected the child; (d) has consistently failed to fulfil his or her parental responsibilities towards the child during the last 12 months; or (e) has failed to reply to a notice of adoption within 30 days of service of notice. Consent is not needed where the child is an orphan.

4.4.2.4 How people are adopted

When people wish to adopt someone the following must be done:

1. The prospective adoptive parents (ie the people wishing to adopt a child) must make an application to the children's court in the district in which the child lives.

investigation by social workers

2. The adoption social worker looks at the application and investigates the suitability of the prospective adoptive parents. The social worker writes a report on whether the parents are suitable to adopt the child.

letter from provincial head of social development

3. The adoption application and social worker's report must also be accompanied by a letter from the provincial head of social development recommending the adoption of the child.

court hearings not open to the public

4. When the clerk of the children's court receives an application, the clerk must submit to the court any information that has been filed regarding consent to the adoption. A formal court hearing takes place. The court will listen to the prospective adoptive parents, read the report written by the social worker, and make a decision. The court hearing is not open to the public.

Problem 2: Would you allow the couple to adopt the child?

Mandla and Zanele wish to adopt Jan

Questions

1. Mandla and Zanele are a black couple whose first language is isiZulu. They have recently moved into one of the formerly white suburbs and have good jobs. They wish to adopt an extra-marital Afrikaans child called Jan. The children's court refuses the application without holding a hearing because the court says the racial and cultural difference between the adoptive parents and the child 'will not be in the best interests of the child'. If this case went on review and you were the judge, would you agree with the children's court? Give reasons for your answer.
2. Kerry and Chantelle are a lesbian couple. Chantelle is an attorney and Kerry is a psychologist. They have lived together in a steady loving relationship for many years. Chantelle applies to the children's court to adopt a child called Jonathan. Should Chantelle be allowed to adopt the child? Will raising a child by a couple of the same sex be in the interests and welfare of the child? Give reasons for your answer.
3. Precious is a stable and loving mother of two children. She has no permanent job and struggles to provide a living for her two children. However, she lives in a decent house which she obtained from her ex-husband after divorce. Precious wants to adopt Tom, aged 8 years. Do you think Precious should be allowed to adopt Tom, given that she has no permanent job? Give reasons for your answer.

4.4.2.5 Effect of adoption

legal status of adopted children

The Children's Act says that an adopted child shall for all purposes be regarded in law as the child of the adoptive parents. The adopted child takes the adoptive parents' family name unless the adoption order says otherwise and the birth register may be changed to record it. The adoptive parents: (a) obtain 'parental power' (see above para 4.3.1) over the child; (b) the parents and child owe each other a duty of support (see above para 4.3.2); and, (c) the adopted child may inherit from his or her adoptive parents even though they have not made a will (see below para 4.6.4.2). All legal rights and duties, including the duty of support, between the child and its natural parents and relatives are ended including any claims of contact with the child. Any previous orders of placement of the child are terminated.

adoptive parents obtain 'parental power'

sex and marriage with natural relatives not allowed

An adoption order, however, does not affect any rights to property the child acquired before adoption. Further, the adoption order does not allow an adopted child to marry, or have sexual intercourse with, his or her natural relatives. This is because such acts would have been illegal (eg 'incest', see above para 2.8.1) if the child had not been adopted.

4.4.2.6 When adoption may be cancelled

application to children's court or High Court for cancellation of adoption order

The natural parent of a child, the person who was the guardian at the time of the adoption, the adoptive parents, or the adopted child may apply to the children's court or the High Court for an adoption to be cancelled. However, one of the following conditions must exist:

1. The natural parent of the child did not consent to the adoption. The parent of the child must apply to the court within two years of hearing that his or her child has been adopted.
2. The adoptive parents did not qualify to be fit and proper persons to adopt a child at the time of making the adoption order. The application must be made within two years from the date of adoption.
3. The adoption is not in the best interests of the child. The application must be made within two years of the adoption.

appeals against cancellation orders

If the people who applied to the children's court are unhappy with the decision of the court they may appeal to the High Court (see above para 1.3.1.7).

effect of cancellation of adoption order

In a case where the adoption order has been cancelled, the effects of adoption no longer apply, and all rights and responsibilities regarding the child's previous status are restored. The court may then make an appropriate placement order for the child or order that the child be kept in temporary safe care until an appropriate order can be made.

Problem 3: The case of the mother who changed her mind

Olive changes her mind and wants her baby back, but her application is refused

Olive, a wealthy 30-year-old single woman from Durban has an affair with Sarel, a 40-year-old married man, and has a child by him. Olive is ashamed and does not tell her parents. The baby is born in Johannesburg. While she is emotionally upset Olive gives the child away in adoption to Elmine and Basil, who already have a 3-year-old adopted boy.

Three months later Olive changes her mind and wants her baby back. She applies to the children's court to have her baby returned, but her application is refused. Olive appeals to the High Court.

Questions

1. If you were Olive's advocate, what would your arguments be?
2. If you were Elmine and Basil's advocate, what would your arguments be?
3. If you were the judge, what would your judgment be?

4.4.2.7 Should adopted children be told that they are adopted?

adopted children should be told they are adopted

Nowadays it is generally accepted that adopted children should be told at an early age that they are adopted. There used to be disagreement, however, as to whether they should have the right to know who their natural parents are. Some adopted children are interested in learning about their natural parents. The law says that adopted children are allowed to look at their adoption records only when they have reached the age of 18 years. The adoptive parent is also entitled to look at the adoption records after the child reaches 18. The biological parents or previous adoptive parents can access the adoption records after the child reaches 18 years and only if the child and the adoptive parents give their consent in writing.

Problem 4: Some questions on adoption

Assume that the South African Law Commission wishes to recommend the following law: 'All adopted persons over the age of 18 years shall have the right to obtain a copy of their original birth certificate and shall be given the first name, family name and address of their natural parents'.

At a Law Commission hearing on the proposed law two people give evidence:

Laura Dunn says: 'When I was 16 years old I became pregnant. The father, a sailor from a visiting ship, was from Greece and I never saw him again. My parents did not have the money to support another child in our family and I did not want to leave school. I was also embarrassed, so I went to another town. I had the baby there and placed him for adoption. I returned to my hometown and finished school. I am now happily married and the mother of two children, aged 11 and 14 years. My husband does not know about my earlier affair or the child put up for adoption. I was promised by the adoption agency that they would never tell anyone my name. I do not wish to see the child I put up for adoption. I believe that it is best if we live our separate lives.'

Karel Kroon says: 'I am 19 years old and last year my adoptive parents told me that I was adopted at birth. I love my adoptive parents but feel the need to find out who my natural parents are and to meet them. I want to know where I came from and who I am. Everyone needs to belong somewhere. It is inhuman not to let me know who my real parents are.'

Questions

1. If you were a member of the Law Commission inquiry and heard the stories of the two witnesses would you vote in favour of the proposed law? Give reasons for your answer. Would the law be better if it allowed adopted children to look at their records only after the natural parents had given their consent? Give reasons for your answer.
2. Would fewer people give their children up for adoption if they knew that their children would later find out their names? Give reasons for your answer.
3. What do you think would happen if the proposed law was to be passed? How would you rewrite the law to improve it?
4. Should Karel's adoptive parents have told him sooner that he was adopted? Give reasons for your answer. If they know, should they tell him who his natural mother is and why he was put up for adoption? Give reasons for your answer.

4.5 Family problems: Divorce and maintenance

Outcomes

After completion of this section learners will be able to:

1. Explain the law relating to divorce or separation.
2. Explain the steps to follow in obtaining a divorce and understand the consequences of divorce.

Assessment criteria

1. Some of the factors that commonly lead to a separation or divorce are identified.
2. The difference between a separation and a divorce is explained.
3. An awareness is created of what spouses or civil union partners should do before they decide to separate.
4. The grounds for a divorce are explained.
5. A set of facts is examined to determine when the courts will regard a marriage or civil union as having irretrievably broken down.
6. The steps to be followed in obtaining a divorce are explained.
7. An explanation is given of how family property may be divided and how maintenance is provided for when a couple become divorced.
8. The factors which influence the courts when awarding custody to a spouse or civil union partner are identified.
9. A set of facts is examined and a decision is taken on which parent is likely to be awarded care of the children of a marriage or civil union.
10. An explanation is given of how a person makes an application for maintenance and what happens if maintenance is not paid.

sometimes marriages and civil unions break down

Many people are happily married or in happy civil unions but sometimes problems occur. Most problems are solved by the couples working them out together. Sometimes, however, marriages and civil unions break down. This section deals with what happens when a marriage or civil union breaks down. It discusses not only how marriages and civil unions are ended, but also how the spouses and civil union partners and children may obtain support after a marriage or union has ended. The husband and wife or civil union partners may decide to separate, but the marriage or union legally ends with divorce, or the death of one of the parties. This section will deal with divorce.

4.5.1 Divorce and separation

obtaining help to prevent divorce

People should never rush into a divorce (see below para 4.5.2.2). Divorce is a serious step that may affect the spouses or civil union partners and children for the rest of their lives. Before seeking a divorce the parties should try to obtain help from social welfare agencies or marriage counsellors. They should contact their local social welfare department to find out where to obtain help.

divorce may be very expensive

Apart from causing emotional problems, divorce may also be very expensive. This is especially so if lawyers have to be involved. Arrangements have to be made for the maintenance (support) of the parties and children. The couple also have to divide their property such as the house, cars, furniture, life insurance, cash, bank accounts and everything else they own (see below para 4.5.2.5).

most problems in a marriage or a civil union can be solved by the couples themselves, but sometimes marriages or civil unions break down

situations that may lead to divorce or separation

There are many situations that may lead to a divorce or separation (see below para 4.5.2.1). Surveys have shown that the most common causes of divorce are:

1. Arguments with in-laws or relatives;
2. Problems at work;
3. Spouses having affairs with other people;
4. Arguments about children;
5. Sexual problems;
6. Spouses failing to talk to each other;
7. Boredom with marriage;
8. Alcohol or drug abuse;
9. Money problems;
10. Loss of shared interests; and
11. Domestic violence.

Problem 1: Problems in marriages and civil unions

Questions

1. List five of the most common problems that lead to separation or divorce. Rank them from 1 to 5 according to which you think are the most important. (Rank the most important as 1, and the least important as 5.)
2. Do you think it is possible to know in advance which problems are likely to occur in a marriage or civil union if a couple marry? Give reasons for your answer.
3. If problems in a marriage or civil union occur, what can spouses or civil union partners do to work them out?
4. What are some of the things that have to be dealt with when a couple decide to obtain a divorce?

4.5.1.1 Separation

judicial separation before 1979

Before 1979, if a marriage broke down and the parties did not want to obtain a divorce they could decide to enter into a 'separation agreement'. This agreement could then be confirmed by the court (these were known as orders for judicial separation). However, orders for judicial separation did not end the marriage, but merely temporarily suspended some of the marital obligations of the spouses, particularly that of living together. For example, the husband could have agreed to pay the wife a certain amount of maintenance each month and let her stay on in the house with the children.

judicial separation abolished in 1979

When the Divorce Act came into operation in 1979, orders for judicial separation were abolished. This means that courts could no longer issue such orders. However, spouses or civil union partners can still agree to an 'extra-judicial separation' (an agreement not ordered by the court) which is an informal agreement between them that they will live apart. The agreement usually sets out the rights and duties of each party. In particular, it records the couple's agreement on maintenance, child care and access, division of property, etc.

informal separation agreement

This separation agreement only applies between the parties and if one of them does not carry out the terms of the agreement, the other cannot take the matter to court. It remains valid only for as long as each of them upholds it, which means that it can be cancelled if the parties live together again.

divorce legally ends a marriage

Unlike a separation, a divorce legally ends a valid marriage or civil union (see below para 4.5.2). Once a divorce has been granted the couple may legally marry or enter into civil unions with other people. For religious reasons some people do not believe in divorce. Sometimes a husband and wife or civil union partners need time to think about their future. In these situations a separation rather than a divorce is the best solution. It is important to understand though that the court cannot make a separation order – it can only grant a divorce separation does not legally end the marriage or civil union

order. If a married or civil union couple separate, they still have legal and financial responsibilities between themselves and their children. They remain husband and wife or civil union partners, and neither may marry or enter into a civil union with somebody else.

Problem 2: The unhappy couple

after two years of marriage Jan and Ansie are very unhappy and are considering living apart

Questions

Jan and Ansie are married when they are both 21 years old. A year later Ansie gives birth to twin daughters. After two years of marriage they are always arguing and are very unhappy. They are unsure about divorce, but think it might be better to live apart for a while. Jan works as a mechanic and earns about R9 000 a month. Ansie used to work as a bank teller earning R6 000 a month but has not worked since she had the twins. Jan and Ansie rent a flat for R2 400 a month. They have R3 000 in a savings account, a car worth R18 000, and furniture and appliances worth R12 000.

1. What should Jan and Ansie do? Should they divorce or separate? Give reasons for your answers.
2. If they agree to separate or divorce, do Jan and Ansie need a lawyer to help them? Give reasons for your answer.
3. List the things that Jan and Ansie should decide before agreeing to a separation. Role-play a meeting between them at which they try to work out a separation agreement.

4.5.2 Divorce

If a marriage or civil union breaks down the couple may legally end their relationship by obtaining a divorce. Within the last 40 years the divorce rate in South Africa has risen significantly.

'fault system'

Until 1979 a divorce was only given to a spouse who could prove that the other spouse had done something wrong. This was known as the 'fault system'. The grounds for a divorce based on fault were that:

1. The guilty spouse had had sexual intercourse with somebody other than the innocent spouse;
2. The other spouse had deserted the innocent spouse;
3. The other spouse had been insane for at least seven years; or
4. The other spouse had been declared a 'habitual criminal' (a person who lives a criminal life) and had been in prison for at least five years.

difficult and embarrassing to prove

Proving one of these grounds was often difficult and embarrassing. Because of this many couples found themselves unable or unwilling to divorce each other, and eventually the divorce laws were changed.

4.5.2.1 Grounds for divorce

'no fault' divorce introduced in 1979

In 1979 the Divorce Act did away with the fault system and introduced 'no fault' divorce. This allows one or other of the spouses, or since 2006 civil union partners, to prove one of two grounds for a divorce:

1. The 'irretrievable breakdown' of the marriage or civil union; or
2. The mental illness or continuous unconsciousness of the other spouse or civil union partner.

The person bringing the divorce action may bring it in the High Court or regional division of the magistrate's court in the area where he or she lives, or in the High Court or regional division of the magistrate's court in the area where his or her spouse or civil union partner lives.

Problem 3: Some questions on divorce

Questions

1. Why do you think the divorce rate has increased so over the last 40 years?
2. Do you think the state should make it more difficult or easier to obtain a divorce? Why?

4.5.2.1.1 'Irretrievable breakdown'

evidence of 'irretrievable breakdown'

An irretrievable breakdown means that the couple can no longer live together as man and wife or civil union partners, and there is no chance of reconciliation. The following may be evidence of an 'irretrievable breakdown':

1. The couple have not lived together as man and wife or civil union partners for a continuous period of at least one year immediately before the date when the divorce was brought.

One of the spouses or civil union partners has had sexual intercourse with someone else and the other spouse or partner finds it impossible to continue living together

One of the spouses or civil union partners continually swears at or insults the other; or always sulks or nags the other

One of the spouses or civil union partners frequently becomes drunk or takes drugs

One of the spouses or civil union partners is too friendly with people of the opposite sex

One of the spouse or civil union partners becomes obsessed with a particular religious or political group

One of the spouses or civil union partners has a sex change operation; or has sexual relations with a member of the same sex

2. One of the spouses or civil union partners has had sexual intercourse with somebody else and the other spouse or partner finds it impossible to continue living with that spouse or partner.
3. One of the spouses or civil union partners has been declared a 'habitual criminal' and is in prison.

4. One of the couple finds it impossible to live with the other as man or wife or civil union partner for any other reason. For example, where the one spouse or civil union partner:

grounds for making it impossible to live with the other spouse or partner

   (a) Fails to support the other spouse or civil union partner;
   (b) Refuses to have sexual intercourse with the other spouse or civil union partner;
   (c) Assaults the other spouse or civil union partner or the children;
   (d) Frequently becomes drunk or takes drugs;
   (e) Always sulks or nags the other spouse or civil union partner;
   (f) Becomes obsessed with a particular religious or political group;
   (g) Is too friendly with people of the opposite sex;
   (h) Has sexual relations with a person of the same sex;
   (i) Has a sex change operation;
   (j) Has an operation to stop having children without the other spouse's or civil union partner's consent;
   (k) Continually swears at and insults the other spouse or civil union partner.

postponement of divorce

If the court is not satisfied that the marriage or civil union has irretrievably broken down the judge may postpone the case to give the parties time to see a marriage counsellor or to think again about their divorce. This may be done, for instance, where the parties are young and have only been married a short time, or where the court is satisfied that the parties can work out their differences.

4.5.2.1.2 Mental illness or unconsciousness

mental illness

A divorce may be granted on the grounds of mental illness if the other spouse or civil union partner has been admitted to, or detained in, a mental institution for a continuous period of at least two years immediately before the divorce action and there is no reasonable chance of the ill spouse or partner getting well again.

unconsciousness

A divorce may also be granted if the other spouse or civil union partner is permanently unconscious. The court must be satisfied, however, that the spouse or partner has been unconscious for a continuous period of at least six months immediately before the divorce action. The court must also be satisfied that there is no reasonable chance of the spouse or partner becoming conscious again.

Problem 4: Would you grant a divorce?

Questions

In the cases below decide whether, if you were the judge, you would grant a divorce. Give reasons for your answers.

1. Sonny and Cheryl are both 18 years old when they marry. A year later Cheryl wants to divorce Sonny, because he always goes out to discos by himself and flirts with other girls. She says that she cannot stand living with him anymore and wants to go and live with her parents.

Sonny says he does not want to get divorced, but needs time for himself away from Cheryl. He does not sleep with the other girls but enjoys flirting with them.

2. Gawie comes home drunk nearly every night. He often assaults his civil union partner Harold and son Stoffie when he has had too much to drink. When he is sober he is very kind to his family, but Harold cannot cope with his continuous drunkenness and violence. Harold wishes to divorce him.

4.5.2.2 Help with divorce

High Court or regional court

undefended divorces

defended divorces

separate lawyers

Divorce cases may be heard in the High Court or in the regional division of the magistrate's court. A divorce may be defended or undefended. Many divorces are undefended. If the divorce is undefended only the person seeking the divorce need appear in court. An undefended divorce takes only a few minutes. In a small number of cases the parties actually go to court and argue about: (a) who should have custody of the children; (b) the amount of maintenance to be awarded; (c) how the property should be divided; or (d) whether a divorce should be granted. In both defended and undefended divorces the parties can suffer emotionally and the legal costs may be high. If the divorce is likely to be complicated the couple should consult separate lawyers.

contribution towards legal costs

maintenance until divorce granted

People who cannot afford a divorce lawyer may obtain legal aid if they are not earning too much (see above para 1.4.1.4). Any party to a divorce who does not have sufficient money to pay for a lawyer may ask his or her lawyer to claim a contribution towards his or her legal costs from the other party. If that spouse or civil union partner needs support for himself or herself and their children, he or she may ask the lawyer also to claim maintenance from the other spouse or partner until the divorce is finalised. A spouse or civil union partner who has been deserted by the other spouse or partner may also claim maintenance at the maintenance court from that other spouse or partner. This may be done without consulting a lawyer (see below para 4.5.2.5.2).

'do it yourself' divorces

In cases where divorces are undefended and there are no complications, the couple can avoid legal expenses by doing the divorce themselves. To find out the procedure for a 'do it yourself' divorce, the parties may: (a) check with the registrar of the High Court; (b) call in at their nearest legal aid clinic or Legal Aid Justice Centre; or (c) consult a book on 'do it yourself' divorce.

before proceeding with a divorce the couple should consult a social worker or marriage guidance counsellor

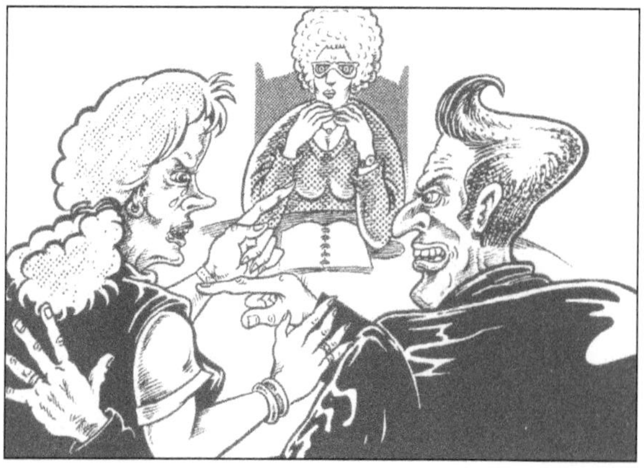

a last resort

counselling

As has been mentioned, married couples or couples in a civil union should only use divorce as a last resort. Before approaching a lawyer or the court for a divorce the couple should try to solve their problems themselves. Social workers and marriage counsellors may act as mediators (see above para 1.3.2.2) to help the parties work out a solution to their problems.

Problem 5: Help before and during divorce

Questions

1. Do you think that couples should be required to see a marriage counsellor before being granted a divorce? Give reasons for your answer.
2. Do you think it is important for spouses or civil union partners to each have their own attorney in a divorce case? Give reasons for your answer.
3. Where may poor people obtain help for a divorce if they cannot afford a lawyer?

Problem 6: If you were the marriage counsellor

Questions

You are a marriage guidance counsellor. The couples in Problem 4 consult you.
1. Role-play an interview between you, Sonny and Cheryl.
2. Role-play an interview between you, Gawie and Harold.

Note: You may consult para 1.3.2.2 above, to see how mediation works.

4.5.2.3 Steps in a divorce action

(For steps in a civil action see above para 1.5.1.2.)

a lawyer is approached

summons

particulars of claim

notice of intention to defend

pleadings

1. One of the spouses or civil union partners approaches a lawyer, or decides to do the divorce himself or herself.
2. The lawyer or divorcing party draws up a *summons* and has it issued by the registrar of the High Court. The *summons* tells the other party about his or her right to defend the divorce.
3. The summons is attached to the *particulars of claim*, which set out the reasons for the breakdown in the marriage or civil union, and what the plaintiff spouse is claiming. Both are served on the other spouse by the sheriff.
4. The party receiving the *summons* usually has 10 days to file a *notice of intention to defend.*
5. If the defending party files a *notice of intention to defend* the case will be heard by a judge after the parties have sent in their '*pleadings*'. *Pleadings* are legal documents used in a court case in which the opposing parties try to clarify their claims and defences. After the pleadings are closed the judge hears the case. Both the husband and wife or civil union partners must attend

the court hearing if the case is defended. After the judge has heard all the evidence he or she will decide whether the plaintiff is entitled to a divorce.

consent paper

6. If the defending party does not file a *notice of intention to defend* and both parties agree on what should happen to the property, children and maintenance, they may record their agreement in a *consent paper*. Then only the party bringing the divorce action need attend the court hearing.

divorce order

7. If the party bringing the action proves his or her case the judge will grant a divorce. The judge will grant a *divorce order* as well as an order about the couple's property, custody of and access to the children, and maintenance. Copies of the *divorce order* are sent to each of the parties.

marriage certificate

8. When suing for a divorce the party bringing the action must hand in a copy of the marriage certificate and give evidence as to why he or she should be granted a divorce.

settlement

9. The parties in a divorce action may enter into a *settlement* (eg by signing a consent paper) at any time during the case.

4.5.2.4 Example of a divorce case

Loshni wishes to divorce Mamoo

Loshni wishes to divorce her husband Mamoo whom she had married in community of property in 2005. Her marriage has irretrievably broken down because Mamoo had an affair with another woman. During the affair Loshni left their home and took their three young children to live with her mother. Loshni has lived away from Mamoo for 18 months. This is what will happen if Loshni brings a divorce action against Mamoo:

Loshni approaches a lawyer

1. Loshni approaches a lawyer and asks for help. The lawyer takes a statement and draws up a *summons*. The *summons* sets out personal information about Loshni and Mamoo. Attached to the summons are *particulars of claim* describing the reasons for the 'irretrievable breakdown' in the marriage, and what Loshni is claiming from Mamoo. She wishes to claim her half-share of the joint estate (see above para 4.2.2.1), custody of the children, and maintenance of R2 500 a month for herself and the children. The *summons* tells Mamoo that he has 10 days to file a *notice of intention to defend*.

a summons is sent

2. When Mamoo receives the *summons* he can do one of the following:
   (a) Defend the case; or
   (b) Agree to the divorce and enter into a *consent paper*.

Mamoo has a choice

3. If Mamoo decides to defend the case he must complete a *notice of intention to defend*. Divorce cases are difficult to defend so Mamoo needs to consult a lawyer.

pleadings

4. After a *notice of intention to defend* has been sent, Loshni's and Mamoo's lawyers will set out the facts in dispute in *pleadings* which have to be drawn up according to the rules of court.
5. At any time during the *pleadings* (or even during the trial) Mamoo may decide to settle the case by signing a *consent paper*. The *consent paper* will set out what Loshni and Mamoo have agreed to about the marriage property,

Mamoo and Loshni may agree to settle

Loshni gives evidence

the trial

witnesses are examined

the advocates try to persuade the court

judgment is given

custody of and access to the children, and maintenance for the children and Loshni. Even if Loshni and Mamoo settle the case, Loshni will still have to go to court on the day of her divorce in order to give evidence of the breakdown of their marriage.

6. If Loshni and Mamoo do not settle their case there will be a *trial*. At the *trial* the parties will present their cases to court. This is done by giving their evidence and calling witnesses. The witnesses may be cross-examined and re-examined (see above para 1.4.2.2).
7. When they think they have led sufficient evidence, the advocates for Loshni and Mamoo will close their clients' cases. They will then try to persuade the judge that their clients should win. Loshni has made up her mind to divorce him and Mamoo will find it very difficult for him to defend the case if their marriage has irretrievably broken down.
8. The judge will decide whether Loshni has proved her case 'on a balance of probabilities' (see above para 1.5.1). If he decides that she has, he will grant her an order for divorce, a half-share of the joint estate, custody of the children, and maintenance for herself and the children. If Loshni does not prove her case she will not be granted a divorce.
9. Copies of the divorce order will be sent to Loshni and Mamoo.

Problem 7: Philamina wants a divorce

Philamina married Adam in 2003 without an ante-nuptial contract. They have two young children. Adam deserts Philamina and goes to live with another woman. Philamina consults a lawyer to sue Adam for divorce. Philamina does not have enough money to pay the lawyer, but Adam earns R12 000 a month. Philamina and the children need R3 600 a month to live.

Questions

1. What will Philamina's lawyer do?
2. What happens if Adam defends the case?
3. What happens if Adam does not defend the case?
4. If you were the judge what order would you make?

4.5.2.5 Arrangements at the time of the divorce

At the time of the divorce a number of arrangements have to be made. The most important are: (a) the division of the family property; (b) maintenance for the parties; and (c) care and maintenance of the children. Care and maintenance of the children will be dealt with below in para 4.5.3.

marriages or civil unions in community of property

4.5.2.5.1 Division of the family property

The way in which the family property is divided between the parties depends upon how they were married or the conditions of their civil union (see above para 4.2.2). If the couple were married before or after 1 November 1984 in community of property, the joint estate is divided into two equal halves. One half belongs to the husband and the other to the wife (see above para 4.2.2.1). If there is a dispute about how the property should be divided, the court must decide and, if necessary, may appoint a 'liquidator' to divide the property.

marriages out of community of property before November 1984

If the couple were married before 1 November 1984 out of community of property, with an ante-nuptial contract which excludes community of property and of profit and loss, each party keeps his or her own property. The parties also take any property to which they are entitled in terms of the ante-nuptial contract (see above para 4.2.2.2). If there is conflict about the ownership of the property, the court must decide how to divide it. When dividing the property the court may take into account that the one spouse helped the other to bring up the children or supported the other spouse in other ways.

marriages or civil unions out of community of property after November 1984 with accrual

If the couple was married or entered into a civil union after 1 November 1984 out of community of property, with an ante-nuptial contract and the accrual system, each party keeps the property that he or she brought into the marriage. In addition, any increase in the value of the property brought into the marriage or union is shared equally between the spouses (see above para 4.2.2.2.1). Each party also takes the property to which he or she is entitled in terms of the ante-nuptial contract.

marriages or civil unions out of community of property after November 1984 excluding accrual

If the couple was married or entered into a civil union after 1 November 1984 out of community of property, with an ante-nuptial contract which excludes the accrual system, each party keeps his or her own property. The parties also take any property to which they are entitled in terms of the ante-nuptial contract. If there is a dispute about the ownership of the property the court will decide how to divide it (see above para 4.2.2.2).

As mentioned, some married or civil union partners may also have chosen to change the legal consequences of their marriage or union by applying to the High Court (see para 4.2.2.3).

4.5.2.5.2 Maintenance for the parties

money paid to a person for support

Maintenance is money paid to a person for support. Previously, when women did not work and were financially dependent on their husbands, it was generally accepted that the husband provided maintenance for his former wife. In recent years this position has changed in that husband and wife and civil union partners are now regarded as equal partners and both work and contribute to the home. It is, therefore, not unusual for the court to order either the husband or wife or any of the civil union partners to pay maintenance to the other. It is important to always make a claim for maintenance at the time of divorce – even if it is just a nominal amount (very small amount), eg one rand a year, which can be increased if something happens to one of the parties after the divorce. Otherwise a party will not be allowed to claim anything from his or her ex-spouse or civil union partner in the future.

claim must be made at time of divorce

The maintenance court will make an order of maintenance only if the person who is requesting it can show that he or she is in need of maintenance, and the person from whom it is being requested can afford to pay it. Once the court has awarded maintenance, the wife or husband or civil union partner may always apply to increase or decrease the amount if his or her position changes. The amount of maintenance may be agreed upon during the divorce negotiations.

parties may apply for increase or decrease of maintenance

The Maintenance Act creates special maintenance courts. These courts deal with applications for maintenance, and increases and decreases in the amount of maintenance. These courts are at every magistrate's court. Maintenance officers work in the courts and assist people who wish to apply for maintenance. We will examine the procedures followed in these courts when we discuss custody and maintenance of children (see below para 4.5.3.2).

maintenance courts

maintenance officers

Problem 8: The ungrateful husband

after 30 years Samson decides to divorce Patricia and marry another woman

Samson and Patricia Ndimande were married in 1983. Their marriage was out of community of property. At the time Patricia had no money or property of her own, but Samson had inherited R20 000. Samson went to university and became a doctor. He opened his own private practice. Patricia stayed at home and gave up her career as a nurse. The couple had five children whom Patricia looked after. After 30 years Samson decides to divorce Patricia and marry another woman. Samson owns all the property.

Questions

1. On divorce, what property is Patricia entitled to?
2. What type of marriage might have been better for Patricia? Give reasons for your answer.
3. On divorce, what do you think Patricia should claim from Samson?

4.5.3 Care and maintenance of children

the court must decide on care, maintenance and access to children

A court will not grant a divorce without first satisfying itself that proper arrangements have been made for the care of the children. The court must decide which parent will have care of the children and who will be responsible for the maintenance of the children. It should also decide what access (visitation rights) the other spouse should have to the children.

4.5.3.1 Care

the best interests of the children

When the court makes a decision about care, it will always take into account the best interests of the children. In the past the care of very small children and young girls used to be given to the mother. However, in recent cases the courts have said that mothers are not always the best parents and fathers may be equally good at looking after small children. In practice it seems that if there is doubt the courts are still likely to give care of small children to mothers. The courts are also reluctant to divide children up between parents by allowing one child to go with one parent and the other with the other parent.

evidence from the 'Family Advocate'

In deciding which parent should have care, the court will look at the 'best interests' of the child. The interests, rights, or wants of parents are less important than the interests of the children. The court may obtain evidence of what is in the best interests of the children from the Family Advocate who, with the assistance of social workers and psychologists, makes a recommendation to the court regarding the children's welfare. Evidence may be obtained from the children's school teachers, doctors and relatives, as well as friends of the family. The court may also interview the children. The court would then decide which parent can best look after the welfare of the child.

the care order may change

The care order may change, however, if circumstances change. For example, if the parent who has been given care of the child becomes addicted to drugs or alcohol the court may change the custody order. The parent who does not have care is usually given the right to visit (access to) the child. This means that he or she can spend time with the child during certain times of the year (eg weekends or holidays). The parent who does not have care may still have to contribute money for the maintenance of the child. A spouse who unreasonably refuses access to the children and disobeys a court order will be guilty of the crime of 'contempt of court'. 'Contempt of court' happens when a person fails to obey a court order or insults a judge in court.

'joint care'

Sometimes the court may make an order of 'joint care' where both parents are given care of the same child for different periods of time. The court will only do this if it is in the child's best interests. Usually a 'parenting plan' is helpful in assisting parents who share parental rights and responsibilities over the same child. A 'parenting plan' is useful because after divorce spouses may not even speak to each other. A 'parenting plan' can also assist unmarried parents who are in a dispute about care of children born outside of marriage. According to

parenting plan

the Children's Act a 'parenting plan' must deal with the following issues: (a) the maintenance of the child; (b) contact between the child and any of the parents; (c) contact between the child and any other person; and (d) the schooling and religious upbringing of the child.

Problem 9: The bad mother

Mrs Samuels drank heavily and often beat her children without good reason

Mr and Mrs Samuels want a divorce. Both claim the care of their two children, a 7-year-old boy and a 14-year-old girl. Mrs Samuels often neglects the children. Once Mrs Samuels left her husband and went to live with another man for a year. During this period her husband looked after the children. At the time Mrs Samuels never visited or enquired about their health. After returning home Mrs Samuels drinks heavily and often beats the children without good reason. Her husband wishes to divorce her.

Questions

1. If you were the judge would you consult the children before awarding care to one of the spouses? What factors would you take into account when awarding care?
2. If you were a judge, to whom would you award care if the children were (a) 7 and 14 years old and (b) 7 and 4 years old? Why?

guardianship

parents have equal guardianship

Apart from a care order, the court may also decide on guardianship of the children (see above para 4.3.1.2). In the past the courts tended to give guardianship of children to the father. Since 1993, the law says that both parents have equal guardianship over their children and so the courts now generally give guardianship to both parents on divorce. But if the one parent is unfit (eg if he or she has neglected to look after the child's interests or leaves the country), guardianship may be given to the other parent.

customary law regarding guardianship

Children born of a customary marriage between Africans used to be governed by the customary law regarding guardianship. Customary law stated that the father or eldest male relative would usually have guardianship of the child. However, the Recognition of Customary Marriages Act (see above para 4.1.5) says that men and women in customary marriages are now equal. For most purposes, customary marriages now resemble civil marriages. If so, it is likely that guardianship of children born of customary marriages is now shared between the father and mother, although this point has not yet been decided by a court.

4.5.3.2 Maintenance of children

both parents have a duty to support children

During a marriage or civil union both parents have a duty to support their children according to what they earn. On divorce this duty does not end and both parents are still obliged to maintain their children. Once care of children is awarded to one parent, the other parent may be ordered to pay money on a weekly or monthly basis as maintenance for the children.

duty to maintain children born of unmarried parents and children of Muslim, Hindu and customary marriages

The Maintenance Act creates ways to force an ex-spouse to pay maintenance if he or she is not doing so. The Act does not only apply to civil law marriages that have come to an end. It applies whenever there is a legal duty to maintain another person. This means that it also applies to children born of unmarried parents and children born of marriages under Muslim or Hindu religion or customary marriages.

Sometimes a father may fail to pay maintenance for children even though he has been ordered to do so by the court. In such a case the mother may apply to a maintenance court for an order against the father. This does not cost anything and can be done without a lawyer.

complaint to maintenance officer

In order to make a maintenance claim, the mother must submit a complaint to the maintenance officer at the maintenance court. She can find out how to go about this by contacting the magistrates' courts where the maintenance courts and maintenance officers are. The complaint will then be investigated by the maintenance officer, who will collect information about the complaint (eg the whereabouts and financial position of the father). The maintenance officer decides whether to take the case to the maintenance court. If the case goes to court, the maintenance officer may summon the people involved in the case to appear before the maintenance court to give evidence. The court may then order the husband to pay the outstanding maintenance.

The Maintenance Act creates important mechanisms to force a person to pay maintenance once a maintenance order has been given.

when maintenance is not paid

If a father, for example, is more than 10 days late with a payment, the ex-wife or civil union partner may ask the court to grant an order for:

1. A warrant of execution against the father's property. (This means that the sheriff of the court may take property belonging to the father and sell it to pay for the maintenance.)

2. An order for the attachment of 'emoluments' (eg salaries, wages or other amounts of money) owed to the father. For example, the father's employer may have to pay part of the father's salary or wages to the ex-wife or civil union partner as maintenance.
3. An order for the attachment of any present or future debt owed or owing to the father. (This means that if the father is owed any money, or will be owed money, the person owing the money will be ordered to pay the money directly to the ex-wife or civil union partner as maintenance.)

guilty of a crime

If a father does not pay maintenance after the court has ordered him to do so he may also be found guilty of a crime and be sentenced to a fine or imprisonment of up to a year.

increase or decrease of maintenance order

It is also possible to ask the court to change maintenance orders. For example, a father might want to pay less maintenance, while a mother might want more maintenance to be paid to her. This can be done by following the same procedure as is mentioned above. The spouse or civil union partner must see a maintenance officer who will investigate the complaint and, if necessary, call the parties to appear before the maintenance court, which may then change the amount of maintenance payable. However, the father or mother would have to show that there are good reasons to change the maintenance payable. For example, the father would have to show that his income has been reduced or that his ex-wife or civil union partner and children can now support themselves, or the mother could show that the children have moved from primary school to secondary school and need more money for fees and clothes.

both parents must support a child born of unmarried parents

Finally, both parents of a child born of unmarried parents may be made to pay maintenance for the support of the children. The children born of unmarried parents requiring maintenance may apply to the maintenance court for maintenance from their parents.

Problem 10: Some questions on maintenance

Questions

1. Vijay and Sheena are divorced. The court grants maintenance to Sheena. Vijay is supposed to give Sheena R1 800 every month. After five years Vijay stops paying Sheena. He says that it is time that she supports herself. What procedure must Sheena follow to claim her maintenance from Vijay?
2. Pauline is a 16-year-old child born of unmarried parents. Who owes Pauline a legal duty of support? If Pauline is not able to support herself financially what can she do to claim maintenance?

4.6 Death and the law

Outcomes

After completion of this section learners will be able to:

1. Demonstrate an understanding of the law relating to death, wills and the winding-up of a dead person's estate.

Assessment criteria

1. The meaning of 'death' is explained.
2. The legal and moral problems involved in cases where a doctor is requested to remove a life-support system from an unconscious patient are discussed.
3. The distinction between a funeral, burial, memorial service and a cremation is explained.
4. An understanding is developed of the costs involved in a funeral and why it is necessary to be careful when approached by a funeral business.
5. A set of facts is examined and a decision is taken whether to order or refuse medical treatment.
6. A description is given of what happens when a person dies without making a will.
7. Advice is given on what has to be done if a person wants to make a will.
8. How to report a death is explained.
9. An explanation is given on the winding-up of an estate and the duties of an executor.

4.6.1 What is the meaning of 'death'?

a person is dead if he or she suffers from 'brain death'

According to the National Health Act a person is regarded as dead if he or she has suffered 'brain death'. Brain death means that all parts of the brain stop working and cannot be made to work again. If a brain-dead person is on a machine which makes him or her 'breathe' by pumping air though the person's lungs, the person is still dead. This means that if the machine is switched off, the person is not killed because he or she is already dead.

'natural deaths'

'unnatural deaths'

Where a person dies from old age or a sickness or injuries not caused by another person, the person is said to have died a 'natural death' and the doctor can issue a death certificate. If the person dies from an anaesthetic (ie the process used to put a person to sleep during an operation), eg while he or she was being operated on or after an operation, the death will be 'unnatural'. It will also be unnatural where a person is killed: (a) by force (eg stabbing, shooting, assault or motor accident); (b) by some physical factor (eg heat, cold or radiation); (c) by a chemical factor (eg snake bites, drugs or poison); or (d) where an act or omission by somebody else causes the death (eg a doctor or nurse failing to treat a person properly).

post-mortem operations

Where the death is unnatural a post-mortem operation (ie an operation after death) must be done on the dead person to find out the cause of death and whether anyone was responsible for it. Sometimes when families collect the body of a person who has died an unnatural death from a mortuary, they may think that certain body parts have been removed because the dead person has wounds that have been sewn up. This usually happens after the body has been examined by the doctor who was trying to find out what caused the person's death. If the wounds have been sewn up again it is usually a sign that a post-mortem was done.

signs of a post-mortem operation

Where, however, obvious body parts are missing, eg hands or feet or arms or legs – unless the person has been in an accident – families need to inquire what has happened. If they are not given a satisfactory answer they must report the case to the police because parts of the body may have been taken for 'muti' purposes and it is a crime for a person to sell body parts. If wounds have not been sewn up again it usually means that those were the wounds found on the body when it was taken to the mortuary or somebody has removed body parts.

missing body parts

Problem 1: What would you do when identifying the body?

You go to the mortuary to identify and collect the body of a relative who has died. What would you do in the following situations?

Questions

1. You are told that your relative had been stabbed in a fight. When you see the body you notice that there is a large wound all along the front of the body that has been sewn up. There is also a wound around the top of the person's head which has been sewn up.
2. You are told that your relative was killed in a taxi accident. When you see the body you notice that one of her hands and a foot are missing.
3. You are told that your relative's body was found lying in the bush. When you see the body you notice that the person's private parts are missing.

4.6.2 Dying and the law

the time of death

The decision concerning death is one that is made by doctors, not lawyers. The courts will usually follow the opinion of doctors when deciding the time of a person's death. Problems arise, however, when people want to die or want others to help them die (see above para 2.2.1.3). For example, a person who is being kept alive on a life-support machine in a hospital may ask a doctor to disconnect the machine. The common law allows people to refuse medical treatment even if it causes their death, provided they understand the nature and effect of what they are consenting to. The Children's Act states that parents may not refuse medical treatment for their children on religious grounds. The National Health Act says that patients have the right to refuse medical treatment, but must be told what the risks are. Sometimes relatives request a doctor to disconnect a life-support

patients may refuse medical treatment even if they will die as a result machine that is keeping an unconscious person alive. The doctor may only do this if the case is hopeless and the patient is not likely to recover. The National Health Act allows patients to appoint in writing somebody to make decisions for them if they are no longer able to make their own decisions. A difficult question is whether people have a right to die. For example, should a pregnant unconscious mother be kept alive until her baby is born or should she be allowed to die before the baby is born?

patients may appoint somebody to make decisions for them

Problem 2: Should the life-support machine be switched off?

One night Karen stops breathing for two fifteen-minute periods. She becomes unconscious and cannot breathe without the assistance of a machine.

Karen's parents ask the doctor to switch off the life-support machine

Her doctors say that she has become a 'vegetable' and will never regain consciousness. She remains like this for six months without recovering. Her parents ask her doctor to disconnect the machine. The doctor refuses to switch off the machine. He says it would go against his oath as a doctor. Karen's parents ask the court to order the doctor to disconnect the machine.

Questions

1. What happened to Karen? Why did her parents ask the doctor to switch off the machine? Why did the doctor refuse?
2. What legal and moral questions are involved in this case?
3. Role-play a conversation between Karen's parents and her doctors.
4. If you were the lawyer for Karen's parents, what arguments would you use? If you were the lawyer for the doctor, what would your arguments be? If you were the judge, how would you decide the case?

Problem 3: If you were the judge would you order, or refuse to order, treatment?

Questions

In each of the following cases imagine that you were the judge and decide whether you would order treatment, or not order treatment. Give reasons for your decisions.

1. Ella, who is 30 years old and whose religion does not allow blood transfusions, is involved in a car accident. She needs a blood transfusion to live but she refuses to have one. Ella's doctor asks the court to decide.
2. Manfred, a 9-year-old boy whose religion does not allow blood transfusions, is unconscious. He will die if he does not have a blood transfusion. The doctor wants to give Manfred a blood transfusion but his parents refuse to allow him to have one on religious grounds. Manfred's doctor says he will give the transfusion and the parents ask the court to stop him.
3. Dube, a professional footballer, is permanently paralysed from the neck down as a result of a car accident. He is connected to a life-support machine. Doctors say that he might not be able to live without the machine. Dube asks for it to be switched off, but the doctor refuses. Dube asks the court to decide.
4. Tollie is born with brain damage and physical problems that will require a difficult and painful operation if he is to live. Her father refuses to consent to the operation. Tollie's doctor asks the court to decide.

4.6.3 Funerals

funeral arrangements

When a member of a family dies the rest of the family suffer grief and sorrow. They may also become involved in major expenses. Often it is not easy to make funeral arrangements and decisions such as whether the dead person should be buried or 'cremated' (burnt to ashes). Other problems are: What kind of service should be held? How much will the funeral cost? How will the funeral be paid for? Some families plan ahead by taking out funeral insurance. Sometimes people who die also plan ahead by stating in their wills how they want to be buried.

Things that need to be dealt with concerning funerals are: (a) planning a funeral; (b) deciding whether to have a burial or cremation; and, (c) the law regarding funerals and other aspects of dying.

one of the first decisions is what type of funeral service should be held

When somebody dies in a family one of the first decisions is to decide what type of funeral service should be held. Funeral services are usually held to pay respect to the dead and their families. They also help to bring people together to comfort one another. Funeral services are held in churches, other religious buildings, funeral homes, and occasionally at public places. Memorial services in memory of the deceased are also sometimes held. They may be held before, or after, a funerals are held to pay respect to the dead and their families, and to bring people together to comfort each other

funeral services, burial services and memorial services

deceased has been buried. A burial service focuses on the burial of the dead person. A funeral service focuses on the deceased's life and is usually held in the deceased's presence at the time of the funeral. A memorial service may be held at any time and the deceased is not usually present.

burial and cremation

The next decision to be made is whether the deceased should be buried or cremated. People who are buried have their bodies placed in the ground. Those who are cremated have their bodies reduced to ashes in an oven (a crematorium). The ashes may then be scattered in a chosen place, stored in a simple jar or container, or buried. Some religions and cultural practices, however, do not allow cremation. Coffins are sometimes not required for a cremation.

A cremation may cost less than a burial. People requesting a cremation should check that the funeral parlour will not charge them for an expensive coffin. There have been reports of people paying for expensive coffins that are removed and resold after the dead person has been burnt in a cheap coffin.

leaving one's body to medical research

Sometimes people decide that instead of being buried or cremated they wish to leave their bodies to a medical school for research. This saves funeral expenses because the medical school pays for all the arrangements. In some cases people choose to donate parts of their bodies (eg eyes, liver or heart) to others or a medical school. In these cases the body is returned to the family for burial once the body parts have been removed.

4.6.3.1 Funeral expenses

most families cannot afford expensive funerals

Some families may be able to afford expensive funerals for their relatives. Most families, however, cannot afford expensive funerals. Families should be careful not to be influenced by people who work for, or advertise, funeral businesses. These people often tell relatives that by paying for an expensive funeral they show that they really care for their deceased relative.

it is difficult for people to behave like careful consumers when they are sad or upset

It is difficult for people to behave like careful consumers when they are sad or upset by the death of a loved person. Consumers should be on their guard against being persuaded to pay for expensive funerals – especially in the townships. People who work as agents for funeral businesses promise fancy coffins with velvet linings and brass handles, but do not ask families whether they can afford to pay for them. Some families find themselves deeply in debt because of expensive funeral arrangements. These families often have to spend many months paying off funeral expenses.

'storage fees' and other costs

caution in funeral matters

Families should enquire whether funeral businesses will charge a 'storage fee' while the dead person is on their premises before being buried. Before families allow funeral businesses to deal with the funeral arrangements, they should make careful inquiries about all the costs involved. Families also should not sign any agreements unless they have read and fully understood them. If members of a family have problems in deciding whether or not to sign an agreement, they should contact their nearest legal aid clinic, or get some advice from a lawyer.

consumers should be on their guard against being persuaded to pay for expensive funerals

Problem 4: Some questions on funerals

Questions

1. Have you ever attended a funeral service? Would you know what to do if there was a sudden death in your family? What are some of the things that must be decided about the funeral when a loved one dies?
2. What is the difference between a funeral service, a burial service and a memorial service?
3. What are the main costs involved in a funeral?

4. Different religions and cultures have different traditions about funeral services, the type of burial, and the period of mourning after a death. Explain the type of funeral service and the burial and mourning period required by your religion or family customs.

4.6.3.2 Death benefit schemes and funeral societies

caution in joining funeral benefit societies

Employers often have death benefit schemes that help to pay for the funeral expenses of their workers and their families. Trade unions may also have these schemes. Families may decide to take out insurance policies and pension plans that help them with funeral expenses. Families should be careful, however, before joining funeral benefit societies or other burial societies that require them to become members and to pay a monthly fee. They should make sure that they understand exactly what they are paying for before they enter into an agreement or become a member.

Problem 5: Vuma is approached by a funeral society

Vuma is approached by a funeral society salesperson, Johannes, who offers to sell him funeral insurance for R100 a month. Vuma is 22 years old and unmarried. Johannes says that if Vuma marries and has children the policy will also cover the funerals of his wife and children.

Role-play a conversation between Vuma and Johannes.

4.6.4 Wills and inheritance

4.6.4.1 What must be done when a person dies

reporting a death

death certificate and 'burial order'

When a person dies, the death must be reported to the Director-General of the Department of Home Affairs. This must be done as soon as the family has received a death certificate from the doctor or from any other person who examined the body after the person's death. The undertaker normally helps the family with the registration of the death. Otherwise, the family must submit the death certificate to the Department of Home Affairs in the area in which the deceased died. The Department will then issue a 'burial order'. The funeral cannot take place before these two documents have been handed over to the undertaker. A burial order is a certificate that says that the dead person may be buried. Usually a burial cannot take place without a burial order. A medical doctor can also issue a death certificate. The death must also be reported to the Master of the High Court (see below para 4.6.5.1).

heirs

When people die their belongings and property are given to people known as 'heirs', who are usually members of their family. The way in which this is done depends upon whether or not the dead person leaves a will. A will is a document that sets out how people wish to distribute their property after death.

dying with or without a will

When a person dies without leaving a will, that person is said to have died 'intestate'. When a person dies with a will, that person is said to have died 'testate'. The property left by a dead person, after his or her debts have been paid, is called an 'estate'.

4.6.4.2 Dying without a will

'intestate succession'

The law of 'intestate succession' is followed if a person dies without a will or if the will that was made was not made properly. These laws apply to the sharing of property that was not provided for in a proper will. The position is as follows:

inheritance by spouse

1. If the dead person leaves a spouse but no children or descendants, the surviving spouse will inherit the property. (A descendant is a person descended from the dead person, such as a child, grandchild, great-grandchild etc.)

spouse and children sharing inheritance

2. If the dead person leaves a spouse, the surviving spouse will receive the same share of the property as a descendant or R125 000, whichever is more, and the children will share the rest.

inheritance by children

3. If the dead person leaves children or descendants and no spouse, the children or descendants will share the property. (If any children died before the dead person, leaving their own children (ie the dead person's grandchildren), the children of the dead child will inherit their dead parent's share.)

inheritance by both parents

4. If the dead person leaves parents but no spouse or descendants (eg children or grandchildren) each parent will inherit half the property.

inheritance by one parent and descendants of other parent

5. If the dead person leaves only one parent and no spouse or descendants, the surviving parent will inherit half of the property and the descendants of the dead parent, the other half (eg brothers and sisters of the dead person). If there are no descendants of the dead parent the surviving parent will inherit all the property.

inheritance by descendants of both parents

6. If the dead person does not leave a spouse, descendant or parent, then half the property will be inherited by the descendants of the dead person's father and the other half by the descendants of the dead person's mother. (This means that brothers and sisters will inherit from each of the dead person's parents while half-brothers and sisters will only inherit from the half-share of their biological parent – unless they were adopted by their step-parent in which case they would be in the same position as the children of the step-parent.)

inheritance by nearest blood relatives

7. If the dead person leaves no spouse, descendant, parents or descendant of parents (eg brothers or sisters) the nearest blood relations of the dead person will inherit the property (eg uncles and aunts).

inheritance by the state

8. If the dead person leaves no blood relatives all the property will go to the state.

Note: Adopted children are regarded as the descendants of their adoptive parents. Children born outside of marriage now inherit in the same way as children born of a marriage. In the case of same-sex couples, it is likely that the definition of a 'spouse' extends to people who are partners in a civil union.

inheritance under African customary law

According to African customary law, the eldest son of the family succeeded the deceased. Where there was no son, the eldest male relative succeeded the deceased. This means that he stepped into the shoes of the deceased and inherited his assets, liabilities and responsibilities. This included the duty to maintain the widow and children of the deceased. The Constitutional Court has held that the customary law rule of allowing only males to inherit on intestacy is unconstitutional because it discriminates against women. The customary law was changed by the Constitutional Court to allow females to inherit.

females may now inherit if no will made

everybody should make a will

Everybody with property should make a will because dying without a will may sometimes cause hardship for the descendants of the dead person. It also means that people who the dead person does not want to inherit may also inherit if they are descendants of the dead person. The minor children of a dead person may claim against that person's property for maintenance and support.

Problem 6: People dying without wills: Who will inherit?

Questions

1. Alan dies leaving a wife Maureen, and two children, Sally and Alfred. Alan forgets to make a will and after his debts have been paid his property is worth R600 000. How much will Maureen, Sally and Alfred inherit? Why?
2. Vish dies after his wife, leaving three sons, Narain, Tony and Karthy, and two grandchildren Sarah and Shaida, the children of his dead daughter, Fariah. Vish does not make a will and his property after his debts have been paid is worth R90 000. How much will Narain, Tony, Karthy, Sarah and Shaida inherit? Why?
3. Thembu dies without making a will. He was married to Bongile in a customary marriage and leaves her and three sons, Alpheus 25, Elias 22 and Proteus 30. Thembu leaves property worth R180 000. Who will inherit? How much? Why? What would be the position if Thembu and Bongile had been married in a civil law marriage?
4. Roelof dies without making a will and leaving no wife, children or parents. His only relatives are two brothers, Tjaart and Braam, and a half-sister Maria, who was the daughter of his mother by a previous marriage. Roelof leaves property worth R120 000. Who will inherit? How much? Why?

4.6.4.3 Dying with a will

the importance of a will

It is important for people to make wills. This is because in a will people can say what they want to happen to their property after they die. People over the age of 16 years may make wills as long as they know and understand what they are doing. In a will people may leave their property to anyone they wish – wives, husbands, choosing an executor

children, relatives, friends or strangers. Once people decide how they want their property to be divided, they must decide who will divide the property when they die. The person who is chosen to divide the property is called an 'executor' (see below para 4.6.5.1).

A will has to meet the following requirements:

1. It must be in writing;
2. It must be signed by two witnesses; and
3. It must be signed by the person making the will.

signing of a will

witnesses to a will

The witnesses and the person making the will must all sign in the presence of each other. The person making the will must sign or initial on every page and must sign in full on the last page as close as possible to the end of the last paragraph. The witnesses need only sign on the last page. However, it is advisable that witnesses sign every page as well. A person signing as a witness must be at least 14 years old.

witnesses may not inherit under a will

A person who signs as witness may not be an 'executor' or take anything under the will. Therefore, people who wish to inherit under a will should not sign as witnesses. Although it is not difficult to draw up a simple will, there are a number of strict rules and technical details that must be followed.

whom to consult to make a will

People should consult an attorney or bank if they wish to make a will. If there is very little property, and the person is poor and wants a simple will, he or she may consult a legal aid clinic or buy a will form from a stationery shop.

Legal Aid South Africa does not help people to write wills. A good lawyer may draft a will that includes ways of saving tax when dividing up a person's estate. A lawyer charges a fee for doing this but in most cases it is not too expensive. A bank may draw up a client's will without charging.

Problem 7: Who inherits from Michael Jack?

Questions

Read Michael Jack's will in para 4.6.4.4 and answer the following questions:

1. Who will inherit Michael's property if he dies the day after he makes a will?
2. Who will inherit his property if Michael and his wife are both killed in a car accident?
3. When will Michael's nephew inherit under Michael's will?
4. Who will take care of Paul if Michael and Jane are killed in an accident?
5. Is a will really necessary? Could not Michael just tell his wife what to do if he dies? Why?

4.6.4.4 An example of a simple will

Last Will and Testament

of

Michael Jack

of 35 Main Street, Newlands East, Durban, Natal.

(1)

I hereby cancel all previous wills made by me.

(2)

I appoint as Executor of my estate, my brother FREDERICK JACK of 30 Church Street, MEREBANK, DURBAN, and direct that he shall not be required by the Master of the High Court to give security for the proper performance of his duties.

(3)

I leave R10 000 to my nephew, JAMES JACK of 50 Loop Street, WENTWORTH, DURBAN, if he completes a B. Com Degree at the University of KwaZulu-Natal in Durban.

(4)

The rest of my estate I leave to my wife, JANE JACK (nee FREDERICKS), to whom I am married out of community of property. If she does not survive me, I leave the rest of my estate to our son, PAUL JACK.

(5)

Should my wife die before me, or at the same time, and should our son at that time still be a minor, I appoint my brother, the said FREDERICK JACK, to be his guardian.

In witness whereof I have set my hand at Durban on this 6th day of March 2010 in the presence of the undersigned witnesses present at the same time and who have witnessed and signed this will in the presence of myself and of each other.

As witnesses:

1. .... **MICHAEL JACK**

2. .... **TESTATOR**

4.6.4.5 Making a will

meaning must be clear

Making a will correctly is very important. Unclear language in a will may cause problems when the will is interpreted. The will may even be disregarded if the language cannot be properly understood. The will may also be disregarded because the legal requirements were not followed (see above para 4.6.4.3). Therefore it is best to consult a lawyer when making a will.

simple and detailed wills

Wills may be simple, like Michael's, or may contain very detailed instructions. Wills indicate what must happen to everything owned by the deceased and may say what must happen at the funeral. They may also contain many other things. For example, people with young children often include a clause naming someone to be the 'guardian' of their children. This clause will usually be followed by the courts.

changing or cancelling a will

A person making a will is free at any time to change it. The usual way of doing this is to state in a later will that all previous wills are cancelled. A person may also cancel a will by tearing it up – as long as he or she has the intention to cancel it. A will may also be changed by adding clauses to it or altering the original wording. These changes or alterations must be signed by the witnesses and the persons making the will. Any large changes in a will should be made by destroying the old will and making a new one.

Problem 8: Have you made a will?

Questions

1. If you die today what will happen to what you own? Who will inherit your property?
2. At what stage in your life do you think you should make a will? Are you old enough to make a will?
3. Do you think people should make wills? Give reasons for your answer.
4. Is it important to consult a lawyer when making a will? Give reasons for your answer.

a will usually states what must happen to everything owned by the deceased

4.6.5 Winding up a dead person's estate

4.6.5.1 Reporting the death

death must be reported within 14 days

death notice and will must be sent to Master of High Court

If a person dies with or without a will, his or her death must be reported within 14 days to the Master of the High Court. There is a Master in each division of the High Court in South Africa (see above para 1.3.1.3). If the person responsible fails to do this, it is a criminal offence. This notice must be given on a special form called a '*death notice*' which is obtained from the Master of the High Court. It is usually filled in by the spouse of the person who died or a relative or close friend. The *death notice* informs the Master that the person has died. In addition to this, any person who has a copy of the will or a document that looks like a will belonging to the dead person must send it to the Master of the High Court.

inventory of the deceased person's belongings

The surviving spouse, the nearest relative, or close friend living in the same district in which the deceased lived must complete an *inventory* form listing all the property that belonged to the deceased person. (The *inventory* form may be obtained from the Master.) This must be done within 14 days of the death. The *inventory* must be sent to the Master.

the Master appoints an executor

The Master will examine the will to see if an executor has been named. The executor is the person who has to administer and '*wind up*' the deceased's estate. If the deceased did not name an executor in his will the Master will call a meeting and appoint someone. The Master usually appoints a member of the family as executor if nobody is named in the will. The Master appoints an executor by giving him or her '*letters of executorship*'. This means that the executor must collect all the deceased's property; pay off all the deceased's debts (by selling some of the property if necessary); and distribute any remaining money or property to the deceased's heirs.

the 'estate' of the deceased includes assets and liabilities

All the deceased's belongings form the '*estate*'. An estate includes '*assets*' and '*liabilities*'. *Assets* are all the things that the person owned while he or she was alive, for example, a car, a house, furniture, etc. *Liabilities* are the deceased person's debts that have to be paid off. The deceased's estate does not go directly to the heirs. It first goes to the executor.

4.6.5.2 The duties of the executor

The executor has several duties:

draw up estate account

1. The executor must draw up an *estate account*. In this account all the person's assets are added up. The debts are then subtracted from the total value of the assets. Afterwards the debts are paid and any assets left over go to the heirs.

pay 'death duties'

2. The executor must pay any income tax owed by the deceased and the '*death duties*' tax on the value of the estate's assets.

account sent to heirs

3. The executor sends a copy of the account to the heirs. They must agree that the balance is the amount that is due to them.

account sent to Master's office

4. The executor sends the account to the Master of the High Court. The account lies at the Master's office for three weeks to allow people to object to it.

if no objections heirs paid

5. If nobody objects to the account, and the Master is satisfied, he or she allows the executor to pay the heirs their share of the property (inheritances).

receipts from heirs sent to Master

6. The executor sends the Master copies of receipts from the heirs showing that they have received their inheritances.

executor released by Master

7. The executor is then released from his or her duties by the Master.

hiring a lawyer to assist executor

The executor will often hire a lawyer to assist with the above duties and responsibilities. Some executors may be able to handle these duties without assistance from lawyers. The executor is entitled to a fixed fee or payment for the work done.

It is advisable for an executor to consult a lawyer if:

when executor should consult a lawyer

1. The deceased did not make a will and minor children will be inheriting;
2. The estate cannot pay all its debts;
3. The deceased set up a 'trust' which will have to be managed by somebody with legal or financial experience after the estate is wound up by the executor; or
4. The estate includes a valuable business.

Problem 9: If you were named executor

Questions

If you were named as an executor in a will, could you perform the duties listed in the text? Would you need a lawyer to help you carry out your duties? Give reasons for your answer.

4.6.5.3 Small estates

executor not necessary

If the value of the dead person's property is less than R120 000 the Master may decide that an executor is not necessary. This is usually done if the surviving spouse is the only heir and he or she is given authority by the Master to collect all the dead person's property, to pay off all the deceased's debts, and to keep any property left over. The death must be reported in the usual way (see above para 4.6.4.1). If it is later found that the dead person's property is worth more than R120 000 the Master will have to appoint an executor.

death reported in usual manner

Further reading

4.1 The family, marriage and civil unions

Cronje DSP & Heaton J *South African Family Law* 3 ed (2010)

Cronje DSP & Heaton J *Casebook on South African Family Law* 3 ed (2010)

Skelton A & Carnelley M (eds) *Family Law in South Africa* (2010)

Van Heerden B (ed) *Schafer's Family Law Service* (loose-leaf)

Civil Union Act 17 of 2006

Marriage Act 25 of 1961

Recognition of Customary Marriages Act 120 of 1998

Daniels v Campbell NO 2004 (5) SA 331 (CC) – limited recognition of Muslim marriages: Maintenance of Surviving Spouses Act and Intestate Succession Act also apply to monogamous Muslim marriages.

Du Plessis v Road Accident Fund 2004 (1) SA 359 (SCA) 12 – common-law right of claim for loss of support extended to same-sex couples in a permanent life partnership.

Fourie v Minister of Home Affairs 2005 (3) SA 429 (SCA) and *Minister of Home Affairs v Fourie* 2006 (1) SA 524 (CC) – common-law definition of marriage as limited to heterosexual persons declared unconstitutional – same-sex partners allowed to marry.

Govender v Ragavayah 2009 (3) SA 178 (D) – limited recognition of Hindu monogamous marriages: Intestate Succession Act was extended to monogamous Hindu marriage.

Hassam v Jacobs NO 2009 (5) SA 572 (CC) – limited recognition of Muslim marriages: inheritance rights of wives in terms of Intestate Succession Act extended to include polygamous wives.

Khan v Khan 2005 (2) SA 272 (T) – limited recognition of Muslim polygamous marriages: enforcement mechanisms of the Maintenance Act extended to wives in polygamous Muslim marriage.

Moola v Aulsebrook NO 1983 (1) SA 687 (N) – a marriage that has not been solemnised by a competent marriage officer may be putative.

Ryland v Edros 1997 (2) SA 690 (C) – limited recognition of Muslim marriage – courts may recognise and enforce between the parties the contractual obligations that flowed from monogamous Muslim marriage.

Singh v Ramparsad 2007 (3) SA 445 (D) – non-recognition of Hindu marriages: courts cannot pronounce parties divorced if they elected to practice a faith that did not allow divorce.

Smith v Smith 1948(4) SA 61 (N) – voidable marriages: marriage set aside after the wife indicated that she had been forced into marriage.

4.2 Husbands and wives and civil union partners

Cronje DSP & Heaton J *South African Family Law* 3 ed (2010)

Hahlo HR *The South African Law of Husband and Wife* 5 ed (1985)

Skelton A & Carnelley M (eds) *Family Law in South Africa* (2010)

Van Zyl L *Handbook of the South African Law of Maintenance* 3 ed (2010)

Constitution of the Republic of South Africa, 1996

Domestic Violence Act 116 of 1998

Maintenance Act 99 of 1998

Marriage Act 25 of 1961

Marriage and Matrimonial Property Law Amendment Act 3 of 1988

Matrimonial Property Act 88 of 1984

Wills Act 7 of 1953

Daniels v Campbell NO 2004 (5) SA 331 (CC) – limited recognition of Muslim marriages: Maintenance of Surviving Spouses Act and Intestate Succession Act also apply to monogamous Muslim marriages.

Du Plessis v Road Accident Fund 2004 (SA 359 (SCA) 12 – common-law right of claim for loss of support extended to same-sex couples in a permanent life partnership.

Govender v Ragavayah 2009 (3) SA 178 (D) – limited recognition of Hindu monogamous marriages: Intestate Succession Act extended to monogamous Hindu marriage.

Gumede v President of the Republic of South Africa 2009 (3) SA 152 (CC) – monogamous customary marriage is regarded as marriage in community of property.

Reloomel v Ramsey 1920 TPD 371 – necessaries of a household depend on the financial position, means and social status of the spouses or the family.

Ryland v Edros 1997 (2) SA 690 (C) – limited recognition of Muslim marriage – courts may recognise and enforce between the parties the contractual obligations that flowed from monogamous Muslim marriage.

Van der Merwe v Road Accident Fund 2006 (4) SA 230 (CC) – a spouse may recover from his or her spouse damages in respect of bodily injuries that are attributable to the negligence of the spouse).

4.3 Parents and children

Boezaart T (ed) *Child Law in South Africa* (2009)

Bosman-Sadie H & Corrie L A *Practical Approach to the Children's Act* (2010)

Cronje DSP & Heaton J *The South African Law of Persons* 3 ed (2008)

Skelton A & Carnelley M (eds) *Family Law in South Africa* (2010)

Spiro E Law *of Parent and Child* 4 ed (1985)

Children's Act 38 of 2005

Choice on Termination of Pregnancy Act 92 of 1996

Constitution of the Republic of South Africa, 1996

Domestic Violence Act 116 of 1998

Christian Lawyers Association of South Africa v The Minister of Health 2005 (1) SA 509 (T); 2004 (4) All SA 31 (T) – minors' ability to consent to termination of pregnancy independently.

F v F 2006 (3) SA 42 (SCA) – children's rights are paramount: relocation of one parent against the best interests of the child.

Fish Hoek Primary School v WG 2010 (2) SA 141 (SCA) – both biological parents of a child are liable for payment of school fees of a child even if the parents were never married, and even if the non-custodial parent did not enrol the child at the school.

HG v CG 2010 (3) SA 352 (ECP) – children have a right to participate in all decisions made about them, taking into account their age and maturity.

J v Director General, Department of Home Affairs 2003 (5) SA 621 (CC) – a child born to a married couple as a result of artificial fertilisation must be regarded as the child of those spouses.

J v J 2008 (6) SA 30 (C) – co-holders of parental rights and responsibilities can make decisions independently of each other.

McCall v McCall 1994 (3) SA 201 (C) – the court prescribed a list of factors that must be taken into account when determining the best interests of the child.

Petersen v Maintenance Officer, Simon's Town Maintenance Court 2004 (2) SA 56 (C) – the court developed the common law to allow extramarital child's claim against paternal grandparents.

S v M (Centre for Child Law as Amicus Curiae) 2008 (3) SA 232 (CC) – best interests of the child can be limited and cannot assume dominance over other constitutional rights.

4.4 Foster care and adoption

Bosman-Sadie H & Corrie L A *Practical Approach to the Children's Act* (2010)

Cronje DSP & Heaton J *South African Family Law* 3 ed 2010

Children's Act 38 of 2005

Wills Act 7 of 1953

AS v Vorster NO and Others 2009 (4) SA 108 (SE) – rescission of adoption order after the mother withdrew consent for the adoption of her baby.

Bester en 'n Ander v Die Meester 1985 (4) SA 70 (T) – adoptive parents included in the term 'natural parents' for the purposes of Administration of Estates Act.

Board of Executors v Vitt and Others 1989 (4) SA 480 (C) – adopted child should be included in the term 'lawful issue' in his adoptive father's will.

C and Another v Commissioner of Child Welfare, Wynberg 1970 (2) SA 76 (C) – matching language, culture and religion are requirements in foster care orders as against adoption orders.

4.5 Family problems: Divorce and maintenance

Bosman-Sadie H & Corrie L *A Practical Approach to the Children's Act* (2010)
Van Zyl L *A Handbook on South African Law of Maintenance* 3 ed (2005)
Cronje DSP & Heaton J South *African Family Law* 3 ed (2010)
Cronje DSP & Heaton J *Casebook on South African Family Law* 3 ed (2010)
Skelton A & Carnelley M *Family Law in South Africa* (2010)
Van Heerden B (ed) *Schafer's Family Law Service* (loose-leaf)
Children's Act 38 of 2005
Divorce Act 70 of 1979
Maintenance Act 99 of 1998
Marriage and Matrimonial Property Law Amendment Act 3 of 1988
Matrimonial Property Act 88 of 1984
Frankel's Estate v The Master 1950 (1) SA 220 (A) – the law of the place where the husband was domiciled at the time of marriage determines the matrimonial property system.
Mngadi v Beacon Sweets & Chocolate Provident Fund 2003 (2) All SA 279 (D) – failure to pay maintenance: court ordered provident fund to retain lump sum withdrawal benefit to secure future children's maintenance.
Reyneke v Reyneke 1990 (3) SA 927 (E) – courts can only make maintenance order if the person against whom it is made is able to pay it.
Schneider-Waterberg v Schneider-Waterberg (2009) JOL 24515 (WCC) – divorce action must be instituted in a court in whose jurisdiction one or both of the parties are domiciled on the date on which the action was lodged.
Schwartz v Schwartz 1984 (4) SA 467 (A) – courts have no discretion not to grant divorce once it has been proved that marriage has broken down irretrievably.
Singh v Ramparsad 2007 (3) SA 445 (D) – non-recognition of Hindu marriages: it is not for the courts to pronounce parties divorced if they elected to practice a faith that did not allow divorce.
Wijker v Wijker 1993 (4) SA 720 (A) – fault principle remains one of the elements that plays a role in determining the patrimonial consequences of divorce.

4.6 Death and the law

Jamneck J & Rautenbach C (eds) *The Law of Succession in South Africa* (2009)
Skelton A & Carnelley M (eds) *Family Law in South Africa* (2010)
Administration of Estates Act 66 of 1965
Constitution of the Republic of South Africa, 1996
Intestate Succession Act 81 of 1987
Maintenance of Surviving Spouses Act 27 of 1990
Wills Act 7 of 1953
Karen Quinlan 355 A 2d 647 (NJ 1976)
Clarke v Hurst NO 1992 (4) SA 630 (D)

Bhe v Magistrate, Khayelitsha 2005 (1) SA 580 (CC) – females' capacity to inherit: Black Administration Act and the customary rule of male primogeniture were declared unconstitutional and the Intestate Succession Act was extended to customary law of intestate succession.

Daniels v Campbell 2004 (5) SA 331 (CC) – the court extended application of the Intestate Succession Act to spouses in Muslim and Hindu marriages.

Gumede v President of the Republic of South Africa 2009 (3) SA 152 (CC); 2009 (3) BCLR 24 (CC) – customary law of succession: the KwaZulu Act on the Code of Zulu law and the Natal Code of Zulu Law were declared unconstitutional insofar as they afford full ownership of property during the marriage to the head of the family only.

Harris v Assumed Administrator, Estate MacGregor 1987 (3) SA 563 (A) – intestate succession: where a deceased dies without having made a will or without leaving a valid will, his or her intestate estate vests on the date of his or her death.

In re Leedham 1901 (18) SC 450 – the deceased's intention to provide for the devolution of his estate was sufficient regardless of whether he intended that the particular document should be his will.

Kidwell v The Master 1983 (1) SA 509 (E) – formalities: a nine centimetre gap between the end of the writing and the testator's signature was held not to be as close as reasonably possible to the concluding words of the will and therefore made the will invalid.

Sim v The Master 1913 CPD 187 – formalities: an unsigned document left by the testator which provided for several charitable bequests was not a valid charitable will.

Spies NO v Smith 1957 (1) SA 539 (A) – where it can be proved that the testator made a will as a result of coercion, fraud, or undue influence, such a will is invalid because it expresses someone else's will.

Street law

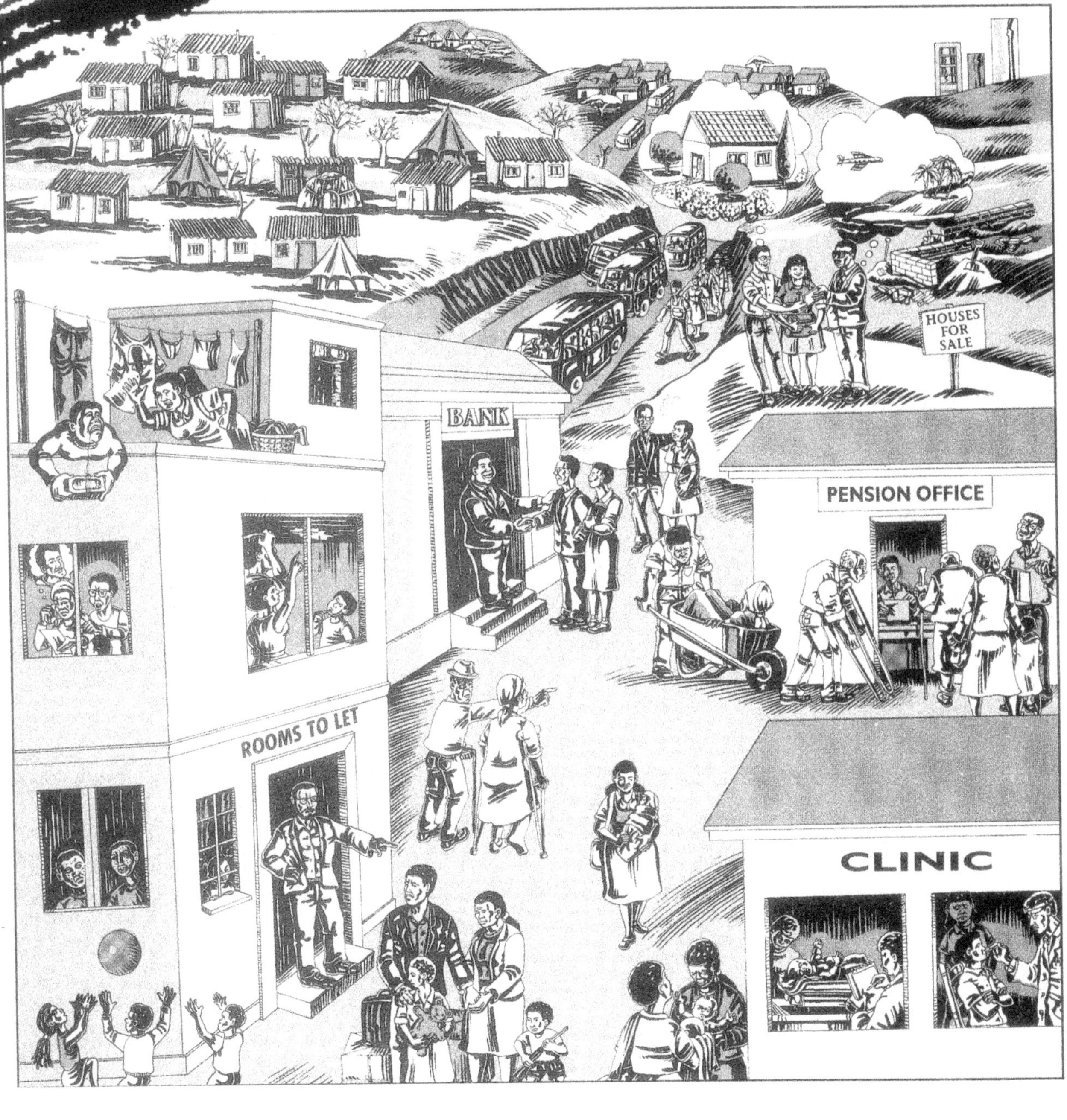

5. Socio-economic rights

CONTENTS

PART FIVE

Socio-economic rights

5.1 Socio-economic rights

Outcomes

After completion of this section learners will be able to:

1. Explain the importance of socio-economic rights.

Assessment criteria

1. The meaning of socio-economic rights and their relationship to the Constitution is explained.
2. A distinction is made between socio-economic rights and civil and political rights.
3. A decision is taken on whether socio-economic rights should be enforceable in the courts.
4. A set of facts is examined and a decision made on the duties of the state towards certain people regarding socio-economic rights.
5. Agencies are identified where people whose socio-economic rights have been violated can seek help.
6. A set of facts is examined and a decision is made on whether the government is entitled to close a school.

5.1.1 Introduction

socio-economic rights are those rights that give people access to certain basic things

civil and political rights are those rights that give people freedom to participate in the political and social life

all human rights are interdependent, indivisible and mutually reinforcing

The 1996 South African Constitution contains a number of economic and social rights (or 'socio-economic rights') together with civil and political rights. Socio-economic rights are those rights that give people access to certain basic things (resources, opportunities and services) needed to lead a dignified life, such as food, shelter, health care, social welfare, etc. Civil and political rights are those rights that give people freedom to participate in political and social life, such as freedom to think, to act, to know, to choose what to do, to join a political party, to vote, etc. South Africa's legacy of apartheid called for active steps to create a new society based on democratic values and social justice. The strong protection given to socio-economic rights in the Bill of Rights shows that South Africa is committed to redressing past wrongs and improving the quality of life of its people. By protecting both sets of rights, it also confirms that all human rights are interdependent, indivisible and mutually reinforcing.

Human rights depend on each other to be effectively protected, eg:

1. Without the right to an education, it is difficult to effectively exercise your civil and political rights, such as to express an opinion and to present a petition;
2. Without the right to food and health care, your right to life as a poor person is threatened; and
3. If you have a right to information and to participate in political decision-making, you have a much better chance of ensuring that the government gives effect to your socio-economic rights.

(Source: Liebenberg S & Pillay K (eds) *Socio-Economic Rights in South Africa: A Resource Book* (2000), p 15)

5.1.2 Which socio-economic rights are included in the Constitution?

socio-economic rights protected by the Constitution

The Constitution protects the following socio-economic rights:

1. Right to a healthy environment;
2. Rights of access to land and to security of tenure;
3. Right to adequate housing and protection against evictions and demolitions;
4. Rights of access to health care services, sufficient food and water, social security, including social assistance, as well as the right not to be refused emergency medical treatment;
5. Children's rights to basic nutrition, shelter, basic health care services and social services;
6. Right to education; and
7. Prisoners' rights to adequate accommodation, nutrition, reading materials and medical treatment.

Problem 1: Some questions on socio-economic rights

Questions

1. Do you think that socio-economic rights should be made enforceable in courts, just like civil and political rights? Give reasons for your answer.
2. List some practical examples which show the interdependence of all human rights (civil and political as well as social and economic rights).

Problem 2: Should there be a right to clothing?

Questions

Given the great poverty levels in South Africa and the fact that many people cannot afford to protect and cover their bodies, do you think that the Constitution should have included the right to clothing, which is recognised at the international level? Give reasons for your answer.

5.1.3 What are the government's duties in respect of socio-economic rights?

According to the Constitution, the government has a duty to respect, protect, promote and fulfil all the rights in the Bill of Rights.

duty to respect

First, the 'duty to respect' means that the government should not take away socio-economic rights or make it difficult for people to exercise to these rights. The government does not respect socio-economic rights if, for example:

1. It demolishes homes or property without a good reason and without a proper order of court.

2. It stops paying a social grant to a person who is eligible for such a grant.

duty to protect

Second, the 'duty to protect' means that the government must pass laws that prevent powerful people or organisations from interfering with people's socio-economic rights. The government is not protecting socio-economic rights if, for example:

1. It does not take action to stop a big oil company from polluting the community's water.
2. It does not make police and welfare authorities respond to cases of child abuse and neglect.

duty to promote

Third, the 'duty to promote' means that the government must take active measures aimed at increasing public awareness and respect for socio-economic rights. It can do so by implementing educational programmes, use of the media, and encouraging and supporting the work of civil society organisations.

duty to fulfil

Fourth, the 'duty to fulfil' means that the government must take positive steps to assist poor people to exercise their socio-economic rights. Largely because of apartheid, not everyone has equal access to resources and opportunities. Many people lack such basic amenities as shelter, sufficient food, clean water, access to good health care services and education.

take reasonable legislative and other measures

According to the Constitution, in order for the government to fulfil these rights, it must 'take reasonable legislative and other measures, within its available resources, to achieve the progressive realisation of each of these rights'. 'Reasonable measures' means that the government must pass laws, and adopt and implement policies and programmes that will give effect to people's right of access to socio-economic rights. During 2013–2014 the government spent R109 billion on social security grants for 16 million people.

progressive realisation

'Progressive realisation' means that the government must ensure that socio-economic rights are realised over time. It may do so through adopting a comprehensive and co-ordinated programme with time-frames, goals and targets, and must be able to monitor its own progress. For example, the government will not realise these rights if it takes away, without good reason, land which people use to produce food, and does not provide alternative means for people to obtain food by themselves.

within available resources

duty to address the needs of desperately poor people

The government must use the resources that it has to ensure that poor people gain access to socio-economic services. The government may not defend itself against the accusation that it has made little progress on the basis that it does not have sufficient resources if it allows large amounts of money to be wasted through corruption and incompetent administration. The Constitutional Court in the case of *Government of the Republic of South Africa v Grootboom (2000)* said that the government must adopt measures that would provide for 'the urgent needs of people in desperate circumstances', eg people without a roof over their head, a daily meal, access to health care services, etc. This means that it must prioritise the provision of services to these people.

Problem 3: Testimony of Emily Mphanya at the Poverty Hearings in the North West Province

'Since my husband died I am suffering. I have four girls and one boy. All the girls are married. I was working as a domestic worker. Then I went to work in the field. Now I stay at home. My son was ill. I moved in with him. He passed away. I am left with a handicapped grandson. There is no money at home. My house has no plaster and no windows. The water is closed. I am dying of hunger and thirst. I ask the government to help me. I have no family. I have no reference book and so no pension. I applied for an identity book, went to fetch it, but it was not there. I went again. They said again that it was not available. I have no more money to go back again. I will ask for money from the neighbours. Now they give me porridge. At present I go out and pick morogo. I eat that.'

(Source: *National 'Speak Out on Poverty' Hearings, March – June 1998, The People's Voices*, 75)

Questions

1. What socio-economic rights are involved in this case study?
2. Describe the duty of the government towards Emily.

5.1.4 How to enforce socio-economic rights

socio-economic rights are enforceable in courts

Socio-economic rights can be enforced in South African courts. This is not common in the legal systems of many other countries. What is common is that socio-economic rights would be regarded as mere guidelines for the government programmes and not enforceable in courts.

courts interpret rights, laws and policies

The Constitutional Court is the highest court in South Africa that deals with cases about the Constitution. It interprets and decides whether a law or policy violates the Constitution. Anyone claiming a violation of socio-economic rights may bring the matter to the High Court first and, if need be, later to the Constitutional Court.

Constitutional Court cases involving socio-economic rights

1. *Soobramoney v Minister of Health, KwaZulu-Natal* (1997) (the right not to be refused emergency medical services);
2. *Government of the Republic of South Africa v Grootboom* (2000) (right of access to adequate housing);
3. *Minister of Health v Treatment Action Campaign* (2002) (right to health care services and anti-retroviral treatment for newborn babies);
4. *Khosa v Minister of Social Development* (2004) (right of non-South African citizens with permanent residence in South Africa to claim social security benefits); and
5. *Mazibuko v City of Johannesburg* (2010) (right of access to sufficient water).

5.1.5 Where can people go for legal assistance if their socio-economic rights are threatened or violated?

SAHRC promotes respect for human rights

the SAHRC may take cases to court

Anyone or any group of people who believe that their socio-economic rights are threatened or have been violated may consult the nearest office of the South African Human Rights Commission (SAHRC) and lodge a complaint. The SAHRC will then investigate the matter and may decide to act on the complainant's behalf by negotiating with the infringing party. The SAHRC may also take the matter to court on the complainant's behalf if the matter is not settled. The SAHRC deals with the complaint at no cost to the complainant. As private lawyers are often expensive, it is advisable that people with complaints relating to human rights, including socio-economic rights, consult the SAHRC.

free legal assistance

People who cannot afford lawyers can also approach their nearest Legal Aid South Africa Justice Centre, the Legal Resource Centre or Legal Aid Clinic for free legal assistance. They can also seek advice from paralegal advice offices in their area. Paralegal offices cannot take cases to court, but they can refer clients to lawyers who can.

People can also contact non-government organisations (NGOs) and community based organisations (CBOs) in the area who may assist in investigating the matter and in getting legal assistance for the community or person.

5.1.6 Can socio-economic rights be limited?

limitation must be reasonable and justifiable

Socio-economic rights can be limited just like any other rights in the Bill of Rights. The Constitution says that a right can be limited on two grounds:

1. The limitation must be made under a law of general application. It is not a valid limitation if the law applies only to identifiable groups of people or individuals (eg it applies to all Zulus in the country).
2. The limitation must be 'reasonable and justifiable in an open and democratic society based on human dignity, equality and freedom'.

The court will look at the following factors to determine if the limitation is reasonable and justifiable:

1. The reason why the right is being limited.
2. The degree to which the right is limited (eg how much of the right is limited).
3. If there are any other ways to achieve the purpose of limitation other than by actually limiting the right.

Problem 4: Socio-economic rights and limited resources

Questions

The Bill of Rights states that people may not be discriminated against on the grounds of nationality.

1. Would the government succeed in an argument that it does not provide social assistance grants to non-nationals on the grounds of resource constraints? Role-play a discussion between groups (a) representing non-nationals and (b) the Department of Social Development.
2. The South African government decided to prioritise the strengthening of the defence system and bought expensive arms in 2001. This decision led to an increase in the budget of the Department of Defence in 2001–2002 and the cutting of social spending in the areas of education, amongst others. As a result of this cut, a number of public schools were forced to close. In Blikkiesdorp, the closure of the only public school providing primary education in the area has serious consequences for pupils. Their only option is to board at the school in the closest town, 50 km from Blikkiesdorp. No subsidised transport is provided. Most parents in Blikkiesdorp are poor and cannot afford the costs of transport and boarding their children at this school. The parents believe that this situation violates their children's rights under the Constitution and want to challenge the government in court.

In court, the government raises the defence of resource constraints and that it has prioritised the need for strengthening the defence system over other needs.

The participants should divide into three groups representing (a) the lawyers for the parents; (b) the lawyers for the government; and (c) judges in the court. The large groups should be subdivided into small groups in order to prepare their roles. Lawyers should prepare their arguments and judges their judgments.

1. Present arguments as lawyers for the parents.
2. Present arguments as lawyers for the government.
3. Give judgments as judges.

5.2 Education rights

Outcomes

After completion of this section learners will be able to:

1. Explain the meaning of education rights and the duties of the state in respect of them.

Assessment criteria

1. Different elements of education rights are identified.
2. A set of facts is examined and a decision made on whether the government is fulfilling its duty regarding school facilities.
3. A decision is taken on the impact a failure by the government to deliver textbooks and workbooks is likely to have on learners.
4. A decision is taken on whether inequalities in the educational system can be addressed by abolishing 'feeder zones' for schools.
5. A set of facts is given and a decision taken on whether certain learners may be turned away from school.
6. The procedure for applying for exemption from paying school fees is explained.
7. A set of facts is examined and a decision made on whether learners may be taught in the language of their choice.

5.2.1 What are education rights?

The Constitution sets out education rights as follows:

1. Everyone has the right to a basic education.
2. Everyone has the right to further education which the state must realise progressively, taking into account available resources.
3. Everyone has the right to receive an education in the official language or language of his or her choice in public education institutions, where this is reasonably practicable.
4. Everyone has the right to establish and maintain, at his or her own expense, independent educational institutions.

Problem 1: Case study: The primary school where learners bring their own chairs

In 2012 the following was reported:

Former United States President Bill Clinton recently donated a container filled with books to a primary school in Qunu, Eastern Cape, the home village of ex-President Nelson Mandela. In the school 228 learners share three classrooms with fewer than 30 desks. The school is one of 1 093 schools in the Eastern Cape that an acute shortage of desks and chairs

has an acute shortage of desks and chairs, with the result that at some of the other schools learners bring their own plastic chairs while others sit on the floor. At the school the principal's office is also used as classroom, staffroom and store room. Teachers combine two different grades in one classroom and when one speaks, the other has to stop and wait. The Lyoness Child and Family Foundation, a charitable trust in Switzerland, has committed to rebuild the school at a cost of R5 million by constructing seven classrooms, a staffroom, toilets, a kitchen and a playground.

(Source: Savides M 'Pupils bring own seat of learning' *Sunday Times* 22 July 2012)

Questions

1. Do you think that the Eastern Cape Department of Education is fulfilling the right of the children of Qunu to basic education? Give reasons for your answer.
2. Does your school experience one or more of the problems that the Qunu school is facing?
3. Who has a duty to fix the problems experienced in schools like the Qunu school?
4. Does South Africa need more schools and better facilities for schools?
5. Does your school have enough resources and facilities to enable you to learn?
6. Does your community protect your school against vandalism and theft?

Problem 2: How does the failure to deliver textbooks and workbooks affect learners?

a severe shortage of textbooks

It was reported during 2012 that in Limpopo, Eastern Cape, Free State and KwaZulu-Natal thousands of students had not received their textbooks and workbooks by mid-year. In Limpopo hundreds of workbooks were found dumped near a dam.

Questions

What is the impact on the right to education if government does not deliver textbooks and workbooks on time at the start of the school year?

5.2.2 What does it mean to have a right to education?

5.2.2.1 The right to basic education, including adult basic education

education develops people's potential

Education becomes more important as time goes by. It is important because it develops people's potential, lays a good foundation for people to be responsible citizens, and gives people skills to be able to compete in the workplace. Society educated people are assets in society

benefits from educating people. For example, society needs doctors, scientists, teachers, engineers, lawyers, judges, politicians, academics, social workers, and so on. These people are assets that enable society to function properly. Without education, people are less able to take part in social and political activities.

children should not be turned away from basic education

In South Africa, the right to basic education means that every child between 7 and 15 years or in grades 1 to 9 must receive compulsory education in public schools. Basic education only covers grades 1 to 9, while other grades are regarded as further education. The right to basic education means that children of 7 to 15 years or in grades 1 to 9 cannot be turned away from school on grounds that may be considered unfair. It also means that parents have a duty to send their children to school. If they cannot afford to pay school fees, for example, their children should not be turned away.

apartheid ensured that black people had low standards of education

The right to adult basic education is aimed at giving opportunities to adults who wish to be educated and skilled. The legacy of apartheid has made the right to education very important. Apartheid laws ensured that the majority of the black population had little education or a low standard of education. Many black children today still go to inferior schools in poor neighbourhoods.

5.2.2.2 How can the inequalities in the schooling system be addressed?

Some people have suggested that the only way to solve the inequalities of the schooling system which results in students in poor communities going to poorly resourced schools is by allowing learners to be admitted to public schools on a first come, first served basis. The South African Schools Act provides for the introduction of defined 'feeder zones' in which students that live closest to a particular school have the right to be enrolled in schools in these zones. However as there are not enough schools in many areas to make sure that the inequalities in the schooling system are addressed, the Government has not defined these zones. This means that learners who live anywhere can attend a school in particular community, provided they apply for admission earlier than learners who live nearby.

It has been argued that to abolish the 'feeder zones' will result in learners living next to a school losing out to learners who live 20 or 30 km away. They say that the way to end the inequalities in education is to provide proper facilities for, and management of, the schools in the disadvantaged areas.

Problem 3: Should 'feeder zones' be abolished or kept?

Questions

1. What are the arguments in favour of 'feeder zones'?
2. What are the arguments against 'feeder zones'?
3. If you were the provincial MEC responsible for education and the need to end the inequalities in schools, would you abolish or keep 'feeder zones'?

high rate of illiteracy

The unequal schooling system under apartheid has led to a high rate of illiteracy among the black adult population. The right to adult education is therefore intended to give disadvantaged people the opportunity to be educated or improve their education. These adults cannot be turned away because they cannot afford to pay for their education.

government must ensure that people are educated

The right to a basic education, including adult education, means that the government must build schools, set up facilities, and provide the necessary materials and equipment for people to have a good education.

The state of education in South Africa

The following was reported regarding education in South Africa in 2010:

There were 24 451 schools in 2010 compared with 26 789 schools in 2000 – ie 2 388 state-funded schools had been shut down since 2000.

Only 3 772 schools had science laboratories.

Only 252 schools had libraries.

3 544 schools had no electricity.

913 schools had no toilets.

11 450 schools had pit latrines.

2 402 schools had no access to water.

9 242 schools depended on boreholes for water.

South African teachers on average spent less than 50% of their teaching time in class each week.

(Source: Report by South African Institute of Race Relations (2012))

Problem 4: How does your school measure up?

Questions

How does your school measure up to the shortages mentioned in the box above? Does it have any of the shortages mentioned?

Problem 5: Can the learners be turned away from school?

Questions

Can the persons in the following circumstances be turned away from school? Give reasons for your answer. What is the government's duty if these people cannot attend schools?

1. A learner living with HIV/AIDS;
2. A pregnant learner and her boyfriend (the father of the child);
3. A learner whose parent cannot afford to pay school fees;
4. A learner who does not have a school uniform;
5. An African learner in a private white school;
6. A learner who is gay;
7. A learner who does not have compulsory school textbooks;
8. A learner who regularly arrives late at school because of the distance between the school and his home;
9. A learner who cannot attend the school because it is too far from her home (more than 30 km) and the parent cannot afford the transport costs every day; and
10. A learner who is doing badly in school because she comes to school hungry most of the time and her family is too poor to provide her with lunch.

5.2.2.3 School fees

exemption from paying school fees

Certain categories of people can be exempted from paying school fees if they cannot afford them. If parents cannot afford to pay and they fall within the category of people who should be exempted, they should make use of the exemption system so that their children are not turned away from school. Children whose parents have been given an exemption should not be discriminated against.

5.2.2.3.1 Guidelines on school fees

The National Education Department sets the amounts that provinces should allocate to each category of school – schools are ranked into five categories with the poorest being category one and the least poor, category five. The category one schools receive a much bigger government subsidy for each student than the category five schools. Depending on their category, each school must receive an 'adequate' amount from their provincial department of education.

Schools in the poorest category will be 'no fee' or 'fee-free' schools if they receive an 'adequate' subsidy allocation per student from their provincial education department. This means that some schools will be completely free and cannot charge school fees. The South African Institute of Race Relations reported that in 2010 60% of schools in the country were 'no fee', compared with 55% in 2008.

(Source: South African Institute of Race Relations Report (2012))

Most of the rural schools fall into category one and most of the Model C schools into category five. While some of the category one schools will be 'fee-free', the category five schools will have to rely on the parents paying adequate school fees to cover most the school's costs.

5.2.2.3.2 Applying for exemptions

applying for exemptions

1. A parent wishing to apply to be exempted from paying school fees for his or her child must send his or her application to the school governing body (SGB).

2. The SGB must consider the application by following the guidelines set out in the School Fees Guidelines in order to make a decision to approve or reject the application.
3. The SGB may change its decision on whether or not a person should qualify for school fees if the person's financial position improves.
4. If the SGB turns down the application, the unsuccessful applicant has the right to appeal against the decision to the Head of Department of Education in the province.

Problem 6: Appealing against a decision not to grant an exemption from school fees

Questions

Draft a letter to the Head of Department in your province in which you appeal against the decision of the SGB not to grant you exemption from school fees for your three children who attend the same school.

5.2.2.3.3 Failure to pay school fees

It is in everyone's interests that parents who can afford to pay school fees should do so. However, if parents have failed to pay school fees, a school may only sue them for the fees if:

1. The school fees were lawfully decided at a general meeting of the parents.
2. The SGB has notified all parents in writing of the annual school fees, and also the criteria and procedure for exemption of school fees.
3. The parents do not qualify for an exemption.

If the above steps have not been followed the parents involved may defend any action against them to pay school fees.

5.2.2.4 The right to further education

higher education depends on the learner's ability to cope with it

The right to further education refers to education from grades 10 to 12 and vocational training (education for a particular skill or training) and tertiary education (universities and universities of technology). Higher education is often based on the learner's ability to cope with studying at universities or universities of technology or any other similar institutions. The state cannot force learners to go and study at these higher learning institutions. However, it has the duty to make it possible for learners who wish to access further education over time to do so. For example, it must pass laws that will ensure that learners are able to attend a further education institution without discrimination. It can provide subsidies to universities and colleges of further education. It can also provide bursaries and loans to learners from poor families so that they can further their studies.

affirmative action programmes

Certain tertiary institutions make it possible for learners from disadvantaged backgrounds to receive education. For example in 2000, the University of the Western Cape adopted a policy that allowed learners to enrol without matriculation exemptions. Other universities have affirmative action programmes to encourage entry by less qualified learners who have the potential.

Case study: The case of the clever learner who was refused admission to the medical school

Questions

In *Motala and another v University of Natal* (1995), the parents of a learner applying to university took the then University of Natal to court to challenge her non-admission to the university's medical school.

The university had an admission policy that gave preference to previously disadvantaged groups. Even though Motala had very good matriculation results, she was refused admission into the medical school, because preference was given to African learners. Motala was an Indian learner. She argued that that the medical school's policy of favouring African learners over Indian learners was unfair discrimination, because Indians were disadvantaged under apartheid.

Motala did not succeed. The court said:

1. Although the Indian group was disadvantaged by the apartheid system, African pupils and learners were at a far greater disadvantage under the four-tier system of education.
2. As Africans were more disadvantaged than Indians under apartheid, the medical school was allowed to have an admission programme that gave preference to African learners over Indian learners.

5.2.2.5 The right to education in a language of your choice

it must be reasonably practicable

Learners have a right to receive education in the official language or language of their choice at a public school to the extent that this is 'reasonably practicable'. To determine what is reasonably practicable in terms of personal choices, the state must consider the following factors:

factors indicating that it is reasonably practicable

1. Is it practically possible to implement?
2. Is it equitable? Is it possible to do it fairly?
3. What would be the purpose of implementing this – is it meant to redress the results of past racially discriminatory laws and practices?

No learner has the right to receive education in the language of his or her choice in a private school.

instruction must be in an official language

The National Education Policy Act says:

1. The language of instruction should be an official language.
2. Learners should be taught in one language during the first two years of school.
3. From the third year of school, learners must learn two languages – one of these must be the language of instruction.

4. Education language policy should aim at promoting multilingualism (being able to speak several languages).

Problem 7: Was the learner entitled to be taught in the language of her choice?

Questions

1. Lebo, a Sotho-speaking girl, attends a public school that is dominated by Afrikaans-speaking learners. The school uses Afrikaans as a medium of instruction and most subjects are taught in Afrikaans. She and other Sotho-speaking learners argue that they also want to be taught in Sotho or English because they cannot understand Afrikaans very well. This results, they say, in their performing badly in their classes.
   Divide into small groups of (a) Lebo's parents; (b) parents of Afrikaans-speaking learners; and (c) the school governing body. Present your arguments for Lebo's parents and the parents of Afrikaans-speaking learners to the school governing body.
2. Tumi, a Tswana-speaking girl, attends a public school in KwaMakhutha near Durban, in KwaZulu-Natal. The school conducts most of the classes in Zulu because the majority of the learners speak it. Tumi can understand some Zulu, but struggles to fully understand what is being taught in class. When she complained to the schoolteachers about this and asked for teachers to teach in English, she was told to go and find another school because the majority of the learners in the school are Zulu-speaking. Tumi has missed classes at times because she feels excluded. She does not feel like attending the school anymore, but does not have much of a choice because the other school is too far away, and her parents cannot afford to pay for transport costs.
   Divide into small groups of (a) Tumi's parents; (b) the school principal; and (c) the school governing body. Present your arguments for Tumi's parents and the school principal to the school governing body.
   In the course of your arguments consider if it is reasonably practicable for the school to implement an English medium option so that Tumi can be accommodated, and whether Tumi can be turned away.

5.3 Social welfare rights

Outcomes

After completion of this section learners will be able to:

1. Explain the law concerning social security and assistance.

Assessment criteria

1. The law and regulations governing social assistance are identified.
2. The requirements for applying and qualifying for different social grants are identified.
3. A set of facts is examined and a decision made on whether certain people qualify for social grants.
4. A set of facts is examined and a decision made on how certain people can access their social grants.
5. A set of facts is examined and a decision made on how to solve certain problems concerning social grants.

5.3.1 Introduction

social security, social assistance and social services

The Constitution says that everyone has the right of access to social security, including, if they are unable to support themselves and their dependants, appropriate social assistance. It says that the government must 'take reasonable legislative and other measures, within its available resources, to achieve the progressive realisation of this right'. It also says that every child has 'the right to social services'. These rights are considered to be social welfare rights.

Examples of social services

The government must take steps to:

1. Protect children from physical or mental violence, injury or abuse, neglect or negligent treatment;
2. Protect and assist children temporarily or permanently separated from their families;
3. Assist children with mental or physical disabilities;
4. Protect children against economic exploitation;
5. Protect children from drug abuse;
6. Protect children from all forms of sexual exploitation and abuse;
7. Promote the recovery and social acceptance of children suffering from any form of abuse; and
8. Promote a variety of alternatives to institutional care of children accused or convicted of crimes.

5.3.2 What is social security?

four types of social security

Social security refers to a number of public and private schemes that give money or in-kind benefits or both, in the event of a person's earning power temporarily or permanently ceasing. There are four types of social security in South Africa.

1. *Private savings* refers to the voluntarily saving of money by a person for unexpected events such as disability, retirement and chronic diseases.
2. *Social insurance* refers to the contribution of both employers and employees to pension or provident funds, or social insurance covering other unexpected events. Government may also contribute to social insurance funds. The most common form of insurance falling within this category is the Unemployment Insurance Fund (UIF), which is paid by the employer and the employee.
3. *Social assistance* refers to non-contributory and means-tested benefits provided by the government to groups such as people living with disabilities, elderly people and unsupported parents and children, who are unable to provide their own minimum needs. In South Africa, social assistance is also called 'social grants'.
4. *Social relief* refers to short-term steps to help people in crisis, for example those affected by such natural disasters as droughts or floods. This is also non-contributory and means tested.

This section focuses on social assistance and social relief of distress.

5.3.3 What types of social grants are available?

different types of grants

The Social Assistance Act of 2004 is the main law which governs social grants. It is also supported by the welfare regulations that set out details of who qualifies for the different grants. The following different types of grants are available:

1. A grant for the aged;
2. A war veteran's grant;
3. A grant for the disabled;
4. A child support grant;
5. A foster child grant;
6. A care dependency grant;
7. A grant in aid; and
8. A social relief of distress grant.

5.3.4 Where do people go to apply for a grant?

All applications must be made to the applicant's nearest social welfare office. Applicants must provide all the necessary documents for applying for a particular grant. If the applicant is too sick to go and apply, it is possible for a family member or friend to go and apply on his or her behalf. The application must be completed in the presence of a social welfare officer. It does not cost money to apply for a grant. It is important to keep proof of the application.

payment within 3 months

After a person has applied, he or she should not wait for longer than three months before getting paid. If it takes longer, a person can contact the social welfare office or provincial Department of Social Development to find out the reason for the delay in payment and approach a Legal Resources Centre, a legal aid clinic or an advice office.

payment from the date of application

An applicant is entitled to payment from the date of application. Social security grants are administered by the South African Social Security Agency.

5.3.5 What do people need to apply and qualify for grants?

a means test

Most social grants require the person applying for them to pass a 'means test'. According to the means test, applications for particular social grants will only be approved if the applicant's income and assets are below a certain level. Therefore, a person applying for social grants that are means-tested will have to provide certain information for evaluation. Assets refer to valuable belongings such as a house, land, money that is saved somewhere, or a pension from retirement or previous employment. A person's financial state is reviewed regularly to check if it is still the same. If a person's financial situation improves, his or her grant may be cancelled.

Note:

1. The 'means test' is not applied to pensioners aged 100 years or more.
2. The grant will be reduced to 25% of the maximum amount if the person is admitted to a state institution that takes care of such person.

pensions are paid to elderly and disabled people who qualify in terms of a 'means test'

5.3.5.1 General requirements for all social grants

Unless stated otherwise, a person applying for any social grant must:

1. Be a South African citizen or a permanent resident;
2. Be resident in South Africa at the time of applying;
3. Have a 13-digit bar-coded identity document ('ID');
4. Not be maintained or cared for in a state institution;
5. Meet the requirements of the 'means test'; and
6. Not be receiving another grant for himself or herself, except in respect of the grants for children (ie child support grant, foster care grant and care dependency grants).

In *Khosa v Minister of Social Development* (2004) the Constitutional Court decided that non-South African permanent residents were entitled to access social grants.

Note: Different requirements apply in the case of social relief of distress grants. See below para 5.3.5.2.8.

In addition to the above general requirements, a person applying for each of the following grants must meet the specific requirements of the grant applied for.

5.3.5.2 Different types of social grants

5.3.5.2.1 A grant for the aged

old age grant

In addition to the requirements mentioned in para 5.3.5.1 above, a person applying for a grant for the aged or an old age grant must:

60 years and older

1. Be a woman or a man of 60 years or older; and
2. If married, provide proof of marriage.

5.3.5.2.2 A grant for war veterans

In addition to the requirements mentioned in para 5.3.5.1 above, a person applying for a war veteran's grant (for people who fought in wars) must:

60 years and older and proof of service

1. Be 60 years and over or must be unable to provide for his or her maintenance due to physical or mental disability resulting from a war; and
2. Provide proof of service (ie must have fought in a war, for example, the Second World War, the Korean War, the Namibian War or the freedom struggle).

5.3.5.2.3 A grant for the disabled

In addition to the requirements mentioned in para 5.3.5.1 above, a person applying for a disability grant must:

18 to 59 years old with a disability

1. Be a woman or a man between the ages of 18 to 59 years; and
2. Have a medical report or certificate confirming the disability (physical or mental or both).

when people apply for a disability pension, the pensions officer will refer them to a district medical officer

5.3.5.2.4 A child support grant

the Department of Social Development has extended the grant to cover children aged up to 18 years

In addition to the requirements mentioned in para 5.3.5.1 above, a person applying for a child support grant must:

1. Be an adult, primary care-giver of the child or children concerned;
2. Have or be caring for a child or children under the age of 18 years;
3. Have a 13-digit birth certificate for the child or children;
4. If the person has a spouse, show that the spouse also meets the means test; and
5. Not have more than six biological children.

5.3.5.2.5 A foster care grant

In addition to the requirements mentioned in para 5.3.5.1 above, people applying for a foster care grant must:

legal foster parents

1. Have a court order confirming that they are legal foster parents;
2. Have a 13-digit birth certificate or 13-digit identity document for the child or children concerned;
3. Show that the foster child meets the means test; and
4. Show that the foster child is also resident in South Africa.

5.3.5.2.6 A care dependency grant

In addition to the requirements mentioned in para 5.3.5.1 above, a person applying for a care dependency grant must:

child between 1 and 18 years

1. Care for a child between 1 and 18 years;
2. Have a medical report or certificate confirming the child's disability;
3. Have a disabled child who is not maintained or cared for in a state institution;

4. Have a 13-digit birth certificate or 13-digit identity document for the child concerned;
5. If the person has a spouse, show that the spouse also meets the means test; and
6. Show that the child meets the means test.

5.3.5.2.7 A grant-in-aid

In addition to the requirements mentioned in para 5.3.5.1 above, a person applying for a grant-in-aid must:

need for full-time help because of physical or mental disability

1. Need full-time help from someone else due to physical or mental disabilities;
2. Be receiving a social grant; and
3. Not be cared for by an institution that receives a subsidy from the state for the care or housing of the beneficiary.

5.3.5.2.8 A social relief of distress grant

desperate need

A social relief of distress grant is a temporary grant that provides financial assistance to people who are in a desperate situation and are unable to meet even the most basic needs of the family. It is issued monthly and for a period of no more than three months. It can also be extended in certain exceptional cases.

Applications for the social relief of distress must be directed to the Director-General of the Department of Social Development.

To qualify for a social relief of distress grant, the applicant must face the following situations:

conditions for social relief of distress grant

1. He or she must be awaiting a permanent social grant or assistance.
2. He or she must be medically unfit to undertake paid work for a period of less than six months.

maintenance grants will be paid to a mother if she becomes a widow

3. The breadwinner is deceased and there are insufficient means for the family to survive.

4. The breadwinner has been admitted to an institution for less than six months (eg in prison, mental institution, or rehabilitation centre).
5. He or she must have been affected by a disaster or any other emergency situation (eg floods, storms or drought) in areas which have not yet been declared a disaster area.
6. He or she is awaiting the result of an appeal against the suspension of his or her grant.
7. He or she is not receiving assistance from any other organisation.
8. He or she is not a member of a household that is already receiving social assistance.
9. He or she is not receiving maintenance from a person who used to maintain him or her. (The applicant must provide proof of efforts that have been made to trace the person who is supposed to maintain him or her.)

5.3.6 What happens if the application is unsuccessful or the grant is suspended or cancelled?

unsuccessful applications

appeal to MEC for social welfare

The success of an application for a grant depends mainly on whether or not all the requirements are met. If one of the requirements is not met, the grant is likely to be unsuccessful. If the grant is not successful, a person has the right to obtain the reasons from the Department of Social Welfare for the decision. A person also has the right to appeal against the decision to the Provincial Minister (MEC) of Social Welfare. An appeal must be lodged within 90 days of knowing that the application was unsuccessful. The aggrieved person may also approach the nearest paralegal office, advice office, legal aid clinic, or Legal Resources Centre, for help.

in some rural areas there are advice offices to help people with pension problems

Note: The same procedure and time frames apply if a person has his or her grant suspended or cancelled.

5.3.6.1 Common reasons for suspending a grant

reasons for suspending grants

A person's grant may be suspended for one or more of the following reasons:

1. A person inherits a lot of money after the death of one of her children.
2. A person has won a huge sum of money from the lottery.
3. The outcomes of a review confirm that a person's disability has improved and he or she will be able undertake remunerative work.
4. A person refuses to co-operate with the review of the grant (ie to provide the information necessary for a review of the grant).

5.3.6.2 Common reasons for cancelling a grant

reasons for cancelling grants

A person's grant may be cancelled for one or more of the following reasons:

1. If a person dies;
2. If a person is admitted to (or is maintained and cared for in) a state institution;
3. If the person does not claim the grant for three consecutive months; and
4. When the period of temporary disability comes to an end.

Problem 1: Does the person qualify for a social grant?

Questions

Consider the following cases and state whether the person qualifies for any of the social grants available. If so, which social grant, why, and what information is needed?

1. Radebe, who is 62 years old and lives in Welkom, served in the South African army in Angola during the Namibian War in the 1980s.
2. Joe, who is 58 years old and lives in Kimberley, was shot and badly wounded while serving in the Umkhonto Wesizwe (MK) during the Struggle. Because of his wound, he can no longer work.
3. Mary Macintosh, who is unmarried and living in Germiston, is about to have a baby. She has to leave her job and the father of her child has deserted her. She needs assistance for living and medical expenses until she can work again.
4. Mr and Mrs Lebo's baby girl was born blind. The child is now 12 years old.
5. Derrick is 67 years old. He has been receiving a pension since he was 65 years old. He has won a lottery prize of R500 000.
6. Betty has her arm cut off as a result of an accident at work. The Compensation Commissioner pays her hospital bills and a monthly pension.
7. Gawie and Jill Abrahamse live in Kroonstad and have four children, the oldest of whom is 14. They are both unemployed and are waiting for a maintenance grant. They cannot afford to pay their bills for food, housing, clothes and medical expenses.

Problem 2: How can the people get their social grants?

Questions

What must the following people do in order to get their social grants?

1. Jama, who is 78 years old and lives in Cape Town, is too sick to collect her old-age grant from the pay point.
2. Fanyana moves from Umlazi outside Durban to Sobantu outside Pietermaritzburg. How can he make sure that he still receives his disability grant?
3. Stoffel, who is 63 years old and lives in Pretoria, has not received his war veteran's grant for the past two months.
4. Jomo Ntuli lives with his family in a flood-stricken area of KwaZulu-Natal. He is self-employed as a farmer, but because there have been several floods during the past year all his crops have been washed away. He and his family have no money for food and clothing.
5. Charlene is 35 years of age. Her ID and her 6-year-old child's birth certificate were destroyed when her house was burnt down two years ago. She wants to apply for a child support grant.
6. Dejewo, a Nigerian citizen and a leader of a refugee movement, has been in South Africa for the last four and a half years. His application for refugee status has been declined.

5.3.7 How to collect a social grant

collecting a social grant

1. Applicants must make sure, before leaving the office of the Social Development Department, that they are aware of where they should go to collect their grants and on what date to go.
2. Many residential areas should have pay points where grantees can collect their grants on the date advised by the social worker.
3. Applicants need to know what they should do if their grants are not paid on the due date, and where they should collect their grants.

Problem 3: How would you solve these problems relating to the payment of social grants?

Questions

1. Sometimes pay-out points are not at convenient places. The beneficiaries of social grants have to travel long distances (more than 20 km) to arrive at them. Bus fares are too expensive for many people, and most have to walk. Some elderly people or people with disabilities have to hire people to push them in wheelbarrows.

pensioners can experience great difficulty in getting their pensions in rural areas

2. Some beneficiaries have to queue outside pay-out points the night before the pay-out to make sure that they receive their grants.
3. There are no toilets, chairs, first aid kits, water, wheelchairs, portable beds and electricity at the pay points.
4. Pay points are not suitable for people with disabilities and some of the elderly pensioners. For example, there are no ramps for wheelchairs.
5. Some beneficiaries do not know when the next date of payment is.
6. Some pensioners are made 'to beg' for their pension money before it is handed over by the pay clerks.
7. Some beneficiaries do not receive a receipt as proof of payment at their pay points.
8. Some people are forced to cook food for social welfare officers.
9. Social welfare officers almost run over old and disabled beneficiaries when they drive up to the pay point. The pensioners have to move away very quickly to avoid being injured.
10. Some beneficiaries are told that social welfare officers have run out of money and that they will have to wait until the next payout for their money.

5.3.8 Private welfare and assistance

disaster relief funds

Sometimes when families suffer as a result of floods or drought, disaster relief funds are set up by the state and private bodies. This is often done during floods and droughts. Usually these are advertised in newspapers and on radio and TV so that people know where to get help. Several private bodies help with the feeding of children, the sheltering of homeless people, and the support of the families of prisoners and detainees.

sometimes disaster relief funds are set up to help families suffering as the result of floods or drought

Problem 4: Private welfare and assistance in your town

Make a list of all the private welfare and assistance organisations in your town that will help families who are no longer able to support themselves. Your nearest Department of Health Services and Welfare should be able to assist you. Your list should include organisations that help people who are poor because of their economic and social position or because their breadwinners have been imprisoned or detained.

5.4 Health rights

Outcomes

After completion of this section learners will be able to:

1. Explain the law concerning the right of access to health care.

Assessment criteria

1. An explanation is given of what people are entitled to in terms of health rights.
2. A set of facts is examined and a decision made on whether certain people are entitled to emergency medical treatment.
3. An explanation is given of when pregnant mothers and prisoners living with HIV are entitled to access anti-retroviral treatment.
4. An explanation is given of the meaning of 'informed consent' by patients.
5. A set of facts is examined and a decision made on whether certain children are entitled to consent to medical treatment.
6. A set of facts is examined and a decision made on whether certain people are entitled to a termination of pregnancy
7. The law governing medical aid schemes is explained.
8. Some questions regarding medical aid schemes are raised and answered.
9. An explanation is given of how to lay a complaint against health workers.
10. A set of facts is examined and a decision made whether certain people qualify for free medical treatment.

5.4.1 What health rights are protected in the Constitution?

The Constitution protects a number of health rights:

1. Everyone has the right of access to health care services, including reproductive health care.
2. Everyone has the right to emergency medical treatment.
3. Every child has the right to basic health care services.
4. Every prisoner has a right to adequate medical treatment.
5. Everyone has the right to bodily and psychological integrity.

components of health rights

Health rights are also linked to a number of other constitutional rights, namely the right to equality, life, privacy, human dignity, education, as well as the rights of access to adequate housing, a pollution free environment, and to sufficient food and water.

The right of access to health care services imposes a duty on the government to take reasonable legislative and other measures to realise the right progressively.

(For the meaning of this duty, see above para 5.1.3.) The government is phasing in a National Health Insurance scheme which it is hoped will make medical treatment accessible for everyone. A number of the critics have argued that until the public health system drastically improves its service delivery the proposed scheme will not work.

5.4.2 What do health rights mean?

poor people can access health care services for free

Health care services are provided by both private and government hospitals and clinics. Most of our discussion, however, will be about government hospitals and clinics as the majority of people cannot afford to attend private ones. People (particularly pregnant women, women who are breastfeeding and children) who are very poor and unable to afford health care services of their own are entitled to get them free from a public hospital or clinic.

People requiring financial assistance for medical equipment like crutches, artificial limbs (eg arms or legs), wheel chairs, leg irons or hearing aids may be able to get them from the hospital, if they cannot afford them. This will apply where the equipment is needed to improve the working of a damaged arm or leg, or where the patient's limbs are damaged. Poor people who need equipment must go to the health clinic or a doctor and get a letter before approaching the hospital.

patients at government hospitals may or may not have to pay the full medical fees depending on their income

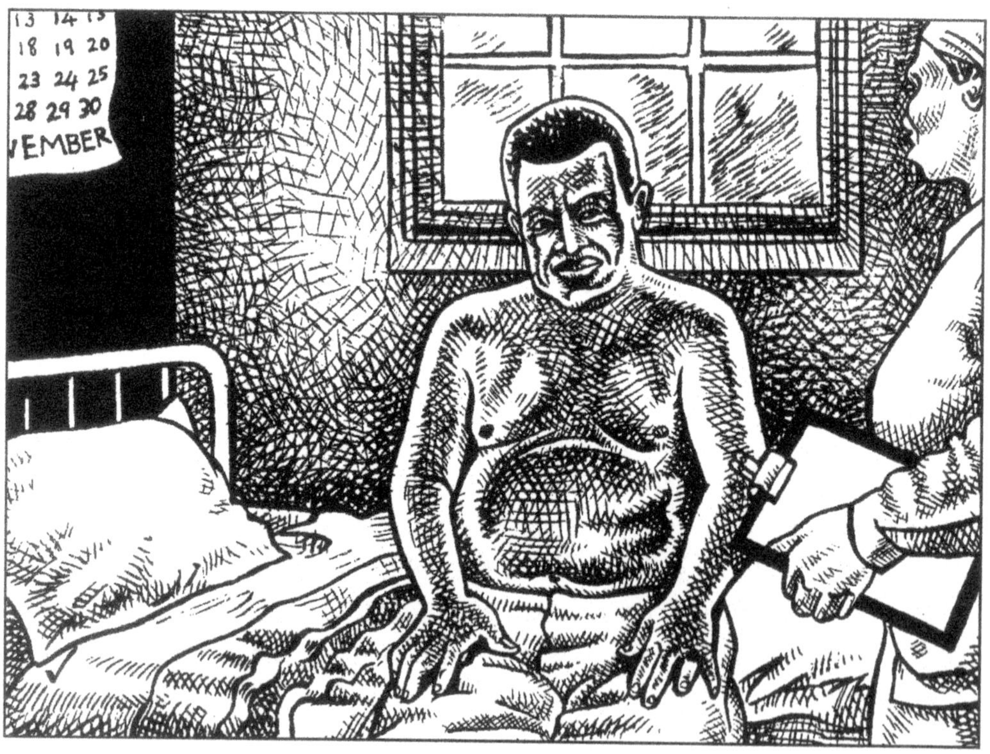

5.4.2.1 The rights to health care services, to emergency medical treatment, and children's rights to basic health care services

nobody may be refused emergency medical treatment

The Constitution states that nobody may be refused emergency medical treatment. A medical emergency occurs when a person's life or health is in serious danger and he or she can be cured if he or she is given treatment immediately. In emergencies treatment cannot be given against the will of the patient (eg against the patient's religious beliefs) – except if it is to protect the public (eg to prevent the spread of a dangerous disease such as drug-resistant TB).

emergency treatment without consent

Emergency treatment without consent is justified provided:

1. It is a real state of emergency;
2. The patient or his or her representative is unable to give consent;
3. The treatment is not against the patient's will unless it is to protect the public; and
4. The treatment is in the best interests of the patient.

The Constitutional Court has given guidance on the meaning of the right of access to health care services and the meaning of 'emergency medical treatment' in the *Soobramoney* and *Treatment Action Campaign* cases (see below).

Problem 1: The case of the kidney patient who is refused dialysis

Soobramoney v Minister of Health, KwaZulu-Natal (1997)

Mr Soobramoney needs kidney dialysis

Mr Soobramoney suffers from a serious kidney disease which requires regular kidney dialysis treatment for his survival. If he is not given treatment he will die. Mr Soobramoney cannot afford treatment from private clinics and approaches a state hospital for dialysis treatment. The hospital refuses to treat him because dialysis treatment is very expensive and it has limited resources to provide such treatment. The hospital says that he does not meet its criteria for treatment.

only good candidates for kidney transplants are given dialysis

The hospital only has a limited number of kidney dialysis machines. The hospital's policy states that patients suffering from irreversible chronic kidney disease will only qualify for dialysis if the patient is a good candidate for a kidney transplant. However, in order to be eligible for a transplant the patient must not have other significant diseases. Unfortunately Mr Soobramoney suffers from other significant diseases.

Mr Soobramoney brings an urgent High Court application

Mr Soobramoney brings an urgent application in the High Court for an order directing the hospital to provide dialysis treatment for him.

He bases his application on two provisions of the Bill of Rights in the Constitution:

(a) Everyone has the right to health care services, within the available resources of the state.

(b) No one may be refused emergency medical treatment.

the hospital opposes Mr Soobramoney's application

The hospital opposes Mr Soobramoney's application on the grounds of the above two provisions of the Bill of Rights in the limitation clause:

The hospital also argues that Mr Soobramoney's condition does not qualify as 'emergency' medical treatment.

Questions

1. If you were the lawyers for Mr Soobramoney what arguments would you make?
2. If you were the lawyers for the hospital what arguments would you make?
3. If you were the judge what would your decision be?

Problem 2: Do the patients require 'emergency medical treatment'?

Questions

Would the following scenarios be considered to be emergency situations within the meaning of the right to 'emergency medical treatment' as set out in the *Soobramoney* case?

Sipho is injured in a car accident

1. Sipho is involved in a car accident and is bleeding heavily. He is rushed to a public hospital by a friend, Sabelo who was an eye-witness to the accident. On arrival at the hospital, the nurses tell Sabelo that there are no doctors to attend to Sipho and that they will only come the next day. As ordinary nurses, they cannot treat him because of his serious condition. Sipho later died as a result of heavy loss of blood. If he had been attended to immediately and the bleeding had been stopped in time, he could have survived.

Bonga has full-blown AIDS

2. Bonga is a patient suffering from an AIDS-related illness. He has full-blown AIDS and is at the critical stage of the disease. He argues that he is entitled to be provided with anti-retroviral drugs at state expense to save his life.

Case study: Anti-retroviral drugs to prevent mother-to-child transmission (MTCT) of HIV/AIDS

Minister of Health v Treatment Action Campaign (2002)

Nevirapine prevents mother-to-child transmission of HIV/AIDS

In 2000, the government adopted and implemented a policy in which it sought to pilot the anti-retroviral drug Nevirapine, which is widely recommended in reducing mother-to-child transmission of HIV/AIDS. Access to Nevirapine was given only to HIV-infected pregnant women in 18 research and training pilot sites. In terms of the policy, doctors in public hospitals could not prescribe Nevirapine to pregnant government policy challenged by the TAC

mothers outside of the pilot sites. In 2001, the Treatment Action Campaign (TAC), an organisation that advocates the treatment of people living with HIV/AIDS, challenged the government's policy in the High Court, arguing that:

1. It violated the rights of access to health care services of pregnant women with HIV/AIDS, including reproductive health care services.
2. It failed to adopt a comprehensive response to the prevention of MTCT of HIV.
3. It violated the right of children to basic health care services.

government ordered to provide Nevirapine

Both the Pretoria High Court and the Constitutional Court decided in the favour of the TAC's arguments. The Constitutional Court ordered the government to allow Nevirapine to be given in hospitals other than those involved in the pilot sites.

HIV-positive women and their new babies are entitled to access to Nevirapine at hospitals

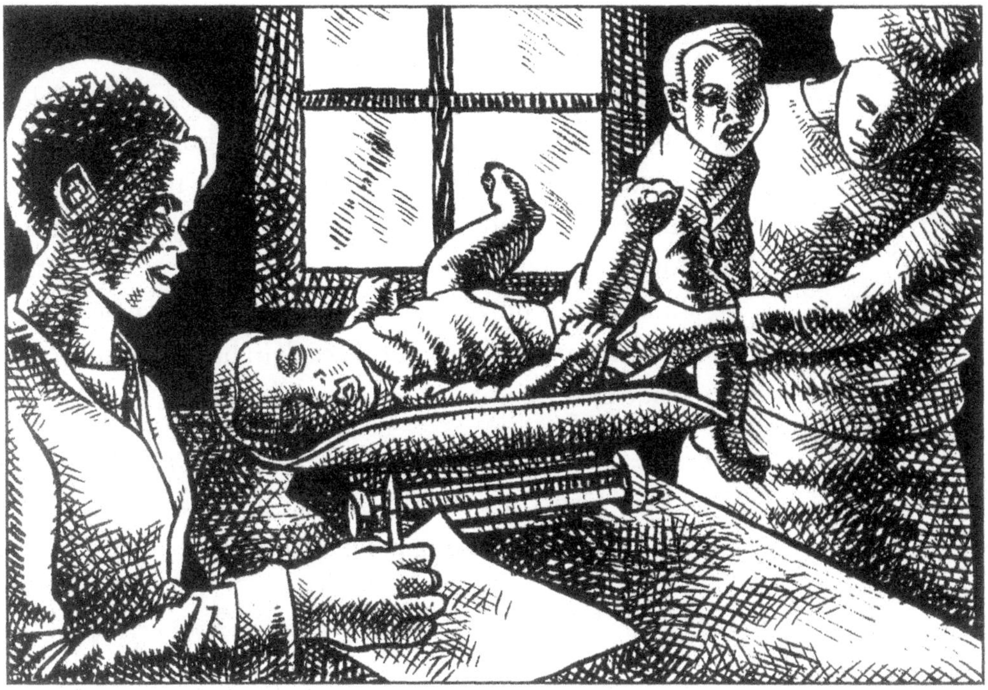

5.4.3 The right to make decisions on reproduction

See above para 4.3.4.

5.4.4 The right of prisoners to adequate medical treatment

prisoners have the same health rights as other patients in hospitals

The meaning of the right of prisoners to adequate medical treatment was tested by the Cape High Court in *B v Minister of Correctional Services* (1997). The applicants, a group of four convicted prisoners who were living with HIV, applied for anti-retroviral medication at state expense under the right to adequate medical treatment. The Department of Correctional Services refused to give them treatment, arguing that prisoners did not have greater rights than other patients at state hospitals who were generally not receiving this treatment, and that the drug for HIV was too expensive.

prisoners have the right to adequate medical treatment

The court decided that:

1. The Constitution did not give prisoners a right to the best medical treatment, but the treatment must be adequate.
2. The meaning of the right to adequate treatment has to be linked to what the state can afford.
3. The state had not proved that, due to budgetary constraints, it could not afford to provide the prisoners with the treatment they claimed.
4. Two of the prisoners living with HIV had a right to get the anti-retroviral treatment at state expense because their infection had developed to a stage where internationally accepted medical standards considered the therapy to be necessary, and this treatment had been prescribed for these prisoners on medical grounds.

government ordered to implement treatment plan for HIV-positive prisoners

In *N v Government of the Republic of South Africa* (2006) prisoners living with HIV in the Westville Correctional Centre challenged the slow implementation of the government's plan to provide ARVs to prisoners living with HIV. The Durban High Court held that the Correctional Centre must:

1. Immediately remove all restrictions that prevented prisoners who needed ARVs from accessing them;
2. Immediately provide all the applicants in the case with access to ARVs; and
3. Submit a plan to the court to explain how it would comply with the orders made by the court.

The state appealed against the above judgment to a full bench of the KwaZulu-Natal High Court, which dismissed the appeal and ordered the state without delay to implement the original court orders.

5.4.5 Privacy and confidentiality

As a general rule, a health care professional may not disclose to any other person information about a patient's health status, treatment or stay in a public or private hospital without the patient's consent.

Case study: Confidentiality and HIV status

Jansen van Vuuren v Kruger (1993)

The decision of the Appellate Division of the Supreme Court (now the Supreme Court of Appeal) in *Jansen van Vuuren v Kruger* ('the *McGeary* case') remains an important one regarding the doctor's duty to respect confidentiality about his or her patient's health status.

doctor sued for disclosing HIV status to other health practitioners while playing golf

Mr McGeary wanted to apply for a life insurance policy. The insurance company required an HIV test first. Mr McGeary was tested and was later informed by his doctor (Dr Kruger) that he was HIV positive. The following day, Dr Kruger played golf with another doctor and dentist. During the game, Dr Kruger disclosed to his colleagues that Mr McGeary had tested positive. Within days, the news spread all over the community. Mr McGeary brought an action against Dr Kruger for breach of confidentiality or privacy.

The Appellate Division said that:

1. Dr Kruger had not respected Mr McGeary's right to privacy or confidentiality, especially the doctor–patient relationship.
2. Dr Kruger had no duty to give the information to his colleagues, who also had no right to receive such information.
3. Mr McGeary died of HIV-related illnesses during the trial and Dr Kruger was ordered to pay compensation of R5 000 to Mr McGeary's estate.

5.4.5.1 Ethical guidelines on HIV/AIDS

According to the *Ethical Guidelines on HIV/AIDS* (1995), the doctor is only allowed to disclose HIV-related information when:

right to privacy and confidentiality upheld

1. The patient consents;
2. A court order or any law says there must be disclosure (eg the limited disclosure allowed under the Criminal Law (Sexual Offences and Related Matters) Amendment Act of 2007 which provides for court ordered HIV testing of alleged sexual offenders); or
3. If the spouse or partner of the person with HIV is at risk and where, even after repeated counselling, the person with HIV refuses to tell the partner. In such circumstances, the doctor is disclosing the information only to protect the partner.

circumstances where it is permissible to disclose

4. The doctor may only tell the partner who is an identifiable sexual partner and only once he has told the patient that she or he will do so after the patient has refused to do so after counselling by the doctor.

5.4.6 Full knowledge and consent ('informed consent')

consent must be free and voluntary

No person may be tested, treated or undergo any other medical procedure without his or her consent. The consent must be given freely and voluntarily after a detailed explanation on the health status and procedure is given (the range of options, the benefits, risks, costs and consequences of each option). Likewise, if a person participates in a research and training study, he or she must be fully informed of his or her rights and the risks as well as the benefits involved in participating in such a study. This is called an 'informed consent'.

5.4.6.1 The meaning of 'informed consent'

According to the Cape High Court case of *Castell v DeGreef* (1994) an 'informed consent' under common law means that:

informed consent means knowledge, appreciation and consent

1. The patient has knowledge of the nature or extent of the harm or risk;
2. The patient appreciates and understands the nature of the harm or risk;
3. The patient has consented to the harm or assumed the risk; and

4. The patient's consent covers everything – all the procedures and their results.

In addition the person giving the consent must be legally capable of doing so (ie not a minor or insane person).

patients must be given information about health status, procedures, benefits, risks, costs and right to refuse treatment

The National Health Act of 2003 requires that the following information must be given to patients to enable them to give an informed consent:

1. The patient's health status – except where it would be against the best interests of the patient;
2. The types of procedures that can be used to find out what is wrong with the patient and the different methods of treatment available to the patient;
3. The benefits, risks, costs and consequences generally associated with each of the methods mentioned above; and
4. The patient's right to refuse health services – including an explanation of the implications, risks and obligations regarding such refusal.

simple language

The health providers are required to inform the patient in a language that the patient understands and in a manner that takes into account the patient's level of literacy.

Problem 3: Was an 'informed consent' obtained?

Questions

Consider the following case and decide whether the patient concerned gave an 'informed consent':

the patient's leg is cut off

A patient consents to having an anaesthetic to put him to sleep and to the doctor operating on him to find out if there is anything wrong with his leg. The doctor finds that he has a cancer in his leg, which, if the leg is not removed, will result in the patient dying after six months. Without waking up the patient to discuss the matter further, the doctor cuts off the patient's leg.

5.4.6.2 Exceptions to the 'informed consent' rule

sudden emergency

There are exceptions to the rule of 'informed consent'. The most common example is where there is a sudden medical emergency (see above para 5.4.2.1)

exceptions to informed consent

Another example of where a health care worker does not have to get an 'informed consent' is when an HIV test is required:

1. In emergency situations where the medical treatment is extremely important to save the patient's life, for example where the patient is unaware of the treatment required because he or she is unconscious;
2. For testing done on blood donations;
3. If a patient is mentally ill and there is no other legally entitled person to give consent;
4. If the test is done anonymously for research purposes to find out how HIV is spreading; and

5. If a patient is tested after a needlestick injury (this should be done with consent; otherwise existing blood samples should be used).

5.4.6.3 Consent by children

the Children's Act has special provisions for consent to medical treatment by children

special provisions for consent by children

The Children's Act of 2005 makes special provision for consent by children for medical treatment and surgical operations, HIV testing and contraception. Consent to male circumcision is also governed by the Children's Act. The Choice on Termination of Pregnancy Act provides that a female of any age (including children) may consent to an abortion provided that she is mature enough to give an 'informed consent':

'of sufficient maturity'

Legal age of consent by children for medical treatment and surgical operations	
Procedure	**Age at which children can legally consent**
Medical treatment	12 years and are 'of sufficient maturity'
Surgical operation	12 years and are 'of sufficient maturity' and assisted by a parent or guardian
HIV testing	12 years
Contraception	12 years
Termination of pregnancy	Any age
Male circumcision	16 years

Notes:
1. *'Of sufficient maturity'*: The term 'of sufficient maturity' is linked to the child also having 'the mental capacity to understand the benefits and risks, and social and other implications' of the medical treatment or surgical operation (see above para 5.4.6.1).
2. *Informed consent*: In all the above instances the child must be able to give an informed consent, which means that the child (a) knows the nature and extent of the harm or risk; (b) appreciates and understands the nature of the harm or risk; (c) consents to the harm or assumed risk; and (d) the child's consent is comprehensive and extends to the entire transaction, including its consequences (see above para 5.4.6.1).
(Source: Dhai A & McQuoid-Mason D *Bioethics, Human Rights and Health Law: Principles and Practice* (2011)).

Problem 4: Are the children able to consent to or refuse the blood transfusions?

Questions

Would the following children be able to consent to or refuse the blood transfusions mentioned?

1. A 15-year-old refuses to have a lifesaving blood transfusion for religious reasons. His parents support his decision. What should the doctors do?
2. A 13-year-old wants to have a blood transfusion to save her life. Her parents refuse to give consent on religious grounds. What should the doctor do?
3. A 12-year-old girl undergoing a termination of pregnancy without her parents' consent requires a blood transfusion. She consents to the transfusion and does not want her parents to know. What should the doctors do?
4. A 16-year-old consents to an operation but says that he does not want any blood transfusions for religious reasons. An emergency arises and he urgently requires blood to save his life. What should the doctors do?

5.4.7 The Patients' Rights Charter

The Patients' Rights Charter

A patient's rights

1. The right to a healthy and safe environment.
2. The right to participate in decision-making on health policies and issues affecting one's heath.
3. The right of access to health care services, including receiving timely emergency care (regardless of one's ability to pay), treatment and rehabilitation, provision for the special health needs of vulnerable groups, counselling without discrimination, a positive attitude by health care workers and the necessary health information in a language understood by the patient.
4. Adequate information about one's health insurance and/or medical aid scheme.
5. The right to choose a particular health facility for treatment.
6. The right to be treated by a named health care provider.
7. The right to privacy and confidentiality.
8. Informed consent – the right to be given full and accurate information so that you can make a decision on testing or treatment.
9. The right to refuse treatment as long as this refusal does not endanger the health of others.
10. The right to be referred for a second opinion.
11. The right not to be abandoned by a health care worker.
12. The right to complain about health care and have these complaints investigated, and to receive a full report of the investigation.

A patient's responsibilities

1. To take care of one's own health.
2. To care for and protect the environment.
3. To respect the rights of other patients, health care workers and health care providers.
4. To use the health care system fully and not to abuse it.
5. To know local health services and what they offer.
6. To provide health workers with relevant and accurate information for diagnostic, treatment rehabilitation or counselling purposes.
7. To advise the health providers of the patient's wishes before he or she dies.
8. To follow the prescribed treatment and or rehabilitation procedures.
9. To enquire about related costs of treatment and or rehabilitation, and to arrange to make payment for these.
10. To take care of health records in a patient's possession.

(Source: Liebenberg S & Pillay K (eds) *Socio-Economic Rights in South Africa: A Resource Book* (2000), p 242)

5.4.8 Termination of pregnancy

The Choice on Termination of Pregnancy Act of 1996 provides that a pregnancy may be terminated by a female of any age:

1. Upon the request of the girl or woman during the first 12 weeks of her pregnancy.
2. From the 13th up to and including the 20th week of her pregnancy if a doctor, after speaking with the pregnant person, thinks that:
   - The continued pregnancy would pose a risk of injury to the person's physical or mental health; or
   - There is a great risk that the unborn baby would suffer from a serious physical or mental defect; or
   - The pregnancy resulted from rape (see above para 2.3.1) or incest (see above para 2.8.1); or
   - The continued pregnancy would seriously affect the social or economic position of the woman.
3. After the 20th week of the pregnancy if a doctor, after speaking with another doctor or a registered midwife, thinks that the continued pregnancy:
   - Would endanger the woman's life;
   - Would result in a serious defect in the unborn baby; or
   - Would pose a risk of injury to the unborn baby.

The termination of a pregnancy may only be done by a doctor or, during the first 12 weeks, by a properly trained registered midwife, and may only be done in a place approved by the Minister of Health.

A girl of any age can consent to a termination of pregnancy and does not need her parents' permission – provided she is mature enough to give an informed consent (see above para 5.4.6.1).

Special provisions in the Termination of Pregnancy Act deal with terminations of pregnancies for people who are mentally disabled.

Problem 5: Does the person qualify for a legal termination of pregnancy?

Questions

Would the following girls or women qualify for a legal termination of pregnancy?

1. A 12-year-old girl is 6 weeks pregnant and asks a midwife to terminate her pregnancy without her parents knowing.
2. A 22-year-old woman who is 15 weeks pregnant asks her doctor to terminate her pregnancy so that she can continue with her modelling career.
3. A 13-year-old schoolgirl who is 17 weeks pregnant asks her doctor to terminate her pregnancy.
4. A 40-year-old woman who is 23 weeks pregnant is told that her baby will be born with mental and physical defects and asks her doctor to terminate her pregnancy.
5. A 15-year-old girl who is 21 weeks pregnant after being raped by her uncle asks her doctor to terminate her pregnancy.

5.4.9 Sterilisation

sterilisation is a medical operation to make a person incapable of having children

Sterilisation is a medical operation to make a person incapable of having children. Everyone has the right to decide whether they want to have children or not. If a person chooses to be sterilised, the hospital must respect that person's decision.

A married person does not need to discuss his or her decision to be sterilised with his or her partner or get the partner's consent.

5.4.9.1 General principles regarding sterilisation

a person must be 18 or older

In order for a woman to have a sterilisation, the following conditions apply:

1. A person must be 18 or older to consent to sterilisation on his or her own.
2. As sterilisation is a medical operation, a person under 18 must have the consent of his or her parents or legal guardian before a hospital will agree to sterilise him or her.
3. The law also allows for the sterilisation of a person with severe mental disability provided their parents, spouse, guardian or close relatives and the hospital also agree.

5.4.10 Protecting against the harmful effects of tobacco on health

prohibition of smoking in public places

The Tobacco Products Control Act of 1993 deals with the harmful effect of tobacco on the health of people. The law prohibits people from smoking in certain places. It also prohibits tobacco companies from:

1. Advertising and promoting tobacco; and
2. Distributing tobacco for free.

5.4.11 Medical schemes

Medical Schemes Act

Medical schemes are governed by the Medical Schemes Act of 1998. The Act protects the interests of members of medical schemes by setting out guidelines on the terms and conditions for membership of schemes. The Act prohibits:

1. Unfair discrimination on a number of grounds; and
2. Risk rating – that is, making people pay more because they are seen as being at higher risk (eg people living with HIV or AIDS).

What is fair and unfair discrimination?

The Constitution declares that certain acts of discrimination may be considered fair and others not. It is fair discrimination if the government implements a policy which provides access to certain opportunities first, or is aimed at redressing the racial discrimination of the past, to the previously disadvantaged groups (Africans, coloureds and Indians).

The Act also says that what people have to pay (premiums) to medical schemes must:

1. Be based on the income and the number of dependants of the medical scheme applicant or holder; and
2. Not be based on any other grounds such as sex, or past or present state of health of the applicant or his or her dependants.

'late joiners'

The Act imposes penalties on 'late joiners' of a scheme. A 'late joiner' refers to an applicant or dependant of the applicant who, at the date of applying for membership, is 40 years or older and has not been a member of another medical scheme during the period of two years before applying for membership. Penalties are set out in the Regulations to the Act. Penalties may include payment of higher premiums.

5.4.11.1 How do medical aid schemes work?

Different medical aid schemes work in different ways. For example, some medical aid schemes cover a member for 80%–100% of the doctor's fees for any treatment. In cases where the scheme does not pay the full amount, the patient will have to pay the rest.

medical aid schemes cover a number of health-related visits to the doctor

Medical aid schemes cover a number of health-related visits to the doctor, including those related to eye and teeth check-ups, pregnancy etc. They also cover hospital fees such as accommodation and medical treatment. However, most medical schemes will pay the hospital fees up to a certain amount.

all private hospitals costs may not be covered

If a person chooses to go to a private hospital, which is more expensive, the medical aid scheme may not cover all hospital fees. It may only pay the amount that the patient would have paid had the person gone to a public hospital.

Patients should find out whether the doctor is 'contracted out' before choosing their doctor. Medical aid schemes cover people who are ill and injured. They do not normally include 'cosmetic surgery' to improve one's looks (eg treatment for lifting a person's breasts or buttocks, or an operation to lift a person's face or stomach).

5.4.11.2 How do you claim under a medical aid scheme?

procedures for claiming under medical aid

There are different procedures for claiming under different medical aid schemes. Depending on the rules:

1. A patient may be able to claim directly by sending the doctor's medical accounts to the medical aid society (or it may be done by the doctor for the patient) if the fees have been charged at the normal rates.
2. A patient may send a claim form with the account, and the medical aid scheme will then pay the hospital or doctor what the patient is owes.
3. A patient may pay the medical doctor or hospital and then claim from the medical aid scheme. This often happens in the case of doctors who are 'contracted out'.
4. A patient must send his or her claim as soon as the account is received.
5. A medical aid scheme may refuse to pay, or reduce the amount that it will pay. For example, many schemes limit the amount that can be claimed for teeth or spectacles in a year, or the time that may be spent in hospitals. Medical schemes may refuse to pay for certain treatment because these drugs are not yet included in the 'prescribed minimum benefits'.
6. Some medical schemes set the amount that can be claimed for different types of treatment during the first year of the scheme.

'prescribed minimum benefits'

many private doctors 'contract out' of medical scheme rates

'contracted out'

7. Many private doctors 'contract out' of the medical scheme rates and their patients are then responsible for paying the full amount to the doctor and then claiming from their medical aid scheme for the amount that the scheme will pay, which is usually much less than what the 'contracted out' doctor charges.

Problem 6: Some questions on medical aid schemes

Questions

1. Does your family belong to a medical aid scheme? If so, how much of the family's medical and hospital expenses does it cover?
2. Do you think that all employers should provide their workers with medical aid? Give reasons for your answer.
3. What happens if medical aid patients choose to consult doctors who have 'contracted out'? How much will the medical aid scheme pay? What might happen if a patient wishes to stay in a private hospital? How much will the medical aid scheme usually pay?
4. What are some of the ways a person may claim from a medical aid scheme?
5. What kinds of limits may be placed on claims against medical aid schemes?
6. Should the state provide free medical aid for everyone or only for the poor? Give reasons for your answer.

5.4.12 How to lay a complaint against health professionals

complaints to HPCSA and SANC

Complaints can be made to the following professional health councils:

1. The Health Professionals Council of South Africa (HPCSA) for medical practitioners, doctors, psychologists, etc; and
2. The South African Nursing Council (SANC), which oversees the training and conduct of nurses.

complaints to Public Protector and Department of Health

In the case of general health workers, complaints can also be made to the nearest offices of the Public Protector or the Department of Health (especially in the case of a health authority's refusal to treat a patient).

5.4.12.1 General guidelines on making complaints

The complaints should be in writing and must give the following details:

1. The name of the complainant;
2. The nature of the complaint;
3. The date and place of the incident; and
4. How the incident happened.

5.4.13 People who cannot afford to pay for medical treatment

affordable and free health care services

No one may be denied access to medical treatment at a public hospital or health clinic simply because he or she cannot afford to pay for it. The right of access to health care services also means that such services must not only be within the reach of the people, but they must also be affordable. Therefore, everyone who is sick and cannot afford medical treatment may approach a public hospital or health clinic for medical attention at state expense. The same applies to people who need dental care.

it is not necessary to remove your own teeth – they may be removed at a hospital or by a private dentist

Most community health care clinics and public hospitals provide free health care services to pregnant and lactating women (women who are breastfeeding) and children, as well as the elderly who cannot afford to pay for their medical treatment.

Problem 7: Do they qualify for free medical treatment?

Questions

1. An old-age pensioner who is 80 years old.
2. Shaida is expecting a baby and requires medical treatment. She cannot afford a doctor.
3. Tembu lives in a rural area and his leg is crushed in an accident in a remote forest. He needs to be transported to a hospital 100 km away but does not have the money for a bus or taxi.
4. Petrus worked in the coal mines for 15 years and suffers from a lung disease. He cannot afford a doctor. What should he do?
5. Thandi is 6 years old and lives with her grandmother who is a pensioner.
6. Daniel has lost all his teeth and needs false teeth.

5.5 Food rights

Outcomes

After completion of this section learners will be able to:

1. Explain the law concerning the right to food.

Assessment criteria

1. The meaning of the right of access to sufficient food is given.
2. Barriers to access to food are identified.
3. Different departments that are responsible for realising the right to food are identified.
4. A set of facts is examined and decision made on whether certain groups of people and their families qualify for free food from the state.

5.5.1 Why is it important to understand food rights?

food needed for survival and healthy development

Everyone needs food to survive, to perform physical activities (eg work), to interact with others, to participate in social and political activities, to prevent infectious diseases and to live a decent life. People without food often find themselves begging for food in the street. This undermines their right to human dignity. They need to be able to get food through their own efforts such as working.

households unable to afford basic subsistence food

Many people in South Africa are poor and cannot afford basic household needs. Some families go hungry every day including going to bed without food, and some do not have enough food to prevent starvation. Children, women, people with disabilities and the elderly are the groups most vulnerable to hunger and malnutrition.

The Constitution protects the right to food in three ways. It protects (a) the right of everyone to have access to sufficient food; (b) the right of children to basic nutrition; and (c) the right of prisoners to adequate nutrition. The state must take reasonable legislative measures to ensure access to food for all South Africans.

access means ability to produce food

The right to food means that people are entitled to produce or obtain food for themselves through work or other income-generating activities, access to productive land, social welfare benefits, etc. It also means that food should be provided to people who have no means of producing or getting food for themselves.

assistance to households with hungry children

The right of 'access' to food means that the state does not have to give everyone food, but must make it possible for people to access food for themselves. The state must ensure that people have access to food over a period of time, subject to available resources. The right to food for children and prisoners is given special protection under the Constitution because they are not in a position to provide food for themselves. The main duty to provide food for children lies with their parents and families.

The state has a duty to provide food to children whose parents cannot afford to do so and to children who do not have, or have been abandoned by their parents and families. For example, the state has a duty to assist orphans or child-headed households who need food or have other basic needs. It also has a duty to provide food to prisoners.

Problem 1: 'I am nothing – I am just a person of God'

Joyce lives in a small rural community in Limpopo. She takes care of both her son and her daughter's children. She has no job and receives no income from relatives living in urban areas. Instead, she derives a very small income from building other people's houses. Her granddaughters also earn money by collecting wood, which they sell for R10 a bundle. The girls are usually out from 06h00 to midday, as the wood is heavy and they cannot carry much at a time. Fetching for their own use and for selling means that they usually go three or four times a week. The wood collecting has already paid for one son's school fees.

Unlike some others, Joyce has no land to plough and no livestock. 'I am nothing – I am just a person of God. My biggest problem is to have enough food for my children.' Joyce has been told that she does not qualify for free mealie meal and soup from Operation Hunger, as the food is only available to orphans.

(Source: NGO Matter, (March 1998) in Liebenberg S & Pillay K (eds) *Socio-Economic Rights in South Africa: A Resource Book* (2000), p 259)

Questions

1. Should the government help Joyce and her family? If not, what kind of assistance should Joyce get from the government or who should help?
2. Does the fact that Joyce has children mean that she is entitled to assistance from the state immediately? If not, does it mean that Joyce should wait for a government programme that provides food in her community?
3. Why do you think people do not have access to food?
4. What rights are linked to the right to food?
5. What do you think the government should do to address hunger and malnutrition amongst children?

5.5.2 What does the right of access to sufficient food mean?

basic amount of food to prevent hunger

The Constitution speaks of 'sufficient food', 'basic nutrition' and 'adequate nutrition'. These words are said to refer to one and the same standard, that is the quantity of food. Everyone must have access to the basic amount of food necessary to prevent hunger.

quality of food to live a healthy and dignified life

Not only should people have a basic amount of food and not go hungry, they must also have access to quality food to prevent vulnerability from diseases. The food people eat should have an adequate mixture of nutrients. It should also be fresh and without harmful substances to enable a person to live a healthy and dignified life.

food must be acceptable to different groups

Further, different groups of people eat different types of food. To be 'adequate', food must not only be sufficient, safe and nutritious, but also be acceptable to those who eat it. For example, a popular meal among African people is mealie meal. Hindu people are not allowed to eat meat. Food must also be culturally and traditionally acceptable to meet the needs of different peoples. It should also be acceptable to meet the special food needs of people such as children, pregnant women, and breastfeeding mothers and people who are ill and elderly.

people who are ill and elderly may need special food

Problem 2: A debate on food security in South Africa

Questions

Government often argues that the right to food is a difficult right to implement because many people are poor, and food insecurity is just one example of this bigger problem. Do you agree with this statement? In two groups, debate the arguments in favour of and against this statement.

5.5.3 What are the common barriers to access to adequate food?

There are many factors that make it difficult for people to have access to sufficient food. People's needs in respect of access to food vary according to their socio-economic conditions:

joblessness and lack of access to resources

1. People do not have access to resources such as land to produce food; jobs or self-employment to generate income to buy food; or any form of financial assistance (eg social grants) to buy food.

impact of HIV on access to food

2. With the toll of HIV/AIDS, many households are affected as their adult family members get sicker and are unable to undertake paid work.

price hike in basic foodstuffs

difficulties in accessing social grants

3. Prices of food are increasing at an alarming rate. The effect of VAT on basic foodstuffs such as bread, sugar, tea, mealie meal, etc is huge. Many poor families cannot afford to buy these basic items.
4. People find it difficult to access social grants and social relief-of-distress funds (see above para 5.3.5.2).
5. The food distribution system often does not reach those who need food the most. It ends up in government warehouses or is illegally taken by the officials responsible for distributing it.
6. Food is often stored for a longer period of time than it is supposed to be, thus resulting in people getting rotten or contaminated food.

Problem 3: Some questions on barriers to sufficient food

Questions

1. Can you think of other reasons why people do not have access to adequate food?
2. Can you think of typical examples of violations of the right to food? What is the role of the state in these examples? Try and provide real life examples.

5.5.4 What food programmes have been implemented?

There are various departments of government that are responsible for realising the right of access to food. These are the Departments of Agriculture, Health, Social Development, and Trade and Industry. These departments run different programmes, some jointly, and some separately, to realise the right to food. These programmes are directed at specific groups of people who face difficulties with access to food.

5.5.4.1 Providing access to opportunities

the Land Bank provides loans for small farmers.

assistance to small farmers

The Department of Agriculture runs programmes that aim to enable people to become farmers in order to produce food for themselves. These are:

1. The Land Bank loan programme makes it possible for previously disadvantaged groups to apply to the Land Bank for loans to assist them in establishing small farming operations.
2. The Department of Agriculture has a programme that helps people who want to start small gardens.

5.5.4.2 Promoting access to adequate food

access to nutrition

The Departments of Health and Education initiated the National School Nutrition Programme aimed at teaching children how to use food effectively and safely. The Department of Health also runs the Integrated Nutrition Programme that seeks to show communities how to improve their own access to nutrition.

5.5.4.3 Providing food

snacks to children in school

The Department of Education, through its Primary School Feeding Scheme originally run by the Department of Health, provides snacks to children every day in certain schools that have been identified as having children in need of adequate food.

> School feeding schemes have been running in more than 15 000 schools. They have reached more than 5 million children.

nutritional supplements for children affected by malnutrition

The Department of Health, through its Infant and Young Child Feeding Scheme, provides nutritional aid to infants at hospitals. For example, children who are affected by malnutrition and end up in hospital can get food through this programme.

The Department of Social Development adopts various ways of providing food to people. It gives social grants to a large number of people (see above para 5.3.3). It also provides cash benefits and food parcels through its Poverty Relief Programme and the Emergency Food Scheme. These programmes are aimed at reducing hunger in certain households and communities. The Department normally uses statistics to determine who will get the food packages. However, any person can assist the government by informing the Department about neighbours who are affected by hunger and malnutrition. This can also be done through organised community structures that are often involved with Department officials in identifying food insecure households. People can also apply for a social relief of distress grant to the Director-General of the Department of Social Development (see above para 5.3.5.2.8).

emergency food schemes

Information on emergency food schemes can be obtained from the Department of Social Development through a toll-free number which the Department announces every time such a programme is about to be implemented. The announcements are made in newspapers and TV programmes, or details can be obtained from the nearest local authority.

Problem 4: What food programmes exist in your area?

Questions

1. Do you know any of the programmes that provide food directly to households?
2. Are these programmes implemented in your area? If so, how?
3. Are there any shortcomings in their implementation?
4. Who is targeted? Do you think the programmes benefit all those who are targeted?
5. Are there households in your area that you think should receive food and who do not? Explain why you think they should benefit.

5.6 Housing rights

Outcomes

After completion of this section learners will be able to:

1. Explain the law regarding access to adequate housing.

Assessment criteria

1. The meaning of the right of access to adequate housing is explained.
2. A set of facts is examined and a decision made on whether or not the people concerned are entitled to be provided with housing by the state.
3. The laws governing evictions are identified and explained.
4. A set of facts is examined and a decision made on whether the landlord may evict the occupiers.
5. An explanation is given on how to access housing subsidies and housing loans.
6. A set of facts is given and a decision made on which persons qualify for a housing subsidy.
7. A set of facts is given and a decision made on whether the persons concerned qualify for a housing loan.
8. Dishonest ways of buying and selling houses are identified.
9. Sets of facts are given and decisions are made on how people exposed to dishonest ways of buying and selling houses should react.
10. An explanation of the nature, context and effect of a deed of sale is given.
11. An explanation is given on what a mortgage bond is and how to apply for one.
12. The law governing the renting of houses is explained.
13. A decision is made on what people should look for when renting houses.
14. An explanation is given on how to lodge a complaint concerning rental agreements.
15. A set of facts is given and a decision made on the rights and duties of landlords and tenants.
16. A set of facts is given and a decision made on whether to rent or buy a house.

5.6.1 What are housing rights?

all families need housing

Everyone and all families need housing. The Constitution says that everyone has a right of access to adequate housing, and not to be evicted from their homes or have their homes demolished unless it is ordered by a court. It also says that every child has the right to shelter and every prisoner 'has a right to adequate accommodation at state expense'. The government must take reasonable steps to ensure that everyone has access to housing.

apartheid is primarily responsible for homelessness

The problem of homelessness or lack of adequate housing is still a major challenge in South Africa. The previous apartheid laws and policies are responsible for this problem. For example, the Group Areas Act was responsible for evicting many people from their homes without any compensation. Often under apartheid people could not choose where to live

these people were relocated to remote areas and townships on the outskirts of cities or towns designated for black South Africans. They could not choose which neighbourhood they were going to live in. This resulted in inadequate housing for many people. The legacy of the apartheid system puts pressure on the current government to address the problem of inadequate housing and homelessness.

under apartheid black people had to live in townships on the outskirts of cities or towns

The constitutional right of access to adequate housing is a useful tool for people and families who are homeless or live in houses that are inadequate for a decent standard of living.

many laws have been passed to enforce the constitutional right of access to adequate housing

Many laws have been passed that seek to achieve the objectives of this constitutional right.

This section will discuss what the law says about people's entitlements to housing. It will also deal with some of the practical issues for people without homes, with inadequate housing and those who rent or cannot own flats or houses.

5.6.2 What does the right of 'access to adequate housing' mean?

5.6.2.1 Housing Act of 1997

the purpose of the National Housing Act

The Housing Act was passed to fulfil the right of access to adequate housing mentioned in the Constitution. The Housing Act:

1. Abolishes the apartheid discriminatory laws on housing.
2. Removes all apartheid housing structures.
3. Creates a new non-racial system of housing rights for everyone in the country.
4. Defines the roles of the national, provincial and local governments regarding housing.
5. Commits municipalities to take reasonable steps to provide access to adequate housing for all the people in their area over a period of time.
6. Places a duty on municipalities to set housing delivery goals and to identify land for housing developments in their areas.

7. Deals with the basic principles that must guide housing developments.
8. Sets limits for how state-subsidised houses may be sold (eg a state-subsidised house may not be sold to a private buyer within eight years from when it was bought without the house first being offered for sale to the provincial government involved).

duties of private and public developers

The Housing Act defines 'housing developments' and requires private and public developers to provide houses that give residents 'convenient access' to:

1. Economic activities (eg jobs);
2. Health, educational and social facilities;
3. Permanent home structures (ie not shacks that can be removed) with secure possession or ownership, inside and outside privacy, and adequate protection against the weather; and
4. Drinkable water, adequate sanitation and a home energy supply (eg electricity).

Case study: Meaning of the right of access to adequate housing and children's rights to shelter

Government of the Republic of South Africa v Grootboom (2000)

the Constitutional Court had to interpret the meaning of access to adequate housing and children's rights to shelter

In the *Government of the Republic of South Africa v Grootboom*, the Constitutional Court had to interpret the meaning of the constitutional right of access to adequate housing and children's rights to shelter as well as the state's duty in respect of these rights. The case involved about 900 adults and children from Wallacedene who were evicted from the private land they were unlawfully occupying. Following the eviction they camped on a sports field. They applied to the Cape High Court claiming that the state had a duty to provide them with adequate temporary shelter or housing. The High Court ruled in their favour on the basis that the state had a duty to provide shelter (including tents, portable latrines and a regular supply of water) to the children and their parents. The state appealed to the Constitutional Court against the judgment and the Court also ruled in favour of Mrs Grootboom and the children.

Problem 1: The case of the sports field squatters

Questions

1. In small groups, half for Mrs Grootboom and her community, and the other half for the state, prepare arguments which you think could have been presented before the Constitutional Court during the appeal hearing.
2. What was the Constitutional Court's decision in the case?
3. Assuming the state provided you and your family with a house, what would you expect to get in order to consider it 'an adequate house'?
   (a) What type of house?

(b) How much should it cost?
(c) What size should the house be?
(d) What quality of building materials should be used?
(e) Where should it be?
(f) What other factors should be considered when deciding what the standard of an adequate house is?

5.6.3 What does the right to protection against arbitrary eviction mean?

Arbitrary eviction means removing people from their homes without a court order. The Constitution says that no one can be evicted from their homes or have their property demolished without an order of court made after all relevant circumstances have been considered. The laws governing evictions are the Extension of Security of Tenure Act of 1997 (ESTA) and the Prevention of Illegal Eviction from and the Unlawful Occupation of Land Act of 1998 (PIE).

people may not be evicted from their homes without a court order

5.6.3.1 Extension of Security of Tenure Act of 1997 (ESTA)

security of tenure

ESTA prohibits unfair evictions, provides security of tenure, and protects against arbitrary eviction for people in rural and peri-urban areas. It is aimed at protecting 'occupiers'.

protection against arbitrary eviction

definition of 'occupier' under ESTA

An 'occupier' is a person living on land belonging to another person and who was on or has since 4 February 1997 been allowed by the owner to continue living on it. The definition does not include the following:

1. A labour tenant under the Land Reform (Labour Tenants) Act;

2. A person using or intending to use the land for industrial or commercial purposes; and
3. A person who has an income of more than R5 000 per month.

ESTA also provides two different procedures for evictions:
1. A procedure for people who occupied land before or on 4 February 1997; and
2. A procedure for people who occupied land after 4 February 1997.

5.6.3.1.1 Procedure for evictions of people who were occupiers on or before 4 February 1997

A court may order an eviction of the above persons if the following conditions are satisfied:

court order granted if suitable alternative accommodation is provided

1. The reason for granting the eviction order is that the occupier has done something wrong.
2. A court may still grant an order of eviction if it is satisfied that suitable alternative accommodation is available for the occupier.
3. Such suitable alternative accommodation must be available to the occupier within a period of nine months after the date of termination of their residence and must be found before the person is evicted.
4. The owner or person in charge provided the house where the occupier lives.
5. Other than the above conditions, a court may still make an eviction order if it is convinced that it will be just and equitable to evict, taking into account:
   (a) The efforts of the owner or person in charge to find suitable alternative accommodation; and
   (b) The interests of both sides (eg it would cause more hardship for the owner if the court were not to grant the eviction).

5.6.3.1.2 Procedure for evictions of people who became occupiers after 4 February 1997

A court may order an eviction of the above if the following conditions are satisfied:
1. There was an express and fair agreement between the occupier and the owner or person in charge on the period of occupation, and the court is of the view that it is just and equitable to grant an eviction order.
2. The court believes, after considering all the circumstances, that it is just and equitable to grant an eviction.

just and equitable factors to be taken into account by the court

To determine what is just and equitable, the court will consider:
(a) How long the occupier has lived on the land;
(b) Whether the agreement between the parties was fair;
(c) Whether the occupier can get suitable alternative accommodation;
(d) The reason for the eviction; and
(e) The interests of the owner or person in charge, the occupier and the remaining occupier on the land.

In deciding on the date of the eviction, the court will also consider what is just and equitable from each side.

5.6.3.2 The Prevention of Illegal Eviction from and Unlawful Occupation of Land Act of 1998 (PIE)

prohibition against unlawful evictions of illegal occupiers

Unlike ESTA, which focuses on 'lawful occupiers', PIE prohibits unlawful evictions of 'illegal occupiers'. It provides procedures for evictions of people by an owner or a person in charge, or by an organ of the state.

5.6.3.2.1 Procedure for evictions of unlawful occupiers by an owner or person in charge

occupation for less than six months

If an occupier has unlawfully occupied the land for less than six months at the time of the start of eviction proceedings, the court may grant an eviction order if it considers it just and equitable to do so, after taking into account all relevant circumstances including the rights and needs of such vulnerable groups as the elderly, children, people living with disabilities and women-headed households.

occupation for more than six months

If an occupier has unlawfully occupied the land for more than six months at the time of the start of eviction proceedings, the court may grant an eviction order if it thinks that is just and equitable, after considering the following circumstances:

1. Whether land has been made available, or can reasonably be made available, by a landowner for the relocation of the unlawful occupier; and
2. The rights of the elderly, children, people living with disabilities and women-headed households.

Case study: Illegal occupation of privately owned land by squatters

people squatted on land owned by Modderklip Boerdery

President of the Republic of South Africa v Modderklip Boerdery (Pty) Ltd (2005)

In *President of the Republic of South Africa v Modderklip Boerdery (Pty) Ltd* about 40 000 people had squatted on land owned by Modderklip Boerdery because of overcrowding and shortage of land in the nearby Daveyton and Chris Hani informal settlements. Despite a court order authorising their evictions, the law enforcement agencies of the state would not help with the eviction. The owners appealed to the Constitutional Court to compel the law enforcement agencies to assist with the evictions.

the state must provide alternative accommodation

private landowners awarded damages

The Constitutional Court held:
1. It was unreasonable for the state to force the private landowners to carry the state's burden of providing the occupiers with accommodation.
2. The unlawful occupiers were entitled to occupy the land until alternative land was made available to them by the state, or by a provincial or local authority.
3. In the meantime the private landowners also deserved protection and could be awarded damages.

Problem 2: The case of the farmland squatters

Questions

Given the facts of the case in the *Modderklip Boerdery* case, divide into groups representing (a) the lawyers for the government; (b) the lawyers for Modderklip Boerdery; and (c) judges in the court. Subdivide the large groups into small groups in order to prepare their roles. Lawyers should prepare their arguments, and judges their judgments.
1. Present arguments as lawyers for the government.
2. Present arguments as lawyers for Modderklip Boerdery.
3. Give judgments as judges.

5.6.3.2.2 Procedure for evictions of unlawful occupiers by an organ of the state

when the court will grant an eviction order

A court may grant an eviction order to remove unlawful occupiers of state land if:
1. It is of the view that this is just and equitable after considering all the relevant circumstances;
2. The unlawful occupier is occupying land without the consent of an organ of state where this consent is needed; and
3. It is in the public interest to grant the eviction order.

just and equitable factors

In deciding what is just and equitable, a court will consider:
1. The circumstances in which the unlawful occupier occupied the land and erected the building or structure;
2. The period that the unlawful occupiers and their families have lived on the land; and
3. The availability of suitable alternative accommodation or land.

5.6.4 How is the right of access to adequate housing being implemented?

5.6.4.1 The housing subsidy scheme

types of housing subsidies

The South African government introduced the housing subsidy scheme in 1995 to address the problem of lack of access to adequate housing. This scheme provides the following types of subsidies:

consolidation subsidies

individual ownership subsidies

project-linked subsidies

institutional subsidies

rural subsidies

1. *Consolidation subsidies* provide people who have already received state housing assistance with financial assistance to improve the standard and quality of their houses.
2. *Individual ownership* subsidies allow people to purchase a site and build their own house.
3. *Project-linked subsidies* allow individuals to own houses in projects that are approved by the Provincial Housing Board.
4. *Institutional subsidies* are available to institutions and agents that build affordable houses for individuals.
5. *Rural subsidies* are for people who enjoy only tenure – not ownership – rights to the state land they occupy.

Housing subsidies vary in amounts. The housing subsidy scheme provides beneficiaries with a set amount of 15% or more in areas where people experience natural, difficult conditions, such as the Western Cape where beneficiaries get an additional amount because of the water table problem.

5.6.4.2 Who qualifies for a housing subsidy scheme?

conditions for qualifying for the housing subsidy scheme

To qualify for the scheme, a person must:

1. Be a South African citizen;
2. Be 21 years or older;
3. Have a total household monthly income that falls within the means test;
4. Be part of a married couple, or a single person living together with another as a couple, or a single person with one or more dependants;
5. Not have received a housing subsidy previously; and
6. Not own or have owned property in South Africa.

People wishing to apply for the housing subsidy scheme must fill in the forms which are available at the nearest office of the Department of Housing. All applications are checked, approved or rejected and recorded on a National Database.

Problem 3: Do the people qualify for a housing subsidy scheme?

Questions

Consider the following cases and decide whether the person(s) involved can qualify for a housing subsidy scheme. Give reasons for your answer.

1. Gerald Smith has been paying for his home for the past seven years. He is now insolvent and cannot afford to continue with the payments. He has also been in arrears for more than three months. He is about to be evicted from the house. Does he qualify for a subsidy?

Mondi is permanently disabled

2. The Motene family have recently been involved in a tragic accident which resulted in their 25-year-old son, Mondi, being permanently disabled. They own a small home. With their poor background, they cannot afford to upgrade the house to suit Mondi's disability needs. Do they qualify for a housing subsidy? Give reasons for your answer.

5.6.4.2.1 Emergency housing

assistance for rural or urban people with urgent housing problems

The Emergency Housing Programme was set up in 2004 after the *Grootboom* case. The Programme assists people in rural and urban areas who have urgent housing problems due to such things as disasters, evictions, threatened evictions, demolition, displacements or immediate threats to life, health or safety.

grants made to municipalities

Grants are made to municipalities to allow them to help people during emergencies by providing land, municipal services, infrastructure and shelter. The people involved may agree to be relocated or settled but cannot be forced to do so. People who receive emergency housing may later apply for permanent housing subsidies under the Housing Subsidy Scheme if they qualify.

5.6.4.2.2 Social housing policy

available for people with low-to-medium incomes

The social housing policy was introduced in 2004 and is aimed at providing housing opportunities on a large scale for everyone in South Africa. Social housing is available from housing institutions for people with low-to-medium incomes, but does not allow for immediate individual ownership. Applicants can choose different tenure options such as cooperative housing and instalment sales.

5.6.4.3 Obtaining a loan or accessing credits

cheaper ways of paying off the loan

The cheapest way to buy a home is to pay for it in cash. If you pay cash for a home you do not have to pay interest or finance charges. Most people, however, do not have large sums of money and usually have to borrow money in order to pay for a home. When a person has obtained a loan for a home, it is cheaper to pay off as much as possible with a high deposit and monthly instalments as high as possible because the buyer will save a lot on interest. The monthly instalments should not, however, take up more than 25% of the buyer's monthly income.

calculating expenses

When calculating the amount to be paid for the home, the buyer should take into account extra expenses such as transfer duty, insurance costs, inspection fees, stamp duty, rates and taxes as well as conveyancing fees. These should be worked out when deciding what deposit and monthly instalments the buyers can afford.

expenses involved in buying a home

Before a person buys a house, he or she should work out the following expenses involved in buying a home:

1. *Transfer duty, which* is a tax that has to be paid to the state when property is transferred from one person to another.
2. *Insurance premiums* that are usually added to the monthly mortgage bond repayments. Banks require buyers to insure the property to cover its value in case it is damaged or destroyed.
3. *Inspection fees*, which are charged by banks when they inspect the property to decide whether or not to make a mortgage bond loan. However, the inspection does not guarantee that the house is free from defects. Usually if there are defects in the property banks will require them to be repaired before the bond is granted.
4. *Stamp duty*, which is a tax that must be paid to the Receiver of Revenue when a mortgage bond is registered over a property.
5. *Rates and taxes*, which must be paid to the relevant municipality for the period up to the date when the property is sold.
6. *Conveyancing fees*, which are fees payable to the attorney who transfers the property into the name of the buyer and registers the mortgage bond. These fees are governed by regulations.

Problem 4: Edward wants to buy a house

Questions

Edward wants to buy a house for R500 000. He sees a house advertised at that price. What other costs should Edward work out before he will know whether he can afford it?

5.6.4.4 Who qualifies for home loans?

Anyone who is capable of repaying a loan qualifies for a home loan. However, different financial institutions have different criteria and procedures for determining to whom they may lend money. High-income earners do not often have a problem borrowing from these institutions, unless they have been blacklisted by a credit bureau. However, financial institutions are sceptical of lending money to low and medium-income earners because they often experience problems with repayments of their home loan from this group of people. The law attempts to strike a balance between the potential risks of lending money to poor communities for the institutions and the need for everyone to access loans for the purposes of buying a house.

The government has different ways of making it possible for people to gain access to adequate housing. It has created mechanisms for people to get credit (borrow money) to buy houses through a number of laws and by developing various programmes.

5.6.4.5 Laws dealing with home loans

The Home Loan and Mortgage Disclosure Act of 2000 promotes fair lending practices among financial institutions that provide home loans. It encourages banks and other financial institutions that provide home loans to focus on marginalised groups of the population in giving such loans. This Act helps the government to determine the progress of each institution in providing access to credit for the purposes of housing. However, it does not interfere with the institution's business of providing home loans. Thus, the institution can approve or decline a person's application on whatever basis the business practice demands.

Problem 5: Should a home loan be granted?

Questions

1. Joyce and her four children live in an informal settlement in Cato Manor in Durban. She applies for a home loan with Boland Company which gives credit to people for the purposes of housing. She has been told that her application was unsuccessful because Boland considers the place where Joyce and her family live to be 'a high risk area'. In small groups discuss whether a loan should be given to Joyce and give reasons for your answers.
2. Kobus is domestic worker who earns R1 500 per month. The combined household income of Kobus's family comes to R6 000 per month. They have been living in a one-room shack in Khayelitsha. He applies for a home loan with Siyathuthuka Bank. His application is refused because he earns too little and the bank is of the view that he cannot afford to repay the loan. In small groups discuss whether a loan should be given to Kobus and give reasons for your answers.

5.6.4.6 Where can people go to borrow money to buy houses?

5.6.4.6.1 Loans from banks and financial institutions

banks give home loans

One of the best ways of getting a loan to buy a home is through a bank. Banks will lend home buyers money in exchange for a mortgage bond.

banks will lend home buyers money in exchange for a mortgage bond

advantages with banks

The advantages of obtaining a loan from a bank are:

1. The loans are usually for a fixed period of time (eg 20, 25 or 30 years).
2. The rates of interest charged are usually very similar because banks compete with each other to give the most economical rates.
3. People can own homes bought through bank loans even though they have not paid the full purchase price.

Sometimes the interest rates are guaranteed for a year at a time.

other financial institutions normally charge higher rates

Loans from private people and other financial organisations are usually more expensive than those from banks because they charge higher interest rates. Higher rates are charged because the loans are often for shorter periods of time. There is also the danger that a private mortgage bond holder may call up the loan after a shorter period of time.

be careful about special agreements with private people and other organisations

Banks usually try to assist buyers who are in trouble with their payments by increasing the period of the loan and reducing the amount that has to be paid each month. Private people and other financial organisations may be prepared to make special arrangements to assist people in trouble. Buyers, however, should be careful about signing 'special' agreements.

the bank will want to know that the buyer has a good financial record

5.6.4.6.2 Loans from employers

getting subsidies from employers

Some employers give loans to their workers. Others help their workers to get bank loans, or give them a 'subsidy' so that they pay less interest on their loans. This usually applies to workers employed by the state. Whether or not an employer will give a loan to a worker may depend upon: (a) what the worker earns; (b) how long the worker has been with the employer; and (c) whether the worker pays into a pension fund. Employers might also help workers to pay the deposit for a housing loan from a bank. In addition, employers may assist workers by giving them a monthly housing allowance (eg a certain amount each month towards the cost of paying off the house). They may also pay part of the interest charged by the bank. For example, if a worker has to pay a bank 19% interest, the employer might agree to pay 10% of the interest to bring the rate down to 9%.

employers may also help to pay the deposit as part of the loan

full-time employees of the state may get loans and subsidies

People employed by the state can also obtain help in buying homes. This is usually done by guaranteeing workers a housing loan and giving them a monthly subsidy towards the cost of paying off the price of the home. In order to qualify for this help workers usually have to have been employed full-time by the state and to have paid into a public service pension fund for at least one year.

Problem 6: How can employers help workers to buy homes?

Questions

Mr Thami is employed by Good Hope Enterprises. He approaches his employer, Mr Hope, and asks him for a loan to buy a house. Role-play a conversation between Mr Thami and Mr Hope.

5.6.4.6.3 Loans from the government

obtaining loans from the state

There are a number of ways in which the state helps people to buy houses. The state has passed laws that encourage financial institutions providing home loans to cater for the needs of everyone (see above para 5.6.4.5). It has also created state agencies that provide home loans and housing subsidy schemes directly to certain groups of people (especially low and medium-income earners (see above para 5.6.4.1). It has also created an agency that will assist people who are at the risk of losing their homes because they are struggling or cannot repay the loan instalments regularly (in arrears) (see below para 5.6.4.9.2).

5.6.4.7 What does a person need to apply for a home loan?

The following information is important when applying for a loan:

1. The person's identity document;
2. The person's proof of income;
3. The value of the person's assets;
4. Previous records of payment by the person (the person will have to disclose other credits held);
5. The person's record with a credit bureau (if any); and
6. The details of the person's guarantor or surety (eg ID, proof of income, value of assets).

5.6.4.8 What happens if an application for a home loan is unsuccessful?

applicants are entitled to reasons for being unsuccessful

Any financial institution that gives credit to people has the right to approve or refuse the applications. It has to protect its business by considering the financial position of the applicants and not lending money to applicants who may not be able to repay their home loans. An applicant is entitled to be given the reasons for the institution's decision not to approve his or her application.

After a person receives a letter or a phone call informing him or her that his or her application was declined, the person should:

1. Ask for the reasons for such a decision.
2. Ask if there are other alternatives within or outside of the institution that may allow him or her to get the home loan.

5.6.4.9 Other housing initiatives to consider when buying a house

5.6.4.9.1 The National Housing Finance Corporation (NHFC)

NHFC is a development finance institution

The National Housing Finance Corporation (NHFC) is a development finance institution established by the South African government to fund and facilitate the development of affordable housing. NHFC's principal mandate is to broaden and deepen access to affordable housing finance and housing structures for the benefit of the low-to-middle income households.

NHFC provides finance to buy, rent or improve houses

The NHFC is committed to ensuring that every South African with a regular source of income has access to finance to buy, rent or improve their house. The Corporation's goal is to enhance the well-being and quality of life of the low-to-middle income households with the security of a home.

a go-between for buyers and lenders

The NHFC provides assistance to people who are looking to buy a house in the price range between R15 000 to R50 000. It gives loans to people who earn between R1 500 and R15 000 a month and acts as a go-between for buyers and lenders who are prepared to offer loans.

5.6.4.9.2 The National Urban Reconstruction and Housing Agency (NURCHA)

guarantees to banks

The NURCHA provides temporary housing finance to households earning less than R1 500 per month. It also provides guarantees to banks that are prepared to make housing loans to low-income borrowers.

5.6.4.9.3 The People's Housing Process

assist people to build

The People's Housing Process aims to assist people to build and organise building their own housing by accessing housing subsidies and technical, financial, logistical and administrative support. This process is driven by the People's Housing Partnership Trust.

5.6.4.10 Dishonest ways of buying and selling homes

dishonesty in the buying and the selling of homes

The shortage and cost of housing means that many dishonest ways of buying and selling homes are used. These involve dishonest agents, builders, developers and estate agents, as well as unfair written agreements that have special clauses that are not drawn to the attention of consumers. They prey on people because very few can afford to pay cash for their homes.

few people can afford to buy a house for cash

5.6.4.10.1 Dishonest agents

be careful before giving agents money for deposits

Dishonest agents who say they are acting for builders approach people who wish to buy homes. They claim that people can immediately buy a house just by giving them a deposit. People who are not careful give these agents large deposits. The agents sometimes give them receipts for the money paid. The people hear nothing more from the agents, and then find out that they are dishonest people who have disappeared with the deposit.

contact the builder and do not pay a deposit until an agreement is signed

People should always check to make sure that an agent is acting for a builder by contacting the builder. A buyer should never pay money 'as a deposit' until a proper agreement has been signed, and the buyer is sure that the builder or seller is genuine.

Problem 7: Mr Nyathi is asked to pay a deposit

Questions

Mr Nyathi is approached by Mrs Kani who tells him that she is acting for Fast Homes, a building and development company that operates in the townships. Mrs Kani says that if Mr Nyathi pays her a R50 000 deposit she will guarantee that Fast Homes will build him a house within three months.

What should Mr Nyathi do? Role-play a conversation between Mr Nyathi and Mrs Kani.

5.6.4.10.2 Dishonest builders and developers

beware of dishonest builders and developers

Builders and developers sometimes contact people who wish to buy homes and offer to build houses for them if they pay large deposits. The builders and developers then fail to build the houses, and may not even have bought sites to build on. This is either because they never intended to build the houses, or because they have gone insolvent after not paying their debts.

be cautious before paying large deposits to builders or agents

get information regarding the developer or builder

People should always make sure that the builder or developer has a good reputation. A useful way of checking this is to ask the builder or developer to point out houses that they have built and to make sure that they are telling the truth. A better ways is to ask the bank that is helping with a loan to check whether the builder has a good reputation.

5.6.4.10.3 'Easy loans'

beware of 'easy loans'

Builders and developers tell people who wish to buy homes, but do not earn enough money to qualify for bank loans, that they will persuade the bank to make a loan. The builders or developers then falsely fill in bond application forms in which they say that the people who wish to buy the homes have more money than they have. Once the house is built, and the owner starts repaying the loan and he or she cannot keep up with the payments, the house may be taken away by the bank after it has followed certain procedures (see below para 5.6.5.2.1).

dangers of 'easy loans'

People should always make sure that they fill in bond forms properly and do not promise to pay more than 25% of their earnings to the bank each month. If they have to pay back more than 25% of their monthly earnings they are likely to fall behind in their payments and lose their homes.

5.6.4.10.4 Reading agreements before signing them

'fly-by-night' builders

'Fly-by-night' builders approach people with offers to build them houses if they pay deposits. Consumers sign agreements which they do not read properly. The agreements often have clauses in them which say that if the buyer does not make the necessary arrangements for a loan, or to obtain a plan passed by the local authority, no building will be done, and the deposit will be kept by the builder. Consumers are not told about these clauses, nor how to apply for a loan or have the plan approved by the local authority. The builder keeps the money when the consumer does not carry out the conditions in the clauses.

never sign agreements without reading them

People should never sign agreements without reading them. If people do not know how to read or do not understand what an agreement says, they should ask somebody to read it and to explain what it means. The person who reads or explains the agreement should not be the person who is trying to persuade the person to sign it. People should never sign an agreement without first having it explained to them.

Problem 8: Mrs Mphahlele is asked to sign an agreement

Questions

Mrs Mphahlele, who cannot read, is approached by Mr Fingo, a builder, who offers to build her a house for R300 000 if she pays a R30 000 deposit and signs an agreement. What should Mrs Mphahlele do? Role-play a conversation between Mrs Mphahlele and Mr Fingo.

5.6.4.10.5 Offers to make alterations or additions to homes

builders do not always disclose everything

Builders sometimes approach people who own council houses and persuade them to make alterations by adding extra bedrooms or a garage for a 'spaza' shop. Finance can be obtained by having a mortgage bond registered over the whole property which is worth much more than the alterations. The builders do not tell the owners that if they are unable to repay their bonds they will not only have to pay for the alterations or garages, but may lose the whole property if it is sold by the bank.

a bond registered over a whole property will be worth much more than the cost of the alterations

For example, a house may be worth R300 000 and the alterations may cost another R100 000. If a bond for R80 000 is taken out and repayments are not made, the home worth R300 000 may be sold by the bank.

an owner may lose their house if payment for the alterations is not made

The owner will lose the house, but will be paid any money not needed to pay off the rest of the bond. Therefore if R50 000 is still owing on the bond and house is sold for R300 000, the owner will receive R250 000 (R300 000 less R50 000). It may be difficult to buy the same kind of house for R250 000, especially if there are other costs involved.

people should not be talked into making alterations unless they can pay for them

People should not be persuaded to make alterations or additions to their homes unless they are able to pay for them. The total repayments for a loan, including the original loan for the house, and the extra money needed to make the alterations or additions, should not cost more than 25% of the homeowner's monthly wages.

5.6.4.10.6 Dishonest estate agents

many people have lost their homes to dishonest estate agents

Estate agents sometimes contact homeowners who are struggling to meet their bond repayments. They offer to buy their homes at a low price (eg half the market value), and to allow the owners to stay on in the houses after they have been sold. The owners will no longer own the houses but can rent them from the agents. The owners sell their houses to the estate agents who allow them and their family to stay on for a few months. The estate agents then find people who are desperate to buy houses and prepared to pay high prices because of the housing shortage. The estate agents sell the houses to the new owners for two or three times the prices paid to the previous owners. The previous owners are then evicted from the houses and the estate agents make a large profit. Many people have lost their houses in this way.

people should be careful about selling their property to people who promise to let them stay in their homes

People should be very careful about selling their property to people who promise to let them stay on in their homes. The chances are that eventually the new owners will want to evict the previous owners. If people are struggling to make payments on their bonds they should approach their banks to see if they will increase the period of the bond so that they can pay a smaller amount each month.

Problem 9: Mrs Luthuli is approached by Ms Batha, an estate agent

Questions

Mrs Luthuli, who is struggling to pay off the bond on her house, is approached by Ms Batha, an estate agent, who offers to buy it. Ms Batha says that she will buy Mrs Luthuli's house for R140 000 even though it is probably worth R250 000. In exchange she will allow Mrs Luthuli to stay on in the house and pay rent.

What should Mrs Luthuli do? Role-play a conversation between Mrs Luthuli and Ms Batha.

5.6.4.10.7 Offers to help with repaying loans

beware of people who offer to help buyers repay their home loans

Some builders and developers advertise that they will help home buyers repay their bonds if they buy houses from the developers. The builders and developers then sell the houses at prices much higher than they are worth. They do this so that when the home buyers apply for loans they are given larger loans than they need. The contractors or developers then put part of the money received from the buyers into banking accounts and use it to help pay off the bonds for two or three years.

people can lose their homes and money paid by them

While the builders or contractors are helping to pay off the bonds, the homeowners pay less than people who are not being assisted. When the builders or developers stop helping with the bond repayments the buyers have to pay the full amount each month. If this is too much for them and they fall behind in their payments they will lose their homes. These schemes look as if they help people who cannot afford to buy houses. Usually, however, people who buy under these schemes lose both their homes and the money paid by them.

people should ask the bank how much their home is worth

People should be very careful about signing agreements in which other people promise to help them pay off loans or mortgage bonds. If such an offer is made they should make sure that the price at which the house is being sold is the proper price, and not higher than it should be. They can do this by asking the bank to tell them how much the house is worth. They can also compare the prices of similar houses in the same neighbourhood. This can be done by reading newspaper advertisements or asking sellers. They should never enter into bond agreements unless the amount that they have to repay is less than 25% of their monthly income.

Problem 10: Mr Marivati is offered help in paying off his bond

Questions

Mr Marivati is approached by Miss Suni who offers to help him pay off his bond if he buys a house from her. Mr Marivati earns R6 000 a month and the repayments on the bond will be R1 000 a month. Miss Suni offers to help Mr Marivati by paying off R500 of the R1 000 each month.

What should Mr Marivati do? Role-play a conversation between Mr Marivati and Miss Suni.

5.6.4.10.8 Buying a home

People often think that buying a home is impossible because houses are so expensive. However, even though people are not very wealthy they may be able to buy a home by getting a mortgage bond (see below para 5.6.4.11) from a bank or with help from the state's national housing scheme. Buying a home is one of the most important decisions people make in their lives and everybody should know what is involved. This section deals with the steps to be taken when buying a home, signing an agreement of sale, and trying to obtain a loan.

5.6.4.10.8.1 Steps to take when buying a home

There are several things that should be done before a person decides whether or not to buy a home. Some of these will be discussed in the section dealing with what to look for before renting (see below para 5.6.5.1.2).

The best way for people to decide whether or not they would like to live in an area is for them to drive or walk around the neighbourhood. This should be done on different days and at different times in order to get an idea of what the neighbourhood is like. Things to look out for are the following:

1. Is there a good public transport system (eg buses, trains, taxis)?
2. Are there good schools in the neighbourhood?
3. Are there recreation facilities (eg parks, playgrounds, sportsfields, swimming pools etc)?
4. Are any large developments planned which will change the nature of the neighbourhood (eg new roads or public buildings)?
5. Is the neighbourhood polluted (eg from oil refineries or factories)?
6. Is there a danger of flooding because the neighbourhood is in a low-lying area or near a river?
7. What is the crime rate like in the neighbourhood?

before moving into an area, you should try to find out whether the neighbours are friendly

8. Are the neighbours friendly?

Most of these questions can be answered by talking to people who live in the area and asking them about its advantages and disadvantages. The best way of finding out about development plans is to visit the planning department of the local town council.

5.6.4.10.8.2 What to look for when buying a home

Many of the things people should look for when buying a house are the same as what people should look for when renting a house (see below para 5.6.5.1.2). People wishing to buy a house should not rely only on what the estate agents tell them but should make sure that:

1. The paint on the walls is not flaking and the plaster is not damp or cracked.
2. There are no signs of borers or other insects attacking the woodwork and the wood is not rotten or damp.
3. The windows and doors open and close easily. If they do not, it may be due to damp or because the house has moved on its foundations.
4. The baths, toilets and basins are not chipped, cracked or stained. Tiles are not missing or cracked.
5. Toilets and taps work properly. The water pressure is high enough to fill the bath and kitchen sink at the same time.
6. The electrical wiring is in good condition and all the lights and plug switches work.
7. There are no signs of damp or leaks. The gutters and drain pipes are not broken or blocked.
8. The drains from the bathrooms, toilets and kitchens are not blocked.
9. The monthly electricity and water accounts have been looked at to see how much they cost each month.
10. The roof and ceiling do not leak. Leaks are shown by stained patches on the ceiling paintwork and down the walls.

Problem 11: What to look out for when buying houses

Questions

1. Before deciding to live in an area, what are the things that a buyer should look out for? Role-play a conversation with a person who wishes to buy in your neighbourhood. Play yourself as the neighbour answering the questions about your neighbourhood.
2. Make a list of the things that a buyer should look out for when inspecting a house.

buying a house is one of the most important decisions people make in their lives

5.6.4.10.9 Signing a 'deed of sale'

deed of sale must be in writing

A deed of sale is an agreement between the buyer and seller of the property and must be in writing. It must be signed by the buyer and seller or their agents. Until both parties have signed the deed of sale it will not be binding on them, even if they agreed that it should be. This means that they may change their mind and decide not to buy or sell the property before the agreement is signed.

'offers to purchase'

Deeds of sale are sometimes called 'offers to purchase'. It does not really matter what they are called. Once they have been signed by the buyer and seller they are binding on both. A deed of sale or offer to purchase usually sets out the conditions of the sale as well as the price to be paid. Usually the buyer offers to pay a lesser price than that asked by the seller. If the seller refuses to accept the lower price, the buyer will have to complete another offer to purchase with a new price in it. Usually sellers are given a certain period in which to accept the offer.

consult an attorney before signing

It is a good idea to show a copy of the deed of sale to an attorney before signing it. The attorney can point out the exact meaning of the complicated clauses in the agreement. An honest seller or estate agent will not object if a buyer asks for time for this to be done. Most agreements of sale are printed forms used by estate agents or attorneys.

deeds of sale may have complicated conditions

Deeds of sale can be very simple agreements in which the seller offers to sell and the buyer agrees to buy the property at a certain price. However, usually deeds of sale or offers to purchase are long agreements with many complicated conditions.

Most deeds of sale or offers to purchase include the following:

1. A description of the full name and address of the buyer and the seller;
2. A full description of the property;
3. The amount of the purchase price, the deposit and how it will be paid;
4. A clause that says that the sale is conditional upon the buyer obtaining a bank or finance house loan to cover the rest of the purchase price (payment);

5. The date when the seller will give the buyer possession of the property (date of possession);
6. The amount of 'occupational interest' that will be paid by the buyer to the seller if the buyer takes occupation before the property has been transferred into his or her name at the deeds office (Occupational interest is like a rent that the buyer has to pay when he or she lives in the house while the seller is still the owner of the property.);
7. The name and address of the 'conveyancers' (The conveyancers are the lawyers who transfer the property out of the seller's name and into the name of the buyer (see above para 1.4.1.2.3).);
8. A reference to the fact that the property is sold together with all its fixtures and fittings (eg built in cupboards, light fittings, fitted carpets etc);
9. The cost of the transfer fees that have to be paid by the buyer;
10. The rates and taxes on the property that will have to be paid by the buyer from the date of occupying the property;
11. A statement that the risk of damage to the property will pass to the buyer from the date that the buyer obtains possession of the property;
12. A statement that the property is sold 'voetstoots' and that the seller will not be liable if there is anything wrong with it;
13. A statement that the seller will be responsible for the estate agent's commission and the amount of commission;
14. A statement that the seller will arrange for a 'beetle-free certificate' to be obtained and will replace any woodwork damaged by beetles and insects;
15. A statement about what the seller may do if the buyer does not carry out the conditions of the agreement; and
16. The date when the offer to buy ends and when it was accepted by the seller. (Usually sellers are given 48 hours to accept the offer but this may be extended.)

transfer of ownership when buyer's name on title deed

Buyers of property only become owners when the deed of transfer shows that the property has been transferred into their names. Transfer takes place when the deed of transfer or title deeds of the property include the buyer's name and are registered with the Registrar of Deeds in the deeds office. Deeds of transfer or title deeds are legal documents which record who is the owner of immovable property. The registration of the transfer has to be done by a conveyancer. Transfer costs are usually paid by the buyer. Buyers should make sure that they have enough money to pay the transfer costs.

the buyer should not sign a deed of sale if he or she does not understand what is in it

At common law the risk of property being damaged passes to the buyer as soon as the contract of sale has been entered into. This means that as soon as the buyer and seller have signed the deed of sale the risk will pass to the buyer. Usually, however, the deed of sale states that the risk will only pass to the buyer once he or she has taken possession of the property. Buyers should never sign a deed of sale if they have not read it and they do not understand any clauses in the agreement. It is a good idea for a buyer to consult an attorney if he or she does not understand something in a deed of sale.

a bank making a loan will check the title deeds

When a property is bought with the assistance of a bank loan, a building inspector will be sent to examine the property. The bank making the loan will check the title deeds of the property to make sure that there are no conditions on it that may affect the value of the property.

a buyer should ask the seller to show them a copy of the title deeds or deed of transfer

For example, somebody may have the right to build a road on the property, or somebody else may have a legal right to use the driveway. Before asking for a loan, buyers should make sure that there are no conditions that will make the property less valuable. They can do this by asking the seller to show them a copy of the title deeds or deed of transfer.

Problem 12: Some questions on buying and selling a house

Questions

1. What is the main difference between a deed of sale for buying a house or land and most other agreements?
2. When do buyers of land or houses become owners of the property?
3. What kind of clauses protecting sellers are usually found in deeds of sale?
4. When does the risk of damage to the property usually pass to the buyer?
5. Who usually pays the transfer costs in a deed of sale?
6. What conditions in a title deed may make land less valuable? How can buyers find out about them?

5.6.4.11 Mortgage bond loans

a mortgage bond is registered on the title deeds of the property as security for the loan

A mortgage bond is a claim against a person's property which is registered on the title deeds to provide security for a loan. If the loan is not paid, the person holding the bond may have the property sold to repay the loan. Usually a person gives a mortgage bond to a bank or financial organisation, or company which lends money to the buyer. The bond is registered against the title deeds of the property as security for the loan. This means that the property cannot be sold until the mortgage bond has been cancelled or paid in full.

'collateral security'

Banks can lend buyers up to 90% of the value of the property. This means that a buyer may only have to pay 10% of the purchase price as a deposit. Sometimes if the buyer can provide 'collateral security', the bank may ask for a smaller deposit. Collateral security means that the buyer is able to offer the bank something valuable like an insurance policy, shares, or a guarantee from an employer as security.

pay off the interest

Usually a mortgage bond is paid off in monthly amounts that reduce the amount of money borrowed as well as the interest that must be paid for the loan. During the first few years of a mortgage loan, most of the monthly payments are used to pay off the interest. It is only after a few years that the repayments start to pay off the amount actually borrowed.

do not promise to pay back more than can be afforded

People should not spend more than 25% of their monthly income on bond repayments. If, however, the buyer is married and the other person is earning a regular income, the bank may be prepared to lend more money. Extra loans may also be given if the buyer has a relative or employer who will guarantee that the loan will be repaid. People must be careful, however, to make sure that they do not promise to pay back more than they can afford each month.

interest rates change over time

Banks may charge different interest rates although their rates are usually the same. Interest rates may go up or down, and if they do the monthly repayments will be adjusted up or down by the bank or person lending the money.

When deciding to lend money, a bank or finance organisation will want to know that:

1. the buyer has a regular income;
2. the borrower has a good credit record and pays debts on time; and
3. the property to be bought is worth the price to be paid.

5.6.4.11.1 What to do before applying for a mortgage bond loan

Before applying for a mortgage bond, people should decide the following:

1. How much money they have in cash savings or will have from the sale of a property.
2. How much of their cash will have to be used for legal fees and extra expenses and how much can be used for a deposit on the property.
3. How much they wish to borrow.
4. How much they can afford to pay in monthly bond repayments.

Problem 13: Mr Truro wishes to buy a house

Questions

Mr Truro wishes to buy a house for R1 000 000. He has R200 000 in a bank savings account, and earns R50 000 a month. The bank says that it will give him a mortgage bond for R900 000 with interest at 20,75% over 20 years. He will have to repay the bond at R10 000 a month. Legal expenses for transferring the property will be another R30 000.

Can Mr Truro afford to buy the house? If so, why? If not, why not?

5.6.4.11.2 Second bonds

'second bond' over the property

Sometimes if a bank will not lend enough money to cover the price of a home, a buyer might wish to borrow money from somebody else. The other person would usually require security to be given by registering a 'second bond' over the property. Often the person who gives the second bond is the person who sells the property, an estate agent or attorney. Interest on second bonds is usually higher than that of banks and the period of the loan is usually shorter (eg five years).

People who take out second loans should make sure that they are able to repay them over the period promised. The monthly repayments of the first mortgage bond together with the second bond should not be more than 25% of the buyer's income. If a person fails to pay off the second bond, or falls behind in the repayments of the second bond, the whole property can be sold. The first bond holder will receive any money owing first, and then the second bond holder. The buyer will receive any money left over once all the debts have been paid. When people take out bank loans, they should obtain life insurance for the amount of the bond to make sure that the bond is paid off if they die. Many banks make this a condition of giving a mortgage bond.

life insurance

Problem 14: Some questions on second bonds

Questions

1. What is a second bond? When do people usually obtain a second bond?
2. What should buyers look out for when deciding whether or not to take out a second bond?

5.6.5 Promoting and protecting access to adequate housing

5.6.5.1 What does the law say about the rental and leasing of houses?

rental accommodation and leases

The Rental Housing Act of 1999 governs all rental accommodation and leases in South Africa. It seeks to create mechanisms to ensure the proper functioning of the rental housing market. It also aims at regulating the relationship between landlords and tenants, protecting them against unfair practices and exploitation. It also provides the mechanisms for conflict resolution between tenants and landlords.

people protected by the Act

The Act protects people who are staying in dwellings which include houses, hostel rooms, huts, shacks, flats, apartments, rooms, outbuildings, garages or similar structures, or parking spaces which form part of the lease. Some local authorities have set up Rental Housing Information Offices to advise landlords and tenants.

5.6.5.1.1 What is a lease?

What is a lease?

A tenant who rents a dwelling pays the landlord (the person who hires it out) a certain amount of rent. In return the landlord gives the tenant the right to live in the dwelling for a certain period of time. The landlord is the person who owns the dwelling leased or the person who is in charge of the property. The landlord and tenant enter into a contract called a 'lease'. The lease sets out the amount of rent that must be paid and the length of time the house or flat may be rented. It also mentions the rights and duties of the landlord and tenant.

5.6.5.1.2 What to look for when leasing a property

A checklist of what to do and what to look for before agreeing on the lease:

1. What is the condition of the house, flat or room?
2. If it is a flat or room, are the passages, entrances, and shared areas clean?
3. Who will be responsible for repairs to the property?
4. Are the taps, toilets, and drains in good working order?
5. Do the lights, plugs and electrical equipment work properly?
6. If they are to be rented, are the kitchen stove and fridge clean and in good working order?
7. Is there evidence of leaks (eg water stains, peeling paint or damp patches)?
8. Are there burglar guards?
9. Is the accommodation furnished or unfurnished? If furnished, is the furniture clean and in good condition?
10. Do the windows and doors open and close easily?
11. Are there any broken window panes, window latches or door locks?
12. Are there any rules about animals or children?
13. Are there keys for all the doors?
14. In the case of a flat, is it serviced?
15. In the case of a house, who looks after the garden?
16. Is the house, flat or room big enough?
17. What is the condition of the paintwork?
18. Is the 'key deposit' refundable?

Note: If things are wrong with the place to be rented, make a list of all the faults and ask the landlord to have them repaired.

tenants should inspect the flat or house before signing a lease

most leases are written

Tenants who wish to rent a flat or house should always do the following before signing a lease:

1. Carefully inspect the flat or house to make sure that it is what they want.

2. Carefully read the lease. If they cannot read or understand the lease they should ask an independent person to explain it to them before they sign it. Most leases are written in favour of the landlord. Therefore a person wishing to rent should read the lease carefully.

Problem 15: The Chitris look for a house to rent

Questions

Mr and Mrs Chitri are looking for a house to rent. They have four children.

1. Make a list of things you think they should look for when inspecting the house.
2. What questions should they ask the landlord? Role-play a conversation between the Chitris and the landlord.

5.6.5.1.3 Rights of tenants and landlords under the Rental Housing Act of 1999

rights of tenants and landlords

The Rental Housing Act outlines the rights of tenants and landlords as follows:

The tenant has the right:

privacy on inspection

1. To privacy from intrusion by the landlord during the lease period. For example, the landlord may only inspect the premises during reasonable times and upon reasonable notice.

no search without a court order

2. Not to have his or her person or home or property searched, and his or her possessions taken away from him or her, unless the landlord obtains a court order.

privacy of communication

3. Not to have the privacy of his or her communications violated. For example, the landlord is not allowed to listen to private conversations between the tenant and tenant's family or friends or read their letters.

Note: The rights of tenants apply equally to other members of the tenant's household or/and visitors.

The landlord has the right

1. To regular payment based on the terms of the lease agreement. Most lease agreements say that payment should be made by the 30th of the month or before the 7th of the following month.
2. To recover unpaid rental or any other amount that is due and payable after getting a decision from the Rental Housing Tribunal or a court order.
3. To terminate the lease for reasons that do not amount to an unfair practice and that are also expressly stated in the lease. For example, it may not be considered an unfair practice for the landlord to decide not to renew the lease after it has lapsed.
4. On termination of the lease, to receive the property leased out in a good condition and to repossess the property after having first obtained an order of court.

5. To claim compensation for damages to his or her property caused by the tenant or a member of the tenant's household or a visitor of the tenants.

5.6.5.1.4 Duties of tenants and landlords

duties of tenants and landlords

Duties of tenants

1. Tenants have to pay rent in return for the use and enjoyment of the landlord's property.
2. Tenants and landlords agree on a fixed date for the payment of rent. Under a periodic lease the rent must be paid at the end of each period (ie at the end of the day, week, month or year). If this is the case the law says that the rent is payable 'in arrears'. The parties, however, may agree that the rent will be payable 'in advance' (ie at the beginning of the day, week, month or year). Under a fixed time period lease the rent must be paid when the lease ends. The parties, however, usually agree that the rent will be paid at the beginning of each month.
3. The rent must be paid on the date, and at the place, that the parties have agreed upon. (If a place for payment has not been agreed upon, the tenant must find the landlord and pay the rent to him. Or the tenant must find a way of making sure that the rent reaches the landlord.)
4. The tenant may only use the property for the purposes for which it is rented. (For example, if the tenant rents the property to live in he or she cannot use it for business, or sub-let it or allow more than a certain number of people to live in it. If the parties do not agree on the purpose of the lease, it may be used in the way it was previously used or to which it is most suited.)

a lease may state that only a certain number of people may live on the property

5. The tenant must look after the premises. (At the end of the lease, the tenant must leave the house in the same condition it was when it was first rented. Damage caused by fair wear and tear, however, need not be repaired. Fair wear and tear means wear to things through ordinary use. For example, carpets or paintwork may wear after being used for a long period of time.)

Duties of landlords

1. The landlord must hand over the property to the tenants for their use. (This is usually done by the landlord handing over the keys of the house, flat or room to the tenant.)
2. The property should be rented out for a particular purpose. (The landlord must hand over the property in a suitable condition so that it can be used for the purpose for which it was rented.)
3. A landlord must keep the property in good condition so that it can continue to be used for the purpose for which it was rented. (This is not necessary, however, if the landlord and tenant agree that the landlord need not do this.)
4. The landlord may not do anything to disturb the tenant's use of the property. (The landlord must also not allow anyone else to do so. The landlord, however, may have the right to inspect the property at all reasonable times.)

the landlord may not do anything to disturb the tenant's use of the property

Problem 16: What are the rights and duties of landlords and tenants?

Questions

Examine the following cases and state (a) whether any right has been violated and (b) who has the duty to address what has happened.

1. A tenant's child smashes some windows and dirties the walls of a home. Who should be responsible for fixing the windows and painting the walls?
2. During a heavy thunderstorm the roof of a rented house leaks. The leak causes damage to the paint on the walls and stains the wooden floors. Who do you think should fix the leak, repaint the walls, and repair the floors?
3. The paint on the walls of a flat is peeling off and fixed carpets are worn out. Who do you think should repaint the walls and replace the carpets?

4. Joseph rents a room in Duma's house for R400 a month. Duma's brother, Paulus, throws Joseph out of the room after saying that the room is his.

5.6.5.1.5 What rules apply to leases?

According to the Rental Housing Act, the following rules apply to leases:

lease may be in writing or verbal

1. The lease between the tenant and landlord may be in writing or verbal. However, the landlord must reduce it to writing upon request by the tenant.
2. For all payments, receipts must be issued and must:
   (a) Be dated and clearly indicate the address of the leased dwelling;
   (b) Include the street number;
   (c) Clearly indicate the month(s) for which payment is made; and
   (d) Specify the period for payment.

payment of deposit before moving in

3. The landlord may require the tenant, before moving into a property, to pay a deposit of a certain amount not exceeding one month's rent. (This deposit is meant to provide security for the landlord in the case of arrears or damage to the property when the lease ends, or any other liabilities of the tenant resulting from the lease. Therefore, the deposit must be fully refundable with interest. The Act requires the landlord to save or invest the deposit in a bank or other financial institution. The tenant may request the landlord to provide proof of the interest accruing from the savings or investment.)
4. The tenant and landlord must jointly, before moving into the property, and also when the lease expires, inspect it to check whether or not it is in a good state. (If the landlord fails to inspect the property before the tenant moves out, it will be assumed that the landlord is satisfied with the state of the property.)

inspection

5. If the tenant does not respond to the landlord's request to inspect the property, the landlord has the right to inspect the property, without further notice to the tenant, within seven days from the expiry of the lease, to assess whether there are any damages and losses.

termination of lease is assumed

6. If the tenant vacates the property, without notice to the landlord, the lease will be assumed to have expired on the date the landlord discovered that the tenant had vacated. (In other words, it is assumed that the tenant has terminated the lease.)

periodic lease

7. If the tenant stays in the property after the lease agreement has ended, and the landlord does not object (agrees impliedly), it will be assumed that the tenant and the landlord had entered into a periodic lease (a monthly lease).

5.6.5.1.6 Lodging a complaint about an unfair rental practice

unfair rental practice

An unfair rental practice occurs when a party to the lease conducts himself or herself in a manner that is not fair to the other party. For example, if the landlord keeps on changing the terms of the lease and such changes affect the tenant, this may be considered as an unfair rental practice.

complaints lodged with the Tribunal

Any tenant, group of tenants, landlord or interested groups may lodge a complaint concerning an unfair rental practice. The complaint must be lodged with the Rental Housing Tribunal which will:

1. Investigate and determine whether there was an unfair practice;
2. In cases of a dispute, refer the matter for mediation; and
3. In cases of the dispute not resolved through mediation, conduct a hearing and make a ruling that is just and fair in the circumstances.

If the matter is set down for a hearing, the Rental Housing Tribunal may request reports from the Rental Housing Information Office in respect of the dispute.

no eviction until the Tribunal decides

The landlord may not evict any tenant who has lodged a complaint with the Tribunal until a ruling has been made, or after three months have expired. When the complaint is lodged, the terms and conditions of the lease continue to apply. For example, the landlord will still have to maintain the dwelling and the tenant will have to continue paying rent etc.

Note: Orders made by the Rental Housing Tribunal may be appealed against in the High Court.

Tenants and landlords can get advice on their rights and duties from the Rental Housing Information Office at their local authority.

Problem 17: The Phalas are evicted

Questions

Mrs Lizzie Phala lives in a house in Kliptown with her husband, Mr Ernest Phala. The house is privately owned by Mr Landu. Mr Phala earns R5 000 a month. The rent for the house is R1 000 a month. Mr Phala is retrenched from his job and can no longer afford to pay the rent. Mr Landu physically evicts the Phalas from the house without a court order. He removes all their furniture and places it on the pavement. He also locks the doors of the house so that the Phalas cannot get in. Mrs Phala wants to break the lock in order to get back into the house. What should she do?

Mr Landu physically removes the Phalas and throws their possessions onto the pavement

5.6.5.2 Deciding whether to rent or buy

There are advantages and disadvantages to both buying and renting homes.

5.6.5.2.1 Buying

The advantages of buying are:

advantages of buying

1. Monthly mortgage repayments are like savings and can be used as savings if the house is sold.
2. Buying a house is a good way of fighting the increasing cost of living over the years because properties usually increase in value much quicker than other things.

The disadvantages of buying are:

disadvantages of buying

1. People who buy houses and cannot afford cash usually have to pay a large deposit and transfer fees that may cost thousands of rands.
2. People who take out 'mortgage bonds' to pay off their loans usually have to pay off the loans for 20, 25 or 30 years. This means that they pay much more for the houses than they would have if they had paid in cash, because they pay interest for many years.
3. People who fail to keep up their monthly mortgage bond repayments may have their house taken away and sold by the bank that made the loan.
4. People who buy houses not only have to pay for electricity and water, but also for maintenance, repairs, insurance, and home improvements.
5. Mortgage repayments may have to be increased if the cost of money increases.

5.6.5.2.2 Renting

The advantages of renting are:

advantages of renting

1. People who rent houses (tenants) have fewer responsibilities than people who buy houses.
2. Tenants may ask their landlords (the people who rent out the property) to make repairs and do not have to worry about insuring the building.
3. Renting allows people to move out of the building at short notice. (People who own a home usually have to sell it before they can move out.)
4. If tenants earn less money they only have to pay the rent for as long as the lease lasts. (If they own houses, they have to keep up mortgage repayments until the bond is paid off or the house is sold.)

The disadvantages of renting are:

disadvantages of renting

1. In the long run a tenant has nothing to show except receipts for rent payments. (A person who buys a home will own the property and the mortgage repayments will help to pay it off.)
2. Monthly rents may increase if there is a shortage of property for renting.
3. Tenants have to agree to more rules and have less privacy than people who own their own homes. (This is because landlords are usually allowed to visit the property at reasonable times to make sure that it is being looked after.)

electricity and water costs may also have to be paid

Depending on the agreements with their landlords, tenants may have to pay electricity and water costs in addition to rent. These costs should be taken into account when tenants work out how much they can afford to pay each month. Before renting or buying flats or houses, tenants or buyers should find out the average monthly cost of electricity and water because if they do not pay their accounts their electricity and water will be cut off. This can be done by asking for copies of accounts from previous tenants or owners of the building. People renting sometimes have to pay a 'key deposit' to cover any damage to the property.

if a tenant does not pay the electricity or water account, the services may be cut off

Problem 18: Should Dawie and Koekie buy or rent the house?

Dawie and Koekie, both 23 years old, decide to get married. Each earns R12 400 a month (R24 800 total). Between them they have R100 000 in savings. They are trying to decide if they should rent or buy a house. They visit an estate agent who takes them to see a small two-bedroomed house. The agent says the owner is willing to rent the house or to sell it to them. If they rent the house the owner wants R5 000 a month rent, plus R700 a month for water and electricity. The owner will give them a one-year lease and make the necessary repairs. If they wish to buy the house the price is R800 000, including a deposit of R100 000. They will then have to obtain a mortgage bond for R700 000 from a bank. The monthly repayments on the mortgage bond will be R12 000. They will have to spend an extra R10 000 a year on rates and taxes, R4 000 a year on insurance, and R900 a month for electricity and water.

Questions

1. List all the reasons why Dawie and Koekie should buy the house.
2. List all the reasons why Dawie and Koekie should not buy the house.
3. Role-play a conversation between Dawie and Koekie in which they discuss whether to rent or buy the house.
4. Where might Dawie and Koekie get help to buy the house?

Landlords renting a house will usually want to know the following about their tenants:

1. Do the tenants have a steady income that is likely to continue?
2. Are the incomes of the tenants high enough and their expenses low enough to allow them to pay the rent?
3. Do the tenants have a good record for paying off previous debts or loans?
4. Will the tenants take good care of the property?

5.6.5.2.3 Problems in renting a house or flat

increased rent and service charges

possessions taken without a court order

movable property not owned by the tenant may not be attached

Type of problem	What can be done about it
i) Rent and service charges increase (eg sewerage, rubbish removal, water, community facilities, maintenance and administration).	i) Often nothing can be done to prevent increases in rent and service charges. The Rental Housing Act says the rent can be increased by 10% every year. But eviction of tenants because they cannot pay may be challenged in court or a Tribunal.
ii) The tenant's possessions are taken by the landlord without a court order because the tenant has not paid the rent.	ii) The landlord may lock the possessions in the premises for a short time, but must apply to court to attach the tenant's possessions. If the landlord does not, the tenant may take legal action against the landlord. The landlord may not use force to prevent the tenant from recovering the possessions. The tenant should consult a Rental Housing Information Office, a lawyer or legal aid clinic in this situation.
iii) Movable property that is still being paid for under a credit agreement or 'hire purchase' is attached by the landlord or sheriff.	iii) This property does not belong to the tenant and may not be attached. The owner of the goods being paid for under a credit agreement must tell the landlord that he or she is the owner of the goods. The tenant may lodge a complaint with the Tribunal, or contact the Rental Housing Information Office, or should immediately consult a lawyer, legal aid clinic, or paralegal advice office.

	Type of problem	What can be done about it
leased property not in a good condition	iv) The landlord fails to keep the leased property in the condition promised.	iv) It is the duty of the landlord to do general maintenance of the property. However, it is also a duty of the tenant not to cause damage to the property. The tenant should consult the Rental Housing Information Office or a lawyer, legal aid clinic, or paralegal advice office for help.
eviction without a court order	v) The landlord evicts a tenant who has not paid the rent, without obtaining a court order.	v) The tenant may obtain a 'spoliation order' from the court to be put back in the house or flat. The landlord will then have to go to court to obtain an eviction order. If the property belongs to a local authority the landlord need not go to court but must give the tenant seven days' written notice.
inspection of the property without reasonable notice	vi) The landlord decides to do an inspection in the property without giving the tenant reasonable notice.	vi) The Rental Housing Act prohibits the landlord from violating the tenant's right to privacy and says that inspection must be done at a reasonable time and upon reasonable notice being given. The tenant may lodge a complaint with the Tribunal, or consult a lawyer or legal aid clinic.

5.7 Water rights

Outcomes

After completion of this section learners will be able to:

1. Explain the law concerning water and water rights.

Assessment criteria

1. The laws that protect the right to water are discussed.
2. The rules relating to licensing for the use of river water are identified.
3. A decision is made on whether people in the townships should pay different rates for water than people in other residential areas.
4. An explanation is given on what can be done if access to a basic water supply is limited.

5.7.1 Introduction

water is a basic human need

Water and sanitation are the most basic human needs and essential for leading a dignified life. People must have access to sufficient water for important human activities such as drinking, cooking, food production and the maintenance of personal and household hygiene. Without access to clean water, people will become sick.

without access to clean water people will become sick

many people do not have access to safe and clean water

Under apartheid, access to water was linked to land ownership. Landowners had the right to use water sources. Yet the majority of the population were removed from productive land to small and remote areas. The result was a lack of clean and safe water for more than 10 million people. In 1997, it was also estimated that over 20 million people did not have adequate sanitation (eg toilets). In 2010 just under 10% of all schools (2 402 out of 24 451 schools) had no access to water, over 900 had no toilets, over 11 000 had pit latrines and over 150 relied on the bucket system (see above para 5.2.1). The effects of not having access to water and sanitation are huge.

Case study: The primary school where educators and learners carry their own water

a primary school has no proper toilets or washrooms

A primary school has no proper toilets or washrooms. Until three years ago, when the local town council donated long-drop toilets, learners and teachers relieved themselves in the surrounding bush. Learners and educators at the school bring their own water to school. Many walk almost 10 km to school, carrying their water.

(Source: Makoe A 'Farm schools in dire state of neglect' *The Sunday Independent*, 11 July 1999, 5 in Liebenberg S & Pillay K (eds) *Socio-Economic Rights in South Africa: A Resource Book* (2000), p 293)

Problem 1: Some questions on the lack of access to water

Questions

There are still many other schools and communities who experience the same difficulties as the schools mentioned above (see above para 5.2.2.2).

1. Discuss the effects of lack of access to sufficient and clean water and sanitation for your area, school, and certain groups of people.
2. What are the barriers to people accessing sufficient water?
3. Do you think the government is moving speedily enough to provide water to underdeveloped communities? Give reasons for your answer.

5.7.2 What is the right of access to sufficient water?

everyone has a right of access to sufficient water

The Constitution says that everyone has a right of access to sufficient water. It also says that the state has the duty to take reasonable legislative and other measures to ensure access to water for all.

water is linked to other rights

Access to water is closely linked to many other rights. It is regarded as part of primary health care, food, environmental and land rights. Access to water is also linked to equality and human dignity.

Case study: *City Council of Pretoria v Walker* (1998)

Questions

it is not unfair discrimination for different areas to be charged different rates

The Constitutional Court, in *City Council of Pretoria v Walker* held that it was not unfair discrimination for the local authority to charge different rates for different areas. People in the townships were paying a flat rate for the use of water and electricity whereas people in the former white areas (suburbs) were paying on the basis of what they consumed per month. The result was that people in the township were paying lower rates than those in the former white areas.

Problem 2: Should different rates be charged in different areas for water and electricity?

Questions

What is the effect of the Constitutional Court's decision in the case of *Walker*? Do you agree with the court that people in townships should pay different rates to those in residential areas? Give reasons for your answer.

5.7.3 How does the law protect access to water?

There are two laws that regulate access to water: the National Water Act of 1998 and the Water Services Act of 1997. These laws seek to make it possible for people to access water.

5.7.3.1 National Water Act

water resources should be conserved for present and future generations

The National Water Act aims to ensure that water resources are conserved and used to meet the needs of present and future generations. It also seeks to:

1. Promote equitable access to water;
2. Facilitate social and economic development; and
3. Reduce and prevent pollution of water resources.

The law also says that the use of water must be authorised through a licensing system.

5.7.3.1.1 What are the rules on licensing for the use of water?

rules on the licensing of water

The rules on the licensing of water are as follows:

1. A person who wants to use water (from a nearby river) for commercial farming or irrigation of crops must apply to the local office of a Catchment Management Agency (CMA).
2. Certain people are allowed to use water without a licence if it is for:
   (a) Reasonable domestic use;
   (b) Gardening that is not for commercial purposes; and
   (c) The watering of animals that graze on the person's land.
3. The licence period may not be longer than 40 years.
4. The person granting licences must consider such factors as the need to redress the results of past racial and other discrimination and the efficient use of water in the public interest.
5. The charges for licences or use of water vary according to geographic area and water use, depending on the socio-economic conditions of the user. (This is to provide emerging farmers from the previously disadvantaged groups with access to water.)
6. If a person or group of persons are members of a previously disadvantaged group (eg black farmers, rural women), they can request that they be given special consideration in the issuing of licences for water use. They can also request financial assistance from the Minister of Water Affairs to make a licence application.

factors to be considered for granting licences

7. The applicant has the right to appeal against the decision of the Catchment Management Agency to the Water Tribunal. If the decision of the Tribunal decision is also not satisfactory, the applicant may appeal to the High Court.

5.7.3.2 Water Services Act

The Water Services Act seeks to give effect to the right of access to sufficient water. It aims at regulating access to basic water and sanitation. It defines 'basic water supply' as the prescribed minimum standard of water supply services necessary for the reliable supply of a sufficient quantity and quality of water to households, including informal households, to support life and personal hygiene.

current minimum is six kilolitres per household per month

The current minimum stated for access to water is six kilolitres per household per month. This minimum is to be reviewed over time. This is calculated at 25 litres per person per day for a family of eight. Free basic water is universal – children and poor people are not specifically targeted. Local authorities are responsible for providing a minimum supply of water and sanitation. They must also take steps to ensure that people have access to water during emergencies.

Recently, in the case of *Federation for a Sustainable Environment v Minister of Water Affairs* (2012), the Pretoria High Court ordered the Gert Sibanda District Municipality to provide the residents of Carolina in Mpumalanga with drinkable water within 72 hours.

5.7.4 Can access to the water supply be limited or cut?

limits to the basic water supply must be on fair and equitable basis

A local authority can cut or limit access to the supply of water services under certain conditions. Procedures for cutting or limiting the water supply must be fair and equitable. The affected user of water must be given reasonable notice about the possibility of the cut and a chance to say why this should not happen. Also, procedures should not result in people being deprived of access to basic water due to not having paid if they can prove that they were unable to pay for basic services. If the water is cut off, the local authority has the responsibility of providing a supply of basic water and sanitation to the affected communities.

'water services development plan'

If the local authority unreasonably refuses to consider the circumstances of those affected by the cuts and limits of the water supplied, the affected persons may challenge the decision of the local authority in court. They can also approach the SA Human Rights Commission for help.

Everyone should be able to participate in the drafting of the 'water services development plan' prepared by their local authorities to ensure that it includes effective and reasonable steps for improving access to water in all in their communities.

Problem 3: Some questions on access to water

Questions

1. Do you think that people should have to pay for water? Give reasons for your answer.
2. Is six kilolitres of free water supply per household a month (ie 25 litres per person a day) enough for people to enjoy their right of access water?
3. Can the local authority cut the water supply to individuals who cannot pay for it? Give reasons for your answer.
4. Where can a person or community whose water supply has been cut go for help?

(This section is based on Khoza S (ed) *Socio-Economic Rights in South Africa: A Resource Book* 2 ed (2007).)

5.8 Land rights

Outcomes

After completion of this section learners will be able to:

1. Explain the law concerning land and property rights.

Assessment criteria

1. The meaning of the right of access to land and property is explained.
2. The components of the land programme in South Africa are identified and explained.
3. People who qualify for the Land Redistribution for Agricultural Development (LRAD) grant are identified.
4. Different ways in which people can access land (ie land restitution, land redistribution, and land reform) are explained.
5. A set of facts is given and a decision made on how the people concerned can access land.
6. Guidelines are drawn up for inclusion in the constitution of a communal property association.
7. A set of facts is given and a decision made on whether a person living on a farm can be protected from eviction.

5.8.1 Introduction

racially biased land policies and laws are responsible for inequalities and poverty

During apartheid, white people owned most of the land. The African people were allocated 13% of South Africa's total land to live in and the rest (87%) belonged to whites. Many African people were forced to leave their land and were relocated to overcrowded, underdeveloped and remote areas which were specifically reserved for blacks. For example, they could not stay permanently in many cities because these were reserved for whites. These racially biased land policies and laws are responsible for much of the inequality and poverty that face South Africa today.

black farmers were forced to use old methods of farming and production

The black groups who had access to land did not have proper agricultural infrastructures and services. Without this, they were forced to use old methods of farming and production. Also, although they had access to land, they could not own it.

process of restitution is slow and confusing

The problem of access to land is a difficult one to address quickly. The process of restitution is slow and confusing for many people who have claimed the land they lost during apartheid. Restitution means giving land back to the people who owned it before, or compensating people for what they had lost during apartheid.

Problem 1: Is South Africa dealing with the problem of landlessness effectively?

Questions

Do you think that South Africa is dealing with the problem of landlessness effectively and efficiently? Give reasons for your answer.

5.8.2 What are land rights?

people may not be deprived of their property

The Constitution says that everyone has a right to property, including access to land on an equitable basis. It also says that the right to property may not be limited unless it is done through a law that applies to everyone. People may not be deprived of their property or have their property unlawfully taken away from them. Property can only be taken away (expropriated) from a person if:

1. It is done through a law that applies to everyone (ie law of general application).
2. It is for a public purpose or in the public interest (eg if it is done for land reform purposes or to redress past racial deprivation of property or land).
3. The person is compensated.

the state does not have to provide everyone with free land

The state has a duty to pass laws and implement programmes to ensure that people have access to land on an equitable basis. This does not mean that the state has to provide everyone with free land. It means that the state must create conditions that make it possible for previously disadvantaged groups to have access to land. People who lost their property as a result of racially discriminatory laws and policies have a right to claim their property or land back (a right to restitution).

Problem 2: Is the right to property a limitation on land reform?

Questions

Do you think that the property rights clause limits land reform in South Africa? Give reasons for your answer.

5.8.3 What do land policies say?

The land programme in South African is divided into three components:

restitution

1. *Land restitution*, which means returning land or compensating victims for land rights lost because of racially discriminatory practices;

redistribution

2. *Land redistribution*, which means achieving a fairer distribution of land by making it possible for previously disadvantaged groups to buy land with help from acquisition grants; and

tenure reform

3. *Land tenure reform*, which allows certain land occupiers to remain on the land on which they are living.

5.8.4 How can people access land?

5.8.4.1 Land restitution

Any person or group of persons can get restitution if they lost possession of land and were not compensated for the value of the lost land. All claims for land restitution during the first period for claims had to be made to the Commission for Restitution of Land by 31 December 1998. Before the end of that cut-off date 67 531 land claims were lodged. The government has reopened the period for land claims.

5.8.4.2 Land redistribution

The land redistribution programme is further divided into three components:

settlement

1. *Settlement programmes*, which focus on providing people with land for settlement purposes;

agricultural

2. *Agricultural development*, which focuses on making land available to people for agricultural purposes; and

non-agricultural

3. *Non-agricultural enterprises*, which aim at providing people with land for non-agricultural enterprises, for example, eco-tourism projects.

This section deals with the first two components.

5.8.4.2.1 Settlement programmes

grants to assist previously disadvantaged people

The Department of Rural Development and Land Reform established a settlement/land acquisition grant which is aimed at assisting people from the disadvantaged groups to acquire, enhance tenure rights, and make investments in infrastructure, and improve homes. The following persons may qualify for the grant:

people who qualify for settlement grants

1. Landless people or people who have limited access to land, especially women.
2. Farm workers and their families who wish to acquire land, and improve their settlement and tenure conditions.
3. Labour tenants and their families who wish to acquire and improve the land they hold or alternative land (under the Land Reform (Labour Tenants) Act).
4. Residents who wish to secure and upgrade the conditions of tenure they live under.
5. Successful claimants under the Restitution of Land Rights Act who need additional funds to pay for basic costs on restored land.
6. A group of people can get together and apply to jointly buy a farm.

5.8.4.2.2 Agricultural development

land to be used for agricultural purposes

The Department of Rural Development and Land Reform developed the Land Redistribution for Agricultural Development sub-programme (LRAD) to make land available for people to use for agricultural purposes. The LRAD aims to transfer land to specific individuals or groups. It is also aimed at improving people's access to municipal and tribal land for grazing purposes (the so-called commonage projects). This section focuses on the first part of the programme.

designed to provide grants

The LRAD was designed to provide grants (financial assistance) to black South African citizens (Africans, coloureds and Indians) to access land specifically for agricultural purposes.

objectives of LRAD programme

The objectives of the programme include:

- Helping previously disadvantaged people in rural areas to improve their living standard, by enabling them to run their own large or small farms effectively;
- Broadening the opportunities available to young people who live in rural areas; and
- Stimulating agricultural production – which will be to the benefit of the entire country.

5.8.4.2.2.1 Who qualifies for the LRAD grant?

minimum grant of R20 000

Beneficiaries can access grants under the LRAD on a sliding scale, depending on how much they contribute in cash, kind or labour. Those who make a minimum contribution of R5 000 receive a minimum grant of R20 000. Those who can make a higher contribution of their own assets, cash or labour receive a higher grant based on what they contribute.

qualifications for an LRAD grant

To apply for the LRAD grant, a person or group must:

- Be a member of a previously disadvantaged group (ie African, coloured or Indian);
- Be 18 years or older;
- Intend to use the land for agricultural purposes only;
- Intend to farm on a full-time basis;
- Not hold any position within government structures;
- Be prepared to participate in a training programme after they have acquired land;
- Be in a position to make an own contribution;
- Be an organised entity if applying as a group; and
- Have a bank account.

The applicant identifies the land he or she wishes to buy or develop. Alternatively, the applicant might already have access to land, such as communal land or tribal land.

grant to help applicants with few resources to become farmers

The size of the grant is intended to help applicants with small resources to become farmers. If the applicant can afford to make a bigger input to buy a larger piece of land, the proportional size of the grant in relation to his or her input will be smaller than that provided to help the less well-off person.

People who already live on agricultural land in communal areas, and who need a grant only to develop the land (not to buy it), may also apply for an LRAD grant.

Small farmers may apply in groups for grants for the purpose of buying agricultural land.

All applications should be sent to the Provincial Grant Committee, which may either reject or approve the grant.

Problem 3: How can they access land?

Questions

How can the following people access land? (In your answer, state the programme they may benefit from and what they need to have and do to receive their benefits.)

1. A coloured woman wants to extend her house.
2. A labour tenant wants to buy the land he lives on for agricultural purposes.
3. A group of people want to buy a farm.
4. A group of people who received land under the restitution programme now need money to pay some expenses for the land they received.

5.8.4.3 Land tenure reform

5.8.4.3.1 The Interim Protection of Informal Land Rights Act of 1996 (IPILRA)

the IPILRA protects people who have no legal protection against eviction

The Interim Protection of Informal Land Rights Act (IPILRA) protects people who live on, use or have occupied land for years but who have no legal protection against eviction, especially those in the former bantustan homelands. The following persons are protected under this law:

1. People who have beneficial occupation. For example:
   (a) A person who has been occupying the land as if it were his or her own, openly and without having used force to occupy it.
   (b) A person who is on the land without the permission of the registered owner and has occupied the land for a continuous period of five years or more prior to 7 December 1997.
2. People who obtain rights in terms of tribal practices, or customary or indigenous law. For example, a person who uses, occupies or has access to land in terms of customary law or custom, where the land is vested in the South African Development Trust (SADT).
3. People who obtained rights as beneficiaries under a trust arrangement such as the SADT.
4. People who use or occupy a plot of land.

people not protected by IPILRA

Owners, tenants, labour tenants, share croppers, farm workers and anyone who has temporary permission to be on, use or occupy land, are not protected by the Act.

People who have rights on land in terms of a contract or with permission are protected under the Extension of Security of Tenure Act (ESTA) (see above para 5.6.3.1).

right to legal representation or legal aid

In *Nkuzi Development Association v Government of the Republic of South Africa* (2001) the Land Claims Court held that people who have land tenure under ESTA (see below para 5.8.4.3.3) and the Land Reform (Labour Tenants) Act of 1996 (see below para 5.8.4.3.6), whose security of tenure is threatened or has been breached, have a right to legal representation or legal aid paid for by the state if:

1. A substantial injustice would otherwise result if they are not represented; and
2. They cannot reasonably afford the cost of legal representation from their own resources.

> **Land tenure definitions**
>
> A 'share cropper' is a person who shares in the harvest in proportion to the economic input that he or she has made to the crop.
>
> A 'labour tenant' is a person who gives labour in return for the right to occupy a farm and grows crops or grazes livestock on the farm.
>
> A 'tenant' is a person who has a lease agreement with the owner of the property.

5.8.4.3.1.1 When can the informal land rights of people protected under the IPILRA be taken away?

loss of rights protected under the IPILRA

The rights of people with informal land rights can only be taken away in the following circumstances:

1. If the person holding the informal land rights gives his or her consent;
2. If the land is expropriated under the expropriation act or any other law that provides for expropriation; and
3. If the land is used for communal purposes.

legal assistance

People who are threatened with eviction and are protected under the IPILRA should seek help from the nearest office of the Department of Land Affairs, Legal Aid South Africa, legal aid clinics or any NGO involved in land work, or an attorney (see above para 1.4.1).

5.8.4.3.2 The Restitution of Land Rights Act of 1994

The Restitution of Land Rights Act deals with the restitution of land that was taken away under race-based policies and provides restitution for:

1. Loss of possession leading to landlessness; and
2. No or little compensation for the value of land taken away.

The Act also established the Commission for the Restitution of Land Rights and the Land Claims Court. The deadline for submitting land restitution claims was extended from 31 December 1998 to 31 March 2008 and has been extended again. The Act allows the Minister of Land Affairs to expropriate property for restitution or other land reform purposes.

5.8.4.3.3 The Extension of Security of Tenure Act of 1997 (ESTA)

ESTA provides security of tenure for vulnerable people who live on rural and peri-urban land and allows them to get ownership of land under certain conditions.

The Act:

1. Protects occupiers against unfair evictions by the landowners.
2. Provides for legal evictions under certain circumstances.
3. Sets out the rights and duties of owners and occupiers.
4. Protects people living on land belonging to somebody else by giving them a basic level of security of tenure.
5. Provides special protection for people who have lived on the land for 10 years or more and who are 60 or older, or who are living with a disability.
6. Allows occupiers to bury family members on the land where they lived.

5.8.4.3.4 The Prevention of Illegal Eviction from and Unlawful Occupation of Land Act of 1998 (PIE)

PIE provides for the following:

1. It prohibits unlawful evictions and sets out fair procedures for the eviction of unlawful occupiers.
2. It recognises that special treatment must be given to the rights of old people, children, people living with disabilities, and households headed by women.

5.8.4.3.5 The Communal Property Associations Act of 1996

communal property associations

The Communal Property Associations Act helps any group of people to legally buy, keep and use land together as a group (communally). It establishes a legal body called a 'communal property association' (CPA) for people from previously disadvantaged communities who want to own and use land together. The CPA can:

powers of the CPA

1. Own property and equipment;
2. Buy and sell property;
3. Borrow money from financial institutions like banks (using the property as a guarantee that it will pay the money back);
4. Take someone to court; and
5. Develop rules that will apply to all members of the group.

constitution of the CPA

The CPA must develop a constitution which will set up:

1. A democratic process;
2. A system of equal representation of men and women;
3. Methods that promote transparency, accountability and consultation; and
4. Resource management systems.

assistance to form a CPA

People wanting to form a CPA should seek help from NGOs or contact the Department of Rural Development and Land Reform, which will appoint an official or service provider to help them.

5.8.4.3.5.1 Guidelines to forming a CPA

People wanting to form a CPA should do the following:

intention to form a CPA

1. Inform the Department of Land Affairs that the group intends forming a CPA.

preparation workshop

2. Run a preparation workshop which will be facilitated by the Department's officials or service providers. This is when the group should write down all the information that will be used for the application to form the CPA.

get legal expertise

3. Draft the constitution of the CPA. Get help from NGOs or from other offices in the location with legal expertise.

adopt the constitution

4. Adopt the constitution, meaning that all members of the group must agree to the constitution.

registering the CPA

5. Apply to register the CPA. When applying for registration, the following information will be needed:
   (a) The draft constitution;
   (b) A formal agreement to follow the principles of the Act;
   (c) The names of the committee members;
   (d) Information about who lives on the land and how it is used;
   (e) What services are needed (eg roads, electricity and water);
   (f) The name of the nearest town or settlement; and
   (g) An explanation of any agreements with services providers who are responsible for social or development services.

complaints about the CPA

appointment of mediator

After the CPA is formed, all sorts of problems can be expected. If individual members of the CPA have complaints against other members, they must lodge such complaints with the Department of Rural Development and Land Reform. The Department may either appoint a mediator (see above para 1.3.2) to settle the disputes between members or hold an inquiry into the matter. The inquiry may result in the CPA being placed under the control of the Director General of the Department for a particular period of time or closed down. The CPA can also be closed down by an order of court or if the members of the group decide to de-register it.

Problem 4: Forming a communal property association

Questions

Simulate a group which intends to form a communal property association (CPA) and is having a workshop where it discusses the details of its intention. Amongst the things on the agenda are developing rules that will guide and bind the CPA members. Discuss and decide on the rules that your group wants to adopt and include in the Constitution of the CPA.

5.8.4.3.6 The Land Reform (Labour Tenants) Act of 1996

protection of labour tenants

The Land Reform Act protects labour tenants and their families from eviction. It also assists labour tenants to acquire land rights.

definition of labour tenant

residing on a farm in return for working for the farmer

The Act defines a labour tenant as:

1. A person who resides on or has the right to reside on a farm; has or had the right to use cropping or grazing land on the farm (or another farm of the owner), and in return works or has worked for the owner or lessee; whose parent or grandparent resided on a farm, and had the use of cropping or grazing land on the farm (or another farm of the owner or lessee), and in return works or worked for the owner or lessee of the farm or another farm.
2. A person appointed as a successor to a labour tenant under the Land Reform Act is also a labour tenant.

Note: A farm worker is not a labour tenant.

eviction of labour tenants only by Land Claims Court

Labour tenants can be evicted in limited situations and such eviction must be just and equitable (eg the labour tenant breaks the employment contract, or is guilty of misconduct, or when the owner has specific needs for the land). Only the Land Claims Court can order an eviction. If it does, the owner may be ordered to pay compensation to the labour tenant or to allow the labour tenant to be on the farm until his or her crops are ripe enough to reap and remove. Labour tenants can buy land. They can also get subsidies to buy land.

impounding livestock of labour tenant is considered as eviction

The Land Claims Court in *Zulu and Others v Van Rensburg and Others* (1996) said that impounding a labour tenant's livestock was the same as an eviction even though the tenant was not physically evicted. It based its decision on the definition of 'labour tenant' in the Act, which made it clear that the right to use land for grazing and cropping was part of the labour tenant's right to occupy land.

5.8.5 Mobilising people to enforce the right of access to land

The Rural People's Charter was adopted and the Rural Development Initiative launched at the Bloemfontein Rural People's Convention in April 1999.
The Charter was a response to the declining political weight given to rural issues reflected in the government's budget allocation. The aims of the Rural Development Initiative are to:

1. Mobilise rural communities and build NGO networks to jointly lobby government about issues affecting rural communities.
2. Work with rural people to develop a clear rural development strategy which also highlights gender issues.
3. Work on issues such as rural economic development, land tenure and reform, gender and development, agriculture and food security, planning and rural communication.

The Charter may be accessed at the offices of the National Land Committee, the co-ordinating organisation of the Rural Development Initiative.

Problem 5: What are Mvuso's rights?

Questions

Read the following case study and discuss the questions in small groups.

Mrs Mvuso is 78. She has been employed as a domestic worker for Mrs Wattle on the farm Riversend since 1965. In 1966, the owner of the farm, Mr Wattle died and Mrs Wattle left the farm. Mrs Mvuso remained on the farm where she built a house and lived with her children. She also grazed her livestock on the farm. Mrs Mvuso was given an eviction summons by the new owner of the farm on 9 July 1998. The notice said that she was occupying the land unlawfully.

1. What legislation protects Mrs Mvusa from being evicted from the farm?
2. Are the correct procedures being followed in this eviction?
3. What are Mrs Mvusa's rights under the law and Constitution?

(This section is based on Khoza S (ed) *Socio-Economic Rights in South Africa: A Resource Book* 2 ed (2007).)

5.9 Environmental rights

Outcomes

After completion of this section learners will be able to:

1. Explain the law relating to environmental rights.

Assessment criteria

1. The law governing environmental rights is discussed.
2. The principles of the National Environmental Management Act (NEMA) are applied to a case of pollution.
3. Methods of protecting the environment against new developments are identified.
4. A set of facts is examined and a decision made on how to protect the community against dust pollution using the NEMA principles.

5.9.1 Introduction

pollution of the environment has harmful effects on the health of humans

Apart from the problems of climate change and global warming, the environment today is experiencing problems of air pollution and contamination of water. This has led, in some parts of the country, to such diseases as cholera and tuberculosis. The Constitution says that everyone has the right to an environment that is not harmful to their health or well-being. It also says that the state must act reasonably to ensure that air pollution is prevented, conservation is promoted, and sustainable development is secured. The right to a healthy and safe environment is closely linked to other rights, such as the right to just administrative action and access to information. The violation of environmental rights often results in the violation of other rights. For example:

the right to a healthy and safe environment is closely linked to other rights

1. If people live in a polluted area, their health and well-being will be threatened.
2. If they live in an area that has contaminated water or unhealthy conditions (common in informal settlements), there is the likelihood of an outbreak of diseases such as cholera and tuberculosis that may threaten their right to life.
3. The right to dignity and privacy is violated if people have no toilets and the local authority does not supply them.

the state must prevent companies from polluting the environment

The state has a duty to prevent powerful companies from causing harm to the health and well-being of people (eg by polluting the environment or contaminating water). In protecting people against pollution, the state must not discriminate against anyone directly or indirectly. It will be direct discrimination if the state allows a toxic waste company to operate in a residential area where people live. Indirect discrimination may happen if the state passes laws that appear to be aimed at everyone but which in fact affect only a particular group of people.

Problem 1: Some questions on environmental pollution

Questions

1. What are the health effects of pollution of the environment?
2. In small groups, make a list of real life cases of environmental pollution in or around your area or of cases you have read about.

5.9.2 What do environmental laws say?

laws protecting environmental rights

The government has passed laws that give effect to the right to a safe and healthy environment. The main law in this regard is the National Environmental Management Act of 1998 (NEMA). The other relevant laws are the Environment Conservation Act of 1989, the Promotion of Access to Information Act of 2000 and the Promotion of Administrative Justice Act of 2000.

5.9.2.1 How does NEMA help protect environmental rights?

NEMA protects the environment in the following ways:

set of principles

1. NEMA creates a set of principles to be followed when protecting the environment. For example, it states that the public must be involved when decisions are made that affect their environment.

'environmental impact'

2. NEMA compels the state to look at the immediate and long-term effects ('environmental impact') of a particular development in the area before approving that it may go ahead.

access to information

3. NEMA also states that people must be allowed to have access to certain information about the environment and public health in their area. This section is now dealt with under the Promotion of Access to Information Act. NEMA states, for example, that information about pollution and waste products from industry is not private information and should be accessed by the public upon request and through following proper channels.

resolution of disputes

4. NEMA also makes it easy to resolve disputes on environmental issues by allowing for conciliation, mediation and arbitration (see above para 1.3.2). It also makes it less financially risky for people to go to court to defend the environment.

environmental crimes

5. NEMA states that the complainant can charge the violator through a private prosecution if the government is not willing to prosecute an environmental crime.

Sometimes communities set up organisations to help them deal with environmental problems in their areas when the law enforcement authorities are slow to use the provisions of NEMA to protect them.

Case study: Setting up an organisation to protect communities from pollution

Bayne's Spruit River is near Sobantu township in Pietermaritzburg and its water is used by local communities for irrigation, swimming and the washing of clothes. For many years oil companies upstream from the township illegally polluted the river by pouring oily water into it. The polluted water blocked the irrigation pipes and made the water unsuitable for swimming and washing. In order to protect themselves the community took the following action:

1. The community members formed an organisation to deal with the pollution and other issues.
2. The organisation helped to set up a multi-stakeholder forum with representatives from the oil companies, the Department of Water Affairs and Forestry, the Department of Agriculture and Environmental Affairs and the Msunduzi Municipality.
3. The aim of the forum was to stop the pollution by investigating pollution incidents, identifying the polluters and collecting samples to assist in the prosecution of individual companies.
4. The forum's activities helped to decrease the pollution of the river because there was the real threat of successfully prosecuting the polluters.

(Source: Legal Resources Centre *Environmental Justice Project Report* (2002); cf Khoza S (ed) *Socio-Economic Rights in South Africa: A Resource Book* 2 ed (2007).)

5.9.2.2 Guidelines on using NEMA's key environmental principles

The following are the key environmental principles of NEMA:

1. People have a right to be consulted before their environment can be harmed.
2. All important aspects of the environment that might be affected by a development must be studied before it is allowed to begin.
3. Women and other vulnerable and disadvantaged groups must be helped to become involved in decisions about their environment.
4. The polluter must pay for harm done to the environment.
5. There must be fair access to environmental resources.

Problem 2: Applying the NEMA principles to a case of environmental pollution

Questions

In the same groups as in Problem 1 above, apply the NEMA principles to one of the examples of environmental pollution you mentioned. How would you resolve the problem?

5.9.3 How can environmental rights be protected before a development begins?

an environmental impact assessment should be conducted before a new development starts

NEMA says that an environmental impact assessment must be done before the government gives permission for a new development to start. This assessment must be made to determine whether there will be harm to the environment if the development were to continue. If so, to what extent? The government must find a way to lessen the harm or find alternative ways of allowing the development without harm. The information about the impact assessment must be made accessible to the public so that they can participate meaningfully in the decision-making processes.

EIA is compulsory under the Environment Conservation Act

An environmental impact assessment is also compulsory under the regulations of the Environment Conservation Act before certain projects in an area can take place. Not all projects or developments in the area require an impact assessment. Developments that are not covered in the regulations do not require an impact assessment. However, if people are of the view that a particular development will 'seriously' or 'significantly' affect their environment, they can try to persuade the government to conduct an impact assessment. If the government ignores the request to conduct an assessment, people have the right to take the case to a court, which may decide in favour of or against the impact assessment. The Environment Conservation Act says that the assessment should also focus on whether the society and the country's cultural heritage will be affected.

the government should not ignore the outcomes of the assessment

If people think that the government has ignored the outcomes of the impact assessment, they can take legal action and ask the court to stop the development.

environmental rights often clash with economic development issues

5.9.3.1 Guidelines for taking steps against new developments

steps that can be taken against a development

contact interested and affected parties

check the qualifications of consultants

research the likely harm

seek help

work out the likely impact of the activity

ask for an independent review of consultants' reports

obtain information about possible harm to environment

government must consider all recommendations

seek help from a local NGO or approach court

People wishing to take steps against a development can:

1. Find out from the developer which government department it has approached for permission;
2. Ask for a list of interested and affected parties and make sure that they are included on the list;
3. Ensure that other interested and affected parties in their areas are included on the list;
4. Ask who the independent consultants are and what their qualifications are;
5. Find out from the local university or university of technology or the Internet if there have been any similar developments elsewhere in the country or in the world, and what kinds of harm they caused to the environment and to human health;
6. Find out what important issues need to be raised in the impact assessment;
7. Ask to see all the scientific studies done on the impact assessment;
8. Ask for 'mitigation measures' in each impact to be studied (in other words, what can be done to make the impact less harmful);
9. Work out the likely impact that the activity might have on the socio-economic environment or cultural heritage;
10. Ask the independent consultants to state when they do not have scientific answers to questions or where they are not qualified enough to answer scientific questions;
11. Ask for an independent review of the reports by another consultant to be paid for by the developer;
12. Make sure all their comments are included and recorded in the review;
13. If not happy at this stage, ask for conciliation, mediation or arbitration (see above para 1.3.2);
14. Make sure that at all stages of the process all the information is obtained from the developer about possible harm to the environment or human health and well-being;
15. Ask if arrangements have been made for the monitoring and managing of the harm that the development might cause to the environment or to people's health; and
16. Make sure that the government considers all the recommendations from the report of the impact assessment.

People may also wish to consider asking for help in getting the above information from a local NGO that works in the field of environmental law. If they are not satisfied after this process, they can approach the court to try and stop the development from going ahead.

5.9.4 How to stop actions that harm the environment and health

Under South Africa's environmental management laws, people can organise themselves in order to protect their environmental rights in the following situations:

1. When a law that protects the environment has been broken (eg a person has been dumping used motor oil in a river, see above para 5.9.2.1).
2. When a principle of NEMA has not been followed by the government. For example, the government has made no attempt to get a mining company to cover a dusty mine-dump next to a community and says that it is too expensive for the mine. This goes against the principle that environmental management must put people and their needs first, and be fair.
3. When there is serious pollution of the environment (eg a local authority is dumping sewerage into a river used by a community for drinking water).
4. If a person is punished for refusing to do work that could harm the environment or for giving information about risks to the environment.

failure to give information about environmental risks

The options a person chooses in these circumstances will depend on what kind of harm is being caused to the environment or how it has affected people's health and well-being. These options include:

1. Complaining to local or provincial authorities, or to the director-general of the relevant department;
2. Asking for conciliation, mediation or arbitration (see above para 1.3.2) the government will pay for them; and
3. Going to court.

options for stopping environmental harm

5.9.4.1 Guidelines on what to do before taking action

Before starting an action people should:

1. Prepare as much evidence as they can (eg photographs, soil and water samples), and record complaints by the people affected.
2. Write letters to the authorities, including as many details as possible, and keep copies of what they have sent.
3. Try to approach local universities and universities of technology and ask them to help with scientific information and support.
4. Get legal advice about whether the law has been broken from law clinics, advice offices, the Legal Resource Centre or private human rights lawyers (see above para 1.4.1).
5. Contact other environmental groups locally and internationally for support and advice.

prepare evidence

approach local universities

get legal advice

contact other environmental groups

5.9.4.2 Taking action

1. People can lodge their complaints with the local government health or environmental department or with the Provincial Department of Environmental Affairs and Tourism.

lodge a complaint with government

lay a charge with the police

approach SA Human Rights Commission

2. In certain cases, they may even lay a charge with the police (eg if a person is dumping toxic material in a river that people use to get water from).
3. They may also approach the South African Human Rights Commission if their constitutional rights are being violated, including their right to an environment that is not harmful to their health or well-being.

Case study: Reporting environmental violations to the Human Rights Commission

An oil refinery in Table View in Cape Town, less than 3 km from poor communities in De Noon and Joe Slovo, was polluting the air. Many of the residents from the poor communities complained of breathing problems, chest-related illnesses, coughs, sore throats, weak immune systems, sinus complications, headaches, eye infections, ear infections and allergies. The communities suspected that their health problems were linked to the air pollution caused by the oil refinery. In order to protect themselves the residents:

1. Started to take air samples that showed that 31 chemicals were in the air, of which 12 were classified as dangerous air pollutants by the United States Environmental Protection Agency; and
2. Approached the South African Human Rights Commission using the air samples to show that they were experiencing human rights abuses as a result of the operations of the oil refinery.

(Source: National Report on Community-based Air Pollution Monitoring in South Africa – Air Pollution in Selected Industrial Areas in South Africa, *GroundWork* (2003) 34; cf Khoza S (ed) *Socio-Economic Rights in South Africa: A Resource Book* 2 ed (2007).)

Problem 3: Taking action against the mining companies

Questions

Communities living near mine-dumps in Johannesburg were exposed to high levels of dust blowing off the gold mine-dumps which got into their houses, clothes, food and cars, and made them sick. They had to stay indoors and sweep their homes regularly. They were always cleaning everything because of the dust. They asked the mining companies to cover the dumps with grass. The companies refused, claiming that it would cost them too much money.

1. Discuss the constitutional rights of the community in this case.
2. Discuss possible options for taking action in this case. In your action plan, state against whom the action will be taken and on what grounds. Follow the NEMA principles and guidelines for taking action.

(This section is based on Liebenberg S & Pillay K (eds) *Socio-Economic Rights in South Africa: A Resource Book* (2000).)

Further reading

5.1 The Constitution and socio-economic rights

Khoza S (ed) *Socio-Economic Rights in South Africa: A Resource Book* 2 ed (2007) 13–86

Liebenberg S & Pillay K (eds) *Socio-Economic Rights in South Africa: A Resource Book* (2000)

Constitution of the Republic of South Africa, 1996

Soobramoney v Minister of Health, KwaZulu-Natal 1998 (1) SA 765 (CC); 1997 (12) BCLR 1696 (CC)

Government of the Republic of South Africa v Grootboom 2001 (1) SA 46 (CC); 2000 (11) BCLR 1169 (CC)

Minister of Health v Treatment Action Campaign (No 1) 2002 (5) SA 703 (CC); 2002 (10) BCLR 1075 (CC)

Khosa v Minister of Social Development 2004 (6) SA 505 (CC); 2004 (6) BCLR 569 (CC)

President of the Republic of South Africa and Another v Modderklip Boerdery (Pty) Ltd 2005 (5) SA 3 (CC); 2005 (8) BCLR 786 (CC)

Mazibuko v City of Johannesburg 2010 (4) SA 1 (CC)

5.2 Education rights

Khoza S (ed) *Socio-Economic Rights in South Africa: A Resource Book* 2 ed (2007) 407–439

Liebenberg S & Pillay K (eds) *Socio-Economic Rights in South Africa: A Resource Book* (2000)

Motala v University of Natal 1995 (3) BCLR 374 (D)

Christian Education South Africa v Minister of Education 2000 (4) SA 757 (CC); 2000 (10) BCLR 1051

5.3 Social welfare rights

Khoza S (ed) *Socio-Economic Rights in South Africa: A Resource Book* 2 ed (2007) 375–406

Liebenberg S & Pillay K (eds) *Socio-Economic Rights in South Africa: A Resource Book* (2000)

Social Assistance Act 13 of 2004

Khosa v Minister of Social Development 2004 (6) SA 505 (CC); 2004 (6) BCLR 569 (CC)

5.4 Health rights

Dhai A & McQuoid-Mason D *Bioethics, Human Rights and Health Law* (2011)

Khoza S (ed) *Socio-Economic Rights in South Africa: A Resource Book* 2ed (2007) 371–310

Liebenberg S & Pillay K (eds) *Socio-Economic Rights in South Africa: A Resource Book* (2000)
Children's Act 38 of 2005
Choice on Termination of Pregnancy Act 92 of 1996
Criminal Law (Sexual Offences and Related Matters) Amendment Act 32 of 2007
Medical Schemes Act 131 of 1998
National Health Act 61 of 2003
Tobacco Products Control Act 83 of 1993
Jansen van Vuuren v Kruger 1993 (4) SA 842 (A)
Castell v De Greef 1994 (4) SA 408 (C)
Soobramoney v Minister of Health, KwaZulu-Natal 1998 (1) SA 765 (CC); 1997 (12) BCLR 1696 (CC)
B v Minister of Correctional Services 1997 (4) SA 441 (C); 1997 (6) BCLR 789 (C)
Minister of Health v Treatment Action Campaign (No 1) 2002 (5) SA 703 (CC); 2002 (10) BCLR 1075 (CC)
N v Government of the Republic of South Africa (No 1) 2006 (6) SA 543 (D); 2007 (1) BCLR 84 (D)

5.5 Food rights

Khoza S (ed) *Socio-Economic Rights in South Africa: A Resource Book* 2 ed (2007) 311–342
Brand D 'Right to food' in Brand D & Heyns C *Socio-Economic Rights in South Africa* (2005) 153

5.6 Housing rights

Khoza S (ed) *Socio-Economic Rights in South Africa: A Resource Book* 2 ed (2007) 229–270
De Vos P 'Right to housing' in Brand D & Heyns C *Socio-Economic Rights in South Africa* (2005) 85
Extension of Security of Tenure Act 62 of 1997
Home Loan and Mortgage Disclosure Act 63 of 2000
Housing Act 107 of 1997
Prevention of Illegal Eviction from and the Unlawful Occupation of Land Act 19 of 1998
Rental Housing Act 50 of 1999
Government of the Republic of South Africa v Grootboom 2001 (1) SA 46 (CC); 2000 (11) BCLR 1169 (CC)
President of the Republic of South Africa and Another v Modderklip Boerdery (Pty) Ltd 2005 (5) SA 3 (CC); 2005 (8) BCLR 786 (CC)

5.7 Water rights

Khoza S (ed) *Socio-Economic Rights in South Africa: A Resource Book* 2 ed (2007) 343–374

National Water Act 36 of 1998

Water Services Act 108 of 1997

City Council of Pretoria v Walker 1998 (2) SA 363 (CC)

Federation for a Sustainable Environment v Minister of Water Affairs case no 35672/12 [2012] ZAGPPHC 128, 10 July 2012, North Gauteng High Court (unreported)

5.8 Land rights

Khoza S (ed) *Socio-Economic Rights in South Africa: A Resource Book* 2 ed (2007) 193–228

Communal Property Associations Act 28 of 1996

Extension of Security of Tenure Act 62 of 1997

Interim Protection of Informal Land Rights Act 31 of 1996

Land Reform (Labour Tenants) Act 3 of 1996

Prevention of Illegal Eviction from and the Unlawful Occupation of Land Act 19 of 1998

Restitution of Land Rights Act 22 of 1994

Zulu v Van Rensburg 1996 (4) SA 1236 (LCC)

Nkuzi Development Association v Government of the Republic of South Africa 2002 (2) SA 733 (LCC)

President of the Republic of South Africa and Another v Modderklip Boerdery (Pty) Ltd 2005 (5) SA 3 (CC); 2005 (8) BCLR 786 (CC)

5.9 Environmental rights

Khoza S (ed) *Socio-Economic Rights in South Africa: A Resource Book* 2 ed (2007) 163–192

Legal Resources Centre *Environmental Justice Project Report* (2002)

Environment Conservation Act 73 of 1989

National Environmental Management Act 107 of 1998

Promotion of Access to Information Act 2 of 2000

Promotion of Administrative Justice Act 3 of 2000

Street law

6. Employment law

CONTENTS

PART SIX

Employment law

6.1 Employment and applying for a job

Outcomes

After completion of this section learners will be able to:

1. Explain the laws affecting workers or employees who apply for a job.

Assessment criteria

1. A set of facts is examined and a decision is made on whether a job advertisement is discriminatory.
2. A set of facts is examined and a decision is made on whether certain questions during a job interview were discriminatory.
3. Sets of facts are examined and decisions are made on whether the testing of job applicants should be allowed.
4. A set of facts is examined and a decision is made on whether affirmative action should be allowed.

6.1.1 Applying for a job

6.1.1.1 Advertising a job

advertising a job

A job can be 'advertised' in a number of different ways:

The employer can:

1. Place an advertisement in a national and local newspaper;
2. Advise potential employees by word of mouth;
3. Put up a notice on the company's notice board; and
4. Recruit candidates through an employment agency.

6.1.1.1.1 Unfair discrimination in advertisements

preventing unfair discrimination in the workplace

The Employment Equity Act of 1998 is a very important piece of legislation that aims at the promotion of equal opportunity and fair treatment of employees and job applicants by preventing unfair discrimination in the workplace.
The Employment Equity Act of 1998 states that recruitment practices and advertising should not be discriminatory. It stipulates that 'no person may unfairly discriminate, directly or indirectly' against an employee or potential employee on the grounds of 'race, gender, sex, pregnancy, marital status, family responsibility, ethnic or social origin, colour, sexual orientation, age, disability, religion, HIV status, conscience, belief, political opinion, culture, language and birth'. These are known as the 'listed grounds'. It is important that the wording of an employment advertisement is not discriminatory.

wording of advertisements must not be discriminatory

Unfair discrimination may occur when the employer uses one of the listed grounds to:

- Demote or promote an employee or job applicant;
- Prevent an employee from accessing training and development; or
- Make an unfair distribution of employee benefits.

Problem 1: Are these advertisements discriminatory?

Questions

Consider whether the following advertisements placed in a local newspaper are discriminatory and on what grounds:

1. A 'young man' is required for the position of computer consultant.
2. 'Zulu-speaking employees' are required to work at a busy butchery in KwaZulu-Natal.
3. 'Attractive young women' are required to work at an exotic dance club.
4. 'A person with a BCom degree' is required for the position of accounts manager at a company.
5. A waitressing position is available to employees 'between the ages of 18 and 28 years'.
6. The position of electrical engineer is available to an applicant with a 'minimum of 5 years' practical experience.'
7. An employee is required to work at a busy all-night take-away: 'Single persons with no family responsibilities' are invited to apply for the position.
8. 'HIV-positive persons are required to work at an HIV Learner Counselling Centre.'

6.1.1.2 The job interview

conduct in job interviews

Once a person has been selected for a job interview it is very important to be prepared for it. The person's appearance and how he or she conducts himself or herself at the interview may affect whether they get the job. It is also a good opportunity for the person being interviewed to find out as much as he or she can about the job and whether it is what they are looking for.

Case study 1: Robert 'Marley' Makhaya applies for a job

Robert 'Marley' Makhaya is applying for a position as a salesman for a large business. He knows he can do the work but people don't take him seriously because he is a Rastafarian. Robert is being unfairly discriminated against.

Robert 'Marley' Makhaya is unfairly discriminated against because he is a Rastafarian

questions at job interviews

At the interview the person being interviewed will be asked many questions by the employers. These questions are aimed at assisting employers in finding out as much information about the person as possible in order to assess whether he or she is suitable for the position.

inappropriate questions may not be asked

The Employment Equity Act of 1998 prohibits discriminatory selection procedures. This means that employees have to be very careful about the questions that they ask during interviews so that they do not have a discriminatory effect or result in an invasion of the job applicant's privacy. Questions that refer inappropriately to a person's race, gender, religion, marital status, or HIV status may be considered to be discriminatory. An applicant who feels that he or she has been refused a position because of a discriminatory question that has been asked may sue the employer for discrimination in the Labour Court. However, the person will have to show that the reason that he or she was not offered the job was based on discrimination. For example, it may be discriminatory to ask an applicant for a secretarial position if she is married. The applicant would have to prove that it was due to her marital status that she was not offered the job and not, for example, due to her lack of typing experience.

Case study 2: *Hoffman v South African Airways* (2000)

discrimination on the grounds of HIV/AIDS status

Mr Hoffman applied for a job at SAA as an air steward. He was required to undergo an HIV/AIDS test and when it was discovered that he was HIV positive, he was not given the job. He decided to sue SAA for unfair discrimination. The reason given by SAA for not appointing him was that, as all air stewards had to have yellow fever inoculations which were 'dangerous' if a person was HIV positive, it was not possible to employ someone who was HIV positive. The court rejected this argument and held that it was discrimination on the grounds of HIV/AIDS.

Problem 2: The job interview

Questions

Joan Smith, age 22, is applying for the position of sales assistant at Ace Retail in Durban. She has a job interview with a Company Director, Mr Naidoo.

1. During the interview Mr Naidoo asks the following questions: Consider which questions are appropriate and which are inappropriate and give reasons for your answers:
   1. What is your name?
   2. How old are you?
   3. Are you a South African citizen?
   4. Are you married?

    5. Are you pregnant or do you plan to have children in the future?
    6. Are you willing to move to another city?
    7. Have you ever been arrested?
    8. How tall are you and how much do you weigh?
    9. What religion are you?
    10. Do you speak Xhosa?
    11. Have you ever been tested for HIV/AIDS?
    12. Will you have dinner with me tonight?
    13. What is your financial situation?
2. Role-play the interview and get Joan Smith to decide whether and how to answer each question. Which questions were inappropriate? How should she respond to them? Decide whether any of her answers were incorrect or improper and decide what would have been a better answer. Which answers were particularly good and why?
3. Evaluate how well Joan Smith did in the interview.

6.1.1.3 Testing job applicants

there can be no psychological or medical testing unless they are necessary for the job and legally valid

A controversial legal issue that arises in the job application process is whether employers can require job applicants to take psychological or medical tests. While aptitude, personality and psychological tests can be useful to establish an applicant's ability to do a job, the Employment Equity Act states that psychological tests are prohibited unless they are scientifically valid and reliable, can be applied fairly to all employees, and are not biased against any employee or group.

Medical testing is also prohibited unless: (a) there is a law that requires it or permits it; (b) it is justifiable in the light of the medical facts, the conditions of employment and the requirements of a benefit scheme (for example a medical aid scheme or pension plan); or (c) is a requirement of the job. For example some companies may require employees to take drug tests.

Cast study 3: Mr Nxumalo is medically tested

Mr Nxumalo is subjected to tests fit for an astronaut

Medical testing is only allowed if legislation permits it and the job's requirements justify it. Mr Nxumalo is subjected to tests fit for an astronaut but he is a receptionist. His duties include answering the phone and dealing with customers. This testing will be illegal.

types of testing not allowed

An employer is not allowed to:

- Ask a job applicant to have an HIV test when applying for a job;
- Ask existing employees to undergo annual HIV testing; and
- Ask employees to have an HIV test before being promoted.

Labour Court must approve HIV/AIDS testing

Testing a job applicant for HIV/AIDS is prohibited unless the Labour Court permits it. The Employment Equity Act provides that the Labour Court will only grant permission for HIV testing of employees if it finds that testing is justifiable. The Labour Court may include the following provisions when granting an order for testing:

conditions for granting permission to test for HIV

- The employees are provided with counselling before and after testing;
- The HIV status of all employees is kept confidential;
- A specified period will be named during which the employees may be tested; and
- The categories of jobs for which testing is permitted will be stated.

Problem 3: When should aptitude and medical tests be allowed?

Questions

Do you think that aptitude tests or medical tests should be allowed in the following situations? Give reasons for your answers.

1. All applicants for a job as an airplane pilot are required to take an eye test.
2. All applicants for the job of ambulance drivers, paramedics and fire-fighters are required to submit to a drug and alcohol use test.
3. All applicants for the position of nursing sister are required to be tested for HIV/AIDS and Hepatitis C (a virus transmitted by the blood).
4. All applicants for the position of copywriter at an advertising company are required to do a creative writing assignment to assess their creative abilities.
5. All applicants for the position of accountant are required to do an IQ test.

6.1.1.4 Selecting an employee

6.1.1.4.1 Affirmative action

affirmative action

The employer is entitled to choose the best employee for the job. However, the Employment Equity Act requires the employer to implement affirmative action measures in the workplace so that the workforce becomes more representative of the different race groups in South Africa. Thus employers are required to appoint suitably qualified persons from within the 'designated groups' into the employment sector.

A person may be suitably qualified for a particular job because of his or her:

- Formal qualifications;
- Relevant experience;
- Capacity to acquire the skills needed for the job.

Case study: Mr Smit and Mr Gumede are interviewed for a job

Fidelity Insurance Brokers Ltd needs a new salesperson. Mr Smit and Mr Gumede are being interviewed for the position but Mr Smit is concerned, as he doesn't fit the company's affirmative action criteria.

Mr Smit is concerned, as he doesn't fit the company's affirmative action criteria

'designated groups'

A 'designated group' means black people, women, and people with disabilities. Affirmative action measures are aimed at ensuring that suitably qualified people from designated groups are given equal opportunities and are fairly represented in all categories at the workplace. This requires the employer to: (a) identify and eliminate barriers that exist to the advancement of people from designated groups; (b) take steps to make the workplace more representative; and (c) to make reasonable accommodation for designated groups to ensure that they are able to enjoy equal opportunities. For example, a company that employs only white male managers would have to identify obstacles at the workplace that prevent black employees from becoming managers. The company would have to take steps to accommodate black employees by giving them training and assistance and take steps towards increasing the number of black managers at the company.

employers must ensure equal opportunities for designated groups

employers with more than 50 employees must implement affirmative action

The Employment Equity Act now requires all employers with more than 50 employees, or those having an annual turnover of more than a specified amount (depending on the type of business), to implement affirmative action measures. They are required to: (a) consult with employees; (b) examine their practices at the workplace and the working environment that might have a discriminatory effect; (c) draw up an employment equity plan; and (d) report to the Department of Labour with regard to the implementing of this plan (see below para 6.7.2.4).

affirmative action objectives to promote equity

An affirmative action programme will not be regarded as unfair as long as the objectives of the affirmative action measures are to promote and advance equity in the workplace and to redress the injustices of the past.

An employer must prove that the specific affirmative action measures are designed to protect and advance those disadvantaged by unfair discrimination.

An important factor when judging the fairness of a discriminatory act is the extent to which the discrimination has affected the rights or interests of the people complaining about it.

affirmative action may affect non-designated groups

Affirmative action may take many forms that may affect the rights of non-designated groups. The extent to which affirmative action affects the rights or interests of non-designated groups will also depend on the type of employment rights or interests that are affected.

equal opportunity by removing unfair discrimination

The Employment Equity Act is concerned with achieving equality by removing unfair discrimination. It requires the employer to take positive steps to promote equal opportunity through removing unfair discrimination in any employment policy or practice. The Act also prohibits the employer from unfairly discriminating against employees on certain grounds.

'rational connection'

The courts, when deciding cases under the Employment Equity Act, have relied on the Constitution and stated that 'there must be a rational connection between the measures and the aim they are designed to achieve'. 'Rational connection' means that the connection is based on reasons that can be justified.

Problem 4: Is affirmative action necessary?

Questions

1. Fast Sales Co Ltd advertises the position of manager in its retail division. Two people apply for the job – Mandla, a black male who has two years' experience in the retail industry and no tertiary education, and Sarie, a white female who has eight years' experience and a BCom degree. The company has an affirmative action policy in which it commits to increasing the number of black and women managers at the company over a 5-year period. Who do you think the company should give the job to? Why?
2. Do you think that affirmative action measures are necessary in the South African work-place? Divide into small groups and prepare to debate the advantages and disadvantages of affirmative action.

6.2 Contracts of employment

Outcomes

After completion of this section learners will be able to:

1. Explain the law relating to contracts of employment.

Assessment criteria

1. The laws regarding employment contracts are identified.
2. A set of facts is examined and a decision is made on whether a person is an employee or an independent contractor.
3. The duties of employees and employers are identified.

employment contracts must be in writing

All employment contracts have to be in writing and must specify all the terms and conditions of employment. The contract has to be signed by both parties. Once the contract is entered into, it cannot be changed by either party, except with the consent of the other.

Problem 1: Drawing up an employment contract

Questions

Make a note of all the information that you think should be included in an employment contract. Think of things that you regard as important for both employees and employers.

6.2.1 Who is an employee?

6.2.1.1 Employee versus independent contractor

employee versus independent contractor

an employee can be told what to do and how to do it

an independent contractor is told what to do – not how to do it

The first question that needs to be answered when solving a labour dispute is whether the parties involved are an employee and employer. In most cases this is not difficult to decide. However, difficulties may arise if it is not clear whether there is an employee–employer or an employee–independent contractor relationship. An employee is defined in the Labour Relations Act and other labour legislation as 'any person, excluding an independent contractor, who works for another person or for the state and who receives or is entitled to receive, any remuneration and any other person who in any manner assists in carrying on or conducting the business of an employer'. In simple terms an employee can be told what to do and how to do the work by an employer. An independent contractor can only be told what to do – not how to do the work. In other words an employee enters into a contract of employment while an independent contractor enters into a contract of work. It is very important to be able to tell whether a person is an employee or an independent contractor, because independent contractors are not protected by labour legislation.

6.2.1.2 Presumption of employment relationship

presumption of employment relationship

A recent amendment to the Labour Relations Act creates a presumption that the following are employees if these factors are present:

factors leading to the presumption

1. The way the person works is subject to the control of another person.
2. The person's hours of work are subject to the control of another person.
3. The person works for an organisation and is part of the organisation (eg he or she wears the organisation's uniform and is subject to the organisation's working times or rules).
4. A person has worked for another person for an average of 40 hours per month over the last three months.
5. The person is economically dependent on the other person for whom he or she is working (eg the person has no other income).
6. The person is provided with tools of trade or work equipment by the other person.

employer may disprove the presumption

This section merely creates a presumption that can be disproved by the employer. The employer is entitled to prove that – despite some of these factors being present – the person is still an independent contractor.

6.2.1.3 Dominant impression test

'dominant impression' test

factors relevant to the 'dominant impression' test

Many tests have been used to try to decide whether a person is an employee or not. The most popular test is called the 'dominant impression' test, which looks at the main impression created by the contract and the working relationship. In other words: would an ordinary, reasonable person have thought that the person was an employee? Some of the factors relevant to this test are: (a) the employer's right to select who will do the work; (b) the employer's power to dismiss; (c) the employee's obligation to work for a given time and given hours; (d) whether remuneration is paid for the time worked or for a particular result (eg the completion of a building); and (e) whether the employer provides the employee with tools, equipment and office space.

6.2.1.4 Differences between employees and independent contractors

differences between employees and independent contractors

As has been previously mentioned, generally an employee is a person whom the employer can tell what to do and how to do it. An independent contractor is a person whom the person hiring his or her services can tell what to do but not how to do it. In an important case the Labour Appeal Court pointed out some of the important differences between an employee and independent contractor as follows:

1. The object of the employment contact is the rendering of personal services by the employee to the employer. The object of hiring an independent contractor is to get certain work done (eg a toilet fixed).
2. In an employment contract the employee will usually be at the beck and call of the employer. An independent contractor is not obliged to do the work himself or herself and may use other persons to do the work.
3. The employee is under the control of the employer and is required to obey the employer's instructions. The independent contractor is required to produce a particular piece of work and may do so however he or she sees fit.
4. An employment relationship is terminated on the death of the employee but a contract with an independent contractor may continue until the work is complete.
5. A contract of service ends when the period of service ends (eg if a person is employed for three months, the contract will end at the end of that time period), but a contract with an independent contractor ends when the work is complete.

Case study: Joe employs an independent contractor

Joe employs an independent contractor

Joe employs an independent contractor to fix a leak in a women's bathroom. The independent contractor completes the job and gives an invoice to Joe for the work done.

Problem 2: Identifying a person as an employee or an independent contractor

Questions

Consider the following examples, using the 'dominant impression' test to decide whether the following people are employees or independent contractors. Discuss why you reached the conclusion that you did.

1. Barry is employed as a computer consultant at a company for six months. He is given an office to work from and is told to restructure the company's website. He can work his own hours and is not supervised. He is required to submit a report to the company once a month. It is agreed that he will be paid R9 000 at the end of the job.
2. Jabu is a plumber. He enters into a contract where it is agreed that he will fix Sam's bath and shower. He leaves his workers at Sam's house in the morning and they do the work. It takes them a week to finish the job. Jabu then gives Sam an account for R3 000.
3. Peter is a gardener. He works for Mrs Smith three times a week. Mrs Smith is at work during the day and is not able to supervise Peter. Peter is provided with gardening equipment (eg a lawnmower and spades etc) by Mrs Smith. Peter is paid monthly.

6.2.2 Duties of employees and employers

6.2.2.1 Duties of employees

common-law duties of employees

In addition to the statutory obligations a number of common-law duties apply to the employee. They are under a duty to:

1. *Enter and remain in service*

   enter and remain in service

   Employees have to enter and remain in service of the employer. If they do not do this, they are not entitled to be paid (eg an employee who absents himself from work).
2. *Maintain reasonable efficiency*

   maintain reasonable efficiency

   Employees are expected to be competent and maintain reasonable efficiency and will be bound by the information given in their testimonials. For example, if employees tell employers that they are trained to operate a computer and this is untrue, they will be in breach of this duty and can be dismissed.
3. *Further the employer's business interests*

   further the employer's business interests

   Employees are under a duty to use all their working hours to further the employer's business interests. In other words they cannot compete with the employer's business or take on a second job during normal working hours – unless with the permission of the employer.
4. *Be respectful and obedient*

   be respectful and obedient

   It is necessary for an employee to show the employer respect and obedience – a failure to do so would undermine the employment relationship.

refrain from misconduct generally

5. *Refrain from misconduct generally*
   Employers must refrain from misconduct generally. Misconduct that makes the continuation of the employment relationship unworkable is sufficient to justify dismissal. Examples of misconduct that justifies dismissal are dishonesty, drunkenness, gross negligence, insolence, fighting and absenteeism (see below para 6.9.2.2).

6.2.2.2 Duties of employers

According to the common law there are three main duties of employers:

to receive the employee into service

1. *To receive the employee into service*
   As service is a pre-requisite for being paid, it is the duty of the employer to receive the employee into service.

to remunerate the employee

2. *To pay the employee*
   The employer is under a duty to pay employees for their services.

to provide safe working conditions

3. *To ensure safe working conditions*
   In terms of the common law and the Constitution the employer must provide the employee with safe and healthy working conditions. This is also governed by the Occupational Health and Safety Act (see below para 6.3.2).

6.3 Labour laws and social benefits

Outcomes

After completion of this section learners will be able to:

1. Explain the laws that apply to skills, health and safety and benefits of the workplace.

Assessment criteria

1. The purpose and application of the Basic Conditions of Employment Act is explained.
2. The concept of paternity leave is discussed.
3. The purpose and application of the Occupational Health and Safety Act is explained.
4. The principle of minimum wages is discussed.
5. The purpose and application of the Skills Development Act is explained.
6. A set of facts is examined and a decision is made on the most appropriate benefits for an employee.
7. The purpose and application of the Compensation for Occupational Injuries and Diseases Act is explained.

laws affecting employers and employees

Once a person is employed there are a large number of laws that apply to both the employee and the employer. These laws deal with hours of work and conditions at the workplace, unions, health and safety at the workplace and protecting employees against unfair labour practices.

6.3.1 Basic conditions of employment

working conditions

The Basic Conditions of Employment Act of 1997 sets out the basic working conditions to which an employee is entitled. It applies to all employees. It imposes the following working conditions, amongst others:

maximum working hours and overtime

1. Maximum working hours (45 hours a week);
2. Maximum overtime (10 hours a week);
3. Sick leave (1 day for every 26 days worked during the first four months of employment; thereafter the employee is entitled to 6 weeks during every 36 month cycle);

different types of leave

4. Annual leave (21 consecutive days a year);
5. Maternity leave (4 months); and
6. Family responsibility leave (3 days a year).

It also states that employees have a right to be paid for services rendered and a right to be given a certificate of service when they leave the service of an employer.

Problem 1: Understanding the Basic Conditions of Employment Act

Questions

1. Do you think that it is necessary to have a Basic Conditions of Employment Act? What about the situation where an employee would like to work more than the maximum hours permitted by the Act and is prevented from doing so?
2. Maternity leave is special leave that is granted to women who give birth. They are entitled to four months' unpaid leave. Many people argue that the law should also provide for paternity leave – leave granted to a father as a result of the birth of his child. Do you think that fathers should be entitled to paternity leave?

6.3.2 Health and safety

safe and healthy working conditions

health and safety representatives

employees must take reasonable care of themselves

health and safety inspectors

Employees are entitled to safe and healthy working conditions. The Occupational Health and Safety Act requires employers to provide a safe working environment for employees. Employers are required to make sure that: (a) machinery and equipment is safe; (b) employees are provided with protective equipment (eg safety hats) where necessary; and (c) employees are not exposed to dangerous substances. Employers are required to appoint health and safety representatives (where there are at least 20 employees at the workplace), who are required to identify potential hazards, investigate the causes of accidents and investigate complaints by employees. Employees are also required to take reasonable care of themselves, obey the employer's health and safety rules and report unsafe working conditions to the employer. Employees are obliged to report any accident at the workplace to their employers or the health and safety representatives at the workplace. The Act also provides for health and safety inspectors (who are appointed by the government) to inspect workplaces for safety hazards and to investigate accidents at the workplace.

Case study: The unsafe working environment

There is a leak in a bathroom at a hotel. The leaking pipes are next to an electrical box and a contractor has been called in to fix the leak. Instead of ensuring that the contractor is not electrocuted, Joe shouts at him. This is an unsafe working environment.

leaking pipes are next to an electrical box

6.3.3 Minimum wages

minimum wages

extended to domestic workers

Employees are entitled to be paid (remunerated) for their services. The Basic Conditions of Employment Act makes provision for the government to set minimum wages for certain industries. A minimum wage has been extended to domestic workers.

Problem 2: Do you agree with minimum wages?

Questions

Should all workers be covered by a minimum wage? Give reasons for your answer. Some people are concerned that the minimum wage that has been imposed with regard to domestic workers will result in domestic workers losing their jobs. Do you agree? Give reasons for your answer.

6.3.4 Skills development

Skills Development Act

Many workers are unskilled and uneducated. As a result it is difficult for them to advance themselves or to be promoted at the workplace. Parliament has passed the Skills Development Act, which requires employers to pay a levy of 1% of their payroll to finance the training and development of employees.

Sector Education and Training Authorities (SETAs)

Sector Education and Training Authorities (SETAs) have been set up and their main tasks are to: (a) establish 'learnerships'; (b) approve workplace skills plans; (c) allocate grants and monitor education and training in the sector; and (d) collect and disburse skills development levies. 'Learnerships' consist of structured courses, including practical work. Employers are obliged to enter into agreements with learners, in terms of which they must undertake to: (a) employ the learner for the time specified in the agreement; (b) provide the learner with specified practical work experience; and (c) release the learner to attend education and training courses specified in the agreement. The Act prohibits employers from terminating learnership agreements before the learner has successfully completed the programme, unless the termination is approved by a SETA, or the learner is fairly dismissed for reasons relating to his or her conduct or capacity.

employers must enter into agreements with learners

Case study: Nicole needs training

Nicole has been working at Speedy Print for a week and has learnt from her colleagues when and if she needed to do something. Now Nicole has to do the cutting and is in serious danger of hurting herself unless her manager shows her how to do it properly.

Nicole's manager needs to show her how to work properly

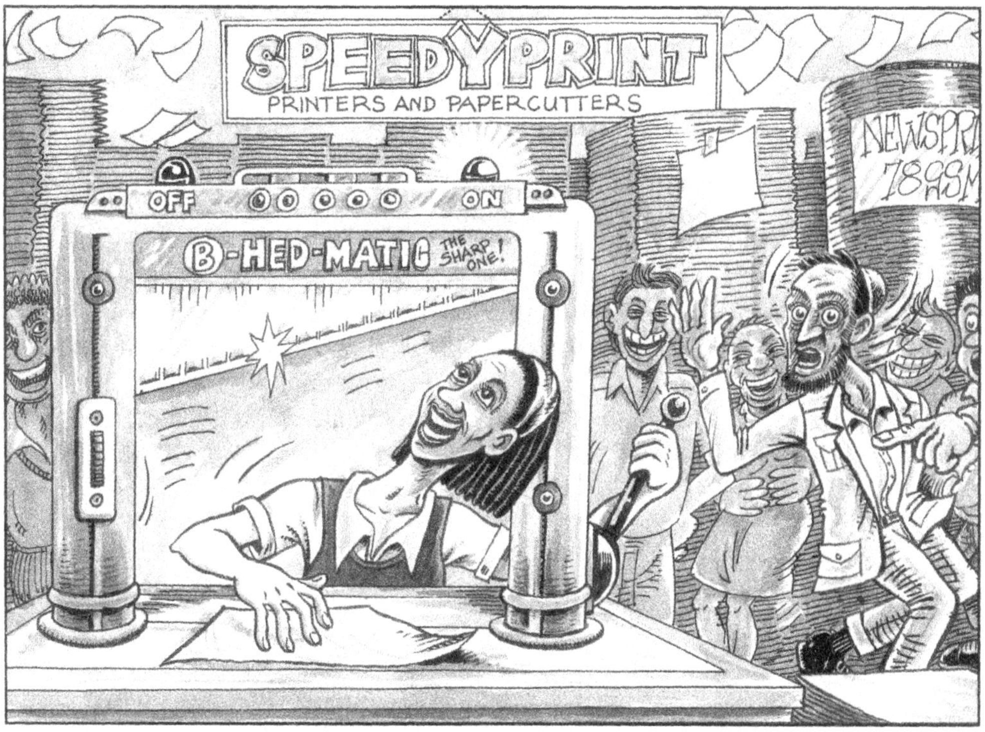

6.3.5 Compensation for occupational injuries

Compensation for Occupational Injuries and Diseases Act

If an employee is injured at work or becomes ill as a result of an industrial disease (eg from being exposed to asbestos, which can cause a disease of the lungs), the employee is entitled to claim compensation for his or her injuries or illness from the Compensation for Occupational Injuries and Diseases Fund. This is provided for in terms of the Compensation for Occupational Injuries and Diseases Act (commonly referred to as COIDA). If there is an accident at work the employer is obliged to report it to the Compensation Commissioner within 12 months

employers must report accidents

of the incident. Claims for compensation must be made by the employee to the Compensation for Occupational Injuries and Diseases Fund. This fund is financed by compulsory contributions made by employers and is a form of insurance for employees. If an employee is killed at work his or her dependants may claim from the Fund. Employees are entitled to be compensated from the fund for any workplace-related injury or illness. To claim compensation it is not necessary to prove negligence on the part of the employee or the employer. However, employees cannot claim from their employers for any injury or illness covered by COIDA.

dependants may claim

employees may not claim from employers

6.3.6 Social benefits

additional workplace benefits

depends upon the employment contract

The employer may provide additional benefits to an employee, over and above the employee's salary. Examples of these benefits are medical aid schemes, pension funds, free parking, education funds, insurance, an entertainment allowance and housing benefits. The employer is not obliged to provide these benefits and whether they are given depends upon the contract of employment that is entered into between the employer and the employee.

employers must register employees with the Unemployment Insurance Fund

It is compulsory for the employer to register employees with, and contribute towards, the Unemployment Insurance Fund. This is governed by the Unemployment Insurance Act. This Act aims to provide benefits to employees who have lost their jobs as a result of pregnancy or circumstances beyond their control. Both employers and employees are required to pay 1% of the employee's salary into the Unemployment Insurance Fund. The money in the Fund is used to pay benefits to employees when they become unemployed. For example, women are entitled to claim unemployment benefits during their maternity leave.

Problem 3: What benefits are appropriate?

Questions

Kim, age 22, has just graduated from university and is going to work for a computer company. Kim is unmarried and lives with her parents. She hopes to be able to study further while working. What company benefits would most interest her? Why?

6.4 Collective bargaining and trade unions

Outcomes

After completion of this section learners will be able to:

1. Explain the meaning of collective bargaining and how trade unions work.

Assessment criteria

1. The concept of collective bargaining is explained.
2. The advantages and disadvantages of belonging to a trade union are discussed.
3. The rules that apply to strikes are identified.
4. A set of facts is examined and a decision made on whether the conduct during a strike was lawful or unlawful.
5. A negotiation exercise is undertaken and an agreement reached.

6.4.1 Collective bargaining

a trade union is an association of workers

When someone starts a job it is important to find out if the company has a trade union. A trade union is an association of workers that seeks to resolve disputes between the employer and employees, secures wage increases for the employees and seeks to improve working conditions. Unions engage in collective bargaining, which is the process of settling labour disputes through negotiations between the employer and representatives of the employees. It is a process of making demands and giving concessions in order to reach agreement. In other words they negotiate as a group with the employer. For example, if the employees would like a wage increase, the union will enter into collective bargaining with the employer on behalf of the employees. If the employer refuses to give a wage increase the union can call for the workers to go on strike. In this way unions are very effective in putting pressure on employers. As a result it is often thought that employees who belong to unions are better protected, earn higher wages and have better working conditions.

unions enter into collective bargaining with employers

only registered trade unions may enter into collective agreements

The first point to note is that only registered trade unions may enter into a collective agreement – unregistered trade unions may not enter into such agreements. Secondly, the collective agreement must be reduced to writing. It should also take the form of an agreement where the parties are named and the terms of the agreement are clearly set out. Thirdly, there must be agreement between the parties authorised to enter into the collective agreement. Finally, the content of a collective agreement must regulate the terms and conditions of employment.

Case study: Phindi joins a trade union

Phindi becomes a trade union representative

When Phindi started working at a shoe factory in her area, she realised that becoming a member of a trade union was very important. The trade union negotiates with the employer around issues such as pay and working conditions. Now Phindi is one of the trade union's representatives so she is able to help other employees.

6.4.2. Collective agreements

collective agreements set out the rights of employees

Unions can conclude an agreement with the employer, called a collective agreement, where the rights of the employees are negotiated and agreed to by the employer. Those who criticise unions say that they result in more strikes at the workplace and less harmony between employers and employees. The right to strike and freedom of association is protected in the Constitution.

6.4.3 Union representatives

union representatives are protected against victimisation

union members pay union fees

The Labour Relations Act protects the union's rights to represent employees and protects union members from being victimised for exercising their rights. Unions are entitled to appoint an employee at the workplace to be a shop steward (union representative). Shop stewards assist employees in disciplinary hearings and grievance proceedings and monitor the employer's conduct to make sure that the employer is complying with the Act. If an employee joins a union the person will have to pay union dues (membership fees).

6.4.4 Negotiating wages and working conditions

unions negotiate better wages and working conditions for employees

Unions negotiate better wages and working conditions for employees. Negotiation is a process whereby either party tries to persuade the other party to agree with their point of view. In order to have a successful negotiation it is very important that both sides listen to the other party's views and are prepared to reach some form of compromise. A successful negotiator will exercise patience and control during negotiations. Union representatives are often very experienced negotiators. An unsuccessful negotiation may result in a strike, which is damaging to both employers and employees.

6.4.4.1 Negotiation

negotiation involves parties talking to each other

Negotiation is a process whereby the parties involved in a dispute talk to each other about their problems and try to reach an agreement.

Steps in a negotiation

preparing for negotiation

Preparing for negotiation:
Before going into a negotiation the parties should be prepared. Each side should understand all the relevant facts and laws. They should decide what their bottom lines are and what is not negotiable. They should try to put themselves in the shoes of the other side and think about the other side's demands.

the negotiation process

The negotiation process:
The two sides should try to establish a good working relationship with each other and try to be as polite and friendly as possible. Good negotiators are good listeners and should let the other party know that they are listening to them. Parties to a negotiation should brainstorm all the different possible solutions to the dispute. They should not make unrealistic demands and should think of creative solutions. They should not be abusive, demanding or threatening. They should not give away things without getting something in return. They should use words like 'if I give you this, will you give me that?'

reaching an agreement

Reaching an agreement:
The parties must show each other that they are ready to reach a compromise. Agreements must be as fair as possible to both sides. Both sides should feel that they came away with something that they wanted.

Problem 1: The annual wage negotiation

Questions

Ace Mining Company employs 400 employees. The union that represents them is the Mine Workers Union. During the annual wage negotiations the employees demand the following:

1. A wage increase of 15% bringing the minimum wage up to R3 400 per month.
2. A transport allowance of R200.
3. Maternity leave of five months.
4. Paternity leave of two weeks.

5. Tea and coffee to be provided by the employer.
6. Provision of new uniforms.
7. A contribution towards a pension scheme.

The employer has experienced a very difficult year financially and offers the following:

1. A wage increase of 7% with a minimum wage of R2 800 per month.
2. No transport allowance, as this has never been offered before. They are, however, prepared to offer an annual transport award of R600.
3. Maternity leave of four months.
4. No paternity leave.
5. No tea and coffee.
6. New uniforms when the old ones are worn out.
7. No pension contributions.

Divide the learners into two large groups:

(a) Representatives of the employees; and
(b) Representatives of the employers.

Each large group should be further divided into smaller groups of not more than five each containing the same representatives.

negotiate a settlement between the employees and employers

You are required to negotiate a settlement between the union and the employer. Use your powers of persuasion to try to reach a settlement between the employer's offers and the employees' demands. Remember that if a settlement is not reached, the employees will go on strike and this will be damaging to both the employer's business (which will not be able to operate) and to the employees (who will not be paid). For how to conduct a negotiation, see above para 1.3.2.1.

draw up a collective agreement

Try to draw up a collective agreement that is a compromise between the employer and the employees.

6.4.5 Strikes

strikes result in the withholding of their labour by employees

certain procedures must be followed for a lawful strike

Unions make it easier for employees to go on strike. Strikes result in the withholding of labour, even partially, by the employees for the purpose of resolving a grievance or dispute between the employer and employees. Even a 'go-slow' (where the employees continue working but work much slower than usual so as to hold up production) constitutes a strike. Strikes are very useful weapons in the hands of the employees as they can financially cripple the business of an employer. As a result they can put pressure on the employer to agree to the employees' demands. The Labour Relations Act sets out the procedures that have to be followed for employees to go on strike. If the union and employees do not follow these procedures the strike will be an unlawful strike and the employees can be dismissed. In addition the union and employees may have to pay financial compensation to the employer for the losses as a result of the strike.

the Labour Relations Act sets out the procedures that have to be followed for a lawful strike

Workers strike for various reasons, eg more overtime, higher wages and better working conditions.

6.4.5.1 Procedures for a lawful strike

the dispute must first be referred to a bargaining council or the CCMA

The Labour Relations Act sets out the procedures that have to be followed for a lawful strike. First the union has to refer the dispute to a bargaining council or the CCMA, which will attempt to try to resolve the dispute. (The CCMA is the Commission for Conciliation, Mediation and Arbitration which was set up to deal with labour disputes, see below para 6.10.1.) The union must wait for a certificate to be issued by the CCMA or the Bargaining Council stating that the dispute remains unresolved. The purpose is to firstly ensure that employees do not engage in strikes unnecessarily and secondly to compel the parties to the dispute to undergo conciliation.

if a dispute is not resolved a 'strike notice' must be given to the employer

If the dispute is not resolved within 30 days the union will have to give 48 hours' notice to the employer (called a 'strike notice') that it intends to call a strike. The strike notice must specify the exact day on which the strike will commence. The exact time, ie minute and hour, is not necessary. It is important to note that the employees are not obliged to commence the strike at the exact time stipulated in the strike notice. The right to strike is not waived if the strike procedure has been followed and the employees commence the strike within a reasonable period.

48 hours after the strike notice is given the employees may go on strike

After the 48 hours have passed the employees can go on strike. In other words the workers will stop working and as a result the business will be unable to operate. The workers can either stay at home during the strike or they 'can picket' at the workplace. When strikers picket they are allowed to stand at the entrance picketing must be peaceful and non-violent

to the workplace and hold placards and toyi-toyi. It is important for the picket to be peaceful and non-violent. If it is not, the employees can be dismissed for misconduct during the strike. If employees strike, the employer is allowed to employ 'scab' labourers (replacement labourers) during the strike so as to keep its business open.

6.4.5.2 No work, no pay

'no work, no pay' applies during a strike

Employees who go on strike are not entitled to be paid because of the rule of 'no work, no pay'. The strike will continue until one of the sides gives up – either the employer agreeing to the employees' demands or vice versa.

6.4.5.3 Essential services and maintenance services

essential services employees are not allowed to strike

Some employees are not allowed to strike. These are employees who work for essential services such as the police, the ambulance services, the fire brigade and maintenance services. An 'essential service' is defined as 'a service, the interruption of which endangers the life, personal safety or health of the whole or part of the population', and includes the Parliamentary service and the SAPS. A service is regarded as a maintenance service if the interruption of the service results in the physical destruction of the working area, plant or machinery.

Problem 2: The role of unions

Questions

1. What are the advantages and disadvantages of having a union at a workplace?
2. Draw up a list of the employees that you think should be classified as 'essential services'. Give reasons for including them on your list.
3. Examine the following examples and decide whether the conduct is lawful:
   (a) The employees decide to work slowly to show their dissatisfaction about working conditions.
   (b) While the employees are picketing outside the employer's business they throw stones at cars driving past.
   (c) The employees follow proper strike procedure yet the employer decides to dismiss them.
   (d) The employer does not pay the employees while they are on strike.
   (e) The nurses in the maternity ward of a hospital go on strike.
   (f) All the employees of a company leave work early to attend a funeral – without the permission of their employer.

6.5 Disciplinary codes

Outcomes

After completion of this section learners will be able to:

1. Explain the purpose and application of disciplinary codes.

Assessment criteria

1. The purpose of a disciplinary code is explained.
2. The concept of progressive and corrective discipline is explained.
3. An example of a disciplinary code is given.
4. A disciplinary code is drafted.

6.5.1 Standards of conduct expected of employees

employees must follow the rules of their employers and not misconduct themselves

It is very important for the efficient running of a business that employees follow the rules laid down by the employer and do not misconduct themselves. Very often employers draw up a set of rules known as a disciplinary code. This is drawn up in consultation with the union or the employee representatives. A disciplinary code sets out the standards of conduct required of an employee and indicates the punishment that will be imposed on an employee if the rule is broken. The form and content of the code will depend upon the particular workplace. For example, drinking alcohol on duty at a workplace that uses dangerous machinery will be regarded as more serious than drinking alcohol in other work situations.

Case study: Alfonso blows his nose into the casserole he is cooking

Alfonso blows his nose into the casserole he is cooking

Carlos owns an Italian restaurant. It is his pride and joy and he runs it very well. He has the Disciplinary Rules on the kitchen wall and has discussed them with his employees. Alfonso doesn't care about these rules and blows his nose into the casserole that he is cooking. Carlos is very angry.

6.5.2 Larger businesses and acts of misconduct

large businesses have more formal codes than small businesses

Large businesses may have a more formal disciplinary code than small businesses. Depending on the seriousness of the misconduct the punishment will vary. Very serious acts of misconduct (eg theft or assault) may result in dismissal. Less serious offences (eg smoking in the workplace) may result in a lesser punishment such as a written warning – except if the employee is working in a fire hazard environment (eg smoking at a petrol service station). If an employee repeats an offence the punishment may increase accordingly. For example, if an employee is late for work once it is likely that he or she will be given a first written warning. If the person is late again (before the warning lapses – which is usually after six months), he or she may get a more serious punishment such as a final written warning. If the employee is late yet again for work within this period, he or she may be dismissed for this offence, even though the misconduct itself is not so serious.

if an employee repeats an offence the punishment may increase

6.5.3 Corrective and progressive discipline

corrective and progressive discipline

This is an example of what a disciplinary code may look like:

Offence	1st	2nd	3rd	4th
Theft	Dismissal			
Assault	Final written warning/ Dismissal			
Smoking	First Written warning	Final written warning	Dismissal	
Lateness	Verbal warning	First written warning	Final written warning	Dismissal
Failure to wear hard hat	Final written warning	Dismissal		

the purpose of disciplinary codes is to make sure that employees know what conduct is expected of them

The purpose of disciplinary codes is to make sure that the employees know what conduct is expected of them and what punishment they may receive if they break these rules. All employees must be made aware of the disciplinary rules. This can be done by placing the rules on a company notice board or by giving a copy to each employee. The rules provide the employer with a way of correcting the employees' conduct by initially giving them a chance (for less serious offences). Employees can be dismissed either for repeated acts of less serious misconduct or for acts of serious misconduct.

not all businesses have disciplinary codes

Not all businesses have disciplinary codes (particularly smaller businesses). The difficulty with this is that employers must first prove that the misconduct was very serious and that the employee was aware of the seriousness of it, before dismissing the employee.

Problem 1: Drafting a disciplinary code

Questions

Imagine that you are the employer at a manufacturing plant. The factory uses very expensive and dangerous machinery and is manned by 100 factory workers. The machines are switched on at 8 am daily and are switched off every day at 5 pm.

Draw up a disciplinary code in respect of the following offences: You will need to decide which offences are more serious and less serious and the appropriate punishment for each offence:

1. Drinking on duty.
2. Insubordination (failure to obey a lawful instruction).
3. Lateness (poor timekeeping).
4. Absenteeism.
5. Theft.
6. Assault.
7. Smoking on duty.
8. Not wearing a proper uniform.
9. Leaving a workstation untidy.
10. Leaving a workstation unattended.
11. Sexual harassment of co-workers.
12. Negligent work.

If the business was a retail store, would your views change? Draw up a disciplinary code in respect of the above offences for a retail store such as a supermarket.

6.6 Privacy at work and protected disclosures

Outcomes

After completion of this section learners will be able to:

1. Explain the meaning of privacy and its application in the workplace.
2. Explain the law regarding 'whistle blowing'.

Assessment criteria

1. The meaning of privacy and its limits at the workplace are discussed.
2. The employer's right to perform drug tests and searches at the workplace is discussed.
3. The employer's right to perform polygraph tests on employees is discussed.
4. The employer's right to regulate an employee's use of e-mail and the Internet at work is discussed.
5. A set of facts is examined and a decision taken on whether the employee's rights to privacy were infringed.
6. A set of facts is examined and a decision made on whether the disclosures by the 'whistle-blower' are protected by the Protected Disclosures Act.

6.6.1 Constitutional and common-law rights

the right to privacy is often referred to as the 'right to be left alone'

The right to privacy is often referred to as the 'right to be left alone' and is protected by the Constitution and the common law. This means that individuals should be free to decide how much of their personal lives they wish to share with others. Many people say that privacy is not possible at work because an employer has the right to monitor, supervise and evaluate his or her employees' work in order to see that they are doing their job properly. However many people believe that they do not give up their right to privacy when they take a job. For example, if an employee is required to be medically tested, the results of those tests should be regarded as private and confidential.

Case study: The manager is searched on his way home

Mr Robert is searched on his way out of the office even though he is a manager. His firm's policy is to search all employees when they arrive and leave work. The security guard finds a gun in Mr Robert's briefcase and will have to report it to the directors.

the security guard finds a gun in Mr Robert's briefcase

6.6.2 Security cameras and searches

the use of security cameras and searches must be reasonable

Employers who are concerned about security at the workplace often install security cameras and undertake searches of employees (and their bags) when they leave the workplace. This is acceptable, provided that the measures taken are reasonable.

6.6.3 E-mail and Internet use

e-mail and Internet use may be monitored if there is an e-mail/Internet policy in force

A controversial question that has arisen recently is whether employers can monitor, and read if necessary, private e-mail correspondence of employees. The general view taken is that employers are only entitled to do this if they have an e-mail/Internet policy in force so that employees are aware of the rules and the consequences of breaking them. This policy is to prevent employees from abusing these facilities for their private use during working hours.

6.6.4 Dress code

the dress code and hairstyles of employees may be regulated

Employers can also generally regulate how employees dress on the job. Employers can require employees to abide by a dress code or even to wear their hair in a certain style. They may also require them to wear certain clothing for safety or health reasons.

6.6.5 Drug testing

drug testing may be justifiable if it is relevant to employment conditions

One of the most controversial issues involving privacy at the workplace is the drug testing of employees. Although the Employment Equity Act does not specifically mention drug testing it is clear that medical testing will only be allowed if legislation permits it. It may be regarded as justifiable in the light of medical facts where it is relevant to employment conditions, social policy, the fair distribution of employee benefits or the inherent requirements of a job.

6.6.6 Polygraph tests

polygraph tests are lie detector tests

If an employee is suspected of having committed misconduct, (for example theft), the employer may require the person to undertake a polygraph test. A polygraph test is a lie detector test. Employees are strapped up to equipment that can detect an increased heartbeat and increased nervousness (such as sweating palms). The employees are then asked questions and if they give a dishonest answer the machine is able to detect it. These tests are not 100% conclusive and as a result employees cannot be dismissed solely on the basis of a failed polygraph test. (Some people, however, say that they are 98% accurate). Employees also cannot be forced to take the test, but a refusal to do so will often result in a negative inference being drawn about them.

polygraph tests are not 100% accurate

Problem 1: Were the employees' rights to privacy infringed?

Questions

Decide whether the employee's right to privacy was infringed in each of the following situations and explain your answers:

1. Vasentha, who works for a construction company, has applied for a new job with a cement company. The manager of the cement company phones the manager of the construction company to get a reference. The manager of the construction company reads the contents of Vasentha's personal file to him, including negative comments about her working abilities.
2. Tshepo is missing some expensive jewellery from his store. He asks the police to come and search all the handbags of the employees before they leave work.
3. To reduce theft at the company Mr Jones installs security cameras to watch his employees.
4. Pat owns a company. She begins to monitor the electronic mail between her employees. She fires Jim after discovering that he has sent an e-mail to another employee which contained jokes.
5. Lionel works in a bakery and wears his hair in dreadlocks. His employer tells him to cut his hair if he wishes to continue working at the company.
6. Due to huge stock losses at the company all the employees are required to take a polygraph test. They are advised by their employer that if they refuse to take the test they will be fired.

6.6.7 'Whistle blowing'

6.6.7.1 Who is a 'whistle-blower'?

'whistle-blowers' report people who break the law

A whistle-blower is a person who 'blows the whistle' on another person by reporting him or her for breaking a law. For example, if the employer requires employees to work for more than the maximum number of hours a week, an employee may 'blow the whistle' on the employer by reporting him or her to the Department of Labour.

whistle-blowers may not be subjected to 'occupational detriment'

Situations where whistle-blowers have been prejudiced at work because of their activities are known as 'occupational detriment' and have been included in the definition of unfair labour practice. Neither the common law nor Acts of Parliament provides procedures for how employees may disclose information on suspected criminal or irregular conduct of the employer without fear. The Protected Disclosures Act provides that such criminal or irregular conduct is bad for good governance in South Africa. The Act promotes a culture of openness and accountability without fear of reprisal (being punished) and the ending of criminal and other conduct. The Act protects employees in the public and private sector from being subjected to an occupational detriment (prejudice in the workplace) on account of having made a protected disclosure.

information that whistle-blowers may disclose without being subjected to 'occupational detriment'

Disclosure refers to any disclosure of information regarding any conduct of an employer or employee of that employer, made by any employee who has reason to believe that the information shows or tends to show one of the following:

- That a criminal offence has been committed, is being committed or is likely to be committed;
- That a person has failed, is failing or is likely to fail to comply with any legal obligation to which that person is subject;
- A miscarriage of justice has occurred, is occurring or is likely to occur;
- the health and safety of an individual has been, is being or is likely to be endangered;
- The environment has been, is being or is likely to be damaged;
- Unfair discrimination is occurring in the workplace; or
- Any matter referred to above has been, is being or is likely to be deliberately concealed.

types of 'occupational detriment'

'Occupational detriment' refers to prejudice to the whistle blowing employee in the working environment. It involves the employee being subjected to:

- Any disciplinary action;
- Dismissal, suspension, demotion, harassment or intimidation;
- Transferral against the will of the employee;
- Refusal of a transfer or promotion etc.

protected disclosures are made to specific persons, bodies or regulators

A protected disclosure is a disclosure which has been made to specific persons, bodies or regulators. These include a legal advisor; an employer; a member of cabinet; the executive council of a province; specified persons; bodies such as the public protector, etc.

requirements for an unfair labour practice based on 'occupational detriment'

An employee has to satisfy three requirements in order to establish an unfair labour practice based on 'occupational detriment':

- The employee must have made a protected disclosure in terms of the Protected Disclosure Act;
- The employer must have taken action against the employee which amounts to 'occupational detriment' in terms of the Protected Disclosures Act; and
- The 'detriment' suffered must be on account of or partly on account of having made the protected disclosure – ie there must be a link between the disclosure and the detrimental action of the employer.

Critics of the Protection of Information Bill of 2013 are worried that it will undermine the Protected Disclosures Act and lead to whistle-blowers who publish information about corruption or abuses by state officials being prosecuted and sentenced to terms of imprisonment.

Problem 2: Were the disclosures protected?

Questions

Do you think that the following disclosures should be protected by the Protected Disclosures Act?

1. Stephen has an argument with his employer and reports him to the Receiver of Revenue for tax evasion.
2. Temba reports his employer to the CCMA for alleged racist behaviour.
3. Tina tells her friend, who is a manager at a competing company, that her company is about to launch an exclusive product.
4. Fanie is concerned about his safety at work as there is inadequate ventilation in the factory. He decides to report his employer to the Health and Safety Commission.
5. Sue and Premilla, both employees at the company, voice their dissatisfaction with their annual bonuses. They write a letter to a local newspaper complaining about their 'poor' bonuses.

6.7 Employment equity

Outcomes

After completion of this section learners will be able to:

1. Explain the purpose and application of the Employment Equity Act.

Assessment criteria

1. The Employment Equity Act is explained.
2. Different forms of discrimination are identified.
3. The purpose and nature of employment equity plans are discussed.
4. An arbitration exercise involving discrimination is undertaken.

6.7.1 Employment Equity Act

The Employment Equity Act has two main functions:

1. To eliminate discriminatory practices at the workplace; and
2. To introduce affirmative action measures, to achieve a diverse and representative workforce by advancing previously disadvantaged employees.

discriminatory workplace practices are prohibited

Workplace practices include recruitment, appointments, job classification or grading, wages, benefits and terms of employment, job assignments, the working environment, training and development, performance evaluation systems, promotion, transfer, demotion, disciplinary measures and dismissal. Any workplace practice that has a discriminatory effect is prohibited.

6.7.2 Forms of discrimination

There are two types of discrimination – direct and indirect discrimination.

6.7.2.1 Direct discrimination

direct discrimination is based on a protected or listed ground

Direct discrimination is discrimination on a protected ground or listed ground. A protected ground is one of the grounds listed in both the Constitution and the Employment Equity Act, namely 'race, gender, sex, pregnancy, marital status, family responsibility, ethnic or social origin, colour, sexual orientation, age, disability, religion, HIV status (only in the Employment Equity Act), conscience, belief, political opinion, culture, language or birth.'

Direct discrimination can occur when an employer treats a woman less favourably than a man on the basis of her sex. Motive or intention does not need to be proved in order to establish direct discrimination.

Problem 1: Examples of discrimination

Questions

Using the protected grounds listed above, think of an example of each type of discrimination mentioned above (eg racial discrimination – promoting only white employees).

6.7.2.2 Indirect discrimination

indirect discrimination uses neutral criteria to disadvantage a specific group of employees

Indirect discrimination is when neutral criteria are used but are materially disadvantageous to a specific group of employees. For example, requiring all employees to have a beard seems to be non-discriminatory on the face of it, but actually indirectly discriminates against all women and so is indirect discrimination on the grounds of gender.

contravention of the Employment Equity Act

If an employer discriminates unfairly against an employee, whether it is direct or indirect discrimination, the employer will be acting in contravention of the Employment Equity Act.

Problem 2: Examples of indirect discrimination

Questions

List two examples of what you think could be regarded as indirect discrimination.

6.7.2.3 Pay discrimination

pay discrimination occurs where two employees earn different salaries for the same work

A typical type of discrimination is pay discrimination where two people, who are performing the same or similar work, are paid different salaries. Unless there is a good reason for the difference (for example where one of the employees is better qualified, or has worked longer at the company), this will be regarded as pay discrimination. The employer will then have to give a good reason why one of the employees is being paid a higher salary.

6.7.2.4 Employment equity plan and report

employers must draw up an employment equity plan and report

As discussed earlier the Employment Equity Act requires employers to draw up an employment equity plan and report. The employer is required to draw up a profile of the workforce (for example the race and gender of each employee and the rank and job he or she has). The employer is then expected to look at the company's policies and practices to try and see which might be discriminatory. The employer must then draw up an employment equity plan which sets out how he or she intends to make progress towards employment equity (ie the equitable representation of all race groups and genders).

Case study: Mr Dlamini is paid less than Mr Smith

Mr Dlamini is paid less than Mr Smith

Mr Dlamini and Mr Smith are both senior managers. Their boss prefers Mr Smith so he pays him more than Mr Dlamini. Unless there is good reason for this, it is direct discrimination and contravenes the Employment Equity Act.

The employment equity plan must set out the following:

1. The plan for the next year;
2. Affirmative action measures to be adopted or implemented;
3. Where there is under-representation of a particular group, a strategy to correct this;
4. A timetable for the achievement of these goals;
5. The procedures to be used to monitor and implement the plan; and
6. The persons responsible for the monitoring and implementation (eg which senior manager will be responsible).

Case study: ABC Company has problems with employment equity

no black or women senior managers

An examination of the workforce of ABC Company reveals that 90% of senior managers are white males, and the remaining 10% are Indian males. There are no black or women senior managers. The unskilled employees consist of the following: 70% black female, 15% Indian female, 10% black male and 5% Indian male. There is clearly a problem with employment equity, and the company will have to consider:

1. What policies or practices led to this situation;

2. What steps can be taken to rectify the problem;
3. What procedures will be used (eg training, promotions); and
4. Which senior employees or employers will be responsible for overseeing the changes.

the employment equity plan must be reported to the Department of Labour

Once a company has drawn up an employment equity plan it must file a report with the Department of Labour. It must then report annually to the Department on the implementation of the plan.

6.7.2.5 Using arbitration to settle employment equity issues

Arbitration happens when a third party (the arbitrator) listens to the arguments of both sides and makes a decision that is binding on them. It may be used to settle employment equity disputes.

Steps in an arbitration

- **Both sides prepare:**
  Representatives from both sides will have an opportunity tell their sides of the story. They should prepare questions to ask the other side.
- **Telling the stories:**
  The complaining side first tells its side of the story. The arbitrator can ask questions to make sure that he or she understands the facts clearly. The other side can also ask questions of (cross-examine) the complaining side. The other side then tells its side of the story and the arbitrator and the other side can also ask questions.
- **The arbitrator makes a decision: (making a decision)**
  Once the arbitrator has heard all the information, he or she can make a decision that is binding on both parties. There is no right of appeal.

Problem 3: An arbitration between mineworkers and their employer

Black workers in a mine complain that, because of the time taken to lift workers to the surface, they have to spend two to three hours longer in the mines each day than white supervisors. The decision about who is brought up to the surface first at the end of the shift is based on whether the person is a supervisor and who has worked there the longest (seniority). Workers claim that this is discriminatory. The management says that it is justified in the case of supervisors because they need to do paperwork in the office after they come up.

Most mineworkers are black and most supervisors are white. Until recently all the supervisory jobs were reserved for whites. Black workers have recently been promoted to supervisory jobs but are still less senior than white supervisors and continue to be the last supervisors to be brought up out of the mines each day.

Conduct an arbitration between the mineworkers and management using the steps in the box above.

6.8 Unfair labour practices and sexual harassment

Outcomes

After completion of this section learners will be able to:

1. Understand what is meant by unfair labour practices and sexual harassment.

Assessment criteria

1. The concept of an unfair labour practice and the different forms of sexual harassment are identified.
2. An employer's obligations in respect of sexual harassment at the workplace are discussed.
3. A set of facts is examined and a decision taken on whether or not the conduct was sexual harassment.

6.8.1 Unfair labour practices

unfair labour practices usually occur where employees are unfairly promoted, demoted or trained

The Labour Relations Act sets out what an unfair labour practice is. An unfair labour practice arises where an employer treats an employee unfairly with regard to promotion, demotion or training. For example, if an employer promoted an employee because he or she was a friend, and not because of the employee's abilities, the other employees would be able to claim that they were the victims of an unfair labour practice and refer the matter to the CCMA for a decision. The same applies if the employer unfairly suspends an employee.

requirements for an unfair labour practice

In order for there to be an unfair labour practice:

- The labour practice must arise between the employer and the employee.
- The conduct (whether an act or omission) must be unfair.
- The unfair labour practice must happen while the employees are working for the employer.

6.8.2 Sexual harassment

6.8.2.1 Unwanted conduct of a sexual nature

unwanted conduct of a sexual nature

behaviour stated to be offensive or should be known to be offensive

Employees are entitled to be protected against sexual harassment at the workplace. Sexual harassment has been defined as 'unwanted conduct of a sexual nature'. Sexual attention becomes sexual harassment when the behaviour is persisted in and/or the recipient (the harassed employee) has made it clear that the behaviour is considered offensive and/or the perpetrator should have known that the behaviour is regarded as unacceptable. A single case of harassment can be regarded as sexual harassment. For example, if a manager puts his hand on an employee's bottom, then it will be sexual harassment even if the employee did not tell him that the conduct was offensive. In other words he should have known that his conduct would offend the employee.

6.8.2.2 Forms of sexual harassment

Sexual harassment can take many forms:

physical

1. Physical conduct of a sexual nature;

verbal

2. Verbal forms of harassment that include unwelcome innuendos (words that have a secondary meaning) and suggestions; sexual jokes; unwelcome comments about a person's body or sex-life; sexual advances; and unwelcome whistling at a person;

non-verbal

3. Non-verbal sexual harassment including unwelcome gestures; indecent exposure; and the unwelcome showing of sexually explicit pictures; and

promotion in exchange for sexual favours

4. The promotion of an employee or the giving of an increase or some other advantage to an employee in response to a sexual favour.

6.8.2.3 Employer's duty to protect employees

protection against sexual harassment

An employer is under a duty to protect his or her employees from sexual harassment by other employees and by clients of the employer.

workplace policies on sexual harassment

All employers are required to adopt policies with regard to sexual harassment which must state clearly that sexual harassment at the workplace will not be tolerated and that perpetrators will be severely disciplined. They also have to set up a procedure whereby an employee can lodge a complaint. The problem with sexual harassment at the workplace is that employees sometimes feel too embarrassed or intimidated to report the harassment. The policy must be communicated to all employees. Employers are required to take complaints very seriously and to take action against the perpetrator.

complaints must be taken very seriously

6.8.2.4 Alleging sexual harassment

offensive conduct is objectively assessed

The person who alleges that he or she was sexually harassed must have subjectively (in their own mind) felt that the conduct in question was offensive. However, these feelings must be able to be assessed against an objective standard (ie a reasonable person would agree that the conduct was offensive).

6.8.2.5 Sexual harassment prohibited

sexual harassment is a type of discrimination

Sexual harassment is prohibited by the Employment Equity Act and is a type of discrimination. Also if an employee resigns because he or she feels harassed, the resignation will be regarded as a constructive dismissal (see para 6.9.1.1) and will constitute an unfair dismissal.

6.8.2.6. Code of Good Practice

Code of Good Practice on sexual harassment

The Department of Labour has produced a Code of Good Practice on the handling of sexual harassment cases, which aims to remove sexual harassment from the workplace. The Code requires the employers to develop sexual harassment policies which state that:

- Sexual harassment is a form of unfair discrimination.
- Sexual harassment in the workplace will not be tolerated.

- People complaining of sexual harassment can use formal and informal procedures when raising a complaint.
- An employee who lodges a complaint of sexual harassment cannot be victimised.

Case study: Mbali is constantly whistled at by Edward and Xolani

Mbali is constantly whistled at by Edward and Xolani

Mbali is constantly whistled at by Edward and Xolani even though she has asked them to stop it. She is tired of it as it demeans her, so she has decided to report her co-workers for sexual harassment.

Problem 1: Was it a case of sexual harassment?

Questions

Do you think that the following examples of conduct amount to sexual harassment? Give reasons for your answer.

1. A group of male workers read a pornographic magazine during their lunch break. Sally, a secretary, sees them and feels embarrassed.
2. A senior manager tells a female employee that she is looking 'very sexy today'.
3. A male employee swears in front of a female employee.
4. A female employee jokingly pinches a male employee's bottom.
5. A male employee puts a poster of a sexy model in a bikini costume up on the wall of his office.
6. An employer offers to promote a female employee if she goes out on a date with him.
7. A female employee sends an e-mail around the office containing a picture of a nude male. Another female employee reads it and feels very uncomfortable.

6.9 Termination of employment through dismissal

Outcomes

After completion of this section learners will be able to:

1. Explain the law regarding the termination of employment through dismissal.

Assessment criteria

1. The different types and meanings of dismissal are identified.
2. A set of facts is examined and a decision made on whether the termination of employment was a constructive dismissal.
3. A set of facts is examined and a decision made on whether the dismissals were automatically unfair.
4. A set of facts is examined and a decision made on whether the dismissals were substantially unfair.
5. A set of facts is examined and a decision made on whether the dismissals were procedurally fair.
6. A set of facts is examined and a decision made on what would be a suitable punishment for different acts of misconduct.
7. A set of facts is examined and a decision made on whether the dismissals for incapacity were fair.
8. The rules that apply to retrenchments are identified.
9. A set of facts is given and a decision taken on what types of dismissals have occurred.

6.9.1 The meaning of dismissal

dismissal must be substantively and procedurally fair

This section examines the many different types of dismissal. The Labour Relations Act protects employees against unfair dismissal. This does not mean that an employee may never be dismissed but rather that the dismissal must be both for a fair reason (substantively fair) and in accordance with a fair procedure (procedurally fair). Dismissal can take many different forms.

The Labour Relations Act sets out the meaning of unfair dismissal as follows:

termination of employment contract

1. The termination of an employment contract, with or without notice (where the contract is terminated without a fair reason and without following a fair procedure).

non-renewal of a fixed term contract

a fixed term contract must be renewed if an employee is given a reasonable expectation that the contract will be renewed

2. The non-renewal of a fixed term contract where the employee had a reasonable expectation of renewal.
   A 'fixed term contract' is a contract for a limited period of time (eg where a temporary employee is employed to replace someone on maternity leave). When the time of the contract comes to an end so does the employment relationship. Where, however, the employee is given a reasonable expectation that the contract will be renewed (eg if he or she is promised this by an employer) and it is not renewed, this will also be a dismissal. The employee has to prove that he or she had a reasonable expectation that the contract would be renewed in order to establish that an unfair dismissal occurred.

refusing employment after maternity leave

3. The refusal to allow an employee to come back to work after maternity leave is regarded as an unfair dismissal. However, if an employee commits serious misconduct either before or during the maternity leave the employee may be dismissed for misconduct.

selective re-employment of employees

4. Selective re-employment of employees.
Selective re-employment of employees happens where all the employees are fairly dismissed and the employer then chooses to re-employ only some of them. If the employees are chosen on unfair grounds (eg if only the male employees are re-employed), this will be unfair dismissal. For example, if an employer dismisses several employees for participating in an unlawful strike, and the employer later changes his mind and decides to re-employ some of the employees dismissed, the employees who were not re-employed may be able to claim that they were unfairly dismissed.
5. Constructive dismissal.

6.9.1.1 Constructive dismissal

constructive dismissal is where an employee resigns because of conditions at the workplace

A constructive dismissal is where an employee resigns from employment because he or she cannot continue with the working relationship because of the conditions at the workplace. In other words where the employee cannot be expected to put up with the employer's conduct and is 'forced' to resign as a result. For example, if an employee is sexually harassed and resigns as a result, this will be constructive dismissal. The feature of a constructive dismissal is that the employee, not the employer, ends the contract of employment with or without notice.

requirements for constructive dismissal

When proving constructive dismissal the employee must show that:
- The employee brought the employment contract to an end.
- The reason for the employee terminating the employment contract was that the employer made continued employment intolerable for the employee.
- The employee had no reasonable alternative except to terminate the employment contract.

Problem 1: Was it constructive dismissal?

Questions

Do you think the following examples amount to constructive dismissal? Give reasons for your answers.
1. Sandy's employer is constantly shouting at her for working slowly. Sandy resigns as a result.
2. Sandile's employer constantly makes racist remarks about Sandile in his presence. Sandile is fed up with this and decides to resign.
3. Mandy is suspected of theft and her employers wish to search her handbag. She refuses to let them and then resigns in anger.

4. Sue's employer tries to kiss her at an office party. She resigns the following morning.

6.9.2 Types of dismissals

The four types of dismissals recognised by the Labour Relations Act are:

1. Automatically unfair dismissals;
2. Dismissal for misconduct;
3. Dismissal for incapacity; and
4. Dismissal for operational requirements.

Code of Good Practice: Dismissal

NEDLAC (the organisation that drafted the Labour Relations Act) has published a Code of Good Practice: Dismissal that gives guidelines to employers, employees and arbitrators regarding unfair dismissals.

6.9.2.1 Automatically unfair dismissals

The Labour Relations Act sets out a category of dismissal known as 'automatically unfair dismissal'. If a dismissal falls within this section, the dismissal will be automatically regarded as unfair.

6.9.2.1.1 Types of automatically unfair dismissals

An automatically unfair dismissal occurs where:

victimisation

1. An employee is dismissed as a result of victimisation (eg for being a member of a trade union).

for taking part in a strike

2. An employee is dismissed for taking part in a lawful strike.

refusing to be scab labour

3. An employee refuses to be a scab labourer and is dismissed as a result.
4. An employee is dismissed by the employer for exercising a right in terms of the Act.

pregnancy

5. An employee is dismissed as a result of her pregnancy or intended pregnancy.

unreasonable grounds for dismissal

6. An employee is dismissed and the dismissal constitutes unfair discrimination against an employee on arbitrary grounds (ie grounds that are not reasonable). These grounds include, but are not limited to, race, gender, sex, ethnic or social origin, colour, sexual orientation, age, disability, religion, conscience, belief, political opinion, culture, language, marital status or family responsibility. An example of a person being automatically unfairly dismissed on the grounds of gender happened when a person was dismissed because he said that he was going to have a sex change operation.

All the dismissed employees have to prove is that they were dismissed for one of the above reasons and the dismissal will be regarded as automatically unfair. The employer will then have to prove that the dismissal was not based on one of the above grounds.

exceptions to the automatically unfair rule

Exceptions to the automatically unfair rule are where employees are dismissed because they have reached retirement age or where the dismissal is based on the requirements of the job.

Case study: Nonhlanhla is fired because she is pregnant

Nonhlanhla is fired because she is pregnant

Her boss fires Nonhlanhla because she is pregnant. Nonhlanhla's work has not suffered as a result of her pregnancy so she cannot understand why she has to leave.

Problem 2: Were the dismissals automatically unfair?

Questions

Do you think that the following dismissals could be automatically unfair? Why or why not?

1. Mary misses 20 days of work during her pregnancy as she is very weak and nauseous. She is dismissed as a result.
2. Sipho leaves work early to attend a union meeting, without the permission of his employer. He is dismissed.
3. The workers at the company embark upon a strike, without following proper procedures. They are all dismissed.
4. Anand reports his employer to the Department of Labour as he is required to work more than the maximum working hours. He is dismissed when his employer finds out.
5. When Jose tells his employer that he is homosexual he is dismissed.
6. Sarah is dismissed when she reaches the age of 65. She feels that this is discrimination on the grounds of age.

6.9.2.2 Dismissal for misconduct

6.9.2.2.1 Breaching a disciplinary rule

misconduct occurs where an employee deliberately breaches a disciplinary rule

disciplinary codes should describe misconduct and punishments for it

Employees can be dismissed for misconduct. Misconduct is where an employee deliberately and intentionally breaks a rule of conduct at the workplace. All employers should adopt disciplinary codes (as discussed earlier) that set out the standards of conduct required of the employees. These codes vary according to the type of employment and the nature of the workplace. Employees must be made aware of what conduct will be treated seriously and what punishment will be imposed on them as a result of the misconduct. Even if there is no disciplinary code at a workplace, some misconduct is so serious that an employee can be dismissed anyway. For example, if employees steal from employers they can be dismissed even if there is no disciplinary code.

6.9.2.2.2 Corrective and progressive discipline

employees should be given a chance to correct their behaviour

When an employee breaches a disciplinary rule the employer can take disciplinary action against him. The Code of Good Practice: Dismissal supports a corrective or progressive approach to discipline, which means that employees should be given a chance to correct their behaviour. For example, if they are late for work they should be made aware that their conduct is unacceptable by being given a warning. Only if they repeat the misconduct can they be dismissed. In fact dismissal is not appropriate for a first offence unless the misconduct is very serious.

dismissal if a good reason and procedural fairness

If employees are guilty of misconduct they can only be dismissed if there is both a good reason for the dismissal (substantive fairness) and the employer has followed a fair procedure (procedural fairness).

6.9.2.2.3 Substantive fairness

fair reason

The Code of Good Practice: Dismissal sets out the guidelines for deciding whether the reason for the dismissal is fair.

In terms of the Code, the employer needs to show that:

employee breached a workplace rule

1. The employee broke a disciplinary rule at the workplace.
   This is very easy for employers to prove if they have a disciplinary code that sets out what conduct is acceptable. An employer need not spell out every workplace rule. It is sufficient for the employer to make the employees aware that certain types of misconduct are not allowed and of the consequences for such misconduct.

the rule was reasonable and valid

2. The rule was a reasonable and valid rule.
   This means that the rule is in place for a good reason. For example, a rule preventing drunkenness is for a very good reason at a workplace that uses dangerous machinery.

the employee was aware of rule

3. The employee was aware of the rule.
   It is important that employees be made aware of the rules of the workplace either by being given copies of the disciplinary code or by a copy of the code

being placed on the notice board. Employees cannot be held responsible for breaking a rule if they do not know about it.

rule consistently applied to all employees

4. The rule was consistently applied to all employees.
   All employees must be treated equally or else this will be unfair. For example, if an employee is given a warning for absenteeism, it is only fair that other employees found guilty of the same offence be treated in the same manner.

dismissal is an appropriate punishment

5. Dismissal is an appropriate punishment.
   Employers need to consider whether the employees had a good reason for breaking the rule. For example, if they assaulted a fellow employee in self-defence. The employer also needs to take into account mitigating circumstances to reduce the punishment, such as: how long the employee has worked for the employer; how many times the employee has been guilty of misconduct in the past; and personal facts about the employee, such as whether the person is the sole breadwinner. For example, if an employee is absent from work for one day without a good reason, and it is the first time that he or she has been guilty of misconduct in the six years he or she has worked for the employer, it is likely that the dismissal will not be a fair punishment.

Case study: Richard breaks his employer's no smoking rule

Richard breaks his employer's no smoking rule

Richard was aware of the 'No smoking' policy at his office but really needed a cigarette. He went into the bathroom to have a quick smoke but was caught by his manager. Richard had been warned of this rule before.

Problem 3: Were the dismissals substantively fair?

Questions

Do you think that the following dismissals are substantively fair (for a good reason)? Give reasons for your answer.

1. Jim has a fight with one of his co-employees at a pub one night. He is dismissed as a result.
2. Bheki is fired for not wearing his safety hat on the construction site. He says that he was not aware of the rule and that the dismissal was unfair.
3. Zama works in a bakery. She is fired for eating a donut without her employer's permission. She is the sole breadwinner and supports her husband and three children.
4. Nazreen worked for her employer for 12 years. She is found guilty of theft and is dismissed.
5. Doris gets to work late again. She has done this in the past and has a final written warning for lateness. She is dismissed. All the other employees in the past have received written warnings for lateness.

6.9.2.2.4 Procedural fairness

there must be fair procedure at the disciplinary hearing

Even if there is a good reason for dismissing an employee, there still has to be compliance with a fair procedure. The employee is entitled to a disciplinary hearing to see whether he or she was guilty of misconduct.

The law states that a pre-hearing investigation must be conducted by the employer to decide whether formal disciplinary action should be taken. At the formal hearing the employee is entitled to:

1. Be represented by a shop steward (union representative) or colleague;
2. Know what he or she is being charged with so as to be able to prepare a defence. The Code of Good Practice requires the employer to notify the employee of the charges and allegations against him or her in a form and language the employee understands;
3. Be given sufficient time to prepare a defence;
4. Be present at the hearing;
5. Call witnesses, if there are any;
6. Have an impartial presiding officer hear the case. The presiding officer must be objective and must not have already made the decision in advance. Presiding officers are the people who conduct the disciplinary hearing and are usually senior managers at the company; and
7. Be notified of the decision in writing and given reasons for the dismissal.

If there is procedural unfairness the dismissal will be unfair even if there is a very good reason for the dismissal. It is therefore very important that proper procedures are followed, even if it seems obvious that the employee should be dismissed.

Case study: The workplace fight

the workplace fight

After a fight breaks out between two employees, a hearing is held to determine the facts surrounding the incident. The managers follow the correct disciplinary procedures and give the employees involved a chance to tell their side of the story.

Problem 4: Were the dismissals procedurally fair?

Questions

Would you say that there has been procedural fairness in the following examples? Give reasons for your answer.

1. Riaan is caught red-handed stealing company property. He is fired on the spot.
2. Mandla is called to a disciplinary hearing for assaulting a fellow worker. The presiding officer is the person that caught him assaulting the other worker.
3. Talia is absent from work three times. On the third occasion a disciplinary hearing is held in her absence and she is dismissed.
4. Neil is called to a disciplinary hearing to answer a charge of insubordination (he is disrespectful and disobeys the instructions of his employer). He brings his cousin to represent him but the presiding officer refuses to let his cousin assist him.
5. Mary is told to attend a disciplinary hearing. She is unsure of the exact charge against her.

6.9.2.2.5. Types of misconduct

There are many different types of misconduct. Some of the more serious types of misconduct are:

gross dishonesty eg theft or fraud

1. Gross dishonesty such as theft or fraud. This is particularly serious, as the employer is no longer able to trust the employee.

drunkenness and drinking on duty

2. Drunkenness and drinking on duty. This is particularly serious where being drunk could endanger the lives of other people, for example if the employee is a driver.

insubordination

3. Insubordination, where, as has been previously mentioned, the employee is disrespectful to the employer and refuses to obey the employer's lawful instructions.

absenteeism

4. Absenteeism, where the employee does not go to work.
   A distinction must be drawn between absenteeism, abscondment and desertion. Absenteeism can refer to absence from the employee's workstation or absence from the workplace. Abscondment happens when the employee is absent from work and it seems from the employee's conduct that the employee does not intend to return to work. Desertion happens when the employee expressly or impliedly indicates that he or she does intend to return to work.

assault

5. Assault.

abusive language

6. Abusive language. Whether language is considered abusive depends on the extent and the practice in the workplace.

drug-use

7. Drug-use.

6.9.2.2.6. Punishment for misconduct

Dismissal is not always the best way of dealing with misconduct, especially if the misconduct was not very serious. Other steps that can be taken against an employee for acts of misconduct are:

verbal warning

1. A verbal warning;

written warning

2. A written warning;

suspension

3. Suspension without pay: the employee is prevented from working for a period of time and does not receive a salary; and

loss of benefits

4. Loss of benefits: the employee might be deprived of a benefit, for example a bonus.

Problem 5: What is a suitable punishment?

Questions

What do you think would be a suitable punishment for the following employees? Give reasons for your answers.

1. An employee is late for work once.
2. An employee assaults a fellow employee.
3. An employee talks too much and works too slowly as a result.
4. An employee is drunk at work. This is the second time this has happened in four months.
5. An employee is sick and does not come to work.
6. An employee is rude to a supervisor.
7. An employee crashes a company car. This is the first time the employee has done anything wrong in seven years.

6.9.2.3 Dismissal for incapacity

6.9.2.3.1 No-fault dismissal

employee cannot do the job because of sickness or incompetence

Dismissal for incapacity is very different from dismissal for misconduct and different rules and procedures apply. Misconduct is where an employee intentionally breaks a rule at the workplace. When an employee is dismissed for incapacity, it is through no fault on the part of the employee but rather an inability to do the job – either as a result of sickness or simply not knowing how to perform the work properly. Incapacity is not intentional wrongdoing and as a result the Code of Good Practice: Dismissal requires the employees to be given a chance to improve their work or, in the case of ill-health, to get better.

6.9.2.3.2 Incapacity due to poor work performance

employees must be given a chance to improve their performance

Where employees are performing badly at work they cannot be dismissed unless they are given a chance to improve their performance.

Often it is not the fault of the employee, but rather the fault of the employer who has not provided the employee with adequate training or equipment. For example, if a secretary has poor typing skills it may be as a result of the computer being faulty, or her not having been trained in the use of a particular computer programme.

6.9.2.3.2.1 Probation

probation is a testing period to see if an employee is suitable

Sometimes new employees are placed on 'probation', which is a short period of time (testing period) during which their suitability can be assessed. Employees on probation are also entitled to training and assistance during this time. However, if they are found to be unsuitable they can be dismissed much more easily than ordinary employees.

probationers are entitled to training and guidance

probation must be for a reasonable period of time

There are many important and distinguishing factors regarding employees on probation. Firstly, probationers, like other employees, are entitled to evaluation, training, instruction, guidance or counselling in respect of the work. They are allowed to make representations prior to dismissal and they are entitled to representation by a trade union representative or a fellow employee. Secondly, the period of the probation should be determined in advance and should be for a reasonable time, taking into account the nature of the job and the length of time needed by the employer to decide whether the employee is suitable. Where a probationary period is not mentioned a newly hired employee cannot be said to be on probation. Lastly, the Code states that probations should not be used for purposes not provided for in the Code, ie to deprive employees of the status of permanent employees.

the probationer's performance must be evaluated

The employer is required to evaluate the performance of the employee and if the employee fails to meet the performance standards the employer should advise the employee of this. The employer should then either extend the probationary period or dismiss the employee. Dismissal can only take place after the employee has been given the opportunity to make representations to the employer. Once the employer makes the decision to dismiss the employee he or she must inform the employee of his or her right to refer the matter to the CCMA.

6.9.2.3.2.2 Dismissal under the Code of Good Practice: Dismissal

requirements before dismissal

Before an employee can be dismissed for poor work performance the Code of Good Practice: Dismissal requires the employer to consider the following:

investigation

1. Whether the employee failed to meet a performance standard (eg an employee who is a salesman might be required to sell four products a month). The Code requires an employer to conduct an investigation when allegations of poor work performance arise in order to find out the reasons for this. This investigation should establish whether there are any weaknesses in the support system and whether any steps can be taken by the employer to correct the situation

employees must have been warned about their conduct

2. If employees fail to reach the performance standard, whether they were aware of what conduct was expected of them. In other words the employer must have explained to the employees what conduct was expected of them, and must have warned them that if they did not improve their work, they would be dismissed. Employers must also check to see whether they can do anything to help employees improve their poor work.

employees must have been given an opportunity to improve

3. Whether the employees were given a fair opportunity to improve their work. In other words, if they require training or assistance they must receive the training first and then be given a chance to improve their performance.

decide if dismissal is appropriate

4. Whether dismissal is an appropriate punishment. After all of the above considerations have been taken into account, the employer must then decide whether there is some punishment other than dismissal that might be more appropriate.

Case study: Samantha does not have many skills

Samantha does not have many skills

Samantha is not very neat and does not have many skills. She does not seem to know how to complete the simplest of tasks. Gideon, her boss, realises that he may have to relieve her of her duties if she does not improve. But Samantha thinks that she just needs more training.

6.9.2.3.2.3 Fair procedures

employees entitled to a 'hearing' and representation

The employer is required to follow fair procedures and, as in the case of misconduct, employees are entitled to have a 'hearing', where they can explain what the problem is that is causing the poor work performance. Employees are entitled to be represented at their hearings by a shop steward (a trade union representative) or a colleague, and should be given a proper chance to present their side of the story to an impartial person.

6.9.2.3.3 Incapacity due to ill-health or injury

6.9.2.3.3.1 Ill-health or injury

employees who are unable to work because of illness or injury must be given a fair chance to get better

Employees will be unable to do their work properly if they are ill or injured. They may be unable to work at all during this time or they may not be able to do their particular job. For example, an employee who has a job that involves manual labour may be unable to do his or her job while she or he has a sore back. Because this illness or injury is not due to the fault of the employee it is only fair that the employer gives the employee a fair chance to get better.

6.9.2.3.3.2 Injuries under the Code of Good Practice: Dismissal

The Code of Good Practice: Dismissal sets out the following requirements:

employer must consider alternatives to dismissal

1. If an employee is temporarily unable to work (eg he or she has to have an operation and will be unable to work for a limited period of time), the employer is required to try and accommodate the employee by considering all alternatives other than dismissal. The employer can, for example, hire a temporary replacement during this time.

when Thulani is injured whilst doing his job, his employers give him time off to get better

if the employee cannot be accommodated he or she may be dismissed

2. If the employee is permanently injured or ill (eg the employee has a leg injury and is unable to stand for long periods of time), the employer has to try to accommodate the employee by adapting the person's duties or changing the job. If the employer cannot do this, the employee may be dismissed.

employer has greater duty to accommodate

3. If the employee is injured at work or catches a workplace-related illness the employer is under a greater duty to accommodate the employee.

investigation to see if accommodation possible

4. The employer should conduct an investigation to find out the seriousness of the employee's condition and to consider ways to accommodate the employee. The employee should be given a chance to state his or her case and also to be represented by a shop steward or co-employee.

Problem 6: Some questions on dismissals for incapacity

Questions

1. Why should dismissals for incapacity be treated differently from dismissals for misconduct? What is the reason for placing an employee on probation?
2. Sue is employed as a secretary to the managing director of a large company. She is employed to answer the phone of her employer, take messages, do general typing and administration duties. After she has worked at the company for three weeks, her employer is very dissatisfied with her work. He does not receive some very important messages and finds many mistakes in Sue's typing. What steps does the employer have to take if he wants to dismiss Sue?
3. Jabu has worked at the company for 10 years. He injures his back while moving heavy boxes at work and as a result has to have a back operation. He is off work for six months. His employer wants to dismiss him and employ someone in his place. Can the employer do this? Give reasons for your answer.
4. Mira is a machinist at a clothing factory. After working there for 25 years, she gets arthritis in her hands and cannot operate the sewing machine. She is dismissed. Is this fair? Give reasons for your answer.

6.9.2.4 Dismissal for operational requirements

6.9.2.4.1 Retrenchments

retrenchments are dismissals for operational requirements

If an employer's business starts experiencing financial problems then he or she might have to consider reducing expenses at the workplace. One of the ways to do this is to dismiss some employees. This is known as dismissal for operational requirements or retrenchment. Retrenchments also occur where new technology is introduced into a workplace or a workplace is restructured and jobs are lost. For example, where a factory is automated and labourers are no longer needed, they will have to be retrenched. Because retrenchments are not due to any fault of the employees the Labour Relations Act and the Code of Good Practice: Dismissal sets out detailed requirements for the fair treatment of employees.

economic, technological, or structural reason

First, there has to be a genuine reason for the retrenchments (ie there must be an economic, technological, or structural reason for the dismissals). Secondly, the employer must follow fair procedures.

6.9.2.4.2 Fair procedures

consultation with employees and their representatives

1. The employer must consult with the employees or their representatives (usually the union) to try and find a way to prevent the retrenchments. The employer must try to consider alternatives such as reducing other expenses, cutting out overtime work, voluntary retrenchments, etc. The employer must discuss this with the employee's representatives before making a decision to retrench. If the employer has no option but to retrench, then he or she must try to keep the number of retrenchments to a minimum and do whatever he or she can to try and help the employees to find other jobs.

selection of employees to be retrenched in a fair way

'last in – first out'

2. The employer has to choose the employees to be retrenched in a fair way. It is very difficult to decide which employees must be dismissed. The employer would probably like to dismiss his least favourite employees but this is unfair. The method of choosing the employees must be fair and objective. One of the fairest selection criteria used is LIFO (last in – first out) which means that the employees who have worked there the shortest time should be dismissed first.

severance pay must be paid

3. Employees who are retrenched are entitled to financial compensation called 'severance pay'. The minimum severance pay that has to be paid is one week's salary for every completed year of service. For example, an employee who has worked for three years is entitled to a minimum of three weeks' salary.

duty to consult with and reply to employee's representatives

4. When the employer consults with the employee's representative, he or she has to reach a compromise with them and must listen to, and seriously consider, their suggestions. If the employer disagrees with the employee's representations he or she has to reply to them in writing to say why he or she disagrees.

Case study: ABC Construction automate their work

ABC Construction recently automated much of their work. They therefore retrenched many of their labourers. Because retrenchments are not due to any fault of the employees they must be treated fairly.

ABC Construction automate their work

6.9.2.4.3 Major retrenchments

large-scale retrenchments allow employees to go on strike

In workplaces where there are large numbers of employees being retrenched (eg 10 employees if the company employs up to 200 employees, 20 employees if the company employs up to 300 employees, etc), other rules also apply. These large-scale retrenchments or major retrenchments have an added provision that allows the employees to go on strike if they are retrenched. This does not apply to smaller retrenchments where the employees can only take the matter to the Labour Court if they are unhappy with their dismissals.

Problem 7: Testing the fairness of retrenchments

Questions

1. Can you think of examples of retrenchments for (a) economic reasons; (b) technological reasons; and (c) structural reasons?
2. How can an employer try to avoid retrenching employees?
3. What do you think are fair criteria for choosing which employees to retrench?

Problem 8: What is the reason for the dismissal?

Questions

Consider the following examples and decide whether you think that the dismissals are for misconduct, incapacity, operational requirements or are automatically unfair dismissals.

1. Lizzie is employed by ABC Butcheries as a till operator. She is extremely slow in operating the tills and as a result causes large queues to build up when the butchery is busy. Despite on-the-job training and several warnings Lizzie fails to improve. Lizzie is dismissed.
2. Joe is employed at the Pinetown branch of XYZ Ltd. Due to an economic recession the Pinetown branch is forced to close down. He is offered a job at either the Durban or the Ladysmith branches but refuses them. Joe is dismissed.
3. Premilla is a secretary at S. Mile Co. In keeping with her nickname of 'Battle-axe' she is rude to her colleagues and uncooperative with clients. Despite several warnings her conduct remains unchanged. Premilla is dismissed.
4. Sipho is employed to promote a product that appeals to heterosexual men. Despite a discreet private life it is revealed in a gossip column that Sipho is the lover of a well-known gay actor. Sipho's employers now feel that Sipho's image is unsuitable for the product and dismiss him.
5. Hanalie is an alcoholic. As a result of this problem she is absent from work on a regular basis. Her employers warn her on several occasions to sort out her problem yet her absenteeism continues. She is then dismissed.
6. Sandile is employed by Progress Co as part of an affirmative action programme. The company experiences financial problems and is forced to dismiss him as he was the last employee appointed.
7. Jane is employed in the catering division of ABC Ltd. The employees in the administrative division go on a lawful strike and Jane is asked by her employers to step in and help in that department until the strike is resolved. Jane refuses and is dismissed.
8. Boetie is one of many workers participating in a lawful strike. During the strike negotiations Boetie throws a brick at a car crossing the picket line and causes damage to the car and its occupants. Boetie is dismissed.
9. Grace is employed in the radiology department at a hospital. She falls pregnant and as a result of the dangers of exposure to radiology to pregnant women, she is dismissed.
10. Rajen and Peter have an argument at work. Peter punches Rajen and Rajen lays a charge of assault against him. Peter is dismissed.

6.10 Resolving labour disputes

Outcomes

After completion of this section learners will be able to:

1. Explain how to resolve a labour dispute and the dispute resolution mechanism available to unfairly dismissed employees.

Assessment criteria

1. An explanation is given about the CCMA and its functions.
2. Methods of dispute resolution such as mediation, conciliation and arbitration are explained.
3. A negotiation and mediation exercise is undertaken.

6.10.1 Referring disputes to the CCMA

the CCMA aims to resolve labour disputes in an informal and non-legal manner

If an employee has a labour dispute or is unhappy about being unfairly dismissed, he or she may refer the matter to the CCMA (the Commission for Conciliation, Mediation and Arbitration). This is a forum that aims at resolving labour disputes in an informal and non-legal manner. The CCMA has been described as a 'one-stop shop' for resolving labour disputes.

conciliation and mediation is used by CCMA commissioners to resolve disputes

All dismissal disputes referred to the CCMA are firstly conciliated or mediated. The CCMA commissioner is a trained conciliator/mediator who uses his or her skills to help the parties reach a settlement. In a conciliation, the commissioner cannot force the parties to reach a settlement and cannot make an order binding on the parties, but can merely use his or her skills to try to persuade the parties to reach a settlement. A mediator will try to make the parties consider alternatives, encourage the parties to assess their points of views, and help the parties rank issues, eliminate demands and come to their own solution. A mediator is neutral and merely helps the parties reach a settlement. The CCMA commissioner must try to resolve the dispute, using his or her conciliation skills, for a period of 30 days.

Case study: The disputed dismissal

An employee is dismissed by her line manager but she is disputing the dismissal. The employee decides to take the case to the CCMA. The commissioner is a trained conciliator/mediator who uses her skills to help parties reach a settlement.

the disputed dismissal

in arbitration the commissioner hears both sides and makes a final binding decision

If the parties cannot reach an agreement through conciliation or mediation the matter will go to arbitration if it is a dismissal for incapacity or misconduct. Arbitration is where the commissioner hears all the evidence of both sides and makes a final and binding decision (see above para 6.7.2.5). It is much less formal than a court and arbitrators can run the proceedings as informally as they like. Matters at the CCMA do not cost the parties money and the parties are not allowed to be represented by a lawyer unless special permission is granted. If the dispute is a dismissal for misconduct or incapacity the CCMA commissioner will arbitrate the dispute.

approaching the Labour Court

If the conciliation fails and it is a dismissal for operational requirements or an automatically unfair dismissal, the dissatisfied parties can go to the Labour Court, where a judge will hear the matter and make a decision.

6.10.2 Negotiation

negotiation involves talking to each other

Negotiation is a process where the parties involved in a dispute talk to each other about their problems and try to reach a solution or agreement (see above para 6.4.4.1).

6.10.3 Mediation

mediation is an extension of negotiation

Mediation is an extension of negotiation. It takes place where a third party (the mediator) helps the disputing parties talk about their problem and settle their differences. The parties themselves decide what their dispute is about and how they want to settle it (see above para 1.3.2.2).

Case study: Sandile and Bert cannot agree on anything

Sandile and Bert cannot agree on anything. When Sandile disciplined Bert for poor performance, a conflict began that they have not been able to solve. They could not reach an agreement by themselves so their manager appointed a mediator to help them come to an agreement.

Sandile and Bert cannot agree on anything

6.10.4 Arbitration

in arbitration the arbitrator makes the decision

Arbitration happens when a third party (the arbitrator) listens to the arguments of both sides and makes a decision that is binding on them (see above para 6.7.2.5).

Problem 1: Negotiation and mediation exercise

Questions

You are to engage in a negotiation exercise. Read the following scenario and rank the five people from least favourite (1) to most favourite (5), without showing your ranking to anyone else. Once you have ranked the five people then get into pairs and try to negotiate a combined ranking. If you are unable to reach an agreement, get a third party to try to mediate the dispute. (Use the information in para 6.4.4.1 above to prepare for the negotiation, and that in para 1.3.2.2 above to prepare for the mediation.)

Sue is a 30-year-old woman who has been in a relationship with Brian for eight years. One day she meets John, a smooth-talking bachelor who convinces Sue to leave Brian and start a relationship with him. Sue immediately breaks off her relationship with Brian and phones John to tell him the good news. John tells her he has since changed his mind and that he does not ever want to see her again. In the meantime Brian is so angry that he finds John and badly assaults him. Sue is so upset she cannot stop crying. She goes to Frank, a psychologist, for therapy. Frank tells Sue that she is immoral and that he is not prepared to help her.

6.11 Remedies for unfair dismissals

Outcomes

After completion of this section learners will be able to:

1. Explain the remedies that are available to unfairly dismissed employees.

Assessment criteria

1. The remedies that are appropriate for unfairly dismissed employees are discussed.
2. A set of facts is examined and a decision is made on the appropriate remedies for dismissal.

6.11.1 Appropriate remedies

If the CCMA commissioners or the Labour Court judges decide that employees have been unfairly dismissed, they can make the following orders:

reinstatement

1. They can order that employees be reinstated in their jobs – that is that they get their jobs back as if they had not been dismissed. This is the most likely remedy that will be granted unless:
   (a) The employee does not want the job back (eg he or she has found another job);
   (b) If the relationship between the employer and employee is so bad that it is not possible to order reinstatement;
   (c) If it is not possible to order reinstatement (eg the employee's position has been filled by another employee); or
   (d) If the dismissal was only procedurally unfair (ie there was a fair reason to dismiss the employee but a proper procedure was not followed).

compensation

2. They can order that financial compensation be paid to employees for the loss of their jobs. The Labour Relations Act stipulates that the maximum amount of compensation that can be paid is 12 months' wages for dismissal for misconduct, incapacity or operational requirements, and 24 months' wages for an automatically unfair dismissal. This is the maximum that can be awarded and it is up to the commissioner or the judge to decide how much compensation to give.

Problem 1: What remedy is suitable?

Questions

What do you think is the most suitable remedy in the following examples? Give reasons for your answers:

1. Jason is caught red-handed stealing company property. He is immediately thrown out of the company and dismissed. He is not given any form of disciplinary hearing and as a result is found to have been unfairly dismissed.

2. Corne is unfairly dismissed. He refers the matter to the CCMA and immediately finds a new job. The CCMA finds that his dismissal is both substantively and procedurally unfair.
3. Pretty and her employer have an angry argument. She is dismissed for insubordination after badly insulting her employer. The CCMA decide that she should not have been dismissed as this was her first offence during the eight years that she has worked at the company.
4. Thandi is dismissed for absenteeism. She mentions during the disciplinary hearing that she had tried to contact her employer to explain her absence but failed. The CCMA Commissioner finds her dismissal to be unfair.

Further reading

6.1 Employment and applying for a job

Code of Good Practice on Key Aspects of HIV/AIDS, Item 7.1.5

Constitution of the Republic of South Africa Act, 1996, section 9

Employment Equity Act 55 of 1998, sections 6 and 7

6.2 Contracts of employment

Du Toit D et al *Labour Relations Law* 3 ed (2000)

Grogan J *Dismissal* (2010)

Grogan J *Workplace Law* 7 ed (2003)

Van Niekerk A, Christianson MA, McGregor M, Smit N & Van Eck BPS *Law@work* (2008)

Code of Good Practice: Who is an employee?

Labour Relations Act 66 of 1995, section 213

Labour Relations Amendment Act 42 of 2002, section 200A

Denel (Pty) Ltd v Gerber (2005) 26 *ILJ* 1256 (LAC); [2005] 9 BLLR 849 (LAC)

SA *Broadcasting Corporation v McKenzie* (1999) 20 *ILJ* 585 (LAC)

6.3 Labour laws and social benefits

Basic Conditions of Employment Act 75 of 1997, sections 9, 16, 18, 20, 21, 22, 23, 25, 26, 27, 32, 33, 34, 35 and 42

Compensation for Occupational Injuries and Diseases Act 130 of 1993, section 47 and Schedule 4

Occupational Health and Safety Act 85 of 1993, section 8

Skills Development Act 97 of 1998

6.4 Collective bargaining and trade unions

Cohen T, Rycroft AJ & Whitcher B *Trade Unions and the Law in South Africa* (2009)

Du Toit D et al *Labour Relations Law* 3 ed (2000)

Grogan J *Collective Labour Law* (2010)

Grogan J *Dismissal* (2010)

Van Niekerk A, Christianson MA, McGregor M, Smit N & Van Eck BPS *Law@work* (2008)

Labour Relations Act 66 of 1995, sections 4, 5, 6, 21, 23, 64(2), 64(3), 65, 66, 68, 71, 75, 95–106 and 213

NUM v East Rand Gold & Uranium Co Ltd 1992 (1) SA 700 (A); 1991 *ILJ* 1221 (A)

East Rand Gold & Uranium Co Ltd v National Union of Mineworkers (1989) 10 *ILJ* 683 (LAC)

SACTWU *v Sheraton Textiles* (1997) 18 *ILJ* 1412 (CCMA); (1997) 5 BLLR 662 (CCMA)

SACTWU *v Marley Flooring (SA) (Pty) Ltd t/a Marley Flooring (Mobeni)* (2000) 21 *ILJ* 425 (CCMA)

Gobile v BP Southern Africa (Pty) Ltd & others (1999) 20 *ILJ* 2027 (LAC)
Picardi Hotels Ltd v FGWU & others (1999) 20 *ILJ* 1915 (LC); [1999] 6 BLLR 601 (LC)
FAWU & others v Rainbow Chicken Farms (2000) 21 *ILJ* 615 (LC); [2000] 1 BLLR 70 (LC)
Ceramic Industries Ltd t/a Betta Sanitary Ware v National Construction Building & Allied Workers Union (2) (1997) 18 *ILJ* 671 (LAC)
Public Servants Association of South Africa v Minister of Justice and Constitutional Development & others [2001] 11 BLLR 1250 (LC)
Tiger Wheels Babelegi (Pty) Ltd t/a TSW International v National Union of Metalworkers of SA & others (1999) 20 *ILJ* 677 (LC)
SACWU & others v Afrox Ltd (1999) 20 *ILJ* 1718 (LAC); [1999] 10 BLLR 1005 (LAC)
Modise & others v Steve's Spar Blackheath 2001 (2) SA 406 (LAC); (2000) 21 *ILJ* 519 (LAC); [2000] 5 BLLR 496 (LAC)
Mzeku & others v Volkswagen SA (Pty) Ltd & others 2001 (4) SA 1009 (LAC); (2001) 22 *ILJ* 1575 (LAC); [2001] 8 BLLR 857 (LAC)

6.6 Privacy at work and protected disclosures

Constitution of South Africa, 1996, section 14
Protected Disclosures Act 26 of 2000

6.7 Employment equity

Dupper O, Garbers C, Landman A, Christianson M & Basson A *Essential Employment Discrimination Law* (2004)
Grogan J *Dismissal, Discrimination and Unfair Labour Practices* (2005)
Van Niekerk A, Christianson MA, McGregor M, Smit N & Van Eck BPS *Law@work* (2008)
Constitution of the Republic of South Africa Act, 1996, section 9
Employment Equity Act 55 of 1998, sections 6(1), 6(2), 13 and 15
Association of Professional Teachers & another v Minister of Education & others (1995) 16 *ILJ* 1048 (IC)
Swart v Mr Video (Pty) Ltd (1998) 19 *ILJ* 1315 (CCMA)
Leonard Dingler Employee Representative Council & others v Leonard Dingler (Pty) Ltd & others (1998) 19 *ILJ* 285 (LC)
Louw v Golden Arrow Bus Services (Pty) Ltd 2001 (1) SA 218 (LC); (2000) 21 *ILJ* 188 (LC)
Louw v Golden Arrow Bus Services (Pty) Ltd (2001) 22 *ILJ* 2628 (LAC)
Stojce v UKZN & another (2006) 27 *ILJ* 2696 (LC); 2007 (3) BLLR 246 (LC)

6.8 Unfair labour practices and sexual harassment

6.8.1 Unfair labour practices

Du Toit D et al *Labour Relations Law* 3 ed (2000)
Grogan J *Dismissal* (2010)

Grogan J *Workplace Law* 7 ed (2003)

Van Niekerk A, Christianson MA, McGregor M, Smit N & Van Eck BPS *Law@work* (2008)

Labour Relations Act 66 of 1995, section 186(2)

Department of Justice v CCMA & others (2004) 25 *ILJ* 248 (LAC); [2004] 4 BLLR 297 (LAC)

Dlamini v Toyota SA Manufacturing [2004] 25 *ILJ* 1513 (CCMA)

6.8.2 Sexual harassment

Dupper O, Garbers C, Landman A, Christianson M & Basson A *Essential Employment Discrimination Law* (2004)

Grogan J *Dismissal* (2010)

Code of Good Practice on the Handling of Sexual Harassment Cases in the Workplace Employment Equity Act 55 of 1998, section 6(1) and 6(3)

Grobler v Naspers Bpk & 'n ander 2004 (4) SA 220 (C); (2004) 25 *ILJ* 439 (C)

Ntsabo v Real Security CC (2003) 24 *ILJ* 2341 (LC)

6.9 Termination of employment through dismissal

6.9.1 The meaning of dismissal

Du Toit D et al *Labour Relations Law* 3 ed (2000)

Grogan J *Dismissal* (2010)

Grogan J *Dismissal, Discrimination and Unfair Labour Practices* (2005)

Grogan J *Workplace Law* 7 ed (2003)

Van Niekerk A, Christianson MA, McGregor M, Smit N & Van Eck BPS *Law@work* (2008)

Labour Relations Act 66 of 1995, section 186(1)

National Automobile and Allied Workers Union v Borg Warner SA (Pty) Ltd 1994 (3) SA 15 (A); (1994) 15 *ILJ* 509 (A)

Pretoria Society for the Care of the Retarded v Loots (1997) 18 *ILJ* 981 (LAC)

Ouwehand v Hout Bay Fishing Industries (2004) 25 *ILJ* 731 (LC)

Owen & others v Department of Health, KwaZulu-Natal (2009) 30 *ILJ* 2461 (LC)

Solid Doors (Pty) Ltd v Commission Theron & others (2004) 25 *ILJ* 2337 (LAC)

6.9.2 Types of dismissals

6.9.2.1 Automatically unfair dismissals

Du Toit D et al *Labour Relations Law* 3 ed (2000)

Grogan J *Dismissal* (2010)

Grogan J *Dismissal, Discrimination and Unfair Labour Practices* (2005)

Grogan J *Workplace Law* 7 ed (2003)

Van Niekerk A, Christianson MA, McGregor M, Smit N & Van Eck BPS *Law@work* (2008)

Labour Relations Act 66 of 1995, sections 185 and 187

Protected Disclosures Act 26 of 2000

Adcock Ingram Critical Care v CCMA & others (2001) 22 *ILJ* 1799 (LAC)
CWIU v Algorax (Pty) Ltd (2003) 24 *ILJ* 1917 (LAC)
Fry's Metals (Pty) Ltd v NUMSA (2003) 24 *ILJ* 133 (LAC)
Mashava v Cuzen & Woods Attorneys (2000) 21 *ILJ* 402 (LC)
SA *Rugby (Pty) Ltd v CCMA & others* (2006) 27 *ILJ* 1041 (LC); [2006] 1 BLLR 27 (LC) 30

6.9.2.2 Dismissal for misconduct

Cohen T, Rycroft AJ & Whitcher B *Trade Unions and the Law in South Africa* (2009)
Du Toit D et al *Labour Relations Law* 3 ed (2000)
Grogan J *Collective Labour Law* (2010)
Grogan J *Dismissal* (2010)
Grogan J *Dismissal, Discrimination and Unfair Labour Practices* (2005)
Grogan J *Workplace Law* 7 ed (2003)
Van Niekerk A, Christianson MA, McGregor M, Smit N & Van Eck BPS *Law@work* (2008)
Labour Relations Act 66 of 1995, section 188
Code of Good Practice: Dismissal, items 3, 4 and 7
Engen Petroleum Ltd v Commission for Conciliation, Mediation & Arbitration (2007) 28 *ILJ* 1507 (LAC); (2007) 8 BLLR 707 (LAC)
Sidumo & another v Rustenburg Platinum Mines Ltd & others 2008 (2) SA 24 (CC); (2007) 28 *ILJ* 2405 (CC)
Toyota SA Motors (Pty) Ltd v Radebe & others (2000) 21 *ILJ* 340 (LAC); [2000] 3 BLLR 243 (LAC)

6.9.2.2.5 Types of misconduct

Grogan J *Dismissal* (2010)
Van Niekerk A, Christianson MA, McGregor M, Smit N & Van Eck BPS *Law@work* (2008)
Adcock Ingram Critical Care v CCMA & others [2001] 22 *ILJ* 1799 (LAC)
Anglo American Farms t/a Boschendal Restaurant v Komjwayo (1992) 13 *ILJ* 573 (LAC)
Dauth and Brown & Weir's Cash & Carry (2002) 23 *ILJ* 1472 (CCMA)
Hoch v Mustek Electronics (Pty) Ltd [2000] 21 *ILJ* 365 (LC)
Lebowa Platinum Mines Ltd v CCMA [2002] 5 BLLR 429 (LC)

6.9.2.3 Dismissal for incapacity

Du Toit D et al *Labour Relations Law* 3 ed (2000)
Grogan J *Dismissal* (2010)
Grogan J *Workplace Law* 7 ed (2003)
Van Niekerk A, Christianson MA, McGregor M, Smit N & Van Eck BPS *Law@work* (2008)
Labour Relations Act 66 of 1995, section 188
Lebowa Platinum Mines Ltd v CCMA [2002] 5 BLLR 429 (LC)

6.9.2.4 Dismissal for operational requirements

Cohen T, Rycroft AJ & Whitcher B *Trade Unions and the Law in South Africa* (2009)

Du Toit D et al *Labour Relations Law* 3 ed (2000)

Grogan J *Collective Labour Law* (2010)

Grogan J *Dismissal* (2010)

Grogan J *Dismissal, Discrimination and Unfair Labour Practices* (2005)

Grogan J *Labour Litigation and Dispute Resolution* (2010)

Grogan J *Workplace Law* 7 ed (2003)

Van Niekerk A, Christianson MA, McGregor M, Smit N & Van Eck BPS *Law@work* (2008)

Labour Relations Act 66 of 1995, sections 189 and 189A

BMD Knitting Mills (Pty) Ltd v SACTWU (2001) 22 *ILJ* 2264 (LAC); [2001] 7 BLLR 705 (LAC)

CWIU v Algorax (Pty) Ltd [2003] 24 *ILJ* 1917 (LAC)

Decision Surveys International (Pty) Ltd v Dlamini [1999] 5 BLLR 413 (LAC)

Fry's Metals (Pty) Ltd v NUMSA (2003) 24 *ILJ* 133 (LAC)

Mazista Tiles (Pty) Ltd v NUM & others (2004) 25 *ILJ* 2156 (LAC); [2005] 3 BLLR 219 (LAC)

National Union of Metalworkers of SA v Atlantis Diesel Engines (Pty) Ltd (1993) 14 *ILJ* 642 (LAC)

Rustenburg Platinum Mines Ltd (Rustenburg Section) v Commission for Conciliation, Mediation & Arbitration & others 2007 (1) SA 576 (SCA); (2006) 27 *ILJ* 2076 (SCA)

SATAWU v Old Mutual Life Assurance Company South Africa Ltd (2005) 26 *ILJ* 293 (LC); [2005] 4 BLLR 378 (LC)

SACCAWU & others v Gallo Africa (2005) 26 *ILJ* 2397 (LC)

SACTWU & others v Discreto (A Division of Trump & Springbok Holdings) (1998) 19 *ILJ* 1451 (LAC); [1998] 12 BLLR 1228 (LAC)

SACWU & others v Afrox Ltd (1999) 20 *ILJ* 1718 (LAC); [1999] 10 BLLR 1005 (LAC)

6.11 Remedies for unfair dismissals

Grogan J *Labour Litigation and Dispute Resolution* (2010)

Van Niekerk A, Christianson MA, McGregor M, Smit N & Van Eck BPS *Law@work* (2008)

Labour Relations Act 66 of 1995

CWIU & others v Latex Surgical Products (Pty) Ltd (2006) 27 *ILJ* 292 (LAC); [2006] 2 BLLR 142 (LAC)

INDEX AND SIMPLE LEGAL DICTIONARY

This is a list of simplified meanings of some of the more difficult legal words in the text. The words in **bold** are defined in the dictionary. Paragraph number references to the words are given in brackets. Where no reference appears after the word the word is not mentioned in the text, but is relevant in order to understand legal terminology.

Abduction:	The unlawful and intentional removal of unmarried **minors** from their parents' control in order to marry or to have sexual intercourse with them. (Para: 2.2.4; 2.3.6.9)
Abortion:	The unlawful termination of a woman's **pregnancy**. (Para: 2.8; 2.8.6; 2.8.6.1; 2.8.6.2; 4.3.2.4)
Abortion and Sterilization Act:	Act 2 of 1975. (Para: 4.3.4)
Abscondment:	Where the **employee** is absent from work and it seems from the **employee's** conduct that the **employee** does not intend to return to work. (Para: 6.9.2.2.5)
Absenteeism:	Absenteeism occurs where the employee is absent from the workstation or the workplace. (Para: 6.5.3 problem 1; 6.2.2.1; 6.9.2.2.3; 6.9.2.2.5)
Access:	Able to get, have or use something. (Paras: 1.2.2.1 problem 2; 1.3.2.3 problem 7; 2.3.9.1; 2.14.5.3; 3.2.2; 3.2.10; 3.2.13.2; 4.5.3; 4.5.3.1; 5.1.2; 5.4.1; 5.4.2.1; 5.4.2.1 problem 1, 5.4.13; 5.5.1; 5.5.1 problem 1; 5.5.2; 5.5.3; 5.5.4; 5.5.4.1; 5.5.4.2; 5.5.4.3 problem 3; 5.6.1; 5.6.5; 5.7.1; 5.7.1 problem 1; 5.7.4; 5.7.4 problem 3; 5.8.1; 5.8.4; 5.8.4.2.2.1 problem 3)
Accessory after the fact:	Someone who, after learning that a **crime** has been committed, helps the **perpetrator to** avoid capture or helps the perpetrator to escape. (Paras: 2.1.5; 2.6.6)
Accident:	The layman's term for a motor collision. (Paras: 1.2.2.1 problem 3; 1.2.2.3 problem 7; 1.3.2.1; 1.4.1.1; 1.4.1.2.2; 1.4.1.3.1; 1.4.1.4.5 problem 6; 1.5.2.1; 2.1.6; 2.1.6 problem 5; 2.2.1.2; 3.5.5; 3.5.9.1; 3.5.9.1 problem 6; 3.5.9.5 problem 7; 3.5.9.6 problem 8; 3.5.10; 3.5.10.1; 3.5.10.2; 3.5.10.2 problem 9; 4.6.1; 4.6.1 problem 1; 4.6.2 problem 3; 4.6.4.3 problem 7; 5.4.2.1 problem 2)
Accomplice:	A person who assists or who helps the **perpetrator** commit the **crime.** (Para: 2.1.5)
Accountable:	Having to report and be answerable for your action. (Paras: 2.14.5; 2.14.7.1)
Accrual system:	When the **marriage** or **civil union** ends, any increase in the value of both estates is shared by the parties equally. (Para: 4.2.2.2; 4.2.2.2.1; 4.2.2.2.1 case study; 4.2.2.2.1 problem 3; 4.2.2.2.2)

Accused:	A person brought before the **court** and charged with committing a **crime**. (Paras: 1.1.1; 1.2.2.1 problem 3; 1.3.1.7.2 case study; 1.3.1.7.3; 1.4.1; 1.4.1.4.1; 1.4.1.4.2; 1.4.2; 1.4.2.2; 2.10.2; 2.10.3; 2.11.3.2.2; 2.11.3.3; 2.13.1.1; 2.13.2.1; 2.13.2.3; 2.13.4; 2.13.4 problem 6)
Accused, justification of action of:	An accused's act will be excused or justified if he or she acted out of private defence, defence of property, defence of other people, necessity or was forced by someone to commit the crime). (Para: 2.10.3)
Acquire:	To get or gain something with the possibility of keeping it permanently. (Paras: 4.3.2.3.1; 4.4.2.5; 5.8.4.2.1; 5.8.4.2.2.1; 5.8.4.3.6; 6.1.1.4.1)
Acquittal:	Where an **accused** person is found not guilty by the court. (Para: 2.13.2.2; 2.13.3.1; 2.13.4)
Act:	A **statute** passed by **Parliament** or a law made by **Parliament**. Also means conduct, deed, something that is done, to perform a function. (Paras:1.2.2; 1.2.2.3; 1.3.1.2; 1.3.1.3; 2.1.4; 2.9.2.1)
Adjudication:	The process whereby a **court** makes a decision about a dispute. (Para: 6.10.1)
Admission of guilt:	Where a person who has committed a **crime** admits that he or she is guilty.
Adopt:	Formally accept something, for example, a **Constitution**. (Paras: 2.2.1.3 problem 3; 3.1.4; 5.8.4.3.5.1; 5.8.4.3.5.1 problem 4; 5.8.5; 6.7.2.4 case study; 6.8.2.3; 6.9.2.2.1)
Adoption of children:	The placement of a child in the permanent care of a person after which the adopted **children** have the same legal relationship with their adoptive **parents** that a natural child has with his or her **parents** and their relatives. (Paras: 2.3.6.9; 2.8.1; 2.8.6.2 problem 2; 4.1.1; 4.3.1.2; 4.4.1.4; 4.4.2; 4.4.2.1; 4.4.2.2; 4.4.2; 4.4.2.1; 4.4.2.2; 4.4.2.3; 4.4.2.4; 4.4.2.5; 4.4.2.6; 4.4.2.6 problem 3; 4.4.2.7; 4.4.2.7 problem 4; 4.6.4.2)
Adult basic education:	Aimed at **adults** who want to finish their **basic education** and be provided with a nationally recognised qualification. (Para: 5.2.2.1)
Adultery:	A **civil wrong** where one, or both, of the people having sexual intercourse is, or are, married to somebody else. (Para: 1.4.1.4.2)
Adversarial system:	A court procedure where the **judge** or **magistrate** plays a neutral role and the contesting parties must prove their cases. (Paras: 1.2.1; 1.4.2; 1.4.2 problem 7; 1.5.2.1)
Advertisement:	Written or spoken words or pictures used to persuade **consumers** to buy things. See also **Job advertisement**. (Paras: 2.3.6.9; 3.2.6 problem 6; 3.2.7.4; 3.2.8.1; 3.2.8.1; 3.2.8.1 problem 11; 3.2.8.2; 3.2.8.2 problems 12, 13, 14 & 15; 3.4.1; 3.5.2; 3.5.4 problem 1; 5.6.4.10.7; 6.1.1.1; 6.1.1.1.1; 6.1.1.1.1 problem 1)
Advertising Standards Authority:	The organisation established by the profession to control its ethical standards. (Paras: 3.2.8.1 problem 11; 3.2.14.2)

Advice office:	An office run by non-lawyers, usually people with experience in dealing with practical problems, who refer people to **lawyers** or legal assistance agencies when necessary. (Paras: 1.3.2.2; 1.4.1.4; 1.4.1.4.5; 2.3.2; 3.4.5.1; 5.1.5; 5.3.4; 5.3.6; 5.6.5.2.3; 5.9.4.1)
Advocate:	A **lawyer** who can appear in any court except the **Small Claims Court**. Advocates do not deal directly with the public. They are instructed by **attorneys** on behalf of their clients. (Para: 1.3.1.3; 1.3.1.5; 1.4.1; 1.4.1.2; 1.4.1.2.1; 1.4.1.3.2; 1.4.1.3.2 problem 3; 1.4.1.4.4; 1.4.1.6; 2.12.1 problem 1; 4.5.2.4)
Affirmative action:	Preferential treatment given to persons from a **designated group** in appointments and promotions. (Paras: 5.2.2.4; 6.1.1.4.1; 6.1.1.4.1 case study; 6.1.1.4.1 problem 4; 6.7.2.4 case study; 6.9.2.4.3 problem 8)
Affordability assessment:	An assessment that will help decide whether a consumer will be able to afford his or her repayments. (Paras: 3.3.2; 3.3.3; 3.3.3.1; 3.3.3.2)
Aged, social grants for:	Is a non-contributory and means-tested benefits provided by the government to elderly people who are unable to provide their own minimum needs. (Para: 5.3.5.2.1)
Agricultural development:	Land Redistribution for Agricultural Development sub-programme (LRAD) makes land available for people to use for agricultural purposes (Para: 5.8.4.2; 5.8.4.2.2; 5.8.4.2.2.1)
Alcohol, abuse of:	Is the habitual excessive use of alcohol (Para: 2.9; 4.5.1)
Alcohol, driving under the influence of:	Driving under the influence, also known as driving while intoxicated, is drunk driving or driving of a motor vehicle while impaired by alcohol or to such an extent that renders a driver incapable from operating a motor vehicle safely. (Para: 2.9.1; 3.5.9.5)
Alibi:	A **plea** by an **accused** that he or she was somewhere else when the **crime** was committed. (Para: 2.10.2)
Allocation:	How resources are divided up and distributed. (Para: 5.8.5)
Alternative dispute resolution agent:	Are people or organisations that can help when a consumer and credit provider have a dispute. (Paras: 3.2.15; 3.3.2.15)
Annulment:	Declaration of invalidity of **marriage** or **civil union**. (Para: 4.1.4.2)
Ante-nuptial contract:	A **contract** entered into before a **marriage** by people intending to become **husband and wife** in which they set out how they will share their income and property. It may also record gifts they wish to make to each other. (Para: 1.4.1.2.4; 3.4.4; 4.1.4.3; 4.1.5; 4.2; 4.2.2.2; 4.5.2.4 problem 7; 4.5.2.5.1)
Anti-retroviral drugs:	**Medications** for the treatment of infection by retroviruses, primarily HIV. *See also* **HIV/AIDS**.
Apartheid:	A policy of segregation of races or "separate development" that was introduced by the National Party in 1948. In 1990 a program of reform was introduced, thereby bringing apartheid to an end. (Paras: 1.2.1; 1.2.2.3; 1.3.1.3; 5.1.1; 5.2.2.1; 5.8.1)

Appeal:	When a person takes a decision of a lower court to a higher court. The person bringing the **appeal** hopes to persuade the higher court to change the decision of the lower court. (Paras: 1.3.1; 1.3.1.1; 1.3.1.2; 1.3.1.3; 1.3.1.4.2 problem 1; 1.3.1.7.2; 1.3.1.7.2 case study; 1.3.2.3; 1.5.1.2; 1.5.2.2; 2.11.3.2.2; 2.13.2.2; 4.4.2.6; 5.2.2.3.2; 5.2.2.3.2 problem 6; 5.3.6; 5.4.4; 5.6.2.1 case study; 5.6.2.1 problem 1; 5.6.3.2.1 case study; 5.6.5.1.6; 5.7.3.1.1; 6.7.2.5)
Applicant:	Person applying for something, for example, **social grant**. *See also* **Job applicant**. (Paras: 5.3.4; 5.3.7; 5.6.4.7; 5.6.4.8; 6.1.1.1.1 problem 1)
Apprenticeship:	A **contract** between a person who wishes to learn a trade (an apprentice) and the person (a master) who undertakes to teach the trade or profession to the apprentice. (Paras: 3.1.2 problem 1; 3.4.5.1)
Aptitude test:	A test to determine a person's intellectual ability. (Para: 6.1.1.3 problem 3)
Arbitrary:	Without good reason and not following the law. (Paras: 2.13.3.2 problem 4; 5.6.3; 5.6.3.1; 6.9.2.1.1)
Arbitration:	Arbitration occurs where instead of going to court the parties to a dispute ask a third person to listen to their arguments and then make a decision that they agree to follow. (Paras: 1.3.2 problem 4; 1.3.2.3; 1.3.2.4; 1.3.2.4 problem 8; 5.9.2.1; 5.9.3.1; 5.9.4; 6.7.2.5; 6.7.2.5 problem 3; 6.10.1; 6.10.4)
Arbitrator:	A person who does the **arbitration**. (Para: 1.3.2.3)
Arrest:	The taking into **custody** and detention of a person on a criminal charge. (Paras: 2.2.4; 2.10.3.1; 2.11.1.1; 2.11.1.3 problem 1; 2.11.2; 2.11.2.1; 2.11.2.2; 2.11.2.3; 2.11.2.3 problem 2; 2.11.2.4; 2.11.2.4 problem 3; 2.11.2.5; 2.11.2.7; 2.11.3.1; 2.11.3.3 problems 5 & 6; 2.12.1.3 problem 2; 2.13.2.1)
Articled clerk:	Law graduates wishing to become attorneys must serve articles of clerkship for a period of two years at a private law firm (Para1.4.1.2.2) *See also* Candidate attorney.
Articles:	The contract entered into by a **candidate attorney** with an **attorney** in which the **attorney** agrees to train the **candidate attorney** in exchange for his or her services. Articles must be served before a person can become an **attorney**.
Arson:	Unlawful setting fire to buildings or immovable structures (eg houses or factories) with the intention of causing injury to another person's property. (Paras: 2.6; 2.6.1; 2.6.5; 2.6.7 problem 1; 2.11.2.3; 2.11.3.2.1; 2.13.4; 2.14.5.1.2)
As is:	A buyer accepts an object sold with all its faults if a sale is entered into "**as is**". Also called **voetstoots** or "**with all faults**" (Paras: 3.4.2.1; 3.4.2.1 problem 2; 3.4.2.3; 3.5.6; 5.6.4.10.9)

Assault:	An unlawful and intentional physical attack or the threat of such an attack on another person. A very serious **assault** is called "assault with intent to cause **grievous body harm**". (Paras: 1.2.3; 1.2.3 problem 8; 1.4.2; 1.5.1.3 problem 2; 1.5.2.1; 2.1.4; 2.2; 2.2.2; 2.2.3.5; 2.2.3.5.6; 2.10.3.4; 2.10.4.3 problem 2; 2.11.2.6; 2.11.2.7; 2.11.3.2.1; 2.13.4; 2.11.2.7 problem 4; 4.2.4; 6.5.2; 6.5.3 problem 1; 6.9.2.2.4 problem 4; 6.9.2.2.5; 6.9.2.2.6 problem 5; 6.9.2.4.3 problem 8)
Assessors:	People who sit with a **judge** and help arrive at a **judgment**, usually in complex cases. (Para: 1.3.1.3)
Assets:	The things that a person owns. (Paras: 3.3.2.11; 3.4.4; 4.2.2.1; 4.6.4.2; 4.6.5.1; 4.6.5.2; 5.3.5; 5.6.4.7; 5.8.4.2.2.1)
Assisted suicide:	*Suicide* committed with the help of another person, sometimes a doctor. (Para: 4.6.2)
Attachment of emoluments:	Is a court order whereby the judgment creditor is able to attach part of the salary or wages of the judgment debtor (who is referred to as the garnishee) (Para: 4.5.3.2)
Attachment of property:	This occurs when the **sheriff** of the court seizes the property of a person against whom the court has issued a **warrant of execution**. (Paras: 1.5.1.3; 3.3.2.15; 5.6.5.2.3)
Attempt:	Where a person intends to commit a **crime** and takes steps towards committing it even if the attempted **crime** is not committed. (Paras: 2.1.7; 2.1.7 problem 6; 2.2.1.3 problem 3; 2.3.8; 2.6.1; 2.7.4; 2.11.2.7; 2.11.3.2.1; 2.14.3.1 problem 2; 2.14.5.1.1; 2.14.5.1.2)
Attorney:	A lawyer. In general they can appear in any court in South Africa except the **Small Claims Court**, the **High Court**, the **Supreme Court of Appeal** and the **Constitutional Court**. Attorneys may now apply to be granted a right of appearance in the higher courts. Attorneys deal directly with members of the public who need legal advice or representation and may refer them to **advocates**. (Para: 1.3.1.3; 1.3.1.5; 1.4.1; 1.4.1.1; 1.4.1.2; 1.4.1.2.1; 1.4.1.2.2; 1.4.1.3.1; 1.4.1.3.2 problem 3; 1.4.1.4.4; 1.4.1.6; 5.6.4.10.9)
Attorney-client privilege:	A privilege in law which says that whatever a person tells his or her **attorney** is secret and cannot be told to anyone without the client's permission. (Para: 1.4.1.5)
Attorney's admission examination:	The practical examination that all **candidate attorneys** must pass before they can become **attorneys**. (Para: 1.4.1.2.2)
Attorneys, Notaries and Conveyancers' Fidelity Guarantee Fund:	The fund against which clients of **attorneys** may claim if their money is stolen by their **attorneys**. (Para: 1.4.1.6)
Auction:	A public sale of goods to the person who is prepared to pay the highest price. (Paras: 3.3.2.1.5; 3.3.1.1)
Automatically unfair dismissals:	If an employee thinks that the dismissal was unfair, in other words that the employer didn't follow fair procedures or there is not a 'good reason' for the dismissal, then the employee can try to challenge the dismissal. (Para: 6.9.2; 6.9.2.1; 6.9.2.1.1; 6.9.2.1.1 problem 2; 6.10.1)

Bag-snatching:	The stealing of handbags by forcibly removing them from victims. (Para: 2.1.3)
Bail:	Money paid by an **accused** so that he or she may be released from police custody or **prison** until the trial. If the **accused** attends the **trial** the money will be paid back. (Paras: 1.4.1.1; 2.11.3.1; 2.11.3.2; 2.11.3.2.1; 2.11.3.2.2; 2.11.3.3; 2.11.3.3 problem 5; 2.13.1.2; 2.13.2.2; 2.13.4; 2.13.4 problem 6; 2.14.6.2)
Bail receipt:	The receipt issued by the **police** or court when a person is granted **bail**. (Para: 2.11.3.2.1)
Bait and switch marketing:	This usually involves **advertising** something at a very cheap price in order to attract **consumers** into a shop. Once they enter the shop **consumers** are switched to a more expensive **product**. (Para: 3.2.8.3)
Balance of probabilities:	The amount of proof that must be shown by a **plaintiff** in a **civil action** to win the case. (Paras: 1.4.2; 1.5.1; 1.5.1.2; 1.5.2.2; 4.5.2.4)
Balance of the purchase price:	The amount of money that must be paid by a **debtor** to a **creditor** in order to pay off the full purchase price. (Para: 3.3.1)
Balance of third party, fire and theft insurance:	Insurance against damage to the property of a **third party** as well as **fire and theft**. (Para: 3.5.9.4)
Balance of third party insurance:	Insurance against damage to the property of a **third party**. (Paras: 3.5.9; 3.5.9.2)
Bar:	A group of practising **advocates**. (Paras: 1.4.1.3.2)
Bar council:	The controlling body for **advocates**. (Para: 1.4.1.3.2; 1.4.1.6)
Bar examination:	The practical examination which must be passed by **advocates** who wish to join a society of practising **advocates**. (Paras: 1.4.1.2.1)
Barrister:	The **English law** word for **advocate**. (Para: 1.4.1.2.1)
Basic Conditions of Employment Act:	Act 75 of 1997. (Para: 6.3.1; 6.3.1 problem 1; 6.3.3)
Basic education, right to:	The right to basic education means that every child between 7 and 15 years or in grades 1 to 9 must receive compulsory education in public schools (Para: 5.2.2.1)
Beneficiary:	A person who benefits from something, for example, receiving a **social grant**. (Para: 5.3.7 problem 3)
Bestiality:	Sexual intercourse between people and animals. (Para: 2.8; 2.8.4)
Beyond a reasonable doubt:	The amount of proof that is required to be shown by the State in order to obtain the **conviction** of an **accused** in a criminal case. (Paras: 1.4.2; 2.9.2; 2.10; 2.13.2.2)
Bigamy:	Where people who are already married unlawfully and intentionally go through what is thought to be a proper marriage ceremony with somebody else. (Paras: 2.8; 2.8.3; 4.1.4.1)
Bill:	A **Bill** is an **Act** of **Parliament** before it has been passed by Parliament. Bills are usually published in the **Government Gazette** for comments by the public before they are considered by **Parliament**. (Paras: 1.2.2.3)

Bill of Rights:	The Chapter in the **Constitution** that sets out the **human rights** to which all South Africans are entitled. (Paras: 1.1.2 problem 4; 1.2.1; 1.2.2.1; 1.2.2.1 problems 2, 3 & 4; 1.3.1.7.3 problem 3; 2.1.1; 2.1.2; 2.3.6.10; 2.8.6.2 problem 2; 2.9.2; 2.11.3.1; 2.12.1; 2.12.1 problem 1; 2.13.3.2 problem 4; 4.1.3; 4.3.4; 5.1.1; 5.1.3; 5.1.6; 5.1.6 problem 4; 5.4.2.1 problem 1)
Blackmail:	The action, treated as a criminal offence, of demanding money from someone in return for not revealing compromising information which one has about them. *See also* **Extortion**.
Blogs:	Can be used as a form of **cyber bullying**. (Para: 2.5.1.4; 2.5.1.8 problem 1)
Boycott:	Where a group of people join together in order to stop using or buying certain things or attending certain functions or places.
Brand:	A particular make of goods. (Para: 3.2.8.2 problem 2)
Breach of promise to marry:	When a person who promises to marry another (see **Marriage**) decides not to marry that person. This is a **civil wrong**. (Para: 1.5.2; 4.1.4 problem 2)
Budget:	A plan of how much to spend each day, week, month or year based on how much a person earns and how much they spend during those periods. (Paras: 3.3.4 problem 10)
Building inspector:	A person who is employed to inspect buildings to work out their value and quality. (Para: 5.6.4.10.9)
Building society:	An organisation that lends money to people so that they can build or buy houses or buy land. (Paras: 4.3.2.4; 4.3.2.4 problem 7)
Bundling:	When a supplier joins two products together in order to sell them as one unit. (Para: 3.2.4.1)
Burglar:	When a person breaks into and enters a house, shop, storeroom or similar structure with the intention of committing a crime inside the premises. *See also* **Housebreaking**.
Burial order:	A burial order is a certificate that says that the dead person may be buried. (Para: 4.6.4.1)
By-law:	A **statute** passed by a town or city council. (Paras: 1.2.2; 1.2.2.2 problem 5)
Bystander:	A person who is an onlooker. (Para: 2.1.6 problem 5)
Cabinet:	A body consisting of the **President** and Ministers of state departments. The main function of the cabinet is to carry out and apply laws passed by **Parliament**. (Para: 1.2.2.3; 6.6.7.1)
Candidate attorney:	A law student who has entered into an agreement with an **attorney** to gain practical experience while working in a law firm. (Para: 1.4.1.2.2; 1.4.1.4.2 problem 4)
Car dealers:	People who sell cars to make a profit. (Paras: 3.3.2.12 problem 7; 3.5.2; 3.5.3; 3.5.7 problem 3; 3.5.8)
Car purchases:	Buying a motor vehicle. (Para: 3.5.2; 3.5.3; 3.5.4; 3.5.4 problem 1; 3.5.5; 3.5.6; 3.5.7; 3.5.7 problem 3; 3.5.8)
Car registration certificate:	A document issued by the vehicle licensing office that describes the motor vehicle and its registration number.

Car transfer documents:	Documents necessary to transfer a car into the name of the purchaser. (Para: 3.5.7; 3.5.8; 3.5.8 problem 4)
Catchment Management Agency (CMA):	Agency responsible for the area of land collecting rainfall. (Para: 5.7.3.1.1)
Caution and discharge:	Where after **conviction** the **accused** is warned that he or she should not commit the offence again and is discharged without a penalty. (Para: 2.13.3.1)
CCMA:	*See* **Commission for Conciliation, Mediation and Arbitration (CCMA)**
Certificate of roadworthiness (COR):	A certificate issued by the vehicle licensing authorities stating that a motor vehicle is roadworthy. (Para: 3.6.7; 3.5.8)
Chain letter schemes:	A direct or electronic mail promotion that sells advice on how to make money by simply re-selling that advice to other people. (Para: 3.2.9.4.4)
Chain store:	One of a number of shops owned by the same firm and selling the same goods. (Para: 3.3.1)
Chambers:	The office where an **advocate** or **judge** works. (Para: 1.4.1.2.1)
Charge:	An accusation that a person has committed a **crime**. (Paras: 1.1.2 problem 4; 1.2.3; 1.3.1.3; 1.3.1.7.2 case study; 1.3.1.7.3 problem 3; 1.4.1.1; 1.4.1.4.2 problem 4; 2.1.5; 2.1.5 problem 4; 2.1.7; 2.2.1.2 problem 2; 2.2.1.3 problem 3; 2.2.2 problem 4; 2.2.3.1; 2.2.3.5; 2.2.3.5.7; 2.3.1; 2.3.2; 2.3.2 problem 2; 2.3.4; 2.3.6.1; 2.3.6.2; 2.3.9; 2.3.9.1; 2.5.1.10; 2.6.1; 2.7.5 problem 1; 3.9.1; 2.9.2.2; 2.10.1; 2.10.3.2 problem 1; 2.11.2.1; 2.11.2.6; 2.11.3.2.1; 2.11.3.3 problem 5; 2.12.1.3; 2.13.1.1; 2.13.2.1; 2.13.2.2; 2.13.2.3; 2.13.3.1; 2.13.4; 2.14.3; 2.14.6.1; 2.14.6.2; 3.3.12.2; 3.4.6.1.2; 4.2.4 problem 6; 5.9.4.2; 6.9.2.4.3 problem 8)
Chief's court:	A court in which a chief sits to decide cases affecting African people in communities that live according to **customary law**. (Paras: 1.3.1; 1.3.1.6; 1.4.1.1; 1.4.1.2.1)
Child and youth care centre:	A Child and Youth Care Centre is a facility that provides residential care to more than six children outside the child's family environment in accordance with a residential care programme suited for the children in the facility. (Paras: 2.14.6.2; 2.14.7; 2.14.7.4; 4.3.3.2)
Child-headed households:	A child over the age of 16 years has assumed the role of a caregiver in respect of the rest of the children in the house. (Paras: 3.4.3; 4.3.3.2; 5.5.1)
Child justice:	Children in conflict with the law. This means that children under the age of 18, who are suspected to have committed crime, will not be dealt with in terms of the **Child Justice Act**. (Para 2.14)
Child Justice Act:	Act 75 of 2008. (Paras: 2.10.4.1; 2.14.1; 4.3.1.3)
Child justice court:	Any court that deals with a child alleged to have committed an offence and applies the provisions of the **Child Justice Act** to the case regarding the child. (Paras: 2.14.5.1.2; 2.14.5.2; 2.14.6; 2.14.6.2; 2.14.6.3; 2.14.8 problem 6)

Children:	People under 18 years of age. Children under the age of 10 years cannot form a guilty intention. Children aged 10-14 are presumed unable to form a guilty intention, but this can be challenged by the **prosecutor**. Children over the age of 14 years are treated as adults. (Paras: 2.10.1; 2.10.4.1; 3.3.2.4; 4.3.1.3; 4.3.2.3.1)
Children, abuse of:	A form of **domestic violence,** including abuse causing physical injury, sexual abuse or deliberate neglect of children. (Paras: 2.4.1; 2.4.2; 4.3.3.2; 4.3.3.4; 4.3.3.4 problem 9)
Children, actions without parental assistance:	Law allows children to do some things without their parents' assistance. (Paras: 4.3.2.4; 4.3.2.4 problem 7)
Children, adoptability of:	A child is adoptable if the adoption is in the best interests of the child and the child is living in unsuitable conditions that would lead to his/her detriment. (Para: 4.4.2.1)
Children, assessment of:	Every child who is alleged to have committed a crime must be assessed by a probation officer, if required. (Paras: 2.14.3; 2.14.3.1; 2.14.3.1 problem 2)
Children, bail applications:	If the arrested persons are under 18 years old a senior police officer may release them 'on warning' into the care of their parents. The parents will be told when to bring the children to court. (Para: 2.14.6.2; 2.11.3.2.1)
Children, best interests of:	Is meant to describe the set of principles or factors that guide a court's deliberations when assessing what decisions would keep a child safe and how best to meet a child's needs, including custody. (Paras: 2.3.6.10; 2.13.3.1; 2.14.2.1; 2.14.3.1; 2.14.4; 2.14.6.1; 2.14.7; 4.3; 4.3.1.4; 4.4.2.4 problem 2; 4.4.2.6; 4.5.3.1)
Children born from customary marriages:	Children born from a customary marriage which took place without a civil marriage officer. The court will decide who will have custody of children born into a customary marriage. (Paras: 4.3.1.5; 4.5.3.1; 4.5.3.2)
Children born of unmarried parents:	Children born from parents who do get married. These parents choose either to cohabit as if they are married or to continue live separate lives. (Paras: 4.1.1.2; 4.3.1.1; 4.3.1.2; 4.3.1.4; 4.3.1.4 problem 4)
Children, care dependency grants for:	A monthly payment from the government to a parent, guardian, foster parent or custodian of any child between the ages of 1 year old and 18 years old who needs full-time care because of mental or physical disability. (Para: 5.3.5.2.6)
Children, consent by to adoption:	If consent is given if he or she is 10 years or older or if below 10 years of age, the child is of sufficient maturity and stage of development to understand the implications of such consent. (Para: 4.4.2.3)
Children, consent by to medical treatment:	Children's Act makes special provision for consent by children (Paras: 5.4.6.3; 5.4.6.3 problem 4)
Children, criminal capacity of:	A child who commits an offence.(Paras: 2.10.4.1; 2.14.1; 2.14.2; 2.14.2.1; 2.14.2.2; 2.14.2.2 problem 1; 2.14.4.1; 4.3.1.3)

Children, detention of:	A child has the right not to be lawfully held or have his or her freedom of liberty taken away at the time of pending criminal charge that is raised against the individual as part of a prosecution. Such child shall be detained as a measure of last resort where it is unavoidable (Para: 2.14.1)
Children, diversion of:	Diversion of a case involving a child away from the formal court procedures in a criminal case. (Paras: 2.14.1; 2.14.4; 2.14.4.1; 2.14.5; 2.14.5.1; 2.14.5.1.1; 2.14.5.1.2; 2.14.5.2; 2.14.5.3; 2.14.6.3; 2.14.6.3 problem 4; 2.14.7)
Children, flashing to:	The unlawful and intentional exposure or display of sexual organs. (Para: 2.3.6.8)
Children, guardianship of:	A legal relationship between a minor child and a guardian that has certain rights and obligations regarding the child. Note a **guardianship** does not sever the legal relationship that exists between a child and his or her biological parents. (Para: 4.3.1.4; 4.3.1.5). *See also* **Guardians**.
Children, independence of:	Children who are mature for their age, responsible and self-reliant. (Para: 4.3.2.3)
Children in need of care and protection:	When a child's basic physical, intellectual, emotional or social needs are being threatened or neglected (Paras: 2.14.8; 4.3.3; 4.3.3.2 problem 8)
Children, joint care of:	Where both parents care for the same child for different periods of time. (Para: 4.5.3.1)
Children, pornography:	The unlawful and intentional use of a child, with or without the child's consent, for the purposes of producing any image, publication, depiction, description or sequence to produce sexual excitement. (Paras: 2.3.6.5; 2.3.6.6; 2.3.6.6.1; 2.3.6.6.2; 2.3.6.6.2 problem 7; 2.3.6.9)
Children, preliminary inquiry	An informal pre-trial procedure which is inquisitorial. (Paras: 2.14.4; 2.14.4.1; 2.14.5.1.2 problem 3)
Children, punishment of:	Parents may use a reasonable amount of physical force to punish their children. A parent who administers unreasonable punishment may be liable for civil damages or a criminal charge of assault. (Paras: 4.3.3.3; 4.4.1.1)
Children, reporting of abuse of:	Certain persons who have become aware of any type of abuse of a child have a duty to report the abuse to a designated child protection organisation, the provincial department of social development or a police official and any other person may report such suspicion. (Paras: 2.4.2; 2.4.3 problem 1; 4.3.3.4; 4.3.3.4 problem 9)
Children, reporting of sexual offences against:	Any person who has knowledge that a sexual offence has been committed against a child must report this information to the police. (Para: 2.3.6.10)
Children, right to participate in decision-making:	In terms of the Children's Act children have a right to participate in all decisions made about them, taking into account their age and maturity. (Para: 4.3.1)

Children, self-supporting:	Children have the right to be supported until the age of 18 years after which they may be able to support themselves but a parent may be legally obliged to support sick or crippled adult children over the age of 18 years if the children are unable to support themselves. (Paras: 4.3.2.1; 4.3.2.3)
Children, sentencing of:	The sentences are similar to those that can be imposed on adults but there are special factors to be taken into account.(Para: 2.14.7)
Children, sexual exploitation of:	Offences are: (a) sexual exploitation of children; (b) being involved in the sexual exploitation of children; (c) furthering the sexual exploitation of children; (d) benefiting from the sexual exploitation of children; (e) living from the earnings of the sexual exploitation of children; and (f) promoting sex tours. (Paras: 2.3.6.3; 2.3.6.3.1; 2.3.6.3.2; 2.3.6.3.3; 2.3.6.3.4; 2.3.6.3.5; 2.3.6.3.6; 2.3.6.3.7 problem 6)
Children, sexual grooming of:	Supplies, exposes or displays to a child an article which is intended to be used in the performance of a sexual act; with the intention to encourage, enable, instruct or persuade such child to perform a sexual act. (Paras: 2.3.6.4; 2.3.6.4.1; 2.3.6.4.2; 2.3.6.6.2 problem 7)
Children, support grants for:	Social grants to help maintain the child. (Para: 5.3.5.2.4)
Children, support of parents by:	Children whose parents do not provide them with a reasonable standard of care. (Paras: 4.3.2.1; 4.3.2.2 problem 5; 4.4.2.5; 4.5.3; 4.5.3.1)
Children, trafficking of:	The crime of commercial sexual exploitation of a child; recruiting, selling, supplying, transporting, transferring, harbouring (keeping) or receiving children. (Paras: 2.3.6.9; 2.3.6.10)
Children, trials involving:	Any court that deals with a child who is alleged to have committed an offence and applies the provisions of the child justice act ss 63-67 to the case regarding the child. (Para: 2.14.6.1)
Children, witnessing certain acts of a sexual nature:	A person who unlawfully or intentionally compels or causes a child to witness a sexual offence is guilty of the crime. (Paras: 2.3.6.7; 2.3.6.7.1; 2.3.6.7.2; 2.3.6.7.3)
Children's Act:	Act 38 of 2005. (Paras: 2.3.6.9; 2.3.6.10; 2.10.1; 2.14.7.4; 3.4.3; 4.1.1.2; 4.3; 4.3.1.4; 4.3.3; 4.3.3.3; 4.4.1.2; 4.4.2.5; 4.6.2; 5.4.6.3)
Children's Amendment Act:	Act 41 of 2007. (Paras: 2.3.6.10; 2.4.1; 2.4.2; 4.3.3.4)
Children's court:	A special court designed to protect the welfare of **children**. (Paras: 2.10.4.1; 2.14.3; 2.14.4; 2.14.8; 2.14.8 problem 6; 4.3.3.1; 4.3.3.2; 4.4.1; 4.4.1.2; 4.4.1.4 problem 1; 4.4.2.4; 4.4.2.6 problem 3)
Children's home:	A special home where **children** are housed when they are unable to be cared for by their **parents** or **guardians** or have been removed from the custody of their **parents** or **guardians**. (Paras: 2.13.3.1; 4.3.2.1)

Children's rights:	Human rights of children with particular attention to the rights of special protection and care afforded to minors. (Paras: 4.3; 5.1.2; 5.5.1; 5.6.1; 5.6.2.1 case study)
Childstealing:	Child abduction or child theft is the unauthorised removal of a minor (a child under the age of legal adulthood) from the custody of the child's natural parents or legally appointed guardians. (Para: 2.11.3.2.1)
Choice on Termination of Pregnancy Act	Act 92 of 1996. (Paras: 2.8.6.2; 4.3.4; 4.3.4 problem 10; 5.4.6.3; 5.4 8)
Christian marriage:	Religious ceremony carried out by an ordained Minister of the Christian faith who is a marriage officer authorised to carry out marriages according to the Christianity. (Para: 4.1.4.3)
Citizen's arrest:	The **arrest** by a private person of people who commit or attempt to commit serious **crimes** in their presence or who are reasonably suspected of having committed serious **crimes**. (Paras: 2.11.2.7; 2.11.2.7 problem 4)
Civil action:	An action brought by a person who feels a wrong was committed against him or her in terms of the law. These actions usually involve damage to property, injury to people, commercial disputes about **contracts**, the renting of houses, **consumer** problems, employment troubles, **family** problems, etc. (Paras: 1.2.3; 1.3.1;1.3.1.4.2; 1.3.1.4.2 problem 1; 1.4.1.1; 1.5.1; 1.5.1.2; 2.2.3.1; 2.11.3.1)
Civil and political rights:	**Human rights** that protect people against oppression by the State (eg freedom from cruel, inhuman and degrading treatment) and rights that enable citizens to participate in the political life of their country. (eg the right to vote). (Paras: 1.2.2.1 problem 2; 5.1.1; 5.1.2 problem 1)
Civil court:	The court that hears **civil actions** and proceedings to force people to stop doing certain things which may harm others. (Paras: 1.3.1,4; 1.3.1.4.2; 1.3.1.3; 1.5.1; 1.5.2.1)
Civil law:	The law dealing with **civil wrongs**. (Para: 1.2.3)
Civil union:	The monogamous voluntary union of two people who are at least 18 years of age, which is solemnised and registered in terms of the procedures set out in the **Civil Union Act**. (Paras: 3.4.4; 4.1.3; 4.1.4; 4.1.4 problem 2; 4.1.4.1; 4.1.4.2; 4.1.4.2 problem 4; 4.1.4.3; 4.1.4.4; 4.3.1.1; 4.3.1.2; 4.5.1 problem 1; 4.5.2.1; 4.5.2.5.1)
Civil Union Act:	Act 17 of 2006. (Paras: 4.1.2; 4.1.3)
Civil union partners:	A couple who wish to get married or enter into a civil union *See also* **Marriage**. (Paras: 4.2; 4.2.1; 4.2.2.1; 4.2.2.2; 4.2.3; 4.2.3 problem 5; 4.2.4; 4.5.2.1; 4.5.2.2; 4.5.2.2 problem 5; 4.5.2.3; 4.5.2.5.2; 4.5.3.2; 4.6.4.2)
Civil union regime, change of:	Husband and wife or civil union partners must apply to the High Court together explaining the type of marriage or civil union they want. (Para: 4.2.2.3)

Civil wrong:	A wrong against a private individual for which the wrongdoer must pay compensation to the injured person as opposed to a criminal wrong that is a wrong against the **State**. (Paras: 1.2.3; 1.2.3 problem 8; 2.1.4; 2.2.1; 3.1.4; 3.4; 3.4.2.9)
Code of Good Practice: Dismissal:	Guidelines to employers, employees and arbitrators regarding unfair dismissals. (Paras: 6.9.2; 6.9.2.2.2; 6.9.2.2.3; 6.9.2.3.1; 6.9.2.3.2.2; 6.9.2.3.3.2; 6.9.2.4.1)
Code of Good Practice on the handling of sexual harassment cases:	Guidelines to employers, employees on handling of sexual harassment cases, which aims to remove sexual harassment from the workplace. (Para: 6.8.2.6)
Co-habitation:	Couples who choose to live together, without getting legally married or entering into a **civil union**. (Para: 4.1.1.2)
Collateral security:	Means that the buyer is able to offer the bank something valuable as security against a home loan. (Para: 5.6.4.11)
Collection costs:	Costs that the credit provider may charge when having to take steps to recover payment from the consumer. (Para: 3.3.5.5)
Clerk of the court:	The court official who receives and issues legal documents and **pleadings** in the **magistrates' courts** in **civil actions**. (Paras: 1.3.1.7.3; 1.5.2.2)
Collective agreement:	An agreement in which the rights of the employees are agreed upon by the employer. (Para: 6.4.2)
Collective bargaining:	A process whereby the **employees**, collectively represented by a **trade union**, negotiate/bargain with an **employer**. (Para: 6.4.1)
Collision:	When vehicles collide as a result of negligent or careless driving. *See also* **Accident**.
Commission for Conciliation, Mediation and Arbitration (CCMA):	A State-funded but independent body established to resolve labour disputes through **conciliation**, **mediation** and **arbitration**. (Paras: 1.3.2.4; 6.4.5.1; 6.6.7.1 problem 2; 6.8.1; 6.9.2.3.2.1; 6.10.1; 6.10.1 case study; 6.11.1)
Commission for Gender Equality:	A state institution set up in terms of the Constitution to promote and strengthen democracy and a culture of human rights in the country. (Para: 3.2.2)
Commission for the Restitution of Land Rights:	A state institution set up to restore People who were dispossessed of their land rights after 1913 as a result of the Native Land Act of 1913 and related racially discriminatory laws. (Para: 5.8.4.3.2)
Commissioner:	The court official, usually an attorney or advocate, who hears and decides cases in the **Small Claims Court**. (Paras: 1.3.1.5; 1.5.2; 1.5.2.1; 1.5.2.2; 4.1.4.3)
Committal to a mental institution:	If the court finds that a person was legally insane at the time of the offence, that person will not be convicted and will not be sent to **prison**, but will be committed to a mental institution. (Para: 2.10.4.2)
Committal to an institution:	The placing of a convicted person who is addicted to **alcohol** or **drugs** and who is a danger to peace in a **rehabilitation** centre. (Para: 2.13.3.1)

Common law:	The law that comes from **Roman-Dutch law**. It sometimes has **English law** influences. (Paras: 1.2.1; 1.2.2; 1.2.2.2; 1.2.2.2 problem 5; 1.4.1.4.1; 2.1.1; 2.2.3.1; 2.3.1; 2.3.3; 2.3.6.3.7; 2.4.2; 2.8.5; 2.8.6.2 problem 2; 2.10.4.1; 2.14.2; 2.14.7; 3.1.4; 3.2; 3.2.8.1 problem 11; 3.4; 3.5.2; 3.5.6; 3.5.7; 4.1.3; 4.1.4.1; 4.1.5; 4.1.6.1; 4.1.6.2; 4.2.4; 4.3.1.4; 4.3.3.3; 4.4.1.1; 4.6.2; 5.4.6.1; 5.6.4.10.9; 6.2.2.1; 6.2.2.2; 6.6.1; 6.6.7.1)
Communal property associations:	Landholding institutions that were established under the Communal Property Associations Act. (Paras: 5.8.4.3.5; 5.8.4.3.5.1; 5.8.4.3.5.1 problem 4)
Communal Property Associations Act:	Act 28 of 1996. (Para: 5.8.4.3.5)
Community of property:	The property and debts of each spouse, from before the **marriage** or **civil union**, are put together in a 'joint estate'. (Paras: 4.2.2.1; 4.5.2.5.1)
Community policing forum (CPF):	A mechanism intended to assist the police in fighting **crime**. (Paras: 2.13.5; 2.13.5 problem 7)
Community service:	A **sentence** that a convicted person may be ordered to serve where they spend so many hours a week or on weekends helping members of the community in organisations like hospitals, old age homes or **children's homes**. The term can also refer to law graduates who render service at the **justice centres** under the supervision of a qualified lawyer. (Paras: 2.13.3.1; 2.14.5.1.1)
Compelled rape:	Compelled rape is defined in the **Criminal Law (Sexual Offences and Related Matters) Amendment Act** as: "Any person ('A') who unlawfully and intentionally compels a third person ('C'), without the **consent** of C, to commit an act of sexual penetration with a complainant ('B'), without the **consent** of B, is guilty of the offence of compelled rape." (Para: 2.3.2)
Compelled self-sexual assault:	Where a person compels a victim to perform any act of sexual violation on the victim himself or herself. (Para: 2.3.5)
Compelled sexual assault:	Compelled rape is defined in the **Criminal Law (Sexual Offences and Related Matters) Amendment Act** as: "A person ('A') who unlawfully and intentionally compels a third person ('C'), without the **consent** of C, to commit an act of sexual violation with a complainant ('B'), without the **consent** of B, is guilty of the offence of compelled sexual assault." (Para: 2.3.4)
Compensation:	The value of the missing money or thing or the amount necessary to repair the damage to the thing. (Paras: 1.1.1; 1.1.2 problem 3; 1.2.3; 1.3.1; 1.3.2.4 problem 8; 1.4.1.6; 1.4.2; 2.1.3; 2.2.1; 2.13.3.1; 2.14.5.1.1; 2.14.7; 3.4.6.1.1; 4.3.1.3; 5.6.1; 5.8.1; 5.8.2; 5.8.4.3.2; 6.4.5)
Compensation Commissioner:	Administer the fund and approves claims against a schedule of common workplace injuries and diseases. (Para: 6.3.5)
Compensation for Occupational Injuries and Diseases Act:	Act 130 of 1993. (Para: 6.3.5)

Competitions, promotional:	Promotional competitions are used to create an interest in a product or service. It does not matter whether a person in the competition has to show any skill or ability before being awarded a prize. (Paras: 3.2.8.8; 3.2.8.8 problem 17)
Complaint:	An accusation that a person has committed a **crime** or a delict. See also **Charge**. (Paras: 1.3.1.5; 1.3.2 problem 4; 1.3.2.2; 1.4.1.6; 1.5.2.2 problem 3; 2.1.3; 3.2.2; 3.2.8.5; 3.2.15; 4.5.3.2; 5.1.5; 5.6.5.1.6; 5.6.5.2.3; 5.9.3.1; 5.9.4; 5.9.4.1; 5.9.4.2; 5.9.4.2 problem 3; 6.8.2.3; 6.8.3.6)
Comprehensive insurance:	**Insurance** against damage to property, **fire and theft** as well as bodily injury. (Paras: 3.5.9; 3.5.9.5)
Compulsory education:	When you have a duty to attend school, and it is a crime for parents not to send their children to school. (Para: 5.2.2.1)
Conciliation:	The act of bringing parties in a dispute together in order to encourage them to settle their differences. (Paras: 1.3.2.4; 5.9.2.1; 5.9.3.1; 5.9.4; 6.4.5.1; 6.10.1)
Confession:	Formal statement admitting guilt to a crime. (Para: 2.11.3.1)
Confidentiality:	Keeping information about a patient private. (Paras: 5.4.5; 5.4.5 case study; 5.4.7; 6.1.1.3; 6.6.1)
Consent:	Where a person knows that something is happening or is about to happen, understands the possible results of what is happening or about to happen, and agrees to let it happen. See also **Informed consent**. (Paras: 1.1.2 problem 4; 2.2.1.3; 2.2.3.1; 2.2.4; 2.3.1; 2.3.2; 2.3.3; 2.3.4; 2.3.5; 2.3.6.1; 2.3.6.2; 2.3.6.3.1; 2.3.6.3.2; 2.3.6.3.3; 2.3.6.3.4; 2.3.6.3.5; 2.3.6.3.7; 2.3.6.4; 2.3.6.5; 2.3.6.6.1; 2.3.6.9; 2.3.7; 2.3.9.2; 2.3.10.1.2; 2.3.10.1.4; 2.10.3.4; 4.2.2.1; 4.4.2.3; 5.4.2.1; 5.4.5.1; 5.4.6; 5.4.6.1; 5.4.6.2; 5.4 8)
Consent paper:	An agreement on what should happen to the property, **children** and **maintenance**, on **divorce**. (Para: 4.5.2.3; 4.5.2.4)
Conspiracy:	An agreement between two or more persons to commit a **crime**. (Paras: 2.1.7; 2.1.7 problem 6; 2.3.8)
Constitution:	A constitution sets out the basic rules according to which a country is governed. A constitution may be unwritten (in which case it is found in different statutes) or written (in which case it is found in a single document, like the South African Constitution). The South African Constitution provides for a **separation of powers**.(Paras: 1.1.2 problem 4; 1.2.1; 1.2.2; 1.2.2.1; 1.2.2.3; 1.3.1.1; 1.3.2.3 problem 7; 1.4.1.4.1; 1.4.1.4.2; 2.1.1; 2.1.2; 2.2.1; 2.2.3.1; 2.3.6.10; 2.4.3; 2.5.1.9.1; 2.5.1.9.2; 2.7.5; 2.8.6.1; 2.11.1.1; 2.11.2; 2.11.2.4; 2.11.3.1; 2.11.3.2; 2.12.1; 2.13.1.1; 2.13.2.3; 2.13.3.2 problem 4; 2.13.4; 2.13.4 problem 6; 2.14.1; 2.14.7; 3.2.2; 3.3.2.4; 4.1.1.2; 4.1.2; 4.1.3; 4.1.6.1; 4.3; 5.1.1; 5.1.2; 5.1.2 problem 2; 5.1.3; 5.1.4; 5.2.1; 5.4.2.1; 5.4.2.1 problem 1; 5.4.11; 5.5.1; 5.6.1; 5.6.2.1; 5.7.2; 5.8.2; 5.9.1; 6.1.1.4.1; 6.2.2.2; 6.4.2; 6.7.2.1)

Constitutional Court:	The highest court with respect to constitutional matters. Its decisions bind all courts, including the **Supreme Court of Appeal**. (Paras: 1.1.2 problem 4; 1.2.2.1 problem 4; 1.2.2.2 problem 5; 1.2.2.3; 1.3.1; 1.3.1.1; 1.3.1.2; 1.3.1.3; 1.3.1.7.2; 1.4.1.2.1; 1.4.1.2.2; 2.2.1.1; 2.2.3.6; 2.3.1; 2.3.6.1; 2.9.2; 2.9.2.2; 2.13.3.2; 2.13.3.2 problem 4; 2.14.7.5; 4.1.3; 4.1.6.1; 4.6.4.2; 5.1.3; 5.1.4; 5.3.5.1; 5.4.2.1; 5.4.2.1 problem 1; 5.4.2.1 problem 2 case study; 5.6.2.1 case study; 5.6.2.1 problem 1; 5.6.3.2.1 case study; 5.7.2 case study); 5.7.2 problem 2)
Constitutionality:	Whether or not laws or conduct go against the **Constitution**. (Paras: 1.3.1.1; 1.3.1.3; 1.3.1.4; 2.8.4; 5.1.4)
Constructive dismissal:	Conduct of the **employer** which is so intolerable that the **employee** is compelled to resign. (Paras: 6.8.2.5; 6.9.1; 6.9.1.1; 6.9.1.1 problem 1)
Consumer:	A person who buys or uses goods or services bought from another. (Paras: 3.1.1; 3.1.1 problem 1)
Consumer affairs offices, provincial:	Offices around the country dealing with consumer complaints lodged (Paras: 3.2.14; 3.2.14.2)
Consumer complaints:	Informal complaints from the public sent to the consumer affairs offices. (Paras: 3.2.14; 3.2.15)
Consumer court:	A court constituted to deal with consumer complaints. (Paras: 3.2.14; 3.2.15; 3.3.2.15)
Consumer law:	The law that governs the relationships between **consumers** and the people who sell goods or services. (Para: 3.1.1)
Consumer protection:	Steps taken by the government and other agencies to protect the rights of individual users of goods or services, who are in a weaker position than the suppliers. (Para: 3.1.4; 3.4)
Consumer Protection Act:	Act 68 of 2008. (Paras: 3.1.4; 3.2; 3.4; 3.4.2.1; 3.4.2.2; 3.4.2.7; 3.4.2.8; 3.4.2.9; 3.4.5; 3.5.2; 3.5.6; 3.5.7)
Consumer rights:	These rights include the protection of safety, information, choice and a fair settlement of just claims. (Paras: 3.2.1; 3.3.2.2)
Consumer, third party:	A consumer who does not enter into a **contract** with the seller, but uses or is injured by the goods bought. (Paras: 3.4.2.9; 3.4.2.9 problem 4)
Consumers, assessment of:	This involves an enquiry into whether a person is able to afford a loan or to pay for goods bought on credit. The applicant must disclose full details of income and other debts and liabilities. (Para: 3.3.2)
Consumers, authorisation of repairs or maintenance:	A consumer cannot be forced to pay for repairs that were done without his or her approval before the repairs were started. (Paras: 3.2.4.3; 3.2.4.3 problem 4)
Consumers, cancellation of advance reservations, bookings or orders:	When a consumer cancels an advance reservation or booking, the supplier may impose a reasonable charge for the cancellation of the booking. (Para: 3.2.4.5)
Consumers, 'customer loyalty programmes':	Programmes' that reward consumers for buying things, very often from the same person or business. (Para: 3.2.8.7)

Consumers, payment in advance:	Payments in advance include prepaid certificates, credits and vouchers, prepaid services and lay-bys. (Para: 3.2.13)
Consumers, promotional offers:	A promotional offer is an offer or promise of any prize, reward, gift, free goods or services, reduction in price or benefit whether or not the person accepting the offer has to enter into an agreement to buy something. (Paras: 3.2.8.6; 3.2.8.6 problem 16)
Consumers, purchase of goods from a catalogue:	This method of shopping takes place when consumers order goods by telephone, fax or postal order after looking through a catalogue which must not be misleading and must indicate all costs, such as delivery charges. (Paras: 3.2.8.5; 3.2.8.5 problem 15)
Consumers, right not to be unfairly discriminated against:	No discriminatory criteria may be used when determining the cost of credit, the terms and conditions under which credit is granted, the grounds that will be used to enforce an agreement and the reason for reporting credit information to the credit bureau. (Para: 3.3.2.4)
Consumers, right to apply for credit:	Every adult has the right to apply for credit. (Para: 3.3.2.3)
Consumers, right to challenge accuracy of credit information:	Challenging credit information is where a consumer logs a dispute with the credit bureau or the National Credit Regulator. (Paras: 3.3.2.11; 3.3.2.11 problem 6)
Consumers, right to choose:	The right to choose means that consumers may shop around for the best price. (Para: 3.2.4)
Consumers, right to confidential treatment of information:	Any person who receives personal information in terms of the NCA about a consumer is forced to protect the secrecy of that information. (Paras: 3.3.2.10; 3.3.2.10 problem 5)
Consumers, right to debt counselling:	Where the consumer's account is in arrears and the consumer has not voluntarily surrendered or returned the goods, the seller must inform the consumer of the right to seek help from a debt counsellor, alternative dispute resolution agent, consumer court or ombudsman. (Para: 3.3.2.15)
Consumers, right to early settlement of account:	A consumer has the right to settle an account earlier than agreed without giving notice to the credit provider but the consumer may ask the credit provider for a statement that contains the settlement amount. (Paras: 3.3.2.9; 3.3.2.9 problem 4)
Consumers, right to equality:	The right to equality means that suppliers may not unfairly limit access to goods and services for certain consumers, nor may they unfairly favour certain consumer groups when they market, sell or distribute their goods or services. (Para: 3.2.2)
Consumers, right to examine or choose goods:	Suppliers must allow consumers a reasonable opportunity to inspect goods that have been purchased or delivered and consumers may return goods that were not examined by them before delivery. (Para: 3.2.5)
Consumers, right to fair and honest dealing:	Honest dealing excludes unacceptable behaviour, false and misleading representations, fraudulent schemes and offers, pyramid, Ponzi, multiplication and other fraudulent schemes, substituted goods being used to change terms of agreements of sale and overselling and overbooking. (Para: 3.2.9)

Consumers, right to fair and responsible marketing:	The right to fair and responsible marketing involves, for example, protection against false and misleading advertising, 'bait' marketing, fake 'free' offers, misleading claims in catalogues, misleading promotional offers, unsupported customer loyalty programmes, misleading promotional competitions and 'referral' selling. (Para: 3.2.8)
Consumers, right to fair, just and reasonable terms and conditions:	Before a consumer enters into an agreement the supplier must give the person written notice of clauses in the agreement that affect the supplier's liability to the consumer and the effects of these risks must be drawn to the consumer's attention in a way that can easily be seen by the consumer and the consumer must accept them. (Paras: 3.2.10; 3.2.10.1; 3.2.10.1 problem 21)
Consumers, right to fair value, quality and safety:	This right includes the quality of the service and the goods which includes repaired goods and the related service, and safety precautions regarding the use of goods as well as the safe disposal of certain goods. (Para: 3.2.11)
Customers, right to implied warranty of quality:	All persons involved in the supply of goods are responsible for their good quality and safety, and defective goods may be returned for replacement, repair or refund at the customer's choice. (Para: 3.2.11.3)
Consumers, right to information:	The consumer is entitled to all information regarding the product which he or she considers buying and all labelling and verbal information must be provided in clear and understandable language. (Paras: 3.2.7; 3.2.7.1; 3.2.7.2; 3.3.2.6; 3.3.2.7)
Consumers, right to information on intermediaries:	People who deliver goods or services or who install things must wear a name badge or identification and consumers may demand such identification. (Para: 3.2.7.6)
Consumers, right to invoices and receipts:	Proof of payment or terms of payment must be provided by all persons who supply goods or services. (Para: 3.2.7.5)
Consumers, right to privacy:	This right means that private information may not be shared with another person or made public without the person's consent. (Para: 3.2.3)
Consumers, right to quotation before incurring credit:	The National Credit Act forces the credit provider to give the debtor a quote before entering into the agreement and the quotation is binding on the credit provider for five days. (Paras: 3.3.2.12; 3.3.2.12 problem 7)
Consumers, right to reasons for refusal of credit:	A consumer whose application for credit was refused may ask the credit provider to give reasons why the application was refused and the reasons must be given in writing. (Paras: 3.3.2.5; 3.3.2.5 problem 3)
Consumers, right to receive documentation:	There are various way in which the documents may be delivered and the consumer makes the choice, (Para: 3.3.2.8)
Consumers, right to receive statements of account:	The general rule is that the consumer must receive monthly statements but the intervals vary according to the type of agreement. (Para: 3.3.2.9)
Consumers, right to return defective goods:	If there is something wrong with the goods that consumers have bought they may return the goods within a reasonable period and ask for a full refund. (Paras: 3.2.6; 3.2.6 problems 6 & 7; 3.4.2.2)

Consumers, right to return goods:	The consumer who enters into a lease, instalment agreement or a secured loan has the right to notify the credit provider that he or she wishes to return the goods so that they can be sold to settle the consumer's account. (Paras: 3.3.2.14; 3.3.2.14 problem 9)
Consumers, right to termination of agreement:	If the place of contracting was not the business premises of the credit provider, the consumer has a right to cancel the agreement within five business days from the date of signing the agreement. (Paras: 3.3.2.13; 3.3.2.13 problem 8)
Consumers, right to warranty on repaired goods:	Suppliers must guarantee the parts and labour used to repair goods for at least three months after the date of repair. (Para: 3.2.11.4)
Consumers, risks to:	If there are any unusual or unexpected risks and risks that could lead to serious injury or death suppliers must inform consumers and labelling on products must include warnings and adequate instructions for the safe handling and use of those goods. (Para: 3.2.11.5)
Consumers, strict liability for harm caused to:	This means that all suppliers are liable for harm caused to consumers, even if there was no negligence on their part, when supplying any unsafe goods, or there was a product failure, defect or danger in any goods, or inadequate instructions or warnings provided to the consumer regarding any danger linked to the use of such goods. (Para: 3.2.12)
Consumers, unacceptable behaviour towards:	Behaviour that includes assaulting consumers, putting pressure on them, harassing them or using unfair tactics to sell goods or services to them or to collect payments owing for goods or services or to get back goods sold. (Para: 3.2.9.1)
Consumers, unordered goods:	If a consumer receives unordered goods he does not have to pay for them nor is he obliged to return them as the seller must have the unsolicited goods collected at the seller's expense. (Paras: 3.2.6.1; 3.2.6.1 problem 8)
Consumer Tribunal:	The role of the Tribunal is to adjudicate on applications made in terms of the National Credit Act 34 of 2005 by and review the decisions of the National Credit Regulator. (Paras: 3.2.13.1; 3.2.14)
Contempt of court:	The **crime** of failing to obey a court order. (Paras: 1.5.1.3; 2.2.4; 3.4.6.1.1; 3.4.6.1.2; 4.5.3.1)
Contingency fees:	The client only pays the **attorney** if the **lawyer** wins the case. (Paras 1.4.1.3.1; 1.4.1.4.2)
Continuous unconsciousness, grounds for divorce:	The court must be satisfied that the spouse or partner has been unconscious for a continuous period of at least six months immediately before the divorce action and that there is no reasonable chance of the spouse or partner becoming conscious again. (Paras: 4.5.2.1; 4.5.2.1.2)
Contract:	An agreement between two or more persons – usually in writing. (Paras: 1.4.1.1; 3.1.1; 3.1.1 problem 1; 3.4; 3.4.1; 3.4.3; 3.4.5; 3.4.5.1; 3.4.5.1 problem 6)
Contract, breach of:	When a person breaks a **contract**. (Paras: 3.4.6; 3.4.6 problem 7; 3.4.6.1)

Contract, cancellation of and damages:	An innocent person may cancel the contract if the wrongdoing person failed to carry out an important part of the contract and claim damages. (Para: 3.4.6.1.4)
Contract, conditions in:	Conditions in a **contract** often limit liability. *See also* "**As is**". (Para: 3.4.2)
Contract, fixed-term:	A **contract** for a fixed period of time. (Para: 3.2.4.2; 3.2.4.2 problem 3)
Contract, law of:	Where such people have entered into agreements they will be governed by the common law of contract. (Para: 3.4)
Contract, requirements for:	The legal requirements that must be proved before there is a **contract**. (Para: 3.4.1)
Contract, termination of:	A contract ends when each party does what he or she promised to do, both parties agree to end the contract, the contract is cancelled as a result of breach of contract or one of the parties dies. (Para: 3.4.6.2)
Contractor:	A person who contracts to build a house – a builder. (Paras: 5.6.4.10.7)
Conveyancer:	An **attorney** who specialises in preparing documents for the transfer of land and other **immovable property**, and the registration of **mortgage bonds**. (Paras: 1.4.1.2; 1.4.1.2.3; 1.4.1.3.2 problem 3; 5.6.4.10.9)
Conveyancing fees:	Fees paid to a **conveyancer**. (Para: 5.6.4.3)
Conviction:	When a **judge** or **magistrate** finds an **accused** guilty in a **criminal court**. (Paras: 2.13.2.2; 2.13.3.1)
Cooling-off period:	The period of five days given to **consumers** who wish to cancel a **credit agreement** signed away from a seller's place of business. (Paras: 3.2.4.4; 3.2.4.4 problem 5; 3.3.2.13; 3.3.2.13 problem 8)
Co-perpetrator:	A person who helps the **perpetrator** of a **crime**. (Para: 2.1.5)
Corporal punishment:	The whipping of juvenile criminals has been declared unconstitutional. (Para: 1.2.2.1 problem 4)
Corpse, sexual acts with:	A crime created by statute when committed intentionally and at common law it is a crime to interfere with a dead body. (Paras: 2.8; 2.8.5)
Correctional supervision:	A community-based form of **punishment** which is the supervision of the offender with the view to correcting the wrongdoer and the wrongdoing. (Paras: 2.13.3.1; 2.14.7; 2.14.7.3)
Corrective discipline:	In the workplace disciplinary codes or rules will vary according to what has been agreed to by the employer and union/employees to enable the employer to deal with breaches of these rules and to treat all employees equally. (Para: 6.5.3)
Court bail:	Bail applied for during a court hearing on application by a person awaiting trial instead of being held in prison until the trial date. (Para: 2.11.3.2.2)
Cover:	The protection given to an **insured** person by an **insurance** company. (Para: 3.5.9)

Credit:	Where a purchaser is allowed to take possession or ownership of a thing without paying for it in full. The **balance of the purchase price** is usually paid in **instalments**. (Paras: 3.3.1; 3.3.2.1; 3.3.4; 3.3.4 problem 10; 3.3.5)
Credit agreement:	A **contract** to buy or hire something by paying a deposit and the **balance of the purchase price** over a fixed period of time. **Credit agreements** have to be in writing. (Paras: 2.13.3.3 problem 5; 3.1.2; 3.2.10; 3.2.10.1 problem 21; 3.3.1; 3.3.2.1; 3.3.2.4; 3.3.2.9; 3.3.2.12 problem 7; 3.3.2.13 problem 8; 3.3.2.15 case study; 3.3.3.1; 3.3.3.2; 3.3.4 problem 10; 3.3.5; 3.3.6; 3.3.6.1; 3.3.7.7; 3.3.7.10; 3.3.8; 3.3.10; 3.3.11; 3.3.12.1; 3.3.12.3; 3.4.2.7; 3.4.3; 3.4.5.1; 3.5.7; 4.2.2.1; 5.6.5.2.3)
Credit agreement, clauses in:	The **Consumer Protection Act** states that certain clauses must not be included in a **credit agreement**. (Paras: 3.2.10; 3.2.10.1)
Credit bureau:	A self-regulatory organisation that assists consumers with complaints. Credit bureaus have information about the creditworthiness of individuals. (Paras: 3.2.14.2; 3.3.2.4; 3.3.2.11; 3.3.2.11 problem 6)
Credit buying:	The buying of goods or services in exchange for a promise to pay the full purchase price in future. (Paras: 3.3.1; 3.3.2; 3.3.2.1)
Credit costs:	If a consumer enters into a credit agreement various costs relating to the granting of the credit can be charged. (Para: 3.3.5)
Credit facilities:	When a **consumer** is given possession or ownership of the thing sold before the full purchase price has been paid. (Para: 3.3.6.2)
Credit guarantee:	Where a person agrees to pay the obligations of another consumer in terms of a credit facility or a credit transaction (Paras: 3.3.2; 3.3.6.3)
Credit insurance:	An **insurance policy** on the life of the consumer that covers the outstanding debt for the duration of the **credit agreement**. (Para: 3.3.5.6)
Credit manager:	The person in a business responsible for deciding whether or not to give a **debtor credit**. (Paras: 3.3.4 problem 10; 3.3.12.3 problem 14)
Credit repair:	Credit repair refers to the situation where the consumer has paid off a debt that created the negative listing and then approaches the credit bureau to remove the information proving that he or she has paid off the debt concerned. (Para: 3.3.2.11)
Credit transactions:	A credit transaction can take on many forms but essentially it is a transaction where payment of the amount owed by one person is delayed and interest is charged. (Para: 3.3.7)
Creditor:	The person who lends money to a **debtor**. (Paras: 3.3.1; 3.3.2.15; 3.3.4; 3.3.8; 3.3.9; 3.3.12; 3.3.12.1; 3.3.12.2; 3.3.12.3; 3.3.12.3 problem 14)
Crime:	A **crime** is a wrong against the **State** for which the **criminal** is punished by the **State** (see Part 2 on **criminal law)**. (Paras: 2.1.1; 2.1.2; 2.1.4; 2.2; 2.2.1.3; 2.6.5; 2.7)
***Crimen injuria*:**	*See* **Criminal insult**.

Crimes against morality:	**Crimes** against what society believes are wrong. They usually include **drug abuse** and sexual relations between consenting adult partners. (Paras: 2.8; 2.8.6.2 problem 1)
Crimes, causes of:	The reason why **crimes** are committed. (Paras: 2.1.2; 2.1.2 problem 2)
Crimes, defences against:	A **criminal** may escape **conviction** if he or she proves that a **crime** was not committed; or that he or she did not commit the **crime**; or that there was a justified excuse for committing the **crime**; or that he or she was not criminally responsible. (Para: 2.10)
Crimes, elements of:	The legal requirements that must be proved by the **State** before a person can be found guilty of a **crime**. (Para: 2.1.4)
Crimes, preliminary	These are acts or omissions by people which take place before **crimes** are committed, but which are still regarded as complete **crimes** in themselves. (Para: 2.1.7)
Crimes, preparation of:	Preparation to commit a **crime** is not sufficient for a **conviction** unless it goes as far as being an **attempt**. (Para: 2.1.7)
Crimes related to alcohol:	There are several crimes relating to alcohol but the most common is driving under the influence of alcohol. (Paras: 2.9.1; 2.9.2.2 problem 1)
Crimes related to drugs:	Use or possession of drugs is not treated in the Drugs and Drug Trafficking Act as two separate offences, but as a single crime, whereas dealing in drugs is a specific crime. (Paras: 2.9.2; 2.9.2.2 problem 1; 2.11.3.2.1)
Crimes, reporting of:	Generally ordinary people have no duty to report crimes but the duty may be and has been placed on all persons in some statutes which entails that the failure to report those crimes constitutes a crime in its own right. (Paras: 2.3.6.10; 2.3.7; 2.4.1; 2.4.2; 2.4.3; 2.4.3 problem 1; 2.7.5)
Crimes, serious:	**Crimes** regarded as serious include **Arson, Culpable Homicide**, **Indecent Assault**, **Murder**, **Rape**, **Robbery, Sedition** and **Treason.** (Paras: 1.3.1.4.1; 2.2; 2.11.2.3; 2.11.2.7; 2.11.3.2.1; 2.13.3.1; 2.14.6.2)
Crimes, victims of:	People who have suffered injuries or lost money or property or had property damaged as a result of actions by **criminals**. (Paras: 2.1.3; 2.3.2; 2.3.2 problem 2; 2.3.6.9; 2.5.1.10; 4.3.1.3)
Criminal:	A person who is found guilty of a **crime**. See also definitions of **criminal courts** and **criminal trial**. (Paras: 1.2.2.1 problem 4; 1.2.3; 1.3.1)
Criminal Bureau:	The records maintained by the **police** to keep a list of all persons convicted of **crimes**. (Para: 2.13.3.1)
Criminal, compensation by:	Where the **criminal** is made to pay over the value of the missing money or thing or the amount necessary to repair the damage to the thing. (Paras: 1.1.2 problem 3; 1.2.2.2 problem 6; 1.2.3; 1.3.1; 2.1.3; 2.2.1; 2.13.3.1; 2.14.7; 4.3.1.3)
Criminal courts:	**Courts** that hear criminal cases. (Paras: 1.2.2.3; 1.3.1.4.1; 1.3.1.4.2 problem 1)

Criminal defamation:	The unlawful and intentional publication of words or behaviour about another which tends to injure his or her reputation. (Paras: 2.2.3.1; 2.2.3.6)
Criminal insult:	The unlawful, intentional and serious **violation** of the dignity or **privacy** of another person. (Paras: 2.2.3.1; 2.2.3.2; 2.2.3.3; 2.2.3.4 problem 5; 2.5.1.10)
Criminal intent:	The intention necessary for a person to be found guilty of committing a **crime**. (Paras: 2.1.4; 2.2.1.1; 2.2.3.1; 2.6.5; 2.10.1; 2.10.4; 2.10.4.2)
Criminal law:	The law dealing with **crimes**. (Para: 1.2.3; Part 2)
Criminal Law Amendment Act:	Criminal Law Amendment Act 105 of 1997 (Para: 2.10.4.3)
Criminal Law (Sexual Offences and Related Matters) Amendment Act:	Act 32 of 2007. (Paras: 2.2.3.1; 2.3.1; 2.3.2; 2.3.3; 2.3.6.1; 2.3.6.2; 2.3.6.3; 2.3.6.3.1; 2.3.6.3.2; 2.3.6.3.3; 2.3.6.3.4; 2.3.6.3.5; 2.3.6.3.6; 2.3.6.4; 2.3.6.5; 2.3.6.6; 2.3.6.7; 2.3.6.7.1; 2.3.6.7.2; 2.3.6.7.3; 2.3.6.8; 2.3.6.10; 2.3.8; 2.3.9.1; 2.3.10.1; 2.8.1; 2.8.2; 2.8.4; 2.8.5; 5.4.5.1)
Criminal omissions:	Where a person is criminally liable for failing to do something which the law requires to be done. (Paras: 2.1.6; 2.2.3.1)
Criminal Procedure Act:	Act 51 of 1977. The **statute** dealing with the administration of criminal justice in South Africa. (Paras: 1.2.2.1 problem 4; 1.2.2.3; 2.11.2; 2.12.1; 2.13.2.3; 2.13.3; 2.14.1; 2.14.6.1; 2.14.6.2; 2.14.7; 2.14.7.3)
Criminal process:	The process is provided for in the Criminal Procedure Act and the Constitution. (Para: 2.13.1)
Criminal records:	The information held by the **Criminal Bureau** which shows that a person has been found guilty of a **crime**. (Paras: 2.13.3; 2.13.3.1)
Criminal responsibility:	An accused may not be criminally liable for committing a crime because of the lack of the intention to commit the crime as a result of, for instance, youth or insanity. (Para: 2.10.4)
Criminal trial:	A **trial** in which the **State** brings an action against an **accused** who has been charged with committing a **crime**. (Paras: 1.4.2.2; 2.1.3; 2.10; 2.13.2)
Cross-examination:	A method of questioning **witnesses** to test the truth of their **evidence** by trying to show that they are not telling the truth or that they are mistaken. (Paras: 1.4.2; 1.4.2.2; 1.5.1.2; 2.13.2.2; 4.5.2.4)
Cross-subsidisation:	Using money from wealthier areas to cover the costs of extending services to poorer areas.
Culpable homicide:	The unlawful negligent killing of another person. (Paras: 2.1.4; 2.2; 2.2.1; 2.2.1.2; 2.11.2.3; 2.11.3.2.1; 2.13.3.3 problem 5; 2.14.5.1.2)
Curfew law:	A law which states that people must not be on the streets during certain hours of the day or night. (Para: 1.3.1.7.2 case study)
Custody, by parents:	When **parents** exercise care and control over their **children** and are responsible for their well-being. (Paras: 2.2.4; 2.11.3.2.1; 2.11.3.3)

Custody, by police:	Where a person is detained by the **police**. (Para: 2.13.2.2 problem 2)
Customary law:	The indigenous African legal system that existed in South Africa before the arrival of the European settlers. In some instances the law has been written down in **statutes**. An example is the Code of Zulu Law. (Paras: 1.2.1; 1.2.1 problem 1; 1.2.2.2; 1.3.1; 1.3.1.6; 2.8.3; 4.1.2; 4.1.4.1; 4.1.4.3; 4.1.5; 4.3.1.2; 4.3.1.5; 4.5.3.1; 4.6.4.2; 5.8.4.3.1)
Customary marriage:	A marriage entered into according to customary law under the Recognition of Customary Marriages Act. (Paras: 4.1.2; 4.1.3; 4.1.4.1; 4.1.4.3; 4.1.4.5; 4.2.4; 4.3.1.5; 4.5.3.1 problem 9)
Customs officials:	Civil servants employed by the **State** to control goods that are brought into or allowed to leave the country. (Para: 2.12.1.2)
Cyber bullying:	The use of information technology on computers and cell phones to harass, threaten, embarrass, or target another person. (Para: 2.5.1; 2.5.1.1; 2.5.1.2; 2.5.1.3; 2.5.1.4; 2.5.1.5; 2.5.1.6; 2.5.1.6 case study; 2.5.1.7; 2.5.1.8; 2.5.1.8 problem 1; 2.5.1.9; 2.5.1.10 problem 2)
Cyber crimes:	These crimes can take many forms such as the violation of privacy and dignity but are all committed using electronic media and applications. (Para: 2.5)
Damages:	**Compensation** for injuries caused to persons or property. (Paras: 1.2.2.2 problem 6; 1.2.3; 1.3.1.5; 1.4.1.1 problem1; 1.4.1.4.2 problem 5; 1.5.1.1; 1.5.1.3 problem 2; 2.1.4; 2.4.2; 2.11.2.3; 2.11.2.5; 2.11.2.6; 3.2.1.2 problem 23; 3.4.2.9; 3.4.2.9 problem 4; 3.4.3; 3.4.6.1.2; 3.4.6.1.3; 3.4.6.1.4; 4.1.4 problem 2; 4.3.1.2)
Deadly force:	Force intended to kill someone or cause serious bodily harm. (Paras: 2.10.3.1; 2.11.2.4; 2.11.2.4 problem 3)
Death:	A person is regarded as dead if he or she has suffered 'brain death', where all parts of the brain stop working and cannot be made to work again. (Paras: 4.6.1; 4.6.1 problem 1; 4.6.4.1; 4.6.5.1)
Death benefit schemes:	Schemes that help to pay for funeral expenses which may be provided by employers or be entered into in a private capacity. (Para: 4.6.3.2)
Death penalty:	A **sentence** by the court in which the judge orders that the convicted criminal be executed. The death penalty was declared unconstitutional in the case of S v Makwanyana. (Paras: 1.1.2 problem 3; 1.2.2.1 problem 3; 2.1.2; 2.2.1.1; 2.13.3.2; 2.13.3.2 problem 4)
Debt:	Money owed by a **debtor** to a **creditor**. (Paras: 1.4.1.2.2; 1.5.1.3)
Debt administrators:	People who help **consumers** who are having problems in paying off their **debts**. (Para: 3.3.2)
Debt collection:	Debt collection must take place in a lawful manner. (Paras: 3.3.2; 3.3.12; 3.3.12.2; 3.3.12.3)
Debt counselling:	Through debt counselling a consumer may rearrange the repayment of his or her debts. (Paras: 3.3.2; 3.3.2.15; 3.3.9)
Debt prescription:	A debt collector may not collect a debt that is older than three years. (Para: 3.3.12.1)

Debtor:	The person who borrows money from a **creditor**. (Paras: 3.3.1; 3.3.2.12; 3.3.7.2; 3.3.9; 3.3.12)
Deed of sale:	A written agreement between a buyer and a seller to buy and sell land and buildings. (Paras: 5.6.4.10.9; 5.6.4.10.9 problem 12)
Deed of transfer:	A legal document used to transfer **immovable property** from one person to another. (Para: 5.6.4.10.9)
Deeds office:	The **State** office where the transfer of land and buildings and registration of **mortgage bonds** is recorded. (Para: 5.6.4.10.9)
Defamation:	The unlawful and intentional publication of statements about another which lowers the reputation of that person in the eyes of others. (Paras: 1.4.1.4.2; 1.4.1.4.2 problem 5; 1.5.1.1; 1.5.2; 2.2.3.1; 2.2.3.6; 2.5.1.9.1)
Default administration fee:	A fee that the credit provider charges to cover the costs that the credit provider incurs when the consumer fails to pay his or her account. (Para: 3.3.5.4)
Default judgment:	A **judgment** given against a **defendant** who does not defend an action. (Paras: 1.5.1.2; 1.5.1.3; 1.5.2.2)
Defect:	Where there is a fault or something wrong with the goods or services sold. (Paras: 1.5.2.2 problem 3; 3.2.6; 3.2.11.1; 3.2.11.2; 3.2.11.3; 3.2.11.7; 3.2.12; 3.4.2.2; 3.4.2.3; 3.4.2.4; 3.4.2.5; 3.4.2.5 problem 3; 3.4.2.7; 3.4.2.9; 3.5.6; 3.5.8; 5.6.4.3)
Defence of other people:	This defence falls under what is termed private defence which allows reasonable force to be used when defending yourself, your property or another person. (Para: 2.10.3; 2.10.3.1)
Defendant:	The person who is **sued** by the **plaintiff** in a **civil action**. (Paras: 1.2.3; 1.3.1; 1.3.1.5; 1.4.2; 1.4.2.2; 1.5.1.2; 1.5.1.3; 1.5.2.2)
Delict:	See **Civil wrong**.
Democracy:	Government by all the people through elected representatives. (Paras: 12.2.1; 2.8; 2.13.5)
Dependence-producing substances:	See **Drugs**.
Deposit:	The small amount paid by a **debtor** to the **creditor** at the time the item or product is bought. (Para: 3.3.1)
Desertion:	Where the employee expressly or impliedly indicates that he or she does intend to return to work. (Para: 6.9.2.2.5)
Designated group:	Black people, women, and people with disabilities. (Para: 6.1.1.4.1)
Detention without trial:	The Protection of Constitutional Democracy against Terrorist and Related Activities Act provides for a 14-day period of detention during which interrogation takes place without the accused being brought to trial. (Para: 2.7.5)
Deterrence:	This is one of the justifications for **punishment**. It means that the **punishment** may discourage the criminal from committing the **crime** again; it may also act as an example that discourages other people from committing **crimes**. (Para: 2.10.3.3)

Developer:	A person who develops land by employing builders to build homes. (Paras: 5.6.2.1; 5.6.4.10; 5.6.4.10.2; 5.6.5.10.3; 5.6.4.10.7; 5.9.3.1)
Direct marketing:	Direct marketing occurs when suppliers contact potential customers individually in their homes in order to promote their goods and services. (Para: 3.2.3)
Director of Public Prosecutions:	The senior public servant in charge of all prosecutions by the **State**. (Para: 2.14.1)
Disability grants:	A grant paid to a person between the ages of 18 to 59 years on application supported by a medical report or certificate confirming the physical and/or mental disability. (Para: 5.3.5.2.3)
Disaster area:	An area declared to be a disaster area by the **President**. (Para: 5.3.5.2.8)
Discharge:	See **Caution and discharge**.
Disciplinary code:	A written set of rules that stipulates which conduct of the **employee** constitutes **misconduct**, the seriousness of this **misconduct** and the sanction to be imposed. (Paras: 6.5.1; 6.5.2; 6.5.3; 6.5.3 problem 1; 6.9.2.2.1; 6.9.2.2.3)
Disciplinary hearing:	These hearings take place when employees are considered to have misbehaved in the workplace to give the employees an opportunity to state their side before action is taken against them. (Paras: 6.9.2; 6.9.2 problem 4)
Discount:	A reduction in the price. (Paras: 3.2.8.7; 3.2.8.8; 3.2.8.9; 3.5.3; 3.5.6 problem 2; 3.5.9.7)
Discrimination:	Being treated differently because you are, for example, a woman, black, gay, not married or living with a disability. (Paras: 1.2.1; 1.2.2.1 problem 2; 1.2.2.3; 2.1.2; 2.8.6.2 problem 2; 3.2.2; 3.3.2.4; 4.1.1.2; 4.3.1.4; 5.2.2.2 problem 5; 5.2.2.3; 5.4.11; 5.7.2; 5.9.1; 6.1.1.1.1; 6.1.1.2; 6.1.1.2 case study; 6.7.2; 6.7.2.1; 6.7.2.1 problem 1; 6.7.2.2; 6.7.2.2. problem 2; 6.7.2.3; 6.8.2.5)
Dismissal:	Termination of employment. (Paras: 6.9; 6.9.1; 6.9.2.2; 6.9.2.2.3; 6.9.2.4.3 problem 8; 6.11.1)
Dismissal, automatically unfair:	See **Automatically unfair dismissal**.
Dismissal for incapacity:	Different considerations apply in the case of incapacity owing to injury or ill health, on the one hand, or poor work performance, on the other. (Paras: 6.9.2.3; 6.9.2.3.1; 6.9.2.3.2; 6.9.2.3.2.2 case study; 6.9.2.3.3; 6.9.2.3.3.2 problem 6; 6.10.1)
Dismissal for misconduct:	See **Misconduct**.
Dismissal for operational requirements:	See retrenchment. (Paras: 6.9.2.4; 6.10.1)
Dismissal, no-fault:	See retrenchment. (Para: 6.9.2.3.1)
Dismissal, unfair:	See **Unfair dismissal**.
Dispute resolution:	Disputes can be settled in court but the process is expensive and not always necessary as many disputes can be settled out of court by, for example negotiation or mediation. (Para: 1.3.2)

District magistrates' courts	Courts presided over by ordinary **magistrates**. (Paras: 1.3.1; 1.3.1.4.1; 1.3.1.4.2)
Diversion:	See **Children, diversion of.**
Divided profession:	A rigid distinction between **attorneys** and **advocates**. (Paras: 1.4.1.2.1; 1.4.1.2.2; 1.4.1.2.2 problem 2)
Divorce:	A legal action to end a **marriage**. The action can only be brought in the **High Court**. (Paras: 1.1.1; 1.3.1.4.2; 1.3.1.7.3 problem 3; 1.3.2.4 problem 8; 1.4.1.1; 1.4.1.1 problem 1; 1.4.1.4.2; 1.4.1.4.2 problem 5; 1.5.1.1; 1.5.2; 4.1.4.2; 4.2.2.2; 4.2.2.2.1 problem 3; 4.2.2.2.2. problem 4; 4.3.1.1; 4.3.1.5; 4.3.2.3.2; 4.4.2.4 problem 2; 4.5; 4.5.1; 4.5.1.1; 4.5.1.1 problem 2; 4.5.2; 4.5.2.1; 4.5.2.1.1; 4.5.2.1.2; 4.5.2.1.2 problem 4; 4.5.2.2; 4.5.2.2 problem 5; 4.5.2.3; 4.5.2.4; 4.5.2.4 problem 7; 4.5.2.5; 4.5.2.5.1; 4.5.2.5.2; 4.5.2.5.2 problem 8; 4.5.3; 4.5.3.1 problem 9; 4.5.3.2)
Domestic violence:	Includes all forms of abuse, intimidation, harassment, stalking, etc, and other controlling behaviour against a person that can cause harm to his or her safety, health or well-being (Paras: 2.2.2 problem 4; 2.4.1; 2.9; 4.2.4; 4.2.4 problem 6; 4.5.1)
Domestic Violence Act:	Act 116 of 1998. (Paras: 2.2.3.5; 2.4.1; 4.2.4; 4.2.4 problem 6)
'Dominant impression' test:	This test is used to decide whether someone is an employee or independent contractor. (Paras: 6.2.1.3; 6.2.1.4 problem 2)
Drivers, police powers to question:	Failure by a driver to stop a vehicle, give his or her name and address, or present a drivers' licence at the request of the police, may result in the driver being prosecuted for committing a crime. (Para: 2.11.1.2)
Drugs, abuse of:	Using or selling illegal drugs, or unlawfully using legal drugs, e.g. without a doctor's prescription. (Paras: 2.8; 2.8.6.2 problem 1; 2.9.2.1; 2.14.5.1.2 problem 3; 4.5.1; 5.3.1; 6.9.2.2.5)
Drugs and Drugs Trafficking Act:	Act 140 of 1992 that creates offences for using, or dealing in, drugs such as cocaine, dagga, LSD and mandrax. (Paras: 2.9.2; 2.9.2.1; 2.9.2.2)
Drugs, dealing in:	In order for a person to be convicted of unlawful dealing in drugs, his or her conduct must be unlawful and unlawfulness in this case includes intent. (Paras: 2.9; 2.9.2; 2.9.2.2)
Drugs, driving under the influence of:	The National Road Traffic Act provides that it is a crime if a person drives a vehicle or sits in the driver's seat of a vehicle with its engine running on a public road, while under the influence of a drug having a narcotic effect. (Paras: 2.9.1; 3.5.9.5)
Drugs, possession of	No person may have in his or her possession any dependence-producing substance, unless an Act of Parliament allows it. (Paras: 2.9; 2.9.2; 2.9.2.1; 2.14.5.1.2 problem 3)
Drunkenness:	See **Intoxication**.
Duress:	Where a person is forced to do something unlawful, normally by threats of violence. (Paras: 2.10.3; 2.10.3.3)
Duty of support:	See **Parents, duty to support children.**

Economic and social rights:	**Human rights** that require the State to provide certain things for its people. Economic rights include the right to fair labour practices, while social rights include rights to education, health, housing and **social security**. See also **Socio-economic rights**. (Paras: 1.2.2.1 problem 2; 1.3.2.3 problem 7; 5.1.1)
Education rights:	The rights are set out in the Constitution but the most important is the right to basic education.(Paras: 5.2.1; 5.2.1 problem 1; 5.2.1 problem 2; 5.2.2; 5.2.2.1; 5.2.2.5; 5.2.2.5 problem 7)
Electronic Communications and Transactions Act:	Act 25 of 2002. (Para: 3.1.1 problem 1)
Emancipation of minors:	Emancipation of minors means that a court agrees that they are financially independent of their parents but this does not mean that they have full legal capacity. (Paras: 3.4.3; 4.3.2.3.3)
Emergency Housing Programme:	The Programme assists people in rural and urban areas who have urgent housing problems due to such things as disasters, evictions, threatened evictions, demolition, displacements or immediate threats to life, health or safety. (Para: 5.6.4.2.1)
Emergency medical treatment, consent to:	In emergencies treatment cannot be given against the will of the patient unless it is to protect the public but there are certain exceptions. (Para: 5.4.2.1)
Emergency medical treatment, right to:	The Constitution states that nobody may be refused emergency medical treatment. (Paras: 5.4.2.1; 5.4.2.1 problem 1)
Employee:	A person who works for another person and who receives a salary or who assists an **employer** in the running of the business. (Paras: 6.1.1.4; 6.2.1; 6.2.1.1; 6.2.1.2; 6.2.1.3; 6.2.1.4; 6.2.1.4 case study; 6.2.1.4 problem 2; 6.2.2; 6.2.2.1; 6.3; 6.3.1; 6.4.5; 6.5.1; 6.5.3; 6.6.1; 6.6.2)
Employee, certificate of service:	(Para: 6.3.1)
Employee, dress code:	It is acceptable for an employer to have a dress code or requirements regarding appearance, including hairstyles but these requirements must be reasonable and necessary, and not discriminatory. (Para: 6.6.4)
Employee, drug testing:	In certain circumstances the employer may perform drug tests. (Para: 6.6.5)
Employee, ill-health or injury of:	Incapacity is not due to fault but rather an inability by the employee to do the job, either as a result of ill health. (Paras: 6.9.2.3.3.1; 6.9.2.3.3.2)
Employee, incapacity of:	This could be as a result of illness or injury, or the inability to perform the work leading to poor work performance. (Paras: 6.9.2.3; 6.9.2.3.3.2 problem 6)
Employee, minimum wage:	The lowest possible lawful wage payable to a worker for performing certain work. (Paras: 6.3.3; 6.3.3 problem 2)
Employee, poor work performance:	See incapacity. (Para: 6.9.2.3.2)

Environment Conservation Act:	Act 73 of 1989. (Para: 5.9.2)
Environment impact assessment (E.I.A.):	A scientific study of the likely effect of a development on the environment – in other words, all the things that can happen when you disturb the environment through a development. (Para: 5.9.3; 5.9.3.1)
Equality court:	Equality courts are established to ensure that reported cases of alleged unfair discrimination are dealt with to ensure justice for all. (Para: 3.2.2)
Equitable:	Fair and reasonable.
Essential service:	A group of **employees** that perform a service that if interrupted will endanger the lives and safety of other people. (Paras: 1.3.2.3 problem 7; 2.7.4; 6.4.5.3; 6.4.5.3 problem 2)
Euthanasia:	Where people ask others to kill them, usually so that it will end suffering by them. (Para: 2.2.1.3)
Eventual intention:	Where a person knows that his or her act or failure to act might cause some event, but does not care whether or not that event takes place. (Para: 2.2.1.1)
Eviction, arbitrary:	Arbitrary eviction means removing people from their homes without a court order. (Paras: 5.6.3; 5.6.3.1; 5.6.5.1.6; 5.6.5.1.6 problem 17)
Eviction, lawful occupiers:	These evictions are ordered by the court after consideration of various factors. (Paras: 5.6.3.1.1; 5.8.4.3.6; 5.8.5 problem 5)
Eviction order:	A court order allowing a **landlord** to have a **tenant** removed from his or her property. Usually when the **tenant** fails to pay the **rent**, is destroying the property, or disturbing the neighbours. (Paras: 1.5.1.1; 5.6.3.1.1; 5.6.3.1.2; 5.6.3.2.1; 5.6.3.2.2; 5.6.5.1.6; 5.6.5.2.3)
Eviction, unlawful occupiers:	A distinction is made between unlawful occupation for less than three months and unlawful occupation exceeding six months but in both cases the courts must take certain factors into consideration. (Paras: 5.6.3.2.1; 5.6.3.2.1 case study; 5.6.3.2.1 problem 2; 5.6.3.2.2)
Evidence:	This is information that is used by the **plaintiff** (or a **prosecutor**) or the **defendant** (or **accused**) to prove or disprove a case. It may consist of statements by **witnesses** or documents used in the case. (Paras: 1.3.1.7.1, 1.3.2 problem 4; 1.4.2; 1.4.2.2; 1.5; 1.5.1.2; 1.5.2.2; 2.11.3.2.2; 2.12.1; 2.12.1 problem 1; 2.13.2.2; 2.13.2.3 problem 3; 4.5.2.4)
Exclusionary rule:	Rule embodied in section 35(5) of the **Constitution**, which states that, if evidence is obtained in a manner that **violates** any of the rights in the **Bill of Rights**, it may be excluded from the trial of the **accused**, if to include the evidence would render the trial unfair or otherwise be detrimental to the administration of justice. (Paras: 2.12.1; 2.12.1 problem 1; 2.12.1.3)
Executive:	The branch of government consisting of the **President** and the Ministers which executes laws. (Para: 1.2.2.1)

Executor of estates:	The person who has to administer and 'wind up' the deceased's estate. (Paras: 4.6.4.3; 4.6.5.2; 4.6.5.2 problem 9)
Exemption clause:	A clause in a **contract** which prevents the buyer from suing the seller if something goes wrong or there is a hidden fault in the thing sold. (Para: 3.4.2.7)
Express warranty:	A statement made in writing or by words or acts that forms part of the **contract**. (Para: 3.4.2.8)
Expropriation:	When property is taken away from a person. (Paras: 5.8.2; 5.8.4.3.2)
Extended warranty:	An extended warranty is a prolonged warranty offered to consumers in addition to the standard warranty on new items at an extra cost to the buyer. (Para: 3.5.6)
Extension of Security of Tenure Act:	Act 62 of 1997. (Paras: 5.6.3; 5.6.3.1; 5.6.3.1.1; 5.6.3.1.2; 5.8.4.3.1; 5.8.4.3.3)
Extenuating circumstances:	Special facts that the courts could take into account to reduce a **sentence**. (Para: 2.2.1.1; 2.13.3.2)
Extortion:	Where people unlawfully and intentionally obtain something they are not entitled to, by forcing another person to hand the thing over to them. (Paras: 2.6.8; 2.14.5.1.1; 2.14.5.1.2)
Extra-judicial separation:	An informal agreement between spouses or **civil union partners** that they will live apart (Paras: 4.5.1.1; 4.5.1.1 problem 2)
Fair trial, right to:	(Paras: 2.7.5; 2.13.1.1; 2.13.4)
Fake 'free' offers:	A supplier offers **consumers** a 'free' sample and assumes the consumer will keep buying more of it. (Paras: 3.2.8; 3.2.8.4)
Family:	A group of people who live together as a unit and care for and support one another, usually related by blood or **marriage**. (Paras: 4.1.1; 4.1.1; 4.1.1.2; 4.1.1.2 problem 1)
Family Advocate:	The role of the Family Advocate is to assist the courts in establishing the best interests of minor children in civil legal disputes. (Para: 4.5.3.1)
Family court:	A High Court sitting in family-related matters. (Para: 4.2.4)
Feeding schemes:	These programmes are aimed at reducing hunger in certain households, communities and schools. (Para: 5.5.4.3)
Films and Publications Act:	Act 65 of 1996. (Para: 2.3.6.5)
Finance charges:	Debtors must usually pay creditors an amount of money in addition to the amount that they lend. (Paras: 3.3.1; 3.3.2.1)
Financial institution:	An institution that specializes in money lending or keeping, e.g. banks. (Paras: 3.2.15; 3.3.2; 5.6.4.4; 5.6.4.5; 5.6.4.6.1; 5.6.4.6.3; 5.6.4.8; 5.6.5.1.5; 5.8.4.3.5)
Fine:	Where a person convicted of a **crime** is ordered to pay money to the **State**. (Paras: 1.2.3; 1.3.1.3; 1.3.1.4.1; 1.3.1.7.3;1.4.1.4.2; 1.4.1.4.2 problem 5; 2.3.6.10; 2.5.1.10; 2.11.1.1; 2.13.3.1; 2.14.6.1; 2.14.7; 3.4.6.1.1; 4.2.4; 4.3.3.2; 4.3.3.4; 4.5.3.2)

Fire and theft insurance:	A person who takes out insurance against fire and theft will be compensated if the car is damaged by fire or stolen. (Para: 3.5.9.3)
Fire–arms:	See **Guns**.
Fixed time period lease:	A lease that runs for a fixed period of time. (Para: 5.6.5.1.4)
Food, adequacy of:	Common barriers to sufficient food are unemployment and lack of resources or social security grants, among others. (Paras: 5.5.3; 5.5.3 problem 3)
Food, right to:	The Constitution protects the right to food and the state must take reasonable legislative measures to ensure access to food for all South Africans. (Paras: 5.5.1; 5.5.2)
Food security:	Access to enough of the right kind and quality of food to live healthy life. (Paras: 5.5.2 problem 2; 5.8.5)
Force, unlawful use of:	In certain circumstances the use of force by a police officer is unlawful and constitutes an assault. See also **deadly force**. (Paras: 2.11.2.6; 2.12.1.3; 2.12.1.4 problem 3)
Forfeiture of benefits and/ or accrual:	The court may order that the party to a marriage or civil union who is guilty of causing the divorce does not benefit from the marriage or civil union. (Paras: 4.2.2.2.2; 4.2.2.2.2 problem 4)
Forgery:	Where a person makes a false document that harms another. (Paras: 2.6.8; 2.14.5.1.1; 2.14.5.1.2)
Foster-parent:	A parent who acts as a parent for somebody else's child. (Paras: 4.1.1; 4.3.3.2; 4.4.1; 4.4.1.1; 4.4.1.2; 4.4.1.3; 4.4.1.4; 4.4.1.4 problem 1; 4.4.2.2; 4.4.2.3; 5.3.5.2.5)
Fraud:	Where a person makes a false statement, which causes harm to another. (Paras: 2.3.6.9; 2.3.10.1.1; 2.6.8; 2.13.3.3 problem 5; 3.1.3; 2.14.5.1.1; 2.14.5.1.2; 3.1.3; 3.2.9; 3.2.9.3; 3.2.9.4; 3.2.9.4.4; 3.2.10.1; 3.4.3; 6.9.2.2.5)
Fraudulent schemes and offers:	People may not knowingly become involved in fraudulent or unlawful financial dealings. (Para: 3.2.9.3)
Freedom of association:	The right of people, protected by the **Bill of Rights** in the **Constitution**, to meet and gather together freely without interference by the **State**. (Paras: 1.2.2.1; 2.1.7; 6.4.2)
Freedom of speech:	The right of people, protected by the **Bill of Rights** in the **Constitution**, to say what they like, without interference by the **State**. This right must, however, be exercised subject to the laws of **defamation** and **privacy**. (Paras: 2.1.7; 2.2.3.1; 2.2.3.6; 2.5.1.9.2; 2.5.1.10 problem 2)
Funerals:	Any wishes expressed by the deceased and the financial means available must be considered when making decisions. (Paras: 4.6.3; 4.6.3.1; 4.6.3.1 problem 4)
Funeral societies:	Families should make sure that they understand exactly what they are paying for before they enter into an agreement or become a member and pay a monthly fee. (Paras: 4.6.3.2; 4.6.3.2 problem 5)

Further education, right to:	The state has the duty to make it possible for learners who wish to access further education over time to do so. (Paras: 5.2.2.4; 5.2.2.4 case study)
Gay men, rights of:	The Bill of Rights also says that the state may not discriminate on the ground of sexual orientation. (Para: 2.8.6.2 problem 2)
Gay relationships:	The family may be broadly defined as people who live together as a unit and care for and support one another without having regard to their gender. (Para: 4.1.1.2)
General Council of the Bar:	The body which co-ordinates the activities for the different **Bar councils**. (Para: 1.4.1.3.2)
Government Gazette:	A newspaper published by the government in which all government notices, legal notices and new **statutes** are published. (Para: 1.2.2.3)
Grant-in-aid:	An additional grant to a person who already receives another social grant to pay the person who takes full-time care of such person who cannot care for himself or herself. (Para: 5.3.5.2.7)
'Grey' goods:	Foreign goods that are imported by a supplier in South Africa which is not the official importer and supplier appointed by the foreign company. (Paras: 3.2.7; 3.2.7.4; 3.2.7.6 problem 10)
Grievous bodily harm:	Where a person **assaults** another with the intention of causing a serious injury. (Paras: 2.2.2; 2.13.3.3 problem 5; 2.14.5.1.2; 4.2.4)
Group Areas Act:	Act 36 of 1966 which has been repealed. (Para: 5.6.1)
Guarantee:	This is a statement by a seller or manufacturer that sets out the conditions under which a thing is sold. Usually it says that the thing will only be repaired or replaced if something goes wrong within a fixed period of time. (Paras: 1.4.1.1 problem 1; 1.5.2.2 problem 3; 3.2.7.4; 3.2.11.3; 3.2.11.4; 3.4.2.2; 3.4.2.3; 3.4.2.4; 3.4.2.6; 3.4.2.8; 3.4.2.9; 3.5.1; 3.5.2; 3.5.6)
Guarantee against hidden faults:	The seller is responsible to the buyer for any hidden faults unless the **contract** has a condition limiting liability for them. (Para: 3.4.2.3)
Guardian:	A person who is legally responsible for the welfare and upbringing of a **minor** child. (Paras: 2.3.6.3.3; 2.3.6.3.4; 2.3.6.3.7; 2.14.6.1; 2.14.8; 3.1.2 problem 2; 3.2.2; 3.4.3; 4.1.3; 4.1.4.3; 4.1.4.4; 4.2.2.1; 4.3.1; 4.3.1.2; 4.3.1.3; 4.3.1.4; 4.3.1.4 problem 4; 4.3.1.5; 4.3.2.3.1; 4.3.2.4; 4.3.3.1; 4.3.3.2; 4.3.4; 4.4.1; 4.4.1.1; 4.4.1.2; 4.4.2.1; 4.4.2.3; 4.4.2.6; 4.5.3.1 problem 9; 4.6.4.5; 5.4.6.3; 5.4.9.1)
Guns:	Ownership without a licence is forbidden by law and strict conditions must be met before a licence is granted. (Paras: 1.3.2 problem 4; 2.1.7; 2.1.7 problem 6)
Harassment:	See also **Sexual harassment**. (Paras: 2.2.3.5; 2.5.1.10; 4.2.4)
Headman's court:	A court in which a Headman sits to decide cases affecting African people, in communities that live according to **customary law**. (Paras: 1.3.1; 1.3.1.6; 1.4.1.1; 1.4.1.2.1)
Health care, access to:	The Constitution protects a number of health rights including the right of access to health care services. (Paras: 5.4.1; 5.4.2; 5.4.2.1; 5.4.2.1 problem 1; 5.4.13; 5.4.13 problem 7)

Health professionals, complaints against:	Complaints can be made to professional health councils. (Paras: 5.4.12; 5.4.12.1)
Health Professionals Council of South Africa (HPCSA):	This council regulates medical practitioners, doctors, psychologists and related health care professionals. (Para: 5.4.12)
Health rights:	The various health rights are protected by the Constitution. (Paras: 5.4.1; 5.4.2)
High courts:	The higher or superior courts which usually hear more serious criminal or civil cases. Precedents set by the **Constitutional Court** and the **Supreme Court of Appeal** must be followed by the **high courts.** (Paras: 1.2.2.2 problem 5; 1.3.1; 1.3.1.1; 1.3.1.3; 1.3.1.7.1; 1.3.1.7.2; 1.4.1.2.1; 1.4.1.2.2; 1.4.1.6; 2.11.3.2.2; 2.13.2.2; 4.1.4.1; 4.2.2.1; 4.3.1.1; 4.3.1.2; 4.3.1.4; 4.4.2.6; 4.5.2.1; 4.5.2.2; 4.5.2.5.1; 4.6.5.1; 5.4.2.1 problem 1; 5.4.2.1 problem 2 case study; 5.6.5.1.6)
High treason:	See **Treason**.
Hindu marriage:	The common law does not recognise Hindu marriages if the religious leader who conducted the ceremony was not a marriage officer and no laws have been passed regarding these marriages. (Paras: 4.1.1.2; 4.1.2; 4.1.4.3; 4.1.6.2; 4.1.6.2 problem 5; 4.2.4; 4.5.3.2)
Hire-purchase agreement:	See **Credit agreement**.
HIV/AIDS, confidentiality of status:	The general rule applies that a health care professional may not disclose to any other person information about a patient's health status without the patient's consent. (Para: 5.4.5 case study)
HIV/AIDS, ethical guidelines on:	The *Ethical Guidelines on HIV/AIDS* (1995). (Para: 5.4.5.1)
HIV/AIDS, mother-to-child transmission of :	The Constitutional Court ordered the government to allow Nevirapine to be given in all hospitals to reduce mother-to-child transmission of HIV/AIDS. (Para: 5.4.2.1 problem 2 case study)
HIV/AIDS, testing:	The HIV/AIDS test would only be allowed if the employer applies to the Labour Court for permission and the Labour Court will give permission if it thinks that the test is necessary and reasonable in order to prevent a threat or danger to patients. (Para: 6.1.1.3; 6.1.1.3 problem 3)
HIV/AIDS, unfair discrimination:	Whether discrimination occurs or not will depend on the circumstances of each case. (Para: 6.1.1.2 case study 1)
Home loan:	Money borrowed from a financial institution to buy a home. (Paras: 5.6.4.4; 5.6.4.5; 5.6.4.5 problem 5; 5.6.4.6; 5.6.4.7; 5.6.4.8)
Home Loan and Mortgage Disclosure Act:	Act 63 of 2000. (Para: 5.6.4.5)
Homes, buying:	Even people who are not very wealthy may be able to buy a home by getting a mortgage bond from a bank or with help from the state's national housing scheme. (Paras: 5.6.4.10.8; 5.6.4.10.8.1; 5.6.4.10.8.2; 5.6.4.10.8.2 problem 11; 5.6.4.10.9; 5.6.4.10.9 problem 12; 5.6.5.2; 5.6.5.2.1)

Homes, dishonest ways of buying and selling:	The shortage and cost of housing means that many dishonest ways of buying and selling homes are used. (Paras: 5.6.4.10; 5.6.4.10.1; 5.6.4.10.1 problem 7; 5.6.4.10.2; 5.6.4.10.3; 5.6.4.10.4; 5.6.4.10.4 problem 8; 5.6.4.10.5; 5.6.4.10.6; 5.6.4.10.7)
Homes, renting:	See also **Housing**; **Landlord**; **Lease**; **Tenant**. (Paras: 5.6.5.2; 5.6.5.2.2; 5.6.5.2.2 problem 18; 5.6.5.2.3)
Homicide:	The unlawful killing of another person. See also **Culpable homicide**. (Para: 2.2.1)
Homosexuality:	The practice of having sexual relations with a person of one's own sex. See also **Gay** and **Lesbian relationships**.
House arrest:	A form of **correctional supervision**. (Para: 2.13.3.1)
Housebreaking:	Breaking into and entering the **immovable property** of another with the intention of committing a **crime** on such property (see Part 2). (Paras: 2.1.3; 2.2.2; 2.6.5; 2.6.7 problem 1; 2.11.3.2.1; 2.11.3.3 problem 5; 2.13.3.2; 2.13.43.3.12.2)
Housing Act:	Act 107 of 1997. The law that governs the provision of housing by the government. (Para: 5.6.2.1)
Housing, emergency:	Urgent housing problems due to such things as disasters, evictions, threatened evictions, demolition, displacements or immediate threats to life, health or safety. (Para: 5.6.4.2.1)
Housing rights:	The Constitution says that everyone has a right of access to adequate housing, and not to be evicted from their homes or have their homes demolished unless it is ordered by a court. (Paras: 5.6.1; 5.6.2; 5.6.2.1; 5.6.2.1 case study)
Housing subsidy:	The South African government introduced the housing subsidy scheme to address the problem of lack of access to adequate housing and some employers also provide housing subsidies as part of an employee's remuneration. (Paras: 5.6.4.1; 5.6.4.2; 5.6.4.2 problem 3; 5.6.4.2.1; 5.6.4.6.3)
Human rights:	**Human rights** are the rights that all human beings have by virtue of being born human. In democratic countries **human rights** are often enshrined in the country's **Bill of Rights**. (Paras: 1.2.2.1 problem 2; 1.4.1.4.4; 2.1.2; 2.2.1; 2.2.3.1; 2.5.1.9; 2.5.1.10 problem 2; 2.8.6.2 problem 2; 2.9.2.2; 2.11.1.1; 2.11.3.1; 2.13.1.1; 2.13.2.1; 2.13.2.3; 2.13.3.2 problem 4; 2.13.4; 5.1.1; 5.1.2 problem 1; 5.1.5; 5.4.1; 5.7.2; 5.9.4.2; 5.9.4.2 problem 3; 6.6.1)
Husband and wife:	See also **Marriage**. (Paras: 4.1.1; 4.1.2; 4.1.5; 4.2; 4.2.1; 4.2.2.1; 4.2.2.2; 4.2.3; 4.2.3 problem 5; 4.2.4; 4.5.1 problem 1; 4.5.2.1; 4.5.2.2; 4.5.2.2 problem 5; 4.5.2.3; 4.5.2.5.2)
Identity document:	The document that must be applied for by all citizens and residents of South Africa over the age of 16 years. (Paras: 2.11.1.1; 2.11.3.3 problem 6; 3.3.4; 3.3.10 problem 12; 4.1.4.3; 5.3.5.1; 5.3.5.2.5; 5.3.5.2.6; 5.6.4.7)
Identity parade:	A line up of people including **suspects** at which **witnesses** try to identify the person or persons they thought they saw commit the **crime**. (Para: 2.11.3.3 problem 6)

Immovable property:	Property which cannot be moved like land, houses, flats and other buildings. (Paras: 1.4.1.2.3; 2.3.6.3.3; 3.3.2; 4.2.2.1; 5.6.4.10.9)
Implied warranty:	A **guarantee** that the law assumes has been given by the seller even though the seller does not say anything about a **guarantee** at the time of the sale. (Para: 3.4.2.2)
Implied warranty against eviction:	An implied guarantee by the seller that nobody else will have the right to take the goods away from the buyer. (Para: 3.4.2.6)
Impossibility:	It is often a good defence for an **accused** to show that it was impossible for him or her to have avoided committing the **crime**. (Paras: 1.3.1.7.2 case study; 2.10.3.4; 3.4.6.1.1)
Imprisonment:	The **sentence** of a **criminal** to a period of time in **prison**. (Paras: 2.13.3.1; 2.14.7; 3.3.1)
Incapacitation:	Where a convicted **criminal** is separated from the community either by being locked up in **prison** or by **execution**. (Para: 2.13.3.3)
Incapacity:	An **employee's** inability to perform his/her job due to poor work performance or ill-health or injury. (Paras: 6.9.2; 6.9.2.3; 6.9.2.3.1; 6.9.2.3.2; 6.9.2.3.3; 6.9.2.3.2 problem 6; 6.9.2.3.2 problem 6; 6.9.2.4.3 problem 8; 6.10.1; 6.11.1)
Incest:	Sexual intercourse between **parents** and **children**, brothers and sisters, or other close relatives. (Paras: 2.8; 2.8.1; 2.8.6.1; 2.8.6.2 problem 1; 4.1.4.1; 4.3.4; 4.4.2.5)
Incidental credit agreement:	Where a consumer buy goods or services and the supplier informs the consumer that if payment is not made within 20 business days a late payment fee or interest will be charged, or where the supplier indicates the amount by which the price of goods increases if payment is not made within 20 business days. (Para: 3.3.7.2)
Incitement:	Where one person encourages another to commit a **crime**. (Paras: 2.1.7; 2.1.7 problem 6; 2.3.8)
Income tax:	The amount of a person's salary or wages which has to be paid to the **State** each year. (Paras: 2.1.1 problem 1; 2.1.6; 4.6.5.2)
Indecent assault:	See **Sexual assault**.
'Independent Bar':	A body consisting of advocates who have not joined the different bar councils. (Para: 1.4.1.3.2)
Independent contractor:	An independent contractor is a person who provides goods or services to another entity under agreed terms, does not work regularly for an employer but works as and when required and is usually paid on a freelance basis. (Paras: 6.2.1.1; 6.2.1.2; 6.2.1.3; 6.2.1.4; 6.2.1.4 case study; 6.2.1.4 problem 2)
Indicators:	Signs or measures used for understanding and evaluating progress.
Indirect discrimination:	Neutral criteria that have a discriminatory effect. (Paras: 5.9.1; 6.7.2; 6.7.2.2; 6.7.2.2 problem 2)
Indivisibility and interdependence of human rights:	Different human rights cannot be separated because they depend on each other. (Paras: 5.1.1; 5.1.2 problem 1)

Informed consent:	Giving permission for a medical procedure or test after receiving full information, including: understanding the benefits, possible harm, and the choices you have. (Paras: 5.4.6; 5.4.6.1; 5.4.6.1 problem 3; 5.4.6.2; 5.4 8)
Initiation fee:	A once-off fee that the credit provider can charge the consumer when a credit agreement is entered into. (Para: 3.3.5.3)
Inquisitorial system:	A court procedure where the **judge** or **magistrate** conducts the case by asking most of the questions. It is different from the "adversarial system" where the **judge** or **magistrate** plays a neutral role and the contesting parties must prove their cases. (Paras: 1.2.1; 1.4.2; 1.4.2 problem 7; 2.14.4)
Insanity:	See **Mentally disabled / incompetent people.**
Inspection fees:	The fees paid to a building inspector who inspects a property about to be sold. (Para: 5.6.4.3)
Instalment:	The amount of money paid in small amounts each week or month by the **debtor** in order to pay off the purchase price. (Paras: 1.5.1.3; 3.2.13.3; 3.3.1; 3.3.2; 3.3.2.9 problem 4; 3.3.2.12; 3.3.2.14 problem 9; 3.3.2.15 case study; 3.3.3.1; 3.3.6.1; 3.3.6.2; 3.3.7.10 problem 11; 3.3.9; 3.3.10 problem 12; 3.3.11; 3.3.12.2 problem 13; 3.3.12.3 problem 14; 3.4.3 problem 5; 5.6.4.3; 5.6.4.6.3)
Instalment agreement:	An agreement that usually requires the buyer to pay off the **balance of the purchase price** and **finance charges** in **instalments** over a period of time. Usually the seller remains owner of the goods until the last **instalment** has been paid. (Paras: 3.3.2.9; 3.3.2.13; 3.3.2.13 problem 8; 3.3.2.14; 3.3.7; 3.3.7.3; 3.3.12.3 problem 14; 3.4.2.6)
Instant short messaging:	Can be used as a form of **cyber bullying**. (Paras: 2.5.1.2; 2.5.1.8 problem 1)
Insubordination:	Defying an **employer's** lawful instruction/ a lack of respect shown to an **employer**. (Paras: 6.5.3 problem 1; 6.9.2.2.4 problem 4; 6.9.2.2.5; 6.11.1 problem 1)
Insult:	A **civil wrong** in which a person's feelings are intentionally harmed. (Paras: 1.1.2 problem 3; 1.4.1.4.2; 1.4.2.1 problem 8; 2.2.3; 2.2.3.1; 2.2.3.2; 2.2.3.4; 2.5.1.5; 2.10.4.3 problem 2; 4.5.2.1.1; 4.5.3.1; 6.11.1 problem 1)
Insurance:	A **contract** in which the **insurer** agrees to compensate the **insured** for loss or damage or injury in exchange for payment of a **premium** in advance. (Paras: 1.3.2.1; 1.4.1.1 problem 1; 1.4.1.4.5 problem 6; 1.4.1.6; 2.1.7 problem 6; 3.3.2.12; 3.3.5.6; 3.5.1; 3.5.3; 3.5.4; 3.5.6 problem 2; 3.5.9; 4.2.2.1; 4.5.1; 4.6.3; 4.6.3.2; 5.3.2; 5.4.5; 5.4.7; 5.6.4.3; 5.6.4.11; 5.6.4.11.2; 5.6.5.2.1; 5.6.5.2.2 problem 18; 6.3.5; 6.3.6)
Insurance, balance of third party:	This type of insurance covers damage to the property of third parties but must be taken out and paid for by the car owner. (Paras: 3.5.9; 3.5.9.2; 3.5.9.4)

Insurance policy:	The **contract** of **insurance** between the **insured** and the **insurance** company. (Paras: 3.3.2; 3.3.5.6; 3.3.7.8; 3.3.7.10 problem 11; 3.5.9; 4.2.2.1; 4.6.3.2; 5.4.5; 5.6.4.11)
Insurance policy, excesses payable:	An excess is the amount that must be paid by the insured if he or she wishes to claim under the policy. (Paras: 3.5.9.6; 3.5.9.6 problem 8)
Insurance, third party:	**Insurance** against people other than the driver of the **insured** vehicle, being injured in a motor vehicle collision. (Paras: 3.5.9; 3.5.9.1)
Insured:	The person who takes out an **insurance policy**. (Paras: 3.5.9; 3.5.9.7)
Integrated Nutrition Programme:	(Para: 5.5.4.2)
Interactive gaming:	Can be used as a form of **cyber bullying**. (Para: 2.5.1.8)
Interdict:	A court order preventing a person from doing something or requiring a person does something. (Paras: 3.4.6.1.2; 4.3.3.2)
Interest:	Debtors must usually pay creditors an amount of money in addition to the amount that they lend. (Paras: 3.3.1; 3.3.2.1; 3.3.5.2; 5.6.4.6.1; 5.6.4.11)
Interest, fixed rate of:	Usually about 60% of the effective rate of interest. (Para: 3.3.5.2)
Interim Protection of Informal Land Rights Act:	Act 31 of 1996. (Paras: 5.8.4.3.1; 5.8.4.3.1.1)
Internet polling:	Can be used as a form of **cyber bullying**. (Paras: 2.5.1.7; 2.5.1.8 problem 1)
Interpretation of statutes:	Courts must look at the intention of **Parliament** or the law-making body in order to apply the **statute** correctly. (Para: 1.2.2.3 problem 7)
Intestate succession:	Dying without a will, or if the will that was made was not made properly (Paras: 4.2.2.1; 4.4.2.5; 4.6.4.2; 4.6.4.2 problem 6)
Intestate Succession Act:	Act 81 of 1987. (Para: 4.1.6.2)
Intoxication:	The state of being drunk. (Para: 2.10.4.3; 2.10.4.3 problem 2)
Irretrievable breakdown of marriage or civil union:	Means that the couple can no longer live together as **husband and wife** or **civil union partners** and there is no chance of reconciliation. (Paras: 4.5.2.1; 4.5.2.1.1; 4.5.2.4)
Jail:	See **Prison**.
Jewish marriage:	A religious ceremony carried out by a rabbi who is a marriage officer authorised to carry out marriages according to the Jewish faith. (Para: 4.1.4.3)
Job advertisement:	An advertisement placed in the media when a position is vacant. (Paras: 6.1.1.1; 6.1.1.1.1)
Job applicant:	A person applying for a job with the prospect of being employed. See also **Employee**. (Paras: 6.1.1.3; 6.1.1.3 case study; 6.1.1.3 problem 3)
Job interview:	A meeting between the prospective employer(s) and applicant. (Paras: 6.1.1.2; 6.1.1.2 case study; 6.1.1.2 problem 2)

Judge:	A court officer who hears and decides cases in the **High Court**, **Supreme Court of Appeal** and **Constitutional Court**. **Judges** are the most important of all court officers who hear cases. (Paras: 1.1.2 problem 4; 1.2.1; 1.2.2.2 problem 5; 1.3.1.1; 1.3.1.2; 1.3.1.3; 1.3.1.4; 1.3.1.7.1; 1.3.1.7.2; 1.3.1.7.3; 1.3.2.3; 1.4.1; 1.4.1.3.2 problem 3; 1.4.2; 1.4.2.2; 1.5; 2.2.1.2 problem 2; 2.13.2.3 problem 3; 2.13.3; 2.13.3.2 problem 4)
Judgment:	The decision of a **judge** or **magistrate** or other judicial officer in a case. (Paras: 1.2.2.2; 1.3.1.7.1; 1.4.2.2; 1.5.1.3; 1.5.2.2; 2.13.2.2)
Judicial separation order:	Order for temporary suspension of some of the marital obligations of spouses, particularly that of living together. (Para: 4.5.1.1)
Judicial Service Commission	An independent body that advises the **President** on the appointment of judges. (Para: 1.3.1.3)
Jury:	The group of ordinary people (usually 6-12) which in England and the United States, decides in a **trial** whether an **accused** is guilty or a **plaintiff** has proved his or her case. (Para: 1.4.2)
Justice Centre:	A centre established by **Legal Aid South Africa** to provide legal services to poor people. Justice Centres act as law firms and are staffed by public defenders, law clinic public defenders, paralegals and administrative staff. (Paras: 1.4.1.2.2; 1.4.1.4.2 problem 4; 2.11.2.5; 2.12.1.2; 4.5.2.2; 5.1.5)
Justifiable:	Something that can be justified or supported with good reasons. (Paras: 1.2.2.1 problems 3 & 4; 1.3.2.2 problem 6; 2.2.1; 2.2.1.1; 2.3.9.2; 3.2.2; 5.1.6; 6.1.1.3; 6.6.5)
Justifiable homicide:	Where the killing of another human being is justified by the law. (Para: 2.2.1)
Juvenile delinquent:	A person under the age of 18 years who commits an **offence** or **crime**. (Paras: 1.2.3 problem 8; 2.14.7.5 problem 5)
Kidnapping:	The unlawful and intentional taking away of a person's freedom of movement. In the case of **children** the taking away of **children** from their **parents**' or **guardian's** control or **custody**. (Paras: 2.2.4; 2.2.4 problem 6; 2.10.3.3; 2.11.3.2.1; 2.13.4)
Labour Appeal Court:	Adjudicates repeals relating to labour disputes. (Para: 6.2.1.4)
Labour Court:	Adjudicates matters relating to labour disputes. (Paras: 1.3.2.3 problem 7; 6.1.1.2 case study; 6.1.1.3; 6.9.2.4.3; 6.10.1; 6.11.1)
Labour practices, unfair:	Where an **employer** treats an **employee** unfairly with regard to promotion, demotion or training. (Paras: 6.8; 6.8.1)
Labour Relations Act:	Act 66 of 1995. (Paras: 1.3.2.3 problem 7; 6.2.1.1; 6.2.1.2; 6.4.3; 6.4.5; 6.8.1; 6.9.1; 6.9.2.1; 6.9.2.4.1; 6.11.1)
Labour tenant:	People allowed to live on and develop land in return for their labour. (Paras: 5.6.3.1; 5.8.4.2.1; 5.8.4.2.2.1 problem 3; 5.8.4.3.1; 5.8.4.3.3; 5.8.4.3.6)
Land Claims Court:	The Land Claims Court specialises in dealing with disputes that arise out of laws that underpin South Africa's land reform initiative and has the same status as any High Court. (Para: 5.8.4.3.2; 5.8.4.3.6)

Landlord:	A person who rents property to a **tenant**. *See also* **Lease.** (Paras: 1.5.1.1; 5.6.5.1; 5.6.5.1.3; 5.6.5.1.11; 5.6.5.1.2; 5.6.5.1.2 problem 15; 5.6.5.1.3; 5.6.5.1.4; 5.6.5.1.4 problem 16; 5.6.5.1.5; 5.6.5.1.6; 5.6.5.2.2; 5.6.5.2.2 problem 18; 5.6.5.2.3)
Land redistribution:	Means achieving a fairer distribution of land by making it possible for previously disadvantaged groups to buy land with help from acquisition grants. (Paras: 5.8.3; 5.8.4.2)
Land Redistribution for Agricultural Development sub-programme:	Makes land available for people to use for agricultural purposes. (Paras: 5.8.4.2.2; 5.8.4.2.2.1)
Land reform:	It involves the changing of laws, regulations or customs regarding land ownership. (Paras: 5.8.2; 5.8.2 problem 2; 5.8.3)
Land Reform (Labour Tenants) Act:	Act 3 of 1996. (Paras: 5.6.3.1; 5.8.4.2.1; 5.8.4.3.1; 5.8.4.3.6)
Land rights:	(Paras: 5.8.1; 5.8.2)
Land rights, informal:	See also **Interim Protection of Informal Land Rights Act**. (Paras: 5.8.4.3.1; 5.8.4.3.1.1)
Land settlement programmes:	Focus on providing people with land for settlement purposes. (Paras: 5.8.4.2; 5.8.4.2.1)
Land tenure reform:	Allows certain land occupiers to remain on the land on which they are living. (Paras: 5.8.3; 5.8.4.3; 5.8.4.3.1)
Latent defects, implied guarantee against:	Where the seller is assumed to have guarantee that there are no hidden faults in the **product**. *See also* **Guarantee against hidden faults**. (Para: 3.4.2.3)
Law:	A set of rules used to control the behaviour of people in society. (Para: 1.1.2)
Law clinic:	Most universities in South Africa now have law clinics that will usually help people who fall within the income limits set by Legal Aid South Africa. (Paras: 1.4.1.1; 1.4.1.2.1; 1.4.1.2.2; 1.4.1.4; 1.4.1.4.2 problem 4; 1.4.1.4.3; 1.4.1.4.5; 1.4.1.6; 2.11.2.5; 2.12.1.2; 4.6.4.3; 5.1.5; 5.3.4; 5.3.6; 5.9.4.1)
Law Society of South Africa:	Co-ordinating body for the four law societies which are responsible for controlling the conduct of attorneys. (Para: 1.4.1.3.1)
Lawyer:	A person who practises law. Usually an **attorney** or an **advocate**. Also called a **legal practitioner**. (Paras: 1.1.1 problem 2; 1.2.1; 1.2.2.1 problem 2; 1.3.1.3; 1.3.1.4.2 problem 1; 1.3.1.5; 1.3.1.7.2; 1.3.1.7.3; 1.3.2; 1.3.2.1; 1.4.1; 1.4.1.1; 1.4.1.2; 1.4.1.4.5; 1.4.1.6; 1.4.2; 1.4.2.1; 2.11.2.5; 2.12.1.2; 2.13.1.1; 2.13.2.3 problem 3; 3.5.9.1; 4.5.2.2; 4.5.2.4 problem 7; 4.6.4.3; 4.6.4.5; 4.6.5.2)
Lay-bys:	An agreement where the seller agrees to keep goods aside for a consumer, in exchange for a deposit and the **balance** in periodic **instalments**, until he or she has paid the full price. (Para: 3.2.13.3)

Lease:	A **contract** between a **landlord** and a **tenant** in which the **tenant** hires the property from the **landlord**. (Paras: 2.3.6.9; 3.1.2; 3.3.2; 3.3.2.9; 3.3.2.13; 3.4.5.1; 5.6.5.1; 5.6.5.1.1; 5.6.5.1.2; 5.6.5.1.2 problem 15; 5.6.5.1.3; 5.6.5.1.4, 5.6.5.1.4 problem 16; 5.6.5.1.5; 5.6.5.1.6; 5.8.4.3.1)
Lease of movable goods:	An agreement in terms of which temporary possession of movable property (eg a car) is given to the consumer. (Para: 3.3.7.4)
Legal aid:	Free legal assistance for poor people given by **Legal Aid South Africa** and legal aid clinics. (Paras: 1.3.2.1; 1.4.1.1; 1.4.1.2.2; 1.4.1.4.1; 1.4.1.4.2; 1.4.1.4.3; 1.4.1.4.5; 1.4.1.6; 2.11.2.5; 2.11.3.3 problem 6; 2.12.1.2; 2.13.1.1; 4.5.2.2; 4.6.3.1; 5.1.5; 5.3.4; 5.3.6; 5.8.4.3.1; 5.8.4.3.1.1)
Legal Aid South Africa:	An independent body that is financed by the **State** and responsible for providing **legal aid** to poor people. (Paras: 1.4.1.1; 1.4.1.4; 1.4.1.4.2; 1.4.1.4.3; 1.4.1.4.5; 2.14.4.1; 4.6.4.3; 5.1.5; 5.8.4.3.1.1)
Legal costs:	Lawyers' fees, court fees and any other costs involved when bringing or defending a legal action or getting legal advice. (Paras: 1.5.1.3; 4.5.2.2)
Legal duty to act:	Generally people are not liable for omissions where there is no legal duty on them to act but if there is a legal duty on them to act they may be criminally and civilly liable. (Paras: 2.1.6; 2.1.6 problem 5)
Legal practitioner:	A **lawyer**. (Para: 1.4.1.2.2)
Legal representation:	The right of an **accused** person to be represented by a lawyer. (Paras: 1.3.1.6; 1.4.1.4.1; 2.13.2.2; 2.14.4.1; 5.8.4.3.1)
Legal Resources Centres:	**Public interest law firms** that usually deal with problems that affect large numbers of people in the community. (Paras: 1.4.1.2.1; 1.4.1.2.2; 1.4.1.4; 1.4.1.4.2 problem 4; 1.4.1.4.4; 1.4.1.4.5; 2.11.2.5; 2.12.1.2; 5.1.5; 5.3.4; 5.3.6; 5.9.4.1)
Legislation:	Law passed by **Parliament**, **provincial legislatures** or **municipal councils**. (Para 1.2.1)
Lesbian relationships:	The family may be broadly defined as people who live together as a unit and care for and support one another irrespective of their gender. (Para: 4.1.1.2)
Lesbians, rights of:	The Bill of Rights provides for all rights pertaining to sexual preferences. (Para: 2.8.6.2 problem 2)
Lessee:	See **Tenant.** *See also* **Lease.**
Lessor:	See **Landlord**. *See also* **Lease.**
Letter of demand:	A letter demanding payment of a claim or some other action in a civil case. (Paras: 1.5.1.2; 1.5.1.3; 1.5.2.2; 1.5.2.2 problem 3)
Letters of executorship:	Appointment of an **executor** by the **Master of the High Court**. (Para: 4.6.5.1)
Liabilities:	Debts of the deceased person that have to be paid off. (Para: 4.6.5.1)

Life policy:	An Insurance policy taken out on the life of the **insured** which will be paid out on the **insured's death**. (Para: 3.5.9)
Lift club:	An agreement in which people give each other or each other's **children** lifts in each other's cars. (Para: 3.5.9.5)
Limitation of rights:	All **human rights** are indivisible and may only be limited under certain circumstances. (Paras: 1.2.2.1 problem 3; 2.12.1; 5.1.6)
Litigation:	Starting a court case, and if necessary, going to court to defend your rights.
LLB degree:	A four year undergraduate law degree. (Paras: 1.4.1.2; 1.4.1.2.1; 1.4.1.2.2)
Lobbying:	Talking to, persuading and influencing a person or body to do, make or change something, for example, a decision, a law.
Local authority:	The local government structure responsible for governing a particular area e.g. city or town. (Paras: 2.1.1; 5.5.4.3; 5.6.3.2.1; 5.6.5.2.3; 5.6.4.10.4; 5.6.5.1.6; 5.6.5.2.3; 5.7.2 case study; 5.7.4; 5.7.4 problem 3; 5.9.1; 5.9.4)
Low income housing agreement:	A low income housing agreement is provided. (Para: 3.3.7.5)
Magistrate:	The court officer who hears and decides cases in the **magistrates' court**. (Paras: 1.2.1; 1.2.2.1 problem 3; 1.3.1; 1.3.1.3; 1.3.1.4.2; 1.3.1.4.2 problem 1; 1.3.1.7.2 case study; 1.4.1.3.2 problem 3; 1.4.2; 1.4.2.2; 1.5; 2.11.3.2.2; 2.11.3.3; 2.12.1.1; 2.13.2.1; 2.13.2.3 problem 3; 2.13.3; 2.14.4)
Magistrates Commission:	Deals with matters such as the appointment or removal from office of magistrates. (Paras: 1.3.1.4.2; 1.3.1.4.2 problem 1)
Magistrates' courts:	The lower or inferior courts which deal with less serious criminal and civil cases. Precedents set by the **Constitutional Court**, the **Supreme Court of Appeal** and **High Courts** must be followed by the **magistrates' courts**. (Paras: 1.2.2.2 problem 5; 1.3.1; 1.3.1.4; 1.3.1.7.1; 1.3.1.7.2; 1.4.1.2.2; 2.13.2.1; 4.2.4; 4.5.2.5.2; 4.5.3.2)
Magistrates' Courts Act:	Act 32 of 1944. (Para: 3.3.8)
Mail order sales:	Goods or services sold by **advertising** in the post. (Para: 3.2.8.5 problem 15)
Maintenance:	Money paid to a **parent** or **children** for their support, usually by a **divorced** or separated spouse, or the father of an illegitimate child (a child whose **parents** are not married). (Paras: 4.1.6.2; 4.2.1; 4.2.1.1; 4.2.1.1 problem 1; 4.3.1.4; 4.4.1.2; 4.4.1.3; 4.5; 4.5.1; 4.5.1.1; 4.5.2.2; 4.5.2.3; 4.5.2.4; 4.5.2.5; 4.5.2.5.2; 4.5.3; 4.5.3.1; 4.5.3.2; 4.5.3.2 problem 10; 4.6.4.2; 5.3.5.2.8; 5.3.6.2 problem 1)
Maintenance Act:	Act 99 of 1998. (Paras: 4.1.6.2; 4.5.2.5.2; 4.5.3.2)
Maintenance court:	A court situated at the magistrate's court that deals with applications for maintenance, and increases and decreases in the amount of maintenance. (Paras: 4.3.1.4; 4.5.2.2; 4.5.2.5.2; 4.5.3.2)
Maintenance of divorced spouse:	The court may order either the husband or wife or any of the civil union partners to pay maintenance to the other. (Para: 4.5.2.5.2)

Maintenance of Surviving Spouses Act:	Act 27 of 1990. (Para: 4.1.6.1)
Maintenance order:	On divorce once care of children is awarded to one parent, the other parent may be ordered to pay money on a weekly or monthly basis as maintenance for the children. (Paras: 4.3.1.4; 4.5.3.2)
Maintenance service:	A service, the interruption of which results in the physical destruction of the working area, plant or machinery. (Para: 6.4.5.3)
Malicious prosecution:	The **civil wrong** of maliciously or spitefully laying a false criminal charge against a person with the **police**. (Para: 1.5.2)
Marital power:	The **husband** acts as his wife's **guardian** and she is treated as a minor. (Paras: 4.2.2.1; 4.2.2.2)
Marriage:	An agreement or **contract** between a man and a woman to live together as **husband and wife**. (Paras: 1.4.1.1; 1.4.1.2.4; 1.4.1.4.2 problem 5; 1.5.1.1; 2.2.2 problem 4; 2.8.1; 2.8.4; 2.8.6.2 problem 2; 3.4.4; 4.1.2; 4.1.3; 4.1.4; 4.1.4.1; 4.1.4.2; 4.1.4.2 problem 4; 4.1.4.3; 4.2.2.1; 4.2.2.2; 4.3.1.1; 4.3.1.2; 4.5.1 problem 1; 4.5.2.1; 4.5.2.5.1)
Marriage Act:	Act 25 of 1961. The **statute law** that deals with **marriage**. (Paras: 4.1.3; 4.1.4.1; 4.1.4.4; 4.1.5)
Marriage guidance counsellor:	Marriage counsellors may act as mediators to help the parties work out a solution to their problems before seeking a divorce. (Paras: 4.5.1; 4.5.2.1.1; 4.5.2.2 problem 6)
Marriage officer:	The Minister of Home Affairs may appoint any officer in the public, diplomatic or consular service as a marriage officer and certain ministers of religion may also be appointed as marriage officers. (Paras: 4.1.4.3; 4.1.4.4; 4.1.5; 4.1.6.1)
Marriage regime, change of:	If a husband and wife or civil union partners want to change the type of marriage or union they have, they may apply to the High Court, asking for the court to let them do so. (Paras: 4.2.2.3; 4.5.2.5.1)
Master of the High Court:	The Master serves the public in respect of deceased estates, liquidations, registration of trusts, tutors and curators, as well as administration of the Guardian's Fund for minors and mentally challenged persons. (Paras: 4.6.5.1; 4.6.5.2; 4.6.5.3)
Matrimonial property:	Property brought into the marriage and accrued by married people and civil union partners. (Paras: 4.5.2.5; 4.5.2.5.1)
Matrimonial Property Act:	Act 88 of 1984. (Paras: 4.1.5; 4.2; 4.2.2.1)
Means test:	The highest amount of money a person may earn in order to qualify for **legal aid** from **Legal Aid South Africa**. (Paras: 1.4.1.4.2; 5.3.5; 5.3.5.1; 5.3.5.2.4; 5.3.5.2.5; 5.3.5.2.6)
Mediation:	The situation when a **Mediator** acts as a "go between" to help people who are arguing to settle their problem. (Paras:1.3.2 problem 4; 1.3.2.2; 1.3.2.4; 1.3.2.4 problem 8; 2.14.5.1.2; 2.14.7; 4.5.2.2; 5.6.5.1.6; 5.9.2.1; 5.9.3.1; 5.9.4; 6.10.1; 6.10.3; 6.10.3 case study; 6.10.4 problem 1)
Mediator:	A person who does **mediation**. (Paras: 1.3.2.2; 4.5.2.2; 5.8.4.3.5.1)

Medical aid schemes:	Schemes whereby people or their **employers** pay into a fund to cover the **medical expenses** of themselves and their families. (Paras: 5.4.7; 5.4.11; 5.4.11.1; 5.4.11.2; 5.4.11.2 problem 6; 6.1.1.3)
Medical aid schemes, contracting out of:	A doctor who has decided to charge fees at a rate higher than the medical aid scheme. (Paras: 5.4.11.1; 5.4.11.2)
Medical expenses:	Expenses arising from medical and health care. (Paras: 1.2.3; 3.4.2.9 problem 4; 5.3.6.2 problem 1)
Medical Schemes Act:	Act 131 of 1998. (Para: 5.4.11)
Mental illness, grounds for divorce:	The concept of 'no fault' in divorce includes the ground or mental illness. (Paras: 4.5.2.1; 4.5.2.1.2)
Mentally disabled / incompetent people, consent	The person giving the consent must be legally capable of doing so ie not a minor or insane person. (Paras: 4.4.2.3; 5.4.6.1; 5.4.6.2; 5.4.8)
Mentally disabled / incompetent people, criminal capacity:	An accused may not be criminally liable for committing a crime because he or she could not form the intention to commit the crime as a result of insanity. (Paras: 2.2.3.2; 2.10.4.2; 2.10.4.3 problem 2)
Mentally disabled / incompetent people, declaration of:	Only the High Court may make a declaration of insanity. (Paras: 1.3.1.3; 1.3.1.4.2; 1.5.2)
Mentally disabled / incompetent people, sexual offences against:	Mentally incompetent persons have the same protection as children under the age of 12 years regarding sexual acts to which they cannot legally consent. (Para: 2.3.7)
Mentally disabled / incompetent people, sterilisation of:	The law allows for the sterilisation of a person with severe mental disability provided their parents, spouse, guardian or close relatives and the hospital also agree. (Para: 5.4.9.1)
Mercy killing:	See **Euthanasia**.
Micro lenders:	People who give small loans to **consumers** who need to borrow money. (Para: 3.3.2)
Minors:	People under 18 years of age who cannot enter into **contracts** without their **parents**' or **guardians' consent**. (Paras: 3.4.3; 3.4.3 problem 5; 4.1.3; 4.1.4.4; 4.1.5; 4.3.1; 4.3.1.5; 4.3.2.2; 4.3.2.3.2; 4.3.2.3.3; 4.3.2.3.3 problem 6; 4.3.2.4; 4.3.4 problem 10; 4.6.4.2; 5.4.6.1)
Minors, High Court as 'upper guardian' of:	The High Court as the 'upper guardian' of all minors has the power to appoint someone who is not the parent of the children as their guardian when circumstances so warrant. (Para: 4.3.1.2)
Misconduct:	An act of intentional wrongdoing by the **employee** that breaches a **disciplinary code**. (Paras: 6.5.1; 6.5.1 case study; 6.5.2; 6.9.2.2; 6.9.2.2.2; 6.9.2.2.4; 6.9.2.2.5; 6.9.2.3.1; 6.9.2.3.3.2 problem 6; 6.10.1)
Misconduct, punishment for:	Punishment for misconduct in the workplace depends on the type of misconduct. (Paras: 6.9.2.2.6; 6.9.2.2.6 problem 5)
Misrepresentations, false or misleading:	The CPA protects consumers against false or misleading statements by suppliers. (Paras: 3.2.9.2; 3.2.9.2 problem 18)

Mock trial:	A simulated trial where people roleplay the different parties – clients, **lawyers**, **witnesses**, **judges**, etc.
Monitoring:	A form of **correctional supervision**. (Para: 2.13.3.1)
Mortgage bond:	A claim over **immovable property** that is registered on the **title deeds**, usually to provide security for a loan. If the loan is not paid the person holding the bond may have the property sold to recover the loan. (Paras: 1.4.1.2.3; 4.2.2.1; 5.6.4.3; 5.6.4.6.1; 5.6.4.10.3; 5.6.4.10.5; 5.6.4.10.6 problem 9; 5.6.4.10.7; 5.6.4.10.7 problem 10; 5.6.4.10.8; 5.6.4.11; 5.6.4.11.1; 5.6.4.11.1 problem 13; 5.6.4.11.2; 5.6.5.2.1)
Mortgage bond agreements:	A mortgage bond agreement is an agreement a consumer enters into when he or she wants a loan to buy a house. (Paras: 3.3.2; 3.3.7.6)
Morality:	Behaviour that a particular society regards as right or wrong. (Paras: 1.1.2; 1.1.2 problems 3, 4 & 5; 2.1.1; 2.1.2; 4.6.2 problem 2)
Motive:	The reason why a person does something. (Paras: 2.1.4; 2.13.3.3 problem 5; 2.13.4; 6.7.2.1)
Mugging:	See **Robbery**.
Multiplication schemes:	Where the supplier offers the investor interest rates of 20% above the Reserve Bank's repo (repurchase) rate. (Para: 3.2.9.4.3)
Municipal council:	A governing body, usually in a town or city, in which member's sit who are elected by all adult South Africans of that particular area. The main function of a municipal council is to govern the communities that fall under its authority. (Paras: 1.2.2; 1.2.2.2)
Murder:	The unlawful and intentional killing of another human being. (Paras: 1.1.2 problems 3 & 4; 1.3.1.4.1; 1.3.1.7; 1.3.1.7.3 problem 3; 1.4, 2.1 problem 8; 2.1.1; 2.1.5; 2.1.7; 2.2; 2.2.1; 2.2.1.1; 2.2.1.2; 2.2.1.2 problem 2; 2.2.1.3; 2.2.2; 2.11.2.3; 2.11.3.2.1; 2.13.3.1; 2.13.3.2; 2.13.4; 2.13.4 problem 6; 2.14.2.2 problem 1; 4.2.4)
Muslim marriage:	Muslim marriages are not recognised in South African common law but Parliament is presently considering whether it will extend full recognition to Muslim marriages, as it has to customary marriages. (Paras: 4.1.1.2; 4.1.2; 4.1.4.3; 4.1.6.1; 4.1.6.2; 4.1.6.2 problem 5; 4.2.4; 4.5.3.2)
National Assembly:	The section of **Parliament** in which members sit who are elected by all adult South Africans. The main function of the **National Assembly** is to debate, pass or reject any legislation placed before it. (Paras: 1.2.2; 1.2.2.3)
National Consumer Commission:	A person who feels that he or she has been discriminated against as a consumer may lay a complaint with the National Consumer Commission. (Paras: 3.2.2; 3.2.13.1; 3.2.14; 3.2.14.1)
National Council of Provinces:	Section of **Parliament** in which members sit who are sent by their provincial legislatures. The primary function of the National Council of Provinces is to debate, reject or pass legislation passed by the **National Assembly**. (Paras: 1.2.2; 1.2.2.3)

National Credit Act:	Act 34 of 2005. (Paras: 3.1.4; 3.3.2; 3.4)
National Credit Regulator:	A body responsible for the regulation of the South African credit industry. (Para: 3.3.2.11)
National Education Policy Act:	Act 27 of 1996. (Para: 5.2.2.5)
National Environmental Management Act:	Act 107 of 1998. (Paras: 5.9.2; 5.9.2.1; 5.9.2.2; 5.9.2.2 problem 2)
National Health Act:	Act 61 of 2003. (Paras: 4.6.1; 4.6.2; 5.4.6.1)
National Health Insurance scheme:	The government is phasing in a National Health Insurance scheme which it is hoped will make medical treatment accessible for everyone. (Para: 5.4.1)
National Housing Finance Corporation (NHFC):	A development finance institution established by the South African government to fund and facilitate the development of affordable housing. (Para: 5.6.4.9.1)
National Register of Credit Agreements (NRCA):	The National Register of Credit Agreements (NRCA) has information about the creditworthiness of individuals. (Paras: 3.3.2.11; 3.3.3.2; 3.3.4)
National Road Traffic Act:	Act 93 of 1996. (Para: 2.9.1)
National Urban Reconstruction and Housing Agency (NURCHA):	Provides temporary housing finance to households earning less than R1 500 per month. (Paras: 5.6.4.6.3; 5.6.4.9.2)
National Water Act:	Act 36 of 1998. (Para: 5.7.3; 5.7.3.1)
Necessity:	Where people harm the person or property of an innocent third person in order to save other people's lives or property. (Paras: 2.10.3; 2.10.3.2; 2.11.2.4)
Negligence:	The failure to act as a reasonable person would in a particular situation (Paras: 1.4.1.3.1; 2.2.1.2; 2.2.2; 2.2.3.1; 3.2.5; 3.2.10.1; 3.2.12; 3.5.9.1; 6.2.2.1; 6.3.5)
Negotiation:	When people in a dispute talk to each other in order to arrive at a solution to their problem. (Paras: 1.3.2; 1.3.2.1; 1.3.2.1 problem 5; 1.3.2.2 problem 6; 1.3.2.4; 1.3.2.4 problem 8; 1.4.1; 1.4.1.4.3; 2.3.6.3.7; 3.3.9; 4.5.2.5.2; 5.1.5; 6.4.1; 6.4.4; 6.4.4.1; 6.4.4.1 problem 1; 6.10.2; 6.10.4 problem 1)
No claim bonus:	A discount on **premiums** given to an **insured** who does not claim against his or her **insurance** company. (Para: 3.5.9.7)
Non-contributory:	When you do not have to pay money in to get a benefit. (Para: 5.3.2)
Notarial contract:	A document which must be submitted to the court where spouses want to change their type of marriage or union. (Para: 4.2.2.3)
Notary public:	An **attorney** who specialises in certifying that the proper people have signed certain legal documents. A notary draws up documents like **ante-nuptial contracts**. (Paras: 1.4.1.2; 1.4.1.2.4; 1.4.1.3.2 problem 3)
Notice of intention to defend:	A notice at the back of a **summons** or drawn up by a lawyer in which the **defendant** in a **civil action** states that he or she intends to defend the case. (Paras: 1.5.1.2; 1.5.1.3; 4.5.2.3; 4.5.2.4)

Obedience to orders:	Where the **accused** persons claim they are not liable for their **crimes** because they were ordered to commit the **crimes** by somebody whom they had lawfully to obey. (Para: 2.10.3.4)
Obligations:	Legal duties and responsibilities. (Paras: 2.3.6.10; 2.7.5; 3.1.4; 3.2.10.1; 3.3.3.1; 3.3.6.3; 3.3.7.3; 3.3.10; 3.4; 4.3.1.4; 4.5.1.1; 5.4.6.1; 6.2.1.3; 6.2.2.1; 6.6.7.1)
Occupational detriment:	Situations where **whistle-blowers** have been prejudiced at work because of their Activities. (Para: 6.6.7.1)
Occupational Health and Safety Act:	Act 85 of 1993. (Paras: 6.2.2.2; 6.3.2; 6.3.2 case study)
Occupier:	A person living on land belonging to another person and who was on or has since 4 February 1997 been allowed by the owner to continue living on it. Paras: 5.6.3.1; 5.6.3.1.1; 5.6.3.1.2; 5.8.5 problem 5)
Occupier, unlawful:	A person who lives on land belonging to another without the latter's permission.(Paras: 5.6.3.2; 5.6.3.2.1)
Offence:	A **crime**.
Offer to purchase:	See **Deed of sale**.
Older persons, abuse of:	Any person who is involved with an older person in a professional capacity and who on personal observation concludes that the older person is in need of care and protection must report such conclusion to the director-general of social development. (Paras: 2.4.3; 2.4.3 problem 1)
Older Persons Act:	Act 13 of 2006. (Paras: 2.4.1; 2.4.3)
Ombudsman:	An official that investigates citizens' complaints.(Paras: 3.2.14.2; 3.2.15; 3.3.2.15)
Opt-out:	The option of asking that you must not be contacted by anyone about direct marketing. (Paras: 3.2.3; 3.2.3 problem 2)
Orphan:	A child whose parents have died.
Oscar Pistorius trial:	Oscar was charged with murder and his trial was broadcast on TV in South Africa and throughout the world. (Paras: 2.2.1.2 problem 2; 2.13.3.3 problem 5)
Over-booking and over-selling:	The CPA also protects consumers against over-selling and over-booking. (Paras: 3.2.9.4.6; 3.2.9.4.6 problem 20)
Paralegal office:	An advice office staffed by people who are not qualified lawyers but who are trained to help people with legal problems. (Paras: 1.4.1.4; 1.4.1.4.2 problem 4; 1.4.1.4.5; 5.1.5; 5.3.4; 5.3.6)
Parental care:	Generally ensuring that the best interests of the child is the most important concern in everything affecting the child, whether the parents live together or are divorced. (Paras: 4.3.1.1; 4.3.3.2; 4.5.3; 4.5.3.1)
Parental control:	The legal authority to make the decisions regarding the child. (Para: 4.3.1.2 problem 2)
Parental power:	As long as parents do not abuse or neglect their children, the law gives them wide powers over their children and the right to control the lives of their children. (Paras: 4.3.1; 4.4.2.5)

Parental punishment:	Parents have a right and a duty, when their children misbehave, to punish them and to correct their behaviour and furthermore, parents may use a reasonable amount of physical force to punish their children. (Para: 4.3.3.3)
Parental responsibility:	The law states that parents are not responsible for the wrongs of their children unless the parent was involved in the commission of the wrong or ought to have foreseen that the child might have done the wrongful act and should have taken steps to prevent it. (Paras: 4.3.1.3; 4.3.1.3 problem 3)
Parenting plan:	A 'parenting plan' must deal with issues such as the maintenance of the child, contact between the child and any of the parents, contact between the child and any other person, and the schooling and religious upbringing of the child. (Para: 4.5.3.1)
Parents, duty to support children:	Parents have a legal duty to feed and clothe their family, as well as to provide a home, medical care and education for their children according to their standard of living. (Paras: 4.3.1; 4.3.1.4; 4.3.2; 4.3.2.1; 4.3.2.3; 4.4.2.5; 4.5.1)
Parents, unmarried:	Unless the parents live together, the mother has care over of the child but the father may apply to the High Court for care to be given to him. (Paras: 4.3.1.1; 4.3.1.2; 4.5.3.1; 4.5.3.2; 4.5.3.2 problem 10)
Parliament:	The highest law-making body in South Africa, consisting of the **National Assembly** and the **National Council of Provinces**. (Paras: 1.1.2 problem 4; 1.2.2; 1.2.2.1; 1.2.2.3; 1.4.1.4.2; 2.1.1; 2.2.1.1; 2.9.2.1; 2.10.4.3; 4.1.1.2; 4.1.3; 4.1.4.3; 4.1.5; 4.1.6.1; 4.1.6.2; 4.2.2.1; 4.2.2.2)
Particulars of claim:	The particulars of claim set out the reasons for the breakdown in the marriage or civil union and what the plaintiff spouse is claiming. (Paras: 4.5.2.3; 4.5.2.4)
Party:	A person involved in a legal case. (Paras: 1.2.2.2; 1.2.3; 1.3.1.7.1; 1.3.1.7.2; 1.3.2.2; 1.4.2; 1.5.2.2; 2.1.5)
Password stealing:	A form of **cyber bullying**. (Paras: 2.5.1.3; 2.5.1.8 problem 1)
Patients' Rights Charter:	The Charter sets out the rights and responsibilities of patients. (Para: 5.4.7)
Pawn transactions:	Where a consumer gives a person (like a pawnbroker) some of his or her property to keep as security for the repayment of money that the person lends to him or her. (Paras: 3.3.2; 3.3.3.2; 3.3.7.1)
Pay discrimination:	Such discrimination takes place where there is not equal pay for equal work. (Paras: 6.7.2.3; 6.7.2.4 case study)
Pension:	A monthly payment to retired, old, disabled persons by the State. (Paras: 1.1.1; 2.4.3; 2.4.3 problem 1; 3.2.9.4.4 problem 19; 4.3.2.2 problem 5; 4.6.3.2; 5.1.3 problem 3; 5.3.2; 5.3.5; 5.3.5.2.3; 5.3.6.2 problem 1; 5.6.4.6.2; 6.1.1.3; 6.3.6; 6.4.4.1 problem 1)
Pensioner:	A person who receives a pension. (Paras: 5.3.5; 5.3.7 problem 3; 5.4.13 problem 7)

People's Housing Process:	Aims to assist people to build and organise building their own housing by accessing housing subsidies and technical, financial, logistical and administrative support. (Para: 5.6.4.9.3)
Periodic lease:	A lease that runs for a period of time that is not fixed. (Para: 5.6.5.1.4)
Periodical imprisonment:	Where a convicted person is required to spend a number of hours in **prison** each week or on weekends. (Para: 2.13.3.1)
Perpetrator:	A person who commits a **crime**. (Paras: 2.1.5; 2.2.3.1; 2.2.3.5; 2.2.3.5.9; 2.3.1; 2.3.3; 2.3.6.1; 2.3.6.2; 2.3.6.3.1; 2.3.6.3.2; 2.3.6.4.2; 2.3.6.6.1; 2.3.6.7.1; 2.3.6.7.2; 2.3.6.7.3; 2.5.1.10; 6.8.2.1; 6.8.2.3)
Person with a disability:	A person who has a physical or mental disability.
Petition:	Formal written statement to claim a right or complain about something. (Para: 5.1.1)
Pirate taxi:	A taxi that is operated illegally without a taxi licence. (Para: 3.5.9.5)
Place of safety:	A home where **children** are sent if their **parents** or **guardians** are unable to look after them or have deserted them. (Paras: 4.3.3.1; 4.3.3.2; 4.3.3.4)
Plaintiff:	The person bringing an action in a civil case. (Paras: 1.2.3; 1.3.1; 1.3.1.5; 1.4.2; 1.4.2.2; 1.5.1; 1.5.1.2; 1.5.1.3; 1.5.2.2; 4.5.2.3)
Plea:	A statement by an **accused** as to whether or not he or she is guilty. (Paras: 2.13.2.1; 2.13.2.2)
Pleadings:	The legal documents used in a court case in which the opposing parties try to clarify their claims and defences. (Paras: 1.5.1.2; 1.5.1.3; 4.5.2.3; 4.5.2.4)
Police:	Public servants employed by the **State** to maintain law and order in the country. (Paras: 1.1.1; 1.2.2.1; 1.2.2.1 problem 3; 1.3.2 problem 4; 2.1.2; 2.1.3; 2.1.7; 2.2.3.1; 2.2.3.5; 2.3.2; 2.3.6.10; 2.3.9; 2.4.2; 2.5.1.10; 2.10.3.1; 2.10.3.4; 2.11; 3.5.10.1; 4.2.4; 4.2.4 problem 6; 4.3.3.1; 4.3.3.4; 4.3.3.4 problem 9; 4.4.1.4; 4.6.1; 5.1.3; 5.9.4.2; 6.4.5.3)
Police, assaults by:	The police are not allowed to assault people for failing to answer questions or refusing to make statements but they may use reasonable force against people who resist arrest. (Para: 2.11.1.3)
Police bail:	**Police** may sometimes release a person on bail decided by them if the charge is not serious. (Paras: 2.11.3.2.1; 2.11.3.3)
Police powers:	The powers laid down by the law which controls the methods of **arrest** and **detention** by the **police**. (Para: 2.11)
Police powers to arrest:	The powers of the **police** to **arrest** people in terms of the **Criminal Procedure Act**. (Para: 2.11.2)
Police powers to question:	The police may question suspects but may not force them to give answers except their name and address but the police may ask a suspect to go to the police station to make a statement. (Paras: 2.11.1; 2.11.1.1; 2.11.1.2; 2.11.1.3 problem 1)

Police powers to search and seize property:	The powers of the **police** to search and seize property in terms of the law. (Paras: 2.12.1; 2.12.1.1; 2.12.1.2; 2.12.1.3; 2.12.1.3 problem 2)
Police, release on warning:	Release of a person without **bail** by warning him or her when to appear in court. (Paras: 2.11.3.2.1; 2.11.3.3)
Pollution:	The Constitution says that everyone has the right to an environment that is not harmful to their health or well-being and that the state must act reasonably to ensure that air pollution is prevented, conservation is promoted and sustainable development is secured. (Paras: 5.9.1; 5.9.1 problem 1; 5.9.2.1 case study; 5.9.2.2 problem 2; 5.9.4)
Polygraph test:	A lie-detector test. (Paras: 6.6.6; 6.6.6 problem 1)
Ponzi schemes:	Where a person hands money over and is promised unrealistically high returns on the investment. (Para: 3.2.9.4.2)
Post exposure prophylaxis (PEP):	Rape survivors can access free anti-retroviral drugs that may stop them from being infected with HIV at a state health care facility if certain conditions are met. (Para: 2.3.9.1)
Postponed sentence:	Where the **sentence** of a convicted person is delayed on condition that he or she agrees to do, or not do, certain things. (Para: 2.13.3.1)
Practical training course:	**Short courses** to train **articled clerks**. The courses run every year by the **Law Society of South Africa**. (Para: 1.4.1.2.2)
Precedent:	A **Judgment** that becomes a rule of law established by the higher courts. (Paras: 1.2.2.2; 1.2.2.2 problem 5; 1.3.1)
Pregnancy, termination of:	South African law recognises that a lawful abortion may take place under certain conditions in terms of the Choice on Termination of Pregnancy Act but it is a crime to terminate a pregnancy outside of the conditions specified in the Act or for any person who is not a doctor or a midwife to end a pregnancy. (Paras: 2.8.6.1; 4.3.2.4; 4.3.4; 4.3.4 problem 10; 5.4 8; 5.4 8 problem 5)
Premium:	The amount of money paid to an **insurance** company each year to provide **cover** against risks. (Paras: 3.3.2; 3.5.9; 3.5.9.5; 3.5.9.7; 5.4.11; 5.6.4.3)
Prepayments, certificates, credits and vouchers:	Payment in advance for goods or services. (Paras: 3.2.13; 3.2.13.1; 3.2.13.1 problem 24)
Prepayments, services:	Prepaid services and access to services is where a consumer agrees to pay a one-time or periodic membership fee or a certain amount for services or access to services that will be provided more than 25 business days after the payment was made. (Paras: 3.2.13.2; 3.2.13.2 problem 25)
Prescribed:	As set out in law, usually by regulations made under an Act. (Paras: 2.4.2; 2.14.3; 2.14.3.1; 5.4.11.2; 5.7.3.2)
Prescription of debt:	A debt collector may not collect a debt that is older than three years. (Para: 3.3.12.1)
President of the Republic of South Africa	Declaration of conduct as unconstitutional. (Paras: 1.3.1.1; 1.3.1.2; 1.3.1.3)

Presumption of innocence:	An accused is innocent of a crime until proved guilty and the onus is not on the accused to prove innocence but on the state to prove guilt. (Paras: 2.7.5; 2.9.2; 2.13.4)
Prevention of Illegal Eviction from and the Unlawful Occupation of Land Act:	Act 19 of 1998. (Paras: 5.6.3; 5.6.3.2; 5.8.4.3.4)
Prison:	The place where people convicted of **crimes** or detained in terms of the security laws are held in **custody**. (Paras: 1.2.1; 2.5.1.10; 2.10.4.2; 2.11.3.2; 2.11.3.2.2; 2.11.3.3; 2.11.3.3 problem 5; 2.13.1.2; 2.13.1.2 problem 1; 2.13.3.1; 2.13.3.3; 2.13.4 problem 6; 2.14.1; 2.14.6.2; 2.14.7; 2.14.7.2; 2.14.7.3; 2.14.7.5; 3.1.2 problem 2; 3.3.1; 4.2.4; 4.5.2; 4.5.2.1.1; 5.3.5.2.8)
Prisoner's friend:	A prison official who helps **accused** people contact **family** or friends if they are not in court. (Para: 2.11.3.2.2)
Prisoners' rights:	Prisoners' rights include adequate accommodation, nutrition, reading materials and medical treatment. (Paras: 5.1.2; 5.4.1; 5.4.4; 5.5.1; 5.6.1)
Private defence:	Where people who are unlawfully attacked by others use reasonable force to defend themselves, their property or other people. (Paras: 2.10.3; 2.10.3.1)
Private sales:	Consumers are not protected by the Consumer Protection Act, but are protected by the common law. (Para: 3.5.7)
Private welfare:	Sometimes when families suffer as a result of floods, fire or drought, disaster relief funds are set up by private bodies and private people often help with hunger relief by setting up 'soup kitchens'. (Paras: 5.3.8; 5.3.8 problem 4)
Privacy and confidentiality:	As a general rule, a health care professional may not disclose to any other person information about a patient's health status, treatment or stay in a public or private hospital without the patient's consent. (Paras: 5.4.5; 6.6.1)
Privacy, invasion of:	An intentional interference with people's private lives by going into their homes, investigating their personal affairs, or publishing facts about them to the outside world, without their consent. (Paras: 1.3.2.2 problem 6;1.4.1.4.2; 2.2.3.1; 2.2.3.3; 2.2.3.4 problem 5; 2.3.9.2; 2.5.1.9.1; 2.5.1.9.3; 2.8.6.2 problem 2; 2.12.1; 2.12.1 problem 1; 3.2.3; 3.3.12.2; 6.6.1; 6.6.1 case study; 6.6.2; 6.6.3; 6.6.5; 6.6.6 problem 1)
Privilege against self-incrimination:	The right of **accused** persons not to be forced to give **evidence** that might lead to a court finding them guilty of a **crime**. (Para: 2.13.2.3)
Probation:	Where a **juvenile** is put under the supervision of a **probation officer**. *See also* **Employee, probation of**.
Probation officer:	A **social worker** who makes sure that **juveniles** who have got into trouble with the law behave themselves. (Paras: 2.14.2.2; 2.14.3; 2.14.3.1; 2.14.3.1 problem 2; 2.14.4; 2.14.5.1.1; 2.14.5.1.2; 2.14.7.2)

Procedural fairness:	The correct procedures must be followed before reaching a decision. (Paras: 6.9.2.2.4; 6.9.2.2.4 problem 4)
Product:	Something made by a manufacturer.(Para: 3.2.6 problem 6)
Product labelling:	The CPA protects consumers against misleading labelling and makes sure that they are given sufficient information in labels on products. (Paras: 3.2.7.3; 3.2.7.3 problem 9)
Product safety and recall:	Consumers have the right to expect that the relevant industries will monitor their products for safety and where necessary ensure that consumers are warned and dangerous products are recalled. (Para: 3.2.11.7)
Products, faulty:	At common law under the law that deals with civil wrongs a consumer or any person who uses a product may recover damages if he or she suffers personal injury, damage to property or economic loss as a result of a defective product or service. (Para: 3.4.2.9)
Progressive discipline:	An **employee** is given an opportunity to correct an act of **misconduct** without being dismissed. (Paras: 6.5.3; 6.9.2.2.2)
Promotion of Access to Information Act:	Act 2 of 2000. (Paras: 5.9.2; 5.9.2.1)
Promotion of Administrative Justice Act:	Act 3 of 2000. Para: 5.9.2)
Promotion of Equality and Prevention of Discrimination Act:	Act 4 of 2000. (Para: 3.2.2)
Property, crimes against:	Crimes against property include cases in which property is destroyed and those in which property is stolen or otherwise taken without the consent of the owner. (Para: 2.6)
Property, damage to:	(Para: 5.6.4.10.9) *See also* **As is**
Property, defence of:	An accused's act, in certain circumstances, will be excused or justified if he or she acted out of defence of property. (Paras: 2.10.3; 2.10.3.1)
Property, malicious injury to:	Where a person unlawfully damages property with the intention of causing injury to another. (Paras: 2.6; 2.6.1; 2.6.2)
Property, receipt of stolen:	A person who receives or buys property that he or she knows, or has reason to believe, is stolen, commits the crime of receiving stolen property. (Paras: 2.6.6; 2.6.7 problem 1)
Prosecute:	Where the **State** brings a case against an **Accused**. (Paras: 1.2.3; 2.1.3; 2.1.4; 2.3.6.1; 2.7.5; 2.8.1; 2.8.2; 2.8.6.2 probem1; 2.10.4.1; 2.11.1.2;2.13.2.3; 2.13.4; 2.14.2; 2.14.5; 3.2.3; 3.2.8.3; 4.3.3.3; 5.9.2.1; 6.6.7.1)
Prosecutor:	The person who represents the **State** in court in a criminal law **trial**. (Paras: 1.1.2 problem 4; 1.3.1.4.2; 1.3.1.4.2 problem 1; 1.4.2; 1.4.2.2; 2.1.3; 2.2.1.2 problem 2; 2.13.2.2; 2.14.4)
Prostitution:	Where a person has sexual intercourse with another person in exchange for money. (Paras. 1.4.2.1 problem 8; 2.1.1 problem 1; 2.3.1; 2.3.1 problem 1; 2.3.10.1.4 problem 9; 2.3.6.9; 2.8; 2.8.2; 2.8.6.2 problem 1; 2.10.4.3 problem 2; 2.14.8 problem 6; 4.4.1.4 problem 1)

Protected disclosure:	A disclosure that is protected in terms of the **Protected Disclosures Act** which has been made to specific persons, bodies or regulators. (Paras: 6.6.7.1; 6.6.7.1 problem 2)
Protected Disclosures Act:	Act 26 of 2000. (Para: 6.6.7.1)
Protection from Harassment Act:	Act 17 of 2011. (Paras: 2.2.3.5; 2.5.1.10)
Protection of Constitutional Democracy against Terrorism and Related Activities Act:	Act 33 of 2004. (Para: 2.7; 2.7.5)
Protection of Information Bill, 2013:	(Para: 6.6.7.1)
Protection of State Information Act:	A proposed Act that has not yet been passed by Parliament and still in Bill form [B 6B—2010]. (Para: 2.7.5)
Protection order:	A court order to protect people from any form of harassment. (Paras: 2.2.3.5; 2.2.3.5.7; 2.5.1.10; 4.2.4; 4.2.4 problem 6)
Provincial Act:	A **statute** passed by a **provincial legislature**. (Paras: 1.2.2; 1.3.1.2, 1.3.1.3)
Provincial legislature:	The provincial body in which members who sit are elected by all adult South Africans in that particular province. The main function of a provincial legislature is to govern its province. (Paras: 1.2.2; 1.2.2.3; 2.1.1)
Provocation:	Where something is done or said which makes people so angry that they do not know what they are doing. (Para: 2.10.4.2)
Public interest law firm:	A firm of lawyers that specialises in accepting cases that affect large numbers of people. These firms usually help disadvantaged people in society. The best known examples are the **Legal Resources Centres** and the Centre for Applied Legal Studies. (Paras: 1.4.1; 1.4.1.2.1; 1.4.1.4.4)
Public violence:	Takes place when a number of people act together unlawfully and intentionally commit disturbances that are so serious that they become dangerous to the rest of the community (Paras: 2.7.2; 2.7.5 problem 1; 2.11.3.2.1)
Puffing:	Advertising based upon the seller's opinion or taste or some obvious exaggeration. (Paras: 3.2.8.2; 3.2.8.2 problem 12; 3.4.2.8; 3.5.6)
Punishment:	Where the courts impose a penalty on a **criminal** for wrong-doing. (Paras: 1.1.2 problems 3 & 4; 1.3.1; 1.3.1.3; 2.1.1; 2.13.3.2 problem 4)
Pupil:	A person in training to become a practising **advocate** entitled to join a **Bar**. (Para: 1.4.1.2.1)
Pupillage:	The period of training required to be served by **pupils**. At present it is 6 months. (Para: 1.4.1.2.1)
Pyramid schemes:	Where a person makes one payment as an initial investment and is paid **compensation** for the recruitment of other participants. (Para: 3.2.9.4.1)

Quality goods:	Consumers are entitled to receive goods or services that are of good quality, in good working order and free of any defects, and that comply with any applicable standards. (Para: 3.2.11.2)
Quality service:	Consumers are entitled to expect high quality services on time. (Para: 3.2.11.1)
Rape:	Unlawful sexual intercourse with another person without his or her consent. Rape is defined in the **Criminal Law (Sexual Offences and Related Matters) Amendment Act** as: "Any person ('A') who unlawfully and intentionally commits an act of sexual penetration with a complainant ('B'), without the consent of B, is guilty of the offence of rape." (Paras: 1.3.1.4.1; 1.3.1.7.3 problem 3; 2.1.1; 2.1.3; 2.2; 2.2.2; 2.3.1; 2.3.1 problem 1; 2.3.2; 2.3.2 problem 2; 2.8.6.1; 2.10.1; 2.11.2.3; 2.11.3.2.1; 2.13.3.1; 2.13.3.2; 4.3.4)
Rape survivors, services for:	Advice centres help rape survivors lay charges at police stations, provide psychological counselling and give them emotional support during the court case. (Para: 2.3.9)
Reasonable suspicion:	A reasonable belief based upon some facts. (Paras: 2.11.2.3; 2.11.3.3 problem 6; 2.12.1.1; 2.12.1.2)
Receipt:	A piece of paper given by a person who receives money that can be used to prove that the money was paid. (Paras: 1.2.2.1 problem 3; 1.5.2.2; 1.5.2.2 problem 3; 2.11.3.2.1; 2.11.3.2.2; 2.11.3.3 problem 6; 3.27; 3.3.7.5; 3.3.2.1 problem 1; 3.4.2; 3.5.7 problem 3; 4.6.5.2; 5.3.7 problem 3)
Receiver of Revenue:	The government office that collects taxes. (Paras: 5.6.4.3, 6.6.7.1 problem 2)
Reckless granting of credit:	The granting of credit to consumers without taking into account the consumers' ability to pay back the money they borrow or pay their accounts. (Paras: 3.3.2; 3.3.10; 3.3.10 problem 12)
Recognition of Customary Marriages Act:	Act 120 of 1998. (Paras: 4.1.5; 4.1.6.2 problem 5; 4.3.1.5; 4.5.3.1 problem 9)
Redress:	To remedy or set right (an undesirable or unfair situation). (Paras: 5.1.1; 5.2.2.5; 5.4.11; 5.7.3.1.1; 5.8.2)
Re-examination:	Questions asked of a **witness** to clear up any confusion or doubt caused by **cross-examination**. (Paras: 1.4.2.2; 1.5.1.2; 2.13.2.2; 4.5.2.4)
Referral selling:	Where **consumers** are told that if they give the seller the names of friends or other people who may buy they will be given a bonus or **discount** on what they buy. (Paras: 3.2.8; 3.2.8.9)
Reformatory:	A place where **juvenile criminals** are sent to be reformed. (Para: 2.11.3.3 problem 5)
Reform school:	*See* **Reformatory**.
Regional magistrates' courts:	Magistrates' courts that hear serious **crimes** like **murder**, **rape**, armed **robbery** and serious **assaults**. (Paras: 1.3.1; 1.3.1.4.1; 1.3.1.4.2; 4.5.2.1; 4.5.2.2)
Registrar of the High Court:	The official who receives and issues legal documents or **pleadings** in the **High Court**. (Paras: 1.4.1.2.2; 4.5.2.2; 4.5.2.3)

Regulate:	Make laws, rules, procedures and standards to control an activity. (Paras: 2.12.1; 3.2; 3.3.2; 3.4.2.1; 3.4.5; 4.1.5; 5.7.3; 6.4.1; 6.6.4)
Regulations:	Rules made under an Act and published in the **Government Gazette** and other newspapers. (Para: 1.2.2.3)
Rehabilitation:	The method by which **criminals** are helped to overcome the social, educational or psychological problems that cause them to commit Crimes. Also refers to an application by an **insolvent** for an order from the **High Court** declaring him or her to be solvent. (Paras: 2.13.3.1; 2.13.3.3)
Release on warning:	See **Police, release on warning**.
Remedy:	An order by a court or other body that prevents a human rights violation or that compensates you when your rights have been violated; or finding solutions in other ways, for example, through negotiation or mediation. (Paras: 6.11.1; 6.11.1 problem 1)
Rent:	An amount of money a **tenant** pays to a **landlord** (Paras: 1.1.1; 1.3.2.4 problem 8; 5.6.5.1.3; 5.6.5.1.4; 5.6.5.1.5; 5.6.5.2.2)
Rental Housing Act:	Act 50 of 1999. The law that deals with renting. (Paras: 5.6.5.1; 5.6.5.1.3; 5.6.5.1.5; 5.6.5.2.3)
Rental Housing Tribunal:	A structure set up to receive **complaints**, investigate them, and make decisions on them. (Paras: 5.6.5.1.3; 5.6.5.1.6)
Repossession:	If the buyer does not pay missing instalments or return the goods, the seller may repossess them. (Paras: 3.3.11; 3.3.12.2; 3.3.12.3)
Repossession order:	A court order allowing the taking back by a **creditor** of goods sold under an **instalment sales agreement**. (Para: 3.3.11)
Reproduction, right to make decisions concerning:	If a woman wants to terminate her pregnancy, she does not need anyone's consent. (Para: 4.3.4)
Restitution:	Where a person asks the court to order the **criminal** to return the thing stolen. (Paras: 2.1.3; 2.13.3.1; 2.14.5.1.1; 2.14.7; 5.8.1; 5.8.2; 5.8.3; 5.8.4.1; 5.8.4.2.2.1 problem 3; 5.8.4.3.2)
Restitution of Land Rights Act:	Act 22 of 1994. (Para: 5.8.4.2.1)
Restorative justice:	Restorative justice sentences, such as family group conferences and victim offender mediation, which result in a recommendation, are particularly important in cases of child offenders. (Paras: 2.14.5.1.2; 2.14.7)
Retrenchment:	A dismissal due to the operational requirements of the business such as for economic, structural or technological reasons. (Paras: 6.9.2.4.1; 6.9.2.4.2; 6.9.2.4.2 case study; 6.9.2.4.3; 6.9.2.4.3 problem 7)
Retribution:	Where **punishment** takes the form of revenge to pay back the **criminal** for his wrongful act and to show society's disapproval of what the **criminal** has done. (Paras: 2.13.3.2 problem 4; 2.13.3.3)

Review:	A case brought from a lower to a higher court when a person believes that the proceedings were irregular or illegal. The person asks the higher court to make sure that justice is done. (Paras: 1.3.1.4.2 problem 1; 1.3.1.5; 1.3.1.7; 1.3.1.7.3; 1.5.1.2; 1.5.2.2; 2.13.1.1; 2.13.2.2)
Right to die:	The common law allows people to refuse medical treatment even if it causes their death, provided they understand the nature and effect of what they are consenting to but the issue remains contentious, especially when patients are kept on life-supporting machines. (Paras: 4.6.2; 4.6.2 problem 2; 4.6.2 problem 3)
Right to remain silent:	This means that an arrested person does not have to give any information to the police except his or her name and address. (Paras: 2.11.1.1; 2.11.3.1; 2.13.1.1; 2.13.2.3)
Road Accident Fund:	The **statute law** that requires all motor vehicles to be covered by **third party insurance**. (Paras: 3.5.9; 3.5.9.1; 3.5.95 problem 7; 3.5.10.2)
Roadblocks:	Police have the power to erect roadblocks, forcing vehicles to stop, and may search vehicles without a search warrant and seize specified articles. (Paras: 2.12.1.2; 2.12.1.4; 2.12.1.4 problem 3)
Robber:	A person who uses or threatens force to steal from another.
Robbery:	**Theft** by the use or threat of force (Paras: 1.2.2.3 problem 7; 1.3.1.4.1; 1.4.1.1 problem 1; 2.1.3; 2.1.4; 2.1.5; 2.1.5 problem 4; 2.1.7; 2.1.7 problem 6; 2.2.2; 2.6.4; 2.6.7 problem 1; 2.11.2.3; 2.11.3.2.1; 2.12.1 problem 1; 2.13.3.1; 2.13.3.2; 2.13.4)
Roman-Dutch law:	The law based on Roman and Dutch law brought from Holland to South Africa by the Dutch settlers in 1652. (Paras: 1.2.1; 1.2.2; 1.2.2.2)
Rural People's Charter:	The Charter was adopted address problems experienced by rural communities. (Para: 5.8.5)
Sabotage:	Intentionally endangering public safety, polluting water supplies, interrupting essential services or industries, and impeding the movement of land, sea or air traffic. (Para: 2.7.4)
SA Direct Marketing Association:	The association to which reputable **mail order** firms belong and which lays down a code of ethics for its members. (Para: 3.2.3)
Same-sex relationships:	Intimate relationships between people of the same sex. (Paras: 2.4.1; 4.1.1; 4.1.1.2; 4.1.3; 4.6.4.2)
Sanitation:	Toilets and sewerage systems. (Paras: 5.6.2.1; 5.7.1; 5.7.1 problem 1; 5.7.3.2; 5.7.4)
School fees:	Fees paid to the school to cover running costs where the parents can afford to pay them but parents who cannot afford to pay may be exempted on certain conditions. (Paras: 5.2.2.3; 5.2.2.3.1; 5.2.2.3.2; 5.2.2.3.2 problem 6; 5.2.2.3.3)
School for Legal Practice:	A practical training school to train **candidate attorneys** run by the **Law Society of South Africa**.

School loan agreement:	A credit agreement in which money is paid for school fees or related costs for the benefit of a child or it is an agreement entered into with the school to delay the payment of fees or related costs until the consumer can afford to pay them. (Para: 3.3.7.7)
School system, inequalities in:	The system is still not equal but attempts are being made to provide equal educational opportunities. (Para: 5.2.2.2)
Search warrant:	An order obtained from a **magistrate** that allows the **police** to search people or property. (Paras: 2.12.1.1; 2.12.1.2; 2.12.1.3 problem 2; 2.12.1.4)
Second bonds:	A bond taken out in addition to the original **mortgage bond** over the property. (Paras: 5.6.4.11.2; 5.6.4.11.2 problem 14)
Secured loan agreement:	An agreement in which one person lends money to another person in return for something valuable as security for the repayment of all money owing in terms of the agreement. (Para: 3.3.7.8)
Security of tenure:	Giving people legally secure rights in land or housing (Paras: 5.6.3; 5.6.3.1; 5.6.3.1.1; 5.6.3.1.2; 5.8.3; 5.8.4.3.1)
Sedition:	Where a number of people join together with the intention of undermining or attacking the authority of the State. (Paras: 2.7.3; 2.7.5 problem 1; 2.11.2.3; 2.11.3.2.1)
Seduction:	Unlawful sexual intercourse with a virgin with her consent. (Paras: 1.4.1.4.2; 1.5.2)
Self-defence:	The act of using force to defend oneself against injury or harm threatened or caused by another. (Paras: 1.3.2; 2.2.1.1; 2.10.3.1; 2.11.2.4)
Self-incrimination:	*See* **Privilege against self-incrimination**.
Sentence:	The penalty imposed by a **criminal court**. (Paras: 1.3.1.4.1; 1.3.1.7.3; 1.4.1.4.1; 1.4.1.4.2; 2.1.5; 2.2; 2.2.1; 2.2.1.1; 2.13.2.2; 2.13.3; 2.13.3.1; 2.14.7)
Separation of powers:	Main branches of government are separated into **Parliament**, the executive and the courts. (Paras: 1.2.2.1; 1.2.2.1 problem 2)
Separation of spouses or civil union partners:	See also **extra-judicial separation**. (Paras: 4.5.1.1; 4.5.1.1 problem 2)
Serve:	To deliver a legal document or **pleading** to a person involved in a legal action. (Para: 1.5.2.2)
Settlement:	An agreement in which the parties to a dispute agree to accept the terms offered by each other and to withdraw the case. (Paras: 1.3.2.1; 1.4.1; 1.4.1.4.3; 1.4.1.5; 1.5.1.2; 1.5.1.3; 4.5.2.3)
Severance pay:	Financial compensation that is paid to employees who are retrenched. (Para: 6.9.2.4.2)
Sex offenders, compulsory testing of for HIV:	The Sexual Offences Amendment Act provides that any victim or any interested person on behalf of a victim may apply to a magistrate for an order that the alleged offender be tested for HIV and that the results of the test be disclosed to the victim or interested person, and to the alleged offender. (Para: 2.3.9.2)
Sexting:	A form of **cyber bullying**. (Para: 2.5.1.6)

Sex workers:	All people involved in the sex industry whether directly or indirectly (such as the staff in an establishment where sex is provided for payment). (Paras: 2.3.8 problem 8; 2.3.10.1.4 problem 9)
Sexual assault:	Where a person unlawfully and intentionally sexually violates a complainant without his or her consent, or unlawfully and intentionally inspires the belief in a complainant that he or she will be sexually violated (Paras: 2.3.3; 2.3.3 problem 3)
Sexual assault, victims of:	Rape crises centres have been established to assist victims of sexual assault. (Para: 2.3.9)
Sexual harassment:	Unwanted conduct of a sexual nature. (Paras: 6.5.3 problem 1; 6.8; 6.8.2; 6.8.2.1; 6.8.2.2; 6.8.2.4; 6.8.2.5; 6.8.2.6 problem 1)
Sexual offences:	These include crimes like **Bigamy**, **Bestiality, Incest and Prostitution**, (Paras: 2.3.6.10; 2.3.7; 2.3.8; 2.3.9.2; 2.3.10)
Sexual offences, commission of:	This crime, apart from the actual commission includes any attempt, conspiring with any other person, and aiding, abetting, inducing, inciting, instigating, instructing, commanding, counselling or procuring another to commit a sexual offence. (Paras: 2.3.8; 2.3.8 problem 8)
Sexual Offences Act:	Act 23 of 1957. (Para: 2.8.6.2 problem 2)
Sexual Offences Amendment Act:	*See* **Criminal Law (Sexual Offences and Related Matters) Amendment Act.**
Share cropper:	A person who shares in the harvest in proportion to the economic input that he or she has made to the crop. (Para: 5.8.4.3.1)
Sheriff:	The court official who delivers legal documents to the parties involved in a case in the **High Court** and **Magistrates' Court**. (Paras: 1.5.1.3; 1.5.2.2; 3.3.11; 3.3.12.3; 4.2.4; 4.5.2.3; 4.5.3.2; 5.6.5.2.3)
Shoplifting:	A common example of theft where goods are unlawfully taken from a shop without paying, with the intention of keeping the goods for own use or enjoyment. (Paras: 1.3.1.7.3 problem 3; 2.6.3; 2.10.3.2 problem 1)
Shop steward:	A union representative that represents **employees** at the workplace. (Paras: 6.4.3; 6.4.4; 6.9.2.2.4; 6.9.2.3.2.3; 6.9.2.3.3.2)
Skills Development Act:	Act 97 of 1998. See also **Employee**. (Para: 6.3.4)
Small Claims Commissioner:	*See* **Commissioner**.
Small Claims Court:	The court where **civil actions** for less than R15 000 are heard by a **commissioner**. (Paras: 1.3.1; 1.3.1.5; 1.4.1.1; 1.4.1.2.1; 1.4.1.4.2; 1.4.2; 1.5; 1.5.1.2; 1.5.2; 1.5.2.1; 1.5.2.2; 1.5.2.2 problem 3; 3.2.14)
SMS:	*See* **Instant short messaging.**
Social assistance:	*See* **Social grants**.
Social Assistance Act:	Act 13 of 2004.The law that governs the administration of **social grants**. (Para: 5.3.3)

Social grants:	Grants paid out of government funds such as a grant for the aged, a war veteran's grant, a grant for the disabled, a child support grant, a foster child grant, a care dependency grant, a grant in aid and a social relief of distress grant. (Paras: 5.1.3; 5.3.2; 5.3.3; 5.3.4; 5.3.5; 5.3.5.1; 5.3.5.2; 5.3.5.2.1; 5.3.5.2.2; 5.3.5.2.3; 5.3.5.2.4; 5.3.5.2.5; 5.3.5.2.6; 5.3.5.2.7; 5.3.5.2.8; 5.3.6; 5.3.6.1; 5.3.6.2; 5.3.6.2 problems 1 & 2; 5.3.7; 5.5.3; 5.5.4.3)
Social housing policy:	A policy aimed at providing housing opportunities on a large scale for everyone in South Africa. (Para: 5.6.4.2.2)
Social insurance:	When you give money to a fund that helps you when you are in need, for example, unemployed. (Para: 5.3.2)
Social media:	Websites and applications that enable users to create and share content or to participate in social networking. (Paras: 2.5.1.9.2; 2.5.1.9.3; 2.5.1.10 problem 2)
Social relief:	Payments made by the **State** to people who are unable to provide **food**, clothing, housing etc. for themselves and their families. (Paras: 5.3.2; 5.3.3; 5.3.5.1; 5.3.5.2.8; 5.5.3; 5.5.4.3)
Social security:	Schemes that give money or in-kind benefits or both, in the event of a person's earning power temporarily or permanently ceasing. (Paras: 5.3.2; 5.3.4)
Social services:	The welfare services that the **State** makes available to assist people in especially difficult circumstances e.g. children suffering from **abuse**. (Paras: 5.1.2; 5.3.1)
Social welfare rights:	Constitutionally protected social rights including social assistance for people who are unable to support themselves.(Para: 5.3.1)
Social worker:	A person trained to help people with social welfare problems. (Paras: 1.3.2.2; 2.4.2; 4.3.3.1; 4.3.3.4; 4.4.1; 4.4.1.2; 4.4.1.4; 4.4.2.1; 4.4.2.2; 4.4.2.1; 4.4.2.2; 4.4.2.4; 4.5.2.2; 4.5.3.1; 5.2.2.1; 5.3.7)
Socio-economic rights:	Social and economic rights, for example, the right of housing, **food**, health care and education. (Paras: 5.1.1; 5.1.2; 5.1.2 problem 1; 5.1.2 problem 2; 5.1.3; 5.1.3 problem 3); 5.1.4; 5.1.5; 5.1.6; 5.1.6 problem 4)
Sodomy:	Sexual intercourse between males. This practice used to be prosecuted as a crime in South Africa. It is no longer regarded as a crime for a male to have sexual intercourse with another male. (Para: 2.8.6.2 problem 2)
Solicitor:	The **English law** word for **attorney**. (Para: 1.4.1.2.1)
South African Bureau of Standards (SABS):	The bureau sets standards for goods and services to which consumers are entitled. (Para: 3.2.11.2)
South Africa Human Rights Commission (SAHRC):	(Paras: 3.2.2; 5.1.5; 5.7.4; 5.9.4.2; 5.9.4.2 A The body that promotes respect for human rights and which may take cases to court or provide free legal assistance. (Para: 5.1.5)
South African law:	Mainly **Roman-Dutch law** with some **English law** influences. It consists of **common law** and **statute law**. (Paras: 1.2.1; 1.2.1 problem 1; 1.2.2; 2.2.1.3; 2.2.1.3 problem 3; 2.10.4.3; 4.3.1.5; 4.4.2.7 problem 4)

South African Nursing Council (SANC):	The council oversees the training and conduct of nurses and to which claims may be made regarding the conduct of nurses. (Para: 5.4.12)
South African Schools Act:	Act 84 of 1996. (Para: 5.2.2.2)
South African Social Security Agency:	The government body that administers social security grants. (Para: 5.3.4)
Specific performance:	A court order requiring a person who breaches a **contract** to do what was promised. (Para: 3.4.6.1.1)
Squatter:	*See* **Eviction**.
Stalkers:	People who use unlawful means to harass their victims. (Paras: 2.2.3.1; 2.2.3.5; 4.2.4)
Stamp duty:	The duty payable to the **State** when a mortgage bond is registered. (Para: 5.6.4.3)
State:	In South Africa the 'state' brings a legal action against a person charged with a **crime**. (Para: 1.2.3)
State, crimes against:	These crimes exist in order to protect the structures and institutions that the state uses to govern and because people should use lawful means, such as elections, if they want to change or influence the government. (Para: 2.7)
State, duties in respect of socio-economic rights:	According to the Constitution, the government has a duty to respect, protect, promote and fulfil all the rights in the Bill of Rights with certain exceptions. (Para: 5.1.3)
Statement of defence:	A written statement by a **defendant** in a **Small Claims Court** action which sets out his or her defence. (Para: 1.5.2.2)
Statute:	A law passed by **Parliament** (*see also* Act). (Paras: 1.2.1; 1.2.2.2 problem 5; 1.2.2.3; 1.3.1.7.3 problem 3)
Statutory authority:	The defence that a **statute** allows a person to do something. (Para: 2.10.3.4)
Statutory rape:	Acts of consensual sexual penetration with certain **children** (Paras: 2.3.6.1; 2.3.6.1 problem 4)
Statutory sexual assault:	Acts of consensual sexual violation with certain **children** (Paras: 2.3.6.2; 2.3.6.2 problem 5)
Stealing:	*See* **Theft**.
Sterilisation:	A medical operation to make a person incapable of having children. (Paras: 5.4.9; 5.4.9.1)
Stokvel:	A formal or informal financial scheme to which members contribute money in order to help each other with entertainment, social, economic or other activities. (Paras: 3.3.2; 3.3.7.9)
Street law:	A practical course in law which teaches people how the law affects them "on the street", how they can use the law, and how the law can be improved. (Paras: 1.1; 1.1.1; 1.1.1 problems 1 & 2)
Strict liability:	Where a person may be found guilty of a **crime** even if he or she did not have the **criminal intent**. (Para: 2.1.4)

Strike:	Withholding of labour by a group of **employees** for the purpose of resolving a dispute or solving a grievance. (Paras: 1.3.2.3 problem 7; 6.4.1; 6.4.2; 6.4.5; 6.4.5.1; 6.4.5.2; 6.4.5.3; 6.4.5.3 problem 2; 6.9.2.1.1 problem 2)
Student loan agreement:	A credit agreement in which money is paid by the credit provider to a university or college as payment for the education fees of the student or where the college or university delays payment of all or part of the student's education fees or related costs until the student is able to pay for them. (Para: 3.3.7.10)
Subsidy:	An amount paid to people to assist them to buy something. (Paras: 5.6.4.1; 5.6.4.2; 5.6.4.2 problem 3; 5.6.4.6.2)
Substantial and compelling reasons:	Special facts that a court takes into account in passing a reduced **sentence**. (Paras: 2.2.1.1; 2.2.1.3)
Substantial injustice:	It may occur where a person accused of a crime cannot afford legal representation and could result in a conviction or harsher sentence unless legal representation is provided by the state.(Paras: 1.4.1.4.1; 1.4.1.4.2; 2.11.3.1; 2.13.1.1; 2.13.2.1)
Substantive fairness:	A fair reason. (Paras: 6.9.2.2.2, 6.9.2.2.3; 6.9.2.2.3 case study; 6.9.2.2.3 problem 3)
Substitution of goods:	Suppliers who substitute goods or services must treat these as changes to existing agreements and not new agreements without making other changes to the original agreements. (Para: 3.2.9.4.5)
Suburbs:	An area of a town or city away from the centre. (Paras: 4.4.2.4 problem 2; 5.7.2 case study)
Sue:	To take a person to court requesting an award of money or some other action. (Paras: 1.2.3; 1.4.1.4.2 problem 5; 1.4.1.5; 1.5.1.1; 1.5.2.1; 1.5.2.2; 2.1.4; 2.2.1; 2.11.2.5; 2.11.2.6; 2.12.1.2; 2.12.1.3; 3.5.10.1; 4.1.4 problem 2; 4.2.2.2; 4.3.1.3; 4.3.2.1; 4.3.2.3.1; 4.3.2.3.3 problem 6; 4.3.3.3; 4.5.2.4 problem 7; 6.1.1.2)
Suicide:	Where a person takes his or her own life. (Paras: 2.2.1.3; 2.2.1.3 problem 3; 2.2.3.5.3; 4.6.2)
Suicide pact:	Where people agree to commit **suicide** together. (Paras: 2.2.1.3; 2.2.1.3 problem 3)
Summons:	A legal document that is used to begin proceedings in a court of law. A summons is not valid unless it has been signed and stamped by the **Clerk of the court**. (Paras: 1.5.1.2; 1.5.1.3 problem 2; 1.5.2.2; 1.5.2.2 problem 3; 2.14.1; 2.14.3; 2.14.4; 3.3.12.1; 4.5.2.3; 4.5.2.4; 5.8.5 problem 5)
Support:	*See* **Maintenance**; **Parents, duty to support children.**
Supreme Court:	*See* **High Court**.
Supreme Court of Appeal:	The highest court of appeal in all matters except constitutional matters. Its decisions must followed by all courts in South Africa, except the **Constitutional Court**. (Paras: 1.2.2.2 problem 5; 1.3.1; 1.3.1.2; 1.3.1.3; 1.3.1.7.2; 1.4.1.2.1; 1.4.1.2.2; 4.1.6.1; 5.4.5)

Supreme law:	The **Constitution** of South Africa. Certain courts can declare laws in conflict with the Constitution invalid (Paras: 1.2.2.1; 1.2.2.3; 2.1.1)
Suspect:	A person who is suspected of committing a **crime**. (Paras: 1.2.2.3 problem 7; 2.1.3; 2.11.2.1; 2.8.2.3 problem 2; 2.11.2.4; 2.13.2.1)
Suspended sentence:	Where a **sentence** is given, but the convicted person is not required to serve all or part of it, provided he or she is not guilty of a similar **crime** during the period of the suspension. (Paras: 2.13.3.1; 2.14.7)
Sustainable development:	Development that is planned to meet the needs of present and future generations. Sustainable development includes using and conserving resources responsibility. (Para: 5.9.1)
Tenant:	A person who **rents** a property from a **landlord**. See also **Lease.** (Paras: 1.1.1; 1.3.2.4 problem 8; 1.5.1.1; 5.6.5.1; 5.6.5.1.3; 5.6.5.1.4; 5.6.5.1.4 problem 16; 5.6.5.1.5; 5.6.5.1.6; 5.6.5.2.2; 5.6.5.2.2 problem 18; 5.8.4.3.1)
Termination penalty:	An amount paid by the customer for ending the agreement before fully paying for the goods or failing to complete the payment for the goods within 60 business days after the agreed date. (Paras: 3.2.13.3; 3.2.13.3 problem 26)
Terrorism:	Intentionally using, or threatening to use, or attempting to use, violence to overthrow the **State**, bring about political change, for the State to do something or not to do something, and to demoralise the public. (Paras: 2.7; 2.7.5; 2.7.5 problem 1)
Theft:	The unlawful taking control of another person's property with the intention of stealing it. (Paras: 1.1.2 problem 5; 1.2.3 problem 8; 1.3.2.2 problem 6; 1.3.2.4 problem 8; 2.1.1; 2.1.3; 2.1.4; 2.1.7 problem 6; 2.6; 2.6.3; 2.6.4; 2.6.6; 2.11.3.2.1; 2.13.2.1; 2.13.4; 6.5.2; 6.5.3 problem 1;)
Third party:	A person who is not the **insured** person. *See* **Insurance, third party**.
Third party insurance:	See **Insurance, third party**.
Title deeds:	The legal documents which record who is the owner of **immovable property**. (Paras: 1.4.1.2.3; 5.6.4.10.9; 5.6.4.11)
Tobacco, harmful effects on health:	The Tobacco Products Control Act deals with the harmful effect of tobacco on the health of people by prohibiting people from smoking in certain places and tobacco companies from advertising and promoting tobacco and distributing tobacco for free. (Para: 5.4.10)
Tobacco Products Control Act:	Act 83 of 1993. (Para: 5.4.10)
Trade union:	An organisation of workers which **negotiates** conditions of employment with **employers** on behalf of its members. Also defined as an association of workers that resolves disputes between the **employer** and **employees** and secures wage increases and improved working conditions for **employees**. (Paras: 1.3.2.3 problem 7; 1.3.2.4 problem 8; 4.6.3.2; 6.4.1; 6.4.1 case study; 6.4.3; 6.4.4; 6.4.4.1; 6.4.4.1 problem 1; 6.4.5; 6.4.5.1; 6.4.5.3 problem 2; 6.5.1; 6.9.2.1.1)

Traditional courts:	Chiefs' and headmen's courts with limits on the type of cases they may hear. (Para: 1.1.1.6 problem 2)
Trafficking:	Means the supply, recruitment, procurement, capture, removal, transportation, transfer, harbouring (keeping), sale, disposal or receiving of a person, within or across the borders of South Africa. (Paras: 2.3.10.1.1; 2.3.10.1.4)
Trafficking for sexual purposes:	The **crime** of trafficking in persons for sexual purposes is committed by any person who traffics another person without consent. (Paras: 2.3.10.1.2; 2.3.10.1.3; 2.3.10.1.4 problem 9)
Trafficking for sexual purposes, involvement in:	The crime of using people for sexual purposes for gain.(Para: 2.3.10.1.3)
Trafficking, meaning of 'consent' and 'coercion':	Consent is given willingly and consciously whereas coercion means being forced to agree. (Para: 2.3.10.1.4)
Transfer duty:	The duty or costs of transferring property from the seller to the buyer. (Paras: 5.6.4.3; 5.6.4.10.9)
Treason:	The **crime** in which a person intentionally commits an unlawful act in order to overthrow the government or force it to do or not to do something. (Paras: 1.3.1.3; 1.3.1.4.1; 2.7; 2.7.1; 2.11.2.3; 2.11.3.2.1; 2.14.5.1.2)
Trespass:	Where people go on to other people's properties without their consent. (Paras: 2.2.3.5.2; 2.6.8; 2.13.2.1; 2.14.5.1.1; 3.3.11; 3.3.12.2)
Trial:	The court proceedings in which the court officer examines the facts of the case by listening to the **evidence** of the **witnesses** and makes a decision. (Paras: 1.1.2 problem 4; 1.2.1; 1.3.1; 1.3.1.2; 1.3.1.7.1; 1.4.2; 1.4.2.2; 1.5.1.2; 2.13.2.2; 4.5.2.4)
***Ubuntu*:**	Term meaning 'humanity to others' or 'I am what I am because of who we all are'. (Paras: 1.2.1; 2.13.3.2 problem 4)
***Ukuthwala*:**	Customary practice involving the abduction of a girl by a suitor or his friends to force her **family** to enter into marriage negotiations with them. (Paras: 2.3.6.3.4; 2.3.6.3.7; 2.3.6.10; 2.4.3 problem 1)
Unauthorised borrowing:	Where a person intentionally removes property from the control of the owner or person in charge without consent. (Paras: 2.6; 2.6.7; 2.6.7 problem 1)
Unconsciousness, continuous	See **Continuous unconsciousness, grounds for divorce.**
Unfair discrimination:	A policy, law, conduct or situation that unfairly disadvantages you, for example, because you are a woman, black, gay or living with a disability. (Paras: 3.2.2 problem 1; 3.3.2.4; 3.3.2.4 problem 2; 4.1.1.2; 5.2.2.2 problem 5; 5.2.2.3; 5.4.11; 5.7.2 case study; 5.8.2; 6.1.1.1.1; 6.1.1.1.1 problem 1; 6.1.1.2 case study; 6.1.1.2 case study 1; 6.1.1.4.1)
Unfair dismissal:	Where a worker is unlawfully dismissed by an employer. (Paras: 1.3.2.4; 1.3.2.4 problem 8; 6.6.7.1; 6.8.2.5; 6.9.1; 6.9.2; 6.9.2.1; 6.9.2.1.1; 6.9.2.4.3 problem 8; 6.10.1; 6.11.1)

Unfair rental practice:	An unfair rental practice occurs when a party to the lease conducts himself or herself in a manner that is not fair to the other party. (Para: 5.6.5.1.6)
Unfair sales practices:	Unfair methods of selling things to **consumers**. (Paras: 3.2.1; 3.2.2)
Unemployment Insurance Act:	Act 63 of 2001. (Para: 6.3.6)
Unemployment Insurance Fund (UIF):	A form of insurance which is paid by the employer and the employee and which the employee may claim on unemployment. (Para: 5.3.2)
University law clinic:	*See* **law clinic**.
Unlawful arrest:	Where a person is arrested without a "**Reasonable suspicion**", or not to be taken to court but to be intimidated; or a person who is not caught committing a **crime** is not told why he or she is being arrested, or is **arrested** without a proper **warrant of arrest**. (Paras: 2.11.2.3; 2.11.2.3 problem 2; 2.11.2.5)
Unnatural sexual relations:	**Sex offences** like **Bestiality** and **Incest**.
Uttering:	Using a false document to harm another. (Paras: 2.6.8; 2.14.5.1.1; 2.14.5.1.2)
Vandalism:	*See* **Property, malicious injury to.**
Voetstoots:	*See* "**As is**".
Vigilantism:	This means that people take the law into their own hands and it has been used by some communities in South Africa to fight crime in their neighbourhoods. (Paras: 1.3.2 problem 4; 2.13.4; 2.13.4 problem 6)
Violation/violate:	Abuse of or no respect for **human rights**, eg violation of your right to human dignity. (Paras: 1.2.2.1 problems 2 & 3; 1.3.2.3 problem 7; 1.4.1.4.2 problem 4; 2.1.2; 2.2.3.1; 2.2.3.2; 2.2.3.3; 2.2.3.4 problem 5; 2.3.9.2; 2.5.1.10 problem 2; 2.11.3.1; 2.13.3.2 problem 4; 5.1.4; 5.1.5; 5.9.1; 5.9.2.1)
Voluntarily:	By choice and without force. (Paras: 2.3.10.1.4; 2.12.1.2; 2.14.5; 3.3.2.14; 3.3.2.15; 4.4.1.3; 5.3.2; 5.4.6)
Voluntary repossession form:	A document signed by a **Debtor** consenting to a **Creditor Repossessing** the goods that were sold. (Para: 3.3.11)
Wage:	Payment in return for work.
Warrant of arrest:	A document giving the **police** the **power** to **arrest** people and bring them to court. It is usually issued by a **magistrate** or a senior **police** officer. (Paras: 2.2.3.5; 2.11.2.1; 2.11.2.2; 2.11.2.3, 2.11.2.3 problem 2; 4.2.4)
Warrant of execution:	A legal document authorising the **sheriff** of the court to **attach property** belonging to a **defendant**. (These are called writs of execution in the **High Court**). (Paras: 1.5.1.3; 3.3.12.3 problem 14; 4.5.3.2)
Warranty:	Terms in a **contract** setting out the conditions under which the thing or service was sold. See also **Express warranty**; **Guarantee; Implied warranty**. (Paras: 3.2.6; 3.2.7; 3.2.7.4; 3.4.2.9; 3.5.2; 3.5.6)

Warranty of quality, implied:	Everyone involved as a supplier is presumed to guarantee that the goods comply with the required standards and are safe, of good quality and durable. (Paras: 3.2.11; 3.2.11.3)
Warranty on repaired goods:	Suppliers must guarantee the parts and labour used to repair goods for at least three months after the date of repair unless the consumer has misused the goods. (Paras: 3.2.11; 3.2.11.4)
War veterans, social grants for:	These grants are available to people who fought in wars and who are 60 years and over or unable to provide for their own maintenance due to physical or mental disability resulting from having fought in certain wars or the freedom struggle. (Para: 5.3.5.2.2)
Waste disposal:	Unlike household waste certain types of waste, such as medicines and hospital waste, require special disposal methods which are prescribed by law. (Para: 3.2.11.6)
Water, licensing for use of:	Certain uses of water do not require licences but licences are generally required for commercial use of water. (Para: 5.7.3.1.1)
Water rights:	Access to an adequate water supply is a constitutional right and no longer linked to land ownership.(Para: 5.7; 5.7.4;)
Water Services Act:	Act 108 of 1997. (Paras: 5.7.3; 5.7.3.2)
Water Tribunal:	A statutory (created by law) body that has jurisdiction over water disputes. (Para: 5.7.3.1.1)
Websites:	Can be used as a form of **cyber bullying**. (Para: 2.5.1.5)
Whipping:	The whipping of juvenile criminals has been declared unconstitutional. (Para: 1.2.2.1 problem 4)
Whistleblower:	A person that makes a disclosure about another person. (Para: 6.6.7.1)
Will:	A legal document, which says how a dead person wants his or her property to be distributed after **death**. (Paras: 1.3.1.3; 1.3.1.4.2; 1.4.1.1; 1.4.1.1 problem 1; 1.4.1.2.2; 1.5.2; 4.2.2.1; 4.3.1.2; 4.3.1.4; 4.3.2.4; 4.3.2.4 problem 7; 4.6.4.1; 4.6.4.3; 4.6.4.3 problem 7; 4.6.4.4; 4.6.4.5; 4.6.4.5 problem 8)
With all faults:	*See* "**As is**".
Witness in court:	A person who comes to court and gives **evidence** for one or other side in a dispute. (Paras: 1.2.2.2; 1.3.1.7.1; 1.4.2; 1.4.2.2; 1.5.1.2; 1.5.2.2; 1.5.2.2 problem 3; 2.1.3; 2.1.3 problem 3; 2.1.5 problem 4; 2.11.3.2.2; 2.11.3.3 problem 6; 2.13.2.2; 2.13.2.3; 4.5.2.4)
Witness to a will:	The witness may not be the executor or a person who stands to inherit under the will, ie the person must be a disinterested party. (Para: 4.6.4.3)
Wrongful imprisonment:	A **civil wrong** whereby a person is wrongfully imprisoned by another. (Para: 1.5.2)

www.ingramcontent.com/pod-product-compliance
Ingram Content Group UK Ltd.
Pitfield, Milton Keynes, MK11 3LW, UK
UKHW052302280926
15471UKWH00007B/1061

9 780702 185540